Lerwick

Kirkwall

Wick

erland

TRY

rk

Kingston
upon Hull

ield

MIDLANDS

ottingham

cester

ntry

Cambridge

Northampton   Ipswich

Luton

rd   LONDON

Dover

UTHEAST ENGLAND

ampton
ortsmouth   Brighton

0 kilometers   100

0 miles   50

EYEWITNESS *TRAVEL GUIDES*

GREAT BRITAIN

EYEWITNESS *TRAVEL GUIDES*

GREAT BRITAIN

Main contributor: MICHAEL LEAPMAN

DORLING KINDERSLEY

LONDON • NEW YORK • STUTTGART • MOSCOW

A DORLING KINDERSLEY BOOK

ART EDITOR Stephen Bere
PROJECT EDITOR Marian Broderick
EDITORS Carey Combe, Sara Harper, Elaine Harries, Kim Inglis,
Ella Milroy, Andrew Szudek, Nia Williams
US EDITOR Mary Sutherland
DESIGNERS Susan Blackburn, Elly King,
Colin Loughrey, Andy Wilkinson
MAP COORDINATORS Michael Ellis, David Pugh
RESEARCHER Pippa Leahy

MANAGING EDITOR Georgina Matthews
SENIOR ART EDITOR Sally Ann Hibbard
DEPUTY EDITORIAL DIRECTOR Douglas Amrine
DEPUTY ART DIRECTOR Gaye Allen

PRODUCTION David Proffit
PICTURE RESEARCH Ellen Root
DTP DESIGNER Ingrid Vienings

CONTRIBUTORS
Josie Barnard, Christopher Catling, Juliet Clough,
Lindsay Hunt, Polly Phillimore, Martin Symington, Roger Thomas

MAPS
Jane Hanson, Phil Rose, Jennifer Skelley (Lovell Johns Ltd)
Gary Bowes (Era-Maptec Ltd)

PHOTOGRAPHERS
Joe Cornish, Paul Harris, Rob Reichenfeld, Kim Sayer

ILLUSTRATORS
Richard Draper, Jared Gilby (Kevin Jones Assocs), Paul Guest,
Roger Hutchins, Chris Orr & Assocs, Maltings Partnership,
Ann Winterbotham, John Woodcock

Film outputting bureau Cooling Brown (London)
Reproduced by Colourscan (Singapore)
Printed by Graphicom (Italy)
Bound by L.E.G.O. (Italy)

First American edition 1995
2 4 6 8 10 9 7 5 3 1
Published in the United States by
Dorling Kindersley Publishing, Inc.,
95 Madison Avenue, New York, NY 10016

Copyright © 1995 Dorling Kindersley Limited, London

Distributed by Houghton Mifflin Company, Boston.

Library of Congress Cataloging-in-Publication Data
Great Britain. – – 1st American ed.
p.   cm. – – (Eyewitness travel guides)
ISBN 0–7894–0187–8
1. Great Britain – – Guidebooks.
I. Series.
DA650.G695   1995   95–7620
914.104'859– – dc20   CIP

Every effort has been made to ensure that the information in this book is as
up-to-date as possible at the time of going to press. However, details such as
telephone numbers, opening hours, prices, gallery hanging arrangements and
travel information are liable to change. The publishers cannot accept
responsibility for any consequences arising from the use of this book.

We would be delighted to receive any corrections and suggestions for
incorporation in the next edition. Please write to:
Deputy Editorial Director, Eyewitness Travel Guides
Dorling Kindersley, 9 Henrietta Street, London WC2E 8PS, UK.

THROUGHOUT THIS BOOK, FLOORS ARE REFERRED TO IN ACCORDANCE WITH EUROPEAN
USAGE, I.E., THE "FIRST FLOOR" IS ONE FLIGHT UP.

CONTENTS

A 14th-century illustration
of two knights jousting

INTRODUCING GREAT BRITAIN

Beefeater at the Tower of London

LONDON

Eilean Donan Castle on Loch Duich in the Scottish Highlands

Jacobean "Old House"
in Hereford

View of the Usk Valley and the
Brecon Beacons, Wales

HOW TO USE THIS GUIDE

THIS GUIDE helps you to get the most from your vacations in Great Britain. It provides detailed practical information and expert recommendations. *Introducing Great Britain* sets the country in its historical and cultural context. The six regional chapters, plus *London*, describe important sights, using maps, illustrations and pictures. Features cover topics from houses and famous gardens to sports. Hotel, restaurant, and pub recommendations are found in *Travelers' Needs*. The *Survival Guide* has practical information on every subject, ranging from transportation to personal safety.

LONDON

The center of London has been divided into four sightseeing areas. Each has its own chapter, which opens with a list of the sights described. The last section, *Farther Afield*, covers the most attractive suburbs. All sights are numbered and plotted on an area map. The information for each sight follows the map's numerical order, making sights easy to locate within the chapter.

Sights at a Glance lists the chapter's sights by category: Historic Streets and Buildings; Museums and Galleries; Churches and Cathedrals; Shops; Parks and Gardens.

All pages relating to London have red thumb tabs.

A locator map shows where you are in relation to other areas of the city center.

1 Area Map
For easy reference, the sights are numbered and located on a map. Sights in the city center are also marked on the Street Finder *on pages 133–41.*

2 Street-by-Street Map
This gives a bird's-eye view of the key areas in each chapter.

Stars indicate the sights that no visitor should miss.

A suggested route for a walk is shown in red.

3 Detailed information
The sights in London are described individually. Addresses, telephone numbers, opening hours, admission charges, tours, photography and wheelchair access are also provided, as well as public transportation links.

1 Introduction
The landscape, history and character of each region is outlined here, showing how the area has developed over the centuries and what it has to offer the visitor today.

GREAT BRITAIN AREA BY AREA

Apart from London, Great Britain has been divided into 14 regions, each of which has a separate chapter. The most interesting towns and places to visit have been numbered on a *Pictorial Map*.

Each area of Great Britain can be identified quickly by its color coding, shown on the inside front cover.

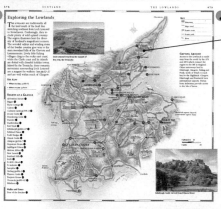

2 Pictorial Map
This shows the main road network and gives an illustrated overview of the whole region. All entries are numbered and there are also useful tips on getting around the region by car, train and other forms of transportation.

3 Detailed information
All the important sights, towns and other places to visit are described individually. They are listed in order, following the numbering on the Pictorial Map. *Within each entry, there is detailed information on important buildings and other sights.*

Story boxes explore related topics.

For all the top sights, a Visitors' Checklist provides the practical information you need to plan your visit.

4 The top sights
These are given one or more full pages. Three-dimensional illustrations reveal the interiors of historic buildings. Interesting town and city centers are given street-by-street maps, featuring individual sights.

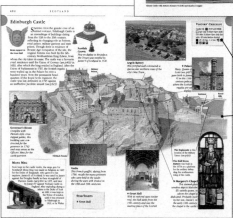

INTRODUCING
GREAT BRITAIN

Putting Great Britain on the Map

LYING IN NORTHWESTERN EUROPE, Great Britain is bounded by the Atlantic Ocean, the North Sea and the English Channel. The island's landscape and climate are varied, and it is this variety that even today affects the pattern of settlement. The remote shores of the West Country peninsula and the inhospitable mountains of Scotland and Wales are less populated than the relatively flat and fertile Midlands and Southeast, where the vast majority of the country's 58 million people live. Due to this population density, the south is today the most built-up part of the country.

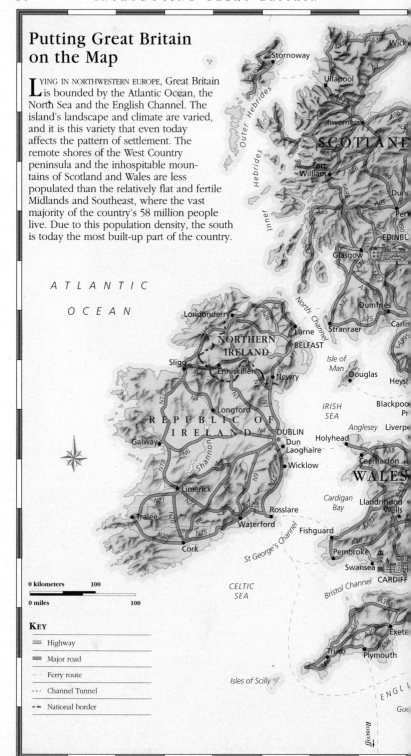

ATLANTIC OCEAN

Stornoway
Wick
Ullapool
Outer Hebrides
Inverness
SCOTLAND
Hebrides
Fort William
Inner
Dunc
Pen
EDINBU
Glasgow
Dumfries
North Channel
Stranraer
Carlis

Londonderry
NORTHERN IRELAND
Larne
BELFAST
Sligo
Enniskillen
Newry
Isle of Man
Douglas
Heyst
IRISH SEA
Blackpoo
Pr
Longford
REPUBLIC OF IRELAND
DUBLIN
Dun Laoghaire
Holyhead
Anglesey
Liverpo
Galway
Shannon
Caernarfon
WALES
Wicklow
Limerick
Cardigan Bay
Llandrindod Wells
Rosslare
Tralee
Waterford
Fishguard
Pembroke
Cork
St George's Channel
Swansea
CARDIFF
CELTIC SEA
Bristol Channel
Exete
Truro
Plymouth
Isles of Scilly
ENGL
Gue
Roscoff

| 0 kilometers | 100 |
| 0 miles | 100 |

KEY

— Highway

— Major road

--- Ferry route

••• Channel Tunnel

-- National border

Shetland and Orkney islands

These islands form the northern-most part of Great Britain, with the Shetlands lying six degrees south of the Arctic Circle. There are transport links to the mainland.

Europe

Great Britain is situated in the northwest corner of Europe. Its nearest neighbors are Ireland to the west, and the Netherlands, Belgium and France across the Channel. Denmark, Norway and Sweden are also easily accessible.

NORTH

SEA

Sunderland

York

Leeds · Kingston upon Hull

Huddersfield

Manchester · Sheffield · Grimsby

ENGLAND

Derby · Nottingham

Peterborough · Norwich

NETHERLANDS

Northampton · Cambridge

AMSTERDAM

Stratford-upon-Avon · Ipswich · Harlow · Harwich · Felixstowe

The Hague · Utrecht · Arnhem

Gloucester · Oxford · Windsor

Rotterdam

Eindhoven · Duisburg · Essen

LONDON · Canterbury · Ramsgate

Zeebrugge · Antwerp

Salisbury · Folkestone · Dover

Ostend

Brighton · Dunkirk · BRUSSELS · Cologne

Portsmouth · Newhaven · Calais

BELGIUM · Liege · Aachen

Bournemouth · Isle of Wight · Boulogne · Lille

GERMANY

CHANNEL

Dieppe · Amiens

LUXEMBOURG

Cherbourg · Le Havre · Rouen · FRANCE

LUXEMBOURG

St Malo · Caen · PARIS · Reims · Metz

Regional Great Britain: London, the South, the Midlands and Wales

GREAT BRITAIN has airline connections with most cities in the world. London is the main transportation hub with two major international airports, including Heathrow, the world's busiest. Southern England, Britain's most populous area, is divided, within this book, into four regions – Southeast England, the West Country, Wales and the Midlands – with a separate chapter for London. Road and train links to the North and Scotland (*see pp14–15*) are plentiful, as are links between all main towns.

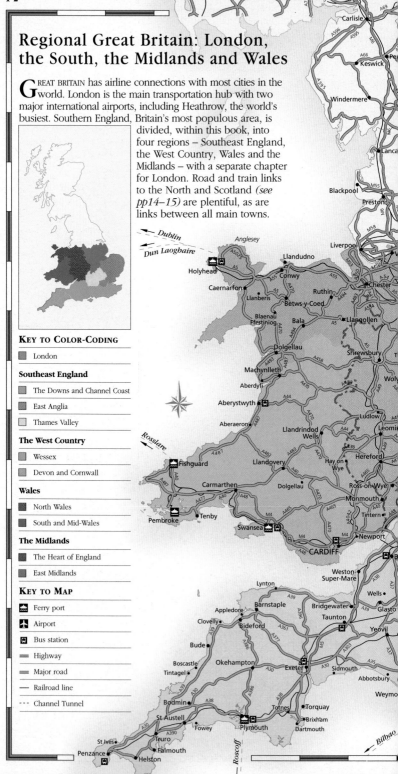

KEY TO COLOR-CODING

- London

Southeast England

- The Downs and Channel Coast
- East Anglia
- Thames Valley

The West Country

- Wessex
- Devon and Cornwall

Wales

- North Wales
- South and Mid-Wales

The Midlands

- The Heart of England
- East Midlands

KEY TO MAP

- Ferry port
- Airport
- Bus station
- Highway
- Major road
- Railroad line
- Channel Tunnel

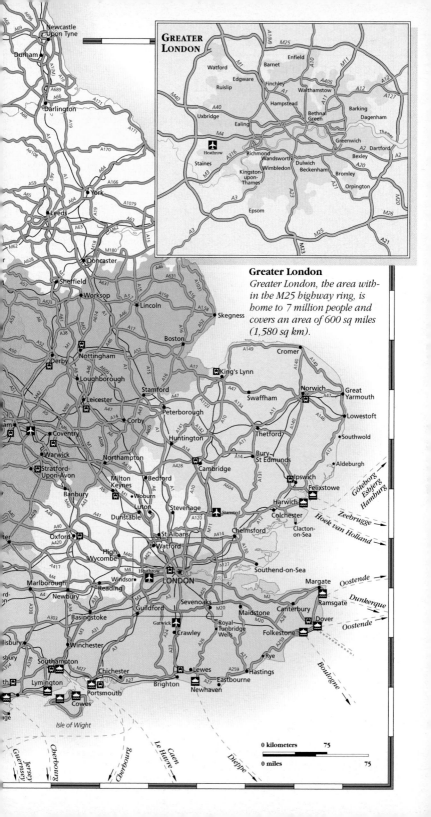

Greater London

Greater London, the area within the M25 highway ring, is home to 7 million people and covers an area of 600 sq miles (1,580 sq km).

GREATER LONDON

Watford
Barnet
Enfield
Edgware
Finchley
Walthamstow
Ruislip
Hampstead
Barking
Uxbridge
Bethnal Green
Dagenham
Ealing
Greenwich
Thames
Heathrow
Richmond
Dartford
Staines
Wandsworth
Bexley
Wimbledon
Dulwich
Kingston-upon-Thames
Beckenham
Bromley
Orpington
Epsom

Newcastle Upon Tyne
Durham
Darlington
York
Leeds
Doncaster
Sheffield
Worksop
Lincoln
Skegness
Boston
Derby
Nottingham
Loughborough
Stamford
King's Lynn
Cromer
Leicester
Swaffham
Norwich
Great Yarmouth
Corby
Peterborough
Thetford
Lowestoft
Huntington
Southwold
Northampton
Bury St Edmunds
Aldeburgh
Coventry
Cambridge
Ipswich
Warwick
Stratford-Upon-Avon
Milton Keynes
Bedford
Felixstowe
Banbury
Woburn
Harwich
Göteborg Esbjerg Hamburg
Luton
Stevenage
Colchester
Zeebrugge
Dunstable
St Albans
Stansted
Clacton-on-Sea
Hoek van Holland
Oxford
Watford
Chelmsford
High Wycombe
Heathrow
Southend-on-Sea
Marlborough
Windsor
LONDON
Margate
Oostende
Newbury
Reading
Ramsgate
Dunkerque
Basingstoke
Guildford
Sevenoaks
Canterbury
Dover
Oostende
Gatwick
Maidstone
Folkestone
Winchester
Crawley
Royal Tunbridge Wells
Southampton
Chichester
Lewes
Rye
Boulogne
Lymington
Portsmouth
Brighton
Hastings
Cowes
Newhaven
Eastbourne

Isle of Wight

Jersey Guernsey
Cherbourg
Cherbourg
Caen
Le Havre
Dieppe

| 0 kilometers | 75 |
| 0 miles | 75 |

Regional Great Britain: The North and Scotland

THIS PART OF GREAT BRITAIN is divided into two sections in this book. Although it is far less populated than the southern sector of the country, there are good road and rail connections, and ferry services link the islands with the mainland.

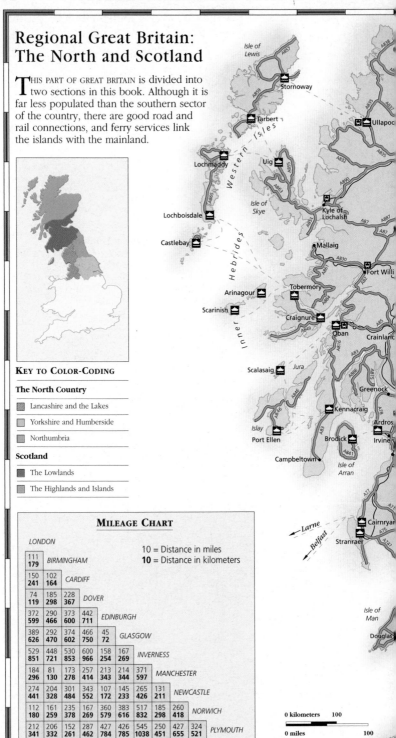

Isle of Lewis

Stornoway

Tarbert

Ullapoc

Lochmaddy

Uig

Western Isles

Lochboisdale

Isle of Skye

Kyle of Lochalsh

Castlebay

Hebrides

Mallaig

Fort Willi

Arinagour

Tobermory

Scarinish

Inner

Craignure

Oban

Crainlaric

Scalasaig

Jura

Greenock

Kennacraig

Ardros

Islay

Irvine

Port Ellen

Brodick

Campbeltown

Isle of Arran

Larne

Cairnryan

Belfast

Stranraer

Isle of Man

Douglas

KEY TO COLOR-CODING

The North Country

- Lancashire and the Lakes
- Yorkshire and Humberside
- Northumbria

Scotland

- The Lowlands
- The Highlands and Islands

MILEAGE CHART

LONDON

10 = Distance in miles
10 = Distance in kilometers

LONDON										
111 **179**	BIRMINGHAM									
150 **241**	102 **164**	CARDIFF								
74 **119**	185 **298**	228 **367**	DOVER							
372 **599**	290 **466**	373 **600**	442 **711**	EDINBURGH						
389 **626**	292 **470**	374 **602**	466 **750**	45 **72**	GLASGOW					
529 **851**	448 **721**	530 **853**	600 **966**	158 **254**	167 **269**	INVERNESS				
184 **296**	81 **130**	173 **278**	257 **414**	213 **343**	214 **344**	371 **597**	MANCHESTER			
274 **441**	204 **328**	301 **484**	343 **552**	107 **172**	145 **233**	265 **426**	131 **211**	NEWCASTLE		
112 **180**	161 **259**	235 **378**	167 **269**	360 **579**	383 **616**	517 **832**	185 **298**	260 **418**	NORWICH	
212 **341**	206 **332**	152 **261**	287 **462**	427 **784**	426 **785**	545 **1038**	250 **451**	427 **655**	324 **521**	PLYMOUTH

0 kilometers   100

0 miles   100

Holyhead

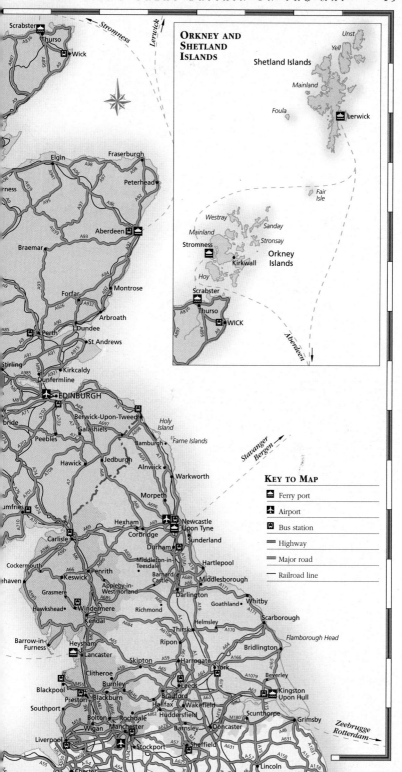

ORKNEY AND SHETLAND ISLANDS

Shetland Islands

Unst
Yell
Mainland
Foula
Lerwick

Fair Isle

Westray
Mainland
Stromness
Kirkwall
Sanday
Stronsay
Orkney Islands
Hoy
Scrabster
Thurso
WICK

KEY TO MAP

- Ferry port
- Airport
- Bus station
- Highway
- Major road
- Railroad line

A PORTRAIT OF GREAT BRITAIN

BRITIAN HAS BEEN ASSIDUOUS *in preserving its traditions, but offers the visitor much more than stately castles and pretty villages. A diversity of landscape, culture, literature, art and architecture, as well as its unique heritage, results in a nation balancing the needs of the present with those of its past.*

Britain's character has been shaped by its geographical position as an island. Never successfully invaded since 1066, its people have developed their own distinctive traditions. The Roman invasion of AD 43 lasted 350 years but Roman culture and language were quickly overlaid with those of the northern European settlers who followed. Ties with Europe were loosened in the 16th century when the Catholic church was replaced by a less dogmatic established church.

Tudor rose

Today a member of the European Union, Britain continues to delight in its nonconformity, even in superficial ways such as driving on the left-hand side of the road instead of the right. The opening of the rail tunnel to France is a topographical adjustment that does not necessarily mark a change in national attitude.

The British heritage is seen in its ancient castles, cathedrals and stately homes with their gardens and Classical parklands. Age-old customs are renewed each year, from royal ceremonies to Morris dancers performing on village greens.

For a small island, Great Britain encompasses a surprising variety in its regions, whose inhabitants have maintained distinct identities. Scotland and Wales, although ruled from London, are separate countries from England.

Walking along the east bank of the River Avon, Bath

◁ **Punting, a popular pastime on the River Cam, Cambridge**

Widecombe-in-the-Moor, a Devon village clustered around a church and set in hills

They have different customs, traditions, and, in the case of Scotland, different legal and educational systems. The Welsh and Scots Gaelic languages survive and are sustained by their own radio and television networks. In northern and West Country areas, English itself is spoken in a rich variety of dialects and accents, and these areas maintain their own regional arts, crafts, architecture and food.

The landscape is varied, too, from the craggy mountains of Wales, Scotland and the north, through the flat expanses of the Midlands and eastern England to the soft, rolling hills of the south and west. The long, broad beaches of East Anglia contrast with the picturesque rocky inlets along much of the west coast.

Scottish coat of arms at Edinburgh Castle

Despite the spread of towns and cities over the last two centuries, rural Britain still flourishes. Nearly three-quarters of Britain's land is used for agriculture. The main commercial crops are wheat, barley, sugar beets and potatoes, though what catches the eye in early summer are the fields of bright yellow rape or slate-blue flax.

The countryside is dotted with farms and charming villages, with picturesque cottages and lovingly tended gardens – a British passion. A typical village is built around an ancient church and a small, friendly pub. Here the pace of life slows. To drink a pint of ale in a cozy, village inn and relax before a fire is a time-honored British custom. Strangers will be welcomed cordially, though perhaps with caution; for even if strict formality is a thing of the past, the British have a tendency to be reserved.

In the 19th and early 20th centuries, trade with the extensive British Empire, fuelled by abundant coal supplies, spurred manufacturing and created wealth. Thousands of people moved from the countryside to towns and cities near mines, mills and factories. By 1900 Britain was the world's strongest industrial nation. Now many

Lake and gardens at Petworth House, Sussex

of these old industrial centers have declined, and today manufacturing employs only 22 percent of the labor force, while 66 percent work in the growing service sector. These service industries are located mainly in the southeast, close to London, where modern office buildings bear witness to comparative prosperity.

Crowds at Petticoat Lane market in London's East End

SOCIETY AND POLITICS

British cities are melting pots for people not just from different parts of the country but also from overseas. Irish immigration has long ensured a flow of labor into the country, and since the 1950s hundreds of thousands have come from former colonies in Africa, Asia and the Caribbean, many of which are now members of the Commonwealth. Nearly five percent of Britain's 58 million inhabitants are from non-white ethnic groups – and about half of these were born in Britain. The result

Priest in the Close at Winchester Cathedral

is a multi-cultural society that can boast a wide range of music, art, food and religions. However, prejudice does exist and in some inner-city areas where poorer members of different communities live, racial tensions can occasionally arise. Even though discrimination in housing and employment on the grounds of race is against the law, it does occur in places. Britain's class structure still intrigues and bewilders many visitors, based as it is on a subtle mixture of heredity and wealth. Even though many of the great inherited fortunes no longer exist, some old landed families still live on their

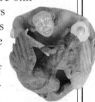

Bosses in Norwich Cathedral cloisters

large estates, and many now open them to the public. Class divisions are further entrenched by the education system. While more than 90 percent of children are educated free by the state, richer parents often opt for private schooling, and the products of these private schools are disproportionately represented in the higher echelons of government and business.

The monarchy's position highlights the dilemma of a people seeking to preserve its most potent symbol of national unity in an age that is suspicious of inherited privilege. Without real political power, but still head of the Church of England, the Queen and her family are subject to increasing public scrutiny. Following a spate of personal scandals, some citizens advocate the abolition of the monarchy.

Democracy has deep foundations in Britain: there was even a parliament of sorts in London in the 13th century.

Yet with the exception of the Civil War in the 17th century, power has gradually passed from the Crown to the people's elected representatives. A series of Reform Acts between 1832 and 1884 gave the vote to all male citizens, though women were not enfranchised on an equal basis until 1928. Margaret Thatcher – Britain's first woman Prime Minister – held office for 12 years from 1979. During the 20th

Afternoon tea on the back lawn at the Thornbury Castle Hotel, Avon

century, the Labour (left wing) and Conservative (right wing) parties have, during their periods in office, favored a mix of public and private ownership for industry and ample funding for the state health and welfare systems.

The position of Ireland has been an intractable political issue since the 17th century. Part of the United Kingdom for 800 years, but divided in 1921, it has seen conflict between Catholics and Protestants for many years. But in 1994 a truce between the two warring factions was agreed and attempts are being made to negotiate a settlement.

CULTURE AND THE ARTS

Britain has a famous theatrical tradition stretching back to the 16th century and William Shakespeare. His plays

The House of Lords, in Parliament

have been performed on stage almost continuously since he wrote them and the works of 17th- and 18th-century writers are frequently revived. Twentieth-century British playwrights such as Tom Stoppard, Alan Ayckbourn and David Hare draw on this long tradition with their vivid language, and by their use of comedy to illustrate serious themes. British actors such as Vanessa Redgrave, Ian McKellen, Alec Guinness and Anthony Hopkins have international reputations.

While London is the focal point of British theater, fine drama is to be seen in many other parts of the country. The Edinburgh Festival and its Fringe are the high point of Great Britain's cultural calendar with theater and music to suit all tastes. Other music festivals are held across the country, chiefly in summer, while there are annual

Schoolboys at Eton, th famous public schoo

festivals of literature at Hay-on-Wye and Cheltenham. Poetry has had an enthusiastic following since Chaucer wrote the *Canterbury Tales* in the 14th century. Poems from all eras can even be read on the London Underground, where they are interspersed with the advertisements in the carriages and on the station platforms.

In the visual arts, Britain has a strong tradition in portraiture, caricature, landscape and watercolor. In modern times, artists David Hockney and Francis Bacon, and sculptors Henry Moore and Barbara Hepworth, have enjoyed worldwide recognition. Architects including

Christopher Wren, Inigo Jones, John Nash and Robert Adam have all created styles that help define many British cities; and nowadays, Terry Farrell and Richard Rogers carry the standard for Post-Modernism. Britain is becoming famous for its fashion designers, many of whom now show their spring and autumn collections in Paris.

Reading the newspaper in Kensington Gardens

The British are avid newspaper readers. There are 11 national newspapers published in London on weekdays; the standard of the broadsheets is very high and newspapers such as *The Times* are read the world over because of their reputation for strong international reporting. Most popular, however, are the tabloid newspapers packed with gossip, crime and sports, which account for some 80 percent of the total.

The indigenous film industry, which flourished briefly in the mid-20th century with a string of light comedies, has been squeezed by Hollywood, but British television is famous for the high quality of its serious news, current affairs and nature programs as well as for its drama. The publicly funded British Broadcasting Corporation, which controls five national radio networks and two television channels, is widely admired.

The British are great sports fans. Soccer, rugby, cricket and golf are popular both to watch and to take part in. An instantly recognizable English image is that of the cricket match on a village green. Nationwide, fishing is the most popular sporting pastime, and

Naomi Campbell, a British supermodel

the British make good use of their national parks as enthusiastic ramblers and walkers.

British food used to be derided for a lack of imagination. The cuisine relied on a limited range of quality ingredients, plainly prepared. But recent influences from abroad have introduced a wider range of ingredients and more adventurous techniques. Typical English food – plain home cooking and regional dishes – can still be found but they are being supplemented by a tastier modern British cuisine.

In this, as in other respects, the British are doing what they have done for centuries: accommodating their own traditions to influences from other cultures, while leaving the essential elements of their national life and character intact.

Whitby harbor, with St. Mary's Church, Yorkshire

Gardens Through the Ages

English red rose

STYLES OF GARDENING in Britain expanded alongside architecture and other evolving fashions. The Elizabethan knot garden became more elaborate and formal in Jacobean times, when the range of plants greatly increased. The 18th century brought a taste for large-scale "natural" landscapes with woods and lakes, some embellished with Classical statuary, while in the 19th century the fierce debate between supporters of the natural and formal gardens reached its peak. In Britain examples of all these styles may be seen today, as well as millions of smaller domestic plots.

RENAISSANCE KNOT GARDEN

THE FIRST BRITISH GARDENERS were monks, who grew medicinal herbs, vegetables and a few flowers within the cloisters of their monasteries. It was not until Tudor times that the fashion for adorning great houses with extravagant gardens began. An early favorite was the knot garden, where plants were divided into intricate patterns by boxwood or lavender hedges. No original knot gardens survive although several have been re-created, including one at Hampton Court *(pp158–9)* and this ornate design at Pitmedden which was first laid out in 1675.

A restored knot garden, Pitmedden, Scotland

Jacobean terrace at Powis Castle, Wales

JACOBEAN GARDEN

DURING THE 17TH CENTURY, gardening became more elaborate, as plant hunters such as the Tradescant family *(p209)* brought plants from abroad. The tulip caused a great sensation in Britain when it was introduced from Turkey, and rare bulbs sold for vast sums. The knot was replaced by the more ambitious parterre, pioneered by French designer André Le Nôtre. Terraces were laid out in geometric patterns and adorned with fountains, topiary and statuary. The gardens at Powis Castle *(p446)* survive largely in their 17th-century form.

LANDSCAPE GARDEN

THE GEORGIAN ERA saw a reaction against the formal designs of the Continent and there was a move towards more "natural" parklands. The early landscape gardens, notably Stowe *(pp216–17)* and Stourhead *(pp252–3)*, with their Greek temples and Palladian bridges, were inspired by mythological themes. Capability Brown, the most prolific new designer, disapproved of such embellishments, and garden design became a controversial topic. Humphrey Repton (1752–1818) later combined naturalism with picturesque "Gothic ruins" and grottoes.

Neo-Classical garden architecture at Stowe, Bucks

CAPABILITY BROWN

Britain's most famous landscape designer, Lancelot Brown (1715–83), pioneered the move away from formal gardens to extensive man-made "natural" pastoral settings, characterized by lakes, clumps of trees and a seeming lack of boundaries. He designed part of Kew Gardens *(see p132)*, while scores of Britain's grandest mansions, including Blenheim Palace *(pp214–15)* and Warwick Castle *(pp308–9)* are still surrounded by parks that he laid out. His nickname came from his habit of telling clients that their land had "great capabilities." Today his reputation is controversial, because in creating his idyllic landscapes he swept away many of the beautiful and historic formal gardens previously in vogue.

VISITORS' CHECKLIST

Apart from the gardens open on a regular schedule in summer, many of which are attached to stately homes, hundreds of gardens throughout Britain are open on occasional days to aid charities. Most are listed in the "yellow book," Gardens of England and Wales, the annual guide to the National Gardens Scheme. Look out for posters advertising the opening of other private gardens.

FORMAL VICTORIAN GARDEN

THE VICTORIANS brought back color to the British garden and reintroduced a stronger element of formal design, distinguished by Italianate fountains, clipped hedges and gravel walks. Greenhouses increased the range of bedding plants available and horticulture became a popular hobby as town houses were built with gardens. Their smaller scale focused interest on individual plants rather than landscape effects. This "gardenesque" style was pioneered by John Claudius Loudon (1783–1843), founder of the first gardening magazine in 1826.

Formal Victorian design, Ascott Wing, Buckinghamshire

A Jekyll border in full flower at Kemerton, Worcester

JEKYLL MIXED BORDER

TRAINED AS AN ARTIST, Gertrude Jekyll (1843–1932) became the most influential garden designer of the early 20th century. Recalling the colorful cottage gardens she knew as a child, she designed broad borders packed with a variety of plants chosen for specific effects of color and height. She worked closely with William Robinson (1838–1935), whose magazine, *The Garden*, advocated informal planting schemes. Some of Jekyll's most famous gardens, such as Hestercombe *(p238)*, were planned in association with the architect Sir Edwin Lutyens *(pp22–3)*.

CONTEMPORARY GARDEN

GARDENS TODAY represent an amalgamation of historic and contemporary styles, and experiments in hybridization and breeding have resulted in many new plant varieties. Concern for the environment has sparked interest in growing wild flowers and creating gardens that attract birds and animals, but highly stylized designs also remain popular. The artist and film director Derek Jarman (1942–94) created this unusual garden combining modern sculpture with mainly white flowering shrubs, tolerant of the sandy soil, to set off his dark-painted seaside home.

Jarman's highly individual garden at Dungeness, Kent

Stately Homes

Adam sketch (c.1760) for ornate panel

THE GRAND COUNTRY HOUSE reached its zenith in the 18th and 19th centuries, when the old landed families and the new captains of industry enjoyed their wealth, looked after by a retinue of servants. The earliest stately homes date from the 14th century, when defense was paramount. By the 16th century, when the opulent taste of the European Renaissance spread to England, houses became centers of pleasure and showplaces for fine art *(see pp288–9)*. The Georgians favored chaste Classical architecture with rich interiors, the Victorians flamboyant Gothic. Due to 20th-century social change many stately homes have been opened to the public, some administered by the National Trust.

The saloon, a domed rotunda based on the Pantheon in Rome, was designed to display the Scarsdale family's Classical sculpture collection to 18th-century society.

The Drawing Room, the main room for entertaining, contains the most important pictures and some exquisite plasterwork.

The Family Wing is a self-contained "pavilion" of private living quarters; the servants lived in rooms above the kitchen. The Scarsdale family still live here.

The Music Room is decorated with musical themes. Music was the main entertainment on social occasions.

TIMELINE OF ARCHITECTS

1650				1750

Sir John Vanbrugh *(see p384)* was helped by **Nicholas Hawksmoor** (1661–1736) on Blenheim Palace *(see pp214–15)*

Colen Campbell (1676–1729) designed Burlington House *(see p83)*

William Kent (1685–1748) built Holkham Hall *(see p182)* in the Palladian style

Robert Adam (1728–92), who often worked with his brother James (1730–94) was as famous for decorative details as for buildings

John Carr (1723–1807) designed the Palladian Harewood House *(see p396)*

Henry Holland (1745–1806) designed the Neo-Classical south range of Woburn Abbey *(see p216)*

Castle Howard (1702) by Sir John Vanbrugh

Adam fireplace, Kedleston Hall, adorned with Classical motifs

NATIONAL TRUST

At the end of the 19th century, there were real fears that burgeoning factories, mines, roads and houses would obliterate much of Britain's historic landscape and finest buildings. In 1895 a group that included the social reformer Octavia Hill formed the National Trust, to preserve the nation's valuable heritage.

National Trust logo with oak leaf design

The first building acquired was the medieval Clergy House at Alfriston in Sussex, in 1896 *(see p166)*. Today the National Trust is a charity that runs many historic houses and gardens, and vast stretches of countryside and coastline *(see p617)*. It is supported by two million members.

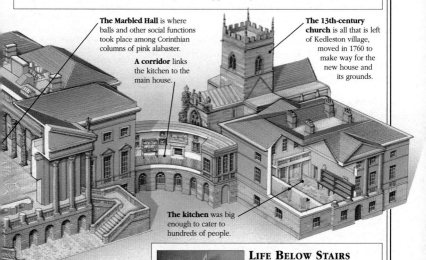

The Marbled Hall is where balls and other social functions took place among Corinthian columns of pink alabaster.

A corridor links the kitchen to the main house.

The 13th-century church is all that is left of Kedleston village, moved in 1760 to make way for the new house and its grounds.

The kitchen was big enough to cater to hundreds of people.

KEDLESTON HALL

This Derbyshire mansion *(see p322)* is an early work of the influential Georgian architect Robert Adam, who was a pioneer of the Neo-Classical style derived from ancient Greece and Rome. It was built for Lord Scardale in the 1760s.

LIFE BELOW STAIRS

A large community of resident staff was essential to run a country house smoothly. The butler was in overall charge, ensuring that meals were served on time. The housekeeper supervised uniformed maids who made sure the place was clean. The cook ran the kitchen, using fresh produce from the estate. Ladies' maids and valets acted as personal servants.

Life Below Stairs by Charles Hunt (c.1890)

1800	1850

Philip Webb (1831–1915) was a leading architect of the influential Arts and Crafts movement *(see p314)*, whose buildings favored the simpler forms of an "Old English" style, instead of flamboyant Victorian Gothic

Sir Edwin Lutyens (1869–1944) designed the elaborate Castle Drogo in Devon *(see p281)*, one of the last grand country houses

Dining Room, Cragside, Northumberland

Norman Shaw (1831–1912) was an exponent of Victorian Gothic, as in Cragside (above), and a pioneer of the Arts and Crafts movement *(see p314)*

Standen, West Sussex (1891–94) by Philip Webb

Heraldry and the Aristocracy

THE BRITISH ARISTOCRACY has evolved over 900 years from the feudal obligations of noblemen to the Norman kings, who conferred privileges of rank and land in return for armed support. Subsequent monarchs bestowed titles and property on their supporters, establishing new aristocratic dynasties. The title of "earl" dates from the 11th century; that of "duke" from the 14th century. Soon the nobility began to choose their own symbols, partly to identify a knight concealed by his armor: these were often painted on the knight's coat (hence the term "coat of arms") and also copied onto his shield.

Order of the Garter medal

The College of Arms, London, contains records of all coats of arms and devises new ones

ROYAL COAT OF ARMS

The most familiar British coat of arms is the sovereign's. It appears on the royal standard, or flag, as well as on official documents and on shops that enjoy royal patronage. Over nearly 900 years, various monarchs have made modifications. The quartered shield in the middle displays the arms of England (twice), Scotland and Ireland. Surrounding it are other traditional images including the lion and unicorn, topped by the crown and the royal helm (helmet).

Edward III (1327–77) was the founder of the chivalric Order of the Garter. The garter, bearing the motto, Honi soit qui mal y pense *(evil be to him who thinks of evil), goes around the central shield.*

The lion is the most common beast in heraldry.

The red lion is the symbol of Scotland.

The unicorn is a mythical beast, generally regarded as a Scottish royal beast in heraldry.

Henry II (1154–89) formalized his coat of arms to include three lions. This was developed by his son Richard I to become the "Gules three lions passant guardant or" seen on today's arms.

Dieu et mon droit (God and my right) has been the royal motto since the reign of Henry V (1413–22).

The royal helm with gold protective bars was introduced to the arms by Elizabeth I (1558–1603).

Henry VII (1485–1509) devised the Tudor rose, joining the white and red roses of York and Lancaster.

ADMIRAL LORD NELSON

When people are ennobled they may choose their own coat of arms if they do not already have one. Britain's naval hero (1758–1805) was made Baron Nelson of the Nile in 1798 and a viscount in 1801. His arms relate to his life and career at sea; but some symbols were added after his death.

A seaman supports the shield.

The motto means "Let him wear the palm (or laurel) who deserves it."

A tropical scene shows the Battle of the Nile (1798).

The San Joseph was a Spanish man o'war that Nelson daringly captured.

TRACING YOUR ANCESTRY

Records of births, deaths and marriages in England and Wales since 1837 are at the **General Register Office**, St. Catherine's House, London (0171-471 4200), and in Scotland at **New Register House**, Edinburgh (0131 334 0380). For help in tracing your family history, consult the **Society of Genealogists**, 14 Charterhouse Buildings, London (0171-251 8799).

Inherited titles usually pass to the eldest son or the closest male relative, but some titles may go to women if there is no male heir.

The Duke of Edinburgh (born 1921), husband of the Queen, is one of several dukes who are members of the Royal Family.

The Marquess of Salisbury (1830–1903), Prime Minister three times between 1885 and 1902, was descended from the Elizabethan statesman Robert Cecil.

Earl Mountbatten of Burma (1900–79) was ennobled in 1947 for diplomatic and military services.

Viscount Montgomery (1887–1976) was raised to the peerage for his military leadership in World War II.

Lord Byron (1788–1824), the Romantic poet, was the 6th Baron Byron: the 1st Baron was an MP ennobled by Charles I in 1625.

PEERS OF THE REALM

There are nearly 1,200 peers of the realm; some titles are hereditary *(see left and below)* and some expire on the death of the recipient, and are known as life peerages. All peers are entitled to sit in the House of Lords, including the Lords Spiritual – archbishops and senior bishops of the Church of England – and the Law Lords. The Law Lords have had life peerages since the 19th century, but in 1958 the Queen expanded the list of life peerages to honor people who had performed notable public service.

KEY TO THE PEERS

☐	25 dukes
☐	35 marquesses
☐	175 earls and countesses
☐	100 viscounts
☐	800+ barons and baronesses

THE QUEEN'S HONORS LIST

Twice a year several hundred men and women nominated by the Prime Minister and political leaders for outstanding public service receive honors from the Queen. Some are made dames or knights, a few receive the prestigious OM (Order of Merit), but far more receive lesser honors such as OBEs or MBEs (Orders or Members of the British Empire).

Mother Theresa received the OM in 1983 for her work in India.

Richard Branson of the Virgin Group was knighted for services to industry.

All four Beatles, the famous musicians, were awarded MBEs in 1965.

Rural Architecture

Fvillages. Their scale and serenity nurture a way of
life envied by those who live in towns and cities. The
pattern of British villages dates back some 1,500 years,
when the Saxons cleared forests and established settlements, usually centered around a green or pond. Most
of today's English villages existed at the time of the
Domesday Book in 1086, though few actual buildings
survive from then. The settlements evolved organically
around a church or manor; the cottages and gardens
were created from local materials. Today, a typical
village will contain structures of various dates,
from the Middle Ages on. The church is usually
the oldest, followed perhaps by a tithe barn,
manor house and cottages.

**Abbotsbury, in Dorset – a typical
village built up around a church**

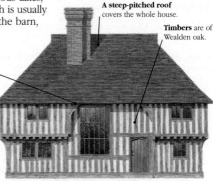

A steep-pitched roof
covers the whole house.

Timbers are of
Wealden oak.

Eaves are supported
by curved braces.

Wealden Hall House *in Sussex is
a medieval timber-framed house,
a type found in southeast
England. It has a tall central open
hall flanked by bays of two storys
and the upper floor is "jettied,"
overhanging the lower story.*

A tiled roof keeps
the grain dry.

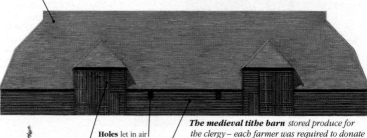

The entrance
is big enough
for oxcarts.

Holes let in air
– and birds.

Walls and doors
are weatherboarded.

The medieval tithe barn *stored produce for
the clergy – each farmer was required to donate
one tenth (tithe) of his annual harvest. The
enormous roofs may be supported by crucks,
large curved timbers extending from the low walls.*

THE PARISH CHURCH

The church is the focal point of the village
and, traditionally, of village life. Its tall spire
could be seen – and its bells heard – by
travelers from a distance. The church is
also a chronicle of local history: a large
church in a tiny village indicates
a once-prosperous settlement. A
typical church contains architectural
features from many centuries,
occasionally as far back as Saxon times.
These may include medieval brasses,
wall paintings, misericords *(see p327),*
and Tudor and Stuart carvings. Many
sell informative guide books inside.

**Slender spire from
the Georgian era**

West elevation

Pinnacled towers
dating from the
15th century are
situated at the
west end.

Bells summon
the congregation.

Buttresses
support
old walls.

**Norman
arches** are
rounded.

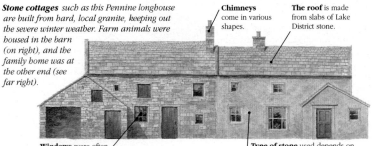

Stone cottages such as this Pennine longhouse are built from hard, local granite, keeping out the severe winter weather. Farm animals were housed in the barn (on right), and the family home was at the other end (see far right).

Chimneys come in various shapes.

The roof is made from slabs of Lake District stone.

Windows were often small in cold areas.

The roof is surfaced with tiles.

Type of stone used depends on locality. In Cumbria blue-gray Pennine stone was used.

Weatherboard houses were built chiefly in southeast England in the 18th and 19th centuries; the timber boarding acted as cladding to keep out the cold and rain.

Bay windows add light and space.

Thatch is made from reeds or straw.

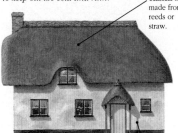

Thatched cob cottages of the 17th century have a cob covering a timber frame. The cob is made from a mixture of wet earth, lime, dung, chopped reed, straw, gravel, sand and stones.

Walls are 1 m (3 ft) thick.

BUILDING MATERIALS

The choice of materials depended on local availability. A stone cottage in east Scotland or Cornwall would be granite, or in the Cotswolds, limestone. Timber for beams was often oak. Flint and pebble were popular in the chalky south and east. Slate is quarried in Wales and brick was widely used since Tudor times.

Welsh slate, making a durable roof

Tiles made from fired clay

Flint and pebble – common in Norfolk

Wood planks used for weatherboarding

Brick, widely used since Tudor times

Local hard granite from South Wales

South elevation

The nave is often the oldest part of the building, with extensions added in later centuries.

Towers are often later additions, due to their tendency to collapse.

Ropes used by bell-ringers.

The font, where babies are baptized, is often a church's oldest feature.

Pointed arches date from the 13th century.

Many pulpits are Jacobean.

A screen separates nave from chancel.

The chancel houses the choir and altar.

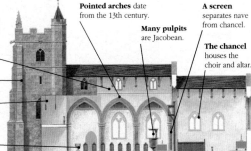

The Countryside

Common Blue butterfly

FOR ITS SIZE, Britain contains an unusual variety of geological and climatic conditions that have shaped diverse landscapes, from treeless windswept moorland to boggy marshes and small hedged cattle pastures. Each terrain nurtures its typical wildlife and displays its own charm through the seasons. With the reduction in farming and the creation of footpaths and nature preserves, the countryside is becoming more of a leisure resource.

INDIGENOUS ANIMALS AND BIRDS

There are no large or dangerous wild animals in Britain but a wealth of small mammals, rodents and insects inhabit the countryside, and the rivers and streams are home to many varieties of fish. For bird-watchers there is a great range of songbirds, birds of prey and seabirds..

Livestock graze on low pastures.

Trees provide shelter and protection for wildlife.

Higher land is uncultivated.

Bushes and trees grow between rocks.

Streams flow over a stony bed from mountain springs.

The highest ground is often covered in snow until spring.

WOODED DOWNLAND

Chalk downland, seen here at Ditchling Beacon on the Downs *(see p167)*, has soil of low fertility and is grazed by sheep. However crops are sometimes grown on the lower slopes. Distinctive wild flowers and butterflies thrive here, while beech and yew predominate in the woods.

WILD HILLSIDE

Large tracts of Britain's uplands remain wild terrain, unsuitable for crops, forestry or even grazing sheep. Purple heather is tough enough to survive in moorland, the haunt of deer and game birds. The highest craggy uplands, such as the Cairngorms *(see p530–31)* in Scotland, pictured here, are the habitat of numerous birds of prey.

Spear thistle has pink heads in summer that attract several species of butterfly.

The dog rose is one of Britain's best-loved wild flowers; its pink single flower is widely seen in hedgerows.

Ling, a low-growing heather with tiny pink bellflowers, adds splashes of color to peaty moors and uplands.

Hogweed has robust stems and leaves with large clusters of white flowers.

Meadow cranesbill is a wild geranium with distinctive purple flowers.

Tormentil resembles wild strawberry plants with its small yellow flowers. It is found near water on heaths and moors in summer

Swallows, swifts and house martins are all summer visitors.

Kestrels are small falcons that prey on mammals such as voles.

Rabbits are often spotted feeding at the edge of fields or near woods.

Robins, common in gardens and hedgerows, have distinctive red breast feathers.

Foxes, little bigger than domestic cats, live in hideaways in woods, near farmland.

Grain crops ripen in small fields.

Hedgerows provide refuge for wildlife.

Small mixed woods break up the field pattern.

Sheep graze on salty marshes.

A culvert drains water from the field.

Reed beds edge the water.

TRADITIONAL FIELDS

The patchwork fields here in the Cotswolds *(see p290)* reflect generations of small-scale farming. A typical farm would produce silage, hay and grain crops, and keep a few dairy cows and sheep in enclosed pastures. The tree-dotted hedgerows mark boundaries that may be centuries old.

MARSHLANDS

Flat and low-lying wetlands, crisscrossed with dikes and drainage canals, provide the scenery of Romney Marsh *(see also p169)* as well as much of East Anglia. Some areas have rich, peaty soil for crops, or salty marshland for sheep, but there are extensive uncultivated sections, where reed beds shelter wildlife.

The oxeye daisy is a larger relative of the common white daisy, found in grassland from spring to late summer.

Sea lavender is a saltmarsh plant that is tolerant of saline soils. It flowers in late summer.

Orchids are among the rarer wild flowers. This species is the Common Spotted Orchid.

Cowslips belong to the primrose family. In spring they are often found in the grass on open meadowlands.

Poppies glow brilliant red in cornfields.

Buttercups are among the most common wild flowers. They brighten meadows in summer.

Walkers' Britain

WALKERS OF ALL LEVELS of ability and enthusiasm are well served in Britain. There is an unrivaled network of long-distance paths through some spectacular scenery, which can be tackled in stages with overnight stays en route, or dipped into for a single day's walking. For shorter walks, Britain is dotted with signs showing public footpaths across common or private land. You will find books of walking trails in local shops and a large map will keep you on track. Choose river routes for easy walking or take to the hills for a greater challenge.

Walker resting on Scafell Pike, Lake District

The West Highland Way is an arduous 95 mile (153 km) route from Milngavie, near Glasgow, to north of Fort William, across mountainous terrain with fine lochs and moorland scenery *(see p480)*.

Fort William

Glasgow

The Pennine Way was Britain's first designated long-distance path. The 256 mile (412 km) route from Edale in Derbyshire to Kirk Yetholm on the Scottish border is a challenging upland hike, with long, lonely stretches of moorland. It is only for experienced hill walkers.

St. Bees Head

Win•

Offa's Dike Footpath *follows the boundary between Wales and England. The 168 mile (270 km) path goes through the beautiful Wye Valley (see p447) in the Welsh borders.*

Dales Way runs from Ilkley in West Yorkshire to Bowness-on-Windermere in the Lake District, 81 miles (130 km) of delightful flat riverside walking and valley scenery.

Prest•

Pembrokeshire Coastal path *is 183 miles (292 km) of rugged cliff-top walking from Amroth on Carmarthen Bay to the west tip of Wales at Cardigan.*

St. Dogmaels •

Amroth •

Minehe•

ORDNANCE SURVEY MAPS

The best maps for walkers are published by the Ordnance Survey, the official mapping agency. Out of a wide range of maps the most useful are the green-covered *Pathfinder* series, on a scale of 1:25,000, and the *Landranger* series at 1:50,000. The *Outdoor Leisure and Explorer* series are maps of the more popular regions and cover a larger area.

The Southwest Coastal Path offers varied scenery from Minehead on the north Somerset coast to Poole in Dorset, via Devon and Cornwall – in all a marathon 600 mile (965 km) round trip.

SIGNPOSTS

Long-distance paths are well marked, some of them with an acorn symbol (or with a thistle in Scotland). Many shorter routes are marked with colored arrows by local authorities or hiking groups. Local councils generally mark public footpaths with yellow arrows. Public bridlepaths, marked by blue arrows, are trails that can be used by both walkers and horseback riders – remember, horses churn up mud. Signs appear on posts, trees and stiles.

TIPS FOR WALKERS

Be prepared: The weather can change very quickly: dress for the worst. Always take a compass, a good walking map and get local advice before undertaking any ambitious walking. Pack some food and drink if the map does not show a pub en route.
On the walk: Always keep to the footpath and close gates behind you. Never feed or upset farm animals, leave litter, pick flowers or damage plants.
Where to stay: The Youth Hostels Association (see pp538–9) has a network of hostels that cater particularly to walkers. Bed-and-breakfast accommodation is also available near most routes (see pp538–9).
Further information: The Ramblers' Association (tel: 0171-582 6878) is a national organization for walkers, with a magazine and a guide to accommodations.

The Coast to Coast Walk crosses the Lake District, Yorkshire Dales and North York Moors, on a 190 mile (306 km) route. This demanding walk covers a spectacular range of North Country landscapes. All cross-country routes are best walked from west to east to take advantage of the prevailing wind.

The Ridgeway is a fairly easy path that follows an ancient track once used by cattle drovers. Starting near Avebury (see p249) it covers 85 miles (137 km) to Ivinghoe Beacon.

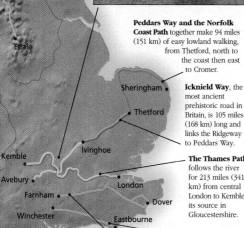

Peddars Way and the Norfolk Coast Path together make 94 miles (151 km) of easy lowland walking, from Thetford, north to the coast then east to Cromer.

Icknield Way, the most ancient prehistoric road in Britain, is 105 miles (168 km) long and links the Ridgeway to Peddars Way.

The Thames Path follows the river for 213 miles (341 km) from central London to Kemble, its source in Gloucestershire.

Robin Hood's Bay
Ilkley
Edale
Sheringham
Thetford
Kemble
Ivinghoe
Avebury
Farnham
London
Winchester
Dover
Eastbourne
Harbour

The Isle of Wight Coastal Path circles the entire island on an easy 65 mile (105 km) footpath.

The North Downs Way is an ancient route through 141 miles (227 km) of low-lying hills from Farnham in Surrey to Dover or Folkestone in Kent.

The South Downs Way is a varied 106 mile (171 km) walk from Eastbourne on the south coast to Winchester (see p156-7). It can be completed in a week.

The Traditional British Pub

EVERY COUNTRY HAS its bars, but Britain is famous for its pubs or "public houses." Ale was brewed in England in Roman times – mostly at home – and by the Middle Ages there were inns and taverns that brewed their own. The 18th century was the heyday of the coaching inn as stage coaches brought more business. In the 19th century came railway taverns for travelers and "gin palaces" for the new industrial workers. Today, pubs come in all styles and sizes and many cater to families, serving food as well as drink *(see pp608–11).*

Beer label c.1900

Early 19th-century coaching inn – also a social center and post office

THE VICTORIAN PUB

A century ago, many pubs in towns and cities had stylish interiors, to contrast with the poor housing of their clients.

Elaborately etched glass is a feature of many Victorian interiors.

Pub games, such as cribbage, bar billiards, pool and dominoes are part of British pub culture. Here some regular customers are competing against a rival pub's darts team.

Pint glasses (containing just over half a liter) are used to serve beer.

The Red Lion pub name is derived from Scottish heraldry *(see p26).*

Beer gardens outside pubs are a favorite place for family summer treats.

Old-fashioned cash register contributes to the period atmosphere of the bar.

Pewter tankards, seldom used by drinkers today, add a traditional touch.

WHAT TO DRINK

Draught bitter is the most traditional British beer. Brewed from malted barley, hops, yeast and water, and usually matured in a wooden cask, it varies from region to region. In the north of England the sweeter mild ale is popular, and lagers served in bottles or on tap are also widely drunk. Stout, made from black malt, is another variation.

Beer pump

Draft bitter is drunk at room temperature.

Draft lager is a light-colored, carbonated beer.

Guinness is a thick, creamy Irish stout.

Pavement tables, crowded with city drinkers during the summer months

A village pub, offering a waterside view and serving drinks in the garden

Bottles of liquor, as well as port and sherry, are arranged behind the bar.

Glass lamps imitate the Victorian style.

Wine, once rarely found in pubs, is now increasingly popular.

A deep-toned mahogany bar forms part of the traditional setting.

Draft beer, served from pumps or taps, comes from national and local brewers.

Optics dispense spirits in precise measures.

Mild may be served by the pint or in a half-pint tankard (as above).

Popular cocktails are gin-and-tonic (right) and Pimm's.

PUB SIGNS

Early medieval inns used vines or evergreens as signs – the symbol of Bacchus, the Roman god of wine. Soon pubs acquired names that showed support for monarchs or noblemen, or celebrated victories in battle. Since many customers were illiterate, signs had vivid images.

The George *derives either from one of six kings of that name, or from the patron saint of England (shown here).*

The Bat and Ball *is one of many pubs celebrating the game of cricket, and is often sited near a village green where it is played.*

The Green Man *is a woodland spirit from pagan mythology, possibly the basis for the legend of Robin Hood (see p322).*

The Magna Carta *sign commemorates and illustrates the "great charter" signed by King John in 1215 (see p48).*

The Bird in Hand *relates to the ancient country sport of falconry, traditionally practiced by noblemen.*

A Flavor of British Food

Britain's unique contributions to gastronomy include its cooked breakfasts, afternoon teas and satisfying puddings. Fast food and take-outs were pioneered here with fish and chips, the sandwich and the Cornish pasty. Modern British cuisine is innovative and varied, but it is also worth seeking out traditional dishes that use first-rate ingredients: beef, lamb and game figure prominently. As an island, Britain has historically been a fish-eating nation, although shellfish, once cheap, have become pricier.

Fish and chips are made from white sea fish such as cod, batter-coated and fried in oil, with fried potatoes, salt and vinegar.

A full English breakfast can include fried bacon and egg, mushrooms, sausage, tomatoes, fried bread and black pudding.

Cockles and whelks remain cheap compared with larger shellfish. They are sold from small stalls outside pubs, and can be awkward to eat.

Laverbread is a Welsh treat made from dark-colored seaweed. It is served cold with seafood, or, as here, hot with bacon, toast and tomato.

Cornish pasties are filled with meat and vegetables baked in a pastry crust. They originated as a handy way for farm laborers to take their lunch to work.

TEA TIME

Afternoon tea, taken at around 4pm, is a British tradition enacted daily in homes, tea-shops and grand hotels. The tea is usually from India or Sri Lanka, served with optional milk and sugar; but it could be scented China or herbal tea served with or without lemon. Small, delicately cut sandwiches are eaten first: fish paste and cucumber are traditional fillings. These may be followed by scones, jam and cream, especially in the west of England *(see p271)*. Other options include buttered toast or crumpets, but leave room for a slice of fruit cake or jam sponge, a chocolate éclair or a regional speciality such as Scottish shortbread.

Eccles cake

Bakewell tart

Barra brith or Welsh tea bread

Welsh cakes

Ginger cake

Victoria sponge

Cucumber sandwiches

Ceylon tea

Lapsang Souchong tea

Plowman's lunch *is served in many pubs. It consists of bread, cheese (often Cheddar), and pickles, garnished with salad. Ham or pâté may be substituted for cheese.*

Horseradish sauce   Roast beef

Gravy   Yorkshire pudding

Broccoli   Roast potatoes

Shepherd's pie *is made from minced lamb baked with a topping of mashed potato. If minced beef is used instead the dish is then called cottage pie.*

Roast beef *is Britain's traditional Sunday lunch. It usually comes with Yorkshire pudding (savory batter baked with the meat), roast potatoes and seasonal vegetables. A rich gravy enhances the flavor, and horseradish sauce is a favorite relish.*

Dover sole *is Britain's most prized flat fish. Served on the bone or filleted, it is firm fleshed and delicately flavored.*

Cumberland sausage, *a regional specialty, is in a coil. Sausages and mashed potatoes are called "bangers and mash."*

Steak and kidney pie *is beef and kidney in gravy, baked in pastry or in a suet crust, when it is known as a pudding.*

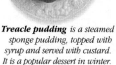

Strawberries and cream *are the delight of early summer, associated with outdoor social occasions of all types. Later, raspberries come into season. Both fruits make excellent jam.*

Cheese *is often served to finish lunch and dinner. Mature Cheddar is one of the most popular regional varieties. Blue-veined cheeses such as Stilton are an acquired taste.*

Treacle pudding *is a steamed sponge pudding, topped with syrup and served with custard. It is a popular dessert in winter.*

Stilton   Cheddar

Cornish Yarg   Sage Derby

Cheshire   Red Leicester

Sherry trifle *was originally sponge cake soaked in sweet sherry and served with custard. Modern versions may include ladyfingers covered with fruit, jelly and a layer of cream, and decorated with angelica and cherries.*

THE HISTORY OF GREAT BRITAIN

RITAIN BEGAN TO assume a cohesive character as early as the 7th century, with the Anglo-Saxon tribes absorbing Celtic and Roman influences and finally achieving supremacy. They suffered repeated Viking incursions and were overcome by the Normans at the Battle of Hastings in 1066. Over centuries, the disparate cultures of the Normans and Anglo-Saxons combined to form the English nation, a process nurtured by Britain's position as an island. The next 400 years saw English kings involved in military expeditions to Europe, but their control over these areas was gradually taken from them. As a result they extended their domain over Scotland and Wales. The Tudor monarchs consolidated this control and laid the foundations for Britain's future commercial success. Henry VIII recognized the vital importance of sea power and under his daughter, Elizabeth I, English sailors ranged far across the world, often coming into conflict with the Spanish. The total defeat of the Spanish Armada in 1588 confirmed Britain's position as a major maritime power. The Stuart period saw a number of internal struggles, most importantly the Civil War in 1641. But by the time of the Act of the Union in 1707 the whole island was united and the foundations for representative government had been laid. The combination of this internal security with continuing maritime strength let Britain seek wealth overseas. By the end of the Napoleonic Wars in 1815, Britain was the leading trading nation in the world. The opportunities offered by industrialization were seized, and by the late 19th century, a colossal empire had been established across the globe. Challenged by Europe and the rise of the US, and drained by its leading role in two world wars, Britain's influence waned after 1945. By the 1970s almost all the colonies had become independent Commonwealth nations.

Medieval knights, masters of the arts of war

Contemporary map showing the defeat of the Armada (1588), making Britain into a world power

◁ **Henry VIII, founder of the British navy, seen here with his children Edward and Mary**

Kings and Queens

ALL ENGLISH MONARCHS since the Norman Conquest in 1066 have been descendants of William the Conqueror. Scottish rulers, until James VI and the Union of Crowns in 1603 (see pp468–9), have been more diverse. When the Crown passes to someone other than the monarch's eldest son, the name of the ruling family usually changes. The rules of succession have been precisely laid down and strongly favor men over women, but Britain has still had six queens since 1553. In Norman times the monarchy enjoyed absolute power, but today the position is largely symbolic.

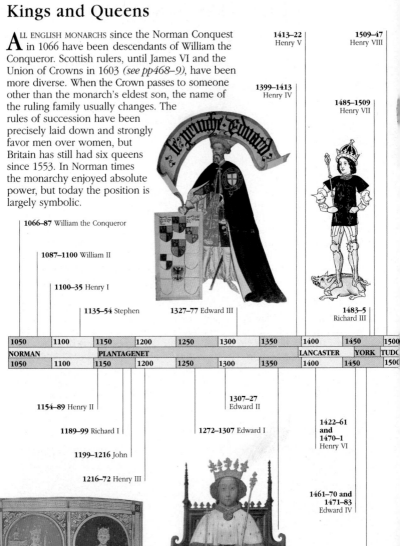

1413–22 Henry V

1509–47 Henry VIII

1399–1413 Henry IV

1485–1509 Henry VII

1066–87 William the Conqueror

1087–1100 William II

1100–35 Henry I

1135–54 Stephen

1327–77 Edward III

1483–5 Richard III

1050	1100	1150	1200	1250	1300	1350	1400	1450	1500
NORMAN		**PLANTAGENET**					**LANCASTER**	**YORK**	**TUDOR**
1050	1100	1150	1200	1250	1300	1350	1400	1450	1500

1154–89 Henry II

1189–99 Richard I

1199–1216 John

1216–72 Henry III

1307–27 Edward II

1272–1307 Edward I

1422–61 and 1470–1 Henry VI

1461–70 and 1471–83 Edward IV

1377–99 Richard II

Matthew Paris's 13th-century chronicle showing clockwise from top left, Richard I, Henry II, John and Henry III

1483 Edward V

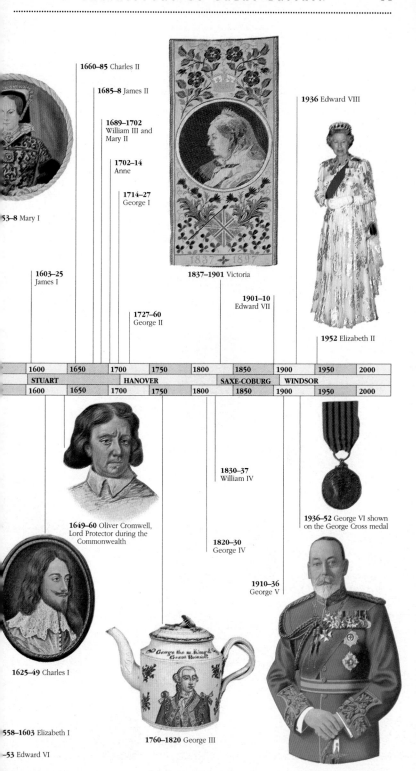

1660–85 Charles II

1685–8 James II

1689–1702 William III and Mary II

1702–14 Anne

1714–27 George I

1936 Edward VIII

53–8 Mary I

1603–25 James I

1837–1901 Victoria

1901–10 Edward VII

1727–60 George II

1952 Elizabeth II

1600	1650	1700	1750	1800	1850	1900	1950	2000
STUART		HANOVER			SAXE-COBURG	WINDSOR		
1600	1650	1700	1750	1800	1850	1900	1950	2000

1830–37 William IV

1649–60 Oliver Cromwell, Lord Protector during the Commonwealth

1936–52 George VI shown on the George Cross medal

1820–30 George IV

1910–36 George V

1625–49 Charles I

558–1603 Elizabeth I

–53 Edward VI

1760–1820 George III

Prehistoric Britain

BRITAIN WAS PART of the European land mass until the end of the last Ice Age, around 6000 BC, when the English Channel was formed by melting ice. The earliest inhabitants lived in limestone caves: settlements and farming skills developed gradually through the Stone Age. The magnificent wooden and stone henges and circles are masterworks from around 3000 BC, but their significance is a mystery. Flint mines and ancient pathways are evidence of early trading and many burial mounds (barrows) survive from the Stone and Bronze Ages.

Axheads
Stone axes, like this one found at Stonehenge, were used by Neolithic men.

Cup and ring marks
were carved on standing stones, such as this one at Ballymeanoch.

Neolithic Tools
Antlers and bones were made into Neolithic leather-working tools. These were found at Avebury (see p249).

MAPPING THE PAST

Monuments from the Neolithic (New Stone), Bronze and Iron Ages, together with artifacts found from these periods, provide a wealth of information about Britain's early settlers, before written history began with the Romans.

Pottery Beaker
The Beaker People, who came from Europe in the early Bronze Age, take their name from these drinking cups often found in their graves.

Gold Breast Plate
Made by Wessex goldsmiths, its spectacular pattern suggests it belonged to an important chieftain.

Pentre Ifan, an impressive Neolithic burial chamber in south Wales, was once covered with a huge earth mound.

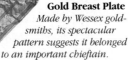

Mold Cape
Gold was mined in Wales and Cornwall in the Bronze Age. This intricately worked warrior's cape was buried in a grave at Mold, Clwyd.

This gold cup, found in a Cornish barrow, is evidence of the wealth of Bronze Age tribes.

TIMELINE

6000–5000 As the Ice Age comes to an end, sea levels rise, submerging the land link between Britain and the Continent

Neolithic flint axes

6000 BC	5500 BC	5000 BC	4500 BC	4000 BC

A gold pendant and button (1700 BC), found in Bronze Age graves

3500 Neolithic Age begins. Long barrows and stone circles built around Britain

Skara Brae is a Neolithic village of about 2500 BC *(see p514).*

Maiden Castle
An impressive Iron Age hill fort in Dorset, its concentric lines of ramparts and ditches follow the contours of the hilltop (see p255).

Iron Age Brochs, round towers with thick stone walls, are found only in Scotland.

Iron Age Ax
The technique of smelting iron came to Britain around 700 BC, brought from Europe by the Celts.

Castlerigg Stone Circle
is one of Britain's earliest Neolithic monuments *(see p347).*

Uffington White Horse
Thought to be 3,000 years old, the shape has to be "scoured" to keep grass at bay (see p207).

A chalk figure, thought to be a fertility goddess, was found at Grimes Graves *(see p180).*

This bronze Celtic helmet (50 BC) was found in the River Thames, London.

Stonehenge was begun around 3,500 years ago *(see pp248–9).*

WHERE TO SEE PREHISTORIC BRITAIN

Wiltshire, with Stonehenge *(p248)* and Avebury *(p249)*, has the best group of Neolithic monuments, and the Uffington White Horse is nearby *(p207)*. The Scottish islands have many early sites and the British Museum *(pp108–9)* houses a huge collection of artifacts.

A circular bank with over 180 stones encloses the Neolithic site at Avebury (see p249).

Snettisham Torc
A torc was a neck ring worn by Celtic men. This one, found in Norfolk, dates from 50 BC and is made from silver and gold.

BC	2500 BC	2000 BC	1500 BC	1000 BC	500 BC
2500 Temples, or henges, are built of wood or stone	**1650–1200** Wessex is at the hub of trading routes between Europe and the mines of Cornwall, Wales and Ireland		**1000** First farmsteads are settled	**550–350** Migration of Celtic people from southern Europe	**500** Iron Age begins. Hill forts are built
	2100–1650 The Bronze Age reaches Britain. Immigration of the Beaker People, who make bronze implements and build ritual temples		*Chieftain's bronze scepter (1700 BC)* **1200** Small, self-sufficient villages start to appear		**150** Tribes from Gaul begin to migrate to Britain

Roman Britain

THROUGHOUT THE 350-YEAR Roman occupation, Britain was ruled as a colony. After the defeat of rebellious local tribes, such as Boadicea's Iceni, the Romans remained an unassimilated occupying power. Their legacy is in military and civil construction: forts, walls, towns and public buildings. Their long, straight roads, built for easy movement of troops, are still a feature of the landscape.

Roman jasper seal

Cavalry Sports Helmet
Found in Lancashire, it was used in tournaments by horsemen. Cavalry races and other sports were held in amphitheaters near towns.

Silver Jug
This 3rd-century jug, the earliest known silver item with Christian symbols, was excavated near Peterborough.

Exercise corridor

Main baths

Fishbourne Palace was built at the site of a natural harbor and ships could moor here.

Entrance hall

Hadrian's Wall
Started in 120 as a defense against the Scots; it marked the northern frontier of the Roman Empire and was guarded by 17 forts housing over 18,500 foot-soldiers and cavalry.

Mithras
This head of the god Mithras was found on the London site of a temple devoted to the cult of Mithraism. The sect demanded of its Roman followers loyalty and discipline.

TIMELINE

54 BC Julius Caesar lands in Britain but withdraws

Julius Caesar (c.102–44 BC)

AD 61 Boadicea rebels against Romans and burns their towns, including St. Albans and Colchester, but is defeated (*see p181*)

AD 70 Romans conquer Wales and the North

Boadicea (1st century), Queen of the Iceni

140–143 Romans occupy southern Scotland and build Antonine Wall to mark the frontier

| 55 BC | AD 1 | AD 50 | | 150 |

AD 43 Claudius invades; Britain becomes part of the Roman Empire

AD 78–84 Agricola advances into Scotland, then retreats

120 Emperor Hadrian builds a wall on the border with Scotland

Flavian Mosaic
*Roman floors of the 1st
century used patterns
in black and white stone.
More mosaics survive
at Fishbourne than at
any other British site.*

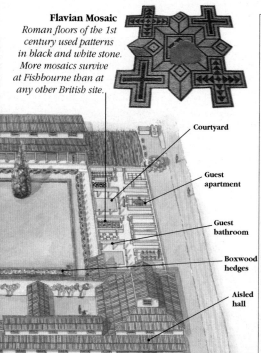

Courtyard

**Guest
apartment**

**Guest
bathroom**

**Boxwood
hedges**

**Aisled
hall**

WHERE TO SEE ROMAN BRITAIN

Many of Britain's main towns
and cities were established
by the Romans and have
Roman remains, including
York *(see pp390–95)*, Chester
(see pp296–7), St. Albans
(see p218), Colchester *(see
p191)*, Bath *(see pp244–7)*,
Lincoln *(see pp326–7)* and
London *(see pp72–121)*.
Several Roman villas were
built in southern England,
favored for its mild climate
and proximity to Europe.

The Roman baths in Bath
*(see pp246–7), known as
Aquae Sulis, were built between
the 1st and 4th centuries
around a natural hot spring.*

Battersea Shield
*Found in the Thames
near Battersea, the
shield bears Celtic
symbols and was
probably made at
about the time of the
first Roman invasion.
Archaeologists suspect
it may have been lost
by a warrior while
crossing the river, or
offered as a sacrifice
to one of the many
river gods. It is now
at the British Museum
(see pp108–9).*

FISHBOURNE PALACE

Built during the 1st century for
Cogidubnus, a pro-Roman governor,
the palace (here reconstructed) had
sophisticated amenities such as under-
floor heating and indoor plumbing
for baths *(see p157)*.

Chi-Rho Symbol
*This early Christian
symbol is from a
3rd-century fresco
at Lullingstone
Roman villa in Kent.*

206 Tribes from
northern Scotland
attack Hadrian's Wall

254 St. Alban is
beheaded, and
becomes Britain's
first Christian
martyr

*Aberlemno Pictish
stone in Scotland*

410 Romans
withdraw
from Britain

200 | 250 | 300 | 350 | 400

209 Septimius Severus
arrives from Rome with
reinforcements

306 Roman troops
in York declare
Constantine emperor

350–69 Border
raids by Picts
and Scots

440–450
Invasions of
Angles, Saxons
and Jutes

Anglo-Saxon Kingdoms

King Canute (1016–35)

BY THE MID-5TH CENTURY, Angles and Saxons from Germany had started to raid the eastern shores of Britain. Increasingly they decided to settle, and within 100 years Saxon kingdoms, including Wessex, Mercia and Northumbria, were established over the entire country. Viking raids throughout the 8th and 9th centuries were largely contained, but in 1066, the last invasion of England saw William the Conqueror from Normandy defeat the Anglo-Saxon King Harold at the Battle of Hastings. William then went on to assume control of the whole country.

Viking Ax
The principal weapons of the Viking warriors were spear, ax and sword. They were skilled metalworkers with an eye for decoration, as seen in this axhead from a Copenhagen museum.

Vikings on a Raiding Expedition
Scandinavian boatbuilding skills were in advance of anything known in Britain. People were terrified by these large, fast boats, with their intimidating figureheads, which sailed up the Thames and along the coasts.

ANGLO-SAXON CALENDAR
These scenes from a chronicle of seasons, made just before the Norman invasion, show life in late Anglo-Saxon Britain. At first people lived in small farming communities, but by the 7th century towns began to spring up and trade increased. Saxon kings were supported by nobles but most of the population were free peasants.

TIMELINE

c.470–495 Saxons and Angles settle in Essex, Sussex and East Anglia	**c.556** Saxons move across Britain and set up seven kingdoms		**635** St. Aidan establishes a monastery on Lindisfarne	*St. Augustine (d.604)* **730–821** Supremacy of Mercia, whose king, Offa (d.796), builds a dike along the Mercia–Wales border

450	500	550	600	650	700	75

450 Saxons first settle in Kent

563 St. Columba lands on Iona

617–85 Supremacy of Northumbrian kingdom

597 St. Augustine sent by Rome to convert English to Christianity

Mercian coin, which bears the name of King Offa

Ox-drawn plow for tilling

Alfred Jewel
This 9th-century gold ornament in the Ashmolean Museum (see p210) *has the inscription: "Alfred ordered me made." This may refer to the Saxon King Alfred.*

WHERE TO SEE ANGLO-SAXON BRITAIN

The best collection of Saxon artifacts is from a burial ship unearthed at Sutton Hoo in Suffolk in 1938 and now on display at the British Museum *(see pp108–9)*. There are fine Saxon churches at Bradwell in Essex and Bosham in Sussex *(see p157)*. In York the Viking town of Jorvik has been excavated *(see pp390–93)* and actual relics are shown alongside models of people and dwellings.

***The Saxon church** of St. Laurence* (see p242) *was built in the late 8th century.*

Minstrels entertaining at a feast

Edward the Confessor
In 1042, Edward – known as "the Confessor" because of his piety – became king. He died in 1066 and William of Normandy claimed the throne.

Hawks, used to kill game

Harold's Death
This 14th-century illustration depicts the victorious William of Normandy after King Harold was killed with an arrow in his eye. The Battle of Hastings (see p167) was the last invasion of Britain.

Legend of King Arthur
Arthur is thought to have been a chieftain who fought the Saxons in the early 6th century. Legends of his knights' exploits appeared in 1155 (see p269).

802–839 After the death of Cenwulf (821), Wessex gains control over most of England

867 Northumbria falls to the Vikings

An invading Norman ship

1016 Danish King Canute *(see p157)* seizes English crown

878 King Alfred defeats Vikings but allows them to settle in eastern England

| 800 | 850 | 900 | 950 | 1000 | 1050 | 1100 |

843 Kenneth McAlpin becomes king of all Scotland

926 Eastern England, the Danelaw, is reconquered by the Saxons

1042 The Anglo-Saxon Edward the Confessor becomes king (d.1066)

1066 William of Normandy claims the throne, and defeats Harold at the Battle of Hastings. He is crowned at Westminster

c.793 Lindisfarne sacked by Viking invaders; first Viking raid on Scotland about a year later

The Middle Ages

Noblemen stag hunting

R EMAINS OF Norman castles on English hilltops bear testimony to the military might used by the invaders to sustain their conquest – in spite of the fact that Wales and Scotland resisted for centuries. The Normans operated a feudal system, creating an aristocracy that treated native Anglo-Saxons as serfs. The ruling class spoke French until the 13th century, when it mixed with the Old English used by the peasants. The medieval church's power is shown in the cathedrals that grace British cities today.

Magna Carta
To protect themselves and the church from arbitrary taxation, the powerful English barons compelled King John to sign a "great charter" in 1215 (see p222). This laid the foundations of an independent legal system.

Becket is received into heaven.

Craft Skills
An illustration from a 14th-century manuscript depicts a weaver and a copper-beater – two of the trades that created a wealthy class of artisans.

Henry II's knights murder Becket in Canterbury Cathedral.

MURDER OF THOMAS À BECKET

The struggle between church and king for ultimate control of the country was brought to a head by the murder of Becket, the Archbishop of Canterbury. After Becket's canonization in 1173, Canterbury became a major center of pilgrimage.

Ecclesiastical Art
Nearly all medieval art had religious themes, such as this window at Canterbury Cathedral (see pp174–5) depicting Jeroboam.

Black Death
A plague swept Britain and Europe several times in the 14th century, killing millions of people. This illustration, in a religious tract, produced about 100 years later, represents death taking its heavy toll.

TIMELINE

1071 Hereward the Wake, leader of the Anglo-Saxon resistance, defeated at Ely

1154 Henry II, the first Plantagenet king, demolishes castles, and exacts money from barons instead of military service

1170 Archbishop of Canterbury, Thomas à Becket, is murdered by four knights after quarreling with Henry II

1100	1150	1200	1250

1086 The *Domesday Book*, a survey of every manor in England, is compiled for tax purposes

Domesday Book

1215 Barons compel King John to sign the *Magna Carta*

1256 Fi Parliament inclu ordina citize

Battle of Agincourt
In 1415, Henry V took an army to France to claim its throne. This 15th-century chronicle depicts Henry beating the French army at Agincourt.

This casket (1190), in a private collection, is said to have contained Becket's remains.

Becket takes his place in Heaven after his canonization.

Two clergymen look on in horror at Becket's murder.

Richard III
Richard, shown in this 16th-century painting, became king during the Wars of the Roses: a bitter struggle for power between two factions of the royal family – the houses of York and Lancaster.

John Wycliffe (1329–84)
This painting by Ford Madox Brown (1821–93) shows Wycliffe with the Bible he translated into English to make it accessible to everyone.

WHERE TO SEE MEDIEVAL BRITAIN

The university cities of Oxford (pp208–13) and Cambridge (pp196–201) contain the largest concentrations of Gothic buildings. Magnificent medieval cathedrals rise high above many historic cities, among them Lincoln (p324) and York (pp390–93). Both cities still retain at least part of their ancient street pattern. Military architecture is best seen in Wales (pp424–5), with the formidable border castles of Edward I.

All Souls College *in Oxford, (see p212), which only takes graduates, is a superb blend of medieval and later architecture.*

Castle Life
Every section of a castle was allotted to a baron whose soldiers helped defend it. This 14th-century illustration shows the coats of arms (see p26) of the barons for each area.

Tudor Renaissance

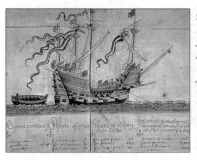

Hawking, a popular pastime

AFTER YEARS OF DEBILITATING civil war, the Tudor monarchs established peace and national self-confidence, reflected in the split from the church of Rome – due to Henry VIII's divorce from Catherine of Aragon – and the consequent closure of the monasteries. Henry's daughter, Mary I, tried to re-establish Catholicism but under her half-sister, Elizabeth I, the Protestant church secured its position. Overseas exploration began, provoking clashes with other European powers seeking to exploit the New World. The Renaissance in arts and learning spread from Europe to Britain, with playwright William Shakespeare adding his own unique contribution.

Curtains behind the queen are open to reveal scenes of the great English victory over the Spanish Armada in 1588.

Sea Power
Henry VIII laid the foundations of the powerful English navy. In 1545, his flagship, the Mary Rose *(see p155), sank before his eyes in Portsmouth harbor on its way to do battle with the French.*

Theater
Some of Shakespeare's plays were first seen in specially designed theaters such as the Globe *(see p119) in south London.*

The globe signifies that the queen reigns supreme far and wide.

Monasteries
With Henry VIII's split from Rome, England's religious houses, like Fountains Abbey (see pp376–7), were dissolved. Henry stole their riches and used them to finance his foreign policy.

TIMELINE

1497 John Colet denounces the corruption of the clergy, supported by Erasmus and Sir Thomas More

1533–4 Henry VIII divorces Catherine of Aragon and is excommunicated by the Pope. He forms the Church of England

1542–1567 Mary, Queen of Scots rules Scotland

1490	1510	1530

1497 John Cabot (*see pp242–3*) becomes the first European to reach Newfoundland

1513 English defeat Scots at Flodden (*see p468*)

Henry VIII (1491–1547)

1535 Act of Union with Wales

1536–40 Dissolution of the Monasteries

1549 First Book Common Pray introduc

Mary, Queen of Scots
As great-granddaughter of Henry VII, she laid claim to the English throne in 1559. But in 1567, Elizabeth I had her imprisoned for 20 years until her execution for treason in 1587.

Jewels symbolize triumph.

WHERE TO SEE TUDOR BRITAIN

Hampton Court Palace *(p159)* has been altered over the centuries but remains a Tudor showpiece. Part of Elizabeth I's former home at Hatfield *(p217)* still survives. In Kent, Leeds Castle, Knole *(p172)* and Hever Castle *(p173)* all have connections with Tudor royalty. Burghley House *(pp328–9)* and Hardwick Hall *(p288)*, both Midlands mansions, retain their 16th-century character.

***This astronomical clock** at Hampton Court (see p158), with its intriguing zodiac symbols, was installed in 1540 by Henry VIII.*

Protestant Martyrs
Catholic Mary I reigned from 1553 to 1558. Protestants who opposed her rule were burned, such as these six churchmen at Canterbury in 1555.

DEFEAT OF THE ARMADA

Spain was England's main rival for supremacy on the seas, and in 1588 Philip II sent 100 powerfully armed galleons towards England, bent on invasion. The English fleet – under Lord Howard, Francis Drake, John Hawkins and Martin Frobisher – sailed from Plymouth and destroyed the Spanish navy in a famous victory. This commemorative portrait of Elizabeth I by George Gower (d.1596) celebrates the triumph.

William Shakespeare 1564–1616)

1570 Sir Francis Drake's first voyage to the West Indies

1584 Sir Walter Raleigh tries to colonize Virginia after Drake's first unsuccessful attempt

1591 First play by Shakespeare performed

1600 East India Company founded, beginning British involvement on the Indian continent

1570

1590

1553 Death of Edward VI; throne passes to the Catholic Mary I

1559 Mary, Queen of Scots lays claim to English throne

1558 Elizabeth I ascends to the throne

1587 Execution of Mary, Queen of Scots on the orders of Elizabeth I

1588 Defeat of the Spanish Armada

Sir Walter Raleigh (1552–1618)

1603 Union of Crowns. James VI of Scotland becomes James I of England

Stuart Britain

THE END of Elizabeth I's reign signaled the start of internal turmoil. The throne passed to James I, whose belief that kings ruled by divine right provoked clashes with Parliament. Under his son, Charles I, the conflict escalated into Civil War that ended with his execution. In 1660 Charles II regained the throne, but after his death James II was ousted for Catholic leanings. Protestantism was reaffirmed with the reign of William and Mary, who suppressed the Catholic Jacobites (see p469).

A 17th-century barber's bowl

Science
Sir Isaac Newton (1642–1727) invented this reflecting telescope, laying the foundation for a greater understanding of the universe, including the law of gravity.

Charles I stayed silent at his trial.

Oliver Cromwell
A strict Protestant and a passionate champion of the rights of Parliament, he led the victorious Parliamentary forces in the Civil War. He became Lord Protector of the Commonwealth from 1653 to 1658.

On the way to his death, the king wore two shirts for warmth, so onlookers should not think he was shivering with fright.

Theater
After the Restoration in 1660 when Parliament restored the monarchy, theater thrived. Plays were performed on temporary outdoor stages.

EXECUTION OF CHARLES I
Cromwell was convinced there would be no peace until the king was dead. At his trial for treason, Charles refused to recognize the authority of the court and offered no defense. He faced his death with dignity on January 30, 1649, the only English king to be executed. His death was followed by a republic known as the Commonwealth.

TIMELINE

1605 "Gunpowder Plot" to blow up Parliament thwarted	**1614** "Addled Parliament" refuses to vote money for James I	**1620** Pilgrim Fathers sail in the *Mayflower* to New England	**1642** Civil war breaks out	**1653–8** Cromwell rules as Lord Protector	
		1625			**1650**
James I (1566–1625)	**1611** New translation of Bible published, known as King James Version	**1638** Scots sign National Covenant, opposing Charles I's Catholic leanings	**1649** Charles I executed outside Banqueting House and Commonwealth declared by Parliament	**1660** Restoration of the monarchy under Charles

Restoration of the Monarchy

This silk embroidery celebrates the fact that Charles II escaped his father's fate by hiding in an oak tree. There was joy at his return from exile in France.

The headless body kneels by the block.

The axman holds the severed head of Charles I.

Plague
Bills of mortality showed the weekly deaths as bubonic plague swept London in 1665. Nearly 100,000 Londoners died.

Onlookers soaked up the king's blood with their hand-kerchiefs to have a memento.

Anatomy
By dissecting corpses, physicians began to gain an understanding of the working of the human body – a crucial step towards modern surgery and medicine.

WHERE TO SEE STUART BRITAIN

The best work of the two leading architects of the time, Inigo Jones and Christopher Wren, is in London, and includes St. Paul's Cathedral *(pp116–17)*. In the southeast two classic Jacobean mansions are Audley End *(p194)* and Hatfield House *(p175)*. The Palace of Holyrood *(p495)* in Edinburgh, is another example.

Hatfield House (p275) *is a splendid Jacobean mansion.*

Pilgrim Fathers
In 1620 a group of Puritans sailed to America. They forged good relations with the native Indians; here they are shown being visited by the chief of the Pokanokets.

1665–6 Great Plague

1666 Great Fire of London

The Great Fire of London

1688 The Glorious Revolution: Catholic James II deposed by Parliament

1707 Act of Union with Scotland

1675

1700

1690 Battle of the Boyne: William's English/Dutch army defeats James II's Irish/French army

1692 Glencoe Massacre of Jacobites (Stuart supporters) by William III's forces

William III (1689–1702)

Georgian Britain

THE 18TH CENTURY saw Britain, now recovered from the trauma of its Civil War, develop as a commercial and industrial powerhouse. London became a center of banking, and a mercantile and professional class grew up. Continuing supremacy at sea laid the foundations of an empire; steam engines, canals and railroads heralded the Industrial Revolution. Growing confidence was reflected in stately architecture and elegant fashions but, as cities became more crowded, conditions for the underclass grew worse.

Slate became the preferred tile for Georgian buildings. Roofs became less steep to achieve an Italian look.

A row of sash windows is one of the most characteristic features of a Georgian house.

Actress Sarah Siddons (1785), Gainsborough

Battle of Bunker Hill

In 1775 American colonists rebelled against British rule. The British won this early battle in Massachusetts, but in 1783 Britain recognised the United States of America.

Oak was used in the best dwellings for doors and stairs, but pine was standard in most houses.

The parlor was covered in wallpaper, a cheaper alternative to hanging walls with tapestries or fabrics.

The drawing room was richly ornamented and used for entertaining visitors.

Watt's Steam Engine
The Scottish engineer James Watt (1736–1819) patented his engine in 1769 and then developed it for locomotion.

The dining room was used for all family meals.

Lord Horatio Nelson
Nelson (see p27) became a hero after his death at the Battle of Trafalgar fighting the French.

Steps led to the servants' entrance in the basement.

TIMELINE

1720 "South Sea Bubble" bursts: many speculators ruined in securities fraud

1746 Bonnie Prince Charlie (see p521), Jacobite claimant to throne, defeated at the Battle of Culloden

1715	1730	1745	1760

1714 George, Elector of Hanover, succeeds Queen Anne, ending the Stuart dynasty and giving Britain a German-speaking monarch

1721 Robert Walpole (1717–97) becomes the first Prime Minister

George I (1660–1727)

Satirical engraving about the South Sea Bubble, 1720

1757 Britain's first canal completed

The attics were where children and servants slept.

The master bedroom often had a mahogany four-poster bed.

Furniture was often carved, depicting animal heads and legs.

Canal Barge *(1827)*
Canals were a cheap way to carry the new industrial goods but were gradually superseded by railroads during the 19th century.

Chippendale Armchair *(1760)*
Thomas Chippendale (1718–79) designed elegant furniture in a style still popular today.

GEORGIAN TOWN HOUSE

Tall, terraced dwellings were built to house wealthy families. The main architects of the time were Robert Adam *(see p24)* and John Nash *(see p107)*.

The servants lived and worked in the basement during the day.

Kitchen

WHERE TO SEE GEORGIAN BRITAIN

Bath *(see pp244–7)* and Edinburgh *(see pp490–7)* are two of Britain's best-preserved Georgian towns. The Building of Bath Museum in Bath *(see p247)* has a real Georgian flavor and Brighton's Royal Pavilion *(see pp164–5)* is a Regency extravaganza by John Nash.

Charlotte Square (see p490) *in Edinburgh has fine examples of Georgian architecture.*

Hogarth's Gin Lane
Conditions in London's slums shocked William Hogarth (1694–1764), who made prints like this to urge social reform.

	1788 First convict ships are sent to Australia	**1811–17** Riots against growing unemployment	**1815** Duke of Wellington beats Napoleon at Waterloo	*Caricature of Wellington (1769–1852)*
1776 American Declaration of Independence	**1805** The British, led by Lord Nelson, beat Napoleon's French fleet at Battle of Trafalgar			
1775	1790	1805	1820	
	1783 Steam-powered cotton mill invented by Sir Richard Arkwright (1732–92)	**1807** Abolition of slave trade	**1811** Prince of Wales made Regent during George III's madness	**1825** Stockton to Darlington railroad opens	**1829** Catholic Emancipation Act passed

Silver tureen, 1774

Victorian Britain

WHEN VICTORIA BECAME QUEEN in 1837, she was only 18. Britain was in the throes of its transformation from an agricultural country to the world's most powerful industrial nation. The growth of the Empire fueled the country's confidence and opened up markets for Britain's manufactured goods. The accelerating growth of cities created problems of health and housing and a powerful Labour movement began to emerge. But by the end of Victoria's long and popular reign in 1901, conditions had begun to improve as more people got the vote and universal education was introduced.

Victoria and Disraeli, 1887

Florence Nightingale *(1820–1910)*
Known as the Lady with the Lamp, she nursed soldiers in the Crimean War and pioneered many improvements in army medical care.

Newcastle Slum *(1880)*
Rows of cheap houses were built for an influx of workers to the major industrial cities. The awful conditions spread disease and social discontent.

Glass walls and ceiling

Prefabricated girders

As well as silk textiles, exhibits included carriages, engines, jewels, glass, plants, cutlery and sculptures.

Union Banner
Trade unions were set up to protect industrial workers against unscrupulous employers.

Ophelia by Sir John Everett Millais *(1829–96)*
The Pre-Raphaelite painters chose Romantic themes, reflecting a desire to escape industrial Britain.

TIMELINE

1832 Great Reform Bill extends the vote to all male property owners

1841 London to Brighton railroad makes resort accessible

Vase made for the Great Exhibition

1851 Great Exhibition

1867 Second Reform Act gives the vote to all male householders in towns

1830	1840	1850	1860

1834 Tolpuddle Martyrs sent to Australia for forming a union

1833 Factory Act forbids employment of children for more than 48 hours per week

1854–6 Britain victorious against Russia in Crimean War

1863 Opening of the London Underground

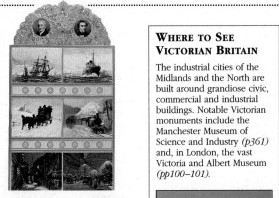

Triumph of Steam and Electricity (1897)
This picture from the Illustrated London News *sums up the optimism engendered by the tremendous industrial advances.*

Elm trees were incorporated into the building along with sparrows, and sparrow hawks to control them.

WHERE TO SEE VICTORIAN BRITAIN

The industrial cities of the Midlands and the North are built around grandiose civic, commercial and industrial buildings. Notable Victorian monuments include the Manchester Museum of Science and Industry *(p361)* and, in London, the vast Victoria and Albert Museum *(pp100–101)*.

The Rotunda, Manchester *is a stately Victorian building.*

GREAT EXHIBITION OF 1851

The brainchild of Prince Albert, Victoria's consort, the exhibition celebrated industry, technology and the expanding British Empire. It was the biggest of its kind held up until then. Between May and October, six million people visited Joseph Paxton's lavish crystal palace, in London's Hyde Park. Nearly 14,000 exhibitors brought 100,000 exhibits from all over the world. In 1852 it was moved to south London, where it burned down in 1936.

Cycling Craze
The bicycle, invented in 1865, became immensely popular with young people, as illustrated by this etching of 1898.

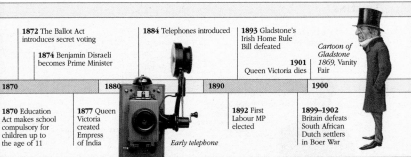

1872 The Ballot Act introduces secret voting

1874 Benjamin Disraeli becomes Prime Minister

1884 Telephones introduced

1893 Gladstone's Irish Home Rule Bill defeated

Cartoon of Gladstone 1869, Vanity Fair

1901 Queen Victoria dies

1870   1880   1890   1900

1870 Education Act makes school compulsory for children up to the age of 11

1877 Queen Victoria created Empress of India

Early telephone

1892 First Labour MP elected

1899–1902 Britain defeats South African Dutch settlers in Boer War

Britain from 1900 to 1950

W̶HEN QUEEN VICTORIA'S REIGN ended in 1901, British society threw off many of its 19th-century inhibitions. An era of gaiety and excitement began. This was interrupted by World War I and the economic troubles that ensued. These culminated in the Depression of the 1930s that brought misery to millions. In 1939 German ambitions provoked World War II from which Britain emerged victorious and embarked on a far-reaching program of social reform.

Playwright Noel Coward

Welwyn Garden City was based on the Utopian idea of Sir Ebenezer Howard (1850–1928), founder of the garden city movement.

Suffragettes
Women marched and chained themselves to railings in their effort to get the vote; many went to prison. Women over 30 won the vote in 1919.

The Roaring Twenties
Young flappers discarded the rigid social codes of their parents and instead discovered jazz, cocktails and the Charleston.

New Towns
A string of new towns was created on the outskirts of London, planned to give residents greenery and fresh air. Welwyn Garden City was originally founded in 1919 as a self-contained community, but fast rail links turned it into a base for London commuters.

World War I
British troops in Europe dug into deep trenches protected by barbed wire and machine guns, only yards from the enemy, in a war of attrition that cost the lives of 17 million.

Wireless
Invented by Guglielmo Marconi, radios brought news and entertainment into homes for the first time.

WE GAR

HOUS £44 OR FOR SALE PART WELWYN or 64.

Timeline

1903 Suffragette movement founded

1911 MPs are given a salary for the first time, allowing working men to be elected

1914–18 World War I

1924 First Labour government

| 1905 | 1910 | 1915 | 1920 |

Henry Asquith (1852–1928), Prime Minister

1908 Asquith's Liberal government introduces old age pensions

1919 Vote given to all women over 30

1922 First national radio service begins

Marching for Jobs
These men were among thousands who marched for their jobs after being put out of work in the 1920s. The stock market crash of 1929 and the ensuing Depression caused even more unemployment.

Garden cities
ll had trees,
onds and
pen spaces.

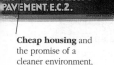

World War II
German nighttime air raids targeted transportation, military and industrial sites and cities, such as Sheffield, in what was known as the "Blitz."

WYN
N CITY

TO LET
PER ANNUM
AL PURCHASE TERMS
M ESTATE OFFICE
EN CITY. HERTS.
PAVEMENT. E.C.2.

Cheap housing and the promise of a cleaner environment, attracted many people to these new cities.

HILLMAN MINX

Family Motoring
By the middle of the century, more families could afford to buy mass-produced automobiles, like the 1950s Hillman Minx pictured in this advertisement.

Modern Homes
Laborsaving devices, such as the vacuum cleaner, invented by William Hoover in 1908, were very popular. This was due to the virtual disappearance of domestic servants, as women took jobs outside the home.

1926 General Strike		**1936** Abdication of Edward VIII	**1944** Education Act; school-leaving age raised to 15; grants provided for university students	**1948** National Health Service introduced

Edward VIII (1894–1972) and Wallis Simpson (1896–1986)

1947 Independence for India and Pakistan

1930	1935	1940	1945

1929 Stock market crashes

1936 First scheduled television service begins

1939–45 Winston Churchill leads Britain to victory in World War II

1928 Votes for all men and women over 21

Food ration book

RATION BOOK

1945 Majority Labour government; nationalization of railroads, trucking, civil aviation, Bank of England, gas, electricity and steel

Britain Today

Designer Vivienne Westwood and Naomi Campbell

WITH THE DEPRIVATIONS of war receding, Britain entered the Swinging Sixties, an explosion of youth culture characterized by the miniskirt and the emergence of pop groups. The Age of Empire came to an end as most colonies gained independence by the 1970s – although Britain went to war again in 1982 when Argentina sought to annex the tiny Falkland Islands.

People were on the move; immigration from the former colonies enriched British culture – though it also gave rise to social problems – and increasing prosperity allowed millions of people to travel abroad. Britain joined the European Community in 1973, and forged a more tangible link when the Channel Tunnel opened in 1994.

1960s The mini-skirt takes British fashion to new heights of daring – and Flower Power arrives from California

1951 Winston Churchill comes back as Prime Minister as Conservatives win general election

1958 Campaign for Nuclear Disarmament launched, reflecting young people's fear of global annihilation

1965 Death penalty is abolished

1950	1955	1960	1965	1970
1950	1955	1960	1965	1970

1953 Elizabeth II crowned in first televised Coronation

1963 The Beatles pop group from Liverpool captures the spirit of the age with numerous chart-topping hits

1959 First highway, the M1, built from London to the Midlands

1957 First immigrants arrive from the Caribbean by boat

1951 Festival of Britain lifts postwar spirits

1973 After years of negotiation, Britain joins the European Community

1970s The outlandish clothes, hair and make-up of Punk Rockers shock the country

1990 Mrs. Thatcher forced to resign by Conservative MPs; replaced by John Major

1982 British troops set sail to drive the Argentinians from the British-owned Falkland Islands

1991 Britain's tallest building, Canada Tower *(see p131)*, erected as part of the huge Docklands development – London's new financial center

1992 Conservative Government elected for fourth term – a record for this century

1976 Supersonic Concorde makes first commercial flight

1984 Year-long miners' strike fails to stop pit closures and heralds decline in trade union power

| '5 | 1980 | 1985 | 1990 | 1995 |

| '5 | 1980 | 1985 | 1990 | 1995 |

1981 Charles, Prince of Wales, marries Lady Diana Spencer in "fairytale" wedding at St. Paul's Cathedral

'5 Drilling ins for th Sea oil

1994 Oil reserves found off west coast of Scotland

1979 The "Iron Lady" Margaret Thatcher becomes Britain's first woman Prime Minister; her right-wing Conservative Government privatizes several state-owned industries

1985 Concern for famine in Africa gives rise to giant Live Aid pop concert to raise money for the starving

1994 Channel Tunnel opens to give direct rail link between Britain and Continental Europe

GREAT BRITAIN THROUGH THE YEAR

Every British season has its particular charms. Most major sights are open all year round, but many secondary attractions may be closed in winter. The weather is changeable in all seasons and the visitor is as likely to experience a crisp, sunny February day as to be caught in a cold, heavy shower in July. Long periods of

Film festival sign

adverse weather and extremes of temperature are rare. Spring is characterized by daffodils and bluebells, summer by roses and autumn by the vivid colors of changing leaves. In wintertime, country vistas are visible through the bare branches of the trees. Annual events and ceremonies, many stemming from age-old traditions, reflect the attributes of each season.

Bluebells in spring in Angrove woodland, Wiltshire

SPRING

As the days get longer and warmer, the countryside starts to come alive. At Easter many stately homes and gardens open their gates to visitors for the first time, and during the week before Whit Sunday, or Whitsun (the seventh Sunday after Easter), the Chelsea Flower Show takes place. This is the focal point of the gardening year and spurs on the nation's gardeners to prepare their summer displays. Outside the capital, many music and arts festivals mark the middle months of the year.

MARCH

Ideal Home Exhibition *(second week)*, Earl's Court, London. New products and ideas for the home.
Crufts Dog Show *(second week)*, National Exhibition Centre, Birmingham.
International Book Fair *(third week)*, Olympia, London.
St. Patrick's Day *(March 17)*. Musical events in major cities celebrate the feast day of Ireland's patron saint.

APRIL

Maundy Thursday (Thursday before Easter), the Queen gives money to the elderly.
St. George's Day *(April 23)*, English patron saint's day.
British International Antiques Fair *(last week)*, National Exhibition Centre, Birmingham.

Water garden exhibited at the Chelsea Flower Show

MAY

Furry Dancing Festival *(May 8)*, Helston, Cornwall. Spring celebration *(see p266)*.
Well-dressing festivals *(Ascension Day)*, Tissington, Derbyshire *(see p323)*.
Chelsea Flower Show *(mid-May)*, Royal Hospital, London.
Brighton Festival *(last three weeks)*. Performing arts.
Glyndebourne Festival Opera Season *(mid-May–end Aug)*, near Lewes, East Sussex. Opera productions.
International Highland Games *(last weekend)*, Blair Atholl, Scotland.

Yeomen of the Guard conducting the Maundy money ceremony

SUMMER

Life moves outdoors in the summer months. Cafés and restaurants place tables on the pavements and pub customers take their drinks outside. The Queen holds garden parties for privileged guests at Buckingham Palace while, more modestly, village fêtes – a combination of a carnival and street party – are organized. Beaches and swimming pools become crowded and office workers picnic in city parks at lunch. The rose, England's national flower, bursts into bloom in millions of gardens. Cultural treats include open-air theater performances, outdoor concerts, the Proms in London, the National Eisteddfod in Wales, Glyndebourne's opera festival, and Edinburgh's festival of the performing arts.

Deck chair at Brighton

Glastonbury music festival, a major event attracting thousands of people

London. The Queen's official birthday parade.

Glastonbury Festival *(June 23–25)*, Somerset.

Aldeburgh Festival *(second and third weeks)*, Suffolk. Arts festival with concerts and opera.

Royal Highland Show *(third week)*, Ingliston, near Edinburgh. Scotland's agricultural show.

Leeds Castle *(last week)*. Open-air concerts.

Glasgow International Jazz Festival *(last weekend)*. Various places.

JULY

Royal Show *(first week)*, near Kenilworth, Warwickshire. National agricultural show.

International Eisteddfod *(first week)*, Llangollen, North Wales. International music and dance competition *(see p436)*.

Hampton Court Flower Show *(early July)*, Hampton Court Palace, Surrey.

Summer Music Festival *(third weekend)*, Stourhead, Wiltshire.

Royal Tournament *(third and fourth weeks)*, Earl's Court, London. Displays by the armed forces.

Cambridge Folk Festival *(last weekend)*. Music festival with top international artists.

Royal Welsh Show *(last weekend)*, Builth Wells, Wales. Agricultural show.

International Festival of Folk Arts *(late Jul–early Aug)*, Sidmouth, Devon *(see p275)*.

JUNE

Royal Academy Summer Exhibitions *(Jun–Aug)*. Large and varied London show of new work by many artists.

Bath International Festival *(May 19–Jun 4)*, various venues. Arts events.

Beaumaris Festival *(May 27–Jun 4)*, various places. Concerts, craft fairs plus fringe activities.

Trooping the Colour *(Sat closest to Jun 10)*, Whitehall,

Assessment of sheep at the Royal Welsh Show, Builth Wells

AUGUST

Royal National Eisteddfod *(early in month)*. Traditional arts competitions, in Welsh *(see p421)*. Various locations.

Reveler in bright costume at the Notting Hill Carnival

Henry Wood Promenade Concerts *(mid-Jul–mid-Sep)*, Royal Albert Hall, London. Famous concert series popularly known as the Proms.

Edinburgh International Festival *(mid-Aug–mid-Sep)*. The largest festival of theater, dance and music in the world *(see p495)*.

Edinburgh Festival Fringe. Alongside the festival, there are 400 shows a day.

Brecon Jazz *(mid-Aug)*, jazz festival in Brecon, Wales.

Beatles Festival *(last weekend)*, Liverpool. Music and entertainment related to the Fab Four *(see p363)*.

Notting Hill Carnival *(last weekend)*, London. West Indian street carnival with floats, bands and stalls.

Boxes of apples from the autumn harvest

AUTUMN

AFTER THE HEADY escapism of summer, the start of the new season is marked by the various party political conferences held in October and the royal opening of Parliament. All over the country on November 5, bonfires are lit and fireworks let off to celebrate the foiling of an attempt to blow up the Houses of Parliament by Guy Fawkes and his co-conspirators in 1605. Cornfields become golden, trees turn fiery yellow through to russet and orchards are heavy with apples and other autumn fruits. In churches throughout the country, thanksgiving festivals mark the harvest. The shops stock up for the rush to Christmas, their busiest time of the year.

Shot putting at Braemar

SEPTEMBER

Blackpool Illuminations *(beg Sep–end Oct)*. A 5-mile (8-km) spectacle of lighting along Blackpool's seafront.
Royal Highland Gathering *(first Sat)*, Braemar, Scotland. Kilted clansmen from all over the country toss cabers, practise shotputting, dance and play the bagpipes. The royal family usually attends.
International Sheepdog Trials *(14–16 Sep)*, all over Britain, with venues changing from year to year.
Great Autumn Flower Show *(third weekend)*, Harrogate, N Yorks. Displays by nurserymen and flower organizations.
Horse of the Year Show *(last weekend)*, Wembley, London *(see p67)*.
Oyster Festival *(Sat at start of season)*, Colchester. Mayor hosts lunch to celebrate the start of the oyster season.

Fireworks over Edinburgh on Guy Fawkes Night

OCTOBER

Harvest Festivals *(whole month)*, all over Britain especially in farming areas.
Nottingham Goose Fair *(second weekend)*. One of Britain's oldest fairs with an amusement park.
Canterbury Festival *(second and third weeks)*. Music, drama and the arts.
Aldeburgh Britten Festival *(third weekend)*. Concerts with music by Britten *(see p189)* and other composers.
Hallowe'en *(Oct 31)*, "trick or treat" games countrywide.

Procession leading to the state opening of Parliament

NOVEMBER

Opening of Parliament *(Oct or Nov)*. The Queen goes from Buckingham Palace to Westminster in a state coach, to open the new parliamentary session.
Lord Mayor's Procession and Show *(second Sat)*. Parade in the City, London.
Remembrance Day *(second Sun)*. Services and parades at the Cenotaph, Whitehall, London and all over Britain.
RAC London to Brighton Veteran Car Rally *(first Sun)*. A 7am start from Hyde Park, London to Brighton, East Sussex.
Guy Fawkes Night *(Nov 5)*, fireworks and bonfires all over the country.
London Film Festival *(first two weeks)*. Forum for new films, various places.
Regent Street Christmas Lights *(mid-Nov)*, London.

Winter landscape in the Scottish Highlands, near Glen Coe

WINTER

BRIGHTLY COLORED fairy lights and Christmas trees decorate Britain's principal shopping streets as shoppers rush to buy their seasonal gifts. Carol services are held in churches across the country, and pantomime, a traditional entertainment for children deriving from the Victorian music hall, fills theaters in major towns.

Brightly lit Christmas tree at the center of Trafalgar Square

Many offices close between Christmas and the New Year. Shops reopen for the January sales on December 27 – a paradise for bargain hunters.

DECEMBER

Christmas Tree *(first Thu)*, Trafalgar Square, London. The tree is donated by the people of Norway and is lit by the Mayor of Oslo; this is followed by carol singing.
Carol concerts *(month)*, all over Britain. **Grand Christmas Parade** *(beg Dec)*, London. Parade with floats to celebrate myth of Santa Claus.
Midnight Mass *(Dec 24)*, in churches everywhere around Britain.
Allendale Baal Festival *(Dec 31)*, Northumberland. Parade by villagers with burning tar barrels on their heads to celebrate the New Year.

Sprig of holly

JANUARY

Hogmanay *(Jan 1)*, Scottish New Year celebrations.
Burns Night *(Jan 14)*. Scots everywhere celebrate poet Robert Burns' birth with poetry, feasting and drinking.

FEBRUARY

Chinese New Year *(late Jan or early Feb)*. Lion dances, firecrackers and processions in Chinatown, London.

PUBLIC HOLIDAYS

New Year's Day (Jan 1).
Jan 2 (Scotland only).
Easter weekend (March or April). In England it begins on **Good Friday** and ends on **Easter Monday**; in Scotland there is no Easter Monday holiday.
May Day (usually first Mon in May).
Late Spring Bank Holiday (last Mon in May).
Bank Holiday (first Mon in August, Scotland only).
August Bank Holiday (last Mon in August, except Scotland).
Christmas and Boxing Day (December 25, 26).

Morris dancing on May Day in Midhurst, Sussex

The Year in Sports

MANY OF THE WORLD'S major competitive sports, including soccer, cricket and tennis, were invented in Britain. Originally devised as recreation for the wealthy, they have entered the arena of mass entertainment. Some, however, such as the Royal Ascot race meeting and Wimbledon tennis tournament, are still valued as much for their social cachet as for the sport itself. Other delightful sporting events in Britain take place on a local level: village cricket, point-to-point racing and the Highland Games are all popular amateur sports events.

Linford Christie

Oxford and Cambridge Boat Race *was first held in 1845 and has become a national event, with the two university eights battling it out between Putney and Mortlake on the Thames.*

Royal Ascot *is the four-day social highlight of the horse racing year. The high class of the thoroughbreds is matched by the high style of the fashion, with royalty attending.*

FA Cup Final *at Wembley is the apex of the soccer season.*

Derby Day horse races, Epsom

January	February	March	April	May	June

Cheltenham Gold Cup steeplechase *(see p314)*

Grand National steeplechase, Aintree *(see p363)* **Liverpool**

Rugby League Cup Final, Wembley

Embassy World Snooker Championship, Sheffield

Wimbledon Lawn Tennis Championships *are the world's most prestigious tennis tournament held on grass.*

Henley Royal Regatta *(see p221) is an international rowing event that takes place on the River Thames. It is also a glamorous social occasion.*

Five Nations Rugby Union *is an annual contest between England (right), France, Ireland, Scotland and Wales (left). This league-based competition runs through the winter months and ends in March.*

London Marathon *attracts thousands of long-distance runners, from the world's best to fancy-dressed fund raisers.*

British Grand Prix, held at Silverstone, is Britain's round of the Formula One World Championship.

TICKETS AND SCALPERS

For many big sporting events, the only official source of tickets is the club concerned. Booking agencies may offer hard-to-get tickets – though often at high prices. Scalpers may lurk at popular events but their expensive tickets are not always valid. Check carefully.

Tickets for the Grand Prix

***British Open Golf Championship**, a major golf event, is held at one of several British courses. Here, Nick Faldo putts.*

***The NatWest Trophy** is the main one-day county cricket competition, with the final held at Lord's, the game's London shrine (see p127).*

Cowes week *(see p154), a yachting festival, covers all classes of racing.*

Horse of the Year Show brings together top showjumpers to compete on a tough indoor course *(see p64).*

Oxford versus Cambridge rugby union, Twickenham

August	September	October	November	December

Silk Cut showjumping, Hickstead

Gold Cup Humber powerboat race, Hull

Braemar High-land Games *(see p64)*

***British Figure Skating and Ice Dance Championships** are a feast of elegance on ice (various places).*

Winmau World Darts Championships, London

KEY TO SPORT SEASONS

- Cricket
- River fishing
- Soccer
- Hunting and shooting
- Rugby (union and league)
- Flat racing
- Jump racing
- Athletics – track and field
- Road running and cross-country
- Polo

Jane Torvill and Christopher Dean

***Cartier International Polo**, at the Guards Club, Windsor (see p221), is one of the main events for this peculiarly British game, played mainly by royalty and army officers.*

The Climate of Great Britain

BRITAIN HAS A TEMPERATE CLIMATE. No region is far from the sea, which exerts a moderating influence on temperatures. Seldom are winter nights colder than -15° C (5° F), even in the far north, or summer days warmer than 30° C (86° F) in the south and west: a much narrower range than in most European countries. Despite Britain's reputation, the average annual rainfall is quite low – less than 100 cm (40 inches) – and heavy rain is rare. The west coast is warmer and wetter than the east.

LANCASHIRE AND THE LAKES

°F			
	66		
53	55	56	
41		46	43
			35

5.5 hrs	6 hrs	3 hrs	1.5 hrs
2.1 in	3.3 in	4.1 in	3.5 in
month	Apr	Jul	Oct	Jan

THE HEART OF ENGLAND

°F			
	68		
54	54.5	55	
40		45	42
			35

4.5 hrs	5.5 hrs	3 hrs	1.5 hrs
2.1 in	2.7 in	2.7 in	2.9 in
month	Apr	Jul	Oct	Jan

Average monthly maximum temperature

Average monthly minimum temperature

Average daily hours of sunshine

Average monthly rainfall

SOUTH AND MID-WALES

°F			
	69		
55	54.5	57	
41		45	44
			36

5.5 hrs	6 hrs	3.5 hrs	1.5 hrs
2.6 in	3.5 in	4.3 in	4.3 in
month	Apr	Jul	Oct	Jan

NORTH WALES

°F			
	63		
52	52	56	
40		46	43
			34

3 hrs	3.5 hrs	2.5 hrs	1.5 hrs
5.7 in	8.1 in	10.3 in	9.9 in
month	Apr	Jul	Oct	Jan

DEVON AND CORNWALL

°F			
	66		
54.5	55	58	
43		48	46
			39

6 hrs	6.5 hrs	3.5 hrs	2 hrs
2.1 in	2.8 in	3.6 in	3.9 in
month	Apr	Jul	Oct	Jan

WEST COUNTRY

°F			
	69		
56	56	59	
42		47	45
			36

5.5 hrs	6.5 hrs	3.5 hrs	2 hrs
1.9 in	2.6 in	3.3 in	2.9 in
month	Apr	Jul	Oct	Jan

THAMES VALLEY

°F			
	71		
56	54.5	58	
40		44	44
			34

5.5 hrs	6 hrs	3 hrs	1.5 hrs
1.6 in	2.2 in	2.5 in	2.4 in
month	Apr	Jul	Oct	Jan

THE HIGHLANDS AND ISLANDS

°F

month	Apr	Jul	Oct	Jan
high °F	52	63	55	44
low °F	37	50	44	34
sun	4.5 hrs	3.5 hrs	2 hrs	1 hrs
rain	4.4 in	5.4 in	8.5 in	7.9 in

THE LOWLANDS

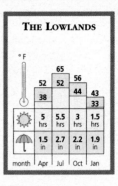

°F

month	Apr	Jul	Oct	Jan
high °F	52	65	56	43
low °F	38	52	44	33
sun	5 hrs	5.5 hrs	3 hrs	1.5 hrs
rain	1.5 in	2.7 in	2.2 in	1.9 in

NORTHUMBRIA

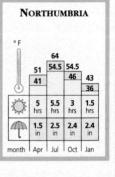

°F

month	Apr	Jul	Oct	Jan
high °F	51	64	54.5	43
low °F	41	54.5	46	36
sun	5 hrs	5.5 hrs	3 hrs	1.5 hrs
rain	1.5 in	2.5 in	2.4 in	2.4 in

YORKSHIRE AND HUMBERSIDE

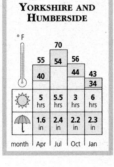

°F

month	Apr	Jul	Oct	Jan
high °F	55	70	56	43
low °F	40	54	44	34
sun	5 hrs	5.5 hrs	3 hrs	6 hrs
rain	1.6 in	2.4 in	2.2 in	2.3 in

EAST MIDLANDS

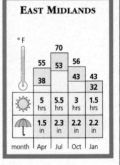

°F

month	Apr	Jul	Oct	Jan
high °F	55	70	56	43
low °F	38	53	43	32
sun	5 hrs	5.5 hrs	3 hrs	1.5 hrs
rain	1.5 in	2.3 in	2.2 in	2.2 in

THE DOWNS AND CHANNEL COAST

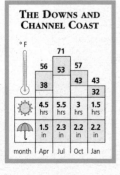

°F

month	Apr	Jul	Oct	Jan
high °F	56	71	57	43
low °F	38	53	43	32
sun	4.5 hrs	5.5 hrs	3 hrs	1.5 hrs
rain	1.5 in	2.3 in	2.2 in	2.2 in

LONDON

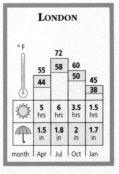

°F

month	Apr	Jul	Oct	Jan
high °F	55	72	60	45
low °F	44	58	50	38
sun	5 hrs	6 hrs	3.5 hrs	1.5 hrs
rain	1.5 in	1.8 in	2 in	1.7 in

EAST ANGLIA

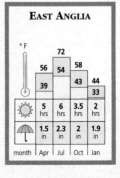

°F

month	Apr	Jul	Oct	Jan
high °F	56	72	58	44
low °F	39	54	43	33
sun	5 hrs	6 hrs	3.5 hrs	2 hrs
rain	1.5 in	2.3 in	2 in	1.9 in

Northumbria

Newcastle upon Tyne

Yorkshire and Humberside
York

Manchester

East Midlands

Birmingham

Norwich

Heart of England

Cambridge

East Anglia

Thames Valley
Oxford

London

Downs and Channel Coast
Portsmouth

Dover

LONDON

London at a Glance

THE LARGEST CITY IN EUROPE, London is home to about seven million people and covers 625 sq miles (1,600 sq km). The capital was founded by the Romans in the first century AD as a convenient administrative and communications center and a port for trade with Continental Europe. For a thousand years it has been the principal residence of British monarchs as well as the center of business and government, and it is rich in historic buildings and treasures from all periods. In addition to its diverse range of museums, galleries and churches, London is an exciting contemporary city, packed with a vast array of entertainments and shops. The attractions offered are virtually endless, but this map highlights the most important of those described in detail in the following pages.

Buckingham Palace (pp88–9) is London home and office to the monarchy. The Changing of the Guard takes place on the palace forecourt.

REGENT'S PARK AND BLOOMSBURY (see pp104–109)

WEST EN AND WESTMINS (see pp78–

SOUTH KENSINGTON AND HYDE PARK (see pp96–103)

Hyde Park (p77), the largest central London park, boasts numerous sports facilities, restaurants, an art gallery and Speakers' Corner. The highlight is the Serpentine Lake.

0 kilometers   1

0 miles   0.5

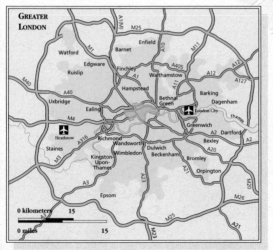
GREATER LONDON

M25, Enfield, Watford, Barnet, Edgware, Finchley, Ruislip, A1, Walthamstow, Hampstead, Uxbridge, Bethnal Green, Barking, Dagenham, Ealing, London City, Greenwich, Thames, Heathrow, Richmond, Wandsworth, Dartford, Staines, Wimbledon, Dulwich, Bexley, Bromley, Kingston-Upon-Thames, Beckenham, Orpington, Epsom, M26, M23, M25

0 kilometers   15

0 miles   15

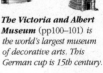
The Victoria and Albert Museum (pp100–101) is the world's largest museum of decorative arts. This German cup is 15th century.

KEY

☐ Main sightseeing area

◁ Nelson's Column (1843) and the National Gallery, Trafalgar Square

The British Museum's (pp108–9) *vast collection of antiquities from all over the world includes this Portland Vase from the 1st century BC.*

The National Gallery's (pp84–5) *world-famous collection of paintings includes works such as* Christ Mocked *(c.1495) by Hieronymus Bosch.*

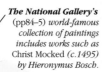

THE CITY AND SOUTHWARK *(see pp110–121)*

THAMES

St. Paul's (pp116–17) *huge dome is the cathedral's most distinctive feature. Three galleries around the dome give spectacular views of London.*

Westminster Abbey (pp94–5) *has glorious medieval architecture and is crammed with impressive tombs and monuments to some of Britain's greatest public figures.*

The Tate Gallery (p93) *has two outstanding collections: British art dating from 1550 and 20th-century international modern art. This explosive image* Whaam! *(1963) is by Roy Lichtenstein.*

The Tower of London (pp120–21) *is most famous as the prison where enemies of the Crown were executed. The Tower houses the Crown Jewels, including the Imperial State Crown.*

A River View of London

THE RIVER THAMES was the artery for much of the country's commerce from Roman times until the 1950s. Today the river is one of London's foremost leisure amenities, with wharves and warehouses converted into riverside marinas, bars and restaurants. One of the most enjoyable ways to see the capital is by boat, and the most popular river trips travel downstream from the Houses of Parliament to Tower Bridge. This 30-minute cruise gives a different perspective on some of London's historic buildings and sights.

St. Paul's Cathedral (pp116–17), *Wren's masterpiece, dominates the north bank of the river.*

Temple and the Inns of Court (p112) *have been the offices of lawyers and barristers for over 500 years.*

Shell Mex House *was built in 1931 on the site of the vast Cecil Hotel.*

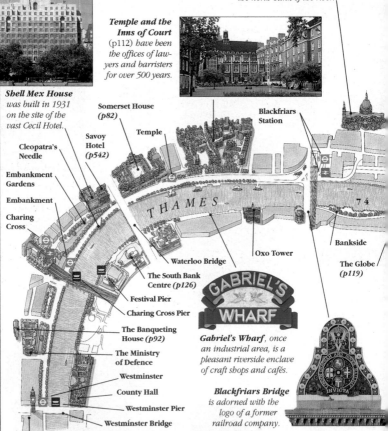

Somerset House (p82)

Savoy Hotel (p542)

Temple

Cleopatra's Needle

Embankment Gardens

Embankment

Charing Cross

Blackfriars Station

THAMES

7 4

Bankside

The Globe (p119)

Oxo Tower

Waterloo Bridge

The South Bank Centre (p126)

Festival Pier

Charing Cross Pier

The Banqueting House (p92)

The Ministry of Defence

Westminster

County Hall

Westminster Pier

Westminster Bridge

GABRIEL'S WHARF

Gabriel's Wharf, *once an industrial area, is a pleasant riverside enclave of craft shops and cafés.*

Blackfriars Bridge *is adorned with the logo of a former railroad company.*

The Houses of Parliament (p92) *were designed by Charles Barry after a fire burned down the 14th-century Palace of Westminster in 1834. The tall tower housing Big Ben dominates the skyline.*

BOAT TOUR OPERATORS

The most popular boat trips run through central London all year, with reduced schedules in winter. In the summer months there are trips downriver to Greenwich *(see p131)* and upriver to Hampton Court *(see p159)*.

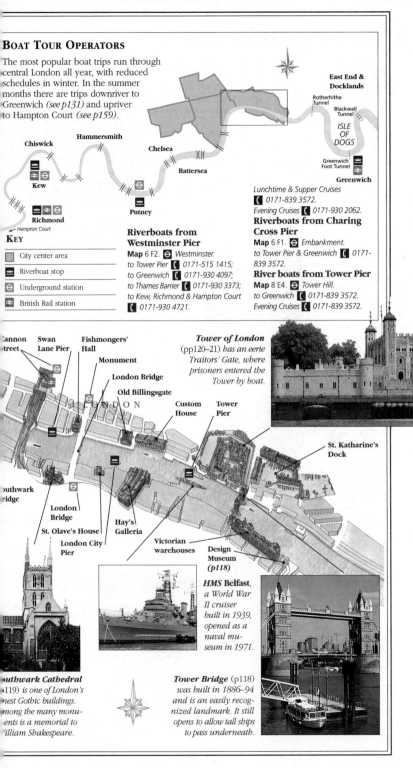

**East End &
Docklands**

Rotherhithe
Tunnel

Blackwall
Tunnel

*ISLE
OF
DOGS*

Greenwich
Foot Tunnel

Greenwich

Chiswick

Hammersmith

Chelsea

Battersea

Kew

Putney

Richmond

Hampton Court

KEY

	City center area
≋	Riverboat stop
⊖	Underground station
≋	British Rail station

Lunchtime & Supper Cruises
[0171-839 3572.
Evening Cruises [0171-930 2062.

Riverboats from Charing Cross Pier

Map 6 F1. ⊖ *Embankment.*
to Tower Pier & Greenwich [0171-839 3572.

River boats from Tower Pier

Map 8 E4. ⊖ *Tower Hill.*
to Greenwich [0171-839 3572.
Evening Cruises [0171-839 3572.

Riverboats from Westminster Pier

Map 6 F2. ⊖ *Westminster.*
to Tower Pier [0171-515 1415;
to Greenwich [0171-930 4097;
to Thames Barrier [0171-930 3373;
to Kew, Richmond & Hampton Court
[0171-930 4721.

Cannon
Street

Swan
Lane Pier

Fishmongers'
Hall

Monument

London Bridge

Old Billingsgate

Custom
House

Tower
Pier

St. Katharine's
Dock

Southwark
Bridge

London
Bridge

St. Olave's House

London City
Pier

Hay's
Galleria

Victorian
warehouses

Design
Museum
(p118)

Tower of London
(pp120–21) *has an eerie
Traitors' Gate, where
prisoners entered the
Tower by boat.*

HMS **Belfast**, *a World War
II cruiser
built in 1939,
opened as a
naval mu-
seum in 1971.*

Southwark Cathedral
(p119) *is one of London's
finest Gothic buildings.
Among the many monu-
ments is a memorial to
William Shakespeare.*

Tower Bridge (p118)
*was built in 1886–94
and is an easily recog-
nized landmark. It still
opens to allow tall ships
to pass underneath.*

London's Parks and Gardens

Camilla japonica

Lreenest ONDON HAS ONE OF THE WORLD'S greenest city centers, full of tree-filled squares and large expanses of grass, some of which have been public lands since medieval times. From the elegant terraces of Regent's Park to the botanic gardens of Kew, every London park and garden has its own charm and character. Some are ancient crown or public lands, while others were created from the grounds of private houses or unused land. Londoners make the most of these open spaces for exercise, listening to music, or simply escaping the bustle of the city.

Holland Park (see pp128–9) *offers acres of peaceful woodland, an open-air theater (see p125) and a café.*

Kew Gardens (see p132) *are the world's premiere botanic gardens. An amazing variety of plants from all over the world is complemented by an array of temples, monuments and a landscaped lake.*

Richmond Park (see p132), *London's largest royal park, remains unspoiled with roaming deer and magnificent river views.*

0 kilometers   1

0 miles   0.5

SEASONAL BEST

As winter draws to a close, spectacular drifts of crocuses, daffodils and tulips are to be found peeping above the ground in Green Park and Kew. Easter weekend marks the start of outdoor events with carnivals on many commons and parks. During the summer months the parks are packed with picnickers and sunbathers. You can often catch a free open-air concert in St. James's or Regent's parks. The energetic can play

Winter in Kensington Gardens, adjoining Hyde Park

tennis in most parks, swim in Hyde Park's Serpentine or the ponds on Hampstead Heath, or take rowboats out on the lakes in Regent's and Battersea parks. Autumn brings a different atmosphere, and on November 5 firework displays and bonfires celebrate Guy Fawkes Night *(see p64)*. Winter is a good time to visit the tropical glasshouses and the colorful outdoor winter garden at Kew. If the weather gets really cold, the Round Pond in Kensington Gardens may be good for ice-skating.

Hampstead Heath (see p130) is a breezy open space embracing a variety of landscapes.

Regent's Park (see p105) *has a large boating lake, an open-air theater* (see p125) *and London Zoo. Surrounded by Nash's graceful Regency buildings, it is one of London's most civilized retreats.*

St. James's Park, in the heart of the city, is a popular escape for office workers. It is also a wildfowl preserve.

THAMES

Green Park, with its shady trees and benches, offers a cool, restful spot in the heart of London.

Battersea Park is a pleasant riverside site with a man-made boating lake.

Greenwich Park (see p131) *is dominated by the National Maritime Museum. There are fine views from the Old Royal Observatory on the hill top.*

Hyde Park and Kensington Gardens (see p103) *are both popular London retreats. There are sporting facilities, a lake and art gallery in Hyde Park. This plaque is from the ornate Italian Garden in Kensington Gardens.*

HISTORIC CEMETERIES

In the late 1830s, a ring of private cemeteries was established around London to ease the pressure on the monstrously overcrowded and unhealthy burial grounds of the inner city. Today the cemeteries, notably **Highgate** *(see p130)* and Kensal Green, are well worth visiting for their flamboyant Victorian monuments.

Kensal Green cemetery on the Harrow Road

WEST END AND WESTMINSTER

THE WEST END is the city's social and cultural center and the London home of the royal family. Stretching from the edge of Hyde Park to Covent Garden, the district bustles all day and late into the night. Whether you're looking for art, history, street- or café-life, it is the most rewarding area in which to begin any exploration of London.

Westminster has been at the center of political and religious power for a thousand years. In the 11th century, King Canute founded Westminster Palace and Edward the Confessor built Westminster Abbey, where all English monarchs have been crowned since 1066. As modern government developed, the great offices of state were established in the area.

Horse Guard on Whitehall

SIGHTS AT A GLANCE

Historic Streets and Buildings
Banqueting House ⑱
Buckingham Palace pp88–9 ⑬
Cabinet War Rooms ⑯
Downing Street ⑰
Houses of Parliament pp92–3 ⑲
Piccadilly Circus ⑦
Ritz Hotel ⑩
Royal Mews ⑮
The Mall ⑫
The Piazza and Central Market ①

Museums and Galleries
Courtauld Institute and Somerset House ④
London Transport Museum ②
Museum of Mankind ⑨
National Gallery pp84–5 ⑥
National Portrait Gallery ⑤
Queen's Gallery ⑭
Royal Academy ⑧

Tate Gallery ㉑
Theatre Museum ③

Churches
Queen's Chapel ⑪
Westminster Abbey pp94–5 ⑳

KEY

	Street-by-Street map *pp80–81*
	Street-by-Street map *pp86–7*
	Street-by-Street map *pp90–91*
⊖	Underground station
⇌	British Rail station
P	Parking
⚓	River boat boarding point

GETTING THERE

This area is the hub of the city's public transportation system, served by many subway lines and buses *(see pp642–3)*. The most convenient subway and railroad station is Charing Cross.

0 meters   500
0 yards   500

◁ **Westminster Bridge, Big Ben and the Houses of Parliament viewed from the South Bank**

Street-by-Street: Covent Garden

UNTIL 1973, COVENT GARDEN was an area of decaying streets and warehouses, which only came alive after dark, when the fruit and vegetable market traders packed up for the day. Since then the Victorian market and elegant buildings nearby have been converted into stylish shops, restaurants, bars and cafés, creating an animated district that attracts a lively young crowd, night and day.

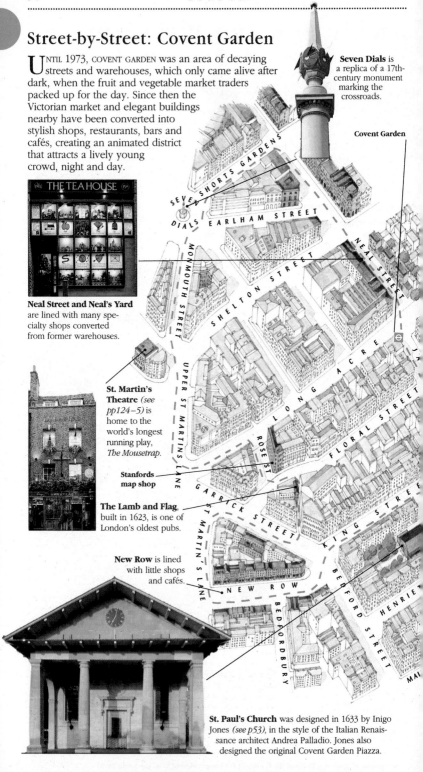

Seven Dials is a replica of a 17th-century monument marking the crossroads.

Covent Garden

Neal Street and Neal's Yard are lined with many specialty shops converted from former warehouses.

St. Martin's Theatre *(see pp124–5)* is home to the world's longest running play, *The Mousetrap.*

Stanfords map shop

The Lamb and Flag, built in 1623, is one of London's oldest pubs.

New Row is lined with little shops and cafés.

St. Paul's Church was designed in 1633 by Inigo Jones *(see p53)*, in the style of the Italian Renaissance architect Andrea Palladio. Jones also designed the original Covent Garden Piazza.

Theatre Museum
This houses a collection of theatrical memorabilia ❸

The Royal Opera House
(see p126), is where many of the greatest opera singers and ballet dancers have performed.

Floral Hall is soon to become an extension to the Opera House.

LOCATOR MAP
See Street Finder map 4

KEY

─ ─ ─ Suggested route

0 meters	100
0 yards	100

London Transport Museum
This museum's intriguing collection brings to life the history of the city's tubes, buses and trains. It also displays examples of 20th-century commercial art ❷

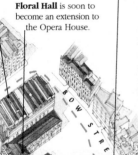

Jubilee Market

★ **Piazza and Central Market**
Street performers entertain passersby in the square ❶

The Piazza and Central Market ❶

Covent Garden WC2. **Map** 4F5.
🚇 Covent Garden. ♿ cobbled streets. **Street performers in Piazza:** 10am–dusk daily.

THE 17TH-CENTURY ARCHITECT Inigo Jones *(see p53)* planned the Piazza in Covent Garden as an elegant residential square, modeled on the piazza in the Tuscan town of Livorno, which he had seen under construction during his travels in Italy. For a brief period, the Piazza became one of the most fashionable addresses in London, but it was superseded by the even grander St. James's Square *(see pp86–7)* which lies to the southwest.

Decline accelerated when a fruit and vegetable market developed. By the mid-18th century, the Piazza had become a haunt of prostitutes and most of its houses had turned into seedy lodgings, gambling dens, brothels and taverns.

A mid-18th-century view of Covent Garden's Piazza

Meanwhile the wholesale produce market became the largest in the country, and in 1828 a market hall was erected to ease congestion. The market, however, soon outgrew its new home and despite the construction of new buildings, such as Floral and Jubilee halls, the congestion grew worse. In 1973 the market moved to a new site in south London, and over the past two decades Covent Garden has been redeveloped. Today only St. Paul's remains of Inigo Jones's buildings, and Covent Garden, with its many small shops, cafés, restaurants, market stalls and street entertainers, is one of central London's liveliest districts.

London Transport Museum ❷

The Piazza, Covent Garden WC2.
Map 4 F5. 📞 0171-379 6344.
🚇 Covent Garden. 🕐 10am–6pm daily. 🚫 Dec 24–26. 🅰 🔴 ♿

THIS COLLECTION of buses, trams and underground trains ranges from the earliest horse-drawn omnibuses to a present-day Hoppa bus. Housed in the iron, glass and brick Victorian Flower Market of Covent Garden, which was built in 1872, the museum is particularly good for children, who can put themselves in the driver's seat of a bus or an underground train, operate signals and chat to one of the actors playing the part of a 19th-century tube-tunnel miner.

London's bus and train companies have long been prolific patrons of artists, and the museum holds a fine collection of 19th- and 20th-century commercial art. Copies of some of the best posters – including the innovative Art Deco designs of E. McKnight Kauffer, and works by artists such as Graham Sutherland and Paul Nash – are on sale at the museum shop.

Poster by Michael Reilly (1929), London Transport Museum

Theatre Museum ❸

7 Russell St WC2. **Map** 4 F5. 📞 0171-836 7891. 🚇 Covent Garden.
🕐 11am–7pm Tue–Sun. 🚫 public hols. 🅰 ♿

A LARGE GOLD STATUE of the Spirit of Gaiety lures you down into the subterranean galleries of this museum. Children can be made up with gruesome wounds and find out how Cyrano de Bergerac's nose was created for the film. An exhibition reveals how a

theater production is organized, from cast readings of the author's original script, through videoed rehearsals and backstage procedures, to the first staged performance.

More conventionally, the intriguing history of show business is traced through a collection of memorabilia – playbills, programs, props and costumes, such as a slinky silver jumpsuit worn by the rock singer Mick Jagger.

Courtauld Institute Galleries and Somerset House ❹

Somerset House, Strand WC2.
Map 4 F5. 📞 0171-873 2526.
🚇 Temple, Embankment. 🕐 10am–6pm Mon–Sat, 2–6pm Sun. 🚫 Dec 24–26, Jan 1, Good Fri. 🅰 🔴 ♿

DESIGNED IN 1770 by William Chambers, Somerset House was the first built to order office block in London. Much of the building is still used by civil servants, but the north block (the original home

Somerset House: Strand façade

of the Royal Academy) now houses a spectacular display of paintings. The collection is based on the textile magnate Samuel Courtauld's collection of Impressionist and Post-Impressionist works, which includes Manet's *Bar at the Folies-Bergère* (1882), a version of *Le Déjeuner sur l'Herbe* (c.1863) and Van Gogh's *Self-Portrait with Bandaged Ear* (1889). There are also earlier 15th- and 16th-century works by Giovanni Bellini, Botticelli and Brueghel, and paintings by 20th-century British artists, such as *Painting 1937* by Ben Nicholson (*see p263*).

SOHO AND CHINATOWN

Soho has been renowned for pleasures of the table, the flesh and the intellect ever since it was first developed in the late 17th century. At first a fashionable residential area, it declined when high society shifted west to Mayfair and immigrants from Europe moved into its narrow streets. Furniture makers and tailors set up shop here and were joined in the late 19th century by pubs, nightclubs, restaurants and brothels. In the 1960s, Hong Kong Chinese moved into the area around Gerrard and Lisle streets and they created an aromatic Chinatown, packed with many restaurants and food shops. Soho's raffish reputation has long attracted artists and writers, ranging from the 18th-century essayist Thomas de Quincey to poet Dylan Thomas and painter Francis Bacon. Although strip joints and peep shows remain, Soho has enjoyed something of a renaissance, and today is full of stylish and lively bars and restaurants.

Lion dancer in February's Chinese New Year celebrations

The opulent Palm Court of the Ritz Hotel

National Portrait Gallery ❺

2 St. Martin's Place WC2. **Map** 6 E1.
📞 0171-306 0055. ➤ Leicester Sq.
⬜ 10am–6pm Mon–Sat, noon–6pm
Sun. ⬤ Dec 24–25, Jan 1, Good Fri,
May Day. ♿ 🖼 Aug.

THIS MUSEUM CELEBRATES
Britain's history through
portraits, photographs and
sculptures; subjects range from
Elizabeth I and Shakespeare
to the Beatles and Margaret
Thatcher. Early works include
a sketch of Henry VIII by
Hans Holbein and aristocratic
portraits by Gainsborough,
Van Dyck and Reynolds. The
most popular part of the
gallery, however, is the 20th-
century section, with paintings
and photographs of the royal
family, politicians, rock stars,
designers, artists and writers.

National Gallery ❻

See pp84–5.

Piccadilly Circus ❼

W1. **Map** 6 D1. ➤ Piccadilly Circus.

DOMINATED BY garish neon
advertising billboards,
Piccadilly Circus is a hectic
traffic junction surrounded by
shopping malls and fast food
outlets. It began as an early
19th-century crossroads
between Piccadilly and John
Nash's (see p107) Regent Street.

It was briefly an elegant space,
edged by curving stucco
façades, but by 1910 the first
electric advertisements had
been installed. The Circus
marks the beginning of London's entertainment district,
and for years people have con-
gregated at its center, beneath
the delicately poised figure of
Eros, the Greek god of love.
Erected in 1892, the figure was
originally intended to be an
angel of Christian mercy.

Royal Academy ❽

Burlington House, Piccadilly W1.
Map 6 D1. 📞 0171-439 7438.
➤ Piccadilly Circus, Green Park.
⬜ 10am–6pm daily. ⬤ Dec 24–26,
Good Fri. 🖼 ♿ 🖼

FOUNDED IN 1768, the Royal
Academy is best known
for its summer exhibition,
which has been an annual
event for over 200 years and
comprises around 1,200 new
works by established and

Vivien Leigh by Angus McBean
(1952), National Portrait Gallery

unknown painters, sculptors
and architects. During the rest
of the year the gallery shows
prestigious touring exhibitions
from around the world.

Museum of Mankind ❾

6 Burlington Gdns W1. **Map** 5 C1.
📞 0171-437 2224. ➤ Green Park,
Piccadilly Circus. ⬜ 10am–5pm Mon–
Sat, 2:30–6pm Sun. ⬤ Dec 24–26,
Jan 1, Good Fri, May Day. 🖼 ♿

THE MUSEUM OF MANKIND is
the ethnographic section
of the British Museum (see
pp 108–109) and shows
many temporary exhibitions
that draw on its collection of
ancient, recent and contemporary artifacts created
by indigenous
groups throughout
the world. Major
exhibitions may last
for a year, and are
often based on
fieldwork carried
out by the muse-
um's staff. The
exhibitions afford
thought-provoking
insights into many
cultures through
a wide variety of
photographs and
objects, useful
information boards **Early 19th-**
and painstaking **century**
reconstructions of **Hawaiian**
sites and buildings. **war god**

Ritz Hotel ❿

Piccadilly W1. **Map** 5 C1. 📞 0171-
493 8181. ➤ Green Park. ♿
See **Where to Stay** p540.

CESAR RITZ, the Swiss hote-
lier who inspired the word
ritzy, had virtually retired by
1906 when this hotel was built
and named after him. The
colonnaded front of the dominant, château-style building
was put up in 1906 to suggest
Paris, where the grandest
hotels were to be found at the
turn of the century. It has managed to maintain its Edwardian
air of opulence and grandeur
and is a popular stop, with
those suitably dressed, for an
extravagant afternoon tea.

National Gallery ⑥

THE NATIONAL GALLERY is London's leading art museum, with over 2,200 paintings, most on permanent display. It has flourished since 1824 when George IV persuaded a reluctant government to purchase 38 major paintings. These became the core of a national collection of European art that now ranges from Giotto in the 13th century to 20th-century Picassos. The gallery's particular strengths are in Dutch, Italian Renaissance and 17th-century Spanish painting. In 1991 the Sainsbury Wing was added to the main Neo-Classical building (1834–8) to hold the Early Renaissance collection.

The Adoration of the Kings *(1564)*
This realisitic work is by Flemish artist Pieter Brueghel the Elder (1520–1569).

Orange Street entrance ♿

Stairs to lower floor

★ The Leonardo Cartoon *(c.1510)*
The genius of Leonardo da Vinci glows through this chalk drawing of the Virgin and Child, St. Anne and John the Baptist.

KEY TO FLOORPLAN

- ☐ Painting 1260–1510
- ☐ Painting 1510–1600
- ☐ Painting 1600–1700
- ☐ Painting 1700–1920
- ☐ Special exhibitions
- ☐ Nonexhibition space

Link to main building

Stairs to lower floors 🔼

Arnolfini Marriage
Jan van Eyck (1389–1441), one of the pioneers of oil painting, shows his mastery of color, texture, and minute detail in this portrait of 1434.

Main entrance to Sainsbury Wing ♿

The Annunciation
This refined work of 1448, by Fra Filippo Lippi, forms part of the gallery's exceptional Italian Renaissance collection.

★ **Rokeby Venus**
This is Velazquez's only surviving female nude (1649).

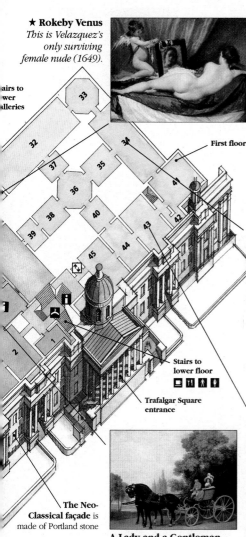

Stairs to lower galleries

32
33
34
35
36
37
38
39
40
41
42
43
44
45

First floor

VISITORS' CHECKLIST

Trafalgar Sq WC2. **Map** 6 E1.
☎ 0171-839 3321. ☎ 0171-747 2885. ☎ Charing Cross, Leicester Sq, Piccadilly Circus.
🚌 3, 6, 9, 11, 12, 13, 15, X15 23, 24, 29, 53, X53, 77A, 88, 91, 94, 109, 139, 159, 176.
🚆 Charing Cross. ◯ 10am–6pm Mon–Sat, 2–6pm Sun. ⬤ Dec 24–26, Jan 1, Good Fri, May Day. ♿ Orange St & Sainsbury Wing. 🎟 🖥 🍴

★ **The Haywain** (*1821*)
The great age of 19th-century landscape painting is represented by Constable and Turner (see p93). This picture shows how Constable caught changing light and shadow.

Stairs to lower floor
🖥 🍴 👶 🚻

Trafalgar Square entrance

The Neo-Classical façade is made of Portland stone

GALLERY GUIDE

Most of the collection is housed on the first floor, divided into four wings. The paintings hang chronologically, with the earliest works, notably the Italian Renaissance collection (1260–1510), in the Sainsbury Wing. Lesser paintings of all periods are displayed on the lower floor of the main building. The better of the two restaurants is on the first floor in the Sainsbury Wing.

A Lady and a Gentleman in a Carriage (*1787*)
George Stubbs was celebrated for his portraits of horses, often shown with their owners. This work displays his versatility.

STAR PAINTINGS

- ★ **Cartoon by Leonardo da Vinci**

- ★ **Rokeby Venus by Diego Velazquez**

- ★ **The Haywain by John Constable**

Umbrellas (*1881–6*)
Renoir was one of the greatest painters to be influenced by the Impressionist movement. In this painting he used the free, flickering touch of Impressionism that captures the fleeting moment.

Street-by-Street: Piccadilly and St. James's

As soon as Henry VIII built St. James's Palace in the 1530s, the surrounding area became the center of fashionable court life. Today Piccadilly is a bustling commercial district with shopping arcades, eateries and movie theaters, while St. James's, to the south, has remained the domain of the wealthy and the influential.

St. James's Church was designed by Sir Christopher Wren in 1684.

★ Museum of Mankind
Exhibitions change regularly at London's main ethnographic museum **9**

★ Royal Academy
The permanent art collection here includes this Michelangelo relief of the Madonna and Child (1505) **8**

Fortnum and Mason *(see p122)* was founded in 1707.

The Ritz
César Ritz founded one of London's most famous hotels in 1906 **10**

Burlington Arcade, an opulent covered walk, has fine shops and beadles on patrol.

St. James's Palace was built on the site of a leper hospital.

To the Mall and Buckingham Palace *(see pp88–9).*

Spencer House, recently restored to its 18th-century splendor, contains fine period furniture and paintings. This Palladian palace was completed in 1766 for the First Earl Spencer, an ancestor of the Princess of Wales.

STAR SIGHTS

★ Royal Academy

★ Museum of Mankind

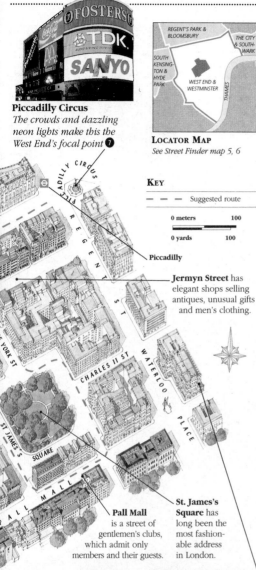

Piccadilly Circus
The crowds and dazzling neon lights make this the West End's focal point ❼

LOCATOR MAP
See Street Finder map 5, 6

KEY

– – – Suggested route

0 meters 100
0 yards 100

Piccadilly

Jermyn Street has elegant shops selling antiques, unusual gifts and men's clothing.

Pall Mall
is a street of gentlemen's clubs, which admit only members and their guests.

St. James's Square has long been the most fashionable address in London.

Queen's Chapel
This was the first Classical church in England ⓫

Royal Opera Arcade is lined with quality shops. Designed by John Nash, it was completed in 1818.

Queen's Chapel ⓫

Marlborough Rd SW1. **Map** 6 D1.
(0171-836 7221. ⊖ Green Park.
◕ 11:30am–3:30pm Tue–Thu. ●
Aug–Sep & during services. ◙ ⓰

THE SUMPTUOUS Queen's Chapel was designed by Inigo Jones for the Infanta of Spain, the intended bride of Charles I (*see p52–3*). Work started in 1623 but ceased when the marriage negotiations were shelved. The chapel was finally completed in 1627 for Charles's eventual queen, Henrietta Maria. It was the first church in England to be built in a Classical style, with a coffered ceiling based on a reconstruction by Palladio of an ancient Roman temple.

Interior of Queen's Chapel ⓰

The Mall ⓬

SW1. **Map** 6 D2. ⊖ Charing Cross, Green Park.

THIS BROAD TRIUMPHAL approach from Trafalgar Square to Buckingham Palace was created by Aston Webb when he redesigned the front of the palace and the Victoria Monument in 1911. The spacious tree-lined avenue follows the course of an old path at the edge of St. James's Park. The path was laid out in the reign of Charles II, when it became London's most fashionable and cosmopolitan promenade. The Mall is used for royal processions on special occasions. Flagpoles down both sides fly the national flags of foreign heads of state during official visits. The Mall is closed to traffic on Sundays.

Buckingham Palace ⓭

OPENED TO VISITORS for the first time in 1993 to raise money for repairing fire damage to Windsor Castle *(see pp222–3)*, the Queen's London home and office is an extremely popular attraction in August and September. John Nash *(see p107)* began converting the 18th-century Buckingham House into a palace for George IV in 1825 but was taken off the job in 1830 for overspending his budget. The first monarch to occupy the palace was Queen Victoria, just after she came to the throne in 1837. The self-guided tour takes visitors up the grand staircase and through the splendor of the state rooms, but not into the royal family's private apartments.

Queen Elizabeth II

Music Room
State guests are presented and royal babies christened in this room.

White Drawing Room

Green Drawing Room

Grand Staircase

Blue Drawing Room

State Dining Room

Entrance to the Queen's Gallery

Public entrance to the palace through Ambassador's Court

Picture Gallery
The valuable collection on display includes this painting by Dutch master Johannes Vermeer:
The Music Lesson *(c.1660).*

Throne Room
The Queen carries out many formal ceremonial duties here, under the richly gilded ceiling.

View over the Mall
On special occasions the Royal Family wave to crowds from the balcony.

VISITORS' CHECKLIST

SW1. **Map** 5 C2. ☎ 0171-839 1377. ⊖ St James's Park, Victoria. 🚌 11, 16, 24, 25, 36, 38, 52, 73, 135, C1. 🚆 Victoria. **State Rooms** ◯ Aug 7– Sep 28: 9:30am–5:30pm daily (last adm: 4:30pm). The ticket office is located in Green Park by Canada Gate. Each ticket is issued for a set entry time. 🈲 ♿ phone first.
Changing of the Guard: 11:30am alternate days throughout the year but subject to change without notice.

The Royal Standard flies while the Queen is in residence.

The East Wing façade was added by Aston Webb in 1913.

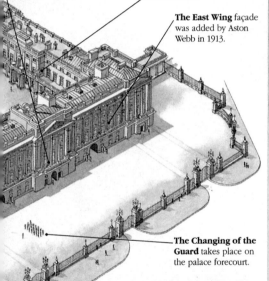

The Changing of the Guard takes place on the palace forecourt.

THE CHANGING OF THE GUARD

Dressed in brilliant red jackets and tall furry hats called bearskins, the palace guards stand in sentry boxes outside the Palace. Crowds gather in front of the gates to watch the colorful and musical military ceremony as the guards march down the Mall from St. James's Palace, parading for half an hour while the palace keys are handed by the old guards to the new.

Queen's Gallery ⑭

Buckingham Palace Rd SW1. **Map** 5 C2. 🛈 0171-799 2331. ⊖ St James's Park, Victoria. ◯ 9:30am–4:30pm daily. ● Dec 25, 26. 🈲

THE QUEEN'S ART COLLECTION is one of the finest and most valuable in the world. A selection of works is displayed here in themed exhibitions that change once or twice a year. This small building at the side of Buckingham Palace was used as a conservatory until 1962; part of it is a private chapel screened from the public. A large and interesting shop sells a selection of royal memorabilia.

Detail: The Gold State Coach (1762), Royal Mews

Royal Mews ⑮

Buckingham Palace Rd SW1. **Map** 5 C3. 🛈 0171-930 4832. ⊖ Victoria. ◯ 12–4pm (Oct–Mar: Wed; Apr–Jul: Tue–Thu; Aug–Sep: Mon–Thu). ● Dec 25, 26, Jan 1. 🈲 ♿

LOVERS OF HORSES and royal pomp should try to fit in with the restricted opening hours of this working stable and coach house. Designed by John Nash in 1825, it accommodates the horses and state coaches used on official occasions. Among them are the Rolls-Royce limousines with transparent tops that allow their royal occupants to be seen, and the glass coach used for royal weddings and foreign ambassadors. The star exhibit is the ornate gold state coach, built for George III in 1762, with panels painted by Giovanni Cipriani.

Street-by-Street: Whitehall and Westminster

THE BROAD AVENUES of Whitehall and Westminster are lined with imposing buildings that serve the historic seat of both government and the established church. On weekdays the streets are crowded with civil servants whose work is based here, while on weekends the area takes on a different atmosphere with a steady flow of tourists.

Downing Street
Sir Robert Walpole was the first Prime Minister to live here in 1732 ⑰

Cabinet War Rooms
Now open to the public, these were Winston Churchill's World War II headquarters ⑯

St. Margaret's Church is a favorite venue for political and society weddings.

★ Westminster Abbey
The abbey is London's oldest and most important church ⑳

Central Hall (1911) is a florid example of the Beaux Arts style.

Richard I's Statue is an 1860 depiction of the king, killed in battle in 1199.

Dean's Yard is a secluded grassy square surrounded by picturesque buildings from different periods, many used by Westminster School.

The Burghers of Calais is a cast of Auguste Rodin's 1886 original in France.

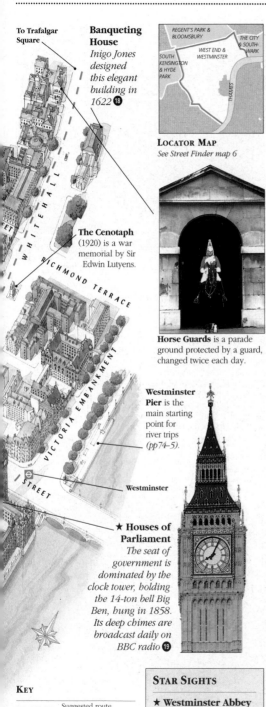

To Trafalgar Square

Banqueting House
Inigo Jones designed this elegant building in 1622 ⓲

LOCATOR MAP
See Street Finder map 6

The Cenotaph
(1920) is a war memorial by Sir Edwin Lutyens.

Horse Guards is a parade ground protected by a guard, changed twice each day.

Westminster Pier is the main starting point for river trips (pp74–5).

Westminster

★ Houses of Parliament
The seat of government is dominated by the clock tower, holding the 14-ton bell Big Ben, hung in 1858. Its deep chimes are broadcast daily on BBC radio ⓳

KEY

– – – Suggested route

0 meters   100

0 yards   100

STAR SIGHTS

★ Westminster Abbey

★ Houses of Parliament

Cabinet War Rooms ⓰

Clive Steps, King Charles St SW1.
Map 6 E2. ◉ *0171-930 6961.*
⊖ *Westminster.* ○ *10am–5:15pm daily.* ● *Dec 24–26.* 🌀 🏬

THIS WARREN OF CELLARS below a government office building is where the War Cabinet – first under Neville Chamberlain, then Winston Churchill from 1940 – met during World War II when German bombs were falling on London. The rooms here include living quarters for key ministers and military leaders and a soundproofed Cabinet Room, where many strategic decisions were made. All the rooms are protected by a concrete layer about a meter (3 ft) thick and are laid out as they were when the war ended in 1945, complete with Churchill's desk, communications equipment, and maps with markers for plotting battles and military strategies.

Telephones in the Map Room, Cabinet War Rooms

Downing Street ⓱

SW1. **Map** 6 E2. ⊖ *Westminster.* ● *to the public.*

NUMBER 10 Downing Street has been the official residence of the British Prime Minister since 1732. It contains a Cabinet Room in which government policy is decided, an impressive State Dining Room and a private apartment; outside is a well-protected garden.

Next door at No. 11 is the official residence of the Chancellor of the Exchequer, who is in charge of the nation's financial affairs. In 1989, iron gates were erected at the Whitehall end of Downing Street for security purposes.

Banqueting House ⑱

Whitehall SW1. **Map** 6 E1. ☎ 0171-839 7569. ⊖ Charing Cross. ◯ 10am–5pm Mon–Sat. ● Dec 25, 26, Jan 1, for functions. 🎦 📷 🚻

COMPLETED BY INIGO JONES (see p53) in 1622, this was the first building in central London to embody the classical Palladian style of Renaissance Italy. In 1629 Charles I commissioned Rubens to paint the ceiling with scenes exalting the reign of his father, James I. They symbolize a belief in the divine nature of kingship, despised by the Parliamentarians, who executed Charles I outside the building in 1649 (see pp52–3).

Panels from the Rubens ceiling (1629–34), Banqueting House

Houses of Parliament ⑲

SW1. **Map** 6 E2. ☎ 0171-219 3000. ⊖ Westminster. **Visitors' Galleries** ◯ 2:30–10:30pm Mon, Tue, Thu, 10am–10:30pm Wed, 9:30am–3pm Fri. Question Time (2:30–3:30pm Mon–Thu): apply in advance to your MP or embassy. ● 2 wks over Christmas, Easter, public hols. 🚻 🎦 by appt.

THERE HAS BEEN a Palace of Westminster on this site since the 11th century, though only Westminster Hall remains from that time. The present Neo-Gothic structure, designed by Sir Charles Barry, was built after the old palace was destroyed by fire in 1834. Since the 16th century it has been the seat of the two Houses of Parliament, the Lords and the Commons. The House of Commons is made up of elected Members of Parliament (MPs) of different political parties. The party with the most MPs forms the Government, and its leader becomes Prime Minister. The House of Lords is made up of peers (see pp58–9), law lords, bishops and archbishops. Draft legislation is debated in both houses before becoming law.

Westminster Abbey ⑳

See pp94–5.

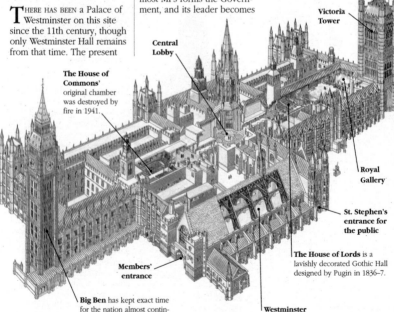

Victoria Tower

Central Lobby

The House of Commons' original chamber was destroyed by fire in 1941.

Royal Gallery

St. Stephen's entrance for the public

The House of Lords is a lavishly decorated Gothic Hall designed by Pugin in 1836–7.

Members' entrance

Big Ben has kept exact time for the nation almost continuously since 1859.

Westminster Hall

Portico of the Tate Gallery

Tate Gallery ㉑

Millbank SW1. **Map** 6 E4. ☎ 0171-
887 8000. ☏ 0171-887 8008.
🚇 Pimlico. ⏰ 10am–5:50pm
Mon–Sat, 2–5:50pm Sun. ⬤ Dec
24–26, Jan 1, Good Fri, May Day.
🎟 for major exhibitions. 📷 ♿ 🛒

FOUNDED IN 1897, the Tate
Gallery is best known for
its magnificent Turner Bequest
and its international collection
of late 19th- and 20th-century
art, but it also has an extensive
range of earlier
British works.
Displays change
annually to high-
light different
aspects of the
collection.

British art was
dominated by
formal portraiture
through the 16th
and 17th centur-
ies. One of the
most exquisite
early works is a
portrait of a be-
jeweled Elizabeth
I (c.1575), by
Nicholas Hilliard. In the 17th
century, the influence of the
Flemish artist Sir Anthony Van
Dyck inspired a grand and
elegant style of portrait painting. Van Dyck's *Lady of the
Spencer Family* (1633–8) and
William Dobson's *Endymion
Porter* (1642–5) are both
superb examples. Van Dyck's
continuing influence
on English portrait
artists can be seen
in works by the
late 18th-century
artist Thomas
Gainsborough.

The Tate holds a
large number of
works by the 19th-
century visionary
poet and artist
William Blake,
which contrast with the reas-
suring landscapes painted
by his contemporary John
Constable (see pp190–91), and
the vibrant, seductive
images created by mid-19th-
century Pre-Raphaelites such
as Millais and Rossetti.

Many of the gallery's best
Impressionist and Post-
Impressionist
paintings were
transferred to the
National Gallery in
1954 (see pp84–5),
but it retains works
by major figures
such as Renoir,
Gauguin, Degas,
Toulouse-Lautrec
and Van Gogh.
Two of the most
innovative are
Claude Monet's
*Poplars on the
Epte* (1891) and
Paul Cézanne's
The Gardener
(c.1906). The artists' radically
new methods of painting had
a crucial influence on artists
such as Kandinsky (1866–
1944), a key figure in the
development of abstract art.

All major movements of
the 20th century are represented: Fauvism by early
Matisse and Derain;

**The Three Dancers
(1925) by Picasso**

Mr. and Mrs. Clark and Percy (1971) by Hockney

Cubism by Picasso, Braque
and Léger; Futurism by
Severini and Boccioni; and
Expressionism by Munch.
Sculpture includes works
by Rodin, Moore and
Hepworth. The vast postwar
collection encompasses the
disquieting images of Francis
Bacon, the worldly works of
David Hockney, splashed
canvases by American artist
Jackson Pollock and a
controversial selection of
contemporary art. There are
also seminal Pop Art works,
including Andy Warhol's
Marilyn Diptych (1962) and
Roy Lichtenstein's
Whaam!
(1963).

**The Kiss
(1901–1904)
by Rodin**

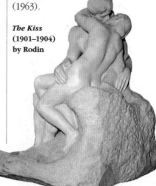

THE TURNER BEQUEST

The landscape artist J.M.W. Turner (1775–
1851) left his works to the nation, on
the condition that they be kept together.
It was not until 1987, with the opening
of the Clore Gallery, an extension of the
Tate, that this became possible. There are
early watercolors, Turner's first exhibited
oilpainting, *Fishermen at Sea* (1796), and
later works in an Impressionistic style that
Constable described as appearing to be
painted with "tinted steam."

A City on a River at Sunset (1832)

Westminster Abbey ⑳

WESTMINSTER ABBEY has been the burial place of Britain's monarchs since the 13th century and the setting for many coronations and royal weddings. It is one of the most beautiful buildings in London, with an exceptionally diverse array of architectural styles, ranging from the austere French Gothic of the nave to the astonishing complexity of Henry VII's chapel. Half national church, half national museum, the abbey aisles and transepts are crammed with an extraordinary collection of tombs and monuments honoring some of Britain's greatest public figures, ranging from politicians to poets.

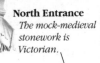

North Entrance
The mock-medieval stonework is Victorian.

Statesmen's Aisle

Flying buttresses help redistribute the great weight of the roof.

★ Nave
At a height of 31 m (102 ft), the nave is the highest in England. The ratio of height to width is 3:1.

Main entrance from Broad Sanctuary

CORONATION

The coronation ceremony is over 1,000 years old and since 1066, with the crowning of William the Conqueror on Christmas Day, the abbey has been its sumptuous setting. The coronation of Queen Elizabeth II, in 1953, was the first to be televised.

Cloisters
Rubbings can be taken from knights' tombs in the Brass Rubbing Centre.

STAR FEATURES
★ Nave
★ Henry VII Chapel
★ Chapter House

★ Henry VII Chapel
The chapel, built in 1503–12, has superb late Perpendicular vaultings and choir stalls dating from 1512.

WILLIAM SHAKESPEARE 1564–1616
BURIED AT STRATFORD-ON-AVON

The Sanctuary, built by Henry III, has been the scene of 38 coronations.

Poets' Corner
A host of great poets are honored here, including Shakespeare, Chaucer and T.S. Eliot.

The Pyx Chamber is where the coinage was tested in medieval times.

The Museum has many of the abbey's treasures including wood, plaster and wax effigies of monarchs.

St. Edward's Chapel
The Coronation Chair, Edward the Confessor's shrine and the tombs of many medieval monarchs are in this chapel.

VISITORS' CHECKLIST

Broad Sanctuary SW1. **Map** 6 E2.
0171-222 5152. St James's Park, Westminster. 3, 11, 12, 24, 29, 53, 70, 77, 77a, 88, 109, 159, 170. Victoria, Waterloo. Westminster Pier. **Nave & cloisters** 8am–6pm daily. **Chapter House, Museum & Pyx Chamber** 10:30am–4pm daily. **Royal Chapels** 9:20am–4:45pm Mon–Fri, 9:20am–2:45pm & 3:45–6pm Sat **Brass Rubbing Centre** 9am–5pm Mon–Sat (last adm: 45 mins before closing). 2nd Mon in Mar. except nave & cloisters. Evensong: 5pm Mon–Fri, 3pm Sat & Sun. only between 6–7:45pm on Wed. limited.

★ Chapter House
A beautiful octagonal room, remarkable for its 13th-century tile floor. It is lit by six huge stained glass windows showing scenes from the abbey's history.

HISTORICAL PLAN OF THE ABBEY

The first abbey church was established as early as the 10th century, but the present French-influenced Gothic structure was begun in 1245 at the behest of Henry III. Because of its unique role as the coronation church, the abbey escaped Henry VIII's mid-16th-century onslaught on Britain's monastic buildings *(see pp50–51)*.

KEY

- ■ Built before 1400
- ■ Added in 15th century
- ■ Built in 1503–19
- ■ Completed by 1745
- ▫ Completed after 1850

SOUTH KENSINGTON AND HYDE PARK

THIS EXCLUSIVE district embraces one of London's largest parks and some of its finest museums, shops, restaurants and hotels. Until the mid-19th century it was a genteel, semirural backwater of large houses and private schools lying to the south of Kensington Palace. In 1851, the Great Exhibition, the largest arts and science event ever staged anywhere *(see p56–7)*, was held in Hyde Park, transforming the area into a celebration of Victorian learning and self-confidence.

Peter Pan statue in Kensington Gardens

The brainchild of Queen Victoria's husband, Prince Albert, the exhibition was a great success and the profits were used to buy 35 ha (87 acres) of land in South Kensington. Here Prince Albert encouraged the construction of a concert hall, museums and colleges devoted to the applied arts and sciences; most of them survive. The neighborhood soon became modish, full of flamboyant red-brick mansion blocks, garden squares and the elite shops still to be found in Knightsbridge.

SIGHTS AT A GLANCE

Historic Buildings
Kensington Palace ❼

Churches
Brompton Oratory ❷

Shops
Harrod's ❶

Parks and Gardens
Hyde Park and Kensington Gardens ❻

Museums and Galleries
Natural History Museum ❺
Science Museum ❹
Victoria and Albert Museum pp100–101 ❸

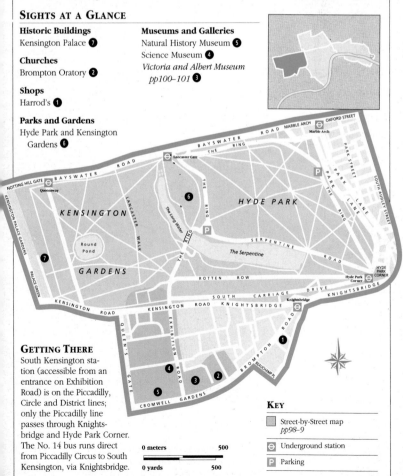

GETTING THERE

South Kensington station (accessible from an entrance on Exhibition Road) is on the Piccadilly, Circle and District lines; only the Piccadilly line passes through Knightsbridge and Hyde Park Corner. The No. 14 bus runs direct from Piccadilly Circus to South Kensington, via Knightsbridge.

| 0 meters | 500 |
| 0 yards | 500 |

KEY

■ Street-by-Street map *pp98–9*

⊖ Underground station

🅿 Parking

◁ **Ennismore Mews in South Kensington, built 1843–6**

Street-by-Street: South Kensington

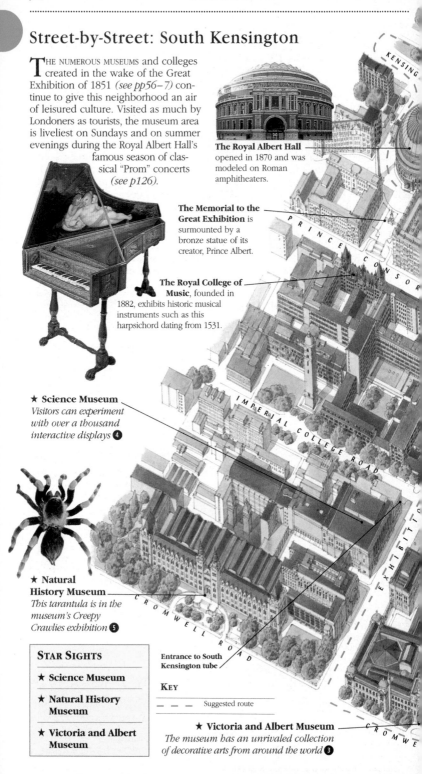

THE NUMEROUS MUSEUMS and colleges created in the wake of the Great Exhibition of 1851 *(see pp56–7)* continue to give this neighborhood an air of leisured culture. Visited as much by Londoners as tourists, the museum area is liveliest on Sundays and on summer evenings during the Royal Albert Hall's famous season of classical "Prom" concerts *(see p126).*

The Royal Albert Hall opened in 1870 and was modeled on Roman amphitheaters.

The Memorial to the Great Exhibition is surmounted by a bronze statue of its creator, Prince Albert.

The Royal College of Music, founded in 1882, exhibits historic musical instruments such as this harpsichord dating from 1531.

★ **Science Museum**
Visitors can experiment with over a thousand interactive displays ❹

★ **Natural History Museum**
This tarantula is in the museum's Creepy Crawlies exhibition ❺

STAR SIGHTS
★ Science Museum
★ Natural History Museum
★ Victoria and Albert Museum

Entrance to South Kensington tube

KEY

– – –　Suggested route

★ **Victoria and Albert Museum**
The museum has an unrivaled collection of decorative arts from around the world ❸

The Albert Memorial was built in memory of Queen Victoria's husband, who died in 1861.

The National Sound Archive is a branch of the British Library containing thousands of disks, tapes and videos, which can be heard or seen by appointment.

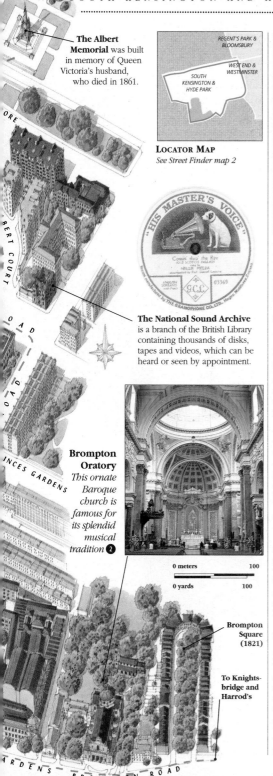

Brompton Oratory
This ornate Baroque church is famous for its splendid musical tradition ②

0 meters 100

0 yards 100

Brompton Square (1821)

To Knightsbridge and Harrod's

Harrod's Food Hall

Harrod's ①

Brompton Rd SW1. **Map** 5 A3.
📞 0171-730 1234. ⊖ *Knightsbridge.*
🕐 *10am–6pm Sat–Tue, 10am–7pm Wed–Fri.* & *See **Shops and Markets** pp122–3.*

IN 1849 HENRY CHARLES HARROD opened a grocery store on Brompton Road, which soon became famous for its impeccable service and quality. The store expanded and in 1905 moved into these extravagant premises in Knightsbridge.

Brompton Oratory ②

Brompton Rd SW7. **Map** 2 F5. 📞
0171-589 4811. ⊖ *South Kensington.*
🕐 *6:30am–8pm daily.* &

THE ITALIANATE ORATORY is a lavish monument to the 19th-century English Catholic revival. It was established as a base for a community of priests by John Henry Newman (later Cardinal Newman), who introduced the Oratorian movement to England in 1848. The church was opened in 1884, and the dome and façade added in the 1890s.

The sumptuous interior holds many fine monuments. The 12 huge 17th-century marble statues of the apostles are from Siena Cathedral, the elaborate Baroque Lady Altar (1693) is from the Dominican church at Brescia, and the 18th-century altar in St. Wilfred's Chapel is from Rochefort in Belgium.

Victoria and Albert Museum ➌

Dᴇsᴄʀɪʙᴇᴅ ᴀs an "extremely capacious handbag" by its former director Sir Roy Strong, the labyrinthine V&A contains one of the world's richest and most eclectic collections of fine and applied arts from all periods and cultures. So broad is the range that it embraces Doc Marten boots, paintings by Constable, Islamic ceramics and the greatest collection of Indian art outside India. The museum was founded as a result of the success of the Great Exhibition (see pp56–7) and since 1909 has been housed in a building designed by Sir Aston Webb.

Textiles

Main entrance

★ **20th-Century Gallery**
This shows modern design such as Daniel Weil's Radio in a Bag (1983).

Musical instruments

Stairs to Levels C and D

British Art and Design 1500–1750
The elaborate Great Bed of Ware (c.1590) is the V&A's most celebrated piece of furniture.

Gᴀʟʟᴇʀʏ Gᴜɪᴅᴇ

The V&A consists of 7 miles (11 km) of galleries occupying four main floor levels. The galleries are divided between those devoted to art and design, and those concentrating on materials and techniques. In the former, a wide variety of artifacts are assembled to illustrate the art and design of a particular period or civilization – such as Europe 1600–1800. These galleries occupy most of Level A and Lower A, with British arts on Levels B and C. The materials and techniques galleries contain collections of particular forms of craft, for example, porcelain, tapestries, metalwork, jewelry and glass. Many are located on Levels C and D. The six-story Henry Cole Wing, on the northwest side of the main building, holds the museum's collection of paintings, drawings, prints and photographs. There is also a gallery devoted to American architect Frank Lloyd Wright (1867–1959).

Exhibition Road entrance

Henry Cole Wing
Highlights here include 200 paintings by John Constable and this graceful portrait, A Young Man Among Roses *(1588), by court miniaturist Nicholas Hilliard.*

Kᴇʏ ᴛᴏ Fʟᴏᴏʀᴘʟᴀɴ

- ☐ Lower A
- ☐ Level A
- ☐ Lower B
- ☐ Level B
- ☐ Henry Cole Wing

Sᴛᴀʀ Exʜɪʙɪᴛs

- ★ **20th-Century Gallery**
- ★ **Morris, Gamble and Poynter Rooms**
- ★ **Medieval Treasury**
- ★ **Nehru Gallery of Indian Art**

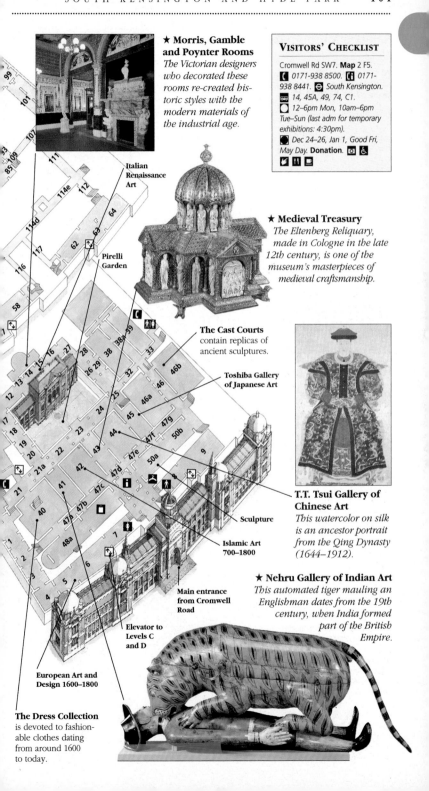

★ **Morris, Gamble and Poynter Rooms**
The Victorian designers who decorated these rooms re-created historic styles with the modern materials of the industrial age.

VISITORS' CHECKLIST

Cromwell Rd SW7. **Map** 2 F5.
0171-938 8500. 0171-938 8441. South Kensington.
14, 45A, 49, 74, C1.
12–6pm Mon, 10am–6pm Tue–Sun (last adm for temporary exhibitions: 4:30pm).
Dec 24–26, Jan 1, Good Fri, May Day. **Donation.**

Italian Renaissance Art

Pirelli Garden

★ **Medieval Treasury**
The Eltenberg Reliquary, made in Cologne in the late 12th century, is one of the museum's masterpieces of medieval craftsmanship.

The Cast Courts contain replicas of ancient sculptures.

Toshiba Gallery of Japanese Art

T.T. Tsui Gallery of Chinese Art
This watercolor on silk is an ancestor portrait from the Qing Dynasty (1644–1912).

Sculpture

Islamic Art 700–1800

Main entrance from Cromwell Road

★ **Nehru Gallery of Indian Art**
This automated tiger mauling an Englishman dates from the 19th century, when India formed part of the British Empire.

Elevator to Levels C and D

European Art and Design 1600–1800

The Dress Collection is devoted to fashionable clothes dating from around 1600 to today.

Science Museum ❹

Exhibition Rd SW7. **Map** 2 E5.
📞 0171-938 8000. ⊖ South
Kensington. ⏱ 10am–6pm daily.
⬤ Dec 24–26. ♿ 🅿 ♿ ✉

CENTURIES OF continuing
scientific and technolog-
ical development lie at the
heart of the Science Museum,
ranging from Ancient Greek
and Roman medicine to space
exploration and nuclear fission.
This huge, impressive
collection brings entertainment to the process of learning, with many interactive
displays, which anyone can

**Newcomen's Steam Engine (1712),
Science Museum**

easily understand. Others are
aimed at children, with staff
on hand to give further
explanations. Of equal importance is the social context of
science: what discoveries and
inventions mean for day-to-
day life, and the process of
discovery itself.

The best of the displays are
Flight, which gives a chance
to experiment with aeronau-
tical principles, and Launch
Pad, designed to give 7- to
13-year-olds a knowledge of
basic scientific principles. The
Exploration of Space displays
the scarred Apollo 10 space-
craft that carried three astro-
nauts to the moon and back
in May 1969. There is also a
video of the Apollo 11 moon
landing which took place a
few weeks later. More down-
to-earth, but just as absorbing, is Food for Thought,
which reveals the impact of
science and technology on
every

aspect of food. You can play
cashier with a laser scanner
cash register, learn about
additives, with a computer
program, and see how eating
habits have changed by
peering into a series of
pantries from 1900 to 1970.
Other popular sections include:
Power and Land Transport,
which displays working steam
engines, vintage trains, cars
and motorbikes; and Optics,
which has holograms, lasers
and colormixing experiments.

The top floors house the
Wellcome Museum of The
History of Medicine, which
charts medical practices, both
scientific and magical, from
ancient times through to the
present day. Exhibits range
from a replica of an Etruscan
dental bridge to an Egyptian
mummified head.

Natural History Museum ❺

Cromwell Rd SW7. **Map** 2 E5.
📞 0171-938 9123. ⊖ South
Kensington. ⏱ 10am–5:50pm
Mon–Sat, 11am–5:50pm Sun & public
hols. ⬤ Dec 23–26. ♿ 🅿 ♿ ✉

THIS VAST CATHEDRAL-LIKE
building is the most archi-
tecturally flamboyant of the
South Kensington museums.
Its richly sculpted stonework
conceals an iron and steel
frame. This building technique
was revolutionary when the
museum opened in 1881. The
imaginative displays tackle
fundamental issues such as
the ecology and evolution of
the planet, the
origin of species
and the develop-
ment of human
beings – all
explained
through a
dynamic

**Relief from a decorative panel in
the Natural History Museum**

combination of the latest
technology, interactive techniques and traditional displays.

The museum is divided into
the Life and Earth Galleries. In
the former, the Ecology exhibition begins its exploration
of the complex web of the
natural world, and man's role
in it, through a convincing replica of a moonlit rain-forest
buzzing with the sounds of
insects. The most popular exhibits here are in the Dinosaur
section, which has a moving,
roaring tableau of three life-
sized, animatronic beasts
devouring a dead Tenonto-
saurus. The Earth Galleries
explore the history of Earth
and its wealth of natural
resources, and offer the opportunity to experience the
rumblings of an earthquake.

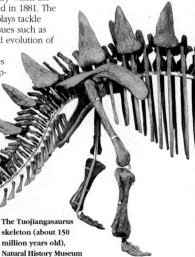

**The Tuojiangasaurus
skeleton (about 150
million years old),
Natural History Museum**

Statue of the young Queen Victoria outside Kensington Palace, sculpted by her daughter, Princess Louise

Hyde Park and Kensington Gardens ⑥

W2. **Map** 2 F2. ☎ 0171-298 2100. **Hyde Park** ⊖ Hyde Park Corner, Knightsbridge, Lancaster Gate, Marble Arch. ◯ 5am–midnight daily. ♿ **Kensington Gardens** ⊖ Queensway, Lancaster Gate. ◯ 5am–dusk daily. ♿ See **Parks and Gardens** pp76–7.

THE ANCIENT MANOR of Hyde was part of the lands of Westminster Abbey seized by Henry VIII at the Dissolution of the Monasteries in 1536 (see pp50–51). James I opened the park to the public in the early 17th century, and it was soon one of the city's most fashionable public spaces. Unfortunately it also became popular with duellers and highwaymen, and consequently William III had 300 lights hung along Rotten Row, the first street in England to be lit up at night.

In 1730, the Westbourne River was dammed by Queen Caroline in order to create the Serpentine, an artificial lake where Britain's victory over the French at Trafalgar was celebrated in 1814 with a re-enactment of the battle to the strains of the National Anthem. Today the Serpentine is used for boating and swimming, and Rotten Row for horse-back riding. The park is also a rallying point for political demonstrations, while at Speaker's Corner, in the northeast, anyone has had the right to address the public since 1872. Sundays are particularly lively, with many budding orators and a number of eccentrics revealing their plans for the betterment of mankind.

Adjoining Hyde Park is Kensington Gardens, the former grounds of Kensington Palace, which were opened to the public in 1841. Two great attractions for children are the bronze statue of J.M. Barrie's fictional Peter Pan (1912), by George Frampton, and the Round Pond where people sail model boats. Also worth seeing is the dignified Orangery (1704), once used by Queen Anne as a "summer supper house" and now used as a summer café.

Detail of the Coalbrookdale Gate, Kensington Gardens

Kensington Palace ⑦

Kensington Palace Gdns W8. **Map** 2 D3. ☎ 0171-937 9561. ⊖ High St Kensington, Queensway. ◯ 9am–5pm Mon–Sat, 11am–5pm Sun. ◯ Dec 24–26, Jan 1, Good Fri. 🎟 ♿ ground floor only. 🎫

KENSINGTON PALACE was the principal residence of the royal family from the 1690s until 1760, when George III moved to Buckingham Palace. Over the years it has seen a number of important royal events. In 1714 Queen Anne died here from a fit of apoplexy brought on by over-eating and in June 1837, Princess Victoria of Kent was awakened to be told that her uncle William IV had died and she was now queen – the beginning of her 64-year reign. Half of the palace still holds royal apartments, but the other half is open to the public. Among the highlights are a display of court dress from 1760 to the present, including Princess Diana's wedding dress, and a series of 18th-century state rooms with intricate ceilings painted by William Kent (see pp24). The most spectacular is the King's Staircase, over-looked by lifelike figures.

REGENT'S PARK AND BLOOMSBURY

CREAM STUCCOED terraces by John Nash *(see p107)* fringe the southern edge of Regent's Park in London's highest concentration of quality Georgian housing. The park, named for the Prince Regent, was also designed by Nash, as the culmination of a triumphal route from the Prince's house in St. James *(see pp86–7)*. Today it is the busiest of the royal parks and boasts a zoo, an open air theater, boating lake, rose garden, cafés and London's largest mosque. To the northeast is Camden Town *(see p130)* with its popular market, stores and cafés, reached by walking, or taking a boat, along the picturesque Regent's Canal.

Ancient Greek vase, British Museum

Bloomsbury, an enclave of attractive garden squares and Georgian brick terraces, was one of the most fashionable areas of the city until the mid-19th century, when the arrival of large hospitals and railroad stations persuaded many of the wealthier residents to move west to Mayfair, Knightsbridge and Kensington. Home to the British Museum since 1753 and the University of London since 1828, Bloomsbury has long been the domain of artists, writers and intellectuals, including the Bloomsbury Group *(see p149)*, George Bernard Shaw, Charles Dickens and Karl Marx. Traditionally a center for the book trade, it remains a good place for literary browsing.

SIGHTS AT A GLANCE

Historic Streets
Bloomsbury ❺

Museums and Galleries
British Museum pp108–109 ❹

Madame Tussaud's and the Planetarium ❶
Sherlock Holmes Museum ❷
Wallace Collection ❸

GETTING THERE
For most of Regent's Park, the nearest tube stations are Regent's Park, Great Portland Street and Baker Street. Buses 13, 139 and 159 run from Trafalgar Square to near Baker Street. The closest station to the zoo is Camden Town. Russell Square tube station is in the heart of Bloomsbury.

KEY

🚇 Underground station

🅿 Parking

0 meters   500
0 yards   500

◁ **St. Andrew's Place, Regent's Park**

Madame Tussaud's and the Planetarium ❶

Marylebone Rd NW1. **Map** 3 B3.
📞 0171-935 6861. ⊖ Baker St.
🕐 10am–5:30pm daily. ⚫ Dec 25.
🏛️ 📷 ♿

MADAME TUSSAUD began her wax-modeling career making death masks of victims of the French Revolution. She moved to England and in 1835 set up an exhibition of her work in Baker Street, near the present site. Traditional techniques are still used to create figures of royalty, politicians, actors, pop stars, and sports heroes. The main sections of the exhibition are: the Garden Party, where visitors mingle with lifelike models of celebrities; Super Stars, devoted to the giants of the entertainment world; and the Grand Hall, a collection of various royalty, statesmen, world leaders, writers and artists, from Lenin and Martin Luther King Jr. to Shakespeare and Pablo Picasso.

Wax figure of Elizabeth II

The Chamber of Horrors is the most renowned part of Madame Tussaud's. Alongside some of the original French Revolution death masks are chilling recreations of murders and executions. The Spirit of

Wax model of Luciano Pavarotti (1990), Madame Tussaud's

Conan Doyle's fictional detective Sherlock Holmes

London finale is a recent addition, where visitors travel in stylized taxicabs through the city's history, to "witness" events, from the Great Fire of 1666 to the Swinging 1960s.

Next door, the Planetarium, built in 1958, is part of the same complex and has spectacular star and laser shows.

Sherlock Holmes Museum ❷

237B Baker St NW1. **Map** 3 A4.
📞 0171-935 8866. ⊖ Baker St. 🕐
10am–6pm daily. ⚫ Dec 25. 🏛️ 📷

SIR ARTHUR CONAN DOYLE'S fictional detective was supposed to live at 221B Baker Street, which did not exist. The museum, labeled 221B, actually stands between Nos. 237 and 239, and is the only surviving Victorian lodging house on the street. There is a reconstruction of Holmes's front room, and memorabilia from the stories decorate the walls. Visitors can buy plaques, Holmes hats, Toby jugs and meerschaum pipes.

Wallace Collection ❸

Hertford House, Manchester Sq W1.
Map 3 B4. 📞 0171-935 0687.
⊖ Bond St. 🕐 10am–5pm Mon–Sat, 2–5pm Sun. ⚫ Dec 24–26, Jan 1, Good Fri, May Day. ♿ phone first. 📷

ONE OF THE WORLD'S finest private collections of art, it has remained intact since 1897. The product of passionate collecting by four generations of the Seymour-Conway family who were Marquesses of Hertford, it was bequeathed to the state on the condition that it would go on permanent public display with nothing added or taken away. The 25 beautiful galleries are a must for anyone with even a passing interest in European art.

The 3rd Marquess (1777–1842), a flamboyant London figure, used his Italian wife's fortune to build on the rich collection of family portraits he had inherited, buying works by Titian and Canaletto, along with numerous 17th-century Dutch paintings including works by Van Dyck. The collection's particular strength, however, is in 18th-century French painting, sculpture, and decorative arts, acquired in France by the 4th Marquess (1800–70) and his natural son, Sir Richard Wallace (1818–90). The Marquess had a taste for lush romanticism rather than realism, a distinct advantage in post-Revolution

A 16th-century Italian majolica dish from the Wallace Collection

France, where most collectors had little time for the dreamy canvases painted for Louis XV and his court. Notable among these are Watteau's *Champs Elysées* (1716–17), Fragonard's *The Swing* (1766) and Boucher's *The Rising and Setting of the Sun* (1753).

Other highlights include Rembrandt's *Titus, the Artist's Son* (1650s), Titian's *Perseus and Andromeda* (1554–6) and Franz Hals's famous *Laughing Cavalier* (1624). There is also an important collection of Renaissance armor, and superb examples of Sèvres porcelain and Italian majolica.

John Nash's Regency London

JOHN NASH, the son of a Lambeth millwright, was designing houses from the 1780s. However, it was not until the 1820s that he also became known as an inspired town planner, when his "royal route" was completed. This took George IV from his Pall Mall palace, through Piccadilly Circus and up the elegant sweep of Regent Street to Regent's Park, which Nash bordered

Statue of John Nash (1752–1835)

with rows of beautiful Neo-Classical villas, such as Park Crescent and Cumberland Terrace. Though many of his plans were never completed, this map of 1851, which unusually places the south at the top, shows Nash's overall architectural impact on London. His other work included revamping Buckingham Palace (see pp88–9), and building theaters and churches.

Pall Mall

Piccadilly Circus (see p83)

St. James's Park (see p76–7)

The Theatre Royal Haymarket has retained Nash's 1821 Corinthian portico, but its interior was totally rebuilt in 1905.

Oxford Circus

Tottenham Court Road

All Souls, Langham Place is shown in this 1824 cartoon that lampoons Nash for his unorthodox design.

Regent Street

Regent's Park (see p105)

Cumberland Terrace, the longest and most ornate of the stuccoed terraces surrounding Regent's Park, was intended to face a royal palace, which was never built.

Park Crescent was designed by Nash to be the southern half of a circle, but the northern half was never built. The interiors were refurbished in the 1960s but the dramatic façade was kept intact.

British Museum ❹

Helmet from Sutton Hoo ship burial

THE OLDEST PUBLIC MUSEUM in the world, the British Museum was established in 1753 to house the extensive collections of the physician Sir Hans Sloane (1660–1753). The main part of the present building (1823–50) is by architect Robert Smirke. Over the years Sloane's collection has been added to by gifts and purchases, and the museum now contains artifacts spanning thousands of years of world culture. The British Library, currently housed in the museum's east wing, is moving to St. Pancras.

★ Egyptian Mummies
Animals such as this cat (30 BC) were preserved alongside humans by the ancient Egyptians.

North stairs

West stairs

Entrance from Montague Place

Bronze Figure Shiva Nataraja
This statue of the Hindu God Shiva Nataraja (c.1100) from South India forms part of the fine collection of Oriental art.

The Mexican Gallery celebrates one of the world's greatest civilizations. Displays include Maya sculptures and Aztec mosaics.

North stairs

West stairs

GALLERY GUIDE
The museum's 94 galleries cover 2.5 miles (4 km). Greek, Roman, Egyptian and Western Asiatic exhibits are on the west side of the ground floor; the Oriental collection on the north side; the British Library exhibits and the new Mexican Gallery are on the east. The rest of the floor is taken up with the Library reading rooms. Collections are continued on the first floor and in the basement. Temporary exhibitions are held throughout the museum and near the entrance in rooms 27 and 28.

★ Elgin Marbles
These 5th-century BC reliefs from the Parthenon in Athens were brought to London by Lord Elgin around 1802 and are the museum's most famous treasure.

Stairs to basement

STAR SIGHTS
★ Egyptian Mummies
★ Elgin Marbles
★ Lindisfarne Gospels

KEY TO FLOORPLAN

- ☐ Early British collections
- ☐ Coins, medals and drawings
- ☐ Medieval, Renaissance and Modern collections
- ☐ Western Asiatic archaeological collections
- ☐ Mexican Gallery
- ☐ Egyptian collections
- ☐ Greek and Roman collections
- ☐ Oriental collections
- ☐ British Library
- ☐ Nonexhibition space
- ☐ Temporary exhibitions

East stairs

The British Library Reading Room has 30,000 reference books and is open to visitors. Karl Marx, Mahatma Gandhi and George Bernard Shaw all used the room.

Private gardens of Bedford Square

Bloomsbury ❺

WC1. **Map** 4 F4. Russell Sq, Tottenham Court Rd. **Dickens House Museum** 0171-405 2127. Mon–Sat. public hols.

First floor

Main stairs

Ground floor

Mildenhall Treasure
The Great Dish was among the 34 pieces of 4th-century Roman silver tableware plowed up in Suffolk in 1942.

Main entrance from Great Russell Street

Main stairs

★ **Lindisfarne Gospels**
These illustrated 7th-century gospels (p405) are among the many manuscripts displayed in the library.

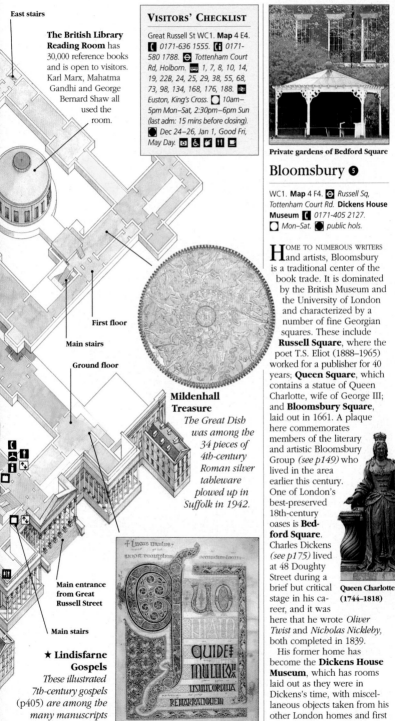

HOME TO NUMEROUS WRITERS and artists, Bloomsbury is a traditional center of the book trade. It is dominated by the British Museum and the University of London and characterized by a number of fine Georgian squares. These include **Russell Square**, where the poet T.S. Eliot (1888–1965) worked for a publisher for 40 years; **Queen Square**, which contains a statue of Queen Charlotte, wife of George III; and **Bloomsbury Square**, laid out in 1661. A plaque here commemorates members of the literary and artistic Bloomsbury Group *(see p149)* who lived in the area earlier this century. One of London's best-preserved 18th-century oases is **Bedford Square**. Charles Dickens *(see p175)* lived at 48 Doughty Street during a brief but critical stage in his career, and it was here that he wrote *Oliver Twist* and *Nicholas Nickleby*, both completed in 1839.

Queen Charlotte (1744–1818)

His former home has become the **Dickens House Museum**, which has rooms laid out as they were in Dickens's time, with miscellaneous objects taken from his other London homes and first editions of many of his works.

THE CITY AND SOUTHWARK

DOMINATED TODAY BY glossy office blocks, the City is the oldest part of the capital. The Great Fire of 1666 obliterated four-fifths of its buildings. Sir Christopher Wren rebuilt much of it and many of his churches survived World War II *(see pp58–9)*. Commerce has always been its lifeblood, and the power of its merchants and bankers secured it a degree of autonomy from state control. Even today the monarch cannot cross its boundaries without permission from the Lord Mayor. Humming with activity in business hours, the City empties at night.

Old bank sign on Lombard Street

In the Middle Ages Southwark, on the south bank of the Thames, was a refuge for pleasure-seekers, prostitutes, gamblers and criminals. Even after 1550, when the area fell under the jurisdiction of the City, its brothels and taverns thrived. There were also several bear-baiting arenas in which plays were staged until the building of theaters such as the Globe (1598), where many of Shakespeare's works were first performed. Relics of old Southwark are mostly on the waterfront, which has been imaginatively redeveloped and provided with a pleasant walkway.

SIGHTS AT A GLANCE

Historic Sights and Buildings
Lloyd's Building ❼
Old St. Thomas's Operating Theatre ⓫
Temple ❷
Tower Bridge ❾
Tower of London pp120–21 ❽

Museums and Galleries
Clink Exhibition ⓭
Design Museum ❿
Museum of London ❹
Shakespeare's Globe ⓮
Sir John Soane's Museum ❷

Churches and Cathedrals
St. Bartholomew-the-Great ❸
St. Paul's Cathedral pp116–17 ❺
St. Stephen Walbrook ❻
Southwark Cathedral ⓬

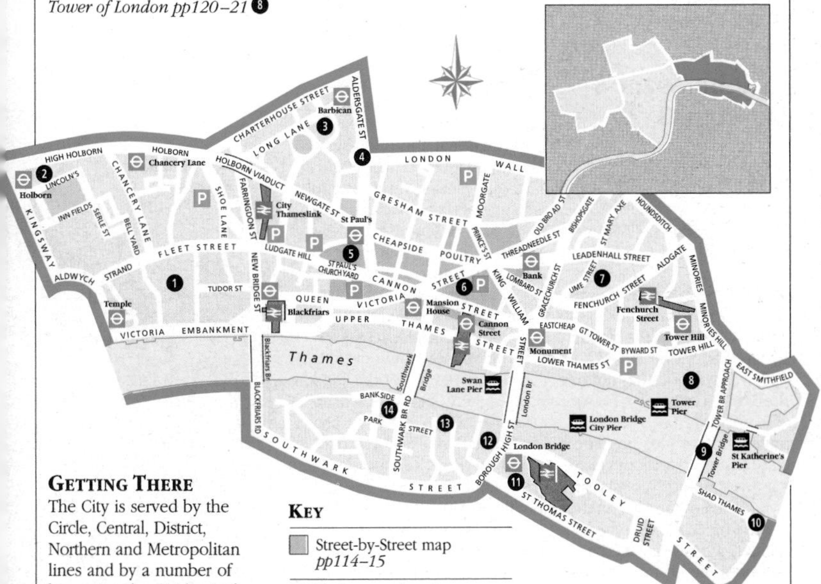

GETTING THERE

The City is served by the Circle, Central, District, Northern and Metropolitan lines and by a number of buses. London Bridge is the main station for Southwark – served by the Northern Line and by BR trains running from Charing Cross, Cannon Street and Waterloo.

KEY

	Street-by-Street map pp114–15
⊖	Underground station
⇒	British Rail station
P	Parking
⛴	River boat stop

0 meters 500
0 yards 500

◁ **St. Paul's Cathedral in the heart of the City, with the NatWest Tower (1980) to its left**

Wigged and robed barristers, Lincoln's Inn

Temple ❶

Middle Temple Lane EC4. **Map** 7 A3.
🚇 *Temple.* **Middle Temple Hall**
📞 *0171-353 4355.* ⏰ *10am–1pm &
2–4pm Mon–Fri.* ● *academic hols,
phone first.* ♿ *phone first.*

A CLUSTER of atmospheric squares form the Inner and Middle Temples, two of London's four Inns of Court, where law students are trained (Lincoln's Inn and Gray's Inn

are the other two). The four Inns fulfil identical functions but each remains conscious of its separate traditions. According to an age-old custom anyone in Britain training to be a trial lawyer has to join one of the Inns and must dine there 24 times – as well as passing exams – before being officially qualified.

The name Temple derives from the medieval Knights Templar, a religious order founded here in 1118 to protect pilgrims going to the Holy Land. The Templars owned this area until 1312 when the order was suppressed on charges of immorality and heresy. But the real reason was that they had become very wealthy, and their power was seen as a threat to the throne. Marble effigies of knights lie on the floor of the circular Temple church, part of which dates from the 12th century.

The finest of the Temple's other ancient buildings is the opulent Middle Temple Hall, which retains a wonderful Elizabethan hammer-beamed roof that was restored after bomb damage in World War II. It is thought that Shakespeare took part in a performance of *Twelfth Night* here in 1601.

St. Bartholomew-the-Great ❸

West Smithfield EC1. **Map** 7 B2.
📞 *0171-606 5171.* 🚇 *Barbican,
Farringdon.* ⏰ *8:30am–4:30pm Mon–
Fri (mid-Nov–mid-Feb: 8:30am–4pm),
10am–4pm Sat, 2–6pm Sun.*
● *Dec 25, 26, Jan 1.* 📷 ♿ ▮

T HE HISTORIC AREA of Smithfield has witnessed a number of bloody events over the years, among them the execution of rebel peasant leader Wat Tyler in 1381, and, in the reign of Mary I (1553–58), the burning of scores of Protestant martyrs.

Hidden in a quiet corner behind Smithfield meat market (central London's only surviving wholesale food market),

Sir John Soane's Museum ❷

13 Lincoln's Inn Fields WC2. **Map** 4
F4. 📞 *0171-405 2107.* 🚇 *Holborn.*
⏰ *10am–5pm Tue–Sat, 6–9pm 1st
Tue of month.* ● *public hols, Dec 24.*
📷 ♿ *limited.*

O NE OF THE MOST eccentric museums in London, this house was left to the nation by Sir John Soane in 1837, with a stipulation that nothing should be changed. The son of a bricklayer, Soane became one of Britain's leading late Georgian architects developing a restrained Neo-Classical style of his own. After marrying the niece of a wealthy builder, whose fortune he inherited, he bought and reconstructed No. 12 Lincoln's Inn Fields. In 1813 he and his wife moved into No. 13 and in 1824 he rebuilt No. 14, adding a picture gallery and the mock medieval Monk's Parlor. Today, true to Soane's

wishes, the collections are much as he left them – an eclectic gathering of beautiful, instructional and often simply peculiar artifacts. There are casts, bronzes, vases, antique fragments, paintings and a selection of bizarre trivia, which ranges from a giant fungus from Sumatra to a scold-bridle, a device designed to silence nagging wives. Highlights include the sarcophagus of Seti I, Soane's own designs, including those for the Bank of England, models by leading Neo-Classical sculptors such as Banks and Flaxman and the *Rake's Progress* series of paintings (1734), by William Hogarth, which Mrs. Soane bought for £520.

The building itself is full of architectural surprises and illusions. In the main ground floor room, cunningly placed mirrors play tricks with light and space, while an atrium stretching from the basement to the glass-domed roof allows light onto every floor.

A glass dome lets light onto all the floors.

A vast sarcophagus (1300 BC) stands on the floor of the crypt.

St. Bartholomew-the-Great is one of London's oldest churches. It once formed part of a priory founded in 1123 by a monk named Rahere, whose tomb is inside. Rahere was Henry I's court jester until he

St. Bartholomew's gatehouse

dreamed that St. Bartholomew had saved him from a winged monster. As prior, he would sometimes revert to his former role, entertaining crowds with juggling tricks at the annual Bartholomew Fair.

The 13th-century arch, now topped by a Tudor gatehouse, used to be the entrance to the church until the old nave was pulled down during the Dissolution of the Monasteries *(see pp50–51)*.

Museum of London ❹

London Wall EC2. **Map** 7 C2.
📞 0171-600 3699. ⊖ Barbican, St Paul's. ☐ 10am–5:50pm Tue–Sat & public hols, noon–5:50pm Sun.
⬤ Dec 25, Jan 1. 🎫 📷 ♿

Tᴴɪꜱ ᴍᴜꜱᴇᴜᴍ traces life in London from prehistoric times to the 20th century. Displays of archaeological finds and original domestic objects alternate with reconstructed street scenes and interiors, culminating in a 1932 broadcasting studio and a counter from Woolworth's.

Delft plate made in London 1602, Museum of London

Objects from Roman London include a brightly colored 2nd-century fresco, which came from a Southwark bath house, while from the Tudor city come a Delft plate and costumes, including leather clothes found on a garbage dump. The 17th-century section holds the shirt Charles I wore on the scaffold *(see pp52–3)*, and an audio-visual display recreating the Great Fire of 1666.

One of the most popular exhibits is the lavishly gilded Lord Mayor's State Coach, built in 1757 and still used for the colorful Lord Mayor's Show in November *(see pp64–5)*.

Every wall is covered and every room filled with artifacts from Soane's voluminous collection.

In the picture gallery, panels covered with paintings unfold to reveal more works of art hidden behind them.

The Monk's Parlor is full of grotesque Gothic casts.

Entrance

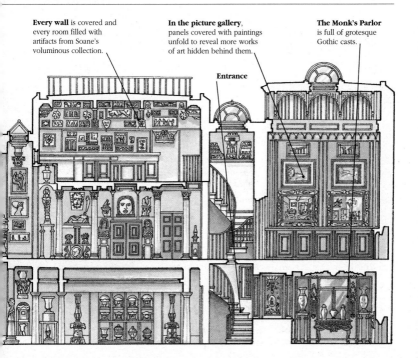

Street-by-Street: The City

Detail: St. Paul's Cathedral

THIS IS THE FINANCIAL HEART of London and
has been ever since the Romans set up a
trading post here 2,000 years ago. For years it
was London's main residential area, but today
very few people live here. The City was
severely bombed in World War II and the
main clues to its past are streets named after
vanished inns and markets. Its numerous
churches, many built after the Great Fire of 1666 by the
architect Sir Christopher Wren *(see p116)*, are now dwarfed
by lavish banks and postmodern developments.

St. Mary-le-Bow takes
its name from the bow
arches in the Norman
crypt. Anyone born
within earshot of its
bells is said to be
a true Cockney.

**The Temple
of Mithras** is
an important
Roman relic
(see p45).

New Change replaces Old
Change, a 13th-century street
destroyed in World War II.

St. Paul's

N E W   C H A N G E

ST PAUL'S CHURCHYARD

W A T L I N G   S T R E E T

C A N N O N   S T R E E T

FRIDAY STREET

BREAD STREET

QUEEN VICTORIA STREET

KING ST

QUEEN

**Mansion
House**

**★ St. Paul's
Cathedral**
*Built after the Great
Fire of 1666, Wren's
masterpiece was funded
by a tax on coal* ❺

Skinners' Hall is an 18th-century
Italianate building constructed
for the ancient guild that controlled trade in fur and leather.

STAR SIGHTS	KEY

- - - Suggested route

STAR SIGHTS

★ St. Paul's Cathedral

★ St. Stephen Walbrook

0 meters   100

0 yards   100

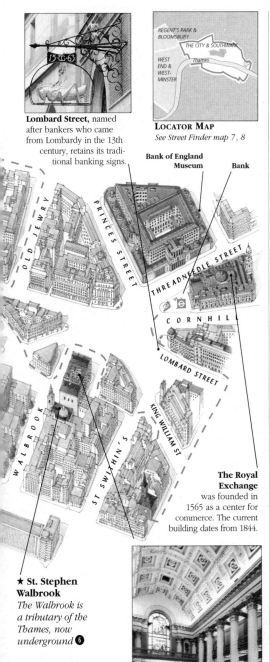

Lombard Street, named after bankers who came from Lombardy in the 13th century, retains its traditional banking signs.

LOCATOR MAP
See Street Finder map 7, 8

Bank of England Museum

Bank

OLD JEWRY

PRINCES STREET

THREADNEEDLE STREET

CORNHILL

LOMBARD STREET

KING WILLIAM ST

WALBROOK

ST SWITHIN'S

The Royal Exchange was founded in 1565 as a center for commerce. The current building dates from 1844.

★ **St. Stephen Walbrook**
The Walbrook is a tributary of the Thames, now underground ⑥

Mansion House (1753), designed by George Dance the Elder, is the official home of the Lord Mayor. One of the most spectacular rooms is the Egyptian Hall.

St. Paul's ⑤

See pp116–17.

St. Stephen Walbrook ⑥

39 Walbrook EC4. **Map** 8 D3.
📞 0171-283 4444. 🚇 Bank, Cannon St. ⏰ 10am–4pm Mon–Thu, 10am–3pm Fri. 📷

THE LORD MAYOR'S parish church was built by Sir Christopher Wren in the 1670s and is among the finest of all his City churches. The bright, airy interior is flooded with light by a huge dome that appears to float above the eight columns and arches that support it. Original fittings, such as the ornate font and rich pulpit, contrast with the stark simplicity of Henry Moore's massive white stone altar (1987). The best way to see the church is during one of its free organ recitals or lunchtime concerts.

Original 17th-century font

Lloyd's Building ⑦

1 Lime St EC3. **Map** 8 E2. 📞 0171-327 6210. 🚇 Monument, Bank, Aldgate. 📷 to the public.

THIS BUILDING, designed by Richard Rogers in 1986 for the world's largest insurance company, echoes his famous Pompidou Center in Paris.
One of London's most interesting modern buildings, it is a vast glass construction, with functional elements, such as stainless steel pipes, high-tech ducts and elevators, on the exterior.

Tower of London ⑧

See pp120–21.

St. Paul's Cathedral ❺

THE GREAT FIRE OF LONDON in 1666 left the medieval cathedral of St. Paul's in ruins. Wren was commissioned to rebuild it, but his design for a church on a Greek Cross plan (where all four arms are equal) met with considerable resistance. The authorities insisted on a conventional Latin cross, with a long nave and short transepts, which was believed to focus the congregation's attention on the altar. Despite the compromises, Wren created a magnificent Baroque cathedral, which was built between 1675 and 1710 and

has since formed the lavish setting for many state ceremonies.

★ **Dome**
At 113 m (360 ft), the elaborate dome is one of the highest in the world.

The balustrade along the top was added in 1718 against Wren's wishes.

★ **West Front and Towers**
Inspired by the Italian Baroque architect, Borromini, the towers were added by Wren in 1707.

The West Portico
consists of two stories of coupled Corinthian columns, topped by a pediment carved with reliefs showing the Conversion of St. Paul.

The Nave
An imposing succession of massive arches and saucer domes open out into the vast space below the cathedral's main dome.

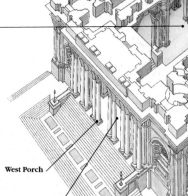

CHRISTOPHER WREN

Trained as a scientist, Sir Christopher Wren (1632–1723) began his impressive architectural career at the age of 31. He became a leading figure in the rebuilding of London after the Great Fire of 1666, building a total of 52 new churches. Although Wren never visited Italy, his work was influenced by Roman, Baroque and Renaissance architecture, as is apparent in his masterpiece, St. Paul's Cathedral.

West Porch

Main entrance approached from Ludgate Hill

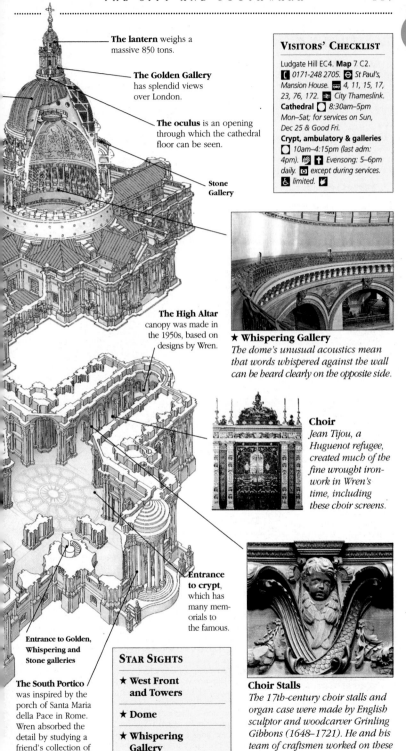

The **lantern** weighs a massive 850 tons.

The **Golden Gallery** has splendid views over London.

The **oculus** is an opening through which the cathedral floor can be seen.

Stone Gallery

The **High Altar** canopy was made in the 1950s, based on designs by Wren.

★ Whispering Gallery
The dome's unusual acoustics mean that words whispered against the wall can be heard clearly on the opposite side.

Choir
Jean Tijou, a Huguenot refugee, created much of the fine wrought iron-work in Wren's time, including these choir screens.

Entrance to crypt, which has many memorials to the famous.

Entrance to Golden, Whispering and Stone galleries

The South Portico was inspired by the porch of Santa Maria della Pace in Rome. Wren absorbed the detail by studying a friend's collection of architectural engravings.

STAR SIGHTS

★ West Front and Towers

★ Dome

★ Whispering Gallery

Choir Stalls
The 17th-century choir stalls and organ case were made by English sculptor and woodcarver Grinling Gibbons (1648–1721). He and his team of craftsmen worked on these intricate carvings for two years.

Tower Bridge ❾

SE1. **Map** 8 F4. 📞 *0171-403 3761.*
🚇 *Tower Hill.* ⏰ *Apr–Oct: 10am–6:30pm daily; Nov–Mar: 10am–4:45pm daily.* ⛔ *Dec 24–26, Jan 1, Good Fri.* 🏛 📷 ♿

T HIS FLAMBOYANT piece of
Victorian engineering,
designed by Sir Horace Jones,
was completed in 1894 and
soon became a symbol of

London. Its two Gothic towers
contain the mechanism for
raising the roadway to permit
large ships to pass through.
The towers are made of a
supporting steel framework
clad in stone to bear the great
weight, and are linked by two
high level walkways, which
were closed between 1909
and 1982 due to their
popularity with

prostitutes and suicides. The
bridge now houses a museum
with a vivid presentation telling
the story of its construction,
featuring lifelike mechanical
talking models. There are fine
river views from the walkways
and a look at the steam engine room that powered the
lifting machinery until
1976, when the system
was electrified.

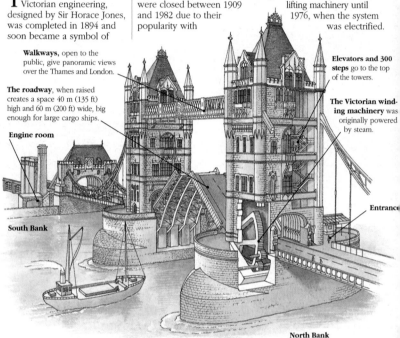

Walkways, open to the
public, give panoramic views
over the Thames and London.

The roadway, when raised
creates a space 40 m (135 ft)
high and 60 m (200 ft) wide, big
enough for large cargo ships.

Engine room

South Bank

**Elevators and 300
steps** go to the top
of the towers.

**The Victorian wind-
ing machinery** was
originally powered
by steam.

Entrance

North Bank

Design Museum ❿

Butlers Wharf, Shad Thames SE1.
Map 8 F4. 📞 *0171-407 6261.*
🚇 *Tower Hill, London Bridge.* ⏰
*11:30am–6pm Mon–Fri, 12–6pm Sat,
Sun.* ⛔ *Dec 24–26, Jan 1.* 🏛 ♿ 📷

T HIS MUSEUM was the first in
the world to be devoted
solely to the design of mass-
produced everyday objects.

**Sculpture by Paolozzi (1986)
outside the Design Museum**

The permanent collection
charts technical innovation,
changes in taste and commercial success or failure through
an eclectic range of furniture,
office equipment, cars, radios,
TV sets and household uten-
sils. Elite design classics such
as chairs by G.T. Rietveld and
a kettle by Philippe Starck
are shown alongside Pyrex
dishes, Tupperware cups and
a Kodak Instamatic camera.
Also worth seeing are proto-
types that disappeared without
a trace, such as a television
designed so that people could
watch it lying down.

Temporary exhibitions of
international design held in
the Review and Collections
galleries give a taste of what
may become familiar in the
future, and a chance to catch
up on various new trends.

Old St. Thomas's Operating Theatre ⓫

9A St. Thomas St SE1. **Map** 8 D4.
📞 *0171-955 4791.* 🚇 *London
Bridge.* ⏰ *10am–4pm Tue–Sun.*
⛔ *Dec 15–Jan 6.* 🏛 📷

M OST OF the old St. Thomas's
hospital was demolished
in 1862 to make room for a
railroad. The women's operating theater (1821) survived
in a garret over the hospital
church, where it lay forgotten
until the 1950s. It has since
been restored and fitted out
exactly as it would have been
in the 19th century, before
the discovery of anesthetics.
Displays show how patients
were blindfolded, gagged and
bound to the operating table.

Southwark Cathedral ⑫

Montague Close SE1. **Map** 8 D4.
📞 0171-407 2939. 🚇 London
Bridge. ⏰ 7:30am–6pm daily.

ALTHOUGH SOME PARTS OF this
building date back to the
12th century, it was not until
1905 that it became a cathedral. Many medieval
features remain, notably the
superb Gothic choir, and the
tomb of John Gower (c.1325–
1408), Chaucer's *(see p172)*
contemporary and fellow poet.

There is a monument to
Shakespeare *(see pp308–309)*,
carved in 1912 and a memorial
window above, installed in
1954. A chapel commemorates
John Harvard, the founder of
Harvard University, who was
born in Southwark and baptized here in 1607.

Clink Prison Museum ⑬

1 Clink St SE1. **Map** 7 C4. 📞 0171-
403 6515. 🚇 London Bridge. ⏰
10am–6pm daily. 🔒 Dec 25, 26. 🏛

THE CLINK RECALLS the notorious prison attached to
Winchester House, the London
residence of the bishops of
Winchester from the 12th century until 1626. Being outside
the range of City authority,
the surrounding area was
under the more lenient jurisdiction of the bishops, and it
was known as "the Liberty of
the Clink." This was London's
red-light district; while con-
demning prostitution, the
bishops licensed and regulated
the brothels, profiting greatly
from their takings – prostitutes commonly became
known as "Winchester geese."

Destroyed by fire in 1780,
the Clink was one of five
prisons in Southwark and the
first in which women were
regularly confined. The recreations of cells and the
grotesque instruments of
torture that are part of the
exhibition vividly evoke the
gruesome life within its walls.

The only surviving part of
Winchester House is a 14th-
century rose window, just
to the east of the museum.

Shakespeare window (1954), Southwark Cathedral

Globe ⑭

Emerson St/New Globe Walk SE1.
Map 7 C3. 📞 0171-928 6406.
🚇 London Bridge. ⏰ 10am–5pm
daily. 🔒 Dec 24–26. 🏛

MANY OF SHAKESPEARE'S plays
were written for and
first produced at the Globe
theater. Originally built in
1599, amid arenas for bear-
baiting and cockfighting, in
order to escape the stricter
jurisdiction of the City, the
theater burned down in 1613
(a common fate of wooden
playhouses). It was rebuilt
in 1614, then closed by the
Puritans in 1642 and finally
demolished two years later.

The Globe is now in the
process of being reconstructed
close to its 16th-century site.
This ambitious project, due to
be completed in 1999, involves
building an entire Elizabethan
complex, including the Globe,
a pub, a permanent exhibition
hall and an indoor theater,
built to a design by Inigo Jones
(see pp52–3), where plays will
take place during the winter.

Today an exhibition explains
the background of the Globe
and the Elizabethan methods
being used to rebuild it.
Guides take you on a tour of
the site, giving an insight into
the project, as well as an idea
of what it will be like to see
Shakespeare's plays produced
in their intended setting. The
first production in the outdoor
Globe is to be staged in 1996.

The site is close to Bankside
Power Station, soon to be a
branch of the Tate *(see p93)*.

Shakespeare's *Henry IV* (performed at the Globe theater around 1600)

Tower of London ❽

SOON AFTER HE BECAME KING in 1066, William the Conqueror built a wooden fortress here to guard the entrance to London from the Thames Estuary. In 1097 the White Tower, standing today at the center of the complex, was completed in sturdy stone, other fine buildings have been added over the centuries. The Tower has served as a royal residence, armory, treasury and most famously as a prison for enemies of the crown. Many were tortured and among those who met their death there were the "princes in the tower", the sons and heirs of Edward IV. Today the tower is a popular attraction, housing the Crown Jewels and countless other exhibits. Its most celebrated residents are six ravens whose presence is protected by the legend that the kingdom will fall if they desert the tower.

Beauchamp Tower
Many high-ranking prisoners were held here, often with their own retinues of servants. The tower was built by Edward I about 1281.

"Beefeaters"
Forty-two Yeoman Warders guard the Tower and live there. Their uniforms hark back to Tudor times.

Two 13th-century curtain walls protect the tower.

Tower Green was the execution site for favored prisoners, away from crowds on Tower Hill, where many had to submit to public execution. Seven people died here, including two of Henry VIII's six wives, Anne Boleyn and Catherine Howard.

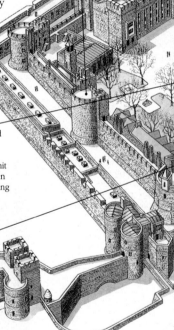

Queen's House
This Tudor building is the sovereign's official residence at the Tower.

Main entrance from Tower Hill

THE CROWN JEWELS

The world's best-known collection of precious objects, now displayed in a splendid exhibition room, includes the gorgeous regalia of crowns, scepters, orbs and swords used at coronations and other state occasions. Most date from 1661, when Charles II commissioned replacements for regalia destroyed by Parliament after the execution of Charles I *(see pp52–3)*. Only a few older pieces survived, hidden by royalist clergymen until the Restoration – notably, Edward the Confessor's sapphire ring, now incorporated into the Imperial State Crown *(see p73)*. The crown was made for Queen Victoria in 1837 and has been used at every coronation since.

The Sovereign's Ring (1831)

The Sovereign's Orb (1661), a hollow gold sphere encrusted with jewels

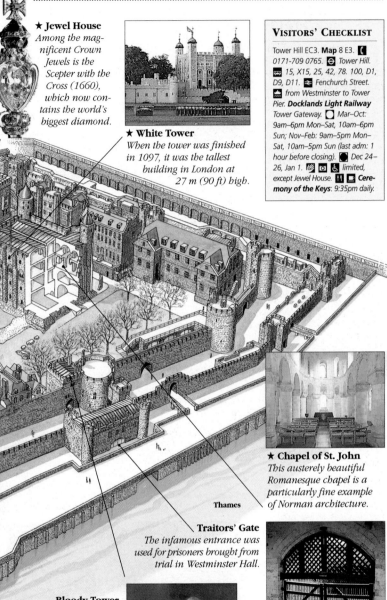

★ Jewel House
*Among the mag-
nificent Crown
Jewels is the
Scepter with the
Cross (1660),
which now con-
tains the world's
biggest diamond.*

★ White Tower
*When the tower was finished
in 1097, it was the tallest
building in London at
27 m (90 ft) high.*

VISITORS' CHECKLIST

Tower Hill EC3. **Map** 8 E3.
0171-709 0765. Tower Hill.
15, X15, 25, 42, 78. 100, D1,
D9, D11. Fenchurch Street.
from Westminster to Tower
Pier. **Docklands Light Railway**
Tower Gateway. Mar–Oct:
9am–6pm Mon–Sat, 10am–6pm
Sun; Nov–Feb: 9am–5pm Mon–
Sat, 10am–5pm Sun (last adm: 1
hour before closing). Dec 24–
26, Jan 1. limited,
except Jewel House. **Ceremony of the Keys**: 9:35pm daily.

★ Chapel of St. John
*This austerely beautiful
Romanesque chapel is a
particularly fine example
of Norman architecture.*

Thames

Traitors' Gate
*The infamous entrance was
used for prisoners brought from
trial in Westminster Hall.*

Bloody Tower
*Edward IV's two sons were
put here by their uncle,
Richard of Gloucester (subsequently Richard III), after
their father died in 1483.
The princes, depicted here
by John Millais (1829–96),
disappeared mysteriously
and Richard was crowned
later that year. In 1674
the skeletons of two children were found nearby.*

STAR SIGHTS

★ Jewel House

★ White Tower

★ Chapel of St. John

SHOPS AND MARKETS

LONDON is one of the great shopping cities of Europe, with bustling, lively street markets, world-famous department stores, and a wide variety of eclectic shops selling clothes, crafts and antiques *(see p627)*. The best shopping areas range from elegant, upmarket districts such as Knightsbridge, which sells expensive clothes, porcelain

Bags from two famous West End shops

and jewelry, to the busy, chaotic stretch of Oxford Street, and the colorful, noisy markets of Covent Garden *(see p81)*, Berwick Street and Brick Lane. The city is best known however, for its inexhaustible range of clothes shops selling everything from traditional tweeds to the latest zany designs of an ever-changing main-street fashion.

CHAIN AND DEPARTMENT STORES

Façade of Liberty (1925)

THE MOST FAMOUS of London's many department stores is **Harrod's**, with 300 departments, 4,000 employees, and a spectacular Edwardian food hall. Nearby **Harvey Nichols** stocks high fashion and boasts the city's most stylish food hall. Gourmets should make a pilgrimage to **Fortnum and Mason**, which has stocked high quality food for nearly 300 years. Traditional teas are available in the top floor café.

Selfridge's sells virtually everything from fine cashmeres to household gadgets, while **John Lewis** and its Chelsea partner **Peter Jones** specialize in fabrics, china, glass and household items. **Liberty**, the West End's last privately owned department store, still sells the hand-blocked silks and Oriental goods for which it was famous when it first opened in 1875. **Marks and Spencer**, long known for its good quality own-label clothes,

began as a market stall in Leeds in 1882, and now has some 700 branches worldwide.

The best chain store record shops are **Virgin Megastore**, **Tower Records** and **HMV**.

CLOTHES AND SHOES

BRITISH DESIGNERS range from elegant **Jasper Conran** to **Vivienne Westwood**, doyenne of the punkish avant-garde. Somewhere between are **Katharine Hamnett** and **Paul Smith**, while an ever-changing host of adventurous young designers produce outrageous clothes for trendy clubbers. You can find these in shops such as **Hyper Hyper**, while the creations of more established international designers are stocked at places such as **Browns**.

Traditional English clothing – waxed Barbour jackets and Burberry trench coats – are

found in outlets such as **The Scotch House, Burberry** and **Gieves & Hawkes**, while **Laura Ashley** is renowned for its floral print dresses.

Shoes range from Oxfords and traditional brogues from **Church's Shoes** and handmade footwear from **John Lobb**, to the stylish, more affordable designs at **Hobbs** and **Pied à Terre**.

MARKETS

LONDON'S MARKETS sell everything from street fashion and vintage clothes to canned food past its sell-by date and cheap household goods. The fashionable markets are **Camden Lock, Greenwich, Portobello Road** and **Covent Garden** where you can find an assortment of handmade crafts, old clothes and antiques. For those more serious about antique collecting, go early

Harrod's at night, illuminated by 11,500 lights

on a Friday to **Bermondsey Market** in South London.

The most famous London market is **Petticoat Lane**, worth a visit for the sheer volume of leather goods and the noisy, cheerful atmosphere created by the many Cockney stallholders. **Brick Lane** is another authentic East End market where dubious characters hustle gold watches and jewelry, and sheds are piled high with shabby furniture and bric-a-brac. For a glimpse of spirited greengrocers in central London head for **Berwick Street**, which is lined with fruit and vegetables, fabrics and household goods.

Bustling Petticoat Lane market, officially known as Middlesex Street

DIRECTORY

CHAIN AND DEPARTMENT STORES

Fortnum and Mason
181 Piccadilly W1.
Map 6 D1.
0171-734 8040.

Harrod's
87–135 Brompton Rd SW1.
Map 5 A3.
0171-730 1234.

Harvey Nichols
109–125 Knightsbridge SW1.
Map 5 B2.
0171-235 5000.

HMV
150 Oxford St W1.
Map 4 D4.
0171-631 3423.

John Lewis
278–306 Oxford St W1.
Map 3 C5.
0171-629 7711.

Liberty
210–20 Regent St W1.
Map 3 C5.
0171-734 1234.

Marks & Spencer
173 & 458 Oxford St W1.
Map 3 C5/3 B5.
0171-935 7954.
Two of many branches.

Peter Jones
Sloane Square SW1.
Map 5 A4.
0171-730 3434.

Selfridge's
400 Oxford St W1.
Map 3 B5.
0171-629 1234.

Tower Records
1 Piccadilly Circus W1.
Map 6 D1.
0171-439 2500.

Virgin Megastore
14–30 Oxford St W1.
Map 4 E4.
0171-631 1234.

CLOTHES AND SHOES

Browns
23 South Molton St W1.
Map 3 B5.
0171-491 7833.
One of several branches.

Burberry
18–22 Haymarket SW1.
Map 6 D1.
0171-930 3343.
One of two branches.

Church's Shoes
163 New Bond St W1.
Map 3 C5.
0171-499 9449.
One of several branches.

Gieves & Hawkes
1 Savile Row W1.
Map 3 C5.
0171-434 2001.

Hobbs
47 South Molton St W1.
Map 3 C5.
0171-629 0750.
One of several branches.

Hyper Hyper
26–40 Kensington High St W8. **Map** 1 C4.
0171-938 4343.
One of two branches.

Jasper Conran
49–50 Great Marlborough St W1.
Map 4 D5.
0171-603 6668.

John Lobb
9 St James's St SW1.
Map 6 D1.
0171-930 3664.

Katharine Hamnett
20 Sloane St SW1.
Map 5 A3.
0171-823 1002.

Laura Ashley
256–258 Regent St W1.
Map 4 D5.
0171-437 9760.
One of several branches.

Paul Smith
41–44 Floral St WC2.
Map 4 E5.
0171-379 7133.

Pied à Terre
19 South Molton St W1
Map 3 B5.
0171-629 1362.
One of several branches.

The Scotch House
2 Brompton Rd SW1.
Map 5 A2.
0171-581 2151.
One of several branches.

Vivienne Westwood
6 Davies St W1.
Map 3 B5.
0171-629 3757.

MARKETS

Bermondsey
Long Lane & Bermondsey St SE1.
Map 8 E5.
5am–2pm Fri.

Berwick Street
Berwick St W1.
Map 4 D5.
9am–6pm Mon–Sat.

Brick Lane
Brick Lane E1.
Shoreditch, Liverpool St, Aldgate East.
dawn–1pm Sun.

Camden Lock
Chalk Farm Rd NW1.
Camden Town.
9am–5pm Thu & Fri, 10am–6pm Sat & Sun.

Covent Garden
The Piazza WC2.
Map 4 F5. 9am–5pm daily (antiques: Mon).

Petticoat Lane
Middlesex St E1.
Liverpool St, Aldgate, Aldgate East.
9am–2pm Sun.

Portobello Road
Portobello Rd W10.
Notting Hill Gate, Ladbrook Grove.
7am–5:30pm Sat (general market: 9am–5pm Fri–Wed, 9am–1pm Thu).

Greenwich
College Approach SE10.
Greenwich.
9am–6pm Sat, Sun.

ENTERTAINMENT IN LONDON

ONDON HAS THE ENORMOUS variety of entertainment that only the great cities of the world can provide. The historical backdrop and the lively bustling atmosphere add to the excitement. Whether dancing the night away at a famous disco or making the most of London's varied arts scene, the visitor faces bewildering choices. A trip to London is not complete without a visit to the theater, which ranges from glamorous West End musicals to experimental Fringe plays. There is world-class ballet and opera in fabled venues such as Sadler's Wells and the Royal Opera House. The musical menu covers everything from classical, jazz and rock to rhythm and

Many London cafés have free live music

blues performed in atmospheric basement clubs, old converted movie theaters and outdoor venues such as Wembley. Movie buffs can choose from hundreds of films each night. Sports fans can watch cricket at Lord's or participate in a host of activities from water sports to ice skating.

Time Out, published every Wednesday, is the most comprehensive guide to what's on in London, with detailed weekly listings and reviews. *The Evening Standard, The Guardian* (Saturday) and *The Independent* also have reviews and information on events. If you buy tickets from booking agencies rather than direct from box offices, do compare prices – and only buy from ticket touts if you're desperate.

WEST END AND NATIONAL THEATERS

Palace Theatre poster (1898)

THE GLAMOROUS, glittering world of West End theaterland, emblazoned with the names of world-famous performers, offers an extraordinary range of entertainment.

West End theaters (see Directory for individual theaters) survive on their profits and rely on an army of financial backers, known as "angels." Consequently, they tend to stage commercial productions with mass appeal:

musicals, classics, comedies and plays by bankable contemporary playwrights that can, if successful, run for years.

The state-subsidized Royal National Theatre is based in the riverside **South Bank Centre** *(see p126)*. Its three auditoriums – the large, open-staged Olivier, the proscenium-arched Lyttelton, and the small but flexible studio space of the Cottesloe – make a diversity of productions possible.

The Royal Shakespeare Company regularly stages plays by Shakespeare, but its large repertoire includes ancient Greek tragedies, Restoration comedies and modern works. Its main base is at Stratford-upon-Avon *(see pp312–13)*, but its major productions also come to its London headquarters at the **Barbican** *(see p126)*, where it performs in the magnificent Barbican Theatre and in the Pit, a more intimate stage in the same complex.

Theater tickets cost from £5 to £30 and can be bought direct from box offices, by telephone or by mail. Many venues offer unsold tickets just before a performance. A ticket booth in Leicester Square, open 2:30–6:30pm (from noon for matinées) Monday to Saturday, sells cheap tickets on the day (cash only) for a wide range of shows.

OFF-WEST END AND FRINGE THEATERS

OFF-WEST END THEATER is a middle category bridging the gap between West End and Fringe theater. It includes venues that, regardless of location, have a permanent management team and often provide the opportunity for established directors and actors to try their hands at more adventurous works in a smaller, more intimate, environment. Fringe theaters, on the other hand, are normally venues rented to visiting companies. Both offer a vast array of innovative productions, serving as an outlet for new, often experimental writing, and for plays by gay, feminist and minority writers.

The Old Vic, the first home of the National Theatre from 1963

Open-air theater at Regent's Park

Venues (too numerous to list – see newspaper listings), range from tiny theaters or rooms above pubs such as the Gate, which has a reputation for high quality productions of neglected European classics, to centrally based theaters such as the Donmar Warehouse, which regularly attracts major directors and actors.

OPEN-AIR THEATER

IN SUMMER, a performance of one of Shakespeare's airier creations such as *Comedy of Errors, A Midsummer Night's Dream* or *As You Like It,* takes on an atmosphere of pure enchantment and magic among the green vistas of Regent's Park or Holland Park. Be sure to take a rug or blanket.

MOVIE THEATERS

THE WEST END abounds with multiplex theater chains (MGM, Odeon, UCI) that show big budget Hollywood films, usually in advance of the rest of the country, although release dates tend to lag well behind the US and many other European countries.

The Odeon Marble Arch has the largest commercial screen in Europe, while the Odeon Leicester Square boasts London's biggest auditorium with almost 2,000 seats.

Londoners are well-informed movie-goers and even the larger theater chains include some low-budget and foreign films in their repertoire. The majority of foreign films are subtitled, rather than dubbed. A number of independent

Life-sized models at the Museum of the Moving Image

theaters, such as the Metro, Renoir and Prince Charles in central London, and the Curzon in Mayfair, show foreign-language and slightly more offbeat art films.

The largest concentration of movie theaters is in and around Leicester Square, although there are local theaters in most areas. Just off Leicester Square, the Prince Charles is the West End's cheapest movie theater. Elsewhere in the area you can expect to pay between £6 and £9 – almost twice the price of the local movie theaters. Monday and after-noon performances in the West End are less pricey.

The National Film Theatre (NFT), on the South Bank, is London's flagship repertory theater. Subsidized by the British Film Institute, it screens a wide range of movies, old and new, from all around the world. Just next door is the fun and innovative Museum of the Moving Image (MOMI), which is an absolute must for movie enthusiasts.

DIRECTORY	Dominion	Lyric	Savoy
WEST END THEATERS	Tottenham Court Rd. **Map** 4 E4. (*0171-416 6060.*	Shaftesbury Ave. **Map** 4 D5. (*0171-494 5045.*	Strand. **Map** 4 F5. (*0171-836 8888.*
Adelphi Strand. **Map** 4 F5. (*0171-344 0055.*	**Duchess** Catherine St. **Map** 4 F5. (*0171-494 5075.*	**New London** Drury Lane. **Map** 4 E5. (*0171-405 0072.*	**Shaftesbury** Shaftesbury Ave. **Map** 4 E4. (*0171-379 5399.*
Albery St. Martin's Lane. **Map** 4 E5. (*0171-369 1730.*	**Duke of York's** St. Martin's Lane. **Map** 4 E5. (*0171-836 5122.*	**Palace** Shaftesbury Ave. **Map** 4 E5. (*0171-434 0909.*	**Strand** Aldwych. **Map** 4 F5. (*0171-240 0300.*
Aldwych Aldwych. **Map** 4 F5. (*0171-416 6003.*	**Fortune** Russell St. **Map** 4 F5. (*0171-836 2238.*	**Phoenix** Charing Cross Rd. **Map** 4 E5. (*0171-867 1044.*	**St Martin's** West St. **Map** 4 E5. (*0171-836 1443.*
Apollo Shaftesbury Ave. **Map** 4 E5. (*0171-494 5070.*	**Garrick** Charing Cross Rd. **Map** 4 E5. (*0171-494 5085.*	**Piccadilly** Denman St. **Map** 4 D5. (*0171-867 1118.*	**Theatre Royal: –Drury Lane** Catherine St. **Map** 4 F5. (*0171-494 5062.*
Cambridge Earlham St. **Map** 4 E5. (*0171-379 5299.*	**Gielgud** Shaftesbury Ave. **Map** 4 D5. (*0171-494 5065.*	**Prince Edward** Old Compton St. **Map** 4 D5. (*0171-734 8951.*	**–Haymarket** Haymarket. **Map** 6 E1. (*0171-930 8800.*
Comedy Panton St. **Map** 6 E1. (*0171-369 1731.*	**Her Majesty's** Haymarket. **Map** 6 E1. (*0171-494 5050.*	**Prince of Wales** Coventry St. **Map** 4 D5. (*0171-839 5972.*	**Vaudeville** Strand. **Map** 4 F5. (*0171-836 9987.*
Criterion Piccadilly Circus. **Map** 4 D5. (*0171-839 4488.*	**London Palladium** Argyll St. **Map** 3 C5. (*0171-494 5040.*	**Queen's** Shaftesbury Ave. **Map** 4 E5. (*0171-494 5040.*	**Wyndham's** Charing Cross Rd. **Map** 4 E5. (*0171-867 1116.*

Royal Festival Hall, South Bank Centre

CLASSICAL MUSIC, OPERA AND DANCE

L ONDON IS ONE of the world's great centers for classical music, with five symphony orchestras, internationally renowned chamber groups such as the Academy of St.-Martin-in-the-Fields and the English Chamber Orchestra, as well as a number of contemporary groups. There are performances virtually every week by major international orchestras and artists, reaching a peak during the summer proms season at the **Royal Albert Hall** *(see pp62–6)*. The newly restored **Wigmore Hall** has excellent acoustics and is a fine setting for chamber music, as is the converted Baroque church (1728) of **St. John's, Smith Square**.

Although televised and outdoor performances by major stars have greatly increased the popularity of opera, prices at the **Royal Opera House** are still aimed at corporate entertainment and many of the tickets never go on general sale. The building (about to close for modernization) is elaborate and productions are often lavish. English National Opera, based at the **London Coliseum**, is more adventurous, appealing to a younger audience (nearly all operas are sung in English). Tickets range from £5 to £200 (about $7.50 to $300) and it is advisable to book well in advance.

The Royal Opera House is also home to the Royal Ballet, and the London Coliseum to the English National Ballet, the two leading classical ballet companies in Britain. Visiting ballets also perform in both. There are numerous young contemporary dance companies that have their own distinctive style, notably the London Contemporary Dance Theatre, based at **The Place Theatre**. Other major dance venues are **Sadler's Wells**, the **ICA**, the **Royalty Theatre** and the **Chisenhale Dance Space**.

The **Barbican** and **South Bank Centre** (comprising the Royal Festival Hall, Queen Elizabeth Hall and Purcell Room) host an impressive variety of events ranging from touring opera performances to free foyer concerts.

Elsewhere in London many outdoor musical events take place in summer *(see p62–3)* at venues such as **Kenwood House**. Events to watch for are: the London Opera Festival (June), with singers from all over the world; the City of London Festival (July), which hosts a range of varied musical events; and two contemporary dance festivals, Spring Loaded (February–April) and Dance Umbrella (October) – see *Time Out* and newspaper listings.

Kenwood House on Hampstead Heath *(see p130)*

DIRECTORY	Archway. 0181-348 1286.	**St. John's, Smith Square** Smith Sq SW1. **Map** 6 E3. 0171-222 1061.	**Brixton Academy** 211 Stockwell Rd SW9. Brixton. 0171-924 9999.
CLASSICAL MUSIC, OPERA AND DANCE	**London Coliseum** St. Martin's Lane W2. **Map** 4 E5. 0171-836 3161.	**South Bank Centre** South Bank SE1. **Map** 6 F1. 0171-928 8800.	**Café de Paris** 3 Coventry St W1. **Map** 4 D5. 0171-287 3481.
Barbican Silk St EC2. **Map** 7 C1. 0171-638 8891.	**Royal Albert Hall** Kensington Gore SW7. **Map** 2 E4. 0171-589 8212.	**The Place Theatre** 17 Duke's Road WC1. **Map** 4 E2. 0171-380 1268.	**Fridge** Town Hall Parade, Brixton Hill SW2. Brixton. 0171-326 5100.
Chisenhale Dance Space 64 Chisenhale Rd E3. Bethnal Green, Mile End. 0181-981 6617.	**Royal Opera House** Floral St WC2. **Map** 4 F5. 0171-240 1066.	**Wigmore Hall** Wigmore St W1. **Map** 3 B4. 0171-935 2141.	**Forum** 9–17 Highgate Rd NW5. Kentish Town. 0171-284 2200.
ICA The Mall SW1. **Map** 6 E1. 0171-930 3647.	**Royalty Theatre** Portugal St WC2. **Map** 4 F5. 0171-494 5090.	**ROCK, POP, JAZZ AND CLUBS**	**Heaven** Underneath the Arches, Villiers St WC2. **Map** 6 E1. 0171-839 3863.
Kenwood House Hampstead Lane NW3.	**Sadler's Wells** Rosebery Ave EC1. Angel. 0171-278 8916.	**100 Club** 100 Oxford St W1. **Map** 4 D5. 0171-636 0933.	

The Hippodrome, Leicester Square

ROCK, POP, JAZZ AND CLUBS

A N ORDINARY WEEKNIGHT in London features scores of concerts, ranging from rock to pop, folk and reggae. Artists guaranteed to fill thousands of seats play large venues such as **Wembley Stadium, Wembley Arena,** or the **Royal Albert Hall**. However, many major bands prefer to play the **Brixton Academy** and the **Forum**, both former movie theaters.

The number of jazz venues has increased over the last few years. Best of the old crop is **Ronnie Scott's**, while the newcomers the **100 Club**, **Jazz Café** and **Pizza on the Park** have good reputations.

London's club scene is one of the most innovative in Europe, particularly since 1990, when all-night clubbing (though not drinking) was legalized. It is dominated by big-name DJs, who host different nights in different clubs and in some of the best clubs are one-nighters (see *Time Out* and newspaper listings). The world-famous mainstream discos **Stringfellows** and **The Hippodrome** are glitzy, expensive and very much part of the tourist circuit, as is the **Limelight** nearby. In contrast the young and trendy **Wag Club**, New York-style **Ministry of Sound**, the camp cabaret of **Madame Jojo's** and a host of other venues ensure that you will never be short of choice. Alternatives are the excellent laser and light shows at **Heaven**, the sleek 1920s

Ticket agency, Shaftesbury Avenue

ballroom **Café de Paris**, where you can waltz and foxtrot all night, or the fun 1970s atmosphere at **Le Scandale** on a Saturday. **Heaven** and **The Fridge** are among the most popular of London's gay clubs.

Business hours are usually 10pm–3am, but on weekends many clubs are open until 6am.

SPORTS

A N IMPRESSIVE variety of public sports facilities are to be found in London, and they are generally inexpensive to use. Swimming pools, squash courts, gyms and sports centers, with an assortment of exercise classes, can be found in most districts, and tennis courts reserved in most parks. Water sports, ice skating and golf are among the variety of activities offered. Spectator sports range from football (soccer) and rugby at **Wembley Stadium** to cricket at **Lord's** or the **Oval**, and tennis at the **All England Lawn Tennis Club**, Wimbledon. Tickets for the most popular matches can often be hard to come by (see p67). More traditional sports include polo at **Guards**, croquet at **Hurlingham** and medieval tennis at **Queen's Club Real Tennis**. See pages 630 to 631 for more information on sporting activities.

Hippodrome
Leicester Square WC2.
Map 4 E5.
0171-437 4311.

Jazz Café
5 Parkway NW1.
Camden Town.
0171-284 4358.

Le Scandale
53–54 Berwick St W1.
Map 4 D5.
0171- 437 6830.

Limelight
136 Shaftesbury Ave,
WC2. **Map** 4 E5.
0171- 434 0572.

Madame Jojo's
8–10 Brewer St W1.
Map 4 D5.
0171-734 2473.

Ministry of Sound
103 Gaunt St SE1.
Map 7 C5.
0171-378 6528.

Pizza on the Park
11 Knightsbridge SW1.
Map 5 B2.
0171-235 5550.

Ronnie Scott's
47 Frith St W1.
Map 4 D5.
0171-439 0747.

Stringfellows
16 Upper St Martin's Lane
SW2. **Map** 4 E5.
0171-240 5534.

Wag Club
35 Wardour St W1. **Map**
4 D5. *0171-437 5534.*

Wembley Stadium and Arena
Empire Way, Wembley,
Middlesex. Wembley
Park. *0181-900 1234.*

SPORTS

General Sports Information Line
0171-222 8000.

All England Lawn Tennis Club
Church Rd, Wimbledon
SW19. Southfields.
0181-946 2244.

Guards Polo Club
Windsor Great Park,
Englefield Green, Egham,
Surrey. Egham.
01784 434212.

Hurlingham Club
Ranelagh Gdns SW6.
Map 5 B5.
0171-736 3148.

Lord's Cricket Ground
St. John's Wood NW8.
St. John's Wood.
0171-289 1611.

Oval Cricket Ground
Kennington Oval SE11.
Oval.
0171-582 6660.

Queen's Club Real Tennis
Palliser Rd W14.
Barons Court.
0171-385 3421.

FARTHER AFIELD

O VER THE CENTURIES London has steadily expanded to embrace the dozens of villages that surrounded it, leaving the City as a reminder of London's original boundaries. Although now linked in an almost unbroken urban sprawl, many of these areas, have kept their old village atmosphere and character. Hampstead and Highgate are still distinct enclaves, as are artistic Chelsea and literary Islington. Greenwich, Chiswick and Richmond have retained features that hark back to the days when the Thames was an important artery for transportation and commerce, while just to the east of the City the wide expanses of the former docks have, in the last 20 years, been imaginatively rebuilt as new commercial and residential areas.

SIGHTS AT A GLANCE

Camden and Islington **7**
Chelsea **1**
Chiswick **10**
East End and Docklands **8**

Greenwich **9**
Hampstead **4**
Hampstead Heath **5**
Highgate **6**

Holland Park **2**
Notting Hill and
   Portobello Road **3**
Richmond and Kew **11**

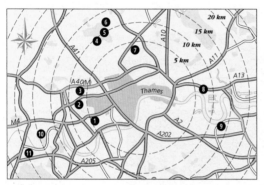

KEY

	Main sightseeing areas
	Greater London
	Parks
=	Highway
=	Major road
=	Minor road

10 miles = 15 km

Chelsea **1**

SW3. 🔵 *Sloane Square.*

R IVERSIDE CHELSEA has been fashionable since Tudor times when Sir Thomas More, Henry VIII's Lord Chancellor

**Statue of Sir Thomas More
(1478–1535), Cheyne Walk**

(see p50), lived here. The river views attracted artists and the arrival of the historian Thomas Carlyle and essayist Leigh Hunt in the 1830s began a literary connection. Blue plaques on the houses of **Cheyne Walk** celebrate former residents such as the painter J.M.W. Turner *(see p93)* and literary giants such as George Eliot, Henry James and T.S. Eliot.

Chelsea's artistic tradition is maintained by its galleries and antique shops, many of them scattered among the clothes boutiques on **King's Road**. This begins at **Sloane Square**, named after the physician Sir Hans Sloane, who bought the manor of Chelsea in 1712. Sloane expanded the **Chelsea Physic Garden** (1673) along Swan Walk to cultivate plants and herbs.

Wren's **Royal Hospital**, on Royal Hospital Road was built in 1692 as a retirement home for old soldiers.

Arab Hall, Leighton House (1866)

Holland Park **2**

W8, W14. 🔵 *Holland Park.*

T HIS SMALL but delightful park is more intimate than the large royal parks such as Hyde Park *(see p103)*. It was opened in 1952 on the grounds of **Holland House**, a center of social and political intrigue in its 19th-century heyday.

Around the park are some magnificent late Victorian

houses. **Linley Sambourne House** was built about 1870 and has hardly changed since Sambourne furnished it in the cluttered Victorian manner, with china ornaments and heavy velvet drapes. He was a political cartoonist for the satirical magazine *Punch*, and drawings, including a number of his own, cram the walls.

Leighton House, built for the Neo-Classical painter Lord Leighton in 1866, has been preserved as an extraordinary monument to the Victorian Aesthetic movement. The highlight is the Arab Hall, which was added in 1879 to house Leighton's stupendous collection of 13th- to 17th-century Islamic tiles. The best paintings include some by Leighton himself and by his contemporaries Edward Burne-Jones and John Millais.

Linley Sambourne House
18 Stafford Terrace W8. *0181-994 1019.* ⊖ *High St Kensington.* ⬭ *Mar–Oct: Wed, Sun.* ✍

Leighton House
12 Holland Park Rd W14. *0171-602 3316.* ⊖ *High St Kensington.* ⬭ *Mon–Sat.* ⬤ *public hols.*

Notting Hill and Portobello Road ❸

W11. ⊖ *Notting Hill Gate.*

IN THE 1950s AND '60s, Notting Hill became a center for the Caribbean community and today it is a vibrant cosmopolitan part of London. It is also home to Europe's largest street carnival *(see p62–3)* which began in 1966 and takes over the entire area on the August bank holiday weekend, when costumed parades flood through the crowded streets.

Nearby, Portóbello Road market *(see p122–3)* has a bustling atmosphere with hundreds of stalls and stores selling a variety of collectables.

Hampstead ❹

NW3, N6. ⊖ *Hampstead.* ⬧ *Hampstead Heath.*

POSITIONED ON A HIGH RIDGE north of the metropolis, Hampstead has always remained apart from London. Essentially a Georgian village with many perfectly maintained mansions and houses, it is one of London's most desirable residential areas, home to a community of artists and writers since Georgian times.

Located in a quiet Hampstead street, **Keats House** (1816) is an evocative and memorable tribute to the life and work of the poet John Keats (1795–1821). Keats lived here for two years before his tragic death from tuberculosis at age 25, and it was under a plum tree in the garden that he wrote his celebrated *Ode to a Nightingale*.

Georgian house, Hampstead

Original manuscripts and books are among the mementos of Keats and of Fanny Brawne, the neighbor to whom he was engaged.

The **Freud Museum**, which opened in 1986, is dedicated to the dramatic life of Sigmund Freud (1856–1939), the founder of psychoanalysis. At the age of 82, Freud fled from Nazi persecution in Vienna to this Hampstead house where he lived and worked for the last year of his life. His daughter Anna, pioneer of child psychoanalysis, continued to live here until her death in 1982. Inside, Freud's rich Viennese-style consulting rooms remain unaltered, and 1930s home movies show moments of Freud's life, including scenes of the Nazi attack on his home in Vienna.

Keats House
Keats Grove NW3. *0171-435 2062.* ⊖ *Hampstead, Belsize Park.* ⬭ *daily.* ⬤ *Dec 24–26, Jan 1, Easter, May Day.*

Freud Museum
20 Maresfield Gdns NW3. *0171-435 2002.* ⊖ *Finchley Rd.* ⬭ *Wed–Sun.* ⬥

Antique store on Portobello Road

View east across Hampstead Heath to Highgate

Hampstead Heath ❺

N6. 🚇 Hampstead, Highgate. 🚉 Hampstead Heath.

SEPARATING the hilltop villages of Hampstead and Highgate, the open spaces of Hampstead Heath are a precious retreat from the city. There are meadows, lakes and ponds for bathing and fishing, and fine views over the capital from **Parliament Hill**, to the east.

Located in landscaped grounds high on the edge of the Heath is the magnificent **Kenwood House**, where classical concerts (see p126) are held by the lake in summer. The house was remodeled by Robert Adam (see p24) in 1764 and most of his interiors have survived, the highlight of which is the library. The

mansion is filled with Old Master paintings, including works by Van Dyck, Vermeer, Turner (see p93) and Romney. The star attraction of this collection is Rembrandt's self-portrait, painted in 1663.

🏛 Kenwood House
Hampstead Lane NW3. 📞 0181-348 1286. ⬤ daily. ⬤ Dec 24–25. ♿

Handmade crafts and antiques, Camden Lock indoor market

Highgate ❻

N6. 🚇 Highgate, Archway.

A SETTLEMENT since the Middle Ages, Highgate, like Hampstead, became a fashionable aristocratic retreat in the 16th century. Today, it still has an exclusive rural feel, away from the urban sprawl below, with a Georgian main street and many expensive houses.

Highgate Cemetery (see p77), with its superb monuments and hidden overgrown corners, has an extraordinary, magical atmosphere. Tour guides (daily in summer, weekends in winter) tell of the many tales of intrigue, mystery and vandalism connected with the cemetery since it opened in 1839. In the newer eastern section is the tomb of Victorian novelist George Eliot (1819–80) and of the cemetery's most famous inhabitant, Karl Marx (1818–83).

🏛 Highgate Cemetery
Swains Lane N6. 📞 0181-340 1834. 🚇 Archway, Highgate. ⬤ daily. ⬤ Dec 25, Jan 1, Good Fri. ♿

Camden and Islington ❼

N1, NW1. 🚇 Angel, Highbury & Islington.

CAMDEN IS A LIVELY AREA packed with restaurants, stores and a busy **market** (see p122–3). Thousands of people come here each weekend to browse among the wide variety of stalls or simply to soak up the atmosphere of the lively cobbled area around the canal, which is enhanced by street musicians.

Neighboring Islington was once a highly fashionable spa but the rich moved out in the late 18th century and the area deteriorated rapidly. In the 20th century, writers such as Evelyn Waugh, George Orwell and Joe Orton lived here. In recent decades, Islington has been rediscovered and is once again fashionable as one of the first areas in London to become "gentrified", with many professionals buying and refurbishing the old houses.

East End and Docklands ❽

E1, E2, E14. 🅴 Aldgate East, Bethnal Green. *Docklands Light Railway*: Canary Wharf.

IN THE MIDDLE AGES the East End was full of craftsmen practising noxious trades such as brewing, bleaching and vinegarmaking, which were banned within the City. The area has also been home to numerous immigrant communities since the 17th century, when French Huguenots, escaping religious persecution, moved into Spitalfields, and made it a silk-weaving center. Even after the decline of the silk industry, textiles and clothing continued to dominate, with Jewish tailors and furriers setting up workshops in the 1880s, and Bengali machinists sewing in cramped premises from the 1950s.

A good way to get a taste of the East End is to explore its Sunday street markets (*see p122–3*), and sample freshly baked bagels and spicy Indian food. For contrast, anyone interested in contemporary architecture should visit the **Docklands**, an ambitious redevelopment of abandoned docks, dominated by the Canada Tower; at 250 m (800 ft) it is London's tallest building. Other attractions include the **Bethnal Green Museum of Childhood,** a toy museum with displays of dollhouses and, **Dennis Severs' House**, where Mr. Dennis Severs takes you on a journey from the 17th to the 19th centuries.

Canada Tower, Canary Wharf

Royal Naval College framing the Queen's House, Greenwich

🏚 **Dennis Severs' House**
Folgate St E1. 📞 *0171-247 4013.* ⏰ *1st Sun of month & eve performances.* 🎫

🏛 **Bethnal Green Museum of Childhood**
Cambridge Heath Rd E2. 📞 *0181-980 3204.* ⏰ *Sat–Thu.* ⚫ *Dec 24, 25, Jan 1, May Day.*

Greenwich ❾

SE10. 🚆 *Greenwich, Maze Hill.*

THE WORLD'S TIME has been measured from the **Old Royal Observatory** (now housing a museum) since 1884. Greenwich avoided the industrialization of its neighbors in the 19th century, and today it makes an enjoyable excursion from London – the most pleasant approach being by boat (*see p74–5*). The area is full of maritime and royal history, with Neo-Classical mansions, a park, many antiques shops and bookstores and various markets (*see p122–3*). The **Queen's House,** designed by Inigo Jones for James I's wife, was completed in 1637 for

Henrietta Maria, Charles I's queen. It has been restored and refurbished as it would have been in the late 17th century. Highlights include the perfectly cubic main hall and the spiral "tulip staircase."

Anyone interested in naval history should visit the adjoining **National Maritime Museum**, with exhibits ranging from primitive canoes through early models of

An 18th-century compass, National Maritime Museum

Elizabethan galleons, to modern cargo, passenger and naval ships. Close by is the **Royal Naval College**, designed by Wren (*see p116*) in two halves so the Queen's House could retain its river view. It began as a royal palace, became a hospital in 1692 and in 1873 the Royal Naval College moved here. The Rococo chapel and the 18th-century *trompe l'oeil* Painted Hall, are open to the public.

🏛 **Old Royal Observatory**
Greenwich Park SE10. 📞 *0181-858 1167.* ⏰ *daily.* 🎫

🏛 **Queen's House and National Maritime Museum**
Romney Rd SE10. 📞 *0181-858 4422.* ⏰ *daily.* ⚫ *Dec 24–26.* 🎫 ♿ *to most of museum.*

🏚 **Royal Naval College**
Greenwich SE10. 📞 *0181-858 2154.* ⏰ *Fri–Wed.*

Chiswick ⑩

W4. 🚇 Chiswick.

CHISWICK IS A PLEASANT suburb of London, with pubs, cottages and a variety of birdlife, such as herons, along the picturesque riverside. One of the main reasons for a visit is **Chiswick House**, a magnificent country villa inspired by the Renaissance architecture of Andrea Palladio. It was designed in the early 18th century by the 3rd Earl of Burlington as an annex to his larger house (demolished in 1758), so that he could display his collection of art and entertain friends. The gardens, with their Classical temples and statues, are being restored to their former glory.

Heron

⚜ Chiswick House

Burlington Lane W4. (0181-995 0508. ◯ Apr–Oct: daily; Nov–Mar: Wed–Sun. ● Dec 24, 25. 🎫

Richmond and Kew ⑪

SW15. 🚇 🚆 Richmond.

THE ATTRACTIVE village of Richmond took its name from a palace built by Henry VII (the former Earl of Richmond in Yorkshire) in 1500, the remains of which can be seen off the green. Nearby is the expansive **Richmond Park** (see p76), which was once Charles I's royal hunting

Chiswick House

ground. In summer, boats sail down the Thames from Westminster Pier, making a pleasant day's excursion from central London (see pp74–5).

The nobility continued to prefer Richmond after royalty had left, and some of their mansions have survived. The Palladian villa, **Marble Hill House**, was built in 1729 for the mistress of George II and has been restored to its elegant original appearance. On the opposite side of the Thames, the brooding **Ham House**, built in 1610, had its heyday later that century when it became the home of the Lauderdales. The Countess of Lauderdale inherited the house from her father, who had been Charles I's "whipping boy" – meaning that he was punished whenever the future king misbehaved. He was rewarded as an adult by being given a peerage and the lease of Ham estate.

A little further north along the Thames, **Syon House** has been inhabited by the Dukes and Earls of Northumberland for over 400 years. Numerous attractions here include a butterfly house, a museum of historic cars and a spectacular conservatory built in 1830. The lavish Neo-Classical interiors of the house, created by Robert Adam in the 1760s (see pp24–5), remain the highlight.

Brewers Lane, Richmond

On the riverbank to the south, **Kew Gardens** (see p76), the most complete botanic gardens in the world, are flawlessly maintained, with examples of nearly every plant that can be grown in Britain. There are also conservatories where thousands of exotic tropical blooms are on display.

⚜ Marble Hill House

Richmond Rd, Twickenham. (0181-892 5115. ◯ daily (Nov–Mar: Wed–Sun). ● Dec 24–26, Jan 1. ♿ limited.

⚜ Ham House

Ham St, Richmond. (0181-940 1950. ◯ Sat–Wed (Nov–Dec: Sat, Sun). 🎫 ♿

⚜ Syon House

London Rd, Brentford. (0181-560 0881. **House** ◯ Oct–Aug: Wed–Sun; Sep: Sun. **Gardens** ◯ Apr–Sep: daily. ● Dec 24–26. 🎫 ♿ gardens only.

♣ Kew Gardens

Kew Rd, Richmond. (0181-940 1171. ◯ daily. ● Dec 25, Jan 1. 🎫 ♿

STREET FINDER

THE MAP REFERENCES given with the sights, hotels, restaurants, shops and entertainment venues based in central London refer to the following four maps. All the main places of interest within the central area are marked on the maps in addition to useful practical information, such as subway, railroad and coach or bus stations. The key map below shows the area of London covered by the *Street Finder*. The four main city center areas (color-coded in pink) are shown in more detail on the inside back cover.

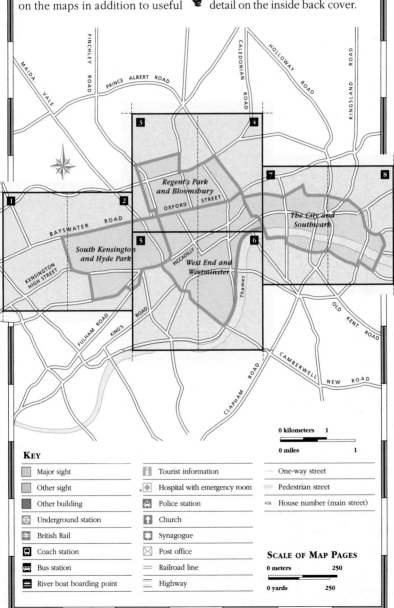

MAIDA VALE

FINCHLEY ROAD

PRINCE ALBERT ROAD

CALEDONIAN ROAD

HOLLOWAY ROAD

KINGSLAND ROAD

3 **4**

7 **8**

1 **2**

BAYSWATER ROAD

OXFORD STREET

Regent's Park and Bloomsbury

The City and Southwark

KENSINGTON HIGH STREET

South Kensington and Hyde Park

5 **6**

PICCADILLY

West End and Westminster

Thames

FULHAM ROAD

KING'S ROAD

ROAD

OLD KENT ROAD

CLAPHAM ROAD

CAMBERWELL NEW ROAD

0 kilometers 1

0 miles 1

KEY

	Major sight
	Other sight
	Other building
⊖	Underground station
⇌	British Rail
🚌	Coach station
🚐	Bus station
⛴	River boat boarding point

ℹ	Tourist information
✚	Hospital with emergency room
🚓	Police station
✝	Church
✡	Synagogue
⊠	Post office
═	Railroad line
═	Highway

—	One-way street
	Pedestrian street
⁵⁶	House number (main street)

SCALE OF MAP PAGES

0 meters 250

0 yards 250

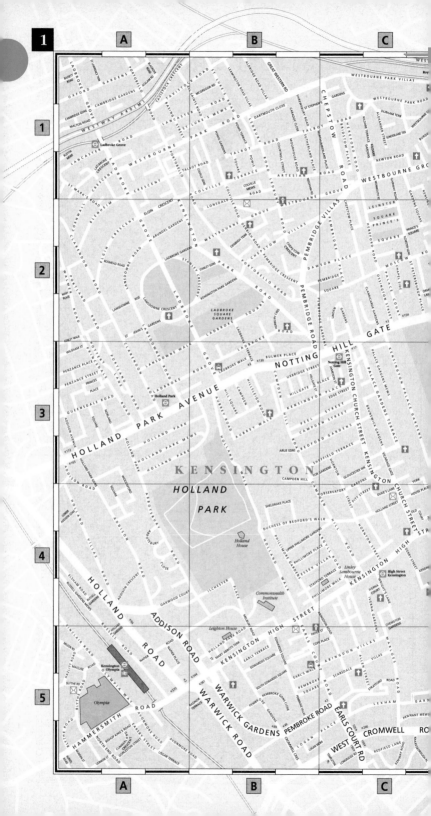

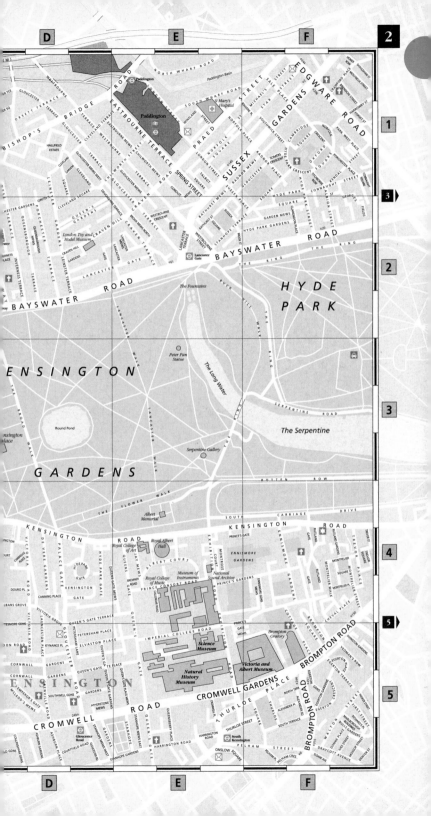

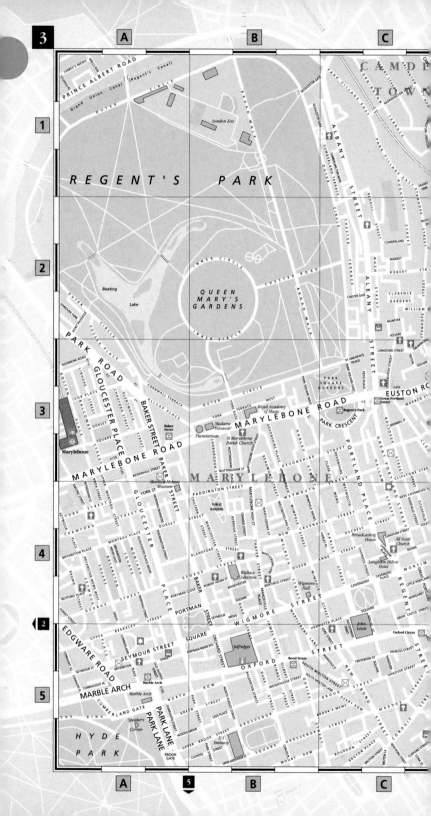

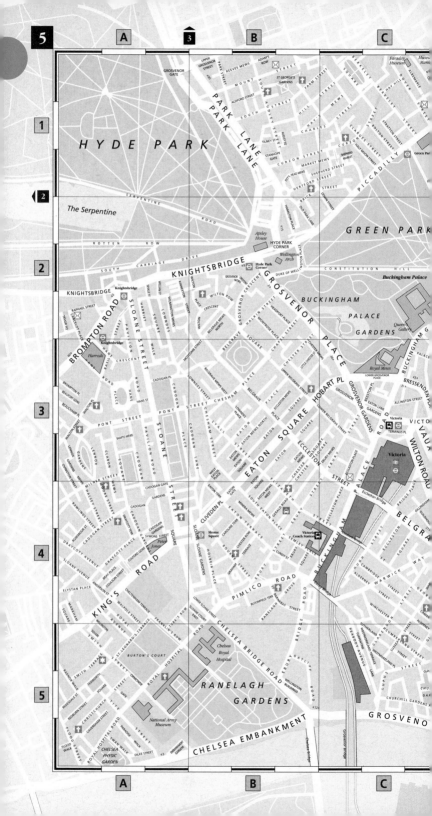

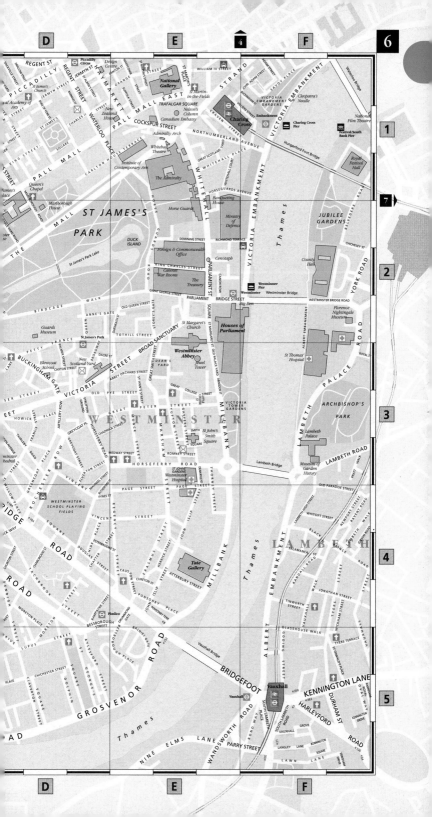

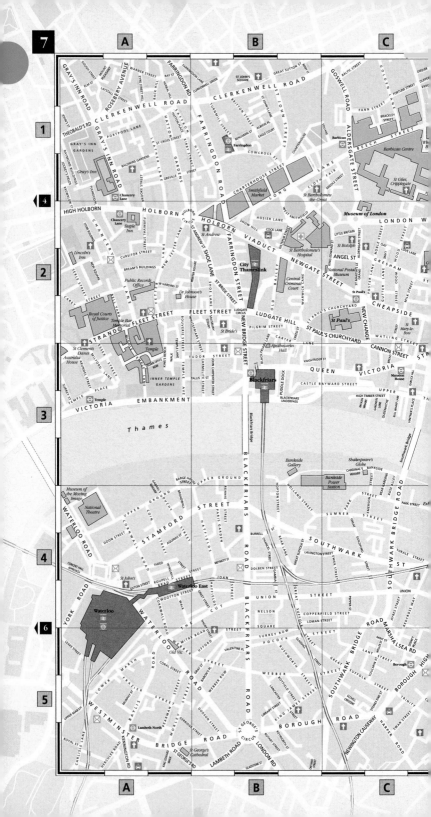

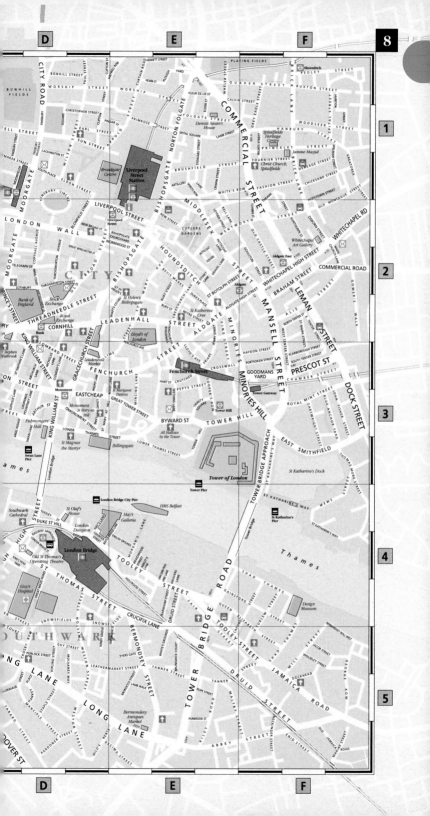

SOUTHEAST
ENGLAND

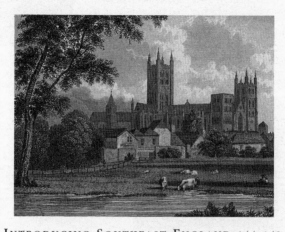

Southeast England at a Glance

THE OLD SAXON KINGDOMS covered the areas surrounding London, and today, while their accessibility to the capital makes them a magnet for commuters, each region retains a character and history of its own. The attractions include England's oldest universities, royal palaces, castles, stately homes and cathedrals, many of which played critical roles in the nation's early history. The landscape is soft, with the green and rounded hills of the south country leveling out to the flat fertile plains and fens of East Anglia, fringed by broad, sandy beaches.

Blenheim Palace *(see pp214–15) is a Baroque masterpiece. The Mermaid Fountain (1892) is part of the spectacular gardens.*

Bedfordshire

Hertfor

Buckinghamshire

THAMES VALLEY *(see pp202–23)*

Oxfordshire

Berkshire

Surrey

Hampshire

West Susse

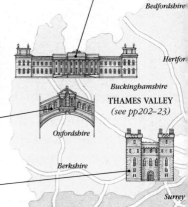

Oxford University's *buildings (see pp208–13) amount to a textbook of English architecture from the Middle Ages to the present. Christ Church College (1525) is the largest in the university.*

Windsor Castle *(see pp222–3) is Britain's oldest royal residence. The Round Tower was built in the 11th century when the palace guarded the western approaches to London.*

Winchester Cathedral *(see pp156–7) was begun in 1097 on the ruins of a Saxon church. But the city was an important center of the Christian church since the 7th century. The northwest door is built in a characteristic medieval style.*

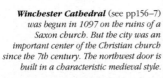

◁ **The white cliffs of Dover, Kent**

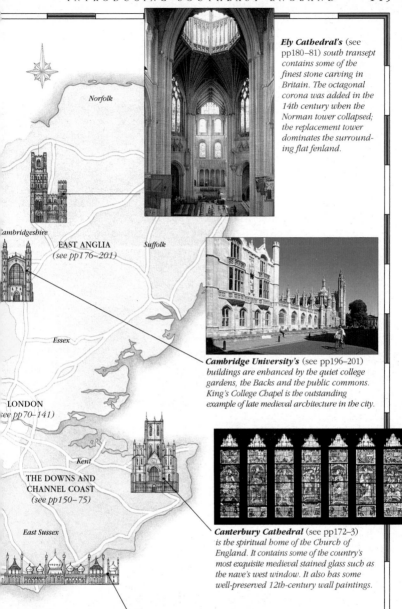

Ely Cathedral's (see pp180–81) *south transept contains some of the finest stone carving in Britain. The octagonal corona was added in the 14th century when the Norman tower collapsed; the replacement tower dominates the surrounding flat fenland.*

Norfolk

Cambridgeshire

EAST ANGLIA (see pp176–201)

Suffolk

Essex

LONDON (see pp70–141)

Kent

THE DOWNS AND CHANNEL COAST (see pp150–75)

East Sussex

Cambridge University's (see pp196–201) *buildings are enhanced by the quiet college gardens, the Backs and the public commons. King's College Chapel is the outstanding example of late medieval architecture in the city.*

Canterbury Cathedral (see pp172–3) *is the spiritual home of the Church of England. It contains some of the country's most exquisite medieval stained glass such as the nave's west window. It also has some well-preserved 12th-century wall paintings.*

Brighton's Royal Pavilion (see pp164–5) *was built for the Prince Regent and is one of the most lavish buildings in the land. Its design by John Nash (see p107) is based on Oriental themes and it has recently been restored to its original splendor.*

0 kilometers 25

0 miles 25

The Garden of England

WITH ITS FERTILE SOIL, mild climate and regular rainfall, the Kentish countryside has flourished as a fruit-growing region ever since its first orchards were planted by the Romans. There has been a recent boom in winemaking, as the vine-covered hillsides around Lamberhurst show, and several vineyards may be visited. The orchards are dazzling in the blossom season, and in the autumn the branches sag with ripening fruit – a familiar sight which inspired William Cobbett (1762–1835) to describe the area as "the very finest as to fertility and diminutive beauty in the whole world." Near Faversham, the fruit research station of Brogdale is open to the public, offering orchard walks, tastings and informative displays.

White wine from the southeast

HOPS AND HOPPING

Hop-picking, a family affair

Oast houses, topped with distinctive angled cowls, are a common feature of the Kentish landscape, and many have now been turned into houses. They were originally

SEASONAL FRUIT

This timeline shows the major crops in each month of the farming year. The first blossoms may appear when the fields are still dusted with snow. As the petals fall, fruit appears among the leaves. After ripening in the summer sun, the fruit is harvested in the autumn.

Peach blossom is usually to be found on south-facing walls, since its fruit requires warm conditions.

Orchards are used to grow plums, pears and apples. The latter (blossoming above) remain Kent's most important orchard crop.

Raspberries are a luscious soft fruit. Many growers allow you to pick your own from the fields, and then pay by weight.

MARCH	APRIL	MAY	JUNE	JULY

Sour cherry blossom is the earliest flower. Its fruit is used for cooking.

Pear blossom has creamy white flowers, which appear two or three weeks before apple blossom.

Cherry plum blossom is one of the most beautiful blossoms; the plum is grown more for its flowers than its fruit.

Srawberries are Britain's favorite and earliest soft fruit. New strains allow them to be picked all summer.

Gooseberries are not always sweet enough to eat raw, though all types are superb in pies and other desserts.

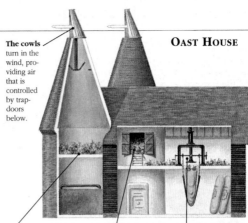

OAST HOUSE

uilt to dry hops, an ingredient brewing beer *(see pp34–5)*. any are still used for that, for though imports have reduced omestic hop-growing, more an four million tons are roduced in Britain annually, ostly in Kent.

In summer, the fruiting plants an be seen climbing the rec- ngular wire frames in fields by e roadside. Until the middle of e 20th century thousands of milies from London's East End ould move to the Kentish hop elds every autumn for working acations harvesting the crop nd camping in barns. That tra- tion has faded, because now e hops are picked by machine.

The cowls turn in the wind, pro- viding air that is controlled by trap- doors below.

Hops are dried above a fan that blows hot air from the underlying radiators.

After drying, the hops are cooled and stored.

A press packs the hops into bags, ready for the breweries.

Cherries are the sweetest of Kent's fruit: two popular varieties are Stella (top) and Duke.

Plums are often served stewed, in pies or dried into prunes. The Victoria plum (left) is the classic English dessert plum and is eatern raw. The Purple plum is also popular.

Greengages are green plums. They have a distinctive taste and can be made into jam.

Bramley Seedling is one of the best cooking apples, but it is not sweet enough to eat raw.

Pears, such as the William (left), should be eaten at the height of ripe- ness. The Conference keeps better.

AUGUST	SEPTEMBER	OCTOBER	NOVEMBER

Currants are among the most assertively flavored fruit and are used in desserts and jams.

Peaches, grown in China 4,000 years ago, came to England in the 19th century.

Dessert apples, such as Cox's Orange Pippin (right), are some of England's best- loved fruits. The newer Discovery is easier to grow.

The Kentish cob, a variety of hazelnut, is undergoing a revival, having been eclipsed by European imports. Unlike many nuts, it is best picked fresh from the tree.

Vineyards are now a familiar sight in Kent (as well as Sussex and Hampshire). Most of the wine produced, such as Lamberhurst, is white.

Houses of Historical Figures

Visiting the homes of artists, writers, politicians and royalty is a rewarding way of gaining an insight into their private lives. Southeast England, near London, boasts many historic houses that have been preserved as they were when their illustrious occupants were alive. All these houses, from large mansions such as Lord Mountbatten's Broadlands to the more modest dwellings, like Jane Austen's House, contain exhibits relating to the life of the famous people who lived there.

Florence Nightingale (1820–1910), the "Lady with the Lamp," was a nurse during the Crimean War (see p56). She stayed at Claydon with her sister, Lady Verney.

Nancy Astor (1879–1964) was the first woman to sit in Parliament in 1919. She lived at Cliveden until her death and made it famous for political hospitality.

Claydon House, Winslow, near Milton Keynes

The Duke of Wellington (1769–1852) was given this house by the nation in 1817, in gratitude for leading the British to victory at Waterloo (see p55).

THAMES VALLEY *(see pp202–23)*

Cliveden House, near Maidenhead

Stratfield Saye, Basingstoke, near Windsor

Jane Austen (1775–1817) wrote three of her novels, including Emma, *and revised the others at this house where she lived for eight years until shortly before her death (see p158).*

Broadlands, Southampton

Jane Austen's House, Chawton, near Winchester

Lord Mountbatten (1900–79), a British naval commander and statesman, was the last Viceroy of India in 1947. He lived here all his married life and remodeled the original house considerably.

Osborne House, Isle of Wight

Queen Victoria (1819–1901) and her husband, Prince Albert, built Osborne House *(see p154)* in 1855 as a seaside retreat for their family because they never truly warmed to the Royal Pavilion in Brighton.

BLOOMSBURY GROUP

A circle of avant-garde artists, designers and writers, many of them friends as students, began to meet at a house in Bloomsbury, London, in 1904 and soon gained a reputation for their Bohemian lifestyle. When Duncan Grant and Vanessa Bell moved to Charleston in 1916, it became a Sussex outpost of the celebrated group. Many of the prominent figures associated with the circle, such as Virginia Woolf, E.M. Forster, Vita Sackville-West and J.M. Keynes paid visits here. The Bloomsbury Group was also known for the Omega Workshops, which made innovative ceramics, furniture and textiles.

Vanessa Bell at Charleston by Duncan Grant (1885–1978)

Gainsborough's House, Sudbury, near Ipswich

EAST ANGLIA
(see pp176–201)

Thomas Gainsborough *(1727–88), one of Britain's greatest painters, was born in this house (see p192). He was best known for his portraits, such as this one of* Mr. and Mrs. Andrews.

Charles Darwin *(1809–82), who developed the theory that man and apes have a common ancestor, wrote his most famous book,* The Origin of the Species, *at the house where he lived.*

Down House, Downe, near Sevenoaks

THE DOWNS AND CHANNEL COAST
(see pp150–75)

Bleak House, Broadstairs, near Margate

Charles Dickens (1812–70), the prolific and popular Victorian novelist *(see p175),* had many connections with Kent. He took holidays at Bleak House, later named after his famous novel.

Chartwell, Westerham, near Sevenoaks

Batemans, Burwash, near Hastings

Winston Churchill (1874–1965), Britain's inspirational Prime Minister in World War II *(see p173),* lived here for 40 years until his death. He relaxed by rebuilding parts of the house.

Rudyard Kipling *(1865–1936), the poet and novelist, was born in India, but lived here for 34 years until his death. His most famous works include* Kim, *the two* Jungle Books *and the* Just So Stories.

Charleston, Lewes

Vanessa Bell (1879–1961), artist and member of the Bloomsbury Group, lived here until her death in 1961. The 18th-century farmhouse reflects her unusual decorative ideas and is filled with murals, paintings and painted furniture.

THE DOWNS AND CHANNEL COAST

HAMPSHIRE · SURREY · EAST SUSSEX · WEST SUSSEX · KENT

WHEN SETTLERS, *invaders and missionaries came from Europe, the southeast coast was their first landfall. The wooded chalk ridges and lower-lying weald beyond them made an ideal base for settlement and proved to be productive farmland.*

The Romans were the first to build major fortifications along the Channel Coast to discourage potential attackers from the European mainland. The remains of many of these can be seen today, and some, like Portchester Castle just outside Portsmouth, were incorporated into more substantial defenses in later centuries. There also exists substantial evidence of Roman domestic buildings, such as Fishbourne Palace, in coastal areas and farther inland.

The magnificence of cathedrals such as Canterbury and Winchester bear witness to their role as important bases of the medieval church, then nearly as powerful as the state. Many Kent and Sussex ports grew prosperous on trade with the Continent – as did the hundreds of smugglers who operated from them. From Tudor times on, monarchs, noblemen and courtiers acquired estates and built manor houses in the countryside between London and the coast, appreciating the area's moderate climate and proximity to the capital. Many of these survive and are popular attractions for visitors. Today the southeast corner of England is its most prosperous and populous region. Parts of Surrey and Kent, up to 20 miles (32 km) from the capital, are known as the Stockbroker Belt: the area has many large, luxurious villas belonging to wealthy people prominent in business and the professions, attracted by the same virtues that appealed to the Tudor gentry.

The fertile area of Kent has long been known as the Garden of England, and despite the incursion of bricks and mortar, it is still a leading area for growing fruit *(see pp146-7)*, being in a prime position for the metropolitan market nearby.

Aerial view of the medieval and moated Leeds Castle

◁ **A lush covering of bluebells in the deciduous woodlands of Kent**

Exploring the Downs and Channel Coast

THE NORTH AND SOUTH DOWNS, separated by the lower-lying Weald are ideal walking country as well as being the site of many stately homes. From Tudor times, wealthy, London-based merchants and courtiers built their country residences in Kent, a day's ride from the capital, and many are open to the public. On the coast are the remains of sturdy castles put up to deter invaders from across the Channel. Today, though, the seashore is largely devoted to pleasure. Some of Britain's earliest resorts were developed along this coast, and ocean swimming is said to have been invented in Brighton.

View of Brighton's Palace Pier from the promenade

Oast houses at Chiddingstone near Royal Tunbridge Wells

GETTING AROUND

The area is well served, with a network of highways and A roads from London to the major towns. The A259 and A27 are picturesque coast roads that offer fine views over the English Channel. Bus and rail travel is also good, with a number of coach companies providing regular tours to the major sites. An InterCity train service runs to all the major towns.

SEE ALSO

SIGHTS AT A GLANCE

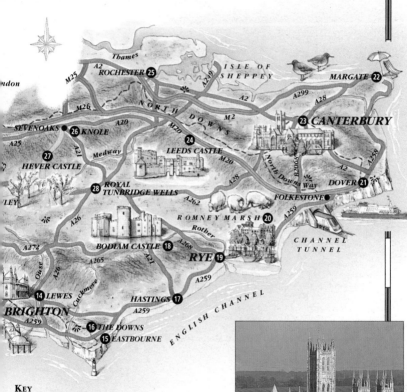

KEY

▰	Highway
▰	Major road
▰	Minor road
▰	Scenic route
▰▰	Scenic path
▰	River
☀	Viewpoint

Canterbury Cathedral's spire, dominating the skyline

The Victorian Osborne House, Isle of Wight

Isle of Wight ❶

Isle of Wight. 🏛 *135,000.* 🚢 *from Lymington, Southampton, Portsmouth.* ℹ *67 High St, Shanklin (01983 862942).*

A VISIT TO **Osborne House**, the favored seaside retreat of Queen Victoria and Prince Albert *(see p148)*, is alone worth the short ferry ride from the mainland. Furnished much as they left it, the house provides a marvelous insight into royal life and is dotted with treasured family mementoes such as sculptures of the children's forearms and group photographs.

The **Swiss Cottage** was built for the royal children to play in. It is now a museum attached to Osborne House. Adjacent to it you can see the bathing machine used by the queen to preserve her modesty while taking her to the edge of the sea *(see p383)*.

The other main sight on the island is **Carisbrooke Castle**, built in the 11th century. A walk on its outer wall and the climb to the top of its keep provide spectacular views. It was here that Charles I *(see pp52–3)* was held prisoner in 1647; an attempt to escape was foiled when he got stuck between the bars of a window.

The island has long been a popular resort for its beaches, coastal walks and as a base for ocean sailing, especially during Cowes Week *(see p67).* The scenic highlight of the

island is the **Needles** – three towers of rock jutting out of the sea at the island's western end. This is only a short walk from Alum Bay, famous for its multicolored cliffs and sand.

🎠 Osborne House
East Cowes. 【 *01983 200022.* ⭕ *Apr–Oct: daily.* 🌙 *Nov–Mar.* 🏷 🛗
🏰 Carisbrooke Castle
Newport. 【 *01983 522107.* ⭕ *daily.* 🌙 *Dec 24–26, Jan 1.* 🏷 🛗

Beaulieu ❷

Brockenhurst, Hampshire. 【 *01590 612345.* 🚄 *Brockenhurst then taxi.* ⭕ *daily.* 🌙 *Dec 25, 26.* 🏷 🛗

P ALACE HOUSE, once the gatehouse of Beaulieu Abbey, has been the home of Lord Montagu's family since 1538. It now contains the finest collection of cars in the country. The **National Motor Museum** has over 250 vintage cars ranging from the 1890s to the present.

There is also an exhibition of monastic life in the ruined ancient **abbey**, founded in 1204 by King John *(see p48)*

for Cistercian monks. The original abbey church now serves as the parish church.

ENVIRONS: Just south is the maritime museum at **Buckler's Hard**, telling the story of shipbuilding in the 18th century. Three of Nelson's fleet were built here. The yard employed 4,000 people at its peak but declined when steel began to be used for shipbuilding.

🏛 Buckler's Hard
Beaulieu. 【 *01590 616203.* ⭕ *daily.* 🌙 *Dec 25.* 🏷 🛗 *limited.*

New Forest ❸

Hampshire. 🚄 *Brockenhurst.* 🚌 *Lymington then bus.* ℹ *main car park, Lyndhurst (01703 282269).*

T HIS UNIQUE EXPANSE of heath and woodland is, at 145 sq miles (375 sq km), the largest area of unenclosed land in southern Britain.

William the Conqueror's "new" forest, despite its name, is one of the few primeval oak woods in England. It was the popular hunting ground of Norman kings, and in 1100 William II was fatally wounded here in a hunting accident.

Today it is enjoyed by about seven million visitors a year who share it with the shaggy New Forest ponies – unique to the area – and over 1,500 fallow deer, which graze here.

Southampton ❹

Hampshire. 🏛 *200,000.* 🚶 🚄 🚌 🚢 ℹ *9 Civic Centre (01703 221106).* 🛍 *Tue–Sat.*

F OR CENTURIES this has been a flourishing port. The *Mayflower* sailed from here to America in 1620 with the

A 1909 Rolls-Royce Silver Ghost at Beaulieu's National Motor Museum

Pilgrim Fathers, as did the supposedly unsinkable *Titanic* at the start of its maiden and ultimately tragic voyage in 1912, when it went down after hitting an iceberg.

The **Maritime Museum** has exhibits about both these ships, along with displays on the huge romantic liners that sailed from the port in the first half of the 20th century, the heyday of ocean travel.

There is a walk around the remains of the medieval city wall. At the head of the High Street stands the old city gate, **Bargate**, the most elaborate gate to survive in England.

Illustration of the luxurious liner the *Titanic*, which sank in 1912

It still has its 13th-century drum towers and is decorated with intricate, 17th-century armorial carvings.

The **Tudor House Museum**, a medieval merchant's house, has exhibits on Victorian and Edwardian domestic life.

🏛 **Maritime Museum**
Town Quay. 📞 01703 635904.
◯ Tue–Sun. ● Dec 25, 26, Jan 1 & public hols. ♿ limited.
🏛 **Tudor House Museum**
St. Michael's Sq. 📞 01703 635904.
◯ Tue–Sun. ● public hols.

Portsmouth ⑤

Hampshire. 🚶 190,000. ⛴ 🚌
ℹ The Hard (01705 826722).
🗓 Thu–Sat.

O NCE A VITAL naval port, with all the nightlife that entails, Portsmouth is today a much quieter town but fascinating for those interested in English naval history.

Under the banner of **Portsmouth Historic Ships**, the city's ancient dockyard is the hub of Portsmouth's most important sights. Among these is the hull of the **Mary Rose**, Henry VIII's flagship *(see p50)*, which capsized on its maiden voyage as it left to fight the French in 1545. It was recovered from the seabed in 1982 along with thousands of 16th-century objects now on display nearby, giving an absorbing insight into life at sea 450 years ago.

Alongside it is HMS *Victory*, the English flagship on which Admiral Nelson was killed at the battle of Trafalgar *(see p27)* and now restored to its former glory. You can also visit the **Royal Naval Museum**, which deals with British naval history from the 16th century to the Falklands War, and the 19th-century ironclad HMS *Warrior*.

Portsmouth's other military memorial is the **D-Day Museum**. This is centered on the *Overlord Embroidery*, a masterpiece of needlework which was commissioned in 1968 from the Royal School of Needlework and took five years to complete. At 83 m

The figurehead on the bow of HMS *Victory* at Portsmouth

(272 ft), its 34 panels are 12 m (41 ft) longer than the *Bayeux Tapestry*, held in France, and it depicts the events surrounding the World War II Allied landing in Normandy in 1944.

Portchester Castle, on the north edge of the harbor, was first fortified in the third century and is presently the best example of Roman sea defenses in northern Europe. The Normans used the Roman walls to enclose a castle and a church. Henry V used the castle as a garrison to assemble his army before the Battle of Agincourt *(see p49)*. In the 18th and 19th centuries the castle was a prisoner-of-war camp and you can still see where the bored prisoners carved their names, initials and dates on the walls.

Among less warlike attractions is the **Charles Dickens Museum** *(see p175)*. The house where the author was born in 1812 – his father was a Navy clerk – is furnished in the style of that time.

🏛 **Portsmouth Historic Ships**
The Hard. 📞 01890 407080.
◯ daily. ● Dec 25, 26. 📷 ♿
🏛 **D-Day Museum**
Clarence Esplanade. 📞 01705 827261. ◯ daily. ● Dec 24–26.
📷 ♿
⛩ **Portchester Castle**
Castle St, Porchester. 📞 01705 378291. ◯ daily. ● Dec 24–26, Jan 1. 📷 ♿ limited.
🏛 **Charles Dickens Museum**
393 Old Commercial Rd. 📞 01705 827261. ◯ Apr–Oct: daily. 📷

A wild pony and her foal roaming freely in the New Forest

Winchester ❻

Hampshire. 🏠 34,000. 🚆 🚌
ℹ️ Guildhall, The Broadway (01962
840500). 🛒 Wed, Fri, Sat.

THE CAPITAL of the ancient
kingdom of Wessex, the
city of Winchester was also
the headquarters of the
Anglo-Saxon kings until the
Norman Conquest (see p47).

William the Conqueror built
one of his first English castles
here. The only surviving part
of the castle is the **Great Hall**,
erected in 1235 to replace the
original. It is now home to

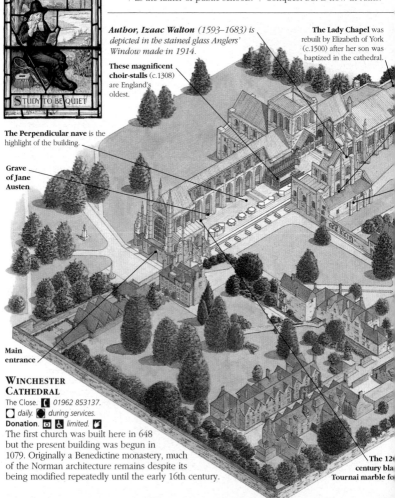

the legendary Round
Table. The story behind
the table is a mix of
history and myth. King
Arthur (see p269) had it
shaped so no knight
could claim precedence.
It was said to have been
built by the wizard
Merlin but was actually
made in the 13th century.

The **Westgate Museum** is
one of the four surviving 12th-
century gatehouses in the city
wall. The room (once a prison)
above the gate has a glorious
16th-century painted ceiling.
The ceiling was moved from
Winchester College, England's
oldest "public," or fee-paying,
school, founded in 1382 by
William of Wykeham – known
as the father of public schools.

**The 13th-century Round Table,
Great Hall, Winchester**

Winchester has been an
ecclesiastical center for many
centuries. **Wolvesey Castle**
(first built around 1110) was
the magnificent home to the
cathedral's bishops before the
Conquest but is now in ruins.

*Author, Izaac Walton (1593–1683) is
depicted in the stained glass Anglers'
Window made in 1914.*

**These magnificent
choir-stalls** (c.1308)
are England's
oldest.

The Perpendicular nave is the
highlight of the building.

**Grave
of Jane
Austen**

The Lady Chapel was
rebuilt by Elizabeth of York
(c.1500) after her son was
baptized in the cathedral.

**Main
entrance**

WINCHESTER
CATHEDRAL

The Close. 📞 01962 853137.
⬜ daily. ⬛ during services.
Donation. 📷 ♿ limited. 📹
The first church was built here in 648
but the present building was begun in
1079. Originally a Benedictine monastery, much
of the Norman architecture remains despite its
being modified repeatedly until the early 16th century.

The 12
century bla
Tournai marble fo

The **Hospital of St. Cross** is an old poorhouse built in 1446. Weary strangers may still claim the "Wayfarer's Dole," a horn (cup) of ale and bread, handed out to the poor here since medieval times.

Great Hall
Castle Ave. 01962 846476.
daily. Dec 25, 26.
Westgate Museum
High St. 01962 869864.
Apr–Sep: daily; Feb–Oct: Tue–Sun.
Hospital of St. Cross
St. Cross Rd. 01962 851375.
Mon–Sat. public hols.

The Library has over 4,000 books. This "B" from Psalm 1 is found in the Winchester Bible, an exquisite work of 12th-century illumination.

The Norman chapter house ceased to be used in 1580. Only the Norman arches survive.

Prior's Hall

The Close originally contained the domestic buildings for the monks of the Priory of St. Swithun's – the name before it became Winchester Cathedral. Most of the buildings, such as the refectory and cloisters, were destroyed during the Dissolution of the Monasteries *(see p50)*.

Chichester ⓻

West Sussex. 26,000.
29A South St (01243 775888).
Wed, Sat.

THIS WONDERFULLY preserved market town, with an elaborate early 16th-century market cross at its center, is dominated by its **cathedral**, consecrated in 1108. The exterior is a lovely mix of greenish limestone and Caen stone and its graceful spire, said to be the only English cathedral spire visible from the sea, dominates the town. Although vandalized in the Civil War *(see p52)*, the cathedral still contains much of interest including a unique detached bell tower (1436).

There are two sculpted stone panels in the choir, dating from 1140. Modern works include paintings by Graham Sutherland (1903–80), and a stained-glass window by Marc Chagall (1889–1985).

ENVIRONS: Just west at Bosham is the Saxon **Holy Trinity Church,** known to have been used by King Canute *(see p46)*. Myth has it that this was where Canute failed to stop the incoming tide and so proved to his courtiers that his powers had limits. The church appears in the *Bayeux Tapestry,* held in France, because Harold heard mass here in 1064 before he was shipwrecked off Normandy and then rescued by William the Conqueror *(see p47)*.

Fishbourne Palace *(see pp44–5),* farther west, is the largest Roman villa in Britain. It covers 3 ha (7 acres) and was discovered in 1960 by a workman digging for drains.

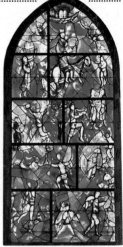

Chagall's stained-glass window (1978), Chichester Cathedral

Constructed from AD 75, it had over 100 rooms built around a formal garden, but was destroyed by fire in 285 – perhaps as a result of a Saxon raid. The north wing has some of the finest mosaics discovered in Britain, including one with Cupid riding a dolphin.

To the north is the 18th-century **Goodwood House**. Its magnificent art collection features works by Canaletto (1697–1768) and Stubbs (1724–1806). This impressive house, home to the Earl of March, has a famous racecourse on the Downs.

Chichester Cathedral
West St. 01243 782595.
daily. during services.
Fishbourne Palace
Fishbourne. 01243 785859.
daily. mid-Dec–mid-Feb.
Goodwood House
Goodwood. 01243 774107.
Easter–Sep: Sun, Mon; Aug: Sun–Thu (pm). special events.

WILLIAM WALKER

At the beginning of the 20th century, the cathedral's east end seemed certain to collapse unless its foundations were underpinned. But because the water table lies just below the surface, the work had to be done under water. From 1906 to 1911, Walker, a deep-sea diver, worked six hours a day laying sacks of cement beneath the unsteady walls.

William Walker in his diving suit

The dominating position of Arundel Castle, West Sussex

Arundel Castle ❽

Arundel, West Sussex. ☎ *01903 883136*. 🚉 *Arundel*. ⬤ *Apr–Oct: Sun–Fri*. ⬤ *Nov–Mar*. 🅿 *limited*.

DOMINATING the small riverside town below, this vast, gray hilltop castle, surrounded by castellated walls, was first built by the Normans but only the keep is from that period.

During the 16th century it was acquired by the powerful Dukes of Norfolk, the country's senior Roman Catholic family, who still live here. They rebuilt it after the original was virtually destroyed by Parliamentarians in 1643 *(see p52)*, and restored it again in the 19th century.

In the castle grounds is the parish church of **St. Nicholas**. Its most unusual feature is the small Catholic Fitzalan chapel (c.1380) built into its east end by the castle's first owners, the Fitzalans. Separated from the church by a superb 14th-century iron grille, it can only be entered from the grounds.

Petworth House ❾

(NT) Petworth, West Sussex. ☎ *01798 342207*. 🚉 *Pulborough then taxi*. **House** ⬤ *Apr–Oct: Tue–Thu, Sat, Sun & public hols*. **Park** ⬤ *daily*. 🅿 ♿

THIS LATE 17th-century house was immortalized in a series of famous views by the painter J.M.W. Turner *(see p93)*, a frequent guest at the house. Some of his best paintings are shown here and are part of Petworth's outstanding art

collection that also includes works by Titian (1488–1576), Van Dyck (1599–1641) and Gainsborough *(see p149)*. Also well represented is ancient Roman and Greek sculpture, such as the 4th-century BC *Leconfield Aphrodite*, thought to be by Praxiteles.

One of the main attractions is the Carved Room, decorated with intricately carved wood panels of birds, flowers and musical instruments, by Grinling Gibbons (1648–1721).

The large deer park includes some of the earliest work of Capability Brown *(see p23)*.

The Restoration clock on the Tudor Guildhall, Guildford

Guildford ❿

Surrey. 🚶 *63,000*. 🚉 🚌 ℹ️ *14 Tunsgate (01483 444333)*. 🅰 *Fri, Sat*.

THE COUNTY TOWN of Surrey, settled since Saxon times, incorporates the remains of a small Norman **castle**. The attractive High Street is lined

with buildings of the Tudor period, such as the impressive **Guildhall**. But it is the huge modern redbrick cathedral, completed in 1954, that dominates the town's skyline.

ENVIRONS: Guildford stands on the end of the North Downs, a range of chalk hills which are popular for walking *(see p33)*. The area also has two famous beauty spots; **Leith Hill** – the highest point in southeast England – and **Box Hill**. The view from the latter is well worth the short, gentle climb from West Humble.

Just to the south of the town is the perfect red brickwork of **Clandon Park**. This 18th-century house has a sumptuous interior, especially the Marble Hall – one of the finest English interiors of the period. It has an intricate Baroque ceiling, and the hall's side lamps are supported by black ivory forearms jutting from the wall, which represent the Park's West Indian servants.

Southwest is Chawton, which contains **Jane Austen's House** *(see p148)*. This small redbrick house is where she wrote most of her gentle, witty comedies of middle-class manners in Georgian England, such as *Pride and Prejudice*.

🏛 **Clandon Park**
West Clandon, Surrey. ☎ *01483 222482*. ⬤ *Apr–Oct: Sat–Wed; Good Fri*. ⬤ *Nov–Mar*. 🅿 ♿ *limited*.
🏛 **Jane Austen's House**
Alton, Hants. ☎ *01420 83262*. ⬤ *Jan–Feb: Sat, Sun; Nov–Dec, Mar: Wed–Sun; Apr–Oct: daily*. ⬤ *Dec 25, 26*. 🅿 ♿ *limited*.

Hampton Court ⓫

East Molesey, Surrey. 0181-781 9500. Hampton Court. daily. Dec 24–26, Jan 1, Good Fri.

THE POWERFUL chief minister and Archbishop of York to Henry VIII *(see p51)*, Cardinal Wolsey, leased Hampton Court in 1514 as his riverside country residence. In 1528, in the hope of retaining royal favor, Wolsey gave it to the king. After the royal takeover, Hampton Court was extended twice, first by Henry himself and then in the 1690s by William and Mary, who used Christopher Wren *(see p116)* as the architect. From the outside the palace is a harmonious blend of Tudor and English Baroque, Inside there is a striking contrast between Wren's Classical royal rooms, which include the King's Apartments, and Tudor architecture, such as the Great Hall. Many of the state apartments are decorated with furniture, paintings and tapestries taken from the Royal Collection *(see p223)*. Also from this period are the Baroque gardens with their radiating avenues of majestic limes, collections of exotic plants and formal plant beds.

Ceiling decoration, Hampton Court

***Wander around** the famous maze and lose yourself in one of the garden's Baroque features.*

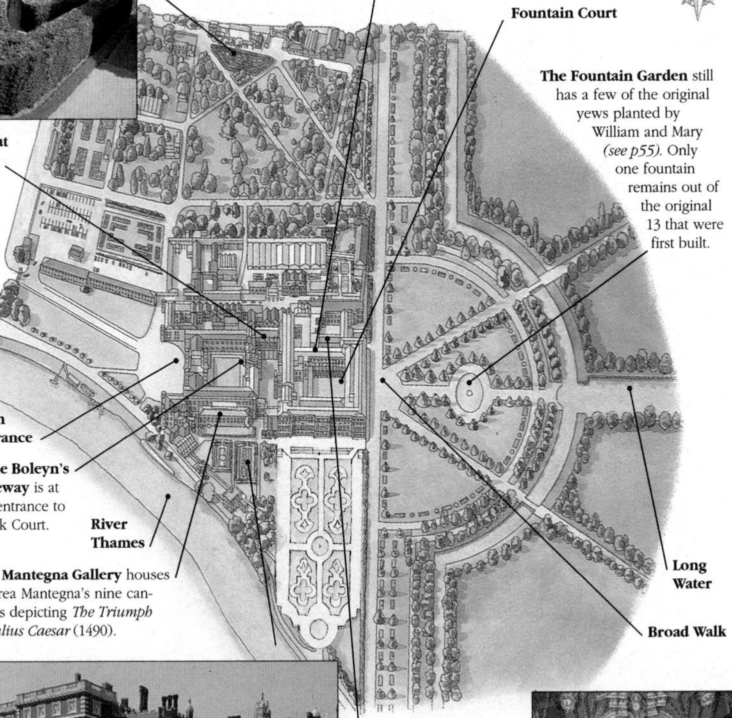
The Queen's Apartments, including the Presence Chamber and Bedchamber, are arranged around the the north and east sides of Fountain Court.
Fountain Court
The Fountain Garden still has a few of the original yews planted by William and Mary *(see p55)*. Only one fountain remains out of the original 13 that were first built.
Great Hall
Main Entrance
Anne Boleyn's Gateway is at the entrance to Clock Court.
River Thames
The Mantegna Gallery houses Andrea Mantegna's nine canvases depicting *The Triumph of Julius Caesar* (1490).
Long Water
Broad Walk

***The pond garden**, a sunken water garden, was part of Henry VIII's elaborate redesigns. The small pond in the middle contains a single-jet fountain.*

***The Tudor Chapel Royal** was completed by Henry VIII. But the superb woodwork, including the massive reredos by Grinling Gibbons, all date from a major refurbishment carried out for Queen Anne (c.1711).*

Steyning ⓬

West Sussex. ⓐ *5,000* ⓔ ⓘ *9 The Causeway, Horsham (01403 211661).*

THIS LOVELY little town in the lee of the Downs is packed with timber-framed houses from the Tudor period and earlier, with some built of flint and others in sandstone.

In Saxon times, Steyning was an important port and ship-building center on the River Adur: King Ethelwulf, father of King Alfred *(see p46),* was buried here in 858; his body was later moved to Winchester. The *Domesday Book (see p48)* records that Steyning had 123 houses, making it one of the largest towns in the south. The 12th-century church is spacious and splendid, evidence of the area's ancient prosperity. The tower, of checkered stone and flint, was added around 1600.

In the 14th century the river silted up and changed course away from the town, putting an end to its days as a port. Later it became an important coach stop on the south coast road: the **Chequer Inn** recalls this prosperous period, with its unusual 18th-century flint and stone façade.

ENVIRONS: The remains of a **Norman castle** can be visited at Bramber, west of Steyning. This small, pretty village also contains the timber-framed **St. Mary's House** (1470). It has fine paneled rooms, including the Elizabethan Painted Room, and one of the oldest trees in the country, a Ginkgo biloba. **Chanctonbury Ring** and **Cissbury Ring**, on the hills west of Steyning, were Iron Age forts and the latter has the remains of a Neolithic flint mine. Worthing is the seaside resort where Oscar Wilde (1854–1900) wrote his play *The Importance of Being Earnest.*

🏛 **St. Mary's House**
Bramber. 【 *01903 816205.*
◯ *Easter–Sep: Mon & Sun (pm).* 🖼

Street-by-Street: Brighton ⓭

A stick of Brighton rock

AS THE NEAREST south coast resort to London, Brighton is perennially popular, but has always been more refined than its boisterous rivals further east, such as Margate *(see p169)* and Southend. The spirit of the Prince Regent *(see p165)* lives on, not only in the magnificence of his Royal Pavilion, but in the town's raffish reputation as a spot for adulterous weekends in small, discreet hotels. Brighton has always attracted actors and variety artists – Laurence Olivier made his final home here.

Old Ship Hotel
Built in 1559, it was later bought by Nicholas Tettersells with the money given to him by Charles II as a reward for taking him to France during the Civil War (see p52).

★ **Palace Pier**
Built in 1899, this typical late-Victorian pier now caters to today's visitors with amusement arcades.

KING'S ROAD

MARKET ST

GRAND JUNCTION ROAD

KEY

– – – Suggested route

STAR SIGHTS

★ **Palace Pier**

★ **Royal Pavilion**

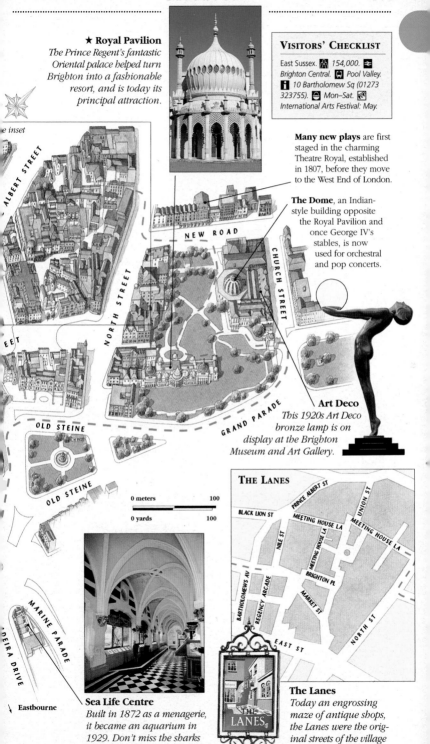

★ **Royal Pavilion**
The Prince Regent's fantastic Oriental palace helped turn Brighton into a fashionable resort, and is today its principal attraction.

VISITORS' CHECKLIST

East Sussex. 🏛 154,000. 🚇
Brighton Central. 🚌 Pool Valley.
🛈 10 Bartholomew Sq (01273 323755). 🛒 Mon–Sat. 🎭
International Arts Festival: May.

Many new plays are first staged in the charming Theatre Royal, established in 1807, before they move to the West End of London.

The Dome, an Indian-style building opposite the Royal Pavilion and once George IV's stables, is now used for orchestral and pop concerts.

e inset

ALBERT STREET

NEW ROAD

NORTH STREET

CHURCH STREET

EET

Art Deco
This 1920s Art Deco bronze lamp is on display at the Brighton Museum and Art Gallery.

GRAND PARADE

OLD STEINE

OLD STEINE

0 meters   100

0 yards   100

THE LANES

BLACK LION ST
PRINCE ALBERT ST
NILE ST
MEETING HOUSE LA
MEETING HOUSE LA
MEETING HOUSE LA
UNION ST
BARTHOLOMEWS AV
REGENCY ARCADE
BRIGHTON PL
MARKET ST
EAST ST
NORTH ST

MARINE PARADE

DEIRA DRIVE

↓ **Eastbourne**

Sea Life Centre
Built in 1872 as a menagerie, it became an aquarium in 1929. Don't miss the sharks and other British marine life.

THE LANES

The Lanes
Today an engrossing maze of antique shops, the Lanes were the original streets of the village of Brightbelmstone.

Brighton: Royal Pavilion

As SWIMMING became fashionable in the mid-18th century, Brighton was transformed into England's first seaside resort. Its gaiety soon appealed to the rakish Prince of Wales, who became George IV in 1820 *(see p55)*. When, in 1785, he secretly married Mrs. Fitzherbert, it was here that they conducted their liaison. He moved to a farmhouse near the shore and had it enlarged by Henry Holland *(see p24)*. As his parties grew more lavish, George needed a suitably extravagant setting for them, and in 1815 he employed John Nash *(see p107)* to transform the house into a lavish Oriental palace. Completed in 1822, the exterior has remained largely unaltered. Queen Victoria sold the Pavilion to the town of Brighton in 1850.

Central Dome
Nash adopted what he called the Hindu Style, as in this delicate tracery on one of the imposing turban domes.

★ **Banqueting Room**
Fiery dragons adorn many of the interior plans. This colorful one dominates the center of the Banqueting Room's extraordinary ceiling, and has a huge crystal chandelier suspended from it.

The exterior is partly built in Bath stone.

Banqueting Room Gallery

South Galleries

The banquet table, which seats 24 people, is laid as for a splendid feast.

The eastern façade of the Pavilion

Standard Lamps
More dragons, along with dolphins and lotus flowers, decorate the Banqueting Room's eight original standard lamps, made of porcelain, ormolu and gilded wood.

STAR SIGHTS
★ **Banqueting Room**
★ **Great Kitchen**

★ **Great Kitchen**
The Prince's epic banquets required a kitchen of huge proportions. The vast stoves and long shelves of gleaming copper pans were used by famous chefs of the day.

◁ **Front façade of George IV's extravagant Royal Pavilion, Brighton**

Saloon (Parlor)
*The gilded wall decorations
were designed on Indian
themes, but the Chinese
wallpaper harks back to an
earlier decorative plan.
The long couch mimics an
Egyptian river boat.*

**Long
Gallery**
*Mandarin
figures,
which can
nod their
heads, line
the pink
and blue
walls of
this 49 m
(162 ft)
gallery.*

Queen Victoria's Bedroom
*This reproduction four-poster is
on display in the upper floor
apartments that were used by
Queen Victoria (see p56).*

The Music Room, with
its crimson and gold
murals, was
where a 70-
piece orchestra
played to the
Prince's guests.

The domes are
made of cast iron.

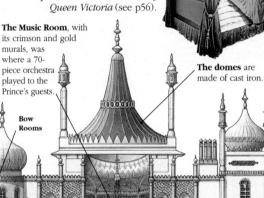

**Music Room
Gallery**

**Bow
Rooms**

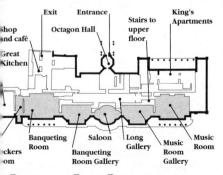

Exit   **Entrance**   **Stairs to
upper
floor**   **King's
Apartments**

Shop
and café
Octagon Hall

Great
Kitchen

ckers
om

**Banqueting
Room**   **Saloon**   **Long
Gallery**   **Music
Room**   **Music
Room**

**Banqueting
Room Gallery**   **Music
Room
Gallery**

PLAN OF THE ROYAL PAVILION
Both Holland and Nash made additions and
changes to the original farmhouse. The upper
floor contains bedrooms, such as the Bow
Rooms, which George's brothers used. The
shaded areas represent the artwork above.

**PRINCE OF WALES
AND MRS.
FITZHERBERT**

The Prince of Wales
was only 23 when
he fell in love with
Maria Fitzherbert, a
29-year-old Catholic
widow, and secretly
married her. They
lived in the farmhouse
together and were the
toast of Brighton
society until George's
official marriage took
place to Caroline of
Brunswick in 1795. Mrs.
Fitzherbert moved into
a small house nearby.

Upstairs interior of Anne of Cleves House, Lewes

Lewes ⓮

East Sussex. 🏠 *16,000.* 🚉 ℹ️ *187 High St (01273 483448).* 🔺 *Tue.*

THE ANCIENT COUNTY TOWN of Sussex was a vital strategic site for the Saxons, because from its vantage point on top of a hill – the name Lewes derives from the Old English word for a hill – you can see a long stretch of coast.

William the Conqueror built a wooden castle here in 1067 but this was soon replaced by a large stone structure whose remains, which include the Barbican, can be visited today.

In 1264 it was the site of a critical battle in which Simon de Montfort and his barons defeated Henry III *(see p48)*, enabling them to establish the first English Parliament.

The Tudor **Anne of Cleves House** is a museum of local history, although Anne of Cleves, Henry VIII's fourth wife, never actually lived here.

On Bonfire Night *(see p64)* lighted tar barrels are rolled to the river and effigies of the Pope are burned instead of the customary Guy Fawkes to commemorate the town's 17 Protestant martyrs burned at the stake by Mary I *(see p52).*

ENVIRONS: Nearby is the 16th-century **Glynde Place**, a handsome courtyard house. It has an extensive display of early 18th-century needle-work and Derby china.

🏛 **Anne of Cleves House**
Lewes. [*01273 474610.* ◯ *Apr–Nov: daily; Dec–Mar: Tue, Thu.* 🈺
♨ **Glynde Place**
Lewes. [*01273 858224.* ◯ *May–Sep: Wed, Thu, Sun & public hols.* 🈺

Eastbourne ⓯

East Sussex. 🏠 *86,000.* 🚉 🈺
ℹ️ *Cornfield Rd (01323 411400).*
🔺 *Wed, Sat.*

THIS VICTORIAN SEASIDE resort is a popular place for retirement, as well as a first-rate center for touring the Downs. The South Downs Way *(see p33)* begins at **Beachy Head**, the spectacular 163 m (536 ft) chalk cliff just on the outskirts of the town. From here it is a bracing walk to the cliff top at Birling Gap, with views to the **Seven Sisters**, the chalk hills that end abruptly as they meet the sea.

ENVIRONS: Just to the west of Eastbourne is **Seven Sisters Country Park**, a 285 ha (700 acre) area of chalk cliffs and Downland marsh. The **Park Visitor's Centre** contains *The Living World* – a display of local wildlife and geology.

To the north is the picture-postcard village of **Alfriston**, with an ancient market cross and a 15th-century inn, **The Star**, on its quaint main street. Near the church is the 14th-century **Clergy House** that, in 1896, was the first building ever bought by the National Trust *(see p25).* To the east is the huge prehistoric chalk carving, the **Long Man of Wilmington** *(see p207).*

ℹ️ **Park Visitor's Centre**
Exceat, Seaford. [*01323 870280.*
◯ *Apr–Oct: daily; Nov–Mar: Sat, Sun.*
● *Dec 25.* 🈺 ♿
♨ **Clergy House**
Alfriston. [*01323 870001.*
◯ *Apr–Oct: daily.* 🈺 ♿

The lighthouse (1902) at the foot of Beachy Head, Eastbourne

The meandering River Cuckmere flowing through the South Downs to the beach at Cuckmere Haven

The Downs ⑯

East Sussex. ⊟ ℗ *Eastbourne.*
🛈 *Cornfield Rd, Eastbourne (01323 411400).*

THE NORTH and South Downs are parallel chalk ridges that run from east to west all the way across Kent, Sussex and Surrey, separated by the lower-lying and fertile Kent and Sussex Weald.

The smooth Downland hills are covered with springy turf, kept short by grazing sheep, making an ideal surface for walkers. The hill above the precipitous **Devil's Dyke**, just north of Brighton, offers spectacular views for miles across the Downs. The legend is that the Devil cut the gorge to let in the sea and flood the countryside, but was foiled by divine intervention. The River Cuckmere runs through one of the most picturesque parts of the South Downs.

Located at the highest point of the Downs is **Uppark House**. This neat square building has been meticulously restored to its mid-18th-century appearance after a fire in 1989.

🏰 **Uppark House**
(NT) Petersfield, West Sussex.
📞 *01730 825317.* ◯ *Jun–Nov: Sun–Thu & public hols (pm).* ▨ ♿

Hastings ⑰

East Sussex. 👥 *83,000.* ⊟ ℗ 🛈
4 Robertson Terrace (01424 781111).

THIS FASCINATING seaside town was one of the first Cinque Ports *(see p168)* and is still a thriving fishing port. The town is characterized by the unique tall wooden "net shops" on the beach, where for hundreds of years, fishermen have stored their nets. In the 19th century, the area to the west of the Old Town was

built up as a seaside resort, which left the narrow streets of the old fishermen's quarter, their half-timbered houses, shops and cozy pubs intact.

The wooden net shops, on Hastings shingle beach

Other attractions include two cliff railroads and a network of former smugglers' caves with a display on smuggling *(see p266)* – once a vital part of the town's economy.

ENVIRONS: Seven miles (11 km) from Hastings is Battle. The center square of this small town is dominated by the gatehouse of **Battle Abbey**. This was built by William the Conqueror on the site of his great victory – he reputedly placed the high altar on the spot where Harold fell. But the abbey was destroyed in the Dissolution *(see p50)*. There is an evocative walk around the actual battlefield.

🏛 **Battle Abbey**
High St, Battle. 📞 *01424 773792.* ◯ *daily.* ● *Dec 24–26, Jan 1.* ▨ ♿

BATTLE OF HASTINGS

In 1066, William the Conqueror's *(see p47)* invading army from Normandy landed on the south coast, aiming to take Winchester and London. Hearing that King Harold and his army were camped just inland from Hastings, William confronted them and won the battle after Harold was killed by an arrow through his eye. This last successful invasion of England is depicted on the *Bayeux Tapestry,* in Normandy, France.

King Harold's death,
Bayeux Tapestry

The fairy-tale 14th-century Bodiam Castle surrounded by its moat

Bodiam Castle ⓲

(NT) Rye, East Sussex. 〖 01580 830436. ≊ Robertsbridge then taxi. ◯ mid-Feb–Oct: daily; Nov–Dec: Tue–Sun. ● Dec 24–26. 🖾 🗓 limited.

SURROUNDED BY its wide, glistening moat, this late 14th-century castle is one of the most romantic in England.

It was originally built as a defense against an anticipated invasion by the French. The attack never came but the castle saw action during the Civil War (see pp52–3) when it was damaged in an assault by Parliamentary soldiers. They removed the roof to reduce its use as a base for Charles I.

It has been uninhabited since, but its gray stone has proved indestructible. With the exception of the roof, it was restored in 1919 by the statesman Lord Curzon who gave it to the nation. The round towers at each corner can be climbed, and offer fine views of the surrounding countryside.

ENVIRONS: To the east is **Great Dixter**, a 15th-century manor house restored by Sir Edwin Lutyens (see pp24–5) in 1910 for the Lloyd family. The writer Christopher Lloyd created a magnificent garden with an Edwardian blend of terraces and borders (see pp22–3).

🏰 Great Dixter
Northiam, Rye. 〖 01797 252878. ◯ Apr–Oct: Tue–Sun & public hols. 🖾

Rye ⓳

See pp170–71.

Romney Marsh ⓴

Kent. ≊ Ashford. 🚌 Ashford, Hythe. 🛈 New Romney (01797 364044).

UNTIL ROMAN TIMES Romney Marsh and its southern neighbor Walland Marsh were entirely covered by the sea at high tide. The Romans drained the Romney section, and Walland Marsh was gradually reclaimed during the Middle Ages. Together they formed a large area of fertile land for arable crops and grazing – particularly suitable for the bulky Romney Marsh sheep bred for the quality and quantity of their wool.

Dungeness, a desolate and lonely spot at the southeastern tip of the area, is dominated by a lighthouse and two nuclear power stations that

COASTAL DEFENSE AND THE CINQUE PORTS

Before the Norman Conquest (see pp46–7), national government was very weak and, with growing threats from Europe, it was important for Saxon kings to keep on good terms with the Channel ports. So, in return for a promise to keep the royal fleet supplied with ships and men, five ports – Hastings, Romney, Sandwich, Hythe and Dover – were granted the right to levy taxes. Cinque – pronounced here as "sink" – came from the French for five. The privileges were revoked during the 17th century. In 1803 the threat from France meant 74 fixed defenses were built along the coast. Only 24 of these Martello towers still exist.

The cliff-top position of Dover Castle

Martello towers were built as part of the Channel's defenses

break up the skyline. It is also the southern terminus of the popular **Romney, Hythe and Dymchurch Light Railway**, which was opened in 1927. During the summer this takes passengers 14 miles (23 km) up the coast to Hythe on trains one third the conventional size.

The northern edge of the marsh is crossed by the Royal Military Canal, built to serve both as a defense and supply line in 1804, when it was feared Napoleon was planning an invasion *(see p55)*.

Dover ㉑

Kent. 🕌 *41,000.* ⊟ 🚉 ⛴
🛈 *Townwall St (01304 205108).*
🏪 *Fri, Sat.*

ITS PROXIMITY to the European mainland makes Dover, with its neighbor Folkestone, the leading port for cross-Channel travel and now the terminal for the Channel Tunnel *(see p632)*. Its famous white cliffs exert a strong pull on returning travelers.

Dover's strategic position and large natural harbor mean the town has always had an important role to play in the nation's defenses.

Built on the original site of an ancient Saxon fortification, **Dover Castle**, superbly positioned on top of the high cliffs, has helped defend the town from 1198, when Henry II first built the keep, right up to World War II, when it was used as the command post for the Dunkirk evacuation. Exhibits in the castle and in the labyrinth of tunnels beneath, made by prisoners in the Napoleonic Wars *(see p55)*, cover all these periods.

ENVIRONS: One of the most significant sites in England's early history is the ruin of **Richborough Castle**. This extensive, grassy site, now 2 miles (3 km) inland, was where, in AD 43, Claudius's Roman invaders *(see p44)* made their first landing. For hundreds of years afterward Rutupiae, as it was known, was one of the most important ports of entry and military encampments in the country.

🏰 **Dover Castle**
Castle Hill. 📞 *01304 211067.* ◯ *daily.* ● *Dec 25, 26, Jan 1.* 🎟
🏛 **Richborough Castle**
Richborough. 📞 *01304 612013.*
◯ *Oct–Mar: Tue–Sun; Apr–Nov: daily.*
● *Dec 25, 26, Jan 1.* ♿ *limited.*

Margate ㉒

Kent. 🕌 *39,000.* 🚉 🚌
🛈 *22 High St (01843 220241).*

TRADITIONALLY THE most boisterous of the three seaside resorts on the Isle of Thanet (the other two are Ramsgate and Broadstairs), Margate has for a long time been a popular destination for day trippers from London, traveling in Victorian times by steam boat and later by train. The town has theme parks and fairground rides.

ENVIRONS: Just south is a 19th-century gentleman's residence **Quex House**, which has two unusual towers in its grounds. The adjoining museum has a fine collection of African and Oriental art, as well as unique dioramas of tropical wildlife.

Visitors relaxing on Margate's popular sandy beach

To the west is a Saxon church, built within the remains of the bleak Roman coastal fort of **Reculver**. Dramatic twin towers, known as the Two Sisters, were added to the church in the 12th century. These were luckily saved from destruction in 1809 because they were a useful navigational aid for shipping. The church now stands at the center of a very pleasant, if rather windy, 37 ha (91 acre) country park.

🏛 **Quex House**
Birchington. 📞 *01843 842168.*
◯ *Apr–Oct: Tue–Thu, Sun. (Museum only: Nov–Dec, Mar: Sun.)* 🎟
♿ *limited.*
🏛 **Reculver Fort**
Reculver. 📞 *01227 361911 (Herne Bay Tourist Information).* ◯ *daily.*

A drainage dike running through the fertile plains of Romney Marsh

Street-by-Street: Rye ⑲

THIS ANCIENT and delightful fortified town was added to the original Cinque ports *(see p168)* in the 11th century. A huge storm in 1287 diverted the River Rother so that it met the sea at Rye, and for more than 300 years it was one of the most important channel ports. However, in the 16th century the harbor began to silt up and the town is now 2 miles (3 km) inland. Rye was frequently attacked by the French, culminating in 1377 when it was burned to the ground.

The Mermaid Inn sign

★ Mermaid Street
This delightful cobbled street, its huddled houses jutting out at unlikely angles, has hardly altered since it was rebuilt in the 14th century.

The Mint
got its name from the 17th-century minting of tokens.

Strand Quay
The brick and timber warehouses survive from the prosperous days when Rye was a thriving port.

The Mermaid Inn, founded in the 11th century, is Rye's largest medieval building. In the 1750s it was the headquarters of a notorious and bloodthirsty smuggling gang called the Hawkhursts.

View over the River Tillingham

STAR SIGHTS

★ Mermaid Street

★ Ypres Tower

Lamb House
This fine Georgian house was built in 1722. George I stayed here when stranded in a storm, and author Henry James (1843–1916) lived here.

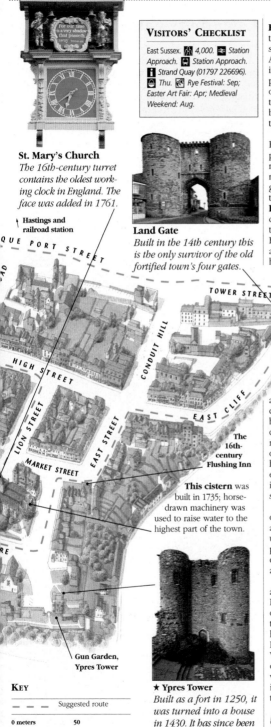

St. Mary's Church
The 16th-century turret contains the oldest working clock in England. The face was added in 1761.

↑ Hastings and railroad station

VISITORS' CHECKLIST

East Sussex. 👥 4,000. 🚉 Station Approach. 🚌 Station Approach. ℹ Strand Quay (01797 226696). 🛒 Thu. 🎭 Rye Festival: Sep; Easter Art Fair: Apr; Medieval Weekend: Aug.

Land Gate
Built in the 14th century this is the only survivor of the old fortified town's four gates.

The 16th-century **Flushing Inn**

This cistern was built in 1735; horse-drawn machinery was used to raise water to the highest part of the town.

Gun Garden, Ypres Tower

KEY

– – – Suggested route

0 meters   50
0 yards   50

★ **Ypres Tower**
Built as a fort in 1250, it was turned into a house in 1430. It has since been a prison and mortuary.

ENVIRONS: Just 2 miles (3 km) to the south of Rye is the small town of **Winchelsea**. At the behest of Edward I, it was moved to its present position in 1288, when most of the old town on lower land to the southeast, was drowned by the same storm that diverted the River Rother in 1287.

Winchelsea is probably Britain's first coherently planned new town. Although not all of it was built as originally planned, its rectangular grid survives today, as does the **Church of St. Thomas Becket** (begun c.1300) at its center. Several raids during the 14th century by the French damaged the church and burned down scores of houses. The church has three tombs that probably predate it, having been rescued from the old town before it was submerged. There are also two well-preserved medieval tombs in the chantry. The three windows (1928–33) in the Lady Chapel were designed by Douglas Strachan as a memorial to those who died in World War I. Just beyond the edges of present-day Winchelsea are the remains of three of the original gates – showing just how big a town was first envisaged. The beach below is one of the finest on the southeast coast.

Camber Sands, to the east of the mouth of the Rother, is another excellent beach. Once used by fishermen it is now popular with swimmers and edged with seaside bungalows and a vacation camp.

The ruins of **Camber Castle** are west of the sands, between Rye and Winchelsea. This was one of the forts built along this coast by Henry VIII when he feared an attack by the French, which never came. When it was first built it was on the edge of the sea but it was abandoned in 1642 when it became stranded inland as the river silted up.

🏛 **Camber Castle**
Camber, Rye. ⬛ for guided tours only: contact Rye tourist office.

**Jesus on Christ Church Gate,
Canterbury Cathedral**

Canterbury ㉓

Kent. 🏛 *50,000.* 🚉 🚌 ℹ *34 St.
Margaret's St (01227 766567).*
🅿 *Wed.*

Its POSITION on the London-to-Dover route meant that Canterbury was an important Roman town even before St. Augustine arrived in 597, sent by the pope to convert the Anglo-Saxons to Christianity. The town rose in importance, soon becoming the center of the Church in England.

With the building of the **cathedral** and the martyrdom of Thomas à Becket *(see p48)*, Canterbury's future as a religious center was assured.

Adjacent to the ruins of **St. Augustine's Abbey**, destroyed in the Dissolution *(see p50)*, is **St. Martin's Church**, one of the oldest in England. This was where St. Augustine first worshiped, and it has impressive Norman and Saxon work.

West Gate Museum, with its round towers, is an imposing medieval gatehouse. It was built in 1381 and contains a display of arms and armory.

The Poor Priests' Hospital, founded in the 12th century, now houses the **Canterbury Heritage Museum**.

🏛 **West Gate Museum**
St. Peter's St. 📞 *01227 452747.*
🕐 *Mon–Sat.* ⬤ *Christmas wk,
Good Fri.* 📷 ♿
🏛 **Canterbury Heritage
Museum**
Stour St. 📞 *01227 452747.*
🕐 *Jun–Oct: daily; Nov–May: Mon–Sat.*
⬤ *Christmas wk, Good Fri.* 📷

Canterbury Cathedral

To MATCH CANTERBURY's growing ecclesiastical rank as a major center of Christianity, the first Norman archbishop, Lanfranc, ordered a new cathedral to be built on the ruins of the Anglo-Saxon cathedral in 1077. It was enlarged and rebuilt many times; as a result it embraces examples of all styles of medieval architecture. The most poignant moment in its history came in 1170 when Thomas à Becket was murdered here *(see p48)*. Four years after his death a fire devastated the cathedral and Trinity Chapel was built to house Becket's remains. The shrine quickly became an important religious site, and until the Dissolution *(see p50)* the cathedral was one of Christendom's chief places of pilgrimage.

The nave at 170 m (556 ft) makes Canterbury Europe's longest medieval church.

The South Porch (1418) may have been built to commemorate the victory at Agincourt *(see p51)*.

Main entrance

★ **Medieval Stained Glass**
This depiction of the 1,000-year-old Methuselah is a detail from the southwest transept window.

GEOFFREY CHAUCER

Considered to be the first great English poet, Geoffrey Chaucer (c.1345–1400), a customs official by profession, wrote a rambunctious and witty account of a group of pilgrims traveling from London to Becket's shrine in 1387 in the *Canterbury Tales*. The pilgrims represent a cross-section of 14th-century English society and the tales remain one of the greatest and most entertaining works of early English literature.

**Wife of Bath,
Canterbury Tales**

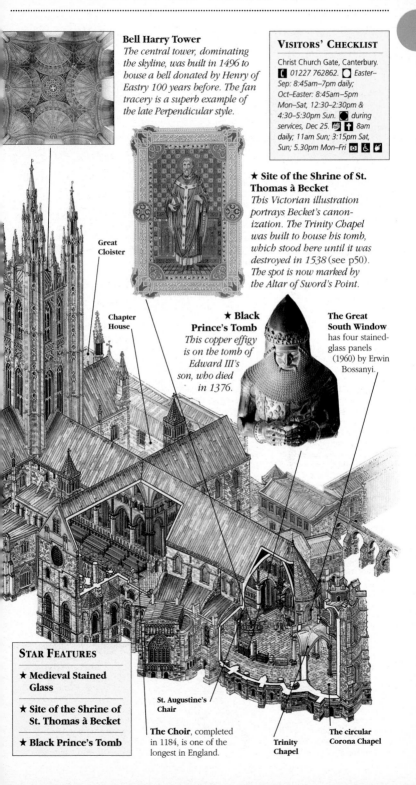

Bell Harry Tower
The central tower, dominating the skyline, was built in 1496 to house a bell donated by Henry of Eastry 100 years before. The fan tracery is a superb example of the late Perpendicular style.

VISITORS' CHECKLIST

Christ Church Gate, Canterbury.
01227 762862. Easter–Sep: 8:45am–7pm daily; Oct–Easter: 8:45am–5pm Mon–Sat, 12:30–2:30pm & 4:30–5:30pm Sun. during services, Dec 25. 8am daily; 11am Sun; 3:15pm Sat, Sun; 5.30pm Mon–Fri

Great Cloister

★ Site of the Shrine of St. Thomas à Becket
This Victorian illustration portrays Becket's canonization. The Trinity Chapel was built to house his tomb, which stood here until it was destroyed in 1538 (see p50). The spot is now marked by the Altar of Sword's Point.

Chapter House

★ Black Prince's Tomb
This copper effigy is on the tomb of Edward III's son, who died in 1376.

The Great South Window has four stained-glass panels (1960) by Erwin Bossanyi.

STAR FEATURES

★ Medieval Stained Glass

★ Site of the Shrine of St. Thomas à Becket

★ Black Prince's Tomb

St. Augustine's Chair

The Choir, completed in 1184, is one of the longest in England.

Trinity Chapel

The circular Corona Chapel

The keep of Rochester Castle, dominating Rochester and the Medway Valley

Leeds Castle ⓜ

Maidstone, Kent. 🅒 *01622 765400.*
🚆 *Maidstone then bus.* 🅞 *daily.*
🅞 *for concerts & Dec 25.* 🈴 🅱

SURROUNDED BY A LAKE that reflects the warm buff stone of its crenellated turrets, Leeds is often considered to be the most beautiful castle in England. Begun in the early 12th century, it has been continuously inhabited and its present appearance is a result of centuries of rebuilding and extensions, most recently in the 1930s. Leeds has royal connections going back to 1278, when it was given to Edward I by a courtier seeking favor.

Henry VIII loved the castle and visited it often, escaping from the plague in London. It contains a life-sized bust of Henry from the late 16th century. Leeds passed out of royal hands when Edward VI gave it to Sir Anthony St. Leger in 1552 as a reward for helping to pacify the Irish. The garden, designed by Capability Brown *(see p23)*, has a maze.

Rochester ㉕

Kent. 🏛 145,000. 🚆 🅗
🅘 *Eastgate Cottage, High St (01634 843666).*

CLUSTERED AT THE MOUTH of the River Medway are the towns of Rochester, Chatham and Gillingham, all rich in

naval history, but none more so than Rochester, which occupied a strategic site on the London to Dover road.

England's tallest Norman keep is at **Rochester Castle**, worth climbing for the views over the Medway. The town's medieval history is still visible, with the original city walls – which followed the lines of the Roman fortifications – on view in the High Street, and some well-preserved wall paintings in the **cathedral**, built in 1088.

ENVIRONS: In Chatham, the **Historic Dockyard** is now a museum of shipbuilding and nautical crafts. **Fort Amherst** nearby was built in 1756 to protect the dockyard and river entrance from attack, and has 1,800 m (5,570 ft) of tunnels to explore that were hewn by Napoleonic prisoners of war.

♣ Rochester Castle
The Esplanade. 🅒 *01634 402276.*
🅞 *daily.* 🅞 *Dec 24–26, Jan 1.* 🈴

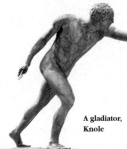

A gladiator,
Knole

🏛 Historic Dockyard
Dock Rd, Chatham. 🅒 *01634 812551.* 🅞 *Easter–Oct: daily; Nov, Feb–Mar: Wed, Sat, Sun.* 🈴 🅱
♪ Fort Amherst
Dock Rd, Chatham. 🅒 *01634 847747.* 🅞 *Mar–Oct: daily; Nov–Feb: Thu–Mon.* 🅞 *Dec 24, 25, Jan 1.* 🈴

Knole ㉖

(NT) Sevenoaks, Kent. 🅒 *01732 450608.* 🚆 *Sevenoaks then taxi.*
House 🅞 *Easter–Oct: Wed–Sun & public hols.* **Garden** 🅞 *May–Sep: first Wed each month.* 🈴 🅱 *limited.*

WITH A DISTINGUISHED royal history, this immense Tudor mansion is also one of the finest houses in the entire country. Built in the late 15th century on the foundations of an older house, it was seized by Henry VIII from the Archbishop of Canterbury, Thomas Cranmer, at the time of the Dissolution *(see p50)*. In 1566 Queen Elizabeth I gave it to her cousin Thomas Sackville. His descendants have lived here ever since, including the writer Vita Sackville-West, (1892–1962) who set her novel, *The Edwardians* (1930) here. Apart from its splendid decorative detail and the valuable collection of paintings, the house is best known for its beautiful 17th-century furniture, such as the elaborate state bed made for James II, and a rare silver table with candlesticks and mirror. The 405 ha (1,000 acre) park and gardens have some lovely walks.

ENVIRONS: A small, square manor house, **Ightham Mote**, situated just east of Knole, is one of the finest examples of medieval architecture in England. Its 14th-century timber-and-stone building encloses a central court and is surrounded by a moat.

♛ Ightham Mote
(NT) Ivy Hatch, Sevenoaks. **[** 01732 810378. **◻** Apr–Oct: Wed–Fri, Sun, Mon & public hols. **⌖** **🔊** limited.

Hever Castle ㉗

Edenbridge, Kent. **[** 01732 865224. **⇄** Edenbridge. **◻** mid-Mar–Oct: daily. **⌖** **🔊** limited.

THIS SMALL, MOATED CASTLE is famous as the 16th-century home of Anne Boleyn, the doomed wife of Henry VIII, executed for adultery. She

CHARLES DICKENS

Charles Dickens (1812–70), a popular writer in his own time, is still widely read today. He was born in Portsmouth but moved to Chatham at age five. As an adult, Dickens lived in London but kept his Kent connections, taking vacations in Broadstairs, just south of Margate – where he wrote *David Copperfield* – and spending his last years at Gad's Hill, near Rochester. The town celebrates the famous connection with an annual Dickens festival.

The façade of Chartwell, Winston Churchill's home

lived here as a young woman and the king often visited her while staying at Leeds Castle. In 1903 Hever was bought by William Waldorf Astor, who undertook extensive restoration, building a Neo-Tudor village alongside it to accommodate guests and servants. The moat and gatehouse remain from when they were first built, around 1270.

ENVIRONS: To the northwest of Hever is **Chartwell**, the home of World War II leader Sir Winston Churchill (*see p58*). It remains furnished as it was when he lived here. To relax, he used to rebuild parts of the house. A few of his paintings are on display.

♛ Chartwell
(NT) Westerham, Kent. **[** 01732 866368. **◻** Mar–Oct: Tue–Thu, Sat, Sun & public hols; Nov: Wed, Sat, Sun. **◐** Tue after public hols. **⌖** **🔊**

Royal Tunbridge Wells ㉘

Kent. **👥** 51,000. **⇄** **🚌** **ℹ** The Old Fish Market, The Pantiles (01892 515675). **🛒** Wed.

HELPED BY ROYAL patronage, the town became a popular spa in the 17th and 18th centuries after mineral springs were discovered in the town in 1606. The Pantiles – the historic colonnade and paved promenade, named after the original square tiles – was laid out in the 1700s.

ENVIRONS: Nearby is a superb example of a medieval manor house, **Penshurst Place**. Built in the 1340s, it has an 18 m (60 ft) high Great Hall.

♛ Penshurst Place
Royal Tunbridge Wells, Kent. **[** 01892 870307. **◻** Mar–Sep: daily; Oct, Feb: Sat, Sun. **⌖** **🔊** limited.

An early 18th-century astrolabe to measure the stars, Hever Castle garden

EAST ANGLIA

NORFOLK · SUFFOLK · ESSEX · CAMBRIDGESHIRE

THE BULGE OF LAND *between the Thames Estuary and the Wash, flat but far from featureless, sits aside from the main north–south axis through Britain, and for that reason it has succeeded in maintaining and preserving its distinctive architecture, traditions and rural character in both cities and countryside.*

East Anglia's name derives from the Angles, the people from northern Germany who settled here during the 5th and 6th centuries. East Anglians have long been a breed of plain-spoken and independent people. Two prominent East Anglians – Queen Boadicea in the 1st century and Oliver Cromwell in the 17th century – were famous for their stubbornness and their refusal to bow to constituted authority. During the Civil War, East Anglia was Cromwell's most reliable source of support. The hardy people who made a difficult living hunting and fishing in the swampy fens, which were drained in the 17th century, were called the Fen Tigers. After draining, the peaty soil proved ideal for arable farming, and today East Anglia grows about a third of Britain's vegetables. The rotation of crops, heralding Britain's agricultural revolution, was perfected in Norfolk in the 18th century. Many of the region's towns and cities grew prosperous on the agricultural wealth, including Norwich. The sea also plays a prominent role in East Anglian life. Coastal towns and villages support the many fishermen who use the North Sea, rich in herring in former days but now known mainly for flatfish.

In modern times, the area has become a center of recreational sailing, both off the coast and on the inland waterway system known as the Norfolk Broads. East Anglia is also home to one of Britain's top universities: Cambridge.

Lavender fields in full bloom in July, Heacham, Norfolk

◁ **Cley windmill overlooking the sea marshes on the north Norfolk coast**

Exploring East Anglia

As you move away from London, you soon reach the countryside immortalized by the painter Constable *(see p190)* and in many ways unchanged since his day, scattered with churches, windmills and medieval agricultural barns. Nature lovers will find it fruitful territory, especially North Norfolk with its bird preserves and seal colonies. Boating enthusiasts, too, are well catered to in this, Britain's driest and sunniest region. Local architecture ranges from medieval to modern. The distinctive pink-washed cottages in Suffolk, flint cottages in Norfolk and thatched roofs everywhere, are also much in evidence.

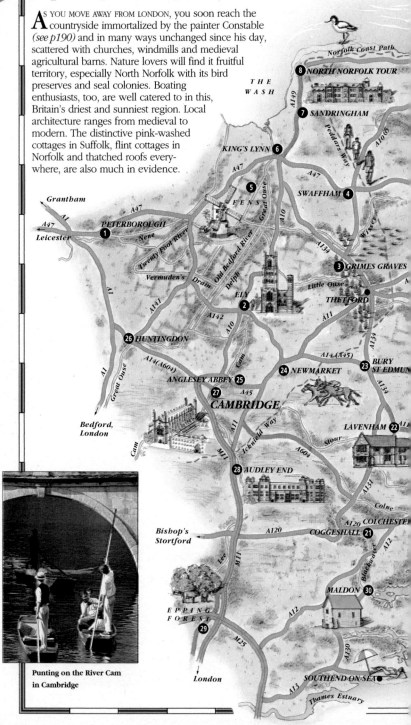

Norfolk Coast Path

THE WASH

8 NORTH NORFOLK TOUR

7 SANDRINGHAM

Peddars Way

A149

A1065

KING'S LYNN 6

A47

A47

5

FENS

SWAFFHAM 4

A134

Wissey

Grantham

A47

A1

A47

Leicester

PETERBOROUGH 1

Nene

Twenty Foot River

Great Ouse

A10

Vermuden's Drain

Old Bedford River

Delph

ELY 2

Little Ouse

3 GRIMES GRAVES

THETFORD

A11

A142

A10

A141

A14(A604)

HUNTINGDON 26

Great Ouse

Cam

A14(A45)

24 NEWMARKET

23 BURY ST EDMUN

A134

ANGLESEY ABBEY 25

A45

27

CAMBRIDGE

Bedford, London

Cam

A11

Icknield Way

A604

Stour

LAVENHAM 22

M11

28 AUDLEY END

A131

Colne

A120 COLCHESTE

Bishop's Stortford

A120

COGGESHALL 21

A12

Lee

M11

Blackwater

A12

EPPING FOREST

MALDON 30

29

A12

A130

M25

London

A13

SOUTHEND-ON-SEA

Thames Estuary

Punting on the River Cam in Cambridge

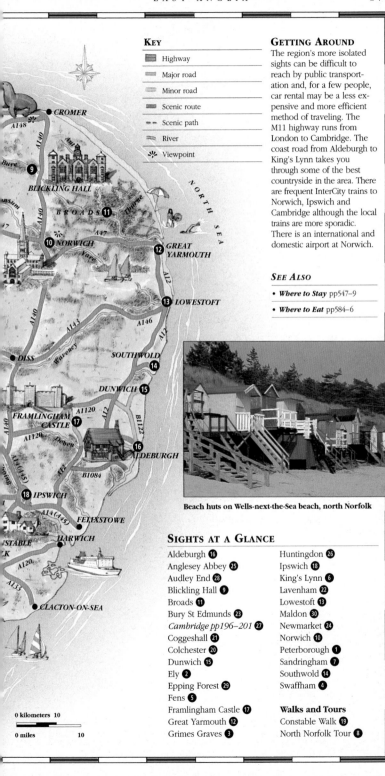

GETTING AROUND

The region's more isolated sights can be difficult to reach by public transportation and, for a few people, car rental may be a less expensive and more efficient method of traveling. The M11 highway runs from London to Cambridge. The coast road from Aldeburgh to King's Lynn takes you through some of the best countryside in the area. There are frequent InterCity trains to Norwich, Ipswich and Cambridge although the local trains are more sporadic. There is an international and domestic airport at Norwich.

SEE ALSO

Beach huts on Wells-next-the-Sea beach, north Norfolk

Peterborough ❶

Cambridgeshire. 🏠 *152,000.* 🚆 🚌
ℹ️ *45 Bridge St (01733 317336).*
🗓️ *Tue–Sat.*

ALTHOUGH ONE OF the oldest
settlements in Britain,
Peterborough was designated
a New Town in 1967 – part of
a plan to move people from
the larger cities – and is now
a mix of ancient and modern.

The city center is dominated
by the 12th-century **St. Peter's
Cathedral**, which gave the city
its name. The interior of this
classic Norman building, with
its vast yet simple nave, was
badly damaged by Cromwell's
troops *(see p52)*, but its unique
painted wooden ceiling (1220)
has survived intact. Catherine
of Aragon, the first wife of

Peterborough's coat of arms with
a Latin inscription: Upon this Rock

Henry VIII, is buried here,
although Cromwell's troops
also destroyed her tomb.

ENVIRONS: The oldest wheel in
Britain (10,000 BC) was found
preserved in peat at **Flag Fen
Bronze Age Excavations**.
The site provides a fascinating
glimpse into prehistory.

⋒ Flag Fen Bronze Age Excavations

Fourth Drove, Fengate, Peterborough.
📞 *01733 313414.* 🕐 *daily.* ⬤ *Dec
25, 26.* 🎦 ♿

Grimes Graves ❸

Brandon, Norfolk. 📞 *01842 810656.*
🚆 *Brandon then taxi.* 🕐 *Easter–Oct:
daily; Nov–Easter: Wed–Sun.*
⬤ *Dec 24–26, Jan 1.* 🎦 ♿ *limited.*

ONE OF THE MOST important
Neolithic sites in England,
this was once an extensive
complex of flint mines – 366
shafts have been located –
dating from before 2000 BC.

Using antlers as pickaxes,
Stone Age miners hacked
through the soft chalk to
extract the hard flint below to
make axes, weapons and tools.
The flint was transported long
distances around England on
the prehistoric network of
paths. You can descend 9 m
(30 ft) by ladder into one of
the shafts and see the galleries

Ely ❷

Cambridgeshire. 🏠 *14,000.* 🚆
ℹ️ *29 St. Mary's St (01353 662062).*
🗓️ *Thu, Sat (craft & antiques).*

BUILT ON A chalk hill, this
small city is thought to be
named after the eels in the
nearby River Ouse.

The hill was once a strategic
and inaccessible island in the
middle of the once marshy and
treacherous Fens *(see p182)*.
It was also the last stronghold
of Anglo-Saxon resistance
under the "Last Englishman,"
Hereward the Wake *(see p46)*,
who hid in the cathedral until
the conquering Normans
crossed the Fens in 1071.

Today this small prosperous
city, totally dominated by the
huge **cathedral**, is the
market center for the rich
agricultural area surrounding it.

The lantern's glass
windows admit light
into the dome.

Octagon

*This painted
wooden angel is
one of hundreds of
bosses that were
carved all over the
south and north
transepts in the 13th
and 14th centuries.*

**Stained-glass
museum**

The tomb is that of
Alan de Walsingham,
designer of the
unique Octagon.

*The Octagon,
made of wood, was built
in 1322 when the Norman
tower collapsed. Its roof,
the lantern, took an extra
24 years to build and
weighs 200 tons.*

Area of cutaway

ELY CATHEDRAL

Ely. 📞 *01353 667735.*
🕐 *daily.* ⬤ *special events.* 🎦 ♿
Begun in 1083, the cathedral took 268 years to
complete. It survived the Dissolution *(see p50)*
but was closed for 17 years by Cromwell *(see
p52)* who lived in Ely for a time.

where the flint was mined. During excavations, unusual chalk models of a fertility goddess *(see p43)* and a phallus were discovered.

ENVIRONS: Nearby, at the center of the once fertile plain known as the Breckland, is the small market town of **Thetford**.

Once prosperous, its fortunes dipped in the 16th century, when the priory was destroyed *(see p51)* and the land deteriorated due to excessive sheep grazing. The area was later planted with pine trees. A mound in the city marks the site of a pre-Norman castle.

The revolutionary writer and philosopher Tom Paine, author of *Common Sense* and *The Rights of Man,* was born here in 1737.

The huge cathedral spire *dominates the flat Fens countryside surrounding Ely.*

Painted ceiling, 19th century

The Prior's Door (c.1150)

The south aisle has 12 classic Norman arches at its foot, with pointed Early English windows above.

Oxburgh Hall surrounded by its medieval moat

Swaffham ❹

Norfolk. 🏘 *6,500.* 🚃 ℹ️ *Market Place (01760 722255).* 🛒 *Sat.*

THE BEST-PRESERVED Georgian town in East Anglia and a fashionable resort during the Regency period, Swaffham is at its liveliest on Saturdays when a market is held in the square around the elegant and unusual market cross of 1783. In the center of the town is the 15th-century **Church of St. Peter and St. Paul**, with a small spire added to the tower in the 19th century. It has a magnificent Tudor north aisle, said to have been paid for by John Chapman, the Pedlar of Swaffham. He is depicted on the unusual two-sided town sign found in the market place. Myth has it that he went to London and met a stranger who told him of hidden treasure at Swaffham. He returned, dug it up and embellished the church on the proceeds. He is shown in a window.

ENVIRONS: Castle Acre, north of the town, has the remains of a massive Cluniac **priory**. Founded in 1090, its stunning Norman front still stands.

A short drive south is **Oxburgh Hall**, built by Sir Edmund Bedingfeld in 1482. The core of the hall, entered through a huge 24 m (80 ft) fortified gatehouse, is a good example of the period when houses were built for comfort as well as defense. The velvet Oxburgh Hangings, embroidered by Mary, Queen of Scots *(see p497),* are displayed.

John Chapman, Swaffham town sign

🏛 **Castle Acre Priory**
Castle Acre. 📞 *01760 755394.*
⭕ *Apr–Oct: daily.* 🎟 🚻 *limited.*
🏛 **Oxburgh Hall**
Oxborough. 📞 *01366 328258.*
⭕ *Apr–Oct: Sat–Wed.* 🎟 🚻 *limited.*

BOADICEA AND THE ICENI

When the Romans invaded Britain, the Iceni, the main tribe in East Anglia, joined forces with them to defeat the Catuvellauni, a rival tribe. But the Romans then turned on the Iceni, torturing Queen Boadicea (or Boudicca). In AD 61, she led a revolt against Roman rule: her followers burned down London, Colchester and St. Albans. The rebellion was put down and the queen took poison rather than submit. At Cockley Cley, near Swaffham, an Iceni camp has been excavated.

Illustration of Queen Boadicea leading her Iceni followers

A windmill on Wicken Fen

The Fens ❺

Cambridgeshire/Norfolk. ⇌ *Ely.* 🛈
29 St. Mary's St, Ely (01353 662062).

THIS IS THE OPEN, flat, fertile expanse that lies between Lincoln, Cambridge, Bedford and King's Lynn. Up until the 17th century it was a swamp, and settlement was possible only on "islands", such as Ely *(see p180)*, raised above their low-lying surroundings.

Through the 17th century, speculators, recognizing the value of the peaty soil for farmland, brought in Dutch experts to drain the fens. However, as the peat dried, it contracted, and the fens have slowly been getting lower. Originally pumped by windmills, the area now needs powerful electric pumps to keep it drained.

Nine miles (14 km) from Ely is Wicken Fen, 243 ha (600 acres) of undrained fen providing a habitat for an abundance of water life, wildfowl and wild flowers.

King's Lynn ❻

Norfolk. 👥 *42,000.* ⇌ 🚌 🛈
🛈 *Saturday Market Place (01553 763044).* 🏠 *Tue, Sat.*

FORMERLY BISHOP'S LYNN, its name was changed at the Reformation *(see p51)* to reflect the changing political reality. In the Middle Ages it was one of England's most prosperous ports, shipping grain and wool from the surrounding countryside to Europe. There are still a few warehouses and merchants' houses by the River Ouse surviving from this period. At the north end of the town is **True's Yard**, a relic of the old fishermen's quarter.

Guild Hall, King's Lynn

North Norfolk Coastal Tour ❽

THIS TOUR TAKES YOU THROUGH some of the most beautiful areas of East Anglia. Nearly all of the north Norfolk coast has been designated an Area of Outstanding Natural Beauty. The sea has dictated the character of the area. With continuing deposits of silt, once-busy ports are now far inland and the shingle-and-sand banks that have been built up are home to a huge variety of wildlife. Along the coast the sea has taken a different toll and eroded great tracts of land, creating spectacular cliffs.

TIPS FOR DRIVERS

Tour length: 28 miles (45 km).
Stopping-off points: Holkham Hall makes a pleasant stop for a picnic lunch. There are some good pubs in Wells-next-the-Sea. (See also pp636–7.)

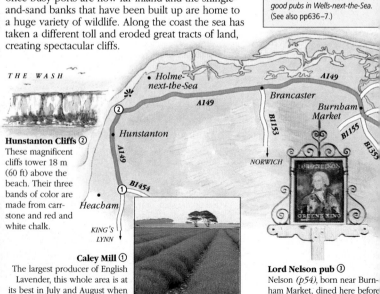

Hunstanton Cliffs ②
These magnificent cliffs tower 18 m (60 ft) above the beach. Their three bands of color are made from carrstone and red and white chalk.

Caley Mill ①
The largest producer of English Lavender, this whole area is at its best in July and August when the fields are a blaze of purple.

Lord Nelson pub ③
Nelson (p54), born near Burnham Market, dined here before he went to sea for the last time.

The **Trinity Guildhall** was built in the 1420s, and among the town regalia on display inside is an early 13th-century sword thought to have been a gift to the town from King John *(see p48),* who visited the town several times. The last occasion was in 1216. He dined here on his way to the north of England to flee rebellious barons. The next day, while crossing the sea, he lost all his treasure – people have been dredging and diving to try and find it ever since.

On the Market Place is **St. Margaret's Church** with work from the 13th-century onward, including a fine Elizabethan screen.

⛪ Trinity Guildhall
Saturday Market Place. **☎** 01553 763044. ◯ Easter–Oct: daily; Nov– Easter: Fri–Tue. ● Dec 24–26. 🎫 ♿

Sandringham House, where the Royal Family spend Christmas

Sandringham ❼

Norfolk. **☎** 01553 772675. 🚌 from King's Lynn. ◯ Easter–Sep: daily. ● three wks Jul–Aug. 🎫 ♿

THIS SIZEABLE NORFOLK estate has been in royal hands since 1862 when it was bought by the Prince of Wales, who later became Edward VII. The 18th-century house was elaborately embellished and refurbished by the Prince and now retains an appropriately Edwardian atmosphere.

The large stables are now a museum and contain several hundred trophies that relate to hunting, shooting and horse racing – all favorite royal activities. A popular feature is an intriguing display of royal motor cars spanning nearly a century. In the country park there are scenic nature trails.

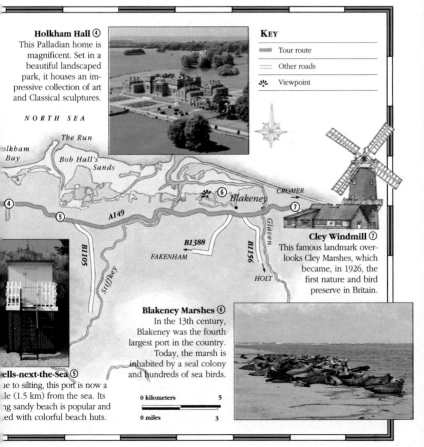

Holkham Hall ④
This Palladian home is magnificent. Set in a beautiful landscaped park, it houses an impressive collection of art and Classical sculptures.

NORTH SEA

The Run

olkham
Bay

*Bob Hall's
Sands*

KEY

━━ Tour route

═══ Other roads

🔆 Viewpoint

④

⑤

A149

Blakeney 🔆 ⑥

CROMER

⑦

Cley Windmill ⑦
This famous landmark overlooks Cley Marshes, which became, in 1926, the first nature and bird preserve in Britain.

B1388

FAKENHAM

B1156

HOLT

Stiffkey

B1105

Glaven

Blakeney Marshes ⑥
In the 13th century, Blakeney was the fourth largest port in the country. Today, the marsh is inhabited by a seal colony and hundreds of sea birds.

ells-next-the-Sea ⑤
ie to silting, this port is now a le (1.5 km) from the sea. Its ng sandy beach is popular and ed with colorful beach huts.

0 kilometers   5

0 miles   3

The symmetrical redbrick façade of the 16th-century Blickling Hall

Blickling Hall ❾

(NT) Aylsham, Norfolk. 📞 *01263 733084.* 🚌 *from Norwich (in summer).* 🕐 *Apr–Oct: Tue, Wed, Fri–Sun.* 🅿️ ♿

Approached from the east, its symmetrical Jacobean front framed by trees and flanked by two yew hedges, Blickling Hall offers one of the most impressive vistas of any country house in the area.

Anne Boleyn, Henry VIII's tragic second queen, spent her childhood here, but very little of the original house remains. Most of the present structure dates from 1628, when it was home to James I's Chief Justice Sir Henry Hobart. Later in 1767 the 2nd Earl of Buckinghamshire, John Hobart, made several alterations. He celebrated the Boleyn connection with reliefs in the Great Hall depicting Anne and her daughter, Elizabeth I.

The Long Gallery is the most spectacular room to survive from the 1620s. Its ceiling depicts symbolic representations of learning mingled with the Hobart coat of arms.

The Peter the Great Room marks the 2nd earl's service as ambassador to Russia and was built to display a huge spectacular tapestry (1764) of the Russian tsar on horseback, a gift from the empress, Catherine the Great. It also has portraits (1760) of the ambassador and his wife by Gainsborough *(see p149).*

Norwich ❿

See pp186–7.

The Broads ⓫

Norfolk. 🚊 *Hoveton, Wroxham.* 🚌 *Norwich, then bus.* ℹ️ *Station Rd, Hoveton (01603 782281).*

These shallow lakes and waterways south and northeast of Norwich, joined by six rivers – the Bure, Thurne, Ant, Yare, Waveney and Chet – were once thought to have been naturally formed, but in actual fact they are medieval peat diggings that flooded when the water level rose in the 13th century.

During summer the 200 km (125 miles) of open waterways, uninterrupted by locks, teem with thousands of boating enthusiasts, from devotees of pure sail to those who prefer motorboats. You can either rent a boat yourself or take one of the many trips offered to view the plants and wildlife of the area. Look out for Britain's largest butterfly, the swallowtail. Wroxham, the unofficial capital of the Broads, is the starting point for many of these excursions.

The waterways support substantial clumps of strong and durable reeds, much in demand for thatching *(see p29).* They are cut in winter and carried to shore in the distinctive Broads punts – also used for hunting wildfowl.

For a more detailed look at the origins of the Broads and their varied wildlife, visit the **Broadland Conservation Centre** – a large thatched floating information center on Ranworth Broad, with displays on all aspects of the area, and a bird-watching gallery.

In the center of Ranworth is **St. Helen's Church** which has a painted medieval screen, a well-preserved 14th-century illuminated manuscript and spectacular views over the entire area from its tower.

🦋 **Broadland Conservation Centre**
Ranworth. 📞 *01603 270479.* 🕐 *Apr–Oct: daily.* ♿

Sail boat, Wroxham Broad, Norfolk

Great Yarmouth ⓬

Norfolk. 👥 *82,000.* 🚂 🚌 ℹ️ *Hall Quay (01493 846345).* 🛒 *Wed, Fri (in summer), Sat.*

HERRING FISHING was once the major industry of this port, with 1,000 boats engaged in it just before World War I. Overfishing led to a depletion of stocks and, for the port to survive without the herring, it started to earn its living from servicing container ships and the North Sea oil rigs.

It is also the most popular seaside resort on the Norfolk coast and has been since the 19th century, when Dickens *(see p173)* gave it useful publicity by setting part of his novel *David Copperfield* here.

The **Elizabethan House Museum** has a large, eclectic display that illustrates the social history of the area.

In the old part of the town, around South Quay, are a number of charming houses including the 17th-century **Old Merchant's House**. It retains its original patterned plaster ceilings as well as examples of old ironwork and architectural fittings from

Fishing trawlers at Lowestoft's quays

nearby houses, which were destroyed during World War II. The guided tour of the house includes a visit to the adjoining cloister of a 13th-century friary.

🏛 Elizabethan House Museum

4 South Quay. 📞 *01493 857900.*
🕐 *Jun–Sep: Sun–Fri; 2 wks over Easter.* ⬤ *Good Fri.* ♿

🪟 Old Merchant's House

South Quay. 📞 *01493 857900.*
🕐 *Apr–Sep: Sun–Fri.* ♿

WINDMILLS ON THE FENS AND BROADS

The flat, open countryside and the stiff breezes from the North Sea made windmills an obvious power source for East Anglia well into the 20th century, and today they are an evocative and recurring feature of the landscape. On the Broads and Fens, some were used for drainage, while others, such as that at Saxtead Green, ground grain. On the boggy fens they were not built on hard foundations, so few survived, but elsewhere, especially on the Broads, many have been restored to working order. The seven-story Berney Arms Windmill is the tallest on the Broads. Thurne Dyke Drainage Mill is the site of an exhibition about the occasionally idiosyncratic mills and their more unusual mechanisms.

Grain mill at Saxtead Green, near Framlingham

Herringfleet Smock Mill, near Lowestoft

Lowestoft ⓭

Suffolk. 👥 *55,000.* 🚂 🚌
ℹ️ *East Point Pavilion, Royal Plain (01502 523000).* 🛒 *Tue, Fri, Sat.*

THE MOST EASTERLY TOWN in Britain was long a rival to Great Yarmouth, both as a holiday resort and a fishing port. Its fishing industry has survived better than that of its neighbor, since it has turned to flat fish, like plaice, to replace the disappearing herring.

The coming of the railroad in the 1840s gave the town an advantage over other seaside towns, and the solid Victorian and Edwardian boarding houses are evidence that it was a popular place to stay.

Lowestoft Museum, in a 17th-century house, has a good display of the fine porcelain made here in the 18th century, as well as exhibits on local archaeology and domestic life.

ENVIRONS: To the northwest is **Somerleyton Hall**, built in a Victorian mock-Tudor style on the foundations of a smaller Elizabethan mansion, parts of which survive. Its gardens are a real delight, and there is a genuinely baffling maze.

🏛 Lowestoft Museum

Oulton Broad. 📞 *01502 565371.*
🕐 *Easter–Whitsun: Sat, Sun; Whitsun–Sep: daily.* ♿ 🅿️ *limited.*

🪟 Somerleyton Hall

On B1074. 📞 *01502 730224.*
🕐 *Apr–Sep: Thu, Sun & public hols (Jul–Aug: Tue–Thu, Sun).* ♿ 🅿️

Norwich ⑩

IN THE HEART of the fertile East Anglian countryside, Norwich, one of the best-preserved cities in Britain, is steeped in a relaxed provincial atmosphere. The town was first fortified by the Saxons in the 9th century and still has the irregular street plan of that time. Flemish settlers arrived in the early 12th century and established a textile industry. The town soon became a prosperous market and was the second most important city of England until the Industrial Revolution in the 19th century *(see pp56–7)*.

One of over a thousand carved bosses in the cathedral cloisters

the **Erpingham Gate** at the west end, built by Sir Thomas Erpingham, who led the triumphant English archers at the Battle of Agincourt in 1415 *(see p49)*.

Beneath the east outer wall is the grave of Edith Cavell, the Norwich-born nurse executed in 1915 by the Germans for helping Allied soldiers escape from occupied Belgium.

🏛 Castle Museum
Castle Meadow. 📞 *01603 223624.* ⭕ *daily.* ⬤ *Dec 25, 26, Good Fri.* 📷 ♿ *limited.*
The brooding keep of this 12th-century castle, refaced in Bath stone in 1834, has been a museum since 1894, when it ended 650 years of service as a prison. The most important Norman feature is a carved door that used to be the main entrance.

Exhibits include medieval armor, pottery, porcelain and the largest collection of ceramic teapots in the world.

The cobbled street, Elm Hill

Exploring Norwich
The oldest parts of the city are Elm Hill, one of the finest medieval streets in England, and Tombland, the old Saxon market place by the cathedral. Both have well-preserved medieval buildings, which are now incorporated into pleasant areas of small stores.

With a trading history spanning hundreds of years, the colorful market in the city center is well worth a visit. A good walk meanders around the surviving sections of the 14th-century flint city wall.

🛉 Norwich Cathedral
The Close. 📞 *01603 764385.* ⭕ *daily.* **Donations.** ♿
This magnificent building was founded in 1096 by Bishop Losinga who had the unusual white stone shipped in from Normandy in France.

The precinct originally included a monastery, and the surviving cloister is the most extensive in England. The thin cathedral spire was added in the 15th century, making it, at 96 m (315 ft), the second tallest in England after Salisbury's *(see pp250–51)*. In the majestic nave, soaring Norman pillars

and arches support a 15th-century vaulted roof whose stone bosses, many of which illustrate well-known Bible stories, have recently been beautifully restored.

Easier to appreciate at close hand is the elaborate wood carving in the choir – the canopies over the stalls and the misericords beneath the seats, one showing a small boy being smacked. Not to be missed is the 14th-century Despenser Reredos in St Luke's Chapel. It was hidden for years under a carpenter's table to prevent its destruction by Puritans.

Two gates to the cathedral close survive: **St. Ethelbert's**, a 13th-century flint arch, and

A view of Norwich Cathedral's spire and tower from the southeast

It's nicer with
MUSTARD

COLMAN'S MUSTARD

It was said of the Colmans that they made their fortune from what diners left on their plate. In 1814 Jeremiah Colman started milling mustard at Norwich because it was at the center of a fertile plain where mustard was grown. Today at Bridewell Alley a shop sells mustard and related items, while a small museum illustrates the history of the company.

**A 1950s advertisement for
Colman's Mustard**

🏛 Strangers' Hall

Charing Cross. 📞 *01603 667229.*
⭘ *Mon–Sat.* ● *Dec 24–27, Jan 1,
Good Fri.* 🎫
This 14th-century merchant's house gives a glimpse into English domestic life through the ages. The costume display features a unique collection of underwear. The house was lived in by immigrant weavers – the "strangers." It has a fine 15th-century Great Hall.

The art gallery is dominated by works from the Norwich School of painters. This was a group of landscape artists active in the first half of the 19th century who painted directly from nature, getting away from the stylized studio landscapes that had been fashionable up to then. Chief among the group were John Crome (1768–1821), who many compare with Constable *(see p190)*, and John Sell Cotman (1782–1842), known for his watercolors.

🔒 Church of St. Peter Mancroft

Market Place. 📞 *01603 610443.*
⭘ *daily.* **Donations.** 🚹
This imposing Perpendicular church, built about 1455, so dominates the city center that many visitors assume it is the cathedral. John Wesley *(see p265)* wrote of it, "I scarcely ever remember to have seen a more beautiful parish church."

The large windows make the church very light, and the dramatic east window still has most of its 15th-century glass. The roof is unusual in having wooden fan tracery – it is normally in stone – covering the hammer-beam construction. The famous peal of 13 bells rang out in 1588 to celebrate the defeat of the Spanish Armada *(see p51)* and is still heard every Sunday.

Its name derives from the Latin *magna crofta* (great meadow) that described the area before the Normans built an earlier church here.

🏛 Bridewell Museum

Bridewell Alley. 📞 *01603 667228.*
⭘ *Mon–Sat.* ● *Dec 24–26, Jan 1,
Good Fri.* 🎫
One of the oldest houses in Norwich, this 14th-century flint-faced building was for years used as a jail. It now houses an exhibition on local industries, with displays of old machines, advertisements and reconstructed shops.

🏛 Guildhall

Gaol Hill. 📞 *01603 666071.*
⭘ *Mon–Fri (pm).* ● *public hols.* 🚹
Above the city's 900-year-old market place is the imposing 15th-century flint and stone Guildhall with its gable of checkered flushwork. A display of civic regalia includes a flamboyant sword presented to Norwich by Nelson *(see p54)*, who captured it from a Spanish admiral in 1797.

🏛 The Sainsbury Centre for Visual Arts

University of East Anglia (on B1108).
📞 *01603 456060.* ⭘ *Tue–Sun.*
● *Dec 24–Jan 1.* 🎫 🚹
This important art gallery was built in 1978 to house the collection of Robert and Lisa Sainsbury given to the University of East Anglia in 1973.

The collection's strength is in its modern European paintings, including works by Modigliani, Picasso and Bacon, and in its scuptures by Giacometti and Moore. There are also displays of ethnographic art from Africa, the Pacific and the Americas.

The center, designed by Sir Norman Foster, one of Britain's leading architects, was among the first to display its steel structure openly. This set an example that was to be copied around the world.

***Back of the New Mills** (1814) by John Crome of the Norwich School*

Purple heather in flower on Dunwich Heath

Southwold ⑭

Suffolk. 👥 *1,400*. 🚉 ❶ *Market Place (01502 724729)*. 🛒 *Mon, Thu.*

THIS PICTURE-POSTCARD seaside resort, with its charming whitewashed villas clustered around grassy slopes, has, largely by historical accident, remained unspoiled. The railroad that connected it with London was closed in 1929, which effectively isolated this pretty Georgian town from an influx of sight-seers.

That this was also once a large port can be judged from the size of the 15th-century **St. Edmund King and Martyr Church**, worth a visit for the 16th-century painted screens. On its tower is a small figure dressed in the uniform of a

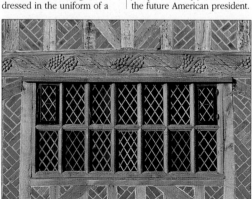

Jack o'the Clock, Southwold

15th-century soldier and known as Jack o'the Clock. **Southwold Museum** tells the story of the bloody Battle of Sole Bay, which was fought offshore between the English and Dutch navies in 1672.

ENVIRONS: The rail closure in Southwold also cut the link with the pretty village of **Walberswick**, across the creek. By road it is a long detour and the only alternative is a rowboat ferry across the harbor. Just inland at Blythburgh, the 15th-century **Holy Trinity Church** dominates the surrounding land. Cromwell's troops *(see p52)* used it as a stable, and you can see the iron rings outside where they tied their horses.

In 1944 a US bomber blew up over the church, killing Joseph Kennedy Jr., brother of the future American president.

🏛 **Southwold Museum**
Bartholomew Green. ❶ *01502 722375*. ◯ *May–Sep: daily*. ♿

Dunwich ⑮

Suffolk. 👥 *1,400*.

THIS TINY VILLAGE with a few cottages and the odd fishing boat is all that remains of a "lost city" consigned to the sea by erosion.

In the 7th century Dunwich was the seat of the powerful East Anglian kings. In the 13th century it was still the biggest port in Suffolk and some 12 churches were constructed during its time of prosperity. But the land was being eroded at about a meter (3 ft) a year, and the last of the original churches collapsed into the sea in 1919.

Dunwich Heath, just to the south, runs down to a sandy beach and is now an important nature reserve. **Minsmere Reserve** has blinds for watching a huge variety of birds such as avocets, marsh harrier and bitterns.

🦅 **Minsmere Reserve**
Westleton. ❶ *01728 648281*. ◯ *Wed–Mon*. ● *Dec 25, 26*. 🖼

Aldeburgh ⑯

Suffolk. 👥 *2,500*. 🚉 ❶ *High St (01728 453637)*.

BEST KNOWN TODAY for the music festivals at Snape Maltings just up the River Alde, Aldeburgh has been a

Intricate carving on the exterior of the Tudor Moot Hall, Aldeburgh

port since Roman times, although the Roman end of the town is now under the sea.

Erosion has resulted in the fine Tudor **Moot Hall**, once far inland, now being close to the beach and promenade. Its ground floor, originally the market, is now a museum. The large timbered court room above can only be reached by the original outside staircase.

The **church**, also Tudor, contains a large stained-glass window placed in 1979 as a memorial to Benjamin Britten.

🏛 **Moot Hall**
Market Cross Pl. 📞 01728 452730. ⬜ Jun–Sep: daily; Apr–May: Sat, Sun. 🅰

Framlingham Castle ⑰

Framlingham, Suffolk. 📞 01728 724189. 🚆 Wickham Market then taxi. ⬜ daily. ⬤ 24–26 Dec, 1 Jan. 🅰

PERCHED ON A HILL, the small village of Framlingham has long been an important strategic site, even before the present castle was built in 1190 by the Earl of Norfolk.

Little of the castle from that period survives except the powerful curtain wall and its turrets; walk around the top for fine views of the town.

Mary Tudor, daughter of Henry VIII, was staying here in 1553 when she heard she was to become queen.

ENVIRONS: To the southeast, on the coast, is the 27 m (90 ft) keep of **Orford Castle**, built for Henry II as a coastal defense at around the same time as Framlingham. It is the earliest known example of an English castle with a five-sided keep; earlier they were square and later round. A short climb to the top of the castle gives fantastic views of the surrounding land.

🏛 **Orford Castle**
Orford. 📞 01394 450472. ⬜ daily. ⬤ Dec 25, 26, Jan 1. 🅰

ALDEBURGH MUSIC FESTIVAL

Composer Benjamin Britten (1913–76), born in Lowestoft, Suffolk, moved to Snape in 1937. In 1945 his opera *Peter Grimes* – inspired by the poet George Crabbe (1754–1832), once a curate at Aldeburgh – was performed in Snape. Since then the area has become the center of musical activity. In 1948, Britten began the Aldeburgh Music Festival, held every June *(see p63)*. He acquired the Maltings at Snape and converted it into a music venue opened by the Queen in 1967. It has since become the focus of an annual series of East Anglian musical events in churches and halls throughout the entire region.

Benjamin Britten in Aldeburgh

Ipswich ⑱

Suffolk. 🏘 102,000. ✈ 🚆 🚌 🛈 St. Stephen's Lane (01473 258070). 🛒 Tue, Fri, Sat.

SUFFOLK'S COUNTY TOWN has a largely modern center but several buildings remain from earlier times. It rose to prominence after the 13th century as a port for the rich Suffolk wool trade *(see p193)*. Later, with the Industrial Revolution, it began to export coal.

The **Ancient House** in Buttermarket has a superb example of pargeting – the ancient craft of ornamental façade plastering. The town's museum and art gallery, **Christchurch Mansion**, is a

Tudor house from 1548, where Elizabeth I stayed in 1561. It also boasts the best collection of Constable's paintings out of London *(see p190)*, including four marvelous Suffolk landscapes, as well as pictures by the Suffolk-born painter Gainsborough *(see p149)*.

Ipswich Museum contains replicas of the locally excavated Mildenhall and Sutton Hoo treasures, the originals of which are held in the British Museum *(see pp108–9)*.

In the center of the town is **St. Margaret's**, a lavish 15th-century church built in flint and stone with a double hammer-beam roof and some beautiful 17th-century painted ceiling panels. A Tudor gateway of 1527 provides a link with Ipswich's most famous son, Cardinal Wolsey *(see p50)*. He started to build an ecclesiastical college in the town, but fell from royal favor before it was completed. Only the gateway remains.

🏛 **Christchurch Mansion**
Soane St. 📞 01473 253246. ⬜ Tue–Sun & public hols. ⬤ Dec 24–26, Jan 1, Good Fri.
🏛 **Ipswich Museum**
High St. 📞 01473 213761. ⬜ Tue–Sat. ⬤ Dec 24–27, Jan 1, Good Fri.

Pargeting on the Ancient House in Ipswich

Constable Walk ⑲

THIS WALK in Constable country follows one of the most picturesque sections of the River Stour. The path followed would have been familiar to the landscape painter John Constable (1776–1837). Constable's father was a wealthy merchant who owned Flatford Mill; the scenery of at least ten of the artist's most important paintings was within view of this much-loved mill. Constable claimed to know and love "every stile and stump, and every lane" around East Bergholt, and the walk encompasses his favorite areas.

The River Stour, used as a backdrop for Constable's *Boatbuilding* (1814)

TIPS FOR WALKERS

Starting point: *Car park off Flatford Lane, East Bergholt.*
H (NT) *Bridge Cottage Information Centre (01206 298260).*
Getting there: *A12 to Ipswich, then B1070 to East Bergholt, follow signs to Flatford Mill.*
Stopping-off point: *Dedham.*
Length: *3 miles (5 km).*
Difficulty: *Flat trail along riverside footpath with stiles.*

Viewpoint ⑤
The view over the valley from the top of the hill shows Constable country at its best.

Car Park ①
Follow the signs to Flatford Mill then cross the footbridge.

Dedham Mill

Stour

A12

Dedham

④

COLCHESTER

EAST BERGHOLT

③

⑤

Gosnalls Farm

P ①

Fen Bridge ③
This modern foot-bridge replaced one that Constable used as a focus for many of his paintings.

Ram Lock •

Flatford Mill •

②

Dedham Church ④
The tall church tower appears in many of Constable's pictures including the *View on the Stour near Dedham* (1822).

KEY

- ▬ ▬ Route
- ▭ B road
- ═ Minor road
- ⚹ Viewpoint
- P Parking

0 meters   500
0 yards   500

Willy Lott's Cottage ②
This cottage remains much the same as it did when featured in Constable's painting *The Haywain* (see p85).

Colchester ⑳

Essex. 🏠 150,000. ✈ 🚌 ℹ️ Queen St (01206 282920). 🛒 Fri, Sat.

THE OLDEST recorded town in Britain, Colchester was the effective capital of southeast England when the Romans invaded in AD 43; it was here that the first permanent Roman colony was established.

After Boadicea *(see p181)* burned the town in AD 60, a 2 mile (3 km) defensive wall was built, 3 m (10 ft) thick and 9 m (30 ft) high, to deter any future attackers. You can still see these walls and the surviving Roman town gate, which is the largest in Britain.

During the Middle Ages Colchester developed into an important weaving center. In the 16th century, a number of immigrant Flemish weavers settled in an area west of the castle, known as the **Dutch Quarter**, which still retains the original tall houses and steep, narrow streets.

Colchester was besieged for 11 weeks during the Civil War *(see p52)* before being captured by Cromwell's troops.

🏛 Tymperleys
Trinity St. 📞 01206 282931. ⭘ Apr–Oct: Tue–Sat.
Clockmaking was an important craft in Colchester, and it is celebrated in this restored half-timbered, 15th-century mansion, also worth visiting for its formal Tudor garden.

🏛 Social History Museum
Trinity St. 📞 01206 282931. ⭘ Apr–Oct: Tue–Sat. ♿ limited.
The town's Saxon inheritance is demonstrated in this marvelous building, originally a church, whose huge tower and west door are classic examples of Saxon architecture. The museum now has exhibits of local social history and the area's rural crafts.

🏛 Castle Museum
High St. 📞 01206 282932. ⭘ Mar–Nov: daily; Dec–Feb: Mon–Sat. ● Dec 24–27. 🎫 ♿
This is the oldest and largest Norman keep still standing in England. Twice the size of the White Tower at the Tower of London *(see pp120–21)*, it was

The Norman keep of the Castle Museum, Colchester

built in 1076 on the platform of a Roman temple dedicated to Claudius I *(see p44)*, using stones and tiles from other Roman buildings. Today, the museum is packed full of exhibits relating the story of the town from prehistoric times to the Civil War. You can also visit the medieval prison.

⛪ Layer Marney Tower
Off B1022. 📞 01206 330784. ⭘ Apr–Sep: Sun–Fri (pm). 🎫 ♿ limited.
This remarkable Tudor gatehouse is the tallest in Britain: its two six-sided, eight-story turrets soar to 24 m (80 ft). It was intended to be part of a larger complex but the designer, Sir Henry Marney, died before it was completed. The brickwork and terra-cotta ornamentation around the roof and windows are models of Tudor craftsmanship. There are fine views of the gardens and deer park from the top.

♣ Beth Chatto Garden
Elmstead Market. 📞 01206 822007. ⭘ Mar–Oct: Mon–Sat; Nov–Feb: Mon–Fri. ● Dec 24–first Mon in Jan, public hols. 🎫
One of Britain's most eminent gardening writers began this experiment in the 1960s to test her belief that it is possible to create a garden in the most adverse conditions. The large garden consists of dry and windy slopes, boggy patches, gravel beds and wooded areas, all of which support an array of plants best suited to that particular environment.

Coggeshall ㉑

Essex. 🏠 4,000. 🛒 Thu.

THIS SMALL TOWN has two of the most important and best-preserved medieval and Tudor buildings in the country. Dating from 1140, **Coggeshall Grange Barn** is the oldest surviving timber-framed barn in Europe. Inside is a display of historic farm wagons. The half-timbered merchant's house, **Paycocke's**, was built around 1500 and has a beautifully paneled interior. There is a display of Coggeshall lace.

⛪ Coggeshall Grange Barn
(NT) Grange Hill. 📞 01376 562226. ⭘ Apr–Oct: Tue, Thu, Sun & public hols (pm). ● Good Fri. 🎫 ♿

⛪ Paycocke's
(NT) West St. 📞 01376 561305. ⭘ Apr–Oct: Tue, Thu, Sun & public hols (pm). ● Good Fri. 🎫 ♿

Beth Chatto Garden, Colchester, in full summer bloom

Lavenham ㉒

Suffolk. 🏠 1,700. 🛈 Lady St
(01787 248207).

OFTEN CONSIDERED the most
perfect of all English small
towns, Lavenham is a treasure
trove of black-and-white
timber-framed houses on
streets whose pattern is
virtually unchanged from
medieval times. For 150 years,
between the 14th and 16th
centuries, Lavenham was the
prosperous center of the
Suffolk wool trade. It still has
many outstanding and well-
preserved buildings; indeed
no less than 300 of the town's
buildings are listed, including
the magnificent **Little Hall**.

**ENVIRONS: Gainsborough's
House**, Sudbury, is a museum
on this painter (see p149).

🏛 **Little Hall**
Market Place. 📞 01787 247179.
⬜ Easter–Nov: Wed, Thu, Sat, Sun &
public hols. 🅿

🏛 **Gainsborough's House**
Sudbury. 📞 01284 735270.
⬜ Tue–Sun. ⬤ public hols. 🅿

LITTLE HALL

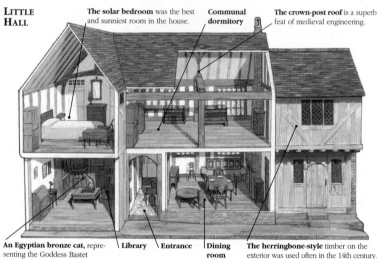

The **solar bedroom** was the best and sunniest room in the house.

Communal dormitory

The **crown-post roof** is a superb feat of medieval engineering.

An Egyptian bronze cat, representing the Goddess Bastet

Library

Entrance

Dining room

The **herringbone-style** timber on the exterior was used often in the 14th century.

Bury St. Edmunds ㉓

Suffolk. 🏠 33,000. 🚃 🚌 🛈
Angel Hill (01284 764667). 🛒 Sat.

ST. EDMUND was the last Saxon
king of East Anglia, decapi-
tated by Danish raiders in 870.
Legend has it that a wolf led
his followers to the body and
picked up the severed head –
an image that appears in a
number of medieval carvings.
Edmund was canonized in 900
and buried in Bury, where in
1014 King Canute (see p157)
built an **abbey** in his honor,
the wealthiest in the country,
until razed by fire in 1347.
The abbey ruins now lie in a
garden in the town center.

Nearby are two large 15th-
century churches, built when
the wool trade made the town
wealthy. **St. James's**
was designated a
cathedral in 1914.
The best features
of **St. Mary's** are
the north porch
and the hammer-
beam roof over
the nave. A stone
slab in the north-
east corner of the
church marks
the tomb of Mary
Tudor (see p50).

Just below the **market cross**
in Cornhill – remodeled by
Robert Adam (see p24) in
1714 – stands the large 12th-
century **Moyse's Hall**, a
merchant's house that serves
as the town museum. It has
Iron Age exhibits, excavated
from West Stowe to the north.

Illustration of St. Edmund

ENVIRONS: Three miles (5 km)
southwest of Bury is the
late-18th-century **Ickworth
House**. This eccentric Neo-
Classical mansion features
an unusual rotunda with a

The 18th-century rotunda of Ickworth House, Bury St. Edmunds

domed roof flanked by two huge wings. The art collection includes works by Reynolds and Titian. There are also fine displays of silver, porcelain and sculpture, for example, John Flaxman's (1755–1826) moving *The Fury of Athamas*. The house is set in a large park.

🏛 **Moyse's Hall**
Cornhill. 📞 *01284 757489.* ◯ *daily.* ● *Dec 25, 26, Good Fri.* ♿ *limited.*
🏠 **Ickworth House**
Horringer. 📞 *01284 735270.* ◯ *Apr–Oct: Tue, Wed, Fri–Sun; public hols (pm).* ● *Good Fri.* 📷 ♿

Newmarket ㉔

Suffolk. 🏘 *1,700.* 🚆 🚌 ℹ *The Rookery (01638 667200).* 🛒 *Tue, Sat.*

A WALK DOWN the short main street tells you all you need to know about this busy and wealthy little town. The stores sell horse feed and all kinds of riding accessories; the clothes on sale are tweeds, jodhpurs and the soft brown hats rarely worn by anyone except racehorse trainers.

Newmarket has been the headquarters of British horse racing since James I decided that its open heaths, where he was fond of hunting, were ideal for testing the mettle of his fastest steeds against those of his friends. The first record-

The stallion unit at the National Stud, Newmarket

ed horse race was held here in 1622. Charles II shared his grandfather's enthusiasm and after the Restoration *(see p53)* would move the whole court to Newmarket, every spring and summer, for the sport – he is the only British king to have ridden a winner.

A horse being exercised on Newmarket Heath

The modern racing industry began to take shape here in the late 18th century. There are now over 2,500 horses in training in and around the town, and two racecourses staging regular race meetings from around April to October *(see p66)*. Training stables are

occasionally open to the public but you can view the horses being exercised on the heath surrounding the town in the early morning.

The **National Stud** can also be visited. You will see the seven or eight stallions on stud, mares in foal and, if you are lucky, a newborn foal – most likely in April or May. Tattersall's, the auction house for thoroughbreds, is also here.

The **National Horseracing Museum** tells the history of the sport and contains many offbeat exhibits such as the skeleton of Eclipse, one of the greatest horses ever, unbeaten in 18 races in 1769 and 1770, and the ancestor of many of today's fastest performers. It also has an interesting and large display of sporting art.

🐎 **National Stud**
Newmarket. 📞 *01638 663464.* ◯ *Mar–Sep: tours daily.* 📷 ♿
🏛 **National Horseracing Museum**
99 High St, Newmarket. 📞 *01638 667333.* ◯ *Apr–Jun & Sep–Nov: Tue–Sun; Jul–Aug: daily.* 📷 ♿

THE RISE AND FALL OF THE WOOL TRADE

St. Mary's Church, Stoke-by-Nayland, southeast of Bury St. Edmunds

Wool was a major English product from the 13th century and by 1310 some ten million fleeces were exported every year. The Black Death *(see p48)*, which swept Britain in 1348, perversely provided a boost for the industry; with labor in short supply, land could not be cultivated and was grassed over for sheep. Around 1350 Edward III decided it was time to establish a home-based cloth industry and encouraged Flemish weavers to come to Britain. Many settled in East Anglia, particularly Suffolk, and their skills helped establish a flourishing trade. This time of prosperity saw the construction of the sumptuous churches, such as the one at Stoke-by-Nayland, that we see today – East Anglia has more than 2,000 churches. The cloth trade here began to decline in the late 16th century with the development of water-powered looms. These were not suited to the area, which never regained its former wealth. Today's visitors are the beneficiaries of this decline, because the wool towns such as Lavenham and Bury St. Edmunds never became rich enough to destroy their magnificent Tudor halls and houses and construct new buildings.

The façade of Anglesey Abbey

Anglesey Abbey ㉕

(NT) Lode, Cambridgeshire. ☎ 01223 811200. ➤ Cambridge then bus. **House** ◯ Apr–Oct: Wed–Sun. **Gardens** ◯ Apr–Oct: Wed–Sun (Jul–Sep: daily). 🅿️ ♿ limited.

THE ORIGINAL ABBEY was built in 1135 for an Augustinian order. But only the crypt – also known as the monks' parlor – with its vaulted ceiling on marble and stone pillars, survived the Dissolution (see p50).

This was later incorporated into a manor house whose treasures include furniture from many periods and a rare

seascape by Gainsborough (see p192). The superb garden was created in the 1930s by Lord Fairhaven as an ambitious, Classical landscape of trees, sculptures and borders.

Huntingdon ㉖

Cambridgeshire. 🚶 18,000. ➤ 🚌 🛈 Princes St (01480 425831). ♿ Wed.

MORE THAN 300 YEARS after his death, Oliver Cromwell (see p52) still dominates this small town. Born here in 1599, a record of his baptism can be seen in **All Saints' and St. John's Church**, off Market Square. You can see his name and traces of ancient graffiti scrawled all over it which says "England's plague for five years." **Cromwell Museum**, his former school, traces his long life with pictures and mementoes including his death mask and medicine chest.

Cromwell remains one of the most disputed figures in British history. An MP before

he was 30, he quickly became embroiled in the disputes between Charles I and Parliament over taxes and religion. In the Civil War (see p52) he proved an inspired general and – after refusing the title of king – was made Lord Protector in 1653, four years after the King was beheaded. But just two years after his death the monarchy was restored by popular demand, and his body was taken out of Westminster Abbey (see pp94–5) to hang on gallows.

There is a 13th-century bridge across the River Ouse that links Huntingdon with Godmanchester, the site of a Roman settlement on the road between London and York.

🏛 **Cromwell Museum**
Grammar School Walk. ☎ 01480 425830. ◯ Tue–Sun. ● Dec 24, public hols. ♿ limited.

Cambridge ㉗

See pp196–201.

Audley End ㉘

Saffron Walden, Essex. ☎ 01799 522399. ➤ Audley End then taxi. ◯ Apr–Sep: Wed–Sun (pm). 🅿️ ♿ limited.

THIS WAS THE largest house in England when built in 1614 for Thomas Howard, Lord Treasurer and 1st Earl of Suffolk. James I joked that Howard's house was too big for a king but not for a Lord Treasurer. Charles II, his grandson, disagreed and bought it in 1667 as an extra palace; but he and his successors seldom went there and in 1701 it was given back to the Howards, who demolished two thirds of it to make it more manageable.

What remains is a Jacobean mansion, retaining its original hall and many fine plaster ceilings. Robert Adam (see p24) remodeled most of the interior in the 1760s and many rooms have been restored to his original designs. At the same time, Capability Brown (see p23) landscaped the magnificent 18th-century park adorned with temples and monuments.

The Chapel was completed in 1772 to a Gothic design. The furniture was made to complement the wooden pillars and vaulting, which are painted to imitate stone.

Main entrance

The painted window, built in 1768, represents the Last Supper.

The Great Hall, hung with family portraits, is the highlight of the house, with the massive oak screen and elaborate hammer-beam roof surviving in their Jacobean form.

Epping Forest 🖤

Essex. 🚆 Chingford. 🚇 Theydon Bois. ℹ️ High Beach, Loughton (0181-508 0028).

A S ONE OF THE LARGE open spaces near London, the 2,400 ha (6,000 acre) forest is popular with walkers, just as, centuries ago, it was a favorite hunting ground for kings and courtiers – the word forest denoted an area for hunting.

Epping Forest contains oaks and beeches almost 400 years old

A depiction of the Battle of Maldon (991) on the *Maldon Embroidery*

Henry VIII had a lodge built in 1543 on the edge of the forest. His daughter Elizabeth I, also a keen hunter, often used the lodge and it soon became known as **Queen Elizabeth's Hunting Lodge**.

This three-story timbered building has been fully renovated and now houses an exhibition explaining the lodge's history and other aspects of the forest's life.

The tracts of open land and woods interspersed with a number of lakes, make an ideal habitat for a variety of plant, bird and animal life: deer roam the northern part, many of a special dark strain introduced by James I. The

Corporation of London bought the forest in the early 19th century to make sure it remained open to the public.

🏫 **Queen Elizabeth's Hunting Lodge**
Rangers Rd, Chingford. 📞 0181-529 6681. ⭕ Wed–Sun (pm). ⬤ Dec 24–26, Jan 1. 🎫 ♿ limited.

Maldon 🖤

Essex. 👥 15,000 🚆 Chelmsford then bus. ℹ️ Coach Lane (01621 856503). 🛒 Thu, Sat.

T HIS DELIGHTFUL old town on the River Blackwater, its High Street lined with shops and inns from the 16th century on, was once an important harbor and is still popular with weekend sailors. One of its main industries is the production of Maldon sea salt, panned in the traditional way.

A fierce battle here in 991, when Viking invaders defeated the Saxon defenders, is told in *The Battle of Maldon,* one of the earliest known Saxon poems. The battle is also celebrated in the *Maldon Embroidery* on display in the **Moot Hall**. This 13 m (42 ft) long embroidery, made by locals, depicts the history of Maldon from 991 to 1991.

ENVIRONS: East of Maldon at Bradwell-on-Sea is the sturdy Saxon church of **St. Peter's-on-the-Wall**, a simple stone box of a building that stands quite isolated on the shore. It was built in 654, from the stones of a former Roman fort, by St. Cedd, who used it as his cathedral. Used as a shed since the 17th century, it was fully restored in the 1920s.

🏛 **Moot Hall**
High St. 📞 01621 851553. ⭕ Mon–Sat. ⬤ Dec 24–26. 🎫 ♿

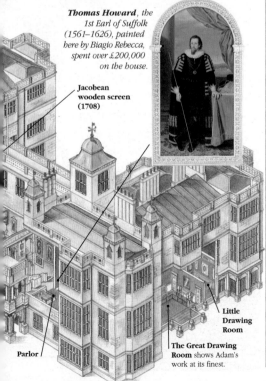

Thomas Howard, *the 1st Earl of Suffolk (1561–1626), painted here by Biagio Rebecca, spent over £200,000 on the house.*

Jacobean wooden screen (1708)

Parlor

Little Drawing Room

The Great Drawing Room shows Adam's work at its finest.

Street-by-Street: Cambridge ㉗

Carving, King's
College Chapel

CAMBRIDGE HAS BEEN an important town since Roman times. It is located at the first navigable point on the River Cam. In the 11th century religious orders began to be established in the town and when, in 1209, a group of religious scholars broke away from Oxford University (*see pp208–213*) after academic and religious disputes, they came here. Student life dominates the city but it is also a thriving market center serving a rich agricultural region.

Cyclists in Cambridge

← Newmarket   BRIDGE STREET

ST JOHN'S STREET

Magdalene Bridge carries Bridge Street across the Cam from the city center to Magdalene College.

St. John's College has superb Tudor and Jacobean architecture.

Kitchen Bridge

★ Bridge of Sighs
Built in 1831 as a copy of its name-sake in Venice, it is best viewed from the Kitchen Bridge.

Trinity College

Trinity Avenue Bridge

The Backs
This is the name given to the grassy strip lying between the backs of the big colleges and the banks of the Cam – a good spot to enjoy this classic view of King's College Chapel.

KEY

– – – Suggested route

STAR SIGHTS

★ Bridge of Sighs

★ King's College Chapel

Clare College

Clare Bridge

Grantchester

0 meters   75

0 yards   75

Round Church
The 12th-century
Church of the Holy
Sepulchre has one of
the few round naves in
the country. Its design
is based on the Holy
Sepulchre in Jerusalem.

Gonville and Caius
(pronounced "keys"),
founded in 1348, is one
of the oldest colleges.

St. Mary's Church
*This clock is over the west door
of the university's official church.
Its tower offers fine views.*

VISITORS' CHECKLIST

Cambridgeshire. 🗺 100,000.
✈ Stansted. ✈ Cambridge. 🚉
Station Rd. 🚌 Drummer St.
ℹ Wheeler St (01223 322640).
🛒 Mon–Sat. 🎪 Folk Festival:
July; Children's Festival: June;
Strawberry Festival: June 10th.

★ **King's College Chapel**
*This late medieval masterpiece took
70 years to build* (see pp198–9).

Market square

Coach station →

King's College
*Henry VIII, king when
the chapel was com-
pleted in 1515, is
commemorated in
this statue near
the main gate.*

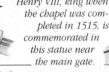

**Queens'
College**
*Its Tudor courts
are among the
university's
finest. This 17th-
century sundial
is over the old
chapel – now a
reading room.*

Corpus Christi College

**London and
railroad station**

Mathematical Bridge
*Linking the two parts of Queens'
College across the Cam, the bridge
was first built without bolts or nuts.*

🏛 Fitzwilliam Museum

Trumpington St. 📞 01223 332900.
⭕ Tue–Sun; public hols. ⬤ Dec 24–
Jan 1. Good Fri, May Day, ♿ limited.
One of Britain's oldest public
museums, this massive Classical building has works of
exceptional quality and rarity,
especially antiquities, ceramics,
paintings and manuscripts.

The core of the collection
was bequeathed in 1816 by
the 7th Viscount Fitzwilliam.
Other gifts have since greatly
added to the exhibits.

Works by Titian (1488–1576)
and the 17th-century Dutch
masters, including Hals, Cuyp
and Hobbema's *Wooded
Landscape* (1866), stand out
among the paintings. French
Impressionist gems include
Monet's *Le Printemps* (1866)
and Renoir's *La Place Clichy*
(1880), while Picasso's *Still
Life* (1923) is notable among
the modern works. Most of
the important British artists
are represented, from
Hogarth in the 18th century
through Constable in the 19th
to Ben Nicholson in the 20th.

The miniatures include the
earliest surviving depiction of
Henry VIII. In the same gallery
are some dazzling illuminated
manuscripts, notably the 15th-
century *Metz Pontifical*, a
sumptuous French liturgical
work produced for a bishop.

The Glaisher collection of
European earthenware and
stoneware is one of the
largest in the country, and
includes a unique display of
English delftware from the
16th and 17th centuries.

Handel's bookcase contains
folios of his work, and nearby
is Keats's original manuscript
for *Ode to a Nightingale* (1819).

**Portrait of Richard James
(c.1740s) by William Hogarth**

Cambridge: King's College

**King's College
Chapel Coat of Arms**

H ENRY VI FOUNDED this college in
1441. Work on the chapel – one
of the most important examples of late
medieval English architecture – began
five years later, and took 70 years to
complete. Henry himself decided that
it should dominate the city and gave
specific instructions about its dimensions: 88 m (289 ft) long, 12 m (40 ft)
wide and 29 m (94 ft) high. The detailed design is
thought to have been by master stonemason Reginald
Ely, although it was altered in later years.

★ **Fan Vaulted Ceiling**
*This awe-inspiring ceiling,
supported by 22 buttresses,
was built by master stonemason John Wastell in 1515.*

The Fellows' Building was
designed in 1724 by James
Gibbs, as part of an
uncompleted design
for a Great Court.

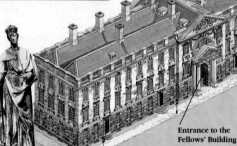

**Entrance to the
Fellows' Building**

Henry VI's statue
*This bronze statue of the college's
founder was erected in 1879.*

KING'S COLLEGE CHOIR

When he founded the chapel,
Henry VI stipulated that a choir
of six lay clerks and 16 boy
choristers – educated at the
College school – should sing
daily at services. This still
happens in term time but today
the choir also gives concerts all
over the world. Its televised
service of carols has become a
much-loved Christmas tradition.

Choristers singing in King's Chapel

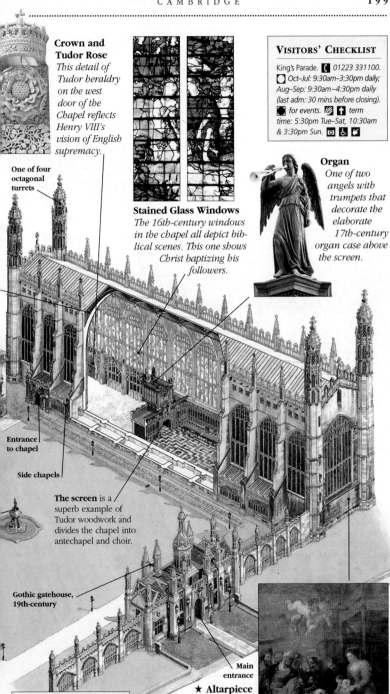

Crown and Tudor Rose
This detail of Tudor heraldry on the west door of the Chapel reflects Henry VIII's vision of English supremacy.

One of four octagonal turrets

Stained Glass Windows
The 16th-century windows in the chapel all depict biblical scenes. This one shows Christ baptizing his followers.

VISITORS' CHECKLIST

King's Parade. ☎ 01223 331100.
◐ Oct–Jul: 9:30am–3:30pm daily;
Aug–Sep: 9:30am–4:30pm daily
(last adm: 30 mins before closing).
◉ for events. ☒ ✝ term
time: 5:30pm Tue–Sat, 10:30am
& 3:30pm Sun. ◙ ☒ ✓

Organ
One of two angels with trumpets that decorate the elaborate 17th-century organ case above the screen.

Entrance to chapel

Side chapels

The screen is a superb example of Tudor woodwork and divides the chapel into antechapel and choir.

Gothic gatehouse, 19th-century

Main entrance

★ Altarpiece by Rubens
Painted in 1634 for the convent of the White Nuns in Belgium, The Adoration of the Magi *was privately donated to King's in 1961.*

STAR SIGHTS

★ **Fan Vaulted Ceiling**

★ **Altarpiece by Rubens**

Exploring Cambridge University

CAMBRIDGE UNIVERSITY HAS 31 COLLEGES *(see pp196–7)*, the oldest being Peterhouse (1284) and the newest being Robinson (1979). Clustered around the city center, many of the older colleges have peaceful gardens backing onto the River Cam, which are known as the "Backs." The layout of the older colleges, as at Oxford *(see pp212–13)*, derives from their early connections with religious institutions, although few escaped heavy-handed modification in the Victorian era. The college buildings are generally grouped around squares called courts and offer an unrivaled mix of over 600 years of architecture *(see pp24–5)* from the late medieval period through Wren's masterpieces *(see p116)* and up to the present day.

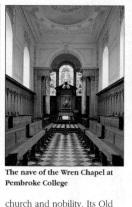

The nave of the Wren Chapel at Pembroke College

The imposing façade of Emmanuel College

Emmanuel College

Built in 1677 on St. Andrew's Street, Sir Christopher Wren's *(see p116)* chapel is the highlight of the college. Some of the intricate interior details, particularly the plaster ceiling and Amigoni's altar rails (1734) are superb. Founded in 1584, the college has a Puritan tradition. A notable graduate was John Harvard, who emigrated to America in 1636, made a fortune and left his money to the Massachusetts college that bears his name.

Senate House

King's Parade is the site of this Palladian building, which is used primarily for university ceremonies. It was designed by James Gibbs in 1722 as part of a grand square of university buildings – but the rest was never built.

Corpus Christi College

Just down from Senate House, this was founded in 1352 by the local trade guilds, anxious to ensure that education was not the sole prerogative of

church and nobility. Its Old Court is well preserved and looks today much as it would have when it was built in the 14th century.

The college is connected by a 15th-century brick gallery to St. Bene't's Church (short for St. Benedict's), whose large Saxon tower is the oldest structure in Cambridge.

King's College

(See pp198–9.)

Pembroke College

The college chapel was the first building completed by Wren *(see p116)*. A formal classical design, it replaced a 14th-century chapel that was turned into a library. The college, just off Trumpington Street, also has fine gardens.

Jesus College

Although founded in 1497, some of its buildings on Jesus Lane are older, as the college took over St. Radegond's nunnery, built in the 12th century. There are traces of Norman columns, windows and a well-preserved hammer-beam roof in the college dining hall.

The chapel keeps the core of the original church but the stained-glass windows are modern. There is a copy of the first American Bible (1663).

Queens' College

Built in 1446 on Queens' Land, the college was endowed in 1448 by Margaret of Anjou, queen of Henry VI, and again in 1465 by Elizabeth Woodville, queen of Edward IV, which explains the position of the apostrophe. Queens' has a

---

PUNTING ON THE CAM

Punting captures the essence of carefree college days: a student leaning on a long pole, lazily guiding the flat-bottomed river craft along, while others stretch out and relax. Punting is still popular both with students and visitors, who can hire punts from boatyards along the river – with a chauffeur if required. Punts do sometimes capsize, and novices should prepare for a dip.

Punting by the King's College "Backs"

marvelous collection of Tudor buildings, notably the half-timbered President's Gallery, built in the mid-16th century on its foundation of brick arches in the Cloister Court. The Principal Court is 15th century, as is Erasmus's Tower, named after the Dutch scholar.

Pepys Library in Magdalene College

The college has buildings on both sides of the Cam, linked by the bizarre Mathematical Bridge, built in 1749 to be held together without using nuts and bolts – although they have had to be used in subsequent repairs.

Magdalene College

Pronounced 'maudlin' – as is the Oxford college *(see p212)* – the college, on Bridge Street, was established in 1482. The diarist Samuel Pepys (1633–1703) was a student here and left his large library to the college at his death. The 12 red-oak bookcases, have over 3,000 books. Magdalene was the last all-male Cambridge college and it admitted women students only in 1987.

St. John's College

Sited on St. John's Street, the imposing turreted brick and stone gatehouse of 1514, with its colorful heraldic symbols, provides a fitting entrance to the second largest Cambridge college and its rich store of 16th- and 17th-century buildings. Its hall, most of it Elizabethan, has portraits of the college's famous alumni, such as the poet William Wordsworth *(see p352)* and the statesman Lord Palmerston. St. John's spans the Cam and boasts two bridges, one built in 1712 and the other, the Bridge of Sighs, in 1831, based on its Venetian namesake.

Peterhouse

The first Cambridge college, on Trumpington Street, is also one of the smallest. The hall has original features from 1286 but its best details are later – a Tudor fireplace, which is backed with 19th-century William Morris tiles *(see p207).* A gallery connects the college to the 12th-century church of St. Mary the Less, which used to be called St. Peter's Church – hence the college's name.

William Morris tiles, Peterhouse

Trinity College

The largest college, situated on Trinity Street, was founded by Henry VIII in 1547 and has a massive court and hall. The entrance gate, with statues of Henry and James I (added later), was built in 1529 for King's Hall, an earlier college incorporated into Trinity. The Great Court features a late Elizabethan fountain – at one time the main water supply. The chapel, built in 1567, has life-size statues of college members, notably Roubiliac's statue of scientist Isaac Newton (1755).

University Botanic Garden

A delightful place for a leisurely stroll, just off Trumpington Street, as well as an important academic resource, the garden has been on this site since 1846. It has a superb collection of trees and a sensational water garden. The winter garden is one of the finest in the country.

The Bridge of Sighs, over the River Cam, links the buildings of St. John's College

THAMES VALLEY

....

BUCKINGHAMSHIRE · OXFORDSHIRE · BERKSHIRE
BEDFORDSHIRE · HERTFORDSHIRE

THE MIGHTY TIDAL RIVER *on which Britain's capital city was founded has modest origins, meandering from its source in the hills of Gloucestershire through the lush countryside toward London. Almost entirely agricultural land in the 19th century, the Thames Valley maintains its pastoral beauty despite the incursion of modern industry.*

There are ancient royal connections with the area. Windsor Castle has been a residence of kings and queens for more than 900 years, and played a critical role in history in 1215, when King John set out from here to sign the *Magna Carta* at Runnymede on the River Thames. Farther north, Queen Anne had Blenheim Palace built for her military commander, the 1st Duke of Marlborough. Elizabeth I spent many years at Hatfield House during her childhood, and part of the Tudor palace still stands.

Several towns in this region, most notably Burford in Oxfordshire, developed as coach staging posts on the important trunk routes between London and the West Country. With the introduction of commuter transportation in the early 20th century, much of the area became an extension of suburbia and saw some imaginative experiments in Utopian town planning such as the garden city of Welwyn and the Quaker settlement at Jordons.

Oxford, Thames Valley's principal city, owes its importance to the foundation of Britain's first university there in 1167; many of its colleges are gems of medieval architecture. In the 17th century, a number of battles during the Civil War *(see pp52–3)* were fought around Oxford, which for a time was the headquarters of King Charles I, who was supported by the students. When the royalists were forced to flee Oxford, Cromwell made himself chancellor of the university.

Punting on the River Cherwell, Oxford

◁ **Medieval staircase in Christchurch College, Oxford**

Exploring the Thames Valley

THE PLEASANT COUNTRYSIDE of the Chiltern Hills and of the Thames Valley itself appealed to aristocrats who built stately homes close to London. Many of these are among the grandest in the country, including Hatfield House and Blenheim. Around these great houses grew picturesque villages, with half-timbered buildings and, as you move toward the Cotswolds, houses built in attractive buff-colored stone. That the area has been inhabited for thousands of years is shown by the number of prehistoric remains, including the most remarkable chalk hillside figure, the White Horse of Uffington.

SIGHTS AT A GLANCE

Blenheim Palace pp214–15 ❻
Burford ❷
Gardens of the Rose ❶❹
Great Tew ❶
Hatfield House ❶❷
Hughendon Manor ❶❺
Kelmscott ❸
Knebworth House ❶❶
Luton Hoo ❶❶
Oxford pp208–13 ❺
St. Albans ❶❸
Stowe ❼
Vale of the White
   Horse ❹
Whipsnade Wild
   Animal Park ❾
Windsor pp221–3 ❶❼
Woburn Abbey ❽

Walks and Tours

Touring the Thames ❶❻

Birmingham

Stratford-upon-Avon

STOWE ❼

GREAT TEW ❶

Cheltenham

Oxford Canal

Cherwell

A361

A44

A361

A40

A361

A40

A40

A418

A34

A329

A417

A420

A417

A44

A40

A4130

Evenlode

Windrush

Isis

Thames

BLENHEIM PALACE ❻

OXFORD ❺

BURFORD ❷

❸ KELMSCOTT

VALE OF THE
WHITE HORSE ❹

Ridgeway

Swindon

M4

A34

A338

A34

A338

HENLEY-ON-THAMES
TOURING THE
❶❻ THAMES
Thames

READING ●

NEWBURY ●

Kennet

A4

Winchester

A thatched cottage, Upper Swarford, Banbury

GETTING AROUND

As an important commuter belt, the Thames Valley is well served by public transportation, as well as a good network of highways and major roads into London. InterCity trains travel to all the major towns and there are many bus services that run from London to the major sights and attractions.

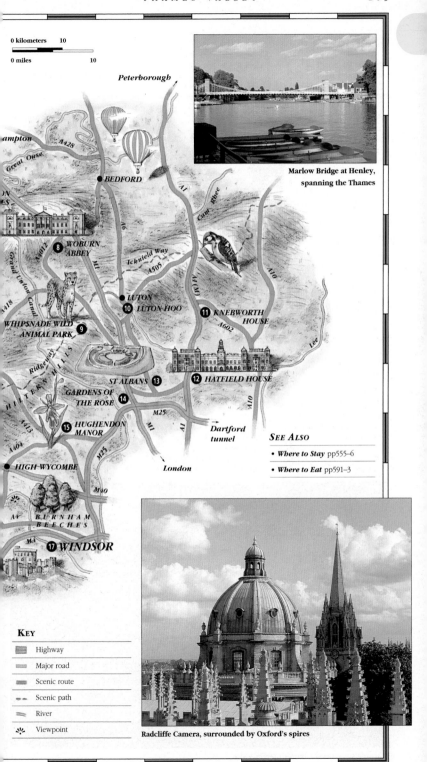

0 kilometers 10

0 miles 10

Peterborough

ampton

Great Ouse.

A428

BEDFORD

Cant River

Marlow Bridge at Henley, spanning the Thames

WOBURN ABBEY 8

Icknield Way

A505

A6

M1

A1

A10

LUTON 10

LUTON-HOO

KNEBWORTH HOUSE 11

A602

WHIPSNADE WILD ANIMAL PARK 9

Grand Union Canal

A418

Lee

Ridgeway

CHILTERN HILLS

ST ALBANS 13

HATFIELD HOUSE 12

GARDENS OF THE ROSE 14

M25

A10

Dartford tunnel

HUGHENDEN MANOR 15

A413

M1

A1

SEE ALSO

- *Where to Stay* pp555–6
- *Where to Eat* pp591–3

HIGH-WYCOMBE

M40

A4

BURNHAM BEECHES

M4

WINDSOR 17

KEY

▬	Highway
▬	Major road
▬	Scenic route
--	Scenic path
～	River
✦	Viewpoint

Radcliffe Camera, surrounded by Oxford's spires

Great Tew ❶

Oxfordshire. 🚶 250. 🚉 Oxford then taxi. 🛈 Banbury (01295 259855).

THIS SECLUDED village of Ironstone, in a small valley surrounded by trees, was founded in the 1630s by Lord Falkland for estate workers. It was heavily restored between 1809 and 1811 in the Gothic style then fashionable. Thatched cottages stand in gardens with clipped boxwood hedges, and in the center of the village is the 17th-century pub, the **Falkland Arms**, which retains its original period atmosphere.

ENVIRONS: 5 miles (8 km) west are the **Rollright Stones**, three Bronze Age monuments. They are: a circle of 77 stones, about 30 m (100 ft) in diameter, known as the King's Men; the remains of a burial chamber called the Whispering Knights; and the solitary King Stone.

Farther north is **Banbury**, well known for its spicy flat cakes and its market cross, immortalized in the nursery rhyme *Ride a Cock-horse to Banbury Cross*. The original medieval cross was destroyed but it was replaced in 1859.

The 19th-century Banbury Cross

🏚 Falkland Arms
Great Tew. ☎ 01608 683653. ◯ Tue–Sun; Mon (eve). ⬤ 25 Dec.

Burford ❷

Oxfordshire. 🚶 1,000. 🛈 Sheep St (01993 823558).

A CHARMING SMALL town, Burford has hardly changed from Georgian times, when it was an important coach stop between Oxford and the West Country. Cotswold stone houses, inns and shops, many built in the 16th century, line its main street. **Tolsey Hall** is a Tudor house with an open ground floor where stalls are still set up. The house is located on the corner of Sheep Street, itself a reminder of the importance of the medieval wool trade *(see p193)*.

ENVIRONS: Just east of Burford is **Swinbrook**, whose church contains the Fettiplace Monuments, six carved figures from the Tudor and Stuart periods.

Two miles (3 km) beyond are the ruins of **Minster Lovell Hall**, a 15th-century manor house whose unusual dovecote survives intact.

Witney, farther west, has a town hall dating from 1730. On its outskirts **Cogges Manor Farm**, founded in the 13th-century, has been restored to its Victorian state and is now a museum of farm life.

🏚 Minster Lovell Hall
Minster Lovell. ☎ 0117 9750700. ◯ daily.
🏚 Cogges Manor Farm
Witney. ☎ 01993 772602. ◯ Apr–Oct: Tue–Sun & public hols. 🅿

Kelmscott ❸

Oxfordshire. 🚶 100. 🛈 Faringdon (01367 242191).

THE IMAGINATIVE designer and writer William Morris lived in this pretty Thameside village from 1871 until his death in 1896. He shared his house, the classic Elizabethan **Kelmscott Manor**, with fellow painter Dante Gabriel Rossetti (1828–82), who left after an affair with Morris's wife Jane – the model for many pre-Raphaelite paintings.

Morris and his followers in the Arts and Crafts movement *(see p25)* were attracted by

Cotswold stone houses, Burford, Oxfordshire

The formal entrance of the Elizabethan Kelmscott Manor

the medieval feel of the village and several cottages were later built in Morris's memory.

Today Kelmscott Manor has works of art by members of the movement – including some William de Morgan tiles. Morris is buried in the village churchyard in a tomb designed by Philip Webb.

Two miles (3 km) to the east is **Radcot Bridge**, the oldest bridge still standing over the Thames. Built in 1160 from the local Taynton stone, it was a strategic river crossing, and in 1387 was badly damaged in a battle between Richard II and his barons. In the 17th and 18th centuries, Taynton stone was shipped from here to London to support the building boom.

⚜ Kelmscott Manor
Kelmscott. 【 01367 252486.
○ Apr–Sep: Wed. 🎫 ♿ limited.

Vale of the White Horse ❹

Oxfordshire. 🚋 Didcot.
ℹ Abingdon (01235 522711).

THIS LOVELY VALLEY gets its name from the huge chalk horse, 100 m (350 ft) from nose to tail, carved into the hillside above Uffington. It is believed to be Britain's oldest hillside carving and has sparked many legends. Some say it was cut by the Saxon leader Hengist (whose name means stallion in German), while others believe it has more to do with Alfred the Great *(see p47)*, thought to have been born nearby.

It is, however, a great deal older than either of these stories suggest, having been dated at around 3000 BC.

Nearby is the Celtic earth ramparts of the Iron Age hill fort, **Uffington Castle**. A mile (1.5 km) west along the Ridgeway, an ancient trade route, *(see p33)*, is an even older monument, a large Stone Age burial mound known as **Wayland's Smithy**. This is immersed in legends that Sir Walter Scott *(see p498)* used in his novel *Kenilworth*.

The best view of the horse is seen from Uffington village, which is also worth visiting for the **Tom Brown's School Museum**. This 17th-century school house contains exhibits devoted to the author Thomas Hughes (1822–96). Hughes set the early chapters of his popular Victorian novel *Tom Brown's Schooldays*, here. The museum also contains material about White Horse Hill.

🏛 Tom Brown's School Museum
Broad St, Uffington. 【 01367 820402. ○ Easter–Oct: Sat, Sun & public hols (pm). 🎫 ♿ limited.

HILLSIDE CHALK FIGURES

It was the Celts who first saw the potential for creating large-scale artworks on the chalk hills of southern England. Horses – held in high regard by both the Celts and later the Saxons, and the objects of cult worship – were often a favorite subject, but people were also depicted, notably Cerne Abbas, Dorset *(see p255)* and the Long Man of Wilmington *(see p166)*. The figures may have served as religious symbols or as landmarks by which tribes identified their territory. Many chalk figures have been obliterated, because without any attention they are quickly overrun by grass. Uffington is "scoured" to prevent encroachment by grass, a tradition once accompanied by a fair and other festivities. There was a second flush of hillside carving in the 18th century, especially in Wiltshire. In some cases – for instance at Bratton Castle near Westbury – an 18th-century carving has been superimposed on an ancient one.

Britain's oldest hillside carving, the White Horse of Uffington

Street-by-Street: Oxford ❺

OXFORD HAS LONG BEEN a strategic point on the western routes into London – its name describes its position as a convenient spot for crossing the river (a ford for oxen). The city's first scholars, who founded the university, came from France in 1167. The development of England's first university created the spectacular skyline of tall towers and "dreaming spires."

Old Ashmolean
Now the Museum of the History of Science, this resplendent building was designed in 1683 to show Elias Ashmole's collection of curiosities. The displays were moved in 1845.

The Ashmolean Museum
displays one of Britain's foremost collections of fine art and antiquities.

St. John's College

Balliol College

ST GILES

BEAUMONT STREET

Swindon

MAGDALEN STREET

BROAD STREET

TURL

BRAS

Martyrs' Memorial
This commemorates the three Protestant martyrs Latimer, Ridley and Cranmer, who were burned at the stake for heresy.

Bus station

Trinity College

CORNMARKET STREET

MARKET STREET

STR

| 0 meters | 100 |
| 0 yards | 100 |

KEY

– – – Suggested route

Oxford Story

Jesus College

Lincoln College

Covered market

Railroad station

All Saints Church

ST AL

Museum of Oxford

PERCY BYSSHE SHELLEY

Shelley (1792–1822), one of the Romantic poets *(see p352),* attended University College, Oxford, but was expelled after writing the revolutionary pamphlet *"The Necessity of Atheism."* Despite that disgrace, the college has put up a marble memorial to him.

Sheldonian Theatre
The first building Wren (see p116) designed is the scene of Oxford University's traditional graduation ceremonies.

STAR SIGHTS

★ **Radcliffe Camera**

★ **Christ Church**

★ **Radcliffe Camera**
*This Classical rotunda is
Oxford's most distinctive
building and is now a
reading room of the
Bodleian. It was one of
the library's original
buildings* (see p213).

VISITORS' CHECKLIST

Oxfordshire. 🏠 *130,000.* 🚄
Botley Rd. 🚌 *Gloucester Green.*
ℹ️ *Gloucester Green (01865
726871).* 🛒 *Wed, Thu (flea
market).* 🎡 *St. Giles Fair: Sep.*

Bridge of Sighs
*A copy of the
steeply arched
bridge in Venice,
this picturesque
landmark, built
in 1914, joins the
old and new
buildings of
Hertford College.*

New College

St. Mary the
Virgin Church

Queen's College

All Souls
College

→ London

University College

Shelley
Memorial

Botanic Gardens
and Magdalen
College

Oriel College

Merton College

QUEEN'S LANE

CATTE STREET

HIGH STREET

LOGIC LANE

ORIEL STREET

MAGPIE LANE

MERTON STREET

BEAR LANE

DEAD MAN'S WALK

Corpus
Christi College

★ **Christ
Church**
*Students still
eat at long
tables in all
the college halls.
Fellows (professors)
sit at the high table and
grace is always said in Latin.*

Exploring Oxford

A bust on the Sheldonian Theatre

OXFORD IS MORE than just a university town; it has one of Britain's most important car factories in the suburb of Cowley. Despite this, Oxford is dominated by institutions related to its huge academic community – like Blackwell's bookstore, which has over 20,000 titles in stock. The two rivers, the Cherwell and the Isis (the name given to the Thames as it flows through the city), provide lovely riverside walks, or you can rent a punt and spend an afternoon on the Cherwell.

🏛 Ashmolean Museum

Beaumont St. 📞 01865 278000.
⭘ Tue–Sun. ⬤ Dec 25–28, Jan 1, Good Fri. ♿ phone first.

One of the best museums in Britain outside London, the Ashmolean – the first specially built museum in England – was opened in 1683, based on a collection of "curiosities" collected by the two John Tradescants, father and son, who were among the first plant hunters and collectors.

On their many voyages to the Orient and the Americas, they collected stuffed animals and tribal artifacts, the like of which had never before been displayed in England. The collection was acquired after their death by the antiquarian Elias Ashmole, who donated it to the university and had a building made for the exhibits on Broad Street – the Old Ashmolean, now the Museum of the History of Science.

During the 19th century part of the Tradescant collection was moved to the University Galleries, a magnificent Neo-Classical building of 1845. This greatly expanded museum is now known as the Ashmolean.

However, what is left of the original curio collection is overshadowed by the other exhibits in the museum, in particular the paintings and drawings. These include Bellini's *St. Jerome Reading in a Landscape* (late 15th century); Raphael's *Heads of Two Apostles* (1519); Turner's *Venice: The Grand Canal* (1840); Rembrandt's *Saskia Asleep* (1635); Michelangelo's *Crucifixion* (1557); Picasso's *Blue Roofs* (1901); and a large group of Pre-Raphaelites, including Rossetti, Millais and Holman Hunt. There are also fine Greek and Roman carvings and a collection of stringed musical instruments.

Items of more local interest include a Rowlandson water-color of Radcliffe Square in about 1790 and the Oxford Crown. This silver coin was minted here during the Civil War in 1644 *(see p52)*, when Charles I was based in Oxford, and forms part of the second-largest coin collection in Britain. Perhaps the single most important item is the gold enameled ring known as the Alfred Jewel *(see p47)*, which is over 1,000 years old.

The entrance to the Ashmolean Museum

🌷 Botanic Gardens

Rose Lane. 📞 01865 276920.
⭘ daily. ⬤ Dec 25, Good Fri.
📷 mid-Jun–Aug. ♿

Britain's oldest botanic garden was founded in 1621 – one ancient yew tree survives from that period. The ornate entrance gates were designed by Nicholas Stone in 1633 and paid for, like the garden itself, by the Earl of Danby. His statue adorns the gate, along with those of Charles I and Charles II. Though small, the garden is a delightful spot for a stroll, with well-labeled flower beds in the original walled garden and a newer section with an herbaceous border and a rock garden.

The 17th-century Botanic Gardens

🔒 Carfax Tower

Carfax Sq. 📞 01865 792653.
⭘ Apr–Oct: daily. 📷

The tower is all that remains of the 14th-century Church of St. Martin, demolished in 1896 so that the adjoining road could be widened. Be there to watch the clock strike the quarter hours, and climb to the top for a panoramic view of the city. Carfax was the crossing point of the original north-to-south and east-to-west routes through Oxford; the word comes from the French *quatre voies*, or "four ways."

🎵 Holywell Music Room

Holywell St. ⭘ concerts only. 📷 ♿

This was the first building in Europe designed, in 1752, specifically for public musical performances. Previously, concerts had been held in private houses for invited guests only. Its two splendid chandeliers originally adorned Westminster Hall at the coronation of George IV in 1820 and were given by the king to Wadham College, of which the music room technically forms a part. The intimate room is used regularly for concerts of both contemporary and classical music.

🏛 Museum of Oxford

St. Aldate. 📞 01865 815559. ◯ Tue–Sat. ● Dec 25, 26, Jan 1. 🎫 🔥
A well-organized display in the Victorian town hall illustrate the long history of Oxford and its university. Exhibits include a Roman pottery kiln and a town seal from 1191.

The main features are a series of well-reconstructed rooms, including one from an Elizabethan inn and an 18th-century student's room.

🏵 Martyrs' Memorial

This commemorates the three Protestants burned at the stake on Broad Street – Bishops Latimer and Ridley in 1555 and Archbishop Cranmer in 1556. On the accession of Queen Mary in 1553 (see p51), they were committed to the Tower of London, then sent to Oxford to defend their views before the doctors of divinity who, after the hearing, condemned them as heretics.

The memorial was designed in 1843 by George Gilbert Scott and based on the Eleanor crosses erected in 12 English towns by Edward I (1239–1307) to honor his queen.

🏛 Oxford Story

6 Broad St. 📞 01865 728822. ◯ daily. ● Dec 25. 🎫 🔥
This audiovisual account of the city's history has a train ride through vivid exhibits which are bought to life with animated, life-size models of major historical characters.

🏵 St. Mary the Virgin Church

High St. 📞 01865 243806. ◯ daily. 🔥 limited.
This, the official church of the university, is said to be the most-visited parish church in England. The oldest parts date from the early 14th century and include the tower, from the top of which you can enjoy a fine view. Its Congregation House, of the same date, served as the university's first library until the Bodleian was founded in 1488 (see p213). The church is where the three Oxford Martyrs were pronounced heretics in 1555. The architectural highlight of the church is the Baroque south porch, constructed in 1637.

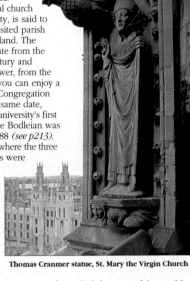

Thomas Cranmer statue, St. Mary the Virgin Church

🏛 University Museum and Pitt Rivers Museum

Parks Rd. 📞 01865 272950. ◯ Mon–Sat. ● Dec 24–26, Easter Thu–Sat. 🔥 limited.
Two of Oxford's most interesting museums adjoin each other. The first is a museum of natural history containing relics of dinosaurs as well as a stuffed dodo. This flightless bird has been extinct since the 17th century, but was immortalized by Lewis Carroll (an Oxford mathematics lecturer whose real name was Charles Dodgson) in his book *Alice in Wonderland (see p387)*. The exhibits are housed in a large Victorian building with cast-iron columns, which support a glass roof leading to a cavernous interior. This leads into the Pitt Rivers Museum,

which has one of the world's most extensive ethnographic collections – masks and tribal totems from Africa and the Far East – and archaeological displays, including exhibits collected by the explorer Captain Cook. An annex on Banbury Road has an unusual collection of musical instruments, with audio equipment so you can hear them playing.

🏵 Sheldonian Theatre

Broad St. 📞 01865 277299. ◯ Mon–Sat. ● Dec 23–Jan 4, Easter & public hols. 🎫 🔥
Completed in 1669, this was the first building designed by Christopher Wren (see p116). It was paid for by Gilbert Sheldon, the Archbishop of Canterbury, as a place to hold university degree ceremonies. The Classical design of the oval building is based on the Theatre of Marcellus in Rome. The octagonal cupola – larger than the original – was built in 1838, and there is a very famous view from its huge Lantern. In the theater the beautifully painted ceiling depicts the triumph of religion, art and science over envy, hatred and malice.

The impressive frontage of the University Museum and Pitt Rivers Museum

Exploring Oxford University

MANY OF THE 36 COLLEGES that make up the university were founded between the 13th and 16th centuries and cluster around the city center. Since scholarship was then the exclusive preserve of the church, the colleges were designed along the lines of monastic buildings but were often surrounded by beautiful gardens. Although most colleges have been altered over the years, many still incorporate a lot of their original features.

The spectacular view of All Souls College from St. Mary's Church

All Souls College
Founded in 1438 on the High Street by Henry VI, the chapel on the college's north side has a classic hammerbeam roof, unusual misericords *(see p327)* on the choir stalls and 15th-century stained glass.

Christ Church College
The best way to view this, the largest of the Oxford colleges, is to approach through the meadows from St. Aldate's. Christ Church dates from 1525 when Cardinal Wolsey founded it as an ecclesiastical college to train cardinals. The upper part of the tower in Tom Quad – a rectangular courtyard – was built by Wren *(see p116)* in 1682 and is the largest in the city. When its bell, Great Tom, was hung in 1648, the college had 101 students, which is why the bell is rung 101 times at 9:05pm, to mark the curfew for students (which has not been enforced since 1963). The odd timing is because night falls here five minutes later than at Greenwich *(see p131).* Christ Church has produced 16 British prime ministers in the last 200 years. Beside the main quad is the 12th-century Christ Church Cathedral, one of the smallest in England.

Lincoln College
One of the best-preserved of the medieval colleges, it was founded in 1427 on Turl Street, and the front quad and façade

are 15th century. The hall still has its original roof, including the gap where smoke used to escape. The Jacobean chapel is notable for its stained glass. John Wesley *(see p265)* was at college here and his rooms, now a chapel, can be visited.

Magdalen College
At the end of the High Street is perhaps the most typical and beautiful Oxford college. Its 15th-century quads in contrasting styles are set in a park by the Cherwell, crossed by Magdalen Bridge. Every May Day at 6am, the college choir sings from the top of Magdalen's bell tower (1508) – a 16th-century custom to mark the start of summer.

New College
One of the grandest colleges, it was founded by William of Wykeham *(see p156)* in 1379 to educate clergy to replace those killed by the Black Death of 1348 *(see p49).*

Magdalen Bridge spanning the River Cherwell

Its magnificent chapel on New College Lane, restored in the 19th century, has vigorous 14th-century misericords and El Greco's (1541–1614) famous painting of *St. James.*

Queen's College
Most of the college buildings date from the 18th century and represent some of the finest work from that period in Oxford. Its superb library was built in 1695 by Henry Aldrich (1647–1710) The front screen with its bell-topped gatehouse is a feature of the High Street.

STUDENT LIFE

Students belong to individual colleges and usually live in them for the duration of their college career. The university gives lectures, sets exams and awards degrees but much of the students' tuition and social life is based around their college. Many traditions date back hundreds of years, like the graduation ceremonies at the Sheldonian that are still held in Latin.

Graduation at the Sheldonian *(see p210)*

Merton College seen from Christ Church Meadows

St. John's College
The impressive frontage on St. Giles dates from 1437, when it was founded for Cistercian scholars. The old library has lovely 17th-century bookcases and stained glass, while the Baylie Chapel has a display of 15th-century vestments.

Trinity College
The oldest part of the college on Broad Street, Durham Quad, is named after the earlier college of 1296, which was incorporated into Trinity in 1555. The late 17th-century chapel has a magnificent reredos and wooden screen.

Corpus Christi College
The whole of the charming front quad on Merton Street dates from 1517, when the college was founded. The quad's sundial, topped by a pelican – the college symbol – bears an early 17th-century calendar. The chapel has a rare 16th-century eagle lectern.

Merton College
Off Merton Street, this is the oldest college (1264) in Oxford. Much of its hall dates from then, including a sturdy decorated door. The chapel choir contains allegorical reliefs representing music, arithmetic, rhetoric and grammar. Merton's Mob Quad served as a model for the later colleges.

BODLEIAN LIBRARY
Founded in 1320, the library was expanded in 1426 by Humphrey, Duke of Gloucester (1391–1447) and brother of Henry VI, when his collection of manuscripts would not fit into the old library. It was refounded in 1602 by Thomas Bodley, a wealthy scholar, who insisted on strict rules: the keeper was forbidden to marry. The library is one of the six copyright deposit libraries in the country – it is entitled to receive a copy of every book published in Britain.

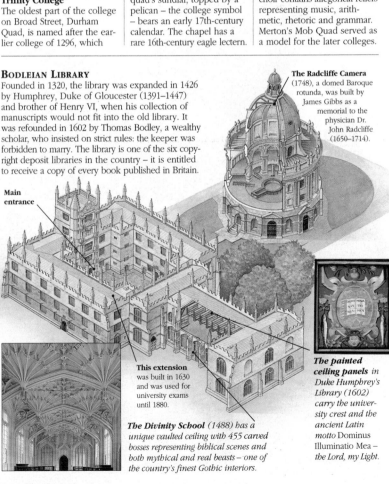

The Radcliffe Camera (1748), a domed Baroque rotunda, was built by James Gibbs as a memorial to the physician Dr. John Radcliffe (1650–1714).

Main entrance

This extension was built in 1630 and was used for university exams until 1880.

The Divinity School (1488) has a unique vaulted ceiling with 455 carved bosses representing biblical scenes and both mythical and real beasts – one of the country's finest Gothic interiors.

The painted ceiling panels in Duke Humphrey's Library (1602) carry the university crest and the ancient Latin motto Dominus Illuminatio Mea – the Lord, my Light.

Blenheim Palace ⑥

AFTER JOHN CHURCHILL, the 1st Duke of Marlborough, defeated the French at the Battle of Blenheim in 1704, Queen Anne gave him the Manor of Woodstock and had this palatial house built for him in gratitude. Designed by both Nicholas Hawksmoor and Sir John Vanbrugh *(see p384)*, it is a Baroque masterpiece. It was also the birthplace of Britain's World War II leader, Winston Churchill, in 1874.

★ **Long Library**
This 55 m (183 f) room was design by Vanbrugh as picture gallery. T portraits include of Queen Anne b Sir Godfrey Knel (1646–1723). Th stucco on the ceiling is by Isaa Mansfield (1725

Winston Churchill and his wife, Clementine

The Grand Bridge was built in 1708. It has a 31 m (101 ft) main span and contains rooms within its structure.

Chapel
The marble monument to the 1st Duke of Marlborough and his family was sculpted by Michael Rysbrack in 1733.

Water Terrace Gardens
These magnificent gardens were laid out in the 1920s by French architect Achille Duchêne in 17th-century style, with detailed patterned beds and fountains.

STAR SIGHTS

★ **Long Library**

★ **Saloon (Parlor)**

★ **Park and Gardens**

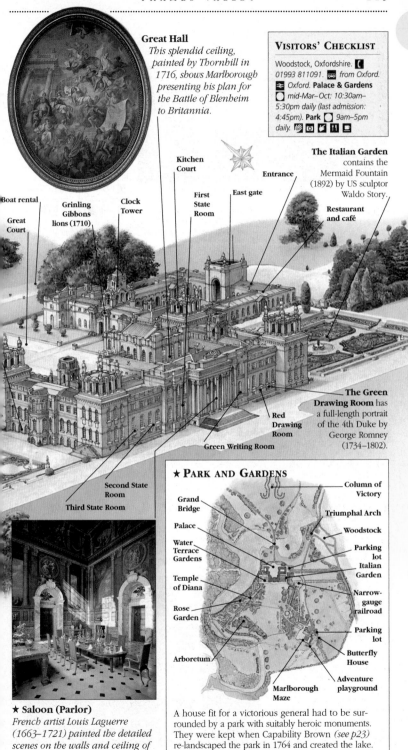

Great Hall
*This splendid ceiling,
painted by Thornhill in
1716, shows Marlborough
presenting his plan for
the Battle of Blenheim
to Britannia.*

VISITORS' CHECKLIST

Woodstock, Oxfordshire. 🛈
01993 811091. 🚌 from Oxford.
🚉 Oxford. **Palace & Gardens**
⏲ mid-Mar–Oct: 10:30am–
5:30pm daily (last admission:
4:45pm). **Park** ⏲ 9am–5pm
daily. 🅿️ 📷 🚻 🍴 ♿

The Italian Garden
contains the
Mermaid Fountain
(1892) by US sculptor
Waldo Story.

**Kitchen
Court**

Entrance

East gate

Boat rental

**Great
Court**

**Grinling
Gibbons
lions (1710)**

**Clock
Tower**

**First
State
Room**

**Restaurant
and café**

**The Green
Drawing Room** has
a full-length portrait
of the 4th Duke by
George Romney
(1734–1802).

**Red
Drawing
Room**

Green Writing Room

**Second State
Room**

Third State Room

★ PARK AND GARDENS

**Grand
Bridge**

Palace

**Water
Terrace
Gardens**

**Temple
of Diana**

**Rose
Garden**

Arboretum

**Marlborough
Maze**

**Column of
Victory**

Triumphal Arch

Woodstock

**Parking
lot**

**Italian
Garden**

**Narrow-
gauge
railroad**

**Parking
lot**

**Butterfly
House**

**Adventure
playground**

★ Saloon (Parlor)
*French artist Louis Laguerre
(1663–1721) painted the detailed
scenes on the walls and ceiling of
the state dining room.*

A house fit for a victorious general had to be surrounded by a park with suitably heroic monuments.
They were kept when Capability Brown *(see p23)*
re-landscaped the park in 1764 and created the lake.

Canaletto's *Entrance to the Arsenal* (1730) hangs at Woburn Abbey

Stowe **⑦**

Buckingham, Buckinghamshire.
📞 *01280 822850.* 🚌 *Milton Keynes
then bus.* ⏰ *school hols: daily;
termtime: Mon, Wed, Fri, & Sun.*
⬤ *Nov–Dec 26.* 📷 ♿ *limited.*

THIS IS THE MOST ambitious
and important landscaped
garden in Britain as well as
also being one of the finest
examples of the 18th-century
passion for trying to shape and
improve on nature to make it
conform to fashionable
notions of taste *(see pp22–3)*.

In the space of nearly 100
years the original garden, first
laid out about 1680, was
enlarged and transformed by
the addition of monuments,
Greek and Gothic temples,
grottoes, statues, ornamental
bridges, artificial lakes and
"natural" tree plantings.

Most of the leading designers
and architects of the period
contributed to the garden,
including Sir John Vanbrugh,
James Gibbs and Capability
Brown *(see pp22–3)* who was
head gardener at Stowe for 10
years, at the start of his career.

From 1593 to 1921 the huge
property was owned outright
by the Temple and Grenville
families – later the Dukes of
Buckingham – until the large
Palladian house at its center
was sold and converted into
an elite boys' "public school."

The family were soldiers
and politicians in the liberal
tradition, and many of the
buildings and sculptures in
the garden symbolize Utopian
ideals of democracy and freedom. There are temples of
British Worthies, of Ancient
Virtue, of Concord and Victory,
the Fane (temple) of Pastoral

Poetry and the Elysian fields.
Some of these features deteriorated in the 19th century, as
the family fortune declined,
and many statues were sold.
But a comprehensive restoration program has meant that
statues have been bought back
and copies made of others.

Woburn Abbey **⑧**

Woburn, Bedfordshire. 📞 *01525
290666.* 🚌 *Bletchley then taxi.*
⏰ *Apr–Oct: daily; Jan–Mar: Sat,
Sun.* ⬤ *Nov–Dec.* 📷 ♿ *call first.*

THE DUKES OF BEDFORD have
lived here for over 350
years and were among the first
owners of an English stately
home to open their house to
the public some 40 years ago.

The abbey was built in the
mid-18th century on the foundations of a large 12th-century
Cistercian monastery. Its mix
of styles range from Henry
Flitcroft and Henry Holland
(see p24). It is now one of the
most popular attractions in the
country, partly due to a 142 ha
(350 acre) safari park and a

deer park with nine species
including the Milu, originally
the imperial herd of China.

The magnificent state apartments house an important
private art collection with
works by Reynolds (1723–92)
and Canaletto (1697–1768).

Whipsnade Wild Animal Park **⑨**

Nr Dunstable, Bedfordshire.
📞 *01582 872171.* 🚌 *Whipsnade.
(Victoria Station, London: May–Oct.)*
⏰ *daily.* ⬤ *Dec 25.* 📷 ♿

THE RURAL BRANCH of London
Zoo, this was one of the
first zoos to minimize the use
of cages and devise areas
where wild animals could be
confined safely but without
too much constriction.

At 240 ha (600 acres), it is
Europe's largest conservation
park, with more than 3,000
species. You can drive through
some areas, or try the steam
train that travels around the
park. Also popular are the
adventure playground and
sea lions' underwater display.

Luton Hoo **⑩**

Luton, Bedfordshire. 📞 *01582 22955.*
🚌 *Luton then taxi.* ⏰ *Easter–mid-
Oct: Fri–Sun & public hols.* 📷 ♿

SINCE ROBERT ADAM designed
it in 1767, the house has
undergone a radical transformation. In 1903 Sir Julius
Wernher, who made a fortune
out of diamond mines in South
Africa, had it rebuilt in a
sumptuous French classical

The 17th-century Palladian bridge over the Octagon Lake in Stowe Park

Hatfield House, one of the largest Jacobean mansions in the country

style, with a strong emphasis on gilt, by the same architects as the Ritz Hotel *(see p83)*.

It is still the home of the Wernher family and much of its interest stems from Sir Julius's daughter-in-law, Lady Zia Wernher, a descendant of the Russian czars. She inherited some items from the royal Russian treasures, including exquisite Fabergé jewelry.

The Wernher art collection includes paintings by Hoppner (1758–1810), Sargent (1856–1925) and Titian (1488–1576) along with medieval ivories. There is a park landscaped by Capability Brown *(see pp22–3)*.

Knebworth House **⑪**

Knebworth, Hertfordshire.
[01438 812661. **≊** *Stevenage then taxi.* **◯** *Jun–Aug, school & public hols: Tue–Sun; Easter–May, Sep: Sat, Sun.* **◪** **&** *limited.*

A NOTABLE TUDOR mansion, with a beautiful Jacobean banqueting hall, Knebworth was extravagantly overlain with a 19th-century Gothic exterior by Lord Lytton, the statesman, novelist and head of one of the most colorful families in Victorian England.

His eldest son, the 1st Earl of Lytton, was Viceroy of India, and several exhibits in the house illustrate the Delhi Durbar of 1877, when Queen Victoria was declared Empress of India. Constance Lytton was a leading member of the suffragette movement during the 1920s *(see p58)*.

Hatfield House **⑫**

Hatfield, Hertfordshire. **[** 01707 262823. **≊** *Hatfield.* **◯** *Apr–mid-Oct: Tue–Sun & public hols.* **◪** **&**

O NE OF ENGLAND's finest Jacobean houses, it was built mainly between 1607 and 1611 for the powerful statesman Robert Cecil, and is still owned by his descendants.

Its chief historical interest, though, lies in the surviving wing of the original Tudor Hatfield Palace, where Queen Elizabeth I *(see pp50–51)* spent much of her childhood. She held her first Council of State here when she was crowned in 1558. The palace, which was partly demolished in 1607 to make way for the new house, contains mementos of her life, including the *Rainbow* portrait painted around 1600 by Isaac Oliver. Visitors can also attend medieval banquets held in its Great Hall.

The house has one of the few 17th-century gardens to survive, laid out by Robert Cecil with help from John Tradescant *(see p210)*.

FAMOUS PURITANS

Three major figures connected with the 17th-century Puritan movement are celebrated in the Thames area. John Bunyan (1628–88), who wrote the allegorical tale *The Pilgrim's Progress*, was born at Elstow, near Bedford. A passionate Puritan orator, he was jailed for his beliefs for 17 years. The Bunyan Museum in Bedford is a

18th-century engraving of John Bunyan

former site of Puritan worship. William Penn (1644–1718), founder of Pennsylvania (1681), lived, worshiped and is buried at Jordans, near Beaconsfield. A bit farther north at Chalfont St. Giles is the cottage where the poet John Milton (1608–74) stayed to escape London's plague. There he completed his greatest work, *Paradise Lost*. The house is now a museum based on his life and works.

William Penn, founder of Pennsylvania

John Milton painted by Pieter van der Plas

St. Albans ⓭

TODAY A THRIVING MARKET TOWN and a base for London commuters, St. Albans was for centuries at the heart of some of the most stirring events in English history. A regional capital of ancient Britain, it became a major Roman settlement and then a key ecclesiastical center – so important that during the Wars of the Roses *(see p49)*, two battles were fought for it. In 1455 the Yorkists drove King Henry VI from the town and six years later the Lancastrians retook it.

The martyr St. Alban

Exploring St. Albans

Part of the appeal of this ancient and fascinating town, little more than an hour's drive from London, is that its 2,000-year history can be traced vividly by visiting a few sites within easy walking distance of one another. There is a large parking lot within the walls of the Roman city of Verulamium, between the museum and St. Michael's Church and across the road from the excavated theater. From there it is a pleasant lakeside walk across the park, passing more Roman sites, Ye Olde Fighting Cocks inn, the massive cathedral and the historic High Street. Marking the center of the town, the High Street is lined with several Tudor buildings and a clock tower dating from 1412, from which the curfew bell used to ring at 4am in the morning and 8:30pm at night.

⋔ Verulamium

Just outside the city center are the walls of Verulamium, one of the first British cities the Romans established after their invasion of Britain in AD 43. Boadicea *(see p181)* razed it

to the ground during her unsuccessful rebellion against the Romans in AD 62, but its position on Watling Street, an important trading route, meant that it was quickly rebuilt on an even larger scale and the city flourished until 410.

🏛 Verulamium Museum

St. Michael's. **(** *01727 819339.*
◯ *daily.* ● *Dec 25, 26.* 🎦 ఊ
This excellent museum tells the story of the city, but its main attraction is its splendid collection of well-preserved Roman artifacts, notably some breathtaking mosaic floors, including one depicting the head of a sea god, and another of a scallop shell with intricate three-dimensional shading. Other finds included burial urns and lead coffins.

On the basis of excavated plaster fragments, a Roman room has been painstakingly recreated, its walls painted in startlingly bright colors and geometric patterns.

Between here and St. Albans Cathedral are a bath house with more mosaics, remnants of the ancient city wall and one of the original gates.

A scallop shell, one of the mosaic floors at the Verulamium Museum

🏮 Ye Olde Fighting Cocks

Abbey Mill Lane. **(** *01727 865830.*
◯ *daily.* ● *Dec 25.* ఊ
Believed to be England's oldest surviving pub, Ye Olde Fighting Cocks is certainly, with its

One of the oldest surviving pubs in England

octagonal shape, one of the most unusual. It originated as the medieval dovecote of the old abbey and moved here after the Dissolution *(see p50)*.

⋔ Roman Theatre

St. Michael's. **(** *01727 835035.*
◯ *daily.* ● *Dec 25, 26.* 🎦 ఊ
Just across the road from the museum are the foundations of the open-air theater, first built around 160 but enlarged several times. It is one of only six known to have been built throughout Roman Britain.

Alongside it are traces of a row of Roman shops and a house, from which many of the museum's treasures – such as a bronze statuette of Venus – were excavated in the 1930s.

⛪ St. Michael's Church

St. Michael's. **(** *01727 835037.*
◯ *May–Sep: daily.* ఊ
This church was first founded during the Saxon reign and was built partly with bricks taken from Verulamium, which by then was in decline. Numerous additions have been made since then, including a truly splendid Jacobean pulpit.

The church contains an early 17th-century monument to the Elizabethan statesman and writer Sir Francis Bacon, whose father owned nearby Gorhambury, a large Tudor house, now in ruins.

🔒 St. Albans Cathedral

Sumpter Yard. 📞 *01727 860780.*
⭕ *daily.* **Donation.** ♿
This outstanding example of
medieval architecture has
some classic features, such as
the 13th- and 14th-century wall
paintings on the Norman piers.

It was begun in 793, when
King Offa of Mercia founded
the abbey in honor of St.
Alban, Britain's first Christian
martyr, put to death by the
Romans in the third century
for sheltering a priest. The
oldest parts, which still stand,

**The imposing west side of
St. Albans Cathedral**

were first built in 1077 and
are easily recognizable as
Norman by the round-headed
arches and windows. They
form part of the 84 m (276 ft)
nave – the longest in England.

The pointed arches farther
east are Early English (13th
century), while the Decorated
work of the 14th century was
added when some of the
Norman arches collapsed.

East of the crossing is
what remains of St. Alban's
shrine – a marble pedestal
made up of more than
2,000 tiny fragments. Next to
it is the tomb of Humphrey,
Duke of Gloucester *(see p213).*

A copy of the *Magna Carta
(see p48)* is displayed on the
wall. It was here that the
English gathered to draw up
this document, which King
John was then forced to sign.

The splendor of the Gardens of the Rose in June

Gardens of the
Rose ⑭

Chiswell Green, Hertfordshire. 📞
01727 850461. 🚆 *St. Albans then bus.*
⭕ *mid-Jun–mid-Oct: daily.* 🖼️ ♿

A S WELL AS BEING England's
national symbol, the rose
is the most popular flower
with British gardeners.

The 5 ha (12 acre) garden
of the Royal National Rose
Society, with over 30,000
plants and 1,700 varieties, is
at its peak in late June. The
gardens trace the history of
the flower, and one bed of
ancient varieties includes the
white rose of York, the red
rose of Lancaster *(see p49)*
and the Rosa Mundi – named
by Henry II for his mistress
Fair Rosamond after she was
poisoned by Queen Eleanor
in 1177. But the nuns who

buried Rosamond wrote on her
tomb a verse implying that,
despite her name, her reputation did not smell of roses.

Hughenden
Manor ⑮

High Wycombe, Buckinghamshire.
📞 *01494 532580.* 🚆 *High Wycombe
then bus.* ⭕ *Mar: Sat, Sun; Apr–Oct:
Wed–Sun & public hols.* ⚫ *Good Fri.*
🖼️ ♿ *limited.*

T HE VICTORIAN STATESMAN and
novelist Benjamin Disraeli,
Prime Minister from 1874 to
1880, lived here for 33 years
until his death. Originally a
Georgian villa, Disraeli adapted
it in 1862 to the Gothic style.
Furnished as it was in his day,
the house gives an idea of
the life of a wealthy Victorian
gentleman and shows some
portraits of his contemporaries.

GEORGE BERNARD SHAW

Although a controversial playwright and known as
a mischievous character, the Irish-born George
Bernard Shaw (1856–1950) was a man of settled
habits. He lived near St. Albans in a house at
Ayot St. Lawrence, now called Shaw's Corner,
for the last 44 years of his life, working
until his last weeks in a summerhouse at the bottom of his large
garden. Shaw's plays, combining
wit with a powerful political and
social message, still seem fresh
today. One of the most enduring
is *Pygmalion* (1913), on which
the musical *My Fair Lady* is
based. The house and garden
are now a museum of
his life and works.

Touring the Thames ⑯

THE THAMES between Pangbourne and Eton is leafy and romantic and best seen by boat. But if time is short, the road keeps close to its bank for much of the way. Swans glide gracefully below ancient bridges, voles dive into the water for cover, and elegant herons stand impassive at the river's edge. Huge beech trees overhang the banks that are lined with fine houses, their gardens sloping to the water. The tranquil scene has inspired many painters and writers well as operating, until recently, as an important transportation link.

Hambledon Mill ⑥
The white weather-boarded mill, which was operational until 1955, is one of the largest on the Thames as well as one of the oldest in origin. There are traces of the original 16th-century mill.

Beale Park ①
The philanthropist Gilbert Beale (1868–1967) created a 10 ha (25 acre) park to preserve this beautiful stretch of river intact and breed endangered birds like owls, ornamental water fowl, pheasants and peacocks.

Henley ⑤
This lovely old river town, with houses and churches dating from the 15th and 16th centuries, is the site for an important regatta (see p66).

Pangbourne ②
Kenneth Grahame (1859–1932), author of *The Wind in the Willows*, lived here until his death. Pangbourne was used as the setting by artist Ernest Shepard (1879–1976) to illustrate the book.

Sonning Bridge ④
The 18th-century bridge is made up of 11 brick arches of varying width.

TIPS FOR DRIVERS

Tour length: 50 miles (75 km).
Stopping-off points: The picturesque town of Henley has a large number of riverside pubs that will make good stops for lunch. If you are boating you can often moor your boat alongside the river bank. (See also pp636–7.)

Whitchurch Mill ③
This charming village, linked to Pangbourne by a Victorian toll bridge, has a picturesque church and one of the many unused watermills that once harnessed the power of this stretch of river.

Cookham ⑦
This is famous as the home of Stanley Spencer (1891–1959), one of Britain's leading 20th-century artists. His old studio is now a museum containing some of his paintings and equipment, including a sign that warned visitors to leave him alone when he was working. This work, titled *Swan Upping* (1914–19), recalls a Thames custom.

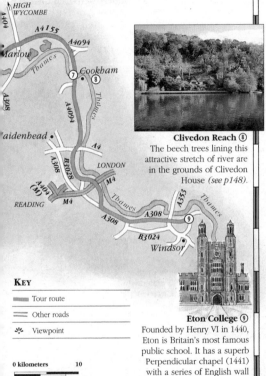

HIGH
WYCOMBE

A404

A4155

A4094

Marlow

Thames

Thames

⑦ ⑧ Cookham

A308

A4094

aidenhead •

A4

B3028

LONDON

M4

A404
(M)

M4

READING

Thames

A353

A308

A308

Thames

B3024

Windsor

⑨

Clivedon Reach ⑧
The beech trees lining this attractive stretch of river are in the grounds of Clivedon House *(see p148)*.

KEY

▬▬▬ Tour route

═══ Other roads

🌿 Viewpoint

0 kilometers   10

0 miles   5

Eton College ⑨
Founded by Henry VI in 1440, Eton is Britain's most famous public school. It has a superb Perpendicular chapel (1441) with a series of English wall paintings (1479–88).

BOATING TOURS

Salter Bros. rental boats, moored at Henley

In summer, scheduled river services run between Henley, Windsor, Runnymede and Marlow. Several companies operate from towns along the route. You can rent boats by the hour or the day or, for a longer tour, you can rent cabin cruisers and sleep on board *(see also p641)*. Ring Salter Bros. on 01753 865 832 for more information.

Windsor ⑰

Berkshire. 🏛 *30,000.* 🚆
ℹ *Central Station, Thames St (01753 852010).* 🛒 *Sat.*

THE TOWN of Windsor is dwarfed by the enormous **castle** *(see p222)* on the hill above – appropriately enough because its original purpose was to serve the castle's needs. The town is full of quaint Georgian shops, houses and inns. The most prominent building on the High Street is the **Guildhall** completed by Wren *(see p116)* in 1689. The **Household Cavalry Museum** has an extensive collection of arms and uniforms.

The 809 ha (2,000 acre) **Windsor Great Park** stretches straight from the castle three miles (5 km) to Snow Hill, where there is a huge statue of George III.

ENVIRONS: Four miles (7 km) to the southeast is the level grassy meadow known as **Runnymede**. This is one of England's most historic sights, where in 1215 King John was forced by his rebellious barons to sign the *Magna Carta (see p48)*, thereby limiting his royal powers. The dainty memorial pavilion at the top of the meadow was erected in 1957.

🏛 Household Cavalry Museum
Leonard's Rd. 📞 *01753 868222.*
🔲 *Mon–Fri.* ⚫ *public hols.* 📷

King John signing the *Magna Carta*, Runnymede

Windsor Castle

Henry II rebuilt the castle

THE OLDEST CONTINUOUSLY inhabited royal residence in Britain, the castle, originally made of wood, was built by William the Conqueror in 1070 to guard the western approaches to London. He chose the site because it was on high ground and just a day's journey from his base in the Tower of London. Successive monarchs have made alterations that render it a remarkable monument to royalty's changing tastes. King George V's affection for it was shown when he chose Windsor for his family surname in 1917. The castle is the primary residence of the Queen and her family who stay here many weekends.

Albert Memorial Chapel
First built in 1240, it was rebuilt in 1485 and finally converted into a memorial for Prince Albert in 1863.

The Curfew Tower has its original medieval interior.

King Henry VIII Gate and main exit

★ St. George's Chapel
The architectural highlight of the castle, it was built between 1475 and 1528 and is one of England's outstanding late Gothic works. Ten monarchs are buried in the chapel.

Entrance

The Round Tower was first built in wood by William the Conqueror. In 1170 it was rebuilt in stone by Henry II *(see p48)*. It now houses the Royal Archives and Photographic Collection.

Statue of Charles II

Albert Memorial Chapel (1485)

The Round Tower (1080)

Waterloo Chamber (1220s)

St. George's Hall (1362–65)

Middle Ward

Lower Ward

St. George's Chapel (1475–1528)

Upper Ward

KEY

▇	11th–13th century
▇	14th century
▇	15th–18th century
▢	19th–20th century

WINDSOR CASTLE'S HISTORY
Founded in 1070 as a motte and bailey (see p472), *Henry II and Edward III were responsible for the bulk of the work until the castle was remodeled by George IV in 1823.*

Royal Collection
This chalk etching of Christ by Michelangelo is part of the Resurrection Series. *The size of the Royal Collection means that the exhibition is always changing and works are often loaned to other museums.*

VISITORS' CHECKLIST

Castle Hill. 01753 868286.
Apr–Oct: 10am–5pm daily;
Nov–Mar: 10am–4pm daily (last adm: one hour before closing).
Dec 25–Jan 1. St. George's Chapel: 5pm Mon–Sat, 11am & 5pm Sun. limited.

The Audience Chamber is where the Queen greets her guests.

The Queen's Ballroom

Queen Mary's Dolls' House was designed by Sir Edwin Lutyens in 1924. Every item was built on a 1:12 ratio. The wine cellar contains genuine vintage wine.

Waterloo Chamber
The walls of this banquet hall, first built in the 13th century, are lined with portraits of the leaders who played a part in Napoleon's defeat (see p55).

Brunswick Tower

The East Terrace Garden was created by Sir Jeffry Wyatville for King George IV in the 1820s.

★ State Apartments
These rooms contain many treasures, including this late 18th-century state bed in the King's State Bedchamber, made for the visit in 1855 of Napoleon III.

STAR SIGHTS

★ **St. George's Chapel**

★ **State Apartments**

The Fire of 1992
A devastating blaze began during maintenance work on the State Apartments. St. George's Hall was destroyed but has been rebuilt.

THE WEST
COUNTRY

The West Country at a Glance

THE WEST COUNTRY forms a long peninsula bounded by the Atlantic to the north and the English Channel to the south, tapering down to Land's End, mainland Britain's westernmost point. Whether exploring the great cities and cathedrals, experiencing the awesome solitude of the moors and their prehistoric monuments, or simply enjoying the miles of coastline and mild climate, this region has an enduring appeal for vacationers.

Exmoor's (see pp236–7) heather-clad moors and wooded valleys, grazed by wild ponies and red deer, lead down to some of Devon's most dramatic cliffs and seaside coves.

Wells (see pp238–9) is a charming town nestling at the foot of the Mendip Hills. It is famous for its exquisite three-towered cathedral with an ornate west façade, featuring an array of statues. Alongside stand the moated Bishop's Palace and the 15th-century Vicar's Close.

St. Ives (see p263) has a branch of the Tate Gallery that shows modern works by artists associated with the area. Patrick Heron's bold colored glass (1993) is on permanent display.

Devon

DEVON AND CORNWALL
(see pp258–81)

Cornwall

Dartmoor (see pp280–81) is a wilderness of great natural beauty covering an area of 365 sq miles (945 sq km). Stone clapper bridges, picturesque villages and weathered granite tors punctuate the landscape.

◁ Stunning views of the Lizard Peninsula

Bath (see pp244–7) is named after the Roman baths that stand at the heart of the old city next to the splendid medieval abbey. It is one of Britain's liveliest and most rewarding cities, full of elegant Georgian terraces, built in local honey-colored limestone by the two John Woods (Elder and Younger).

Stonehenge (see pp248–9), the world-famous prehistoric monument, was built in several stages from 3000 BC. Moving and erecting its massive stones was an extraordinary feat for its time. It is likely that this magical stone circle was a place of worship to the sun.

Avon

WESSEX
(see pp232–57)

Wiltshire

Somerset

Dorset

Salisbury's (see pp250–51) cathedral with its soaring spire, was the inspiration for one of John Constable's best-loved paintings. The picturesque Cathedral Close has a number of fine medieval buildings.

0 kilometers   25

0 miles   25

Stourhead garden (see pp252–3) was inspired by the paintings of Claude and Poussin. Created in the 18th century, the garden is itself a work of art. Contrived vistas, light and shade and a mixture of landscape and gracious buildings, such as the Neo-Classical Pantheon at its center, are vital to the overall effect.

Coastal Wildlife

THE LONG AND VARIED West Country coastline, ranging from the stark, granite cliffs of Land's End to the pebble-strewn stretch of Chesil Bank, is matched with an equally diverse range of wildlife. Beaches are scattered with colorful shells, while rock pools form miniature marine habitats teeming with life. Caves are used by larger creatures, such as gray seals, and cliffs provide nest sites for birds. In the spring and early summer, an astonishing range of plants grow on the foreshore and cliffs, which can be seen at their best from the Southwest Coastal Path *(see p32)*. The plants in turn attract numerous moths and butterflies.

Cliff-tops of Land's End with safe ledges for nesting birds

Chesil Bank is an unusual ridge of pebbles (see p254) stretching 18 miles (29 km) along the Dorset coast. The bank was created by storms and the pebbles increase in size from northwest to southeast due to varying strengths of coastal currents. The bank encloses a lagoon called the Fleet, habitat of the Abbotsbury swans, as well as a large number of wildfowl.

The Painted Lady, often seen on cliff-top coastal plants, migrates to Britai[n] in spring.

High tides wash up shells and driftwoo[d]

Cliff-top turf contains wild flowers of many species.

Thrift, in hummocks of honey-scented flowers, is a familiar sight on cliff ledges in spring.

Yellowhammers are to be seen perched on cliff-top bushes.

Marram grass roots help hold back sand against wind erosion.

Gray seals come on land to give birth to their young. They can be spotted on remote beaches.

A Beachcomber's Guide

The best time to observe the natural life of the sea shore is when the tide begins to roll back, before the scavenging seagulls pick up the stranded crabs, fish and sand fleas, and the seaweed dries up. Much of the plant and marine life can be found in the secure habitat provided by rock pools.

Durdle Door *was formed by waves continually eroding the weaker chalk layers of this cliff (see p256) in Dorset, leaving the stronger oolite to create a striking arch, known in geology as an eyelet.*

COLLECTING SHELLS

Most of the edible mollusks, such as scallops and cockles, are known as bivalves; others, such as whelks and limpets, are known as gastropods.

Great scallop

Common cockle

Common whelk

Common limpet

Seaweed, *such as bladder wrack, can resemble coral or lichen when in water.*

Rocks are colonized by clusters of barnacles, mussels and limpets.

Oystercatchers *have a distinctive orange beak. They hunt along the shore, feeding on all kinds of shellfish.*

Starfish *can be aggressive predators on shellfish. The light-sensitive tips of their tentacles help them to "see" the way.*

Mussels *are widespread and harvested for food.*

Rock pools teem with crabs, mussels, shrimps and plant life.

The Velvet Crab, *often found hiding in seaweed, is covered with fine hair all over its shell.*

Gray mullet, *when newly hatched, can often be seen in rock pools.*

West Country Gardens

GARDENERS HAVE LONG BEEN ATTRACTED to the West Country. Its mild climate is perfect for growing tender and exotic plants, many of which were brought from Asia in the 19th century. As a result, the region has some of England's finest and most varied gardens, covering the whole sweep of garden styles and history *(see pp22–3)*, from the clipped formality of Elizabethan Montacute, to the colorful and crowded cottage-garden style of East Lambrook Manor.

Lanbydrock's (p270) *clipped yews and low boxwood hedges frame a blaze of colorful annuals.*

Trewithen (p267) *is famous for its rare camellias, rhododendrons and magnolias, grown from seed collected in Asia. The huge garden is at its most impressive in March and June.*

Cotehele *(p279)* has a lovely lush valley garden.

DEVON AND CORNWALL *(see pp258–8)*

Trellisick *(p267)* has memorable views over the Fal Estuary through shrub-filled woodland.

Glendurgan *(p267)* is a plant-lover's paradise set in a steep, sheltered valley.

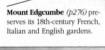

Mount Edgcumbe *(p276)* preserves its 18th-century French, Italian and English gardens.

Trengwainton (p262) *has a fine stream garden, whose banks are crowded with moisture-loving plants, beneath a lush canopy of New Zealand tree ferns.*

Overbecks (near Salcombe) *enjoys a spectacular site overlooking the Salcombe Estuary. There are secret gardens, terraces and rocky dells.*

CREATIVE GARDENING

Gardens are not simply collections of plants; they rely for much of their appeal on man-made features. Whimsical topiary, ornate architecture, fanciful statuary and mazes help to create an atmosphere of adventure or pure escapism. The many gardens dotted around the West Country offer engaging examples of the vivid imagination of designers.

Mazes were created in medieval monasteries to teach patience and persistence. This laurel maze at Glendurgan was planted in 1833.

Fountains and flamboyant statuary have adorned gardens since Roman times. Such eye-catching embellishments add poetic and Classical touches to the design of formal gardens, such as Mount Edgcumbe.

Knightshayes Court (p273) *is designed as a series of formal garden "rooms," planted for scent, color or seasonal effect.*

WESSEX
(see pp232–57)

East Lambrook Manor (near *South Petherton) is a riot of colors, where old-fashioned cottage plants grow unrestrained.*

Stourhead *(see pp252–3)* is a magnificent example of 18th-century landscape gardening.

Athelhampton's *(p255)* gardens make use of fountains, statues, pavilions and columnar yews.

Montacute House *(p254)* has pavilions and a centuries-old yew hedge, and is famous for its collection of old roses.

0 kilometers   25

0 miles   25

Parnham (near Beaminster), like many West Country gardens, has several parts devoted to different themes. Here conical yews complement the formality of the stone balustrade; elsewhere there are woodland, kitchen, shade and Mediterranean gardens.*

Many garden buildings *are linked by an element of fantasy; while country houses had to conform to everyday practicalities, the design of many smaller buildings were more open to imagination. This fanciful Elizabethan pavilion on the forecourt at Montacute House was first and foremost decorative, but sometimes served as a lodging house.*

Topiary *can be traced back to the Greeks. Since that time the sculpting of trees into unusual, often eccentric shapes has been developed over the centuries. The yew topiary of 1920s Knightshayes features a fox being chased by a pack of hounds. The figures form a delightful fantasy and come into their own in winter when little else is in leaf.*

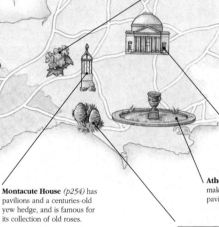

WESSEX

···

AVON · WILTSHIRE · SOMERSET · DORSET

THE NATURAL AND DIVERSE BEAUTY *of this predominantly rural region is characterized by rolling hills and charming villages. The area is enriched by a wealth of historical and architectural attractions, ranging from the prehistoric stone circle of Stonehenge to the Roman baths and magnificent Georgian townscape of Bath.*

Vast swathes of bare windswept downland give way to lush river valleys, and the contrast between the two may explain the origin in medieval times of the saying, "as different as chalk and cheese." The chalk and limestone hills provided pasture for sheep whose wool was exported to Europe or turned to cloth in mill towns such as Bradford-on-Avon. Meanwhile the rich cow-grazed pastures of the valleys produced the Cheddar cheese for which the region has become famous.

The area's potential for wealth was first exploited by prehistoric chieftains whose large, mysterious monuments, such as Stonehenge and Maiden Castle, are striking features of the landscape. From this same soil sprang King Arthur *(see p269)* and King Alfred the Great, about whom there are numerous fascinating legends. It was King Arthur who is thought to have led British resistance to the Saxon invasion in the 6th century. The Saxons finally emerged the victors and one of them, King Alfred, first united the West Country into one political unit, called the Kingdom of Wessex *(see p46)*.

Wilton House and Lacock Abbey, both former monasteries, were turned into splendid stately homes during the 16th century, due to the Dissolution of the Monasteries *(see pp50–51)*. Today, their previous wealth can be gauged by the size and grandeur of their storage barns.

Matching the many man-made splendors of the region, Wessex is rich in rare wildlife and plants.

Two visitors enjoying the Elizabethan gardens of Montacute House, Somerset

◁ Eighteenth-century cottages lining Gold Hill, Shaftesbury

Exploring Wessex

FROM THE ROLLING CHALK PLAINS around Stonehenge
to the rocky cliffs of Cheddar Gorge and the
heather-covered uplands of Exmoor, Wessex is a
scenically varied microcosm of England. Reflecting
the underlying geology, each part of Wessex contributes its own distinctive architecture, with the Neo-
Classically inspired buildings of Bath giving way to the
mellow brick and timber of Salisbury and the thatched
flint-and-chalk cottages of the Dorset landscape.

Wales

BRISTOL 6

WESTON-SUPER-MARE

CHEDDAR GORGE 5

WELL 3

Brue
GLASTONBURY 4

EXMOOR 1

MINEHEAD

TAUNTON 2

Exeter

Tone

SHERBORNE 17

Sidmouth

LYME REGIS

DORCHEST

ABBOTSB

WEYMOU

Bath's abbey and Georgian townscape

0 kilometers 20

0 miles 10

KEY

	Highway
	Major road
	Scenic route
--	Scenic path
	River
⁂	Viewpoint

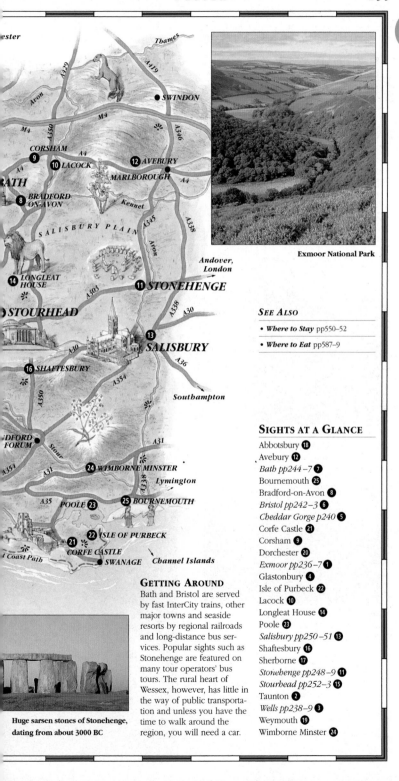

Exmoor National Park

SEE ALSO

• **Where to Stay** pp550–52

• **Where to Eat** pp587–9

SIGHTS AT A GLANCE

GETTING AROUND

Bath and Bristol are served by fast InterCity trains, other major towns and seaside resorts by regional railroads and long-distance bus services. Popular sights such as Stonehenge are featured on many tour operators' bus tours. The rural heart of Wessex, however, has little in the way of public transportation and unless you have the time to walk around the region, you will need a car.

Huge sarsen stones of Stonehenge, dating from about 3000 BC

Exmoor National Park ❶

THE MAJESTIC CLIFFS plunging into the Atlantic along Exmoor's northern coast are interrupted by lush, wooded valleys carrying rivers from the high moorland down to sheltered fishing coves. Inland, wild rolling hills are grazed by sturdy Exmoor ponies, horned sheep and the wild red deer

Curlew that were introduced in the 12th century, when Exmoor was a royal hunting preserve. Curlews and buzzards are a common sight wheeling over the bracken-clad terrain looking for prey. For walkers, Exmoor offers 620 miles (1,000 km) of footpaths and varied, dramatic scenery, while the tamer perimeters of the park have everything from traditional seaside entertainments to picturesque villages and ancient churches.

View east along the Southwest Coastal Path

Combe Martin is a pretty setting for the Pack of Cards Inn *(see p274).*

Parracombe church has a Georgian interior with a complete set of wooden furnishings.

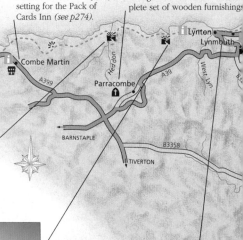

Heddon's Mouth
The River Heddon passes through woodland and meadows down to this attractive point on the coast.

Valley of the Rocks
Sandstone outcrops, eroded into fantastic shapes, characterize this natural gorge.

KEY

🛈	Tourist information
▬▬	A road
▭▭	B road
▭▭	Minor road
- -	Coastal path
☀	Viewpoint

Lynmouth
Above the charming fishing village of Lynmouth stands hill-top Lynton. The two villages are connected by a cliff railroad (see p274).

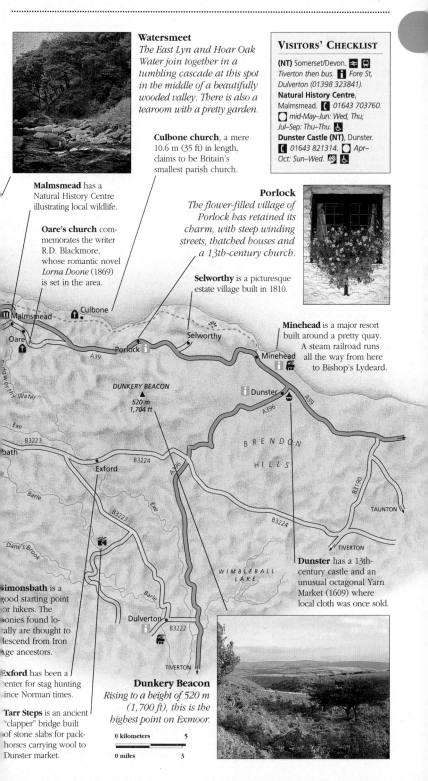

Watersmeet
The East Lyn and Hoar Oak Water join together in a tumbling cascade at this spot in the middle of a beautifully wooded valley. There is also a tearoom with a pretty garden.

Culbone church, a mere 10.6 m (35 ft) in length, claims to be Britain's smallest parish church.

Malmsmead has a Natural History Centre illustrating local wildlife.

Oare's church commemorates the writer R.D. Blackmore, whose romantic novel *Lorna Doone* (1869) is set in the area.

VISITORS' CHECKLIST

(NT) Somerset/Devon. Tiverton then bus. Fore St, Dulverton (01398 323841). **Natural History Centre**, Malmsmead. 01643 703760. mid-May–Jun: Wed, Thu; Jul–Sep: Thu–Thu. **Dunster Castle (NT)**, Dunster. 01643 821314. Apr–Oct: Sun–Wed.

Porlock
The flower-filled village of Porlock has retained its charm, with steep winding streets, thatched houses and a 13th-century church.

Selworthy is a picturesque estate village built in 1810.

Minehead is a major resort built around a pretty quay. A steam railroad runs all the way from here to Bishop's Lydeard.

Dunster has a 13th-century castle and an unusual octagonal Yarn Market (1609) where local cloth was once sold.

Simonsbath is a good starting point for hikers. The ponies found locally are thought to descend from Iron Age ancestors.

Exford has been a center for stag hunting since Norman times.

Tarr Steps is an ancient "clapper" bridge built of stone slabs for pack-horses carrying wool to Dunster market.

Dunkery Beacon
Rising to a height of 520 m (1,700 ft), this is the highest point on Exmoor.

Map labels: Malmsmead, Culbone, Oare, Porlock, A39, Selworthy, Minehead, Dunster, A396, A39, DUNKERY BEACON 520 m 1,704 ft, B3223, Exford, B3224, A396, B R E N D O N H I L L S, B3190, TAUNTON, Barle, B3223, Exe, Dane's Brook, B3224, TIVERTON, WIMBLEBALL LAKE, Barle, Dulverton, B3222, TIVERTON

0 kilometers 5
0 miles 3

Taunton ❷

Somerset. 🏠 77,000. 🚄 🚌
ℹ️ The Library, Corporation St (01823 274 785). 🛒 Tue, Sat (livestock).

TAUNTON LIES at the heart of a fertile region famous for its apples and cider, but it was the prosperous wool industry that financed the massive church of **St. Mary Magdalene** (1488–1514) with its glorious tower. Taunton's **castle** was the setting for the notorious Bloody Assizes of 1685 when "Hanging" Judge Jeffreys dispensed harsh retribution on the Duke of Monmouth and his followers for an uprising against King James II (see pp52–3). The 12th-century building now houses the **Somerset County Museum**, covering local history. A star exhibit is the Roman mosaic from a villa at Low Ham, Somerset, showing the love story of Dido and Aeneas.

ENVIRONS: Created in 1903–8, **Hestercombe Garden** is one of Sir Edwin Lutyens' (see p25) and Gertrude Jekyll's (see p23) greatest surviving masterpieces.

🏛 **Somerset County Museum**
Castle Green. 📞 01823 255504.
🔲 Mon–Sat. 🔴 Dec 25, 26, Jan 1, Good Fri. 📷 ♿ ground floor only.
🌷 **Hestercombe Garden**
Cheddon Fitzpaine. 📞 01823 337222. 🔲 daily. 📷

SOMERSET CIDER

Somerset is one of the few English counties where real farmhouse cider, known as "scrumpy," is still made using the traditional methods. Cider once formed part of the farm worker's wages and local folklore has it that various unsavory additives, such as iron nails, were added to give strength. Cider-making can be seen at **Sheppy's** farm, on the A38 near Taunton.

Scrumpy cider

Wells ❸

Somerset. 🏠 10,000. 🚌 ℹ️ Market Place (01749 672552). 🛒 Wed, Sat.

WELLS IS NAMED after St. Andrew's Well, the sacred spring that bubbles up from the ground near the 14th-century **Bishop's Palace**, residence of the Bishop of Bath and Wells. A tranquil market town, Wells is famous for its magnificent cathedral, which was begun in the late 1100s. Pennyless Porch, where beggars once received alms, leads from the bustling market place to the calm of the cathedral close. **Wells Museum** has prehistoric finds from nearby Wookey Hole caves.

Cathedral clock (1386–92)

ENVIRONS: To the northeast of Wells lies the impressive cave complex of **Wookey Hole**, which has an extensive range of popular amusements.

🏛 **Wells Museum**
8 Cathedral Green. 📞 01749 673477.
🔲 Easter–Sep: daily; Oct–Easter: Wed–Sun. 🔴 Dec 24, 25. 📷
🦇 **Wookey Hole**
Off A371. 📞 01749 672243.
🔲 daily. 🔴 Dec 17–25. 📷 ♿

The West Front features 365 fine medieval statues of kings, knights and saints – many of them life-size.

The Vicars' Close, built in the 14th century for the Vicars' Choir, is one of the oldest complete streets in Europe.

The Chain Gate (1460)

Cloisters

Path leading around the moat

This graceful flight of steps curves up to the octagonal Chapter House, which has delicate fan vaulting dating from 1306. The 32 ribs springing from the central column create a beautiful palm tree effect.

Glastonbury Abbey, left in ruins in 1539 after the Dissolution

Glastonbury ❹

Somerset. 🏘 9,000. 🚉 ℹ Tribunal, High St (01458 832954). 🛒 Tue.

Sᴴʀᴏᴜᴅᴇᴅ in Arthurian myth and rich in mystical association, the town of Glastonbury was once one of the most important destinations for pilgrims in England. Now thousands flock here for the annual rock festival (see p63) and for the summer solstice on Midsummer's Day (June 21).

Over the years history and legend have become intertwined, and the monks who founded **Glastonbury Abbey,** around 700, found it profitable to encourage the association between Glastonbury and the mythical "Blessed Isle" known as Avalon – alleged to be the last resting place of King Arthur and the Holy Grail (see p269).

The great abbey was left in ruins after the Dissolution of the Monasteries (see pp50–51). Even so, some magnificent relics survive, including parts of the vast Norman abbey church, the unusual Abbot's Kitchen with its octagonal roof, and the wonderful abbey barn, now the **Somerset Rural Life Museum**.

Growing in the abbey grounds is a cutting from the famous Glastonbury thorn, which is said to have miraculously grown from the staff of Joseph of Arimathea. According to myth, he was sent in AD 60 to convert England to Christianity. The English hawthorn still astonishes everyone by flowering at Christmas as well as in May.

The **Lake Village Museum** has some interesting finds from the Iron Age lake settlements that once fringed the marshlands around **Glastonbury Tor**. A landmark seen for miles around, the Tor is a natural hill, crowned by the remains of a 14th-century church.

🏛 Somerset Rural Life Museum
Chilkwell St. 📞 01458 831197. ☐ Easter–Oct daily; Nov–Easter: Sun–Fri. ⬤ Dec 24–26, Jan 1, Good Fri. 🎟 ♿ limited.

🏛 Lake Village Museum
Tribunal, High St. 📞 01458 832954. ☐ daily. ⬤ Dec 25, 26. 🎟

Bishops' tombs circle the chancel. This sumptuous marble tomb in the south aisle is that of Bishop Lord Arthur Hervey, who was Bishop of Bath and Wells (1869–94).

The palace moat is home to swans that ring a bell by the gatehouse when they want to be fed. Feeding times are at 11am and 4pm.

The Bishop's Palace (1230–40)

WELLS CATHEDRAL AND THE BISHOP'S PALACE
The Close. 📞 01749 674483. ☐ daily. ♿ limited. **Bishop's Palace** 📞 01749 678691. ☐ Easter–Oct: Tue– Thu, Sun & public hols (Aug: daily). 🎟 ♿

Wells has maintained much of its medieval character with its cathedral, moated Bishop's Palace and other buildings around the close forming a harmonious group. The most striking features of the cathedral are the majestic west front and the massive "scissor arch" installed in 1338 to support the collapsing tower.

13th-century ruins of the Great Hall

Cheddar Gorge ⑤

ESCRIBED AS A "deep frightful chasm" by novelist Daniel Defoe in 1724, Cheddar Gorge is a spectacular ravine cut through the Mendip plateau by fast-flowing streams during the glacial phases of the last Ice Age. Cheddar has given its name to a rich cheese that originated here and is now produced worldwide. The caves in the gorge once provided the perfect environment of constant temperature and high humidity for storing and maturing the cheese.

VISITORS' CHECKLIST

on B3135. **ℹ** Cheddar Gorge
(01934 744071). **🚌** from Wells.
🅿 ♿ 🚻 🏪
**Cheddar Showcaves, Jacob's
Ladder & Museum** **☎** 01934
742343. **◯** daily. **●** Dec 24,
25. **♿** limited.
Chewton Cheese Dairy,
Chewton Mendip. **☎** 01761
241666. **◯** daily. **●** Dec 25,
26, Jan 1. **♿** limited.

*The Chewton Cheese Dairy
(12 km or 7 miles east along
the B3135) has demonstrations
of how traditional Cheddar
cheeses are made by hand (except
on Thursdays and Sundays).*

The B3135
road winds
round the base
of the 5-km
(3-mile) gorge.

"Cheddar Man," a 9,000-
year-old skeleton, is on
display in the museum.

A footpath follows
the top of the
gorge on its
southern edge.

Gough's Cave is
noted for its
cathedral-like
proportions.

**Tourist
information**

*The gorge is a narrow, winding
ravine with limestone rocks rising
almost vertically on either side
to a height of 120 m (400 ft).*

Cox's Cave
contains unusually
shaped stalactites
and stalagmites.

Jacob's Ladder
has 274 steps
leading to the
top of the gorge.

*The rare Cheddar
Pink is among the
astonishing range of
plant and animal life
harbored in the rocks.*

Prospect Tower has
far-reaching views over the
area to the south and west.

Bristol ❻

See pp242–3.

Bath ❼

See pp244–7.

Bradford-on-Avon ❽

Wiltshire. 🏛 9,500. 🚆 ℹ Bridge St (01225 865797). 🛒 Thu.

THIS LOVELY COTSWOLD-STONE town with its steep flagged lanes is full of flamboyant houses built by wealthy wool and cloth merchants in the 17th and 18th centuries. One fine Georgian example is **Church House**, on Church Street. A little farther along, **St. Laurence Church** is a remarkably complete Saxon building founded in 705 (*see p47*). The church was converted to a

Typical Cotswold-stone architecture in Bradford-on-Avon

school and cottage in the 12th century and was rediscovered in the 19th century when a vicar recognized the characteristic cross-shaped roof.

In the middle of the medieval **Town Bridge** is a small stone cell, built as a chapel in the 13th century but later used as a lockup for 17th-century drunks and vagrants. A short walk away, near converted mill buildings and a boat-filled stretch of the Kennet and Avon Canal, is the massive 14th-century **Tithe Barn** (*see pp28–9*).

🍺 **Tithe Barn**
Pound Lane. 🔓 *daily.* 🔴 *Dec 25, 26.* &

Corsham ❾

Wiltshire. 🏛 12,000. ℹ High St (02149 714660). 🛒 Tue.

THE STREETS of Corsham are lined with stately Georgian houses, which make it a delight for connoisseurs of Cotswold-stone architecture. **St. Bartholmew's Church** has an elegant spire and a lovely carved alabaster tomb (1960) to the late Lady Methuen, whose family founded Methuen publishers. The family acquired **Corsham Court** in 1745, with its picture gallery and a remarkable collection of Flemish, Italian and English paintings, including works by Van Dyck, Lippi and Reynolds. Peacocks wander through the grounds, adding their color and elegance to the façade of the 18th-century mansion.

Peacock in grounds, Corsham Court

🍺 **Corsham Court**
off A4. 🎫 *01249 712214.* 🔓 *Easter–Nov: Tue–Sun (pm); Jan–Easter: Tue–Thu, Sat, Sun (pm).* 🗓 &

Lacock ❿

Wiltshire. 🏛 1,000.

MAINTAINED in its pristine state by the National Trust, with very few modern intrusions, Lacock is a picturesque and delightful village to explore. The meandering River Avon forms the boundary to the north side of the churchyard, while humorous stone figures look down from **St. Cyriac Church**. Inside the 15th-century church is the splendid Renaissance-style tomb of Sir William Sharington (1495–1553). He acquired **Lacock Abbey** after the Dissolution of the Monasteries (*see pp50–51*), but it was a later owner, John Ivory Talbot, who had the buildings remodeled in the

Gothic revival style, in vogue in the early 18th century. The abbey is famous for the window (in the south gallery) from which his descendant William Henry Fox Talbot, an early pioneer of photography, took his first picture in 1835, and for the the sheets of snowdrops that cover the abbey grounds in spring. A 16th-century barn at the abbey gates has been converted to the **Fox Talbot Museum**, which has displays on Fox Talbot's experiments.

ENVIRONS: Designed by Robert Adam (*see pp24–5*) in 1769, **Bowood House** includes the laboratory where Joseph Priestley discovered oxygen in 1774, and a rich collection of sculpture, costumes and paintings. Italianate gardens surround the house, while the lake-filled grounds, landscaped by Capability Brown (*see pp22–3*), contain a Doric temple, grotto, cascade and now a large adventure playground.

🏛 **Lacock Abbey**
(NT) High St. 🎫 *01249 730227.* 🔓 *Apr–Oct: Wed–Mon (pm).* 🔴 *Good Fri.* 🗓 & *limited in house.*
🏛 **Fox Talbot Museum**
(NT) High St. 🎫 *01249 730459.* 🔓 *Apr–Oct: daily.* 🔴 *Good Fri.* 🗓 &
🍺 **Bowood House**
Derry Hill, nr Calne. 🎫 *01249 812102.* 🔓 *Mar–Oct: daily.* 🗓 &

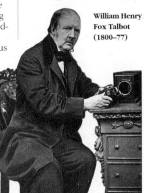

William Henry Fox Talbot (1800–77)

Bristol ❻

IT WAS IN 1497 that John Cabot sailed from Bristol on his historic voyage to North America. The city, at the mouth of the Avon, became the main British port for transatlantic trade, pioneering the era of the ocean-going steam liner with the construction of *S.S. Great Britain*. The city flourished as a major trading center, growing rich on the distribution of wine, tobacco and, in the 17th century, slaves.

King Brennus, St. John's Gate

Because of its docks and engine factories, Bristol was heavily bombed during World War II and the city center bears witness to the ideas of postwar planners. The docks have been shifted to deeper waters at Avonmouth and the old dock area is being transformed, taking on new life characterized by waterside cafés, shops and art galleries.

Exploring Bristol

The most interesting part of the city lies around Broad Street, King Street and Corn Street. There is a lively covered market, part of which occupies the **Corn Exchange**, built by John Wood the Elder *(see p244)* in 1743. Outside are the famous Bristol Nails, four bronze 16th–17th-century pedestals which Bristol merchants used as tables when paying for goods – hence the expression "to pay on the nail." **St. John's Gate**, at the head of Broad Street, has colorful medieval statues of Bristol's two mythical founders, King Brennus and King Benilus. Nearby between Lewins Mead and Colston Street, **Christmas Steps** is a steep lane lined with specialty shops. The **Chapel of the Three Kings** at the top was founded in 1504 and is now adjoined by the flamboyant Burgundian-style Foster's Almshouses of 1861–83.

A striking group of buildings around cobbled King Street include the 17th-century timber-framed **Llandoger Trow** inn.

The Two Sisters (c.1889) by Renoir, City Museum and Art Gallery

It is here that Daniel Defoe is said to have met Alexander Selkirk, whose true-life island exile served as the inspiration for Defoe's novel *Robinson Crusoe* (1719). Just up from here is the **Theatre Royal**, a rare survival of a Georgian playhouse, built in 1766.

Not far away the renowned **Arnolfini Gallery** on Narrow Quay is a showcase for contemporary art, drama, dance and film. In front, a statue of John Cabot (1425– c.1500) looks wistfully across the old Floating Harbour, which is now lined with cafés and pubs.

To the west of the city, the elegant suburbs of **Clifton** revel in ornate Regency crescents, many now used as lodgings or faculties of Bristol University. The impressive structure of **Clifton Suspension Bridge** complements the drama of the steep Avon gorge. Completed in 1864, the bridge is testimony to Brunel's

The bow of S.S. Great Britain

Memorial to William Canynge the Younger (1400–74)

engineering skill. **Bristol Zoo Gardens**, nearby, concentrates on breeding and conserving endangered species.

🛉 St. Mary Redcliffe

Redcliffe Way. 📞 0117 9291487. ⭘ *daily.* ♿

There are few better places to discover the history of Bristol than this magnificent 14th-century church, claimed by Queen Elizabeth I to be "the fairest in England." The church owes much to the generosity of William Canynge the Elder and Younger, both famous mayors of Bristol. Inscriptions on the tombs of merchants and sailors tell of lives devoted to trade in Asia and the West Indies. Look for the Bristol maze in the north aisle.

🏛 S.S. Great Britain

Gas Ferry Rd. 📞 0117 9260680. ⭘ *daily.* ⏺ *Dec 24, 25.* 💷 ♿ *limited.*

The *S.S. Great Britain*, designed by Isambard Kingdom Brunel, is the world's first large iron passenger ship and is a prototype of today's modern vessels. Launched in 1843, it traveled 32 times round the world before it was abandoned in the Falkland Islands in 1886. The wreckage was rescued and brought back to Bristol in 1970, and it now stands, being restored, in the dock where it was originally built. The ship is located next to the Maritime Heritage Centre and is an impressive reminder of the way Brunel revolutionized transportation in the 19th century.

🏚 Georgian House

7 Great George St. 📞 0117 9211362. ⭘ *Tue–Sat.* ⏺ *Dec 25, 26.* 💷

Life in a wealthy Bristol merchant's house of the 1790s is illustrated by Adam-style furnishings in the elegant drawing room and by a miscellany of pots, pans, roasting spits and laundry in the servants' area below stairs.

Warehouses overlooking the Floating Harbour

🏛 Bristol Industrial Museum

Prince's Wharf. 📞 0117 9251470. ◯ Tue–Sun & public hols. ● Dec 25, 26. 🎟 ♿

The museum's diverse collection of vehicles and models illustrate the astonishing range of products made in Bristol over the last 300 years. Among them are luxurious Bristol cars, the once ubiquitous Bristol bus, the world's first touring trailer and Concorde, represented here by a full-scale model of the pilot's cockpit.

🏛 City Museum and Art Gallery

Queen's Rd. 📞 0117 9223571. ◯ daily. ● public hols. 🎟 ♿ limited.

Numerous and varied collections include realistic stuffed tigers, impressive dinosaur fossils, Roman tableware, the largest collection of Chinese glass outside China and a fine collection of European paintings including works by Renoir and Bellini. Bristol artists include Sir Thomas Lawrence and Francis Danby.

✝ Bristol Cathedral

College Green. 📞 0117 9264879. ◯ daily. 🎟 ♿ limited.

Bristol's cathedral took an unusually long time to build. Rapid progress was made between 1298 and 1330, when the wonderfully inventive choir was built; the transepts and tower were finished in 1515, and another 350 years passed before the Victorian architect, G.E. Street, built the nave.

Humorous and eccentric medieval carving abounds – a small snail crawling across the stone foliage in the antechapel, musical monkeys in the 13th-century Elder Lady Chapel, and a famous set of wooden misericords in the choir.

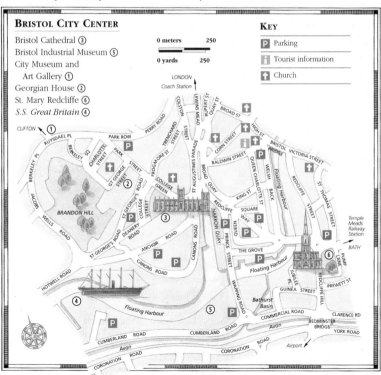

BRISTOL CITY CENTER

Bristol Cathedral ③
Bristol Industrial Museum ⑤
City Museum and Art Gallery ①
Georgian House ②
St. Mary Redcliffe ⑥
S.S. Great Britain ④

KEY

🅿 Parking
ℹ Tourist information
✝ Church

0 meters 250
0 yards 250

Street-by-Street: Bath ❼

BATH OWES ITS MAGNIFICENT Georgian townscape to the bubbling pool of water at the heart of the Roman Baths. The Romans transformed Bath into England's first spa resort and it regained fame as a spa town in the 18th century. At this time the two brilliant John Woods (Elder and Younger), both architects, designed the city's fine Palladian-style buildings. Many houses bear plaques recording the numerous famous people who have resided here.

The Circus
This is a daring departure from the typical Georgian square, by John Wood the Elder (1705–54

No. 1 Royal Crescent

No. 17 is where the 18th-century painter Thomas Gainsborough *(see p149)* lived.

Assembly Rooms and Museum of Costume

★ Royal Crescent
Hailed the most majestic street in Britain, this graceful arc of 30 houses (1767–74) is the masterpiece of John Wood the Younger. West of the Royal Crescent, Royal Victoria Park (1830) is the city's largest open space.

Jane Austen *(see p149)*, the writer, stayed at No. 13 Queen's Square on one of many visits to Bath in her youth.

Milsom Street and New Bond Street contain some of Bath's most elegant stores.

Theatre Royal (1805)

KEY

— — — Suggested route

0 meters   100

0 yards   100

STAR SIGHTS

★ Royal Crescent

★ Roman Baths

★ Bath Abbey

Pump Rooms
These tearooms once formed the social hub of the 18th-century spa community. They contain this decorative drinking fountain.

Pulteney Bridge
This charming bridge (1769–74), designed by Robert Adam, is lined with stores and links the center with the magnificent Great Pulteney Street. Watch out for the rare Victorian pillar-box on the east bank.

The Building of Bath Museum

★ **Roman Baths**
Built in the 1st century, this bathing complex is one of Britain's greatest memorials to the Roman era.

★ **Bath Abbey**
The splendid abbey stands at the heart of the old city in the Abbey Church Yard, a paved piazza enlivened by street musicians. Stone angels climbing Jacob's Ladder to heaven adorn its façade.

Holburne Museum and Crafts Study Centre

Parade Grounds
Courting couples came to this pretty riverside park for secret liaisons in the 18th century.

Sally Lunn's House (1482) is one of Bath's oldest houses.

Rail & coach stations

Exploring Bath

THE BEAUTIFUL AND COMPACT CITY OF BATH is set among the rolling green hills of the Avon valley, and wherever you walk you will enjoy spendid views of the surrounding countryside. The traffic-free heart of this lively city is full of street musicians, museums, cafés and enticing shops, while the elegant honey-colored Georgian houses, so characteristic of Bath, form an elegant backdrop to city life.

Piazza cellist

Bath Abbey, at the heart of the old city, begun in 1499

🔒 Bath Abbey

Abbey Churchyard. 🔳 01225 422462. ☐ daily. **Donation.** ♿
This splendid abbey was supposedly designed by divine agency. According to local legend the form of the church was dictated by God to Bishop Oliver King in a dream that has been immortalized in the wonderfully eccentric carvings on the west front. The bishop began work in 1499, rebuilding a church that had been founded in the 8th century. Memorials cover the walls and the Georgian inscriptions make fascinating reading, encapsulating the whole spectrum of society. The spacious interior is remarkable for the delicate lacelike fan vaulting of the nave, an addition made by Sir George Gilbert Scott in 1874.

🏛 Assembly Rooms and Museum of Costume

Bennett St. 🔳 01225 477789. ☐ daily. ● Dec 25, 26. 🎫 ♿
The Assembly Rooms were built by John Wood Jr. in 1769, as a meeting place for the fashionable elite and as an elegant backdrop for many glittering balls. Jane Austen's novel *Northanger Abbey* (1818) describes the atmosphere of gossip and flirtation here.
In the basements, kept dark to preserve the many precious textiles, is a collection of costumes in authentic period settings. The display illustrates changing fashions from the 16th century to the present day.

🏛 No. 1 Royal Crescent

Royal Crescent. 🔳 01225 428 126. ● mid-Dec–Feb, Good Fri. ☐ Tue–Sun & public hols. 🎫
This museum lets you look inside the first house of Bath's most beautiful terrace, giving a glimpse of what life was like for 18th-century aristocrats, such as the Duke of York, who lived here. The house is furnished down to such details as the dog-powered spit used to roast meat in front of the fire.

🏛 Holburne Museum and Crafts Study Centre

Great Pulteney St. 🔳 01225 466 669. ☐ daily (Nov–Easter: Tue–Sun). ● mid-Dec–mid-Feb. 🎫 ♿
This historic building is named after Thomas Holburne of Menstrie, (1793–1874) whose collections form the nucleus of the museum's impressive display of fine and decorative arts. Paintings by British artists such as Gainsborough and Stubbs can be seen together with 20th-century craftwork.

ROMAN BATHS MUSEUM

Stall St. 🔳 01225 477000. ☐ daily. ● Dec 25, 26. 🎫 ♿ limited.
According to legend, Bath owes its origin to the Celtic King Bladud who discovered the curative properties of its natural hot springs in 860 BC. Cast out from his kingdom as a leper, Bladud cured himself by imitating his swine and rolling in the hot mud at Bath.
In the first century, the Romans built baths around the spring, and a temple dedicated to the goddess Sulis Minerva, who combined the attributes of the water goddess Sulis, worshipped by the Celts, and the Roman goddess Minerva. Among the museum's Roman relics is a gilded bronze head of Sulis Minerva, discovered in 1727.
Medieval monks of Bath Abbey also exploited the springs' properties, but it was when Queen Anne visited in 1702–3 that Bath reached its zenith as a fashionable watering place.

Gilded bronze head of Sulis Minerva

🏛 Building of Bath Museum

The Paragon. 📞 01225 333895. 🕐 Tue–Sun & public hols. ● Dec 11–Feb 2. 🧷 ♿ limited.

This museum, housed in an old Methodist chapel, is an excellent starting point for exploring the city. It shows how, in the 18th century, Bath was transformed from a medieval wool town into one of Europe's most elegant spas. John Wood and his son designed the Classically inspired stone fronts of the Royal Crescent and the Circus, leaving individual property speculators to develop the houses behind. While the façades speak of harmony and order, the houses behind show the result of rampant individualism, with no two houses alike. The museum looks at every aspect of the buildings, from practical issues, such as heating, lighting and cooking, to fashionable whim.

🏛 American Museum

Claverton Manor, Claverton Down. 📞 01225 460503. 🕐 Apr–Oct: Tue–Sun & public hols. 🧷 ♿

Founded in 1961 in an attempt to deepen mutual understanding between Britain and America, this was the first American museum to be established in this country. Rooms in the 1820 manor house are decorated in various styles, from the first rudimentary dwellings of pioneering settlers to the opulent homes of the 19th century. There are special sections on Shaker furniture, quilts and Native American art, and a replica of George Washington's Mount Vernon garden of 1785.

A 19th-century American Indian weathervane

RICHARD "BEAU" NASH (1674–1762)

Elected in 1704 as Master of Ceremonies, "Beau" Nash played a crucial role in transforming Bath into the fashionable center of Georgian society. During his long career, he devised a never-ending round of games, balls and entertainment (including gambling) that kept the idle rich amused and ensured a constant flow of visitors.

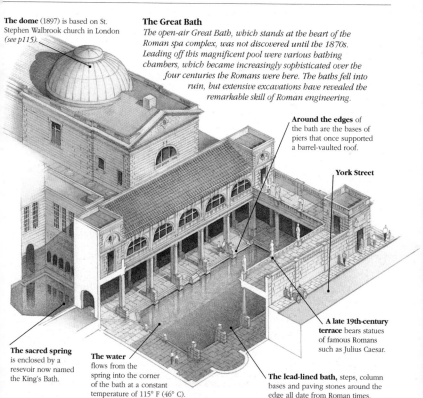

The dome (1897) is based on St. Stephen Walbrook church in London (see p115).

The Great Bath

The open-air Great Bath, which stands at the heart of the Roman spa complex, was not discovered until the 1870s. Leading off this magnificent pool were various bathing chambers, which became increasingly sophisticated over the four centuries the Romans were here. The baths fell into ruin, but extensive excavations have revealed the remarkable skill of Roman engineering.

Around the edges of the bath are the bases of piers that once supported a barrel-vaulted roof.

York Street

A late 19th-century terrace bears statues of famous Romans such as Julius Caesar.

The sacred spring is enclosed by a reservoir now named the King's Bath.

The water flows from the spring into the corner of the bath at a constant temperature of 115° F (46° C).

The lead-lined bath, steps, column bases and paving stones around the edge all date from Roman times.

Stonehenge  ⓫

BUILT IN SEVERAL STAGES from about 3000 BC, Stonehenge is Europe's most famous prehistoric monument. We can only guess at the rituals that took place here, but the alignment of the stones leaves little doubt that the circle is connected with the sun and the passing of the seasons, and that its builders possessed a sophisticated understanding of both arithmetic and astronomy. Despite popular belief, the circle was not built by the Druids, an Iron Age priestly cult that flourished in Britain from about 250 BC – more than 1,000 years after Stonehenge was completed.

Finds from a burial mound near Stonehenge (Devizes Museum)

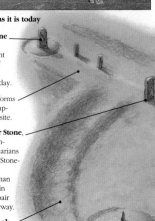

Stonehenge as it is today

The Heal Stone casts a long shadow straight to the heart of the circle on Midsummer's day.

The Avenue forms a ceremonial approach to the site.

The Slaughter Stone, named by 17th-century antiquarians who believed Stonehenge to be a place of human sacrifice, was in fact one of a pair forming a doorway.

The Outer Bank, dug around 3000 BC, is the oldest part of Stonehenge.

BUILDING OF STONEHENGE

Stonehenge's monumental scale is all the more impressive given that the only tools available were made of stone, wood and bone. The labor involved in quarrying, transporting and erecting the huge stones at Stonehenge was such that its builders must have been able to command immense resources, and control vast numbers of people.

RECONSTRUCTION OF STONEHENGE

This illustration shows what Stonehenge probably looked like about 4,000 years ago.

A sarsen stone was moved on rollers and levered into a pit.

With levers supported by timber packing, it was gradually raised.

The stone was then pulled upright by about 200 men hauling on ropes.

The pit round the b̶ was packed tightly w̶ stones and chalk.

WILTSHIRE'S OTHER PREHISTORIC SITES

The open countryside of the Salisbury Plain made this area an important center of prehistoric settlement, and today it is covered with many ancient remains. Ringing the horizon around Stonehenge are scores of circular barrows, or burial mounds, where members of the ruling class were honoured with burial close to the temple site. Ceremonial bronze weapons, jewelry and other finds excavated around Stonehenge and the other prehistoric sites in the area can be seen in the museums at Salisbury *(see pp250–51)* and Devizes.

Silbury Hill (NT) is Europe's largest prehistoric earthwork,

Silbury Hill

but despite extensive excavations its purpose remains a mystery. Built out of chalk blocks about 2750 BC, the hill covers 2 ha (5 acres) and rises to a height of 40 m (131 ft). Nearby **West Kennet Long Barrow** (NT) is the biggest

The Sarsen Circle was erected about 1500 BC and is capped by lintel stones held in place by mortice and tenon joints.

The Bluestone Circle was built about 2000 BC out of some 80 slabs quarried in south Wales. It was never completed.

Sarsen stone forming part of the Avebury Stone Circle

Avebury ⑫

Wiltshire. 600. Swindon then bus. The Great Barn Museum (01672 539425).

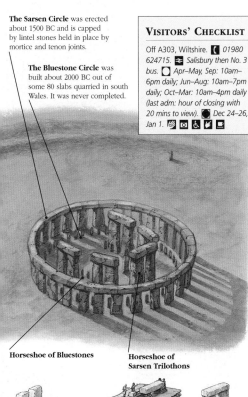

Horseshoe of Bluestones

Horseshoe of Sarsen Trilothons

Alternate ends of the lintel were levered up.

The weight of the lintel was supported by a timber platform.

The lintel was then levered sideways on to the uprights.

chambered tomb in England, with numerous stone-lined "rooms" and a monumental entrance. Built as a communal cemetery about 3250 BC, it was in use for several centuries – old bodies were taken away to make room for newcomers.

Old Sarum is set within the massive ramparts of this 1st-century Romano-British hill fort. The Norman founders of Old Sarum built their own motte and bailey castle inside this ready-made fortification, and the remains of this survive along with the foundations of the huge cathedral of 1075. Above ground nothing remains of the town that once sat within the ramparts. The town's occupants moved to the fertile

river valley site that became Salisbury during the early 12th century (see pp250–51).

Old Sarum
Castle Rd. (01722 335398. daily. Dec 24–26, Jan 1. limited.

The chambered tomb of West Kennet Long Barrow (c.3250 BC)

BUILT ABOUT 2500 BC, the **Avebury Stone Circle** (NT) surrounds the village of Avebury and was probably once some form of religious center. Superstitious villagers smashed many of the stones in the 18th century, believing the circle to have been a place of pagan sacrifice. The original form of the circle is best appreciated by a visit to the excellent **Alexander Keiller Museum**, which illustrates the construction of the circle and its relation to the other monuments in the region. Housed in a splendid thatched barn nearby is the **Museum of Wiltshire Rural Life**, which covers everything from cheese-making to shepherding.

St. James's Church has a Norman font carved with sea monsters and a rare 15th-century choir screen.

ENVIRONS: A few minutes drive east, **Marlborough** is an attractive town with a long and broad High Street lined with colonnaded Georgian shops.

Alexander Keiller Museum
(NT) High St. (01672 539250. daily. Dec 24–26, Jan 1.
Museum of Wiltshire Rural Life
The Great Barn Museum. (01672 539555. daily (mid-Nov–mid-Mar: Sat, Sun). Dec 25, 26.

Salisbury ⓭

S ALISBURY WAS FOUNDED IN 1220, when the old hill-top
settlement of Old Sarum *(see p249)* was abandoned,
being too arid and windswept, in favor of a new site
among the lush water meadows where the rivers Avon,
Nadder and Bourne meet. Creamy white limestone was
floated down the Nadder from Chilmark, 12 miles (20
km) west of Salisbury, for the construction of a new
cathedral which was built mostly in the early 13th
century, over the remarkable short space of 38 years.
Its magnificent landmark spire – the tallest in England –
was an inspired afterthought added in 1280–1310.

The 15th-century house of John
A'Port, Queen's Street

Bishop's Walk and a sculpture by Elisabeth Frink (1930–93), Cathedral Close

network of alleys fans out from
this point with a number of
fine timber-framed houses. In
the large bustling **Market
Place** the **Guildhall** is an unusual gray-brick building from
1788–95, used for civic functions. More attractive are the
brick and tile-hung houses on
the north side of the square,
many with Georgian façades
concealing medieval houses.

Exploring Salisbury
The spacious and tranquil
Close, with its schools, hospitals, theological colleges and
clergy housing, makes a fine
setting for Salisbury's cathedral. Among the numerous
elegant buildings here are the
Matrons' College, built in
1682 as a home for clergy
widows, and 13th-century
Malmesbury House, with its
splendid Queen Anne façade
(1719), fronted by lovely
wrought-iron gates. Other
buildings of interest include
the 13th-century **Deanery**,
the 15th-century **Wardrobe**,
now a regimental museum,
and the **Cathedral School**,
housed in the 13th-century
Bishop's Palace and famous
for the quality of its choristers.
Beyond the walls of the
Cathedral Close, Salisbury
developed its chessboard

layout, with areas devoted to
different trades, perpetuated
in street names such as Fish
Row and Butcher Row.
Leaving the close through
High Street Gate, you
reach the busy High Street
leading to the 13th-
century **Church of St.
Thomas**, which has a
lovely carved timber roof
(1450), and an early
16th-century Doom
painting showing Christ
seated in judgment and
demons seizing the
damned. Nearby on
Silver Street, **Poultry
Cross** was built in the
15th century as a
covered poultry
market. An intricate

The Cloisters are the largest
in England. They were added
between 1263 and 1284 in
the Decorated style.

The Chapter House
displays a copy of the
Magna Carta. Its walls
are decorated with scenes
from the Old Testament.

Choir stalls

The Trinity Chapel
contains the grave of St.
Osmund who was bishop of
Old Sarum from 1078–1099.

Bishop Audley's Chantry, a
magnificent 16th-century monument
to the bishop, is one of several small
chapels clustered around the altar.

FISH ROW

Street signs reflecting trades of
13th-century Salisbury

🏛 Mompesson House
(NT) The Close. ☎ *01722 335659.*
🕐 *Apr–Oct: Sat–Wed (pm).*
🖼 ⛁ limited.

Built by a wealthy Wiltshire family in 1701, the handsomely furnished rooms of this house give an indication of life for the Close's inhabitants in the 18th century. The delightful garden, bounded by the north wall of the Close, has fine herbaceous borders.

The graceful spire
soars to a height of
123 m (404 ft).

The West Front *is decorated by rows of lavish symbolic figures and saints in niches.*

A roof tour takes you up to an external gallery at the base of the spire with views of the town and Old Sarum.

Northwest transept

🏛 Salisbury and South Wiltshire Museum
The Close. ☎ *01722 322151.*
🕐 *Mon–Sat (Jul–Aug: daily).*
● *Dec 24–26.* 🖼 ⛁

In the medieval King's House, this museum has displays on early man, Stonehenge and nearby Old Sarum *(see p249).*

SALISBURY CATHEDRAL
The Close. ☎ *01722 328726.* 🕐 *daily.* **Donation.** ⛁
The cathedral was mostly built between 1220 and 1258. It is a fine example of the Early English style of Gothic architecture, typified by tall, sharply pointed lancet windows, and it is rare in being almost uniform in style.

The clock dating from 1386 is the oldest working clock in Britain.

The nave is divided into ten bays by columns of polished Purbeck marble.

Numerous windows add to the airy and spacious atmosphere of the interior.

ENVIRONS: The town of Wilton is renowned for its carpet industry, founded by the 8th Earl of Pembroke using French Huguenot refugee weavers. The town's ornate **church** (1844) is a brilliant example of Neo-Romanesque architecture, incorporating genuine Roman columns, Flemish Renaissance woodwork, German and Dutch stained glass and Italian mosaics.

Wilton House has been home to the Earls of Pembroke since it was converted from a convent after the Dissolution *(see pp50–51).* The house, largely rebuilt by Inigo Jones in the 17th century, includes one of the original Tudor towers, a fine collection of art and a landscaped park with a Palladian bridge (1737). The two glories of the house are the lavish Single and Double Cube State Rooms. Both have magnificently frescoed ceilings and gilded stucco work and were designed to hang a series of family portraits by Van Dyck.

🏛 Wilton House
Wilton. ☎ *01722 743115.*
🕐 *Easter–Oct: daily.* 🖼 ⛁

Double Cube room, designed by Inigo Jones in 1653

***The Longleat Tree* tapestry (1980) depicting a 400-year history**

Longleat House ⑭

Warminster, Wiltshire. 【 01985 844400. 🚂 Warminster then taxi. **House** ☐ daily. **Park** ☐ Easter–Oct. ☐ Dec 25. 🈲 ♿

THE ARCHITECTURAL HISTORIAN John Summerson coined the term "prodigy house" to describe the exuberance and grandeur of Elizabethan architecture that is so well represented at Longleat. The house was started in 1540, when John Thynn bought the ruins of a priory on the site of Longleat for the sum of £53. The work he began here was continued by each generation, and over the centuries subsequent owners have added their own eccentric touches; such as the Breakfast Room and Lower Dining Room (dating from the 1870s), modeled on the Venetian Ducal Palace, and erotic murals painted by the present owner, the 7th Marquess of Bath. Today, the Great Hall is the only remaining room that belongs to Thynn's time.

In 1948, the 6th Marquess was the first landowner in Britain to open his stately home to the public, in order to fund the maintenance and preservation of the house and its vast estate. The grounds, landscaped by Capability Brown *(see p23)*, were turned into an expansive safari park in 1966, where lions, tigers and other wild animals roam freely. This, along with other commercial additions such as the world's largest maze, the Adventure Castle, and a range of special events now draw even more visitors than the house.

Stourhead ⑮

STOURHEAD IS AMONG THE FINEST EXAMPLES of 18th-century landscape gardening in Britain *(see pp22–3)*. The garden was begun in the 1740s by Henry Hoare (1705–85), who inherited the estate and transformed it into a breathtaking work of art. Hoare created the lake, surrounding it with rare trees and plants, and Neo-Classical Italianate temples, grottoes and bridges. The Palladian-style house, built by Colen Campbell *(see p24)*, dates from 1724.

Pantheon
Hercules is among the statues of Roman gods housed in the elegant Pantheon (1753).

Gothic Cottage (1806)

Iron Bridge

The lake was created from a group of medieval fishponds. Hoare dammed the valley to form a single expanse of water.

Turf Bridge

Temple of Flora (1744)

A walk of 2 miles (3 km) around the lake provides a series of artistically contrived vistas.

★ **Temple of Apollo**
The Classical temples that dot the garden were all designed by architect Henry Flitcroft (1679–1769).

Grotto
Tunnels lead to an artificial cave with a pool and a life-size statue of the guardian of the River Stour, sculpted by John Cheere in 1748.

VISITORS' CHECKLIST

(NT) Stourton, Wiltshire.
01747 840348. Gillingham then taxi. **House** Apr–Oct: noon–5:30pm Sat–Wed (last adm: 5pm). **Gardens** 9am–7pm (or dusk if earlier) daily (last adm: 10 mins before closing). except in house. limited.

★ **Stourhead House**
Reconstructed after a fire in 1902, the house contains fine Chippendale furniture. The art collection reflects Henry Hoare's Classical tastes and includes The Choice of Hercules *(1637) by Nicolas Poussin.*

Colorful shrubs
around the house include fragrant rhododendrons in spring.

Stourton village was incorporated into Hoare's overall design.

The reception contains exhibitions illustrating the story of Stourhead.

Entrance and parking lot

St. Peter's Church
The parish church contains monuments to the Hoare family. The medieval monument nearby was brought from Bristol in 1765.

STAR SIGHTS

★ **Temple of Apollo**

★ **Stourhead House**

Shaftesbury ⑯

Dorset. ⚐ 6,000. ▤ ▯ 8 Bell St
(01747 853514). ⌂ Thu.

HILLTOP SHAFTESBURY, with its
cobbled streets and 18th-
century cottages is often used
as a setting for films and TV
commercials to give a flavor
of Old England. Picturesque
Gold Hill is lined on one side
by the wall of the demolished
abbey, founded by King
Alfred in 888. Only the excavated remains of the abbey
church survive, and a few
masonry fragments found
in the local history museum.

**The Almshouse (1437) adjoining
the Abbey Church, Sherborne**

Sherborne ⑰

Dorset. ⚐ 9,500. ▤ ▤ ▯ Digby
Rd (01935 815341). ⌂ Thu, Sat.

FEW OTHER TOWNS in Britain
have such a wealth of
unspoiled medieval buildings.
Edward VI *(see p40)* founded
the famous Sherborne School
in 1550, saving intact the
splendid **Abbey Church**, the
almshouse and other monastic
buildings that might otherwise
have been demolished after
the Dissolution *(see pp50–51)*.
Remains of the first Saxon
church can still be seen in the
abbey's façade, but the most
striking feature is the 15th-
century fan-vaulted ceiling.

Sherborne Castle, built for
Sir Walter Raleigh *(see pp50–
51)* in 1594, is a wonderfully
varied building that anticipates
the flamboyant Jacobean style.
Raleigh also lived briefly in
the early 12th-century **Old
Castle**, which is largely in
ruins, demolished by
Cromwell's supporters during
the Civil War *(see pp52–3)*.

ENVIRONS: West of Sherborne,
past Yeovil, is the magnificent
Elizabethan **Montacute House**
(see pp230–31), set in 120 ha
(300 acres) of grounds. It is
noted for its collections of
tapestries and 17th-century
samplers and for the Tudor
and Jacobean portraits on display in the vast Long Gallery.

⚜ Sherborne Castle
Off A30. ☎ 01935 813182.
◯ Easter–Sep: Thu, Sat, Sun &
public hols (pm). ⚑
⚜ Old Castle
Off A30. ☎ 01935 812730.
◯ Easter–Oct: daily; Nov–Easter: Wed–
Sun. ● Dec 25, 26, Jan 1. ⚑ ♿
▥ Montacute House
(NT) Montacute. ☎ 01935 823289.
◯ Apr–Oct: Wed–Mon (pm). ⚑

Abbotsbury ⑱

Dorset. ⚐ 400. ▯ West St (01305
871852).

THE NAME ABBOTSBURY recalls
the town's 11th-century
Benedictine abbey of which
little but the huge tithe barn,
built around 1400, remains.
Nobody knows when the
Swannery here was founded,
but the earliest record dates
to 1393. Mute swans come to
nest in the breeding season,
attracted by the reed beds
that spread along the Fleet, a
brackish lagoon protected
from the sea by

The Swannery at Abbotsbury

a high ridge of pebbles called
Chesil Bank *(see p228)*. Its
wild atmosphere makes an
appealing contrast to the south
coast resorts, although strong
currents make swimming too
dangerous. **Abbotsbury Sub-
Tropical Gardens** are the
frost-free home to many new
plants, discovered by botanists
traveling in South America
and Asia in the last 30 years.

⚑ Swannery
New Barn Rd. ☎ 01305 871684.
◯ Apr–Oct: daily. ⚑ ♿
**♣ Abbotsbury Sub-
Tropical Gardens**
Off B3157 ☎ 01305 871387.
◯ daily. ● Dec 25, 26, Jan 1. ⚑ ♿

Weymouth ⑲

Dorset. ⚐ 45,000. ▤ ▤ ▤
▯ Pavilion Complex, The Esplanade
(01305 785747). ⌂ Thu.

WEYMOUTH'S POPULARITY as
one of Britain's earliest
seaside resorts began in 1789
when George III paid the first
of many summer visits here.
The king's bathing machine
can be seen in the **Timewalk**

Weymouth Quay, Dorset's south coast

museum, and his statue is a prominent feature on the seafront esplanade. Here gracious Georgian terraces and hotels look across to the beautiful expanse of Weymouth Bay. Different in character is the old town around Custom House Quay with its fishing boats and old timber-framed seamen's inns.

🏛 **Timewalk**
Hope Sq. 📞 *01305 777622.* ⭕ *daily.* ⚫ *Dec 25, 26, 2 wks in Jan.* 🏷

Dorchester ⑳

Dorset. 👥 *15,000.* 🚊 ℹ *Antelope Walk (01305 267992).* 🏪 *Wed.*

D ORCHESTER, the county town of Dorset, is still recognizably the town that Thomas Hardy used as the background for his novel *The Mayor of Casterbridge* (1886). Here, among the many 17th-century and Georgian houses lining the High Street, is the **Dorset County Museum**, where the original manuscript of the novel is displayed, along with a reconstruction of Hardy's study. There are also finds from Iron Age and Roman sites on the outskirts of the town. **Maumbury Rings** (Weymouth Avenue), is a Roman amphitheatre, originally a Neolithic henge, while to the west of the

A 55 m (180 ft) giant carved on the chalk hillside, Cerne Abbas (NT)

town, many Roman graves have been found in a cemetery below the Iron Age hill fort, **Poundbury Camp**.

ENVIRONS: Just southwest of Dorchester, **Maiden Castle** *(see p43)* is a massive, awe-inspiring monument dating from about 100 BC. In AD 43 it was the scene for a battle as the Romans sought to conquer the Iron Age people of southern England.

To the north lies the charming village of **Cerne Abbas** with its magnificent medieval tithe barn and monastic buildings. The huge chalk-cut figure of a giant on the hillside here is a fertility figure thought to represent either the Roman hero-god Hercules or a 2,000-year-old Iron Age warrior.

East of Dorchester are the churches, thatched villages and rolling hills immortalized in Hardy's novels. Picturesque **Bere Regis** is the Kingsbere of *Tess of the D'Urbervilles*, where the tombs of the family whose name inspired the novel shelter beneath a fine roof in the Saxon **church**.

Hardy's Cottage is where the writer was born and **Max Gate** is the house he designed and lived in from 1885 until his death. Hardy's heart is buried alongside his family in the churchyard at **Stinsford** – his body was given a public funeral at Westminster Abbey in London *(see pp94–5).*

Hardy's statue, Dorchester

There are beautiful gardens *(see p231)* designed in the 1890s and a magnificent medieval hall at 15th-century **Athelhampton House**.

🏛 **Dorset County Museum**
High West St. 📞 *01305 262735.* ⭕ *Mon–Sat (Jul–Aug: daily).* ⚫ *Dec 25, 26.* 🏷 ♿ *ground floor only.*
🏚 **Hardy's Cottage**
(NT) Higher Bockhampton. 📞 *01305 262366.* **Grounds** ⭕ *Apr–Oct: Fri–Wed.* 🏷 ♿ **House** ⭕ *by appt.*
🏚 **Max Gate**
(NT) Arlington Ave, Dorchester. 📞 *01305 262538.* ⭕ *Apr–Sep: Sun, Mon & Wed (pm).* 🏷
🏚 **Athelhampton House**
Athelhampton. 📞 *01305 848363.* ⭕ *Apr–Oct: Tue–Thu, Sun & public hols (Jul–Aug: Sun–Fri).* 🏷 ♿ *to grounds.*

THOMAS HARDY (1840–1928)

The vibrant, descriptive novels and poems of Thomas Hardy, one of England's best-loved writers, are set against the background of his native Dorset. The Wessex country-side provides a constant and familiar stage against which his characters enact their fate. Vivid accounts of rural life record a key moment in history, when mechanization was about to destroy ancient farming methods, just as the Industrial Revolution had done in the towns a century before *(see pp54–5).* Hardy's power-fully visual style has made novels such as *Tess of the D'Urbervilles* (1891) popular with modern film-makers, and has drawn literary pilgrims to the villages and landscapes that inspired his fiction.

Nastassja Kinski in Roman Polanski's film *Tess* (1979)

Corfe Castle ㉑

(NT) Corfe Castle, Dorset. ☎ *01929 481294.* ☴ *Wareham or Swanage then bus.* ◻ *daily.* ● *Dec 25, 26.* ⛶ ♿ *limited.*

THE SPECTACULAR RUINS of Corfe Castle romantically crown a jagged pinnacle of rock above the charming un-spoiled village that shares its name. The castle has domi-nated the landscape since the 11th century, first as a royal fortification, then as the dra-matic ruins seen today. In 1635 the castle was purchased by Sir John Bankes, whose wife and her retainers – mostly women – courageously held out against 600 Parliamentary troops, in a six-week siege during the Civil War *(see pp52–3)*. The castle was eventually taken through trea-chery, and in 1646 Parliament voted to have it "slighted" – deliberately blown up with dynamite to prevent it from being used again. From the shattered ruins there are views over the Isle of Purbeck and its wonderful coastline.

The ruins of Corfe Castle, dating mainly from Norman times

Isle of Purbeck ㉒

Dorset. ☴ *Wareham.* ☴ *Shell Bay.* ℹ *Swanage (01929 422885).*

THE ISLE OF PURBECK, which is in fact a peninsula, is the source of the gray, shelly limestone, known as Purbeck marble, from which the castle and surrounding houses were built. The geology changes to the southwest at **Kimmeridge**, where the muddy shales are rich in fossils and recently discovered oil reserves. The Isle is fringed with wonderful unspoiled beaches. **Studland Bay** (NT)– with its clean white sand spreading in a great arc, and its sand-dune nature reserve, rich in birdlife – has been rated one of Britain's best beaches. Sheltered **Lulworth Cove** is almost encircled by white cliffs and there is a fine clifftop walk to Durdle Door *(see pp228–9)*, a natural chalk arch eroded by the waves.

The main resort in the area is **Swanage**, the port where Purbeck marble was trans-ported by ship to London, to be used for everything from street paving to church build-ing. Unwanted masonry from demolished buildings was shipped back, and this is how Swanage got its wonderfully ornate **Town Hall** façade, de-signed by Wren around 1668.

Poole ㉓

Dorset. ⚏ *135,000.* ☴ ◻ ☴ ℹ *The Quay (01202 673322).*

SITUATED ON ONE of the largest harbors in the world, Poole is an ancient, still thriv-ing, seaport. The quay is lined with old warehouses over-looking a safe sheltered bay, popular for water sports. The **Waterfront Museum**, partly housed in 15th-century cellars on the quay, tells the history of the port and town. A gallery in the museum is devoted to the history of the Boy Scout Movement – founded by Robert Baden-Powell after a trial camp was held on nearby **Brownsea Island** in 1907. Much of this island (reached

Beach adjoining Lulworth Cove, Isle of Purbeck

by boat from the quay) is given over to a woodland nature reserve with a waterfowl and heron sanctuary. Fine views of the Dorset coast add to the island's appeal.

🏛 **Waterfront Museum**
High St. 📞 01202 683138.
◐ daily. ● Dec 25, 26, Jan 1, Good Fri. 📷 ♿

🦋 **Brownsea Island**
(NT) Poole. 📞 01202 707744.
◐ Apr–Oct: daily. 📷 ♿ limited.

Boats in Poole harbor

Wimborne Minster ㉔

Dorset. 🏠 6,500. 🚉 🎫 29 High St (01202 886116). 🚩 Fri–Sun.

THE FINE COLLEGIATE CHURCH of Wimborne's **Minster** was founded in 705 by Cuthburga, sister of King Ina of Wessex. It fell prey to marauding Danish raiders in the 10th century, and the imposing gray church we see today dates from the refounding by Edward the Confessor (see pp48–9) in 1043. Freemasons made use of the local Purbeck marble, carving beasts, biblical scenes, and a mass of zigzag decoration.

The 16th-century **Priest's House Museum**, formerly the clergy's lodgings, has rooms furnished in the style of different periods.

ENVIRONS: Designed for the Bankes family after the destruction of Corfe Castle, **Kingston Lacy** was acquired by the National Trust in 1981. The estate has always been farmed by traditional methods and is astonishingly rich in

wildlife, rare flowers and butterflies. This quiet, forgotten corner of Dorset is grazed by rare Red Devon cattle and can be explored using paths and "green lanes" that date back to Roman and Saxon times. The fine 17th-century house at the center of the estate contains an outstanding collection of paintings, including works by Rubens, Velazquez and Titian.

🏛 **Priest's House Museum**
High St. 📞 01202 882533.
◐ Apr–Oct: Mon–Sat; Jun–Sep: daily; 2 wks over Christmas. 📷 ♿ limited.

🏰 **Kingston Lacy**
(NT) on B3082. 📞 01202 883402.
◐ Apr–Oct: Sat–Wed. ● Good Fri. 📷 ♿ gardens only.

Bournemouth ㉕

Dorset. 🏃 155,000. 🚉 ✈ 🎫 ℹ Westover Rd (01202 789789).

BOURNEMOUTH'S POPULARITY as one of England's favorite seaside resorts is due to an almost unbroken sweep of sandy beach, extending from the mouth of Poole Harbour to Hengistbury Head. Most of the seafront is built up, with many large seaside villas and exclusive hotels. To the west there are numerous clifftop parks and gardens, interrupted by beautiful wooded river ravines, known as "chines." The varied and colorful garden of **Compton Acres** was conceived as a museum of many different garden styles.

In central Bournemouth the amusement arcades, casinos, nightclubs and shops cater to the city's many visitors. During the summer, pop groups, TV comedians and the highly regarded Bournemouth

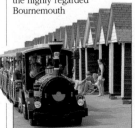

A toy train runs along the popular seafront at Bournemouth

Marchesa Maria Grimaldi **by Sir Peter Paul Rubens (1577–1640), Kingston Lacy**

Symphony Orchestra perform at the **Winter Gardens Theatre**, off Exeter Road. The **Russell-Cotes Art Gallery and Museum**, housed in a late Victorian villa, has an extensive collection with many fine Oriental and Victorian artifacts.

ENVIRONS: The magnificent **Christchurch Priory**, east of Bournemouth, is 95 m (310 ft) in length – the longest church in England. It was rebuilt between the 13th and 16th centuries and presents a sequence of different styles. The original nave, built around 1093, is an impressive example of Norman architecture, but the highlight is the intricate stone reredos, which features a Tree of Jesse, tracing the lineage of Christ. Next to the Priory are the ruins of a Norman **castle**.

Between Bournemouth and Christchurch, **Hengistbury Head** is well worth climbing for grassland flowers, butterflies and far-reaching sea views, while **Stanpit March**, which lies to the west of Bournemouth, is an excellent spot for viewing herons and a variety of other wading birds.

🌸 **Compton Acres**
Canford Cliffs Rd. 📞 01202 700 778. ◐ Mar–Oct: daily. 📷 ♿
🏛 **Russell-Cotes Art Gallery and Museum**
Russell-Cotes Rd. 📞 01202 551009.
◐ Tue–Sun. ● Dec 25, 26, Jan 1, Good Fri. 📷 ♿

DEVON AND CORNWALL

DEVON · CORNWALL

MILES OF MAGNIFICENTLY VARIED COASTLINE *dominate this magical corner of Britain. Popular seaside resorts alternate with secluded coves and unspoiled fishing villages rich in maritime history. In contrast there are lush, exotic gardens and the wild terrain of the moorland interior, dotted with tors and historic remains.*

Geographical neighbors, the counties of Devon and Cornwall are very different in character. Celtic Cornwall, with its numerous villages named after early Christian missionaries, is mostly stark and treeless at its center. In many places it is still scarred by the remains of tin and copper mining that has played an important part in the economy for some 4,000 years. Yet this does not detract from the beauty and variety of the coastline dotted with lighthouses and tiny coves, and penetrated by deep tidal rivers.

Devon, by contrast, is a land of lush pasture divided into a patchwork of tiny fields and threaded with narrow lanes, whose banks support a mass of flowers from the first spring primroses to summer's colorful mixture of campion, foxglove, oxeye daisies and blue cornflowers. The leisurely pace of rural life here, and in Cornwall, contrasts with life in the bustling cities. Exeter with its magnificent cathedral, historic Plymouth, elegant Truro and Elizabethan Totnes are urban centers brimming with life and character.

The spectacular coastline and the mild climate of the region attract families, boating enthusiasts and surfers. For those in search of solitude, the Southwest Coastal Path provides access to the more tranquil areas. There are fishing villages and harbors whose heyday was in the buccaneering age of Drake and Raleigh *(see pp50–51)*, and inland the wild moorland of Bodmin and Dartmoor, which provided inspiration for many romantic tales. Many of these are associated with King Arthur *(see p269)* who, according to legend, was born at Tintagel on Cornwall's dramatically contorted north coast.

Beach huts on Torquay's popular seafront

◁ Fishing boats in Port Isaac, on Cornwall's north coast

Exploring Devon and Cornwall

ROMANTIC MOORLAND dominates the inland parts of Devon and Cornwall, ideal walking country with few roads and magnificent views stretching for miles. By contrast the extensive coastline is indented by hundreds of sheltered river valleys, each one seemingly isolated from the rest of the world – one reason why Devon and Cornwall can absorb so many visitors and yet still seem uncrowded. Wise tourists get to know one small part of Devon or Cornwall intimately, soaking up the atmosphere of the region, rather than rushing to see everything in the space of a week.

KEY

	Highway
	Major road
	Minor road
	Scenic route
‑‑	Scenic path
	River
☼	Viewpoint

SIGHTS AT A GLANCE

Appledore ⑮
Barnstaple ⑯
Bideford ⑭
Bodmin ⑩
Buckfastleigh ㉒
Buckland Abbey ㉕
Bude ⑫
Burgh Island ㉓
Clovelly ⑬
Cotehele ㉖
Dartmoor pp280–81 ㉘
Dartmouth ⑳
Exeter ⑱
Falmouth ⑥
Fowey ⑨
Helston and the
    Lizard Peninsula ⑤
Lynton and Lynmouth ⑰
Morwellham Quay ㉗
Penzance ③
Plymouth ㉔
St. Austell ⑧
St. Ives ②
*St. Michael's Mount
    pp264–5* ④
Tintagel ⑪
Torbay ⑲
Totnes ㉑
Truro ⑦

Walks and Tours
Penwith Tour ①

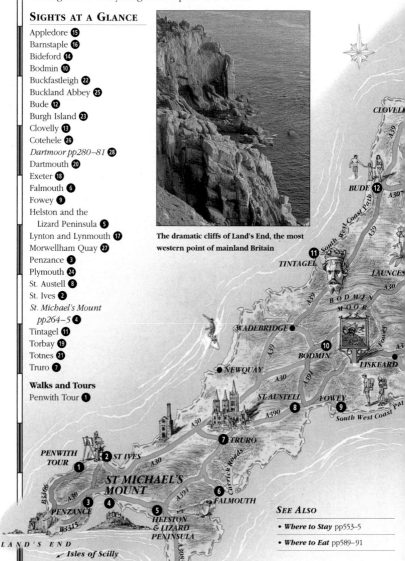

The dramatic cliffs of Land's End, the most western point of mainland Britain

SEE ALSO

- *Where to Stay* pp553–5
- *Where to Eat* pp589–91

Subtropical gardens at Torquay, the popular seaside resort

GETTING AROUND

Large numbers of drivers, many towing trailers, travel along the M5 highway and A30 trunk road from mid-July to early September. Driving here can be slow, especially on Saturdays. Once in Devon and Cornwall, allow plenty of time if you are traveling by car along the region's narrow and high-banked lanes.

The excellent train services, running from Paddington to Penzance, along Brunel's historic Great Western Railway, stop at most major towns. Aside from this, you are dependent on taxis or infrequent local buses.

Typical thatched, stone cottages, Buckland-in-the-Moor, Dartmoor

0 kilometers 15

0 miles 10

Penwith Tour ❶

THIS TOUR PASSES THROUGH a spectacular, remote Cornish landscape, dotted with relics of the tin mining industry, picturesque fishing villages and many prehistoric remains. The magnificent coastline varies between the gentle rolling moorland in the north and the rugged, windswept cliffs that characterize the dramatic south coast. The beauty of the area, combined with the clarity of light, has attracted artists since the late 19th century. Their works can be seen in Newlyn, St. Ives and Penzance.

TIPS FOR DRIVERS

Tour length: 31 miles (50 km)
Stopping-off points: There are pubs and cafés in most villages. Sennen Cove makes a pleasant mid-way stop. (See also pp636–7.)

Zennor ①
The carved mermaid in the church here recalls the legend of the mermaid who lured the local squire's son to her ocean lair.

Lanyon Quoit ②
One of many prehistoric monuments, this chambered tomb is visible on the left from the road to Madron.

Botallack Mine ⑧
Derelict enginehouses clinging to the cliffside are a vivid reminder of the region's former industry of tin-mining.

Trengwainton ③
These gardens are noted for their luxuriance (p230).

Land's End ⑦
Britain's most westerly point is noted for its dramatic and wild landscape. A local exhibition reveals it's history, geology and wildlife.

Minack Theatre ⑥
This Ancient Greek-style theater (1923) overlooks a magical bay of Porthcurno. It forms a magnificent backdrop for productions in summer.

Merry Maidens ⑤
This Bronze Age stone circle is said to be 19 girls turned to stone for dancing on Sunday.

Newlyn ④
Cornwall's largest fishing port gave its name to a school of artists founded in the 1880s (p264). Examples of their work can be seen in the art gallery here.

Map labels: ST IVES, Morvah, B3306, B3318, St Just, Madron, A3071, PENZANCE, A30, B3306, B3283, Sennen Cove, A30, B3283, B3315, Mousehole, Lamorna, B3315, Porthcurno, A30, B3315

KEY

▨▨▨	Tour route
═══	Other roads
☀	Viewpoint

0 kilometers 3
0 miles 2

St. Ives ②

Cornwall. 🚶 11,000. 🚉 🚌
ℹ️ Street-an-Pol (01736 796297).

S⊤. IVES is internationally renowned for the **Barbara Hepworth Museum** and the **Tate Gallery**, which together celebrate the work of a group of young painters, potters and sculptors who set up a seaside art colony here in the 1920s. The Tate, designed to frame a panoramic view of Porthmeor Beach, reminds visitors of the natural surroundings that inspired the art exhibited within. The Barbara Hepworth Museum presents the sculptor's work in the house and garden where she lived and worked for many years. The studios are full of sculptors' paraphernalia, while the subtropical garden is laid out as an art gallery.

The Lower Terrace, Tate Gallery

The town of St. Ives remains a typical English seaside resort, surrounded by a crescent of golden sands. Popular taste rules in the town's many other art galleries tucked down winding alleys with names such as Teetotal Street, a legacy of the town's Methodist heritage. Many galleries are converted cellars and lofts where fish were once salted and packed. In between are whitewashed cottages with tiny gardens brimming with marigolds, geraniums, sunflowers and trailing lobelia, their vibrant colors made all the more intense by the unusually clear light that first attracted artists to St. Ives.

🏛 **Barbara Hepworth Museum**
Barnoon Hill. 📞 01736 796226.
⭕ Apr–Oct: daily; Nov–Mar: Tue–Sun. ⬤ Dec 25, 26, Jan 1. 🎟
🏛 **Tate Gallery**
Porthmeor Beach. 📞 01736 796226.
⭕ Apr–Oct: daily; Nov–Mar: Tue–Sun & public hols. ⬤ Dec 24–26, Jan 1. 🎟 ♿

TWENTIETH-CENTURY ARTISTS OF ST. IVES

Ben Nicholson and Barbara Hepworth formed the nucleus of a group of artists that made a major contribution to the development of abstract art in Europe. In the 1920s, St. Ives together with Newlyn *(see p262)* became a place for aspiring artists. Among the prolific artists associated with the town are the potter Bernard Leach (1887–1979) and the painter Patrick Heron (b.1920) whose *Coloured Glass Window (see p226)* dominates the Tate Gallery entrance. Much of the art displayed at the Tate is abstract and illustrates new responses to the rugged Cornish landscape, the human figure and the everchanging patterns of sunlight on sea.

John Wells's *(b.1907) key interests are in light, curved forms and birds in flight, as revealed in* Aspiring Forms *(1950).*

Barbara Hepworth *(1903–75) was one of the foremost abstract sculptors of her time.* Madonna and Child *(1953) can be seen in the church of St. Ia.*

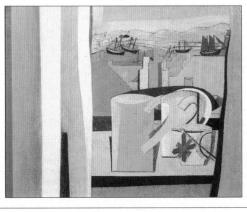

Ben Nicholson's *(1894–1982) work shows a change in style from simple scenes, such as the view from his window, to a preoccupation with shapes – as seen in this painting* St. Ives, Cornwall *(1943–5). Later, his interest moved toward pure geometric blocks of color.*

Penzance ➌

Cornwall. 🚶 15,000. 🚉 🚌 ⛴
ℹ Station Rd (01736 62207).

PENZANCE IS A BUSTLING resort
with a climate so mild that
palm trees and subtropical
plants grow happily in the lush
Morrab Gardens. The town
commands fine views of St.
Michael's Mount and a great
sweep of clean sandy beach.

The main road through the
town is Market Jew Street, at
the top of which stands the
magnificent domed Market
House (1837), fronted by a
statue of Sir Humphrey Davy
(1778–1829). Davy, who came
from Penzance, invented the
miner's safety lamp, which
detected lethal gases.

Chapel Street is lined with
curious buildings, none more
striking than the flamboyant

Egyptian House (1835), with
its richly painted façade and
lotus bud decoration. Just as
curious is **Admiral Benbow
Inn** (1696), on the same street,
which has a pirate looking out
to sea perched on the roof.
Opposite is a small **Maritime
Museum** displaying items
recovered from ancient wrecks.
The town's **Museum and Art
Gallery** has pictures by the
Newlyn School of artists.

ENVIRONS: A short distance
south of Penzance, **Newlyn**
(see p262) is Cornwall's largest
fishing port, which has given
its name to the local school of
artists founded by Stanhope
Forbes (1857–1947). They
painted outdoors, aiming to
capture the fleeting impres-
sions of wind, sun and sea.
Continuing south, the coastal
road ends at **Mousehole**

The Egyptian House (1835)

(pronounced Mowzall), a
pretty, popular village with a
tiny harbor, tiers of cottages
and a maze of narrow alleys.

North of Penzance, over-
looking the magical Cornish
coast, **Chysauster** is an
impressive example of a

St. Michael's Mount ➍

(NT) Marazion, Cornwall. ☎ 01736
710507. 🚢 from Marazion
(Apr–Oct). ◗ Apr–Oct: Mon–Fri;
Jun–mid Sep: daily; Nov–Mar: guided
tours only. ◗ Dec 25, 26. 🎟

ST. MICHAEL'S MOUNT emerges
dramatically from the waters
of Mount Bay, opposite the
small village of Marazion.

According to ancient Roman
historians, the mount was the
island of Ictis, an important
center for the Cornish tin
trade during the Iron Age. It
is dedicated to the archangel
St. Michael, who, according to
legend, appeared here in 495.

When the Normans con-
quered England in 1066 *(see
pp46–7)*, they were struck by
the island's resemblance to
their own Mont-St-Michel,
whose Benedictine monks
were invited to build a small
abbey here. The abbey was
absorbed into a fortress at the
Dissolution of the Monasteries
(see pp50–51), when Henry
VIII set up a chain of coastal
defenses to counter an expected attack from France.

In 1659 St. Michael's Mount
was purchased by Sir John St.
Aubyn whose descendants
subsequently turned the fortress into a magnificent house.

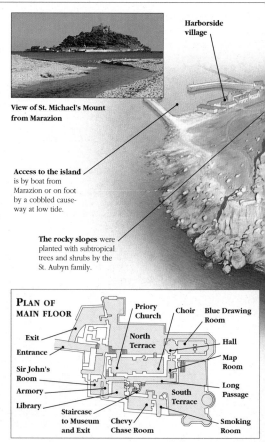

Harborside village

View of St. Michael's Mount
from Marazion

Access to the island
is by boat from
Marazion or on foot
by a cobbled cause-
way at low tide.

The rocky slopes were
planted with subtropical
trees and shrubs by the
St. Aubyn family.

PLAN OF MAIN FLOOR

Priory Church
Choir
Blue Drawing Room
Exit
North Terrace
Hall
Entrance
Map Room
Sir John's Room
Armory
South Terrace
Long Passage
Library
Staircase to Museum and Exit
Chevy Chase Room
Smoking Room

Romano-British village built in the 2nd century. The site has remained almost undisturbed since it was abandoned in the 3rd century. The moorland around the village is carpeted in rare wild flowers in spring.

From Penzance, regular boat and helicopter services depart for the **Isles of Scilly**, a beautiful archipelago forming part of the same granite mass as Land's End, Bodmin Moor and Dartmoor. Along with tourism, flower growing forms the main source of income here.

🏛 **Maritime Museum**
19 Chapel St. 📞 *01736 68890.*
⬤ *Easter–Oct Mon–Sat.* 🎟
🏛 **Museum and Art Gallery**
Morrab Rd. 📞 *01736 63625.* ⬤
Mon–Sat. ⬤ *some public hols.* 🎟 ♿
♟ **Chysauster**
Off B3311. 📞 *01736 61889.*
⬤ *Apr–Oct: daily.* 🎟

THE GROWTH OF METHODISM

The hard working and independent mining and fishing communities of the West Country had little time for the established church, but they were won over by the new Methodist religion, with its emphasis on hymn singing, outdoor preaching and regular or "methodical" Bible reading. When John Wesley, the founder of Methodism, made his first of many visits to the area in 1743, sceptical Cornishmen pelted him with stones. His persistence, however, led to many conversions and by 1762 he was preaching to congregations of up to 30,000 people. Simple places of worship were built throughout the county; one favored spot was the amphitheater **Gwennap Pit**, at Busveal, south of Redruth. Methodist memorabilia can be seen in the Royal Cornwall Museum in Truro *(see p267)*.

John Wesley (1703–91)

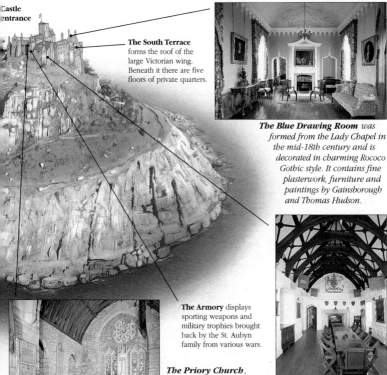

Castle entrance

The South Terrace forms the roof of the large Victorian wing. Beneath it there are five floors of private quarters.

The Blue Drawing Room was formed from the Lady Chapel in the mid-18th century and is decorated in charming Rococo Gothic style. It contains fine plasterwork, furniture and paintings by Gainsborough and Thomas Hudson.

The Armory displays sporting weapons and military trophies brought back by the St. Aubyn family from various wars.

The Priory Church, rebuilt in the late 14th century, forms the summit of the island. Beautiful rose windows are found at both ends.

The Chevy Chase Room takes its name from a plaster frieze (1641) representing hunting scenes.

Pinnacles of serpentine rock at Kynance Cove (NT), Lizard Peninsula

Helston and the Lizard Peninsula ❺

Cornwall. 🚌 from Penzance. 🛈 79 Meneage St (01326 565431).

THE ATTRACTIVE TOWN of Helston makes a good base for exploring the windswept upland and unusual coastline of the Lizard Peninsula. The town is famous for its Furry Dance, which welcomes spring with dancing through the streets *(see p62)*, and the **Folk Museum** explains the history of this ancient custom. The elegant Georgian houses and inns of Coinagehall Street are a reminder that Helston was once a thriving stannary town where tin ingots were brought for weighing and stamping before they could be sold. Locally mined tin was brought down river to a harbor at the bottom of this street until access to the sea was blocked in the 13th century by a sand and shingle bar, which formed across the estuary. The bar created the freshwater lake, Loe Pool, and there is an attractive walk skirting its wooded shores. In 1880, Helston's trade was taken over by a new harbor created to the east on the River Helford, at Gweek. Today, Gweek is the home of the **Cornish Seal Sanctuary**, where sick and injured seals are nursed back to health before being released again into the sea.

Cornwall's tin mining industry, from Roman times to the present day, is exhibited at the **Poldark Mine** where underground tours reveal the working conditions of miners in the 18th century. Another major attraction is **Flambards Village Theme Park,** with its recreation of a Victorian village and of Britain during the Blitz.

Farther south the modernistic receiver dishes of a satellite station rise spectacularly from the heathland. The **BT Satellite Station** visitors' center here explores the world of satellite communications.

Shops in the area sell souvenirs carved from serpentine, a soft greenish stone that forms the pinnacles and unusual shaped rocks that rise from the clean white beach at picturesque **Kynance Cove**.

🏛 **Folk Museum**
Old Butter Market, Helston. 📞 01326 564027. ⬭ Mon–Sat. ⬤ public hols.
🦭 **Cornish Seal Sanctuary**
Gweek. 📞 01326 221361. ⬭ daily. ⬤ Dec 25. 🎦 ⅼ
🏛 **Poldark Mine**
Wendron. 📞 01326 573173.
⬭ Easter–Oct: daily. 🎦
🏛 **Flambards Village Theme Park**
Culdrose Manor, Helston. 📞 01326 573404. ⬭ Easter– Oct: daily. 🎦 ⅼ
🏛 **BT Satellite Station**
Goonhilly Downs, off B3293.
📞 01326 221333. ⬭ Easter–Oct: daily. 🎦 ⅼ

Falmouth ❻

Cornwall. 🏠 18,000. 🚆 🚌 ⛴ 🛈 28 Killigrew St (01326 312300).

FALMOUTH stands at the point where seven rivers flow into a long stretch of water called the **Carrick Roads**. The drowned river valley is so deep that huge ocean-going ships can sail up almost as far as Truro. Numerous creeks are ideal for boating excursions to view the varied scenery and birdlife. Falmouth's beautiful sheltered harbor forms the most interesting part of this popular seaside resort. Its many old houses include the striking **Customs House** and the chimney alongside, known as the "King's Pipe" because it was used for burning contraband tobacco seized from smugglers in the 19th century.

CORNISH SMUGGLERS

In the days before income tax was invented, the main form of government income came from tax on imported luxury goods, such as brandy and perfume. Huge profits were to be made by evading these taxes, which were at their height during the Napoleonic Wars (1780–1815). Remote Cornwall, with its coves and rivers penetrating deep into the mainland, was prime smuggling territory; estimates put the number of people involved, including women and children, at 100,000. Some notorious families resorted to deliberate wrecking, setting up deceptive lights to lure vessels onto the sharp rocks, in the hope of plundering the wreckage.

Pendennis Castle and St. Mawes Castle, which stands opposite, were built by Henry VIII to protect the entrance of Carrick Roads.

ENVIRONS: To the south, **Glendurgan** *(see p230)* and **Trebah** gardens are both set in sheltered valleys leading down to delightful sandy coves on the River Helford.

Ship's figurehead, Falmouth

♠ **Pendennis Castle**
The Headland. 📞 *01326 316594.*
⭘ *daily.* ⬤ *Dec 24–26, Jan 1.* 💷
⬇ *limited*

♣ **Glendurgan**
(NT) Mawnan Smith. 📞 *01326 250906.* ⭘ *Mar–Oct: Tue–Sat & public hols.* ⬤ *Good Fri.* 💷

♣ **Trebah**
Mawnan Smith. 📞 *01326 250448.*
⭘ *daily.* 💷 ⬇

Truro ⑦

Cornwall. 👥 *18,000.* 🚉 🚌
ℹ *Boscawen St (01872 74555).*
🛒 *Wed (cattle).*

ONCE A market town and port, Truro is now the administrative capital of Cornwall. The town's many

gracious Georgian buildings reflect Truro's prosperity during the tin mining boom of the 1800s. In 1876 the new diocese of Truro was created and the 16th-century parish church was rebuilt to create the first new **cathedral** to be built in England since Wren built St. Paul's *(see pp116–17)* in the 17th century. With its noble central tower, tall lancet windows and numerous spires, the cathedral is an exuberant building that looks more French than English.

Truro's cobbled streets and numerous alleys lined with craft shops are a delight to explore. The **Royal Cornwall Museum** provides an excellent introduction to the county with displays on mining, Methodism *(see p265)*, smuggling and archaeology. The art collection includes Impressionist-style pictures by artists of the New-lyn School *(see p263)*.

ENVIRONS: On the outskirts of the city lie **Trewithen** and **Trelissick** gardens *(see pp230–31)*. The former has a rich collection of Asiatic plants.

🏛 **Royal Cornwall Museum**
River St. 📞 *01872 72205.* ⭘ *Mon–Sat.* ⬤ *public hols.* 💷 ⬇

♣ **Trewithen**
Grampound Rd. 📞 *01726 882763.*
⭘ *Mar–Sep: Mon–Sat.* 💷 ⬇

♣ **Trelissick**
(NT) Feock. 📞 *01872 862090.*
⭘ *Mar–Oct: daily.* ⬤ *Dec 24–26.*
💷 ⬇

The "Cornish Alps": china-clay dumps north of St. Austell

St. Austell ⑧

Cornwall. 👥 *20,000.* 🚉 🚌
ℹ *BP Filling Station, Southbourne Rd (01726 76333).* 🛒 *Fri–Sun.*

THE BUSY INDUSTRIAL town of St. Austell is the capital of the local china-clay industry, which rose to importance in the 18th century. Clay is still a vital factor in Cornwall's economy; China is the only other place in the world where such quality and quantity of clay can be found. The dumps are a prominent feature of the surrounding landscape. Viewed on a sunny day they look like snow-covered peaks, meriting the humorous local name, the "Cornish Alps."

ENVIRONS: The process of extracting and refining china-clay is explained at the **Wheal Martyn Museum**. Trails weave through a clay pit and works that operated from 1878 until the 1920s. The water-wheels and pumps have been restored and the old tunnels and dumps have been colonized by a variety of wildlife.

🏛 **Wheal Martyn Museum**
Carthew. 📞 *01726 850362.*
⭘ *Easter–Oct: daily.* 💷 ⬇ *limited.*

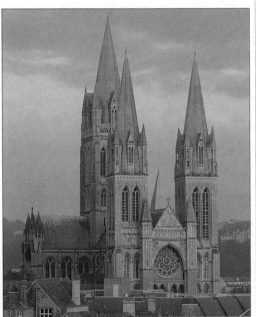

Truro Cathedral, designed by J.L. Pearson and completed in 1910

View of Polruan across the estuary from Fowey

Fowey ⑨

Cornwall. 🏘 2,000. 🚢 🅸 4
Custom House Hill (01726 833616).

FOWEY (pronounced Foy), has been immortalized under the name of Troy Town in the humorous novels of Sir Arthur Quiller-Couch (1863–1944), who lived here in a house called **The Haven**. A resort favored by many wealthy Londoners with a taste for yachting and expensive

DAPHNE DU MAURIER

The period romances of Daphne du Maurier (1907–89) are inextricably linked with the wild Cornish landscape where she grew up. *Jamaica Inn* established her reputation in 1936, and with the publication of *Rebecca* two years later she found herself one of the most popular authors of her day. *Rebecca* was made into a film directed by Alfred Hitchcock, starring Joan Fontaine and Lord Laurence Olivier.

seafood restaurants, Fowey is the most gentrified of the Cornish seaside towns. The picturesque charm of the flower-filled village is undeniable, with its tangle of tiny steep streets and its views across the estuary to Polruan. The church of **St. Fimbarrus** marks the end of the ancient Saint's Way footpath from Padstow – a reminder of the many Celtic missionaries who arrived on the shores of Cornwall to convert people to Christianity. Its flower-lined path leads to a majestic porch and richly carved tower. Inside there are some fine 17th-century memorials to the Rashleigh family whose seat, Menabilly, became Daphne du Maurier's home and featured as Manderley in *Rebecca* (1938).

ENVIRONS: For a closer look at the town of **Polruan** and the ceaseless activity of the harbor, there are a number of river trips up the little creeks. At the mouth of the plaster there is a set of twin towers from which chains were once hung to demast invading ships – a simple but effective form of defense.

A fine stretch of coast leads farther east to the picturesque fishing villages of **Polperro**, nestling in a narrow green ravine, and neighboring **Looe**.

Upriver from Fowey is the tranquil town of **Lostwithiel**. Perched on a hill just to the north are the remains of the Norman **Restormel Castle**.

⚑ Restormel Castle
Lostwithiel. 📞 01208 872687. ◻ Easter–Sep: daily. 🎟

Bodmin Moor ⑩

Cornwall. 🚆 Bodmin Parkway.
🚌 Bodmin. 🅸 Mount Folly Sq, Bodmin (01208 76616).

BODMIN, CORNWALL'S CAPITAL, lies on the sheltered western edge of the great expanse of moorland that shares its name. The history and archaeology of the town and moor is covered by **Bodmin Town Museum**, while **Bodmin Jail**, where public executions took place until 1909, has been turned into a gruesome tourist attraction. The churchyard is watered by the ever-gushing waters of a holy spring, and it was here that St. Guron established a Christian cell in the 6th century. The **church** itself is dedicated to St. Petroc, an influential Welsh missionary who founded a monastery here in the same period, as well as many others in the region. The monastery has disappeared, but the bones of St. Petroc remain, housed in a splendid 12th-century ivory casket in the church.

Jamaica Inn, Bodmin Moor

South of Bodmin is the **Lanhydrock** estate. Amid its extensive wooded acres and formal gardens *(see p231)* lies the massive house, rebuilt after a fire in 1881, but retaining some Jacobean features. The labyrinth of corridors and rooms illustrates life in a Victorian manor house and the fine 17th-century plaster ceiling in the Long Gallery depicts scenes from the Bible.

The lonely, desolate wilderness of Bodmin Moor is noted for its extensive network of prehistoric field boundaries. The main attraction, however, is the 18th-century **Jamaica Inn**, made famous by Daphne du Maurier's well-known tale of smuggling and romance. Today there is a restaurant and bar based on du Maurier's novel, and a small museum.

A 30-minute walk from the Inn is **Dozmary Pool**, reputed to be bottomless until it dried up in the drought of 1976. According to legend, the sword

The ruins of Tintagel Castle on the north coast of Cornwall

Excalibur was thrown into the pool after King Arthur's mortal wounding, when a hand rose from the lake to seize it.

To the east is the charming moorland village of **Altarnun**. Its spacious 15th-century church of **St. Nonna** is known as the "Cathedral of the Moor."

🏛 **Bodmin Town Museum**
Mt. Folly Sq, Bodmin. 📞 01208 74159.
🔘 Easter–Oct: Mon–Sat, Good Fri.
⬤ public hols. 🚻 limited.
🏛 **Bodmin Jail**
Berrycombe Rd, Bodmin. 📞 01208 76292. 🔘 daily. ⬤ Dec 25. 🌃
🏰 **Lanhydrock**
(NT) Bodmin. 📞 01208 73320.
House 🔘 Apr–Oct: Tue–Sun & public hols. **Gardens** 🔘 daily. 🌃 🚻 limited.

Tintagel ⓫

Cornwall. 🚶 1,700. 🚃 Thu (summer).

THE ROMANTIC and mysterious ruins of **Tintagel Castle**, built around 1240 by Earl Richard of Cornwall, sit high on a hilltop surrounded by crumpled slate cliffs and yawning black caves. Access to the castle is by means of two steep staircases clinging to the cliffside where pink thrift and purple sea lavender abound.

The earl was persuaded to build in this isolated, windswept spot by the popular belief, derived from Geoffrey of Monmouth's fictitious

History of the Kings of Britain, that this was the birthplace of the legendary King Arthur.

Large quantities of fine eastern Mediterranean pottery dating from around the 5th century have been discovered, indicating that the site was an important trading center, long before the medieval castle was built. Whoever lived here, perhaps the ancient Kings of Cornwall, could evidently afford a luxurious lifestyle.

A clifftop path leads from the castle to Tintagel's **church** which has Norman and Saxon masonry. In Tintagel village the **Old Post Office** is a rare example of a 14th-century Cornish longhouse, beautifully restored and furnished with 17th-century oak furniture.

ENVIRONS: A short distance to the east, **Boscastle** is another pretty National Trust village. The River Valency runs down the middle of the main street to the fishing harbor, which is sheltered from the sea by high slate cliffs. Access from the harbor to the sea is via a channel cut through the rocks.

🏰 **Tintagel Castle**
Off High St. 📞 01840 770328.
🔘 daily. ⬤ Dec 25, 26, Jan 1. 🌃
🏰 **Old Post Office**
(NT) Fore St. 📞 01840 770024.
🔘 Apr–Oct: daily. 🌃

KING ARTHUR

Historians think the legendary figure of King Arthur has some basis in historical fact. He was probably a Romano-British chieftain or warrior who led British resistance to the Saxon invasion of the 6th century (see pp46–7). Geoffrey of Monmouth's History of the Kings of Britain (1139) introduced Arthur to literature with an account of the many legends connected with him – how he became king by removing the sword Excalibur from a stone, his final battle with the treacherous Mordred, and the story of the Knights of the Round Table (see p156). Other writers, such as Alfred Lord Tennyson, took up these stories and elaborated on them.

King Arthur, from a 14th-century chronicle by Peter of Langtoft

Bude ⓬

Cornwall. 🚶 8,000. ℹ The Crescent car park (01288 354240). 🚃 Fri (summer).

WONDERFUL beaches around this area make Bude a popular resort for families. The expanse of clean golden sand that attracts visitors today once made Bude a bustling port. Shelly, lime-rich sand was transported along a canal to inland farms where it was used to neutralize the acidic soil. The canal was abandoned in 1880 but a short stretch survives, providing a haven for birds such as kingfishers and herons.

Kingfisher

Clovelly ⓭

Devon. 🏠 350. 🕿 01237 431781.
Town & Visitors' Centre 🗓 daily.
⬤ Dec 25. 🎟 ♿ Visitors' Centre.

CLOVELLY has been a noted
beauty spot since the novelist Charles Kingsley (1819–
75) wrote about it in his
stirring story of the Spanish
Armada, *Westward Ho!* (1855).
Today the whole village is
privately owned and has been
turned into a tourist attraction,
with little sign of the flourishing fishing industry to which
it owed its birth. It is a charming, picturesque village with
steep cobbled streets rising
up the cliff from the harborside, gaily painted houses and
gardens brimming with brightly
colored flowers. There are
superb views from the lookout
points and fine coastal paths
to explore from the tiny quay.
The Visitor's Centre offers an
introduction to the village.
   The **Hobby Drive** toll road
(off the A39, near Bucks Cross)
is a scenic approach to the
village, which runs through
woodland along the coast.
The road was constructed in

Bideford's medieval bridge, 203 m (666 ft) long with 24 arches

1811–29 to give employment
to local men who had lost
their jobs at the end of the
Napoleonic Wars *(see pp54–5)*.

Bideford ⓮

Devon. 🏠 13,000. 🚌 ℹ The Quay
(01237 477676). 🛒 Tue, Sat.

STRUNG OUT along the boat-
filled estuary of the River
Torridge, Bideford grew and
thrived from Elizabethan times
on the import of tobacco from
the New World *(see p50–51)*.
Some 17th-century merchants'
houses survive on Bridgeland
Street, including the splendid
bay-windowed house at No. 28

(1693). Beyond is Mill Street,
lined with many shops, leading to the parish church and
the splendid medieval bridge
that has carried traffic across
the Torridge since the 15th
century. The quay stretches
from here to a pleasant park
and a statue commemorating
Charles Kingsley, whose novels
helped revive the local economy by bringing visitors to
the area in the 19th century.

ENVIRONS: To the west of
Bideford, the village **Westward
Ho!** was built in the late 19th
century and named after one
of Kingsley's most popular
novels. The development was
unsuccessful and the Victorian
villas and hotels are now part
of a vacation resort that looks
out across the Taw estuary
onto Braunton Burrows nature
preserve. Rudyard Kipling *(see
p149)* went to school here and
the hill to the south, known as
Kipling Tors, was the setting
for *Stalky & Co* (1899), stories
based on his experiences of
schoolboy life.
   Henry Williamson's literary
classic, *Tarka the Otter* (1927),
describes the otters of the
Torridge Valley and naturalists are hoping to reintroduce
otters to this lovely valley.
Part of a Tarka Trail has been
laid out along the Torridge and
bicycles can be rented from
Bideford railroad station. The
trail passes close to the Royal
Horticultural Society's magnificent **Rosemoor Garden**.
   Day trips run from Bideford
to **Lundy** island, used in the
past as a pirate hideout. The
island is abundant in marine
life, birds, and wildlife.

🌺 **RHS Rosemoor Garden**
Great Torrington. 🕿 01805 624067.
🗓 daily. 🎟 ♿

Fishing boats in Clovelly harbor

Fishermen's cottages, Appledore

Appledore ⓯

Devon. 🏠 3,000.

A PPLEDORE's remote location at the tip of the Torridge estuary has helped to preserve its charms intact. Busy boat-yards line the long riverside quay, which is also the departure point for fishing trips and ferries to the sandy beaches of Braunton Burrows on the opposite shore. Timeworn Regency houses line the main street that runs parallel to the quay, and behind is a network of narrow cobbled lanes with 18th-century fishermen's cottages. Several shops retain their original bow windows and sell an assortment of crafts, antiques and souvenirs.

Uphill from the quay is the **North Devon Maritime Museum**, with an exhibition on the experiences of Devon emigrants in Australia and a selection of models and photographs explaining the work of local shipyards. The tiny **Victorian Schoolroom**, which is affiliated with the museum, shows a selection

of documentary videos on subjects such as fishing, ship-building and local trade.

🏛 **North Devon Maritime Museum**
Odun Rd. ☎ 01237 474852.
⭕ Easter–Oct: daily. ♿ 🅱 limited.

Barnstaple ⓰

Devon. 🏠 33,000. 🚆 🚌 🛈 Tuly St (01271 388584). 🗓 Mon–Sat.

A LTHOUGTH BARNSTAPLE is an important distribution center for the whole region, its town center remains calm due to the exclusion of traffic. The massive glass-roofed **Pannier Market** (1855) has stalls of organic fruit and vegetables, honey and eggs, much of it produced by farmers' wives to supplement their income. Nearby is **St. Peter's Church**, with its twisted broach spire caused by a lightning strike which warped the timbers in 1810.

On the Strand is a wonderful arcade topped with a statue of Queen Anne. It was originally built as an exchange where merchants traded the contents of their cargo boats moored on the River Taw alongside. Nearby is the 15th-century bridge and the **Museum of North Devon**, where displays cover local history and the 700-year-old pottery industry, as well as local wildlife, such as the otters that are returning to rivers in the area. The 180 mile (290 km) Tarka Trail forms a figure of eight circuit centered around Barnstaple, much of which can be cycled.

ENVIRONS: Just to the west of Barnstaple, **Braunton "Great Field"** covers over 120 ha (300 acres) and is a well-preserved relic of medieval open-field cultivation.

Statue of Queen Anne (1708)

DEVONSHIRE CREAM TEAS

Devon people claim all other versions of a cream tea are inferior to their own. The essential ingredient is Devonshire clotted cream, which comes from Jersey cattle fed on rich Devon pasture – anything else is second best, or so it is claimed. Spread thickly on freshly baked scones, with plenty of homemade strawberry jam, this makes a seductive, delicious, but fattening, teatime treat.

A typical cream tea with scones, jam and clotted cream

Beyond lies **Braunton Burrows**, one of the most extensive wild-dune preserves in Britain. It is a must for plant lovers who would like to spot sea kale, sea holly, sea lavender and horned poppies growing in their natural habitat. The sandy beaches and pounding waves at nearby Croyde and Woolacombe, are favorites among surfing enthusiasts, but there are also calmer areas of warm shallow water and rock pools.

Arlington Court, north of Barnstaple, has a collection of Napoleonic model ships, magnificent perennial borders and a lake. The stables are the biggest attraction, housing a collection of horse-drawn vehicles. Carriage rides are available and you can watch the mighty draft horses being fed at the end of the day.

🏛 **Museum of North Devon**
The Square. ☎ 01271 46747. ⭕ Tue–Sat. ● public hols. ♿ 🅱 limited.
🏛 **Arlington Court**
(NT) Arlington. ☎ 01271 850296. ⭕ Apr–Oct: Sun–Fri. ♿ 🅱 limited.

Barnstaple's Pannier Market

The village of Lynmouth

Lynton and Lynmouth ⓱

Devon. 🚶 2,000. 🚌 🛈 Town Hall, Lee Rd (01598 52225). See pp236–7.

SITUATED AT THE POINT where the East and West Lyn rivers meet the sea, Lynmouth is a picturesque, though rather commercialized, fishing village. The pedestrianized main street, lined with shops selling clotted cream and seaside souvenirs, runs parallel to the Lyn, now made into a canal with high embankments as a precaution against flash floods. One flood devastated the town at the height of the holiday season in 1952. The scars caused by the flood, which was fuelled by heavy rain on Exmoor, are now overgrown by trees in the **Glen Lyn Gorge**, which leads north from the village.

Lynmouth's sister town, Lynton, is a mainly Victorian village perched on the clifftop 130 m (427 ft) above, giving lovely views across the Bristol Channel to the Welsh coast. It can be reached from the harbor front by a cliff railroad or by a steep path.

ENVIRONS: Lynmouth makes an excellent starting point for walks on Exmoor. There is a splendid 2 mile (3 km) trail that leads southeast to tranquil **Watersmeet** *(see p237)*.

On the western edge of Exmoor, **Combe Martin** *(see p236)* lies in a lovely sheltered valley. On the main street, lined with Victorian villas, is the 18th-century Pack of Cards Inn, built by a gambler as a folly with 52 windows – one for each card in the pack.

Exeter ⓲

EXETER IS DEVON'S CAPITAL, a bustling and lively city with a great deal of character, despite the World War II bombing that destroyed much of its city center. Built high on a plateau above the River Exe, the city is encircled by substantial sections of Roman and medieval wall, and the street plan has not changed much since the Romans first laid out what is now the High Street. Elsewhere the Cathedral Close forms a pleasant green, and there are cobbled streets and narrow alleys that invite leisurely exploration. For shoppers there is a wide selection of big stores and smaller specialty shops.

Exploring Exeter

The intimate green and the close surrounding Exeter's distinctive cathedral were the setting for Trollope's novel *He Knew He Was Right* (1869). Full of festive crowds listening to street musicians in the summer, the close presents an array of architectural styles. One of the finest buildings here is the Elizabethan **Mol's Coffee House**. Among the other historic buildings that survived World War II are the magnificent **Guildhall** (1330) on the High Street (one of Britain's oldest civic buildings), the opulent **Custom House** (1681) by the quay, and the elegant 18th-century **Rougemont House** that stands near the remains of a Norman **castle** built by William the Conqueror *(see pp46–7)*.

The port area has been transformed into a tourist attraction with its early 19th-century warehouses converted into craft shops, antique galleries and cafés. Boats can be rented for cruising down the short stretch of canal. The **Quay House Interpretation Centre**

The timber-framed Mol's Coffee House (1596), Cathedral Close

West front and south tower, Cathedral Church of St. Peter

(open April–October) has audiovisual and other displays on the history of Exeter.

🏛 Cathedral Church of St. Peter

Cathedral Close. 📞 01392 55573. ⏱ daily. ♿
Exeter's cathedral is one of the most gloriously ornamented in Britain. Except for the two Norman towers, the cathedral is 13th-century and built in the style aptly known as Decorated because of the swirling geometric patterns of the window tracery. The façade, with its hundreds of stone statues, looks like a medieval parliament of knights and nobles, all seated in their stalls and leaning forward in anticipation of a rousing debate.

Inside, the splendid Gothic vaulting sweeps from one end of the church to the other, impressive in its uniformity and punctuated by gaily painted ceiling bosses. Among the numerous tombs around the choir is that of Edward II's treasurer, Walter de Stapledon (1261–1326), who was murdered by a mob in London. Stapledon raised much of the money needed to fund this cathedral

Collection of shells and other objects in the library of A La Ronde

and for Exeter College in Oxford *(see pp208–13)*.

🏛 Underground Passages

Roman Gate Passage. 📞 01392 265887. 🕐 Mon–Sat (winter: pm). ● Dec 25, 26, Jan 1, Good Fri. 🎥
Under the city center lie the remains of Exeter's medieval water-supply system. An excellent video and guided tour explain how the stone-lined tunnels were built in the 14th and 15th centuries on a slight gradient to bring fresh water from springs outside the town into the cathedral district.

🏛 Maritime Museum

The Haven. 📞 01392 58075. 🕐 daily. ● Dec 24–26. 🎥 ♿ ground floor only.
The Maritime Museum has examples of boats from all over the world. The collection includes a Venetian gondola, a Chinese junk and *Bertha* (1844) the world's oldest working steam ship, designed by Isambard Kingdom Brunel in 1844. A number of the larger vessels are moored in the canal basin and visitors can climb aboard most of the exhibits.

🏛 Royal Albert Memorial Museum and Art Gallery

Queen St. 📞 01392 265858. 🕐 Mon–Sat. ● Dec 24–26, Jan 1. ♿
This museum has a wonderfully varied collection, including Roman remains, a zoo of mounted, stuffed animals, examples of West Country art and a particularly good ethnographic display. Highlights include exhibits of silverware, watches and clocks.

19th-century head of an Oba, Royal Albert Museum

ENVIRONS: South of Exeter on the A376, the eccentric **A La Ronde** is a 16-sided house built in 1796 by two spinster sisters, who decorated the interior with shells, feathers and souvenirs gathered while on tour in Europe.

Further east, the unspoiled Regency town of **Sidmouth** lies in a sheltered bay. There is an eclectic array of architecture, the earliest buildings dating from the 1820s when Sidmouth became a popular summer resort. Thatched cottages stand opposite huge Edwardian villas, and elegant terraces line the seafront. In summer the town hosts the famous International Festival of Folk Arts *(see p63)*.

North of Sidmouth lies the magnificent church at **Ottery St. Mary**. Built in 1338–42 by Bishop Grandisson, the church is clearly a scaled-down version of Exeter Cathedral, which he also helped build. The churchyard has a memorial stating that the poet Coleridge was born in the town in 1772.

Nearby **Honiton** is famous for its extraordinarily intricate and delicate lace, made here since Elizabethan times.

To the north of Exeter, just off the M5, **Killerton** is home to the National Trust's costume collection, displayed by means of tableaux illustrating aristocratic lifestyles and fashions from the 18th century to the present day. Exhibits include 19th-century bustles, corsets and crinolines, and the more liberated bead skirts and ostrich feathers of the 1920s.

Farther north near Tiverton, is **Knightshayes Court**, a Victorian Gothic house with fine gardens *(see p230–31)*.

🏛 A La Ronde

(NT) Summer Lane, Exmouth. 📞 01395 265514. 🕐 Apr–Oct: Sun–Thu. 🎥

🏛 Killerton

(NT) Broadclyst. 📞 01392 881345. 🕐 mid-Mar–Oct: Wed–Mon. 🎥 ♿

♣ Knightshayes Court

(NT) Bolham. 📞 01884 254665. 🕐 Apr–Oct: Sat–Thu. 🎥 ♿ limited.

Mexican dancer at Sidmouth's International Festival of Folk Arts

Torbay ⑲

Devon. ≊ 🚆 *Torquay, Paignton.*
ℹ *Vaughan Parade, Torquay (01803 297428).*

THE THREE SEASIDE TOWNS of Torquay, Paignton and Brixham form an almost continuous resort around the great sweep of sandy beach and calm blue waters of Torbay. Because of its mild climate, extensive semitropical gardens and exuberant Victorian hotel architecture, this popular coastline has been dubbed the English Riviera. In its heyday, Torbay was patronized by the wealthy, especially during the Napoleonic Wars *(see p54)*, when touring the continent was neither safe nor patriotic. Today, mass entertainment is the theme and there are plenty of attractions, mostly in and around Torquay.
  Torre Abbey includes the remains of a monastery founded in 1196 and now serves as an art gallery. There is a magnificent barn in the grounds where prisoners captured from the Spanish Armada of 1588 were once held. **Torquay Museum** nearby covers natural history and archaeology, including finds from **Kents Cavern Showcaves**, on the outskirts of the town. This is one of England's most important prehistoric sites and the spectacular caves serve as the background for displays on people and animals who lived here 350,000 years ago.
  The charming miniature town of **Babbacombe Model Village** lies to the north of Torquay, while a mere mile (1.5 km) inland is the lovely little village of **Cockington**. Visitors travel by horse-drawn carriage to view the preserved Tudor manor house, church, thatched cottages and forge.
  In Paignton, the celebrated **Paignton Zoo** teaches children about the planet's wildlife, and from here you can take the steam railroad – an ideal way to visit Dartmouth.
  Continuing south from Paignton, the pretty village of Brixham was once England's most prosperous fishing port.

Bayards Cove, Dartmouth

🏛 **Torre Abbey**
King's Drive, Torquay. 📞 *01803 293593.* ◯ *Easter–Oct: daily.* 🚫

🏛 **Torquay Museum**
Babbacombe Rd, Torquay. 📞 *01803 293975.* ◯ *daily (Nov–Easter: Sun–Fri).* ⬤ *Dec 24–Jan 1, Good Fri.* 🚫

🏛 **Kents Cavern Showcaves**
Ilsham Rd, Torquay. 📞 *01803 294 059.* ◯ *daily.* ⬤ *Dec 25.* 🚫 ♿

🏛 **Babbacombe Model Village**
Hampton Ave, Torquay. 📞 *01803 328 669.* ◯ *daily.* ⬤ *Dec 25.* 🚫 ♿

🐾 **Paignton Zoo**
Totnes Rd, Paignton. 📞 *01803 557 479.* ◯ *daily.* ⬤ *Dec 25.* 🚫 ♿

Dartmouth ⑳

Devon. 🏠 *5,500.* ≊ ℹ *Mayors Ave (01803 834224).* 🛒 *Tue–Fri*

SITTING HIGH ON THE CLIFFTOP above the River Dart is the **Royal Naval College**, where British naval officers have trained since 1905. Long before that, Dartmouth was an important port and it was from here that English fleets set sail to join the Second and Third Crusades *(see pp48–49)*.
  Eighteenth-century houses adorn the cobbled quay of Bayards Cove, while ornately carved timber buildings line the 17th-century Butterwalk; No. 6 houses the **Dartmouth Museum**. To the south, picturesque **Dartmouth Castle** (1481) sits on rocky shores.

🏛 **Dartmouth Museum**
6 Butterwalk. 📞 *01803 832923.* ◯ *Mon–Sat.* ⬤ *25 Dec, 1 Jan.* 🚫

🏰 **Dartmouth Castle**
Castle Rd. 📞 *01803 833588.* ◯ *daily (Nov–Easter: Wed–Sun).* ⬤ *Dec 25, 26, Jan 1.* 🚫

Torquay, on the "English Riviera"

Stained glass window in Blessed Sacrament Chapel, Buckfast Abbey

Totnes ㉑

Devon. 🏘 6,000. 🚊 🚌 🚢 🛈 The Plains (01803 863168). 🗓 Tue (summer), Fri.

Totnes sits at the highest navigable point on the River Dart with a Norman **castle** perched high on the hill above. Linking the two is the steep High Street, lined with bow-windowed Elizabethan houses. Bridging the street is the **Eastgate**, part of the medieval town wall. Life in the town's heyday is explored in the **Totnes Elizabethan Museum**, which also has a room devoted to the mathematician Charles Babbage (1791–1871) known as the pioneer of modern computers. There is a medieval **Guildhall**, and a **church** with a delicately carved and gilded rood screen. On Tuesdays in the summer, market stallholders dress in Elizabethan costume.

ENVIRONS: A short walk north of Totnes, **Dartington Hall** has 10 ha (25 acres) of lovely gardens and a world-famous music school where concerts are held in the heavily timbered 14th-century Great Hall.

Stallholders in Totnes market.

♠ Totnes Castle
Castle St. 📞 01803 864406. 🕐 Apr–Oct: daily; Nov–Mar: Wed–Sun. 🔴 Dec 24–26, Jan 1. 🎫
🏛 Totnes Elizabethan Museum
Fore St. 📞 01803 863821. 🕐 daily (Nov–Mar: Mon & Fri). 🎫 🕭 limited.
🏚 Guildhall
Rampart Walk. 📞 01803 862147. 🕐 Apr–Oct: Mon–Fri. 🎫
🌿 Dartington Hall Gardens
Dartington Hall Rd. 📞 01803 862271. 🕐 daily. 🕭 limited.

Buckfastleigh ㉒

Devon. 🏘 3,300. 🚊

This market town, situated on the edge of Dartmoor (see p280–81), is dominated by **Buckfast Abbey**. The original abbey, founded in Norman times, fell into ruin after the Dissolution of the Monasteries and it was not until 1882 that a small group of French Benedictine monks set up a new abbey here. Work on the present building was financed by donations and carried out by the monks themselves. The abbey was completed in 1938 and now lies at the heart of a thriving community.

The fine mosaics and modern stained glass window are also the work of the monks.

Nearby is the **Buckfast Butterfly Farm and Otter Sanctuary,** and the **South Devon Steam Railway** terminal where steam trains leave for Totnes, chugging down the scenic valley of the River Dart.

🏰 Buckfast Abbey
Buckfastleigh. 📞 01364 642519. 🕐 daily. 🕭
🦋 Buckfast Butterfly Farm and Otter Sanctuary
Buckfastleigh. 📞 01364 642916. 🕐 Easter–Nov: daily. 🎫 🕭

Burgh Island ㉓

Devon. 🚊 Plymouth, then taxi. 🛈 The Barbican, Plymouth (01752 264849).

The short walk across the sands at low tide from Bigbury-on-Sea to Burgh Island takes you back to the decadent era of the 1920s and '30s. It was here that the millionaire Archibald Nettlefold built the luxury **Burgh Island Hotel** in 1929. Created in Art Deco style with a natural rock salt-water pool, this was the exclusive retreat of famous figures, such as the Duke of Windsor and writers Agatha Christie and Noel Coward. The restored hotel is worth a visit for the photographs of its heyday and the Art Deco fittings. You can also explore the island village and **Pilchard Inn** (1336), reputed to be haunted by the ghost of a smuggler.

The Art Deco style bar in Burgh Island Hotel

Plymouth ㉔

Devon. 🏛 250,000. ✈ 🚢 🚉
🚌 🛈 *Island House, The Barbican.*
(01752 264849). 🏪 *daily.*

THE TINY PORT from which
Drake, Raleigh, the Pilgrim
Fathers, Cook and Darwin all
set sail on pioneering voyages
has now grown to a substantial city, much of it boldly
rebuilt after wartime bombing.
Old Plymouth clus-
ters around the
Hoe, the famous
patch of turf on
which Sir Francis
Drake is said to
have calmly fin-
ished his game of
bowls as the in-
vading Spanish
Armada approached
the port in 1588 *(see pp50–
51).* Today the Hoe is a pleasant park and parade ground
surrounded by memorials to
naval men, including Drake
himself. Alongside is Charles
II's massive **Royal Citadel**,
built to guard the harbor in

Drake's coat of arms

the 1660s, and the fascinating
Aquarium. A popular attraction is **Plymouth Dome**, a
visitor center which uses high-
tech display techniques to
explain Plymouth's past and
present, including live satellite
weather pictures and radar
screens for monitoring ships
in the harbor. A short stroll
away, **Mayflower Stone and
Steps** is the spot where the
Pilgrim Fathers set sail for the
New World in
England's third
and successful
attempt at colon-
ization in 1620.

ENVIRONS: A boat
tour of the harbor
is the best way to
see Plymouth's
historic dockyard
complex where warships and
submarines have been built
and equipped since the
Napoleonic Wars *(see pp54–5).*
There are also splendid views
of the numerous fine gardens,
such as **Mount Edgcumbe
Park** *(see pp230–31),* which

**Mid-18th-century carved wood
chimneypiece, Saltram House**

are scattered around the coastline of the Plymouth Sound.
East of the city, the mid-
18th-century **Saltram House**
is remarkable for two opulent
rooms designed by Adam *(see
pp24–5).* There are also portraits by Joshua Reynolds, who
was born nearby in Plympton.

🏰 **Royal Citadel**
The Hoe. 📞 *01752 603300.*
◯ *May–Sep: daily.* 🌊 🚫 *limited.*
🐠 **Aquarium**
Citadel Hill. 📞 *01752 222772.*
◯ *daily.* ● *Dec 25, 26.* 🌊 🚫
🏛 **Plymouth Dome**
The Hoe. 📞 *01752 603300.*
◯ *daily.* ● *Dec 25.* 🌊 🚫
🌷 **Mount Edgcumbe Park**
Cremyll, Torpoint. 📞 *01752 822236.*
◯ *Apr–Oct: Wed–Sun.* 🌊 🚫 *limited.*
🏰 **Saltram House**
(NT) Plympton. 📞 *01752 336546.*
◯ *Apr–Oct: Sun–Thu.* 🌊 🚫

Buckland Abbey ㉕

(NT) Yelverton, Devon. 📞 *01822
853607.* 🚌 *from Yelverton.*
◯ *Fri–Wed (Nov–Mar: Sat & Sun
pm).* ● *Dec 18–29.* 🌊 🚫 *limited.*

FOUNDED BY the Cistercian
monks in 1278, Buckland
Abbey was converted to a
house after the Dissolution of
the Monasteries and became
the home of Drake from 1581
until his death in 1596. Many
of the monastic buildings survive in a delightful garden
setting, the most impressive
being the huge 14th-century
tithe barn *(see pp28–9).* Part
of the house explains Drake's
life and times through paintings, maps and memorabilia.

View of Plymouth Harbour from the Hoe

Cotehele 26

(NT) St. Dominick, Cornwall.
 01579 51346. Calstock.
House *Apr–Oct: Sat–Thu.*
Grounds *daily.* *limited.*

Magnificent woodland and lush river scenery make Cotehele (pronounced Coteal) one of the most delightful spots on the River Tamar and a rewarding day can be spent exploring the estate. Far from civilization, tucked into its wooded fold in the Cornwall countryside, Cotehele has slumbered for 500 years. The main attraction is the house and valley garden at its center. Built mainly between 1489 and 1520, it is a rare example of a medieval house, set around three courtyards with a magnificent open hall, kitchen, chapel and a warren of private parlors and chambers. The romance of the house is enhanced by colorful terraced gardens to the east, leading via a tunnel into a richly planted valley garden. The path through this garden passes a large domed medieval dovecote and descends to a quay, from where lime and coal were once shipped. There are fine views up and down the winding reed-fringed Tamar and a gallery on the quayside specializes in local arts and crafts. The estate includes a village, riverside quay with a small maritime museum, working mill buildings, ancient lime kilns and a number of shops complete with 19th-century equipment.

Medieval dovecote in the gardens of Cotehele estate

Spanish Armada and British fleets in the English Channel, 1588

SIR FRANCIS DRAKE

Sir Francis Drake (c.1540–1596) was the first Englishman to circumnavigate the globe and he was knighted by Elizabeth I in 1580. Four years later he introduced tobacco and potatoes to England, after bringing home 190 colonists who had tried to establish a settlement in Virginia. To many, however, Drake was no more than an opportunistic rogue, renowned for his exploits as a "privateer," the polite name for a pirate. Catholic Spain was the bitter enemy and Drake further endeared himself to queen and people by his part in the victory over Philip II's Armada *(see pp50–51)*, defeated by bad weather and the buccaneering spirit of the English.

Morwellham Quay 27

Off A390, nr Gunnislake, Devon.
 01822 832766. Gunnislake.
 daily. *Dec 24–Jan 1.*
 limited.

Morwellham quay was a neglected and overgrown industrial site until 1970, when members of a local trust began restoring the abandoned cottages, schoolhouse, farmyards, quay and copper mines to the condition they were in at the turn of the century.

Today, Morwellham Quay is a thriving and rewarding industrial museum, where you can easily spend a whole day partaking in the typical activities of a Victorian village, from preparing the shire horses for a day's work hauling carriages, to riding a trolley deep into a copper mine in the hillside behind the village. The museum is brought to life by characters in costumes who give demonstrations throughout the day. You can watch or lend a

Industrial relics at Morwellham Quay in the Tamar Valley

hand to the cooper while he builds a barrel, attend a lesson in the schoolroom, take part in Victorian playground games or dress up in 19th-century hooped skirts, bonnets, top hats or jackets. The staff, who convincingly play the part of villagers, lead you through their lives and impart a huge amount of information about the history of this small copper-mining community.

Dartmoor National Park ㉘

Characteristic moorland near Drewsteignton

THE WILD AND MIST-SODDEN open moorland of Dartmoor's bleak and isolated heart provided the eerie background for Conan Doyle's thriller, *The Hound of the Baskervilles* (1902). Here at Princetown, surrounded by gaunt weathered outcrops of granite tors, is Britain's most secure prison.

Buzzard Also dotting the landscape are scores of prehistoric remains which have survived because of the durability of granite. Elsewhere the mood is very different. Streams tumble through wooded and boulder-strewn ravines forming pretty cascades and waterfalls, and cozy thatched cottages nestle in the sheltered valleys around the margins of the moor offer cream teas and warming fires to weary walkers.

Okehampton has the Museum of Dartmoor Life and a ruined 14th-century castle.

Brentor
This volcanic hill crowned by a tiny church (first built in 1130) is visible for miles.

Lydford Gorge (open Apr–Oct) is a dramatic wooded ravine, leading to a waterfall.

The Ministry of Defence uses much of this area for training. Access is available on weekends.

Main information center

KEY

ℹ️	Tourist information
▬▬	A road
▭▭	B road
══	Minor road
☀	Viewpoint

Map labels: LAUNCESTON · MELDON RESERVOIR · High Willhays 621 m 2,038 ft · West Okement · Okehampton · Lydford · MINISTRY OF DEFENSE FIRING RANGE · Postbridge · Walkham · Two Bridges · A386 · Merrivale · Blackbrook · Tavistock · LISKEARD · Princetown · Mevy · Yelverton · BURRATOR RESERVOIR · PLYMOUTH · Plym · PLYMOUTH · Ivyb...

0 kilometers 5
0 miles 5

Postbridge
Dartmoor's northern fen is best explored from the village of Postbridge. The gently rolling moorland is crossed by many drystone walls.

◁ **Open expanse of central Dartmoor, grazed by wild ponies**

Dartmoor Ponies
These small, tough ponies have lived wild on the moor since at least the 10th century.

Grimspound is the impressive site of Bronze Age huts built nearly 4,000 years ago.

Castle Drogo is a magnificent mock castle built by the architect Sir Edwin Lutyens *(see p25)* in 1910–30.

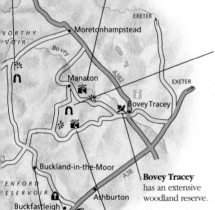

Becky Falls (open Easter–Nov) offers delightful woodland walks and a viewing platform over the 22 m (72 ft) waterfall.

Hound Tor
This site includes the substantial remains of a deserted medieval settlement , inhabited from Saxon times until about 1300.

Bovey Tracey has an extensive woodland reserve.

Haytor Rocks are the most accessible of the many tors.

South Devon Steam Railway

Buckfast Abbey was founded by King Canute *(see p157)* in 1018.

Dartmoor Otter Sanctuary

Dartmeet marks the lovely confluence point of the East and West Dart rivers.

Buckland-in-the-Moor
This is one of the most picturesque thatch-and-granite villages on Dartmoor.

THE MIDLANDS

The Midlands at a Glance

THE MIDLANDS IS AN AREA that embraces wonderful landscapes and massive industrial cities. Visitors come to discover the wild beauty of the rugged Peaks, cruise slowly along the Midlands canals on gaily painted narrowboats and explore varied and enchanting gardens. The area encompasses the full range of English architecture from mighty cathedrals and humble churches to charming spa towns, stately homes and country cottages. There are fascinating industrial museums, many in picturesque settings.

Cheshire

Staffordshi

Shropshire

Tissington Trail *(see p323) combines a walk through scenic Peak District countryside with an entertaining insight into the ancient custom of well-dressing.*

Ironbridge Gorge *(see pp300–1) was the birthplace of the Industrial Revolution (see pp334–5). Now a World Heritage Centre, the site is a reminder of the lovely countryside where the original factories were located.*

THE HEART OF ENGLAND
(see pp290–315)

W Mid

Hereford and Worcester

Gloucestershire

The Cotswolds *(see pp290–91) are full of delightful houses built from local limestone, on the profits of the medieval wool trade. Snowshill Manor (left) is situated near the unspoiled village of Broadway.*

0 kilometers	25
0 miles	25

◁ **The half-timbered Lord Leycester Hospital, Warwick**

Chatsworth House (see pp320–21), *a magnificent Baroque edifice, is famous for its gorgeous gardens. The "Conservative" Wall, a greenhouse for exotic plants, is pictured above.*

Lincoln Cathedral (see p327), *a vast, imposing building, dominates the ancient town. Inside are splendid misericords and the superb 13th-century Angel Choir, which has 30 carved angels.*

Nottinghamshire

Lincolnshire

Derbyshire

EAST MIDLANDS
(see pp316–329)

Leicestershire

Burghley House (see pp328–9) *is a dazzling landmark for miles around in the flat East Midlands landscape, with architectural motifs from the European Renaissance.*

Warwickshire

Northamptonshire

Warwick Castle (see pp308–9) *is an intriguing mixture of medieval power base and country house, complete with massive towers, battlements, a dungeon and state apartments, such as the Queen Anne Bedroom.*

Stratford-upon-Avon (see pp310–13) *has many picturesque houses connected with William Shakespeare's life, some of which are open to visitors. These black and white timber-framed buildings, which abound in the Midlands, are a typical example of Tudor architecture (see pp288–9).*

Canals of the Midlands

ONE OF ENGLAND'S FIRST CANALS was built by the 3rd Duke of Bridgewater in 1761 to link the coal mine on his Worsley estate with Manchester's textile factories. This started a canal-building boom and by 1805, a 3,000 mile (4,800 km) network of waterways had been dug across the country, linking into the natural river system. Canals provided the cheapest, fastest way of transporting goods, until competition began to arrive from the railroads in the 1840s. Cargo transportation ended in 1963, but today nearly 2,000 miles (3,200 km) of canals are still navigable for travelers who wish to take a leisurely cruise on a narrowboat.

The Grand Union Canal (pictured in 1931) is 300 miles (485 km) long and was dug in the 1790s to link London with the Midlands.

Lockkeepers were provided with canalside houses.

Lockside inns cater to narrowboats.

The Farmer's Bridge is a flight of 13 locks in Birmingham. Locks are used to raise or lower boats from one level of the canal to another. The steeper the gradient, the more locks are needed.

Heavy V-shaped timber gates close off the lock.

Water pressing against the gate keeps it shut.

The towpath is where horses pulled the canal boats before engines were invented. They were changed periodically for fresh animals.

Narrowboats have straight sides and flat bottoms and are pointed at both ends. Cargo space took up most of the boat, with a small cabin for the crew. Exteriors were brightly painted.

No 7 BILL O TOMS NEW MARTON LOCK

MIDLANDS CANAL NETWORK

The industrial Midlands was the birthplace of the English canal system and still has the biggest concentration of navigable waterways.

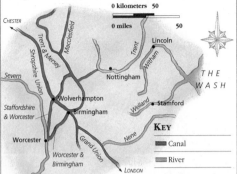

0 kilometers 50
0 miles 50

CHESTER

Trent & Mersey
Macclesfield
Shropshire Union
Severn
Staffordshire & Worcester
Wolverhampton
Birmingham
Worcester
Worcester & Birmingham
Grand Union
Nene
Lincoln
Trent
Witham
Nottingham
Welland
Stamford
THE WASH
LONDON

KEY

▬ Canal
▬ River

VISITORS' CHECKLIST

Companies specializing in canal boat holidays: Blake's Holidays ☏ *0160378 2911;* Hoseasons ☏ *01502 501 010;* Canal Cruising Co ☏ *01785 813982;* Black Prince Holidays ☏ *01527 575115;* Alvechurch Boat Centres Ltd ☏ *0121 4452909;* Rushbrooke Narrow Boats ☏ *01963 78652.*
Canal museums: National Waterways Museum *(see p315);* Canal Museum, Stoke Bruerne, Towcester ☏ *01604 862229;* Boat Museum, South Pier Rd, Ellesmere Port ☏ *0151 355 5017.*

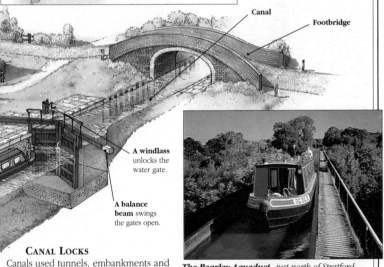

Canal

Footbridge

A windlass unlocks the water gate.

A balance beam swings the gates open.

CANAL LOCKS

Canals used tunnels, embankments and locks for the speedy transportation of goods across the countryside. Locks were used to take boats up or down hills.

***The Bearley Aqueduct**, just north of Stratford-upon-Avon, carries the canal in a cast iron trough. This is supported on brick piers for 180 m (495 ft), over roads and a busy railroad line.*

CANAL ART

Canal boat cabins are very small and every inch of space is utilized to make a comfortable home for the occupants. Interiors were enlivened with colorful paintings and attractive decorations.

Furniture was designed to be functional and to brighten up the cramped cabin.

Narrowboats are often decorated with ornamental brass.

Water cans were also painted. The most common designs were roses and castles, with local variations in style.

Tudor Manor Houses

MANY STRIKING MANOR HOUSES were built in central England during the Tudor Age *(see pp50–51)*, a time of relative peace and prosperity. The abolition of the monasteries meant that vast estates were broken up and sold to secular landowners, who built houses to reflect their new status *(see p24)*. In the Midlands,

The Lucy family arms

wood was the main building material, and the gentry flaunted their wealth by using timber paneling for flamboyant decorative effect.

The decorative molding on the south wing was carved during the late 16th century. Ancient motifs, such as vines and trefoils, are combined with the latest imported Italian Renaissance styles.

The rectangular moat was for decoration rather than defense. It surrounds a re-created knot garden *(see p22)* that was laid out in 1975 using plants known to have been available in Tudor times.

The Long Gallery, the last part of the Hall to be built (1580), was used for exercise. It has original murals portraying Destiny *(left)* and Fortune.

Jetties (overhanging upper stories)

TUDOR MANSIONS AND TUDOR REVIVAL

There are many sumptuously decorated Tudor mansions in the Midlands. In the 19th century Tudor Revival architecture became a very popular "Old English" style, intended to invoke family pride and values rooted in the past.

Hardwick Hall in Derbyshire, whose huge kitchen is pictured, is one of the finest Tudor mansions in the country. These buildings are known as "prodigy" houses *(see p328)* due to their gigantic size.

Charlecote Park, Warwickshire, is a brick mansion built by Sir Thomas Lucy in 1551–59. It was heavily restored in Tudor style in the 19th century, but has a fine original gatehouse. According to legend, the young William Shakespeare *(see pp310–13)* was caught poaching deer in the park.

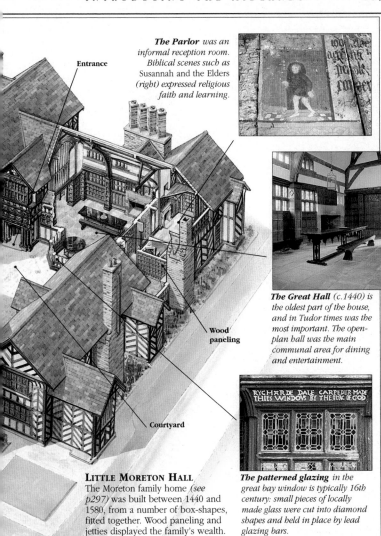

The Parlor *was an informal reception room. Biblical scenes such as Susannah and the Elders (right) expressed religious faith and learning.*

Entrance

Wood paneling

Courtyard

The Great Hall *(c.1440) is the oldest part of the house, and in Tudor times was the most important. The open-plan hall was the main communal area for dining and entertainment.*

RYCHARDE DALE CARPEDER MADE
THIES WINDOWS BY THE GRAC OF GOD

LITTLE MORETON HALL

The Moreton family home *(see p297)* was built between 1440 and 1580, from a number of box-shapes, fitted together. Wood paneling and jetties displayed the family's wealth.

The patterned glazing *in the great bay window is typically 16th century: small pieces of locally made glass were cut into diamond shapes and held in place by lead glazing bars.*

Packwood House *in Warwickshire is a timber-framed mid-Tudor house with extensive 17th-century additions. The unusual garden of clipped yew trees dates from the 17th century and is supposed to represent the Sermon on the Mount.*

Moseley Old Hall, *Staffordshire, has a red brick exterior concealing its early 17th-century timber frame. The King's Room is where Charles II hid after the Battle of Worcester (see pp52–3).*

Wightwick Manor, *West Midlands, was built in 1887–93. It is a fine example of Tudor Revival architecture and has superb late 19th-century furniture and decorations.*

Building with Cotswold Stone

THE COTSWOLDS are a prominent range of limestone hills running over 50 miles (80 km) in a northeasterly direction from Bath *(see p244)*. The thin soils are difficult to plow but ideal for grazing sheep, and the wealth engendered by the medieval wool trade was poured into building majestic churches and opulent town houses. Stone quarried from these hills was used to build London's St. Paul's Cathedral *(see pp116–7)*, as well as the villages, barns and manor houses that make the landscape so picturesque.

Dragon, Deerhurst Church

Arlington Row Cottages *in Bibury, a typical Cotswold village, were built in the 17th century for weavers whose looms were set up in the attics.*

Windows were taxed and glass expensive. Workers' cottages had only a few, not very large windows made of small panes of glass.

A drip mold keeps rain off the chimney.

The roof is steeply pitched to carry the weight of the tiles. These were made by master craftsmen who could split blocks of stone into sheets by using natural fault lines.

COTSWOLD STONE COTTAGE

The two-story Arlington Row Cottages are asymmetrical and built of odd-shaped stones. Small windows and doorways make them quite dark inside.

Timber lintels and doors

Timber framing was cheaper than stone, and was used for the upper rooms in the roof.

VARIATIONS IN STONE

Cotswold stone is warmer-toned in the north, pearly in central areas and light gray in the south. The stone seems to glow with absorbed sunlight. It is a soft stone that is easily carved and can be used for many purposes, from buildings to bridges, headstones and gargoyles.

"Tiddles" *is a cat's gravestone in Fairford churchyard.*

Lower Slaughter *gets its name from the Anglo-Saxon word slough, or muddy place. It has a low stone bridge, over the River Eye.*

COTSWOLD STONE TOWNS AND VILLAGES

The villages and towns on this map are prime examples of places built almost entirely from stone. By the 12th century almost all of the villages in the area were established. Huge deposits of limestone resulted in a wealth of stone buildings. Masons worked from distinctive local designs that were handed down from generation to generation.

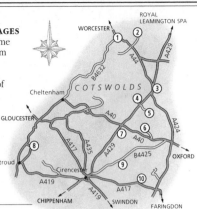

① Winchcombe
② Broadway
③ Stow-on-the-Wold
④ Upper and Lower Slaughter
⑤ Bourton-on-the-Water
⑥ Sherborne
⑦ Northleach
⑧ Painswick
⑨ Bibury
⑩ Fairford

Wool merchants' houses were built of fine ashlar (dressed stone) with ornamental cornerstones, doorframes and windows.

The eaves here have a dentil frieze, so-called because it resembles a row of teeth.

STONE GARGOYLES

In Winchcombe's church, 15th-century gargoyles reflect a combination of pagan and Christian beliefs.

Pagan gods warded off pre-Christian evil spirits.

Fertility figures, always important in rural areas, were incorporated into Christian festivals.

Human faces often caricatured local church dignitaries.

Animal gods represented qualities, such as strength, in pagan times.

COTSWOLD STONE HOUSE

This early Georgian merchant's house in Painswick shows the fully developed Cotswold style, which borrows decorative elements from Classical architecture.

The door frame has a rounded pediment on simple pilasters.

Drystone walling *is an ancient technique used in the Cotswolds. The stones are held in place without mortar.*

A stone cross (16th century) in Stanton village, near Broadway, is one of many found in the Cotswolds.

Table-top and "tea caddy," *fine 18th-century tombs, can be found in Painswick churchyard.*

The Cotswold Arms

Bar Snacks
Restaurant
Beer Garden
Morning Coffee

THE HEART OF ENGLAND

CHESHIRE · HEREFORD & WORCESTER · GLOUCESTERSHIRE
SHROPSHIRE · STAFFORDSHIRE · WARWICKSHIRE · WEST MIDLANDS

BRITAIN'S GREAT ATTRACTION *is its variety, and nowhere is this more true than at the heart of the country, where the Cotswold hills, enfolding stone cottages and churches, give way to the flat, fertile plains of Warwickshire. Shakespeare country borders on the industrial heart of England, once known as the workshop of the world.*

Coventry, Birmingham, the Potteries and their hinterlands have been manufacturing iron, textiles and ceramics since the 18th century. In the 20th century these industries have declined, and a new type of museum has developed to commemorate the towns' industrial heyday and explain the manufacturing processes, which were once taken for granted. Ironbridge Gorge and Quarry Bank Mill, Styal, where the factories are now living museums, are fascinating industrial sites and enjoy beautiful surroundings.

These landscapes may be appreciated from the deck of a narrowboat, making gentle progress along the Midlands canals, to the region on the border with Wales known as the Marches. Here the massive walls of Chester and the castles at Shrewsbury and Ludlow recall the Welsh locked in fierce battle with Norman barons and the Marcher Lords. The Marches are now full of rural communities served by the peaceful market towns of Leominster, Malvern, Ross-on-Wye and Hereford. The cities of Worcester and Gloucester both have modern shopping centers, yet their majestic cathedrals retain the tranquility of an earlier age.

Cheltenham has Regency terraces, Cirencester a rich legacy of Roman art and Tewkesbury a solid Norman abbey. Finally, there is Stratford-upon-Avon, where William Shakespeare, the Elizabethan dramatist, lived and died.

BOWLS CLUB

Leisurely village pastimes, reminiscent of a more tranquil age

◁ **Cotswold stone: an extremely popular building material in the Heart of England**

Exploring the Heart of England

THE HEART OF ENGLAND, more than any other region, takes its character from the landscape. Picturesque houses, pubs and churches, made from timber and Cotswold stone, create a harmonic appearance that delights visitors and adds greatly to the pleasures of exploration. The area around Birmingham and Stoke-on-Trent, however – once the industrial hub of England – contrasts sharply. The bleak concrete skyline may not be appealing but the area has a fascinating history that is reflected in the self-confident Victorian art and architecture, and a series of award-winning industrial heritage museums.

Arlington Row: stone cottages in the Cotswold village of Bibury

SIGHTS AT A GLANCE

GETTING AROUND

The Heart of England is easily reached by train, with InterCity rail services to Cheltenham, Worcester, Birmingham, and Coventry. The M5 and M6 highways are the major road routes but are frequently congested. Coach companies provide regular shuttle services to Cheltenham and Birmingham. Traveling within the region is best done by car. Rural roads are delightfully empty, although major attractions, such as Stratford-upon-Avon, may be very crowded during the summer.

SEE ALSO

0 kilometers 10
0 miles 10

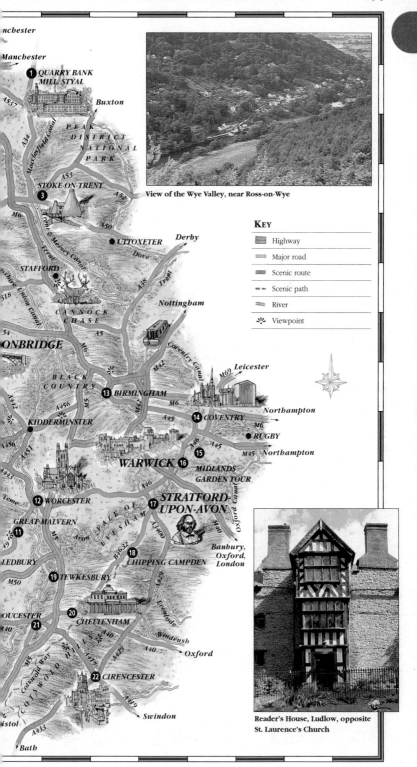

View of the Wye Valley, near Ross-on-Wye

nchester

Manchester

A537

1 QUARRY BANK MILL STYAL

Buxton

*P E A K
D I S T R I C T
N A T I O N A L
P A R K*

A34

Macclesfield Canal

A53

STOKE-ON-TRENT

A54

3

M6

A50

● UTTOXETER

Derby

Dove

Trent & Mersey Canal

STAFFORD ●

Trent

A38

A518

*C A N N O C K
C H A S E*

Nottingham

A5

A54

ONBRIDGE

M6

Coventry Canal

*B L A C K
C O U N T R Y*

Leicester

A456

M42

M69

13 BIRMINGHAM

M6

A442

M5

M6

KIDDERMINSTER ●

A45

14 COVENTRY

Northampton

A456

A451

A46

A45

M6

● RUGBY

M45

Northampton

A413

WARWICK 16

**MIDLANDS
GARDEN TOUR**

15

Teme

12 WORCESTER

A46

**STRATFORD-
UPON-AVON**

17

Oxford Canal

M40

GREAT MALVERN

VALE OF EVESHAM

Avon

A49

11

LEDBURY

M5

M50

A4390

**Banbury,
Oxford,
London**

B4035

18 CHIPPING CAMPDEN

A429

19 TEWKESBURY

A438

Leadon

20

CHELTENHAM

A40

Windrush

Oxford

OUCESTER

A40

21

A417

A429

A40

C O T S W O L D   H I L L S

Cotswold Way

22 CIRENCESTER

A419

A433

Swindon

istol

A433

Bath

KEY

▨	Highway
▬	Major road
▬	Scenic route
‑‑	Scenic path
〜	River
☀	Viewpoint

**Reader's House, Ludlow, opposite
St. Laurence's Church**

Quarry Bank Mill, a working reminder of the Industrial Revolution

Quarry Bank Mill, Styal ❶

Cheshire. 📞 01625 527468.
🚆 Wilmslow then bus. 🕐 Apr–Sep: daily; Oct–Mar: Tue–Sun. ⬛ Dec 25.
🅿️ ♿ limited.

THE HISTORY of the Industrial Revolution (see pp54–5) is brought vividly to life at Quarry Bank Mill, an early factory now transformed into a museum. Here, mill master Samuel Greg first used the waters of the Bollin Valley in 1784 to power the water frame, a machine for spinning raw cotton fibers into thread. By the 1840s, the Greg cotton empire was one of the biggest in Britain, and the mill produced bolts of material to be exported all over the world.

Today the massive old mill buildings have been restored to house a living museum of the cotton industry. This dominated the Manchester area for nearly 200 years, but was finally destroyed by foreign competition.

The entire process, from the spinning and weaving to the bleaching, the printing and dyeing, is shown through a series of reconstructions, demonstrations and many exciting hands-on displays.

The weaving shed is full of clattering looms producing textiles. There are fascinating contraptions that demonstrate how water can be used to drive machinery, including an enormous wheel, 50 tons in weight and 7 m (24 ft) high, still used occasionally to provide power for the looms.

The Greg family realized the importance of having a healthy, loyal and stable work-force. A social history exhibition explains how the mill workers were housed in the specially built village of Styal, in spacious cottages with veg-etable gardens and toilets. Details of their wages, working con-ditions and medical facilities are displayed on information boards.

There are guided tours of the nearby **Apprentice House**. Local orphans lived here, and were sent to work up to 12 hours a day at the mill when they were just six or seven years old. Visitors can try the beds in the house and even sample the medicine they were given. Quarry Bank Mill is surrounded by over 115 ha (284 acres) of woodland.

Chester ❷

Cheshire. 🚶 120,000. 🚆 🅿️
ℹ️ Town Hall, Northgate St (01244 318356). 🕐 daily.

FIRST SETTLED BY THE ROMANS (see pp44–5), who estab-lished a camp in AD 79 to defend fertile land near the River Dee, the main streets of Chester are now lined with timber buildings. These are the **Chester Rows**, which, with their two tiers of stores and continuous upper gallery, anticipate today's high-rise stores by several centuries.

Although their oriel windows and decorative timberwork are mostly 19th century, the Rows were first built in the 13th and 14th centuries, and the original structures can be seen in many places. The façade of the 16th-century **Bishop Lloyd's House** in Watergate Street is the most richly carved in Chester. The Rows are at their most varied and attractive where Eastgate Street meets Bridge Street. Here, views of the cathedral and the town walls give the impres-sion of a perfectly preserved medieval city. This illusion is helped by the Town Crier, who calls the hour and announces news in summer from the Cross, which is a reconstruction of the 15th-century stone crucifix that was destroyed in the Civil War (see pp52–3).

Chester's 1897 clocktower

A **Heritage Centre**, south of the Cross, explains the town's history. To the north is the **cathedral**. The choir stalls have splendid misericords (see p327), with scenes including a sow suckling her litter and

Examples of the intricate carving on Bishop Lloyd's House, a Tudor building in Watergate Street, Chester

The Chester Rows, where stores line the first-floor galleries

a quarreling couple. In sharp contrast are the delicate spirelets on the stall canopies. The cathedral is surrounded on two sides by the high **city walls**, originally Roman but rebuilt at intervals. The best stretch is from the cathedral to Eastgate, where a wrought-iron **clock** was erected in 1897. The route to Newgate leads to a **Roman amphitheatre** built in AD 100.

🏛 **Heritage Centre**
Bridge St Row, Bridge St. 01244 317948. ◯ daily. ● Dec 24–26, Jan 1, Good Fri. limited.
⋔ **Roman Amphitheatre**
Little St John St. 01244 321616.
◯ daily. ● Dec 25, 26, Jan 1, Good Fri.

Stoke-on-Trent ❸

Staffordshire. 250,000. Quadrant Rd, Hanley (01782 284600). Mon–Sat.

FROM THE MID-18TH CENTURY, Staffordshire became a leading center for mass-produced ceramics. Its fame arose from the fine bone china and porcelain products of Wedgwood, Minton, Doulton and Spode,

but the Staffordshire potteries also make a wide range of utilitarian products such as bathtubs, toilets and wall tiles.

In 1910 a group of six towns – Longton, Fenton, Hanley, Burslem, Tunstall and Stoke-upon-Trent – merged to form the conurbation of Stoke-on-Trent, also known as the Potteries. Fans of the writer Arnold Bennett (1867–1931) may recognize this area as the "Five Towns," a term he

used in a series of novels about the region (Fenton was excluded from the stories).

The **Gladstone Pottery Museum** is a Victorian complex of workshops, kilns, galleries and an engine house. There are demonstrations of traditional pottery techniques. The **City Museum and Art Gallery** in Hanley has historic and modern ceramics.

Josiah Wedgwood began his earthenware firm in 1769 and built a workers' village, Etruria (an allusion to Etrurian or Etruscan pottery). The last surviving steam-powered pottery mill is on display at the **Etruria Industrial Museum**.

ENVIRONS: About 10 miles (16 km) north of Stoke-on-Trent is **Little Moreton Hall** (see pp288–9), a half-timbered early Tudor manor house.

🏛 **Gladstone Pottery Museum**
Uttoxeter Rd, Longton. 01782 319232. ◯ daily. ● Dec 25–Jan 1.
🏛 **City Museum and Art Gallery**
Bethesda Rd, Hanley. 01782 202173. ◯ daily. ● Dec 25–Jan 1.
🏛 **Etruria Industrial Museum**
Lower Bedford St, Etruria. 01782 287557. ◯ Wed–Sun. ● Dec 25–Jan 1.
⛪ **Little Moreton Hall**
(NT) off A34. 01260 272018.
◯ Apr–Sep: Wed–Sun & public hols.

STAFFORDSHIRE POTTERY

An abundance of water, marl, clay and easily mined coal to fire the kilns enabled Staffordshire to develop as a ceramics center; and local supplies of iron, copper and lead were used for glazing. In the 18th century, pottery became widely accessible and affordable. English bone china, which used powdered animals' bones for strength and translucence, was shipped all over the world, and Josiah Wedgwood (1730–95) introduced simple, durable crockery – though his best known design is the blue jasperware decorated with white Classical themes. Coal-powered bottle kilns fired the clay until the 1950s Clean Air Acts put them out of business. They have been replaced with electric or gas-fired kilns.

Wedgwood candlesticks, 1785

Timber-framed, gabled mansions in Fish Street, Shrewsbury

Shrewsbury ➍

Shropshire. 🏃 96,000. 🚩 🚌
🛈 The Square (01743 350761).
🛒 Tue, Wed, Fri, Sat.

SHREWSBURY is almost an island, enclosed by a great loop of the River Severn. A gaunt **castle** of red sandstone, first built in 1083, guards the entrance to the town, standing on the only section of land not surrounded by the river. Such defenses were necessary on the frontier between England and the wilder Marches of Wales, whose inhabitants fiercely defied Saxon and Norman invaders *(see pp 46–7)*. The castle, rebuilt over the centuries, now houses the Shropshire Regimental Museum.

In AD 60 the Romans *(see pp44–5)* built the garrison town of *Viroconium*, modern Wroxeter, 5 miles (8 km) east of Shrewsbury. Finds from the excavations are displayed at **Rowley's House Museum**, including a decorated silver mirror from the 2nd century and other luxury goods imported by the Roman army.

The town's other main museum, the **Clive House Museum**, takes its name from Lord Clive *(see p446)*. Clive became the local Member of Parliament upon his return from India until his death,

Roman silver mirror in Rowley's House Museum

and was Mayor of Shrewsbury in 1762, while he lived in this house. The 18th-century brick building has a fine collection of local porcelain, displayed in period settings.

The town's medieval wealth as a center of the wool trade is evident in the many timber-framed buildings found along the High Street, Butcher Row, and Wyle Cop. Two of the finest High Street houses, **Ireland's Mansions** and **Owen's Mansions**, are named after Robert Ireland and Richard Owen, the wealthy wool merchants who built them in 1575 and 1570 respectively. Similarly attractive buildings in Fish Street frame a view of the **Prince Rupert Hotel**, which was briefly the headquarters of the Royalist Prince Rupert in the English Civil War *(see pp52–3)*.

Outside the loop of the river, the **Abbey Church** survives from the medieval monastery. It has a number of interesting memorials, including one to Lieutenant W.E.S. Owen MC, better known as the war poet Wilfred Owen (1893–1918), who taught at the local Wyle Cop school and was killed in the last days of World War I.

ENVIRONS: To the south of Shrewsbury, the road which leads to Ludlow passes through the beautiful landscapes celebrated in the 1896 poem by A.E. Housman (1859–1936), *A Shropshire Lad.* Highlights include the windswept moors of **Long Mynd**, with 15 prehistoric barrows, and the long ridge of **Wenlock Edge**, wonderful walking country with glorious, far-reaching views.

⚜ **Shrewsbury Castle**
Castle St. 【 01743 358516.
◯ Tue–Sun (Oct–Easter: Tue–Sat).
● 2 wks over Christmas. 🖼 🚹
🏛 **Rowley's House Museum**
Barker St. 【 01743 361196.
◯ Tue–Sun (Oct–Easter: Tue–Sat);
public hols. ● 2 wks over Christmas.
🖼 🚹 very limited.
🏛 **Clive House Museum**
College Hill. 【 01743 354811.
◯ Tue–Sun (Oct–Easter: Tue–Sat);
public hols. ● 3 wks over Christmas.
🖼 🚹 limited.

Ironbridge Gorge ➎

See pp300–301.

Ludlow ➏

Shropshire. 🏃 9,000. 🚌 🛈 Castle St (01584 875053).

LUDLOW ATTRACTS large numbers of visitors to its splendid castle, but there is much else to see in this town, with its small shops and its lovely half-timbered Tudor buildings. Ludlow is an important area of geological

The 13th-century south tower and hall of Stokesay Castle, near Ludlow

research and the **museum**, just off the town center, has fossils of the oldest known land animals and plants.

The ruined **castle** is found on cliffs high above the River Teme. Built in 1086, it was damaged in the Civil War *(see pp52–3)* and abandoned in 1689. *Comus,* a court masque using music and drama and a precursor of opera, by John Milton (1608–74), was first performed here in 1634 in the Great Hall. In early summer open-air performances of Shakespeare's plays are held within the castle walls.

Prince Arthur (1486–1502), elder brother of Henry VIII *(see pp50–51),* died at Ludlow Castle. His heart is buried in **St. Laurence Church** at the other end of Castle Square, as are the ashes of the poet A.E. Housman. The east end of the church backs onto the **Bull Ring**, with its ornate timber buildings. Two inns vie for attention across the street: **The Bull**, with its Tudor back yard, and **The Feathers**, with its flamboyant façade, whose name recalls the feathers used in arrow-making, once a local industry.

ENVIRONS: About 5 miles (8 km) north of Ludlow, in a lovely setting, is **Stokesay Castle**, a fortified manor house with a colorful moat garden.

♣ **Ludlow Castle**
The Square. 📞 *01584 873355.*
⬜ *daily.* ⬤ *Dec 24–Feb 1.* 📷
♿ *limited.*

🏛 **Ludlow Museum**
Castle St. 📞 *01584 875384.*
⬜ *Easter–May, Sep: Mon–Sat;*
Jun–Aug: daily. 📷 ♿

♣ **Stokesay Castle**
Craven Arms, A49. 📞 *01588 672544.*
⬜ *Apr–Oct: daily; Nov–Mar: Wed–Sun.*
⬤ *Dec 24–26, Jan 1.* 📷 ♿

Leominster ❼

Herefordshire. 🏠 *10,000.* ✈ 🛈
Corn Sq (01568 616460). 🛍 *Fri.*

FARMERS COME TO LEOMINSTER (pronounced "Lemster") from all over this rural region of England to buy supplies. There are two buildings of note in the town, which has

A view of Leominster, set on the River Lugg in rolling border country

been a wool manufacturing center for 700 years. In the center of the town stands the magnificent **Grange Court**, carved with bold and bizarre figures by the carpenter John Abel in 1633. Nearby is the **priory**, whose imposing Norman portal is carved with an equally strange mixture of mythical birds, beasts and serpents. The lions, at least, can be explained: medieval monks believed the name of Leominster was derived from *monasterium leonis,* "the monastery of the lions." In fact, *leonis* probably comes from medieval, rather than

A Tudor building in Leominster, built with the profits from wool

Classical Latin, and it means "of the marshes." The aptness of this description can readily be seen in the green lanes around the town, following the lush river valleys that come together at Leominster.

ENVIRONS: To the west of the town, along the River Arrow, are the showcase villages of **Eardisland** and **Pembridge**, with their well-kept gardens and timber-framed houses. To the northeast of Leominster is **Tenbury Wells**, which enjoyed a brief popularity as a spa in the 19th century. The River Teme flows through it, full of minnows and spawning salmon and beloved of the composer Sir Edward Elgar *(see p303),* who came to seek inspiration on its banks. The river also feeds **Burford House Gardens**, on the western outskirts of Tenbury Wells, where the water is used to create winding streams, fountains and pools that are rich in a variety of unusual, moisture-loving plants.

♣ **Burford House Gardens**
Tenbury Wells. 📞 *01584 810777.*
⬜ *daily.* ⬤ *Dec 25, 26, Jan 1.* 📷 ♿

Ironbridge Gorge ⑤

IRONBRIDGE GORGE was one of the most important centers of the Industrial Revolution *(see pp54–5)*. It was here, in 1709, that Abraham Darby I (1678–1717) pioneered the use of inexpensive coke, rather than charcoal, to smelt iron ore. The use of iron in bridges, ships and buildings transformed Ironbridge Gorge into one of the world's great ironmaking centers. Industrial decline in the 20th century led to the Gorge's decay, but today it has been restored as an exciting complex of industrial archaeology, with several museums strung along the wooded banks of the River Severn.

VISITORS' CHECKLIST

Shropshire. 🏠 2,900. 🚆 Telford then bus. ☎ 01952 433522. ⏰ Dec–Mar: 10am–4pm; Apr–Jun: 10am–5pm; Jul–Aug: 10am–6pm; Sep–Nov: 10am–5pm daily. ● Dec 24, 25. Some sites closed Nov–Apr, phone for information. ♿ most sites. 🅿️ 🛍 🍴 🎨 Midsummer Fair: Jun (craft workshops and demonstrations throughout the year).

Wrought-iron clock (1843) on the roof of the Museum of Iron

MUSEUM OF IRON

THE HISTORY OF IRON and the men who made it is traced in this remarkable museum. Abraham Darby I's discovery of how to smelt iron ore with coke allowed the mass production of iron, paving the way for the rise of large-scale industry. His original blast furnace forms the museum's centerpiece.

One of the museum's themes is the history of the Darby dynasty, a Quaker family who had a great impact on the Coalbrookdale community. The social and working conditions faced by the laborers, who sometimes had to toil for 24 hours at a stretch, are also illustrated.

Ironbridge led the world in industrial innovation, producing the first iron wheels and cylinders for the first steam engine. A restored locomotive and cast-iron statues, many of them

commissioned for the 1851 Great Exhibition *(see pp56–7)*, are among the many Coalbrookdale Company products on display.

One of the Darby family's homes in the nearby village of Coalbrookdale, **Rosehill House**, has been furnished in mid-Victorian style.

MUSEUM OF THE RIVER

THIS PARTLY CASTELLATED, Victorian building was a warehouse for storing products from the ironworks before they were shipped down the River Severn. The warehouse is now home to the Museum of the River, and has displays illustrating the history of the Severn and the development of the water industry.

Until the arrival of the railroads in the mid-19th century, the Severn was the main form of transportation and communication to and from the Gorge. Sometimes too shallow, at other times flooded, the river was not a particularly reliable means of transportation; by the 1890s river trading had stopped completely. The highlight of the museum is a wonderful 12 m (40 ft) model of the Gorge as it would have appeared in 1796, complete with foundries, cargo boats and growing villages.

Europe (1860), statue in the Museum of Iron

JACKFIELD TILE MUSEUM

THERE HAVE BEEN POTTERIES in this area since the 17th century, but it was not until the Victorian passion for decorative tiles that Jackfield became famous. There were two tile-making factories here – Maw and Craven Dunnill – that produced a tremendous variety of tiles from clay mined nearby.

Peacock Panel (1928), one of the tile museum's star attractions

Talented designers created an astonishing range of images. The Jackfield Tile Museum, in the old Craven Dunnill works, has a collection of the decorative floor and wall tiles that were produced here from the 1850s to the 1960s. Visitors can also watch small-scale demonstrations of traditional methods of tilemaking in the old factory buildings, including the biscuit kilns and the decoration workshops.

IRONBRIDGE GORGE SIGHTS

Blists Hill Museum ⑥
Coalport China
   Museum ⑤
Iron Bridge ③
Jackfield Tile
   Museum ④
Museum of Iron ①
Museum of the River ②

0 kilometers   2

0 miles   1

COALPORT CHINA MUSEUM

IN THE MID-19TH CENTURY the Coalport Works was one of the largest porcelain manufacturers in Britain, and its name was synonymous with fine china. The Coalport Company still makes porcelain but has long since moved its operations to Stoke-on-Trent (*see p297*). Today the china workshops have been converted into a museum, where visitors can watch demonstrations of the various stages of making porcelain, including the skills of pot throwing, painting and gilding. There is a superb collection of 19th-century china housed in one of the museum's distinctive bottle-shaped kilns.

Coalport China Museum with its bottle-shaped kiln

Nearby is the **Tar Tunnel**, an important source of natural bitumen discovered 110 m (360 ft) underground in the 18th century. It once yielded 20,500 liters (5,416 gal) of tar every week; visitors can still explore part of the tunnel.

THE IRON BRIDGE

Abraham Darby III (grandson of the first man to smelt iron with coke) cast the world's first iron bridge in 1779, revolutionizing building methods in the process. Spanning the Severn, the bridge is a monument to the ironmasters' skills. The tollhouse on the south bank charts its construction.

BLISTS HILL MUSEUM

THIS ENORMOUS OPEN-AIR museum re-creates life in Ironbridge Gorge as it was 100 years ago. A group of 19th-century buildings has been reconstructed on the 20 ha (50 acre) site of Blists Hill, an old coal mine that used to supply the ironworks in the Gorge. Here, people in period costume enact roles and perform tasks such as iron forging.

The site has period housing, a church and even a Victorian school. Visitors can change money into old coinage to buy items from the baker or even pay for a drink in the local pub.

The centerpiece of Blists Hill is a complete foundry that still -produces wrought iron. One of the most spectacular sights is the Hay Inclined Plane, which was used to transport canal boats up and down a steep slope. Other attractions include steam engines, a saddlers, a doctors, a drugstore, a candlemakers and a candy store.

Hereford ❽

Herefordshire. 👥 50,000. 🚆 📧
ℹ️ King St (01432 268430).
🛒 Wed (cattle), Sat (general).

O NCE THE CAPITAL of the
Saxon kingdom of West
Mercia, Hereford is today an
attractive town that serves the
needs of a primarily rural
community. A cattle market is
held here every Wednesday,
and local produce is sold at
the covered market in the
town center. Almost opposite,
the timber-framed **Old House**
of 1621 is now a museum of
local history, refurbished with
a mixture of reproduction and
original Jacobean furniture.

In the **cathedral**, only a
short stroll away, interesting
features include the Lady
Chapel, in richly ornamented
Early English style, and the
Chained Library, whose 1,500
books are tethered by iron
chains to bookcases as a
precaution against theft. The
best place for an
overall view of the
cathedral is at the
Bishop's Meadow,
south of the center,
leading down to the
banks of the Wye,
scene of the annual
Hereford Regatta.

Hereford's many
rewarding museums
include the **City
Museum and Art
Gallery**, noted for its
Roman mosaics and
for watercolors by local
artists, and the **Churchill
House Museum** of 18th- and
19th-century furniture and
costume. Set outside the latter

**Detail of figures on
Kilpeck Church**

Hereford's 17th-century Old House, furnished in period style

is Roaring Meg, a cannon used
in the Civil War *(see pp52–3)*.
Visitors to the **Cider Museum
and King Offa Distillery** can
learn how local apples are
turned into 250 million liters
(66 million gal) of
cider a year, by a
range of old and
new methods.

ENVIRONS: During the
12th century, Oliver
de Merlemond made
a pilgrimage from
Hereford to Spain.
Impressed by several
churches he saw on
the way, he brought
French masons over
and introduced their
techniques to this area. One
result was **Kilpeck Church**,
6 miles (10 km) southwest,
covered in lustful figures
showing their genitals, and

tail-biting dragons – all seeming more pagan than Christian.
At **Abbey Dore**, 4 miles (6
km) west, the Cistercian abbey
church is complemented by
the serene riverside gardens
of **Abbey Dore Court**.

🏛 **Old House**
High Town. 📞 01432 268121.
⭕ Jun–Oct: daily; Nov–May: Tue–Sat
& public hols. ⬤ Dec 25, 26, Jan 1,
Good Fri . 📷

🏛 **City Museum and Art
Gallery**
Broad St. 📞 01432 268121.
⭕ May–Sep: Tue–Sun; Oct–Apr:
Tue–Sat & public hols. ⬤ Dec 25, 26,
Jan 1, Good Fri. ♿

🏛 **Churchill House Museum**
Venus Lane. 📞 01432 267409.
⭕ May–Sep: Tue–Sun (pm); Oct–Apr:
Tue–Sat & public hols. ⬤ Dec 25, 26,
Jan 1, Good Fri. 📷 ♿

🏛 **Cider Museum and King
Offa Distillery**
Ryelands St. 📞 01432 354207.
⭕ Apr–Oct: daily; Nov–Mar: Mon–Sat
& public hols. ⬤ Dec 24–26, Jan 1, 2.
📷 ♿ limited.

Ross-on-Wye ❾

Herefordshire. 👥 10,000. 📧
ℹ️ Eddie Cross St (01989 562768).
🛒 Thu, Sat.

T HE FINE TOWN of Ross sits
on a cliff of red sandstone
above the water meadows of
the River Wye. There are wonderful views over the river
from the cliff-top gardens,

MEDIEVAL VIEW

Hereford Cathedral's most
celebrated treasure is the
Mappa Mundi, the Map of
the World, drawn in 1290
by a clergyman, Richard of
Haldingham. The world is
depicted here on Biblical
principles: Jerusalem is at
the center, the Garden of
Eden figures prominently
and monsters inhabit the
margins of the world.

Central detail, *Mappa Mundi*

The wooded Wye Valley near Ross

given to the town by a local benefactor, John Kyrle (1637–1724). Kyrle was lauded by the poet Alexander Pope (1688–1744) in his *Moral Essays on the Uses of Riches* (1732) for using his wealth in a practical way, and he came to be known as "The Man of Ross." There is a memorial to Kyrle in **St. Mary's Church**.

ENVIRONS: From Hereford to Ross, the **Wye Valley Walk** follows 16 miles (26 km) of gentle countryside. From Ross it continues south for 33 miles (54 km), over rocky ground in deep, wooded ravines. **Goodrich Castle**, 5 miles (8 km) south of Ross, is a 12th-century red sandstone fort that sits on the summit of a rock high above the river.

⚜ **Goodrich Castle**
Goodrich. 🕻 *01600 890538.*
⬜ *daily.* ⬤ *Dec 24–26, Jan 1.* 🈺

Ledbury ⑩

Herefordshire. 🏠 *6,500.* 🚉 🚌
🛈 *Church Lane (01531 636147).*

L EDBURY'S MAIN STREET is lined with timbered houses, including the **Market Hall** of 1655. Church Lane, a cobbled alley running up from the High Street, has lovely 16th-century buildings: the **Old Grammar School** and **Butcher Row House** are both now museums. **St. Michael and All Angels Church** has a massive detached bell tower, ornate Early English decoration and interesting monuments.

Medieval tile from the Priory at Great Malvern

🏛 **Old Grammar School**
Church Lane. 🕻 *01531 636147.*
⬜ *Easter–Oct: daily.* ♿
🏛 **Butcher Row House**
Church Lane. 🕻 *01531 632040.*
⬜ *Easter–Oct: daily.*

Great Malvern and the Malverns ⑪

Herefordshire. 🏠 *40,000.* 🚉 🚌
🛈 *Winter Gardens Complex, Grange Rd (01684 892289).* 🛍 *Fri.*

T HE ANCIENT GRANITE ROCK of the Malvern Hills rises from the plain of the River Severn, its 9 miles (15 km) of glorious scenery visible from afar. Composer Sir Edward Elgar (1857–1934) wrote many of his greatest works here, including the oratorio *The Dream of Gerontius* (1900), inspired by what the diarist John Evelyn (1620–1706) described as "one of the goodliest views in England". Elgar's home was in **Little Malvern**, whose truncated Priory Church of St. Giles, set on a steep wooded hill, lost its nave when the stone was stolen during the Dissolution of the Monasteries (*see pp50–51*). **Great Malvern**, capital of the hills, is graced with 19th-century buildings that look like Swiss sanitoriums: patients would stay at institutions such as Doctor Gulley's Water Cure Establishment (now the Tudor Hotel). The water gushing from the hillside at St. Ann's Well, above town, is bottled and sold throughout Britain.

Malvern's highlight is the **Priory**, with its 15th-century stained-glass windows and medieval misericords. The old monastic fishponds below the church form the lake of the **Winter Gardens**. Here the Festival Theatre hosts performances of Elgar's music and plays by George Bernard Shaw (*see p219*) during the Malvern Festival in late May.

A view of the Malverns range, formed of hard Pre-Cambrian rock

Worcester ⑫

Worcestershire. 🏛 86,000. 🚇 🏢
🚊 High St (01905 722480). 🛒 Tue,
Wed, Thu, Sat.

Worcester is one of many English cities whose character has been transformed by modern development. The architectural highlight remains the **cathedral**, off College Yard, which suffered a collapsed tower in 1175 and a disastrous fire in 1203, before the present structure was started in the 13th century.

The nave and central tower were completed in the 1370s, after building was severely interrupted by the Black Death, which decimated the labor force *(see pp48–9)*. The most recent and ornate addition was made in 1874, when Sir George Gilbert Scott *(see p451)* designed the High Gothic choir, incorporating 14th-century carved misericords.

There are many interesting tombs, including King John's *(see pp48–9)*, a masterpiece

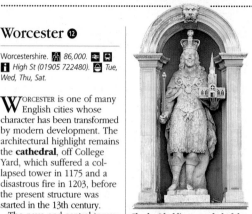

Charles I holding a symbol of the Church on Worcester's Guildhall

of medieval carving, in front of the altar. Prince Arthur, Henry VIII's brother *(see p299)*, who died at the age of 15, is buried in the chantry chapel south of the altar. Underneath, the huge Norman crypt survives from the first cathedral (1084).

From the cathedral cloister, a gate leads to College Green and the cathedral school, and out into Edgar Street and its

Georgian houses. Here the **Dyson Perrins Museum** displays Royal Worcester porcelain dating back to 1751. On the High Street, north of the cathedral, the **Guildhall** of 1723 is adorned with statues of Stuart monarchs, reflecting the city's Royalist allegiances. In Cornmarket you can see **Ye Olde King Charles House**, in which Prince Charles, later Charles II, hid after the Battle of Worcester in 1651 *(see pp52–3)*.

Some of Worcester's finest timber buildings are found in Friar Street: **Greyfriars**, built around 1480, has been newly decorated in period style. The **Commandery** was originally an 11th-century hospital. It was rebuilt in the 15th century and used by Prince Charles as a base during the Civil War. Now a Civil War museum, it has a fine hammer-beam roof and a painted chamber.

Elgar's Birthplace was the home of composer Sir Edward Elgar *(see p303)*. It contains displays of memorabilia relating to his life and works.

🏛 **Dyson Perrins Museum**
Severn St. 📞 01905 23221.
⬜ Mon–Sat. ⬤ Dec 25, 26, Jan 1.
🎫 ♿
🏰 **Greyfriars**
(NT) Friar St. 📞 01905 23571. ⬜
Easter–Oct: Wed, Thu & public hols. 🎫
🏛 **Commandery**
Sidbury. 📞 01905 355071. ⬜ daily.
⬤ Dec 25, 26, Jan 1. 🎫
🏛 **Elgar's Birthplace**
Lower Broadheath. 📞 01905 333224.
⬜ Oct–Apr: Thu–Tue (pm); May–Sep:
Thu–Tue. ⬤ Dec 24–26. 🎫

Birmingham ⑬

West Midlands. 🏛 1,000,000. ✈
🚇 🏢 🏢 City Arcade (0121
6432514). 🛒 Mon–Sat.

Brum, as it is affectionately known to its inhabitants, grew up as a major center of the Industrial Revolution in the 19th century. A vast range of manufacturing trades was based in Birmingham and was responsible for the rapid development of grim factories and cramped housing. Since the clearance of several of these areas after World War II,

Worcester Cathedral, overlooking the River Severn

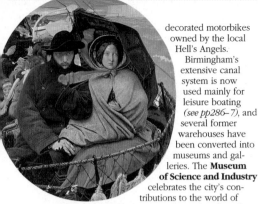

***The Last of England*, Ford Madox Brown, Birmingham Art Gallery**

Birmingham has raised its cultural profile. The city has succeeded in enticing Sir Simon Rattle to conduct the City of Birmingham Symphony Orchestra, and persuaded the former Royal Sadler's Wells Ballet (now the Birmingham Royal Ballet) to leave London for the more up-to-date facilities of Birmingham. The **National Exhibition Centre**, 8 miles (13 km) east of the center, draws thousands of people to its conference, lecture and exhibition halls.

Set away from the massive Bullring shopping center, Birmingham's 19th-century civic buildings are excellent examples of Neo-Classical architecture. Among them are the **City Museum and Art Gallery**, where the collection includes outstanding works by pre-Raphaelite artists such as Sir Edward Burne-Jones (1833–98), who was born here, and Ford Madox Brown (1821–93). The museum also organizes some interesting temporary exhibitions of art, ranging from Canaletto (1697–1768) to the gaudily decorated motorbikes owned by the local Hell's Angels.

Birmingham's extensive canal system is now used mainly for leisure boating *(see pp286–7)*, and several former warehouses have been converted into museums and galleries. The **Museum of Science and Industry** celebrates the city's contributions to the world of train engines, aircraft, and the motor trade. In the old jewelry quarter to the north of the museum, the jewelers continue a traditional craft dating from the 16th century.

Suburban Birmingham has many attractions, including the **Botanical Gardens** at Edgbaston, and the popular **Cadbury World** at Bournville, where there is a visitor center dedicated to chocolate (call ahead to reserve). Bournville village was built in 1890 by the Cadbury brothers, who were Quakers, for their workers and is a pioneering example of a garden suburb.

City Museum and Art Gallery
Chamberlain Sq. 0121 2352834. *daily.* *Dec 23–27, Jan 1, 2.*

Museum of Science and Industry
Newhall St. *0121 2351661.* *daily.* *Dec 23–27, Jan 1, 2.*

Botanical Gardens
Westbourne Rd, Edgbaston. *0121 4541860.* *daily.* *Dec 25.*

Cadbury World
Linden Rd, Bournville. *0121 4514159.* *Apr–Oct: daily; Nov–Mar: Wed, Thu, Sat & Sun.* *Nov 4, 11, Dec 16, 23–25, 31.*

Stately civic office buildings in Victoria Square, Birmingham

Coventry ⓮

West Midlands. *295,000.* *Bayley Lane (01203 832303).* *Mon–Sat.*

As an armaments center, Coventry was a prime target for German bombing raids in World War II, and in 1940 the medieval **cathedral** in the city center was hit. After the war the first totally modern cathedral, designed by Sir Basil Spence (1907–76), was built alongside the ruins of the bombed building. Sir Jacob Epstein (1880–1959) added dramatic sculptures, and Graham Sutherland (1903–80) made the splendid tapestry, *Christ in Majesty*, on the east wall. Benjamin Britten *(see p189)* composed his *War Requiem* for the rededication ceremony, held on May 30, 1962.

Epstein's *St. Michael subduing the Devil*, on Coventry Cathedral

The **Herbert Gallery and Museum** has displays on the 11th-century legend of Lady Godiva, who rode naked through the streets in protest when her husband, the Earl of Mercia, imposed taxes on the town. The city residents remained indoors, except for Peeping Tom, who was struck blind for his curiosity.

Herbert Gallery and Museum
Jordan Well. *01203 832381.* *daily.* *Dec 25, 26, Jan 1, 2.*

Midlands Garden Tour ⑮

Plum tree
in blossom

THE CHARMING COTSWOLD STONE BUILDINGS perfectly complement the lush gardens for which the region is famous. This picturesque route from Warwick to Cheltenham is designed to show every type of garden, from tiny cottage plots, brimming with bell-shaped flowers and hollyhocks, to the deer-filled, landscaped parks of stately homes. The route follows the escarpment of the Cotswold Hills, taking in spectacular scenery and some of the prettiest Midlands villages on the way.

TIPS FOR DRIVERS

Tour length: 35 miles (50 km).
Stopping-off points: Hidcote Manor has excellent lunches and teas; there are refreshments at Kiftsgate Court and Sudeley Castle. Travelers will find a good choice in Broadway, from traditional pubs and tea shops to the deluxe Lygon Arms. (See also pp636–7.)

Cheltenham Imperial Gardens ⑨
These colorful public gardens on the Promenade were laid out in 1817–18 to encourage people to walk from the town to the spa *(see p312)*.

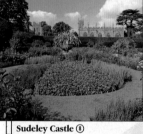

Sudeley Castle ⑧
The restored castle is complemented by boxwood hedges, topiary and a π knot garden *(see p22)*. Catherine Parr, Henry VIII's widow, died here in 1548.

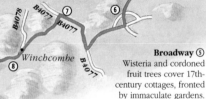

Broadway ⑤
Wisteria and cordoned fruit trees cover 17th-century cottages, fronted by immaculate gardens.

Stanway House ⑦
This Jacobean manor has many lovely trees in its grounds and a pyramid above a cascade of water.

Snowshill Manor ⑥
This Cotswold stone manor contains an extraordinary collection, from bicycles to Japanese armor. There are walled gardens and terraces full of *objets d'art* such as the clock (left). The color blue is a feature.

THE HEART OF ENGLAND

Warwick Castle ①
The castle's gardens
(see pp308–9) include
Mound, planted in
medieval style, with
ass, oaks, yew trees
boxwood hedges.

ne Hathaway's Cottage ②
is has a pretty, informal 16th-
ntury style garden (see p313).

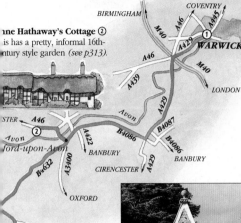

**Hidcote Manor
Gardens ③**
Started in the early
years of this century,
these beautiful gardens
pioneered the idea of a
garden as a series of
outdoor "rooms,"
enclosed by high yew
hedges and planted
according to themes.

Kiftsgate Court Garden ④
This charmingly naturalistic garden
lies opposite Hidcote Manor. It has
many rare and unusual plants on a
series of hillside terraces, including
the enormous "Kiftsgate" Rose, nearly
30 m (100 ft) high.

KEY

▬▬▬	Highway
▬▬▬	Tour route
═══	Other roads
﹡	Viewpoint

0 kilometers   5

0 miles   5

Warwick ⑯

Warwickshire. 👥 28,000. 🚆 🚌
ℹ The Courthouse, Jury St (01926
492212). 🛒 Sat.

THOUGH WARWICK suffered a
major fire in 1694, some
spectacular medieval buildings survived. The **Warwick
Doll Museum** in Castle Street
(1573) displays rare toys and
dolls from all over the world.
At the west end of the High
Street, a row of medieval guild
buildings were transformed in
1571 by the Earl of Leicester
(1532–88), who founded the
Lord Leycester Hospital as
a refuge for his old retainers.
The arcaded **Market Hall**
(1670) in the Market Place is
now part of the Warwickshire
Museum, renowned for its
unusual tapestry map of the
county, woven in 1558.
In Church Street, on the
south side of St. Mary's church,
the **Beauchamp Chapel**
(1443–64) survived the 1694
fire. It is a superb example of
Perpendicular architecture and
has fine tombs of the Earls of
Warwick. There is a bird's-eye
view of **Warwick Castle** (see
pp308–9) from St. Mary's tower.

🏛 **Warwick Doll Museum**
Castle St. 📞 01926 495546.
◻ Easter–Sep: daily (Sun: pm):
(Oct–Easter: Sat). 🎫 🛠 limited.
🏰 **Lord Leycester Hospital**
High St. 📞 01926 491422.
◻ Tue–Sun & public hols. 🚫 Dec
25, Good Fri. 🎫 🛠 limited.
🏛 **Market Hall**
Market Place. 📞 01926 410410.
◻ May–Sep: daily. (Sun: pm).
🚫 Dec 24, 25,
Jan 1. 🛠 limited.

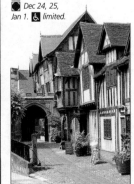

**The Lord Leycester Hospital,
now a home for ex-servicemen**

Warwick Castle

W ARWICK'S MAGNIFICENT CASTLE is a splendid medieval fortress, which is also one of the country's finest stately homes. The original Norman castle was rebuilt in the 14th century, when huge outer walls and towers were added, mainly

Neville family at prayer (c.1460)

to display the power of the great feudal magnates, the Beauchamps and the Nevilles, the Earls of Warwick. The castle passed in 1604 to the Greville family who, in the 17th and 18th centuries, transformed it into a great country house. In 1978 the owners of Madame Tussaud's (see p106) bought the castle and set up tableaux of wax figures to illustrate its history.

Watergate Tower is where the ghost of Sir Fulke Greville, murdered by a servant in 1628, is said to walk.

The Mound has remains of the motte and bailey castle (see p472) and the 13th century keep.

Royal Weekend Exhibition
The waxwork valet is part of the award-winning exhibition of the Prince of Wales's visit in 1898.

★ Great Hall and State Rooms
Medieval apartments were transformed into the Great Hall and State Rooms, and rebuilt after a fire in 1871. The Great Hall is filled with arms, armor, furniture and curiosities.

Kingmaker Exhibition
Dramatic displays re-create medieval life as "Warwick the Kingmaker," Richard Neville, prepared for battle in the Wars of the Roses (see p49).

View of Warwick Castle, south front, by Antonio Canaletto (1697–1768)

VISITORS' CHECKLIST

Castle Lane, Warwick. 01926
495421. Apr–Oct: 10am–6pm
daily; Nov–Mar: 10am–5pm daily
(last adm: 30 mins before closing).
Dec 25. limited.

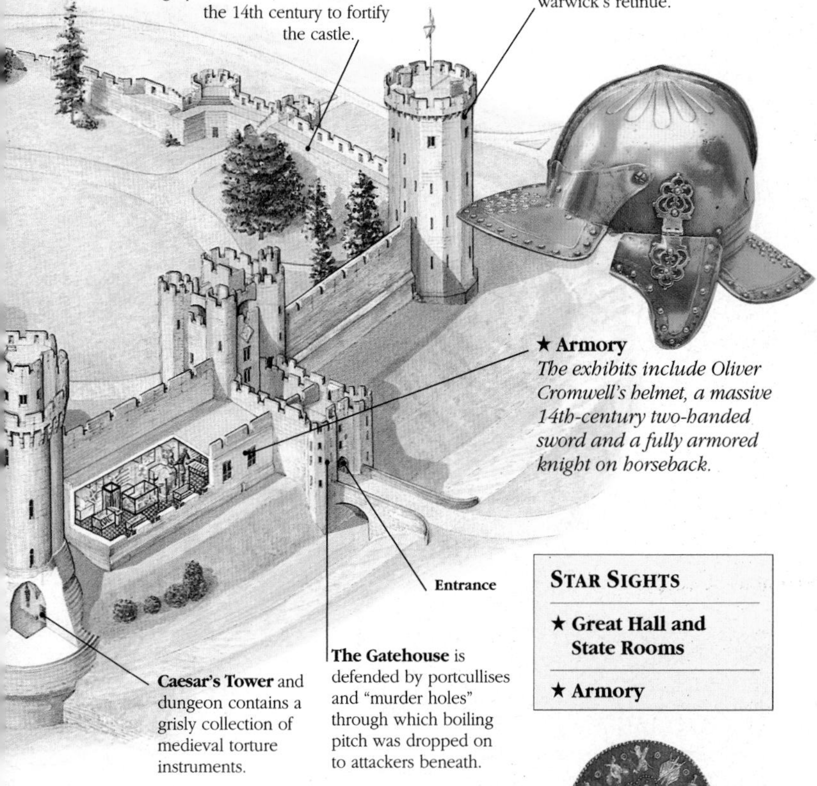

Ramparts and towers, of local
gray sandstone, were added in
the 14th century to fortify
the castle.

Guy's Tower (1393) has
lodgings for guests and
members of the Earl of
Warwick's retinue.

★ Armory
*The exhibits include Oliver
Cromwell's helmet, a massive
14th-century two-handed
sword and a fully armored
knight on horseback.*

Entrance

STAR SIGHTS

**★ Great Hall and
State Rooms**

★ Armory

Caesar's Tower and
dungeon contains a
grisly collection of
medieval torture
instruments.

The Gatehouse is
defended by portcullises
and "murder holes"
through which boiling
pitch was dropped on
to attackers beneath.

TIMELINE

1068 Norman motte and bailey castle built	**1264** Simon de Montfort, champion of Parliament against Henry III, sacks Warwick Castle		*Shield (1745), Great Hall*	**1478** Castle reverts to Crown after murder of Richard Neville's son-in-law	**1893–1910** Visits from future Edward VII
1000	**1200**	**1400**		**1600**	**1800**
	Richard Neville		**1604** James I gives castle to Sir Fulke Greville	**1642** Royalists imprisoned in the castle	**1871** Anthony Salvin (1799–1881) restores Great Hall and State Rooms after fire
	1356–1401 Present castle built by the Beauchamp family, Earls of Warwick			**1600–1800** Interiors remodeled and gardens landscaped	
	1449–1471 Richard Neville, Earl of Warwick, plays leading role in Wars of the Roses				

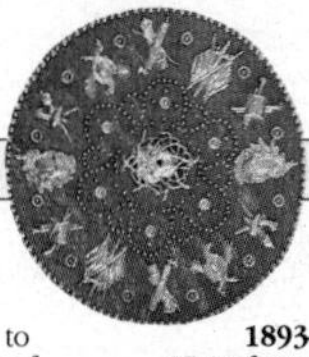

Street-by-Street: Stratford-upon-Avon ⑰

A 1930s jester

SITUATED ON THE WEST BANK of the River Avon, in the heart of the Midlands, is one of the most famous towns in England. Stratford-upon-Avon dates back to at least Roman times but its appearance today is that of a small Tudor market town, with mellow, half-timbered architecture and tranquil walks beside the tree-fringed Avon. This image belies its popularity as the most visited tourist attraction outside London, with eager hordes flocking to see buildings connected to William Shakespeare or his descendants.

Bancroft Gardens
There is an attractive boat-filled canal basin here and a 15th-century causeway.

Tourist information and railroad station

The Cage

WATE

BRIDGE STREET

HIGH STREET

UNION STREET

★ Shakespeare's Birthplace
This building was almost entirely recon-structed in the 19th century, but in the style of the Tudor original.

0 meters	100
0 yards	100

Shakespeare Centre

HENLEY STREET

MEER STREET

WOOD STREET

ELY STREET

Harvard House
The novelist Marie Corelli (1855–1924) had this house restored. Next door is the 16th-century Garrick Inn.

Old Bank

STAR SIGHTS

★ Shakespeare's Birthplace

★ Hall's Croft

★ Holy Trinity Church

Town Hall
Built in 1767, there are traces of 18th-century graffiti on the front of the building saying God Save the King.

Royal Shakespeare Theatre
The highly acclaimed resident theater company, the RSC, has staged all of Shakespeare's plays since it began in 1961.

VISITORS' CHECKLIST

Warwickshire. 🚶 22,000.
✈ 20 miles (32 km) NW of
Stratford-upon-Avon. 🚌 Alcester
Rd. 🚉 Bridge St. 🛈 Bridge Foot
(01789 293127); Shakespeare
Centre, Henley St (01789 204016).
📅 Fri. 🎭 Shakespeare's Birthday:
Apr; Stratford Festival: Jul; Mop
Fair: Oct.

★ **Hall's Croft**
John Hall, Shakespeare's son-in-law, was a doctor. This delightful house has one room fitted out as a dispensary, with original Jacobean furniture.

★ **Holy Trinity Church**
Shakespeare's grave and copies of the parish register entries recording his birth and death are here.

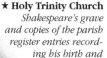

AVON

CHAPEL LANE

SOUTHERN LANE

OLD TOWN

CHURCH STREET

OLD TOWN

→ **Swindon**

Edward VI Grammar School

Nash's House
The foundations of New Place, where Shakespeare died, form the garden beside this house.

Guild Chapel

ane
athaway's
ottage

KEY

– – – Suggested route

Exploring Stratford-upon-Avon

WILLIAM SHAKESPEARE was born in Stratford-upon-Avon on St. George's Day, April 23, 1564. Admirers of his work have been coming to the town since his death in 1616. In 1847 a public appeal successfully raised the money to buy the house in which he was born. As a result Stratford has become a literary shrine to Britain's greatest dramatist. It also has a thriving cultural reputation as the provincial home of the prestigious Royal Shakespeare Company, whose dramas are usually performed in Stratford before playing a second season in London *(see p124)*.

Mosaic of Shakespeare on the beautiful Old Bank (1810)

Anne Hathaway's Cottage, home of Shakespeare's wife

Around Stratford

The center of Stratford-upon-Avon has many buildings that are connected with William Shakespeare and his descendants. On the High Street corner is the **Cage**, a 15th-century prison. It was converted into a house where Shakespeare's daughter Judith lived, and is now a store. At the end of the High Street, the **Town Hall** has a statue of Shakespeare on the façade given by David Garrick (1717–79), the actor who in 1769 organized the first Shakespeare festival.

The High Street leads into Chapel Street where the half-timber **Nash's House** is a museum of local history. It is also the site of **New Place**, where Shakespeare died in 1616, and which is now a herb and knot garden *(see p22)*. On Church Street opposite, the **Guild Chapel** (1496) has a *Last Judgement* painting (c.1500) on the chancel wall. Shakespeare is thought to have attended the **Edward VI Grammar School** (above the former Guildhall) next door.

A left turn into Old Town leads to **Hall's Croft**, home of Shakespeare's daughter Susanna, which has displays of fascinating 16th- and 17th-century medical artifacts. An avenue of lime trees leads to **Holy Trinity Church**, where Shakespeare is buried. A walk along the river from this point follows the Avon to **Bancroft Gardens**, which lies at the junction of the River Avon and the Stratford Canal.

🎭 Shakespeare's Birthplace

Henley St. 📞 *01789 204016.* ⬜ *daily.* ⬤ *Dec 24–26.* 📷 ♿ *limited.* Bought for the nation in 1847, when it was a public house, Shakespeare's Birthplace was converted back to Elizabethan style. Objects associated with Shakespeare's father, John, a glovemaker and wool merchant, are on display. The room in which Shakespeare was supposedly born (arbitrarily chosen by Garrick) has a window etched with visitors' autographs, including that of Sir Walter Scott *(see p498).*

Holy Trinity Church, seen across the River Avon

♜ Harvard House

High St. ☎ 01789 204016. ◯ mid-May–Sep: Mon–Sat. 🎫 ♿ limited.
Built in 1596 and decorated with grotesque carved heads, this was the childhood home of Katherine Rogers. Her son, John Harvard, emigrated to America and in 1638 left his estate to a new college, later renamed Harvard University. The house displays material relating to the family.

ENVIRONS: No tour of Stratford would be complete without a visit to **Anne Hathaway's Cottage**. Before her marriage to William Shakespeare she lived at Shottery, 1 mile (1.5 km) west of Stratford. Despite fire damage in 1969, the cottage is still impressive, with some original 16th-century furniture. The Hathaway descendants lived here until the early 20th century, and there is a fine garden (see p307).

♜ Anne Hathaway's Cottage

Cottage Lane. ☎ 01789 292100.
◯ daily. ◯ Dec 24–26. 🎫

Kenneth Branagh in *Hamlet*

THE ROYAL SHAKESPEARE COMPANY

The Royal Shakespeare Company is renowned for its new interpretations of Shakespeare's work. The company performs at the 1932 Royal Shakespeare Theatre, a windowless brick building adjacent to the Swan Theatre, built in 1986 to a design based on an Elizabethan playhouse. Next to it is a building displaying sets, props and costumes. The RSC also performs at the 150-seat theater, known as the Other Place, and in London (see p124).

Grevel House, the oldest house in Chipping Campden

Chipping Campden ⑱

Gloucestershire. 🚆 2,000.
🅸 Hollis House, Stow-on-the-Wold (01451 831082).

THIS PERFECT Cotswold town is kept in pristine condition by the Campden Trust. Set up in 1929, the Trust has kept alive the traditional skills of stonecarving and repair that make Chipping Campden such a unified picture of golden-colored and lichen-patched stone. Visitors traveling from the northwest along the B4035 first see a group of ruins: the remains of **Campden Manor**, begun around 1613 by Sir Baptist Hicks, 1st Viscount Campden. The manor was burned by Royalist troops to stop it being sequestered by Parliament at the end of the Civil War (see pp52–3), but the poorhouses opposite the gateway were spared. They were designed in the form of the letter "I" (which is Latin for "J"), a symbol of the owner's loyalty to King James I.

The town's **Church of St. James**, one of the finest in the Cotswolds, was built in the 15th century, financed by merchants who bought wool from Cotswold farmers and exported it at a high profit. Inside the church there are many elaborate tombs, and a magnificent brass dedicated to William Grevel, describing him as "the flower of the wool merchants of England." He built **Grevel House** (c.1380) on High Street, the oldest in a fine row of buildings, which is distinguished by a double-story bay window.

Viscount Campden donated the **Market Hall** in 1627. His contemporary, Robert Dover, founded the "Cotswold Olimpicks" in 1612, long before the modern Olympic Games had been established. The 1612 version included such painful events as the shin-kicking contest. It still takes place on the first Friday after each Spring Bank Holiday, followed by a torchlit procession into town, readied for the Scuttlebrook Wake Fair on the next day. The games are set on a natural hollow on **Dover's Hill** above the town, which is worth climbing for the marvelous views over the Vale of Evesham.

The 17th-century Market Hall in Chipping Campden

Tewkesbury's abbey church overlooks the town, crowded onto the bank of the River Severn

Tewkesbury ⑲

Gloucestershire. 🏘 *11,000.*
ℹ *Barton St (01684 295027).*
🗓 *Wed, Sat.*

THIS LOVELY TOWN sits on the confluence of the rivers Severn and Avon. It has one of England's finest Norman abbey churches, **St. Mary the Virgin**. Locals saved it during the Dissolution of the Monasteries *(see p50)* by paying Henry VIII £453 ($693). Around the church, with its bulky tower and Norman façade, timbered buildings are crammed within the river's bend, including once-prosperous ware-houses and wharves. The Borough Mill on Quay Street, the only mill left harnessed to the river's energy, still grinds grain.

Pump Room detail, Cheltenham

ENVIRONS: Boat trips can be taken from the river marina to **Upton-on-Severn**'s riverside pubs, 6 miles (10 km) north.

Cheltenham ⑳

Gloucestershire. 🏘 *107,000.* 🚇 🚌
ℹ *77 Promenade (01242 522878).*
🗓 *Thu, Sun.*

CHELTENHAM'S REPUTATION for elegance was first gained in the late 18th century, when high society flocked to the

spa town to "take the waters", following the example set by George III *(see pp54–5)*. Many gracious terraced houses were built, in a Neo-Classical style, along broad avenues. These survive around the Queen's Hotel, near **Montpellier**, a lovely Regency arcade lined with craft and antique shops, and in the **Promenade**, with its stylish department stores and couturiers. A more modern atmosphere prevails in the new Regency Arcade, where the star attraction is the 1987 **clock** by Kit Williams: visit on the hour to see fish blowing bubbles over the onlookers' heads. The **Museum and Art Gallery** is worth a visit to see its unusual collection of furniture and other crafts made by members of the influential Arts and Crafts Movement *(see p25)*, whose strict principles of utili-tarian design were laid down by William Morris *(see p206)*.

Fashion from the Regency period to the 1960s is dis-played in the domed **Pitville Pump Room** (1825–30), mod-eled on the Greek Temple of Ilissos in Athens and frequently used for performances during the town's famous annual festivals of music (July) and literature (October).

The event that really attracts the crowds, though, is the Cheltenham Gold Cup – the

premier event of the National Hunt season – held annually in March at Prestbury race course to the east of the town *(see p66)*.

🏛 **Museum and Art Gallery**
Clarence St. 📞 *01242 237431.*
⭘ *Mon–Sat.* ⬤ *public hols;*
Dec 24. ♿
♨ **Pitville Pump Room**
Pitville Park. 📞 *01242 523852.*
⭘ *Wed–Mon.* ⬤ *Dec 25, 26, Jan 1.*

Fantasy clock, by Kit Williams, in Cheltenham's Regency Arcade

Gloucester Cathedral's nave

Gloucester ㉑

Gloucestershire. 🏠 110,000. ≋ 🚃
ℹ️ St. Michael's Tower, The Cross
(01452 421188). 🏛 Wed, Sat.

GLOUCESTER has played a prominent role in the history of England. It was here that William the Conqueror ordered a vast survey of all the land in his kingdom, to be recorded in the Domesday Book of 1086 *(see p47)*.

The city was popular with the Norman monarchs and in 1216 Henry III was crowned in its magnificent **cathedral**. The solid, dignified nave was begun in 1089. Edward II *(see p425)*, who was murdered in 1327 at Berkeley Castle, 14 miles (22 km) to the south-west, is buried in a tomb near the high altar. Many pilgrims came to honor Edward's tomb, leaving behind generous donations, and Abbot Thoky was able to begin rebuilding in 1331. The result was the wonderful east window, and the cloisters where the fan vault was developed, a feature that was copied to great effect in other churches all over the country.

The impressive buildings around the cathedral include College Court, with its **Beatrix Potter Museum** in the house used by the children's author *(see p353)* for her illustrations of the story of the *Tailor of Gloucester*. A museum complex has been created in the **Gloucester Docks**, part of which is still a port, linked to the Bristol Channel by the Gloucester and Sharpness Canal (opened in 1827). In the old port, the **National Waterways Museum** relates the history of canals, and the fascinating **Robert Opie Collection – Museum of Advertising and Packaging** looks at the promotion of household goods from 1870 to the present day.

🏛 **Beatrix Potter Museum**
College Court. 📞 01452 422856.
🕐 Mon–Sat. 🔴 public hols.
🏛 **National Waterways Museum**
Llanthony Warehouse, Gloucester Docks. 📞 01452 318054. 🕐 daily.
🔴 Dec 25. 🎫 ♿
🏛 **Robert Opie Collection – Museum of Advertising and Packaging**
Albert Warehouse, Gloucester Docks.
📞 01452 302309. 🕐 daily. 🔴
Dec 25, 26. 🎫 ♿

Cirencester ㉒

Gloucestershire. 🏠 18,000. ≋ 🚃
ℹ️ Market Place (01285 654180).
🏛 Mon–Sat.

KNOWN AS THE CAPITAL of the Cotswolds, Cirencester has as its focus a market place where cheese, fish, flowers, and herbs are sold every Friday. Overlooking the market is the **Church of St. John Baptist**, whose "wineglass" pulpit (1515) is one of the few pre-Reformation pulpits to survive in England. To the west, **Cirencester Park** was laid out by the 1st Earl of Bathurst from 1714, with help from the poet Alexander Pope *(see p303)*. The mansion is surrounded by a massive yew hedge, claimed to be the tallest in the world. Clustering around the park entrance are the 17th- and 18th-century wool merchants' houses of Cecily Hill, built in grand Italianate style. Much humbler Cotswold houses are to be found in Coxwell Street, and underlying all this mellow stonework is a Roman town, evidence of which emerges whenever a spade is put in the ground.

The **Corinium Museum** (*Corinium* was the Latin name) features excavated objects in a series of tableaux illustrating life in a Roman household.

🌿 **Cirencester Park**
Cirencester Park. 📞 01285 653135.
🕐 daily. ♿
🏛 **Corinium Museum**
Park St. 📞 01285 655611.
🕐 daily (Nov–Mar: Tue–Sun).
🔴 Dec 25, 26, Jan 1. 🎫 ♿

Cirencester's fine parish church, one of the largest in England

---

ART AND NATURE IN THE ROMAN WORLD

Cirencester was an important center of mosaic production in Roman days. Fine examples of the local style are shown in the Corinium Museum and mosaics range from Classical subjects, such as Orpheus taming lions and tigers with the music of his lyre, to the naturalistic depiction of a hare. At Chedworth Roman Villa, 8 miles (13 km) north, mosaics are inspired by real life. In the *Four Seasons* mosaic, *Winter* shows a peasant, dressed in a woollen hood and a wind-blown cloak, clutching a recently caught hare in one hand and a branch for fuel in the other.

Hare mosaic, Corinium Museum

EAST MIDLANDS

DERBYSHIRE · LEICESTERSHIRE · LINCOLNSHIRE
NORTHAMPTONSHIRE · NOTTINGHAMSHIRE

THREE VERY DIFFERENT KINDS OF LANDSCAPE *greet visitors to the East Midlands. In the west, wild moors rise to the craggy heights of the Peak District. These give way to the low-lying plain and the massive industrial towns at the region's heart. In the east, hills and limestone villages stretch to a long, flat seaboard.*

The East Midlands owes much of its character to a conjunction of the pastoral with the urban. The spa resorts, historical villages and stately homes coexist within a landscape shaped by industrialization. Throughout the region there are swathes of scenic countryside – and grimy industrial cities.

The area has been settled since prehistoric times. The Romans mined lead and salt, and they built a large network of roads and fortresses. Anglo-Saxon and Viking influence is found in many of the place names. During the Middle Ages profits from the wool industry enabled the development of towns such as Lincoln, which still has many fine old buildings. The East Midlands was the scene of ferocious battles during the Wars of the Roses and the Civil War, and insurgents in the Jacobite Rebellion reached as far as Derby.

In the west of the region is the Peak District, Britain's first National Park. Created in 1951, it draws crowds in search of the wild beauty of the heather-covered moors, or the wooded dales of the River Dove. The peaks are very popular with rock climbers and hikers.

The eastern edge of the Peaks descends through stone-walled meadows to sheltered valleys. The Roman spa of Buxton adds a final note of elegance before the flatlands of Derbyshire, Leicestershire and Nottinghamshire are reached. An area of coal mines and factories since the late 18th century, the landscape is set to be transformed over the next century into a new national forest.

Well-dressing dance, an ancient custom at Stoney Middleton in the Peak District

◁ **West front of Chatsworth House, a superb Baroque stately home in the Peak District**

Exploring the East Midlands

THE EAST MIDLANDS is a popular tourist destination, easily accessible by road, but best explored on foot. Numerous well-marked trails pass through the Peak District National Park. There are superb country houses at Chatsworth and Burghley and the impressive historic towns of Lincoln and Stamford to discover.

SIGHTS AT A GLANCE

GETTING AROUND

The M6, M1 and A1 are the principal road routes to the East Midlands, but they are subject to frequent delays because of the volume of traffic they carry. It can be faster and more interesting to find cross-country routes to the region, going through the attractive countryside and villages around Stamford and Northampton. Roads in the Peak District become very congested during the summer and an early start to the day is advisable. Lincoln and Stamford are well served by fast intercity trains from London. Rail services in the Peak District are far more limited, but local lines run as far as Matlock and Buxton.

SEE ALSO

- *Where to Stay* pp558–559
- *Where to Eat* pp593–595

View of Burghley House from the north courtyard

KEY

▭	Highway
▭	Major road
▭	Scenic route
--	Scenic path
▭	River
❀	Viewpoint

Doncaster

Sheff...

EDALE

BUXTON ❶

Stoke-on-Trent

❷ CHATSWOR...

❸ MATLOCK

❹ TISSINGTON TRAIL

❺ PEAK DISTRICT TOUR

DERBY

Dove

Trent

Coventry

Birmin...

Peak District countryside seen from the Tissington Trail

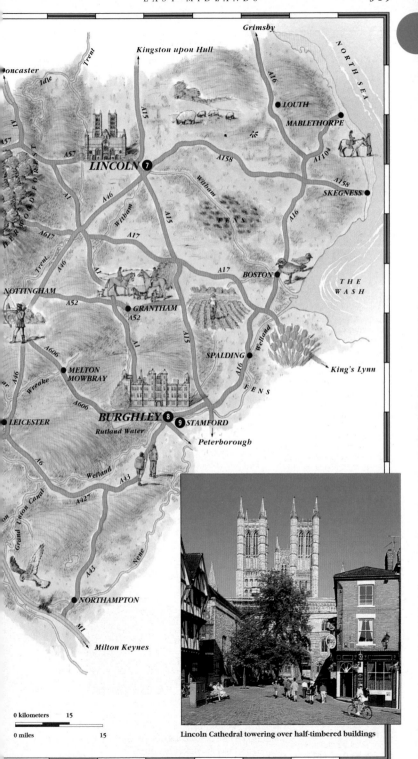

Lincoln Cathedral towering over half-timbered buildings

0 kilometers   15

0 miles   15

Buxton Opera House, a late 19th-century building restored in 1979

Buxton **❶**

Derbyshire. **♛** *20,000.* **☰** **☐**
❖ *The Crescent (01298 25106).*
☐ *Tue, Sat.*

B UXTON was developed as a
  spa town by the 5th Duke
of Devonshire during the late
18th century. It has many fine
Neo-Classical buildings, including the **Devonshire Royal
Hospital** (1790), originally a
stables, at the entrance to the
town. The **Crescent** was built
(1780–90) to rival Bath's
Royal Crescent *(see p244).*
   At its southwest end, the
tourist information office is
housed in the former town
baths. Here, a spring where
water surges from the ground
at a rate of 7,000 liters (1,849
gallons) an hour can be seen.
Buxton water is bottled and
sold commercially but there is
a public fountain at **St. Ann's
Well**, opposite.
   Steep gardens known as the
Slopes lead from the Crescent
to the small, award-winning
Museum and Art Gallery,
with geological and archaeological displays. Behind the
Crescent, overlooking the
Pavilion Gardens, is the striking 19th-century iron and
glass **Pavilion**, and the splendidly restored **Opera House**,
where a Music and Arts
Festival is held in summer.

**🏛 Buxton Museum and
Art Gallery**
Terrace Rd. **☎** *01298 24658.*
☐ *Easter–Sep: Tue–Sun (Oct–Easter:
Tue–Sat).* **●** *Dec 25, 26, Jan 1.* **🎟** **&**
🏛 Pavilion
St. John's Rd. **☎** *01298 23114.*
☐ *daily.* **●** *Dec 25.* **&**

Chatsworth House and Gardens **❷**

C HATSWORTH IS ONE of Britain's
  most impressive stately homes.
Between 1687 and 1707, the 4th
Earl of Devonshire replaced the
old Tudor mansion with this
Baroque palace. The house has
beautiful gardens, landscaped in
the 1760s by Capability Brown
(see p23) and developed by the
head gardener, Joseph Paxton *(see
pp56–7),* in the mid-19th century.

**First house built in 1552
by Bess of Hardwick**

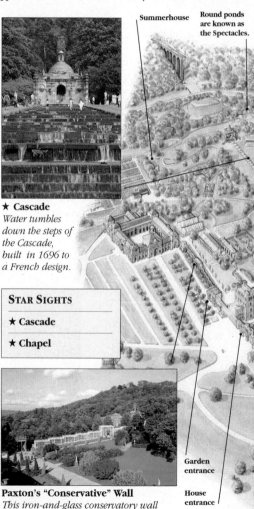

Summerhouse

**Round ponds
are known as
the Spectacles.**

★ **Cascade**
*Water tumbles
down the steps of
the Cascade,
built in 1696 to
a French design.*

STAR SIGHTS
★ **Cascade**
★ **Chapel**

Paxton's "Conservative" Wall
*This iron-and-glass conservatory wall
was designed in 1848 by Joseph Paxton,
the creator of Chatsworth's Great
Conservatory (now demolished).*

**Garden
entrance**

**House
entrance**

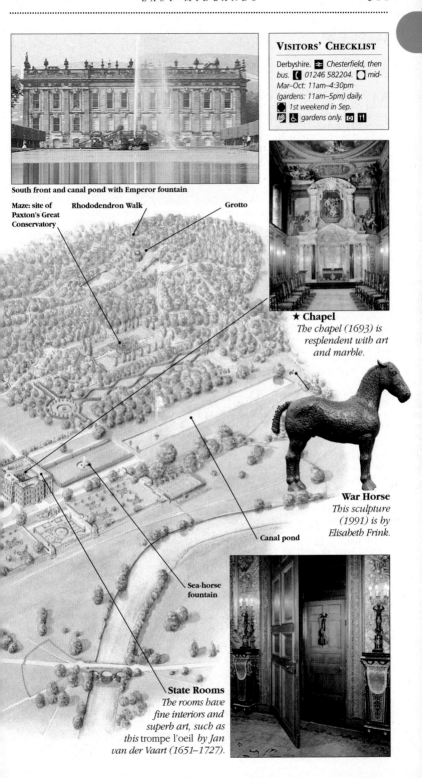

South front and canal pond with Emperor fountain

VISITORS' CHECKLIST

Derbyshire. ⇄ Chesterfield, then bus. 📞 01246 582204. 🕐 mid-Mar–Oct: 11am–4:30pm (gardens: 11am–5pm) daily. 📅 1st weekend in Sep. 🖼 ♿ gardens only. 📷 🍴

Maze: site of Paxton's Great Conservatory

Rhododendron Walk

Grotto

★ **Chapel**
The chapel (1693) is resplendent with art and marble.

War Horse
This sculpture (1991) is by Elisabeth Frink.

Canal pond

Sea-horse fountain

State Rooms
The rooms have fine interiors and superb art, such as this trompe l'oeil by Jan van der Vaart (1651–1727).

Matlock ❸

Derbyshire. 🏘 23,000. 🚊
ℹ *The Pavilion (01629 55082).*

Matlock was developed as a spa in the 1780s. Interesting buildings include the massive **palace** (1853) on the hill above the town, built as a hydrotherapy center but are now council offices. On the hill opposite is the excellent **Riber Castle Wildlife Park**, with a ruined mock-Gothic castle in its grounds.

From Matlock, the A6 winds through the outstandingly beautiful **Derwent Gorge** to **Matlock Bath**. Here, cable cars ascend to the **Heights of Abraham** amusement park, with caves and a nature trail. Lead mining is the subject of the **Peak District Mining Museum**, and visitors can inspect the old **Temple Mine** nearby. **Arkwright's Mill** (1771), the world's first water-powered cotton-spinning mill, is at the southern end of the gorge (*see p325*).

🐾 **Riber Castle Wildlife Park**
Off A615, SE of Matlock. 🅲 *01629 582073.* ◯ *daily.* ● *Dec 25.* 🈶 🅖
🦅 **Heights of Abraham**
On A6. 🅲 *01629 582365.*
◯ *Easter–Oct: daily.* 🈶 🅖
🏛 **Peak District Mining Museum**
The Pavilion, off A6. 🅲 *01629 583834.* ◯ *daily.* ● *Dec 25.* 🈶 🅖
⛏ **Temple Mine**
Temple Rd, off A6. 🅲 *01629 583834.* ◯ *daily (winter: pm).* ● *Dec 25.* 🈶
⛏ **Arkwright's Mill**
Mill Lane, Cromford. 🅲 *01629 824297.* ◯ *daily.* ● *Dec 25.* 🅖

Cable cars taking visitors to the Heights of Abraham

Tissington Trail ❹

See p323.

Peak District Tour ❺

See pp324–5.

Nottingham ❻

Nottinghamshire. 🏘 270,000. 🚊
🚌 ℹ *Smithy Row (0115 9470661).*
🏪 *daily.*

The name of Nottingham often conjures up the image of the evil Sheriff, adversary of Robin Hood. The Sheriff may be fictional but **Nottingham Castle** is real enough, standing on a rock riddled with underground passages. The castle houses a museum, with displays on the city's history, and what was Britain's first municipal art gallery, featuring works by Sir Stanley Spencer (1891–1959)

and Dante Gabriel Rossetti (1828–82). At the foot of the castle, Britain's oldest tavern, the **Trip to Jerusalem** (1189), is still in business. Its name refers to the 12th- and 13th-century crusades, but much of the building dates from the 17th century.

There are several museums near the castle, ranging from the **Tales of Robin Hood**, where special effects are used to tell the story of the outlaw, to the **Museum of Costume and Textiles**. In the latter, Nottingham's role as a leading center for embroidery, lace-making, tapestries and knitted textiles is explained.

Environs: Outstanding stately homes within a few miles' radius of Nottingham include the Neo-Classical **Kedleston Hall** (*see pp24–5*). "Bess of Hardwick," the rapacious Countess of Shrewbury (*see p320*) built the spectacular **Hardwick Hall** (*see p288*).

♠ **Nottingham Castle**
Castle Gate. 🅲 *0115 9483504.*
◯ *daily.* ● *Dec 25, 26.* 🈶 *Sat, Sun & public hols.* 🅖
🏛 **Tales of Robin Hood**
30–38 Maid Marion Way. 🅲 *0115 9414414.* ◯ *daily.* ● *Dec 24–26.* 🈶 🅖
🏛 **Museum of Costume and Textiles**
51 Castle Gate. 🅲 *0115 9483504.* ◯ *daily.* ● *Dec 25, 26.* 🅖 *limited.*
🏰 **Kedleston Hall**
(NT) off A38. 🅲 *01332 842191.*
◯ *Apr–Oct: Sat–Wed.* 🈶 🅗
🏰 **Hardwick Hall**
(NT) off A617. 🅲 *01246 850430.*
◯ *Apr–Oct: Wed, Thu, Sat, Sun & public hols.* 🈶 🅖 *limited.* 🅗

Robin Hood of Sherwood Forest

England's most colorful folk hero was a legendary swordsman, whose adventures are depicted in numerous films and stories. He lived in Sherwood Forest, near Nottingham, with a band of "merry men," robbing the rich to give to the poor. As part of an ancient oral tradition, Robin Hood figured mainly in ballads; the first written records of his exploits date from the 15th century. Today historians think that he was not one person, but a composite of many outlaws who refused to conform to medieval feudal constraints.

Victorian depiction of Friar Tuck and Robin Hood

Tissington Trail ●

THE FULL-LENGTH Tissington Trail runs for 12 miles (20 km), from the village of Ashbourne to Parsley Hay, where it meets the High Peak Trail. This is a short version, taking an easy route along a dismantled railroad line around Tissington village and providing good views of the beautiful White Peak countryside. The Derbyshire custom of well-dressing is thought to have originated in pre-Christian times. It was revived in the early 17th century, when the Tissington village wells were decorated in thanksgiving for deliverance from the plague, in the belief that the fresh water had had a medicinal effect. Well-dressing is still an important event in the Peakland calendar, and can be seen in other villages where the water supplies are prone to dry up.

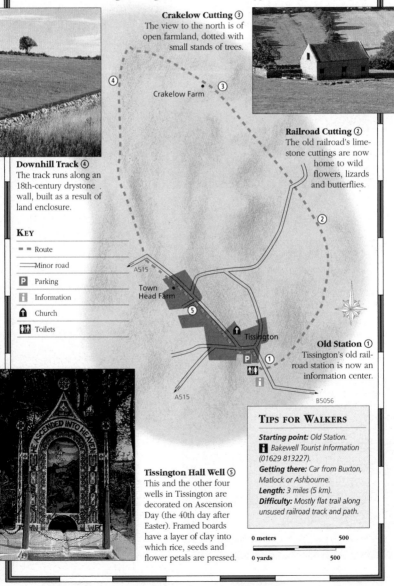

Crakelow Cutting ③
The view to the north is of open farmland, dotted with small stands of trees.

Crakelow Farm

Railroad Cutting ②
The old railroad's limestone cuttings are now home to wild flowers, lizards and butterflies.

Downhill Track ④
The track runs along an 18th-century drystone wall, built as a result of land enclosure.

KEY

- = = Route
- Minor road
- **P** Parking
- **ℹ** Information
- **⌂** Church
- **🚻** Toilets

Town Head Farm

A515

Tissington

Old Station ①
Tissington's old railroad station is now an information center.

B5056

Tissington Hall Well ⑤
This and the other four wells in Tissington are decorated on Ascension Day (the 40th day after Easter). Framed boards have a layer of clay into which rice, seeds and flower petals are pressed.

A515

TIPS FOR WALKERS

Starting point: Old Station.
ℹ Bakewell Tourist Information (01629 813227).
Getting there: Car from Buxton, Matlock or Ashbourne.
Length: 3 miles (5 km).
Difficulty: Mostly flat trail along unsused railroad track and path.

0 meters	500
0 yards	500

Peak District Tour ⑤

Detail, Buxton Opera House

THE PEAK DISTRICT's natural beauty and sheep-grazed crags contrast with the factories of nearby valley towns. Designated Britain's first National Park in 1951, the area has two distinct types of landscape. In the south are the gently rolling hills of the limestone White Peak. To the north, west and east are the wild, heather-clad moorlands of the Dark Peak peat bogs, superimposed on millstone grit.

STOCKPORT, MANCHESTER

⑤

HOLLINS C
410 m
1,345 f
A625

A6

A623

D A R K

A5004

⑥

A53

Wye

A6

A515

A5270

Edale ⑤
The high, dangerous peaks of scenic Edale mark the starting point of the 256-mile (412-km) Pennine Way footpath (*see p32*).

Buxton ⑥
This lovely spa town's opera house (*see p320*) is known as the "theater in the hills" because of its magnificent setting.

TIPS FOR DRIVERS

Tour length: 40 miles (60 km).
Stopping-off points: There are refreshments at Crich National Tramway Museum and Arkwright's Mill in Cromford. Eyam has good old-fashioned tea shops. The Nag's Head in Edale is a charming Tudor inn. Buxton has many pubs and cafés. (See also pp636–7.)

Arbor Low ⑦
This stone circle, known as the "Stonehenge of the North," dates from about 2000 BC and consists of 46 recumbent stones enclosed by a ditch.

KEY

▬▬	Tour route
═══	Other roads
☀	Viewpoint

Dovedale ⑧
Popular Dovedale is the prettiest of the Peak District's river valleys, with its stepping stones, thickly wooded slopes and wind-sculpted rocks. Izaac Walton (1593–1683), author of *The Compleat Angler*, used to fish here.

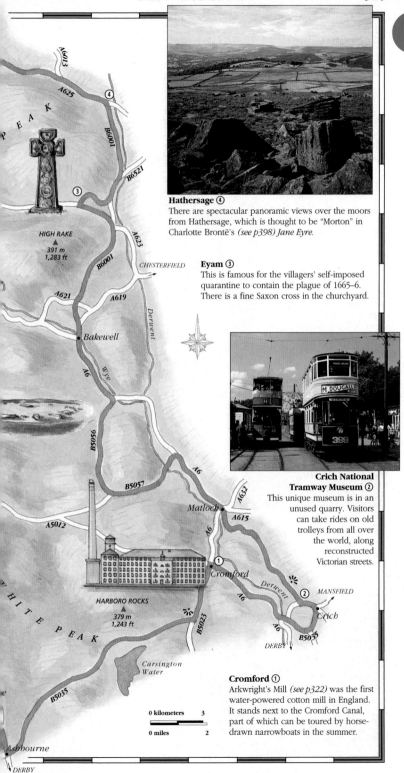

Hathersage ④
There are spectacular panoramic views over the moors from Hathersage, which is thought to be "Morton" in Charlotte Brontë's *(see p398) Jane Eyre*.

Eyam ③
This is famous for the villagers' self-imposed quarantine to contain the plague of 1665–6. There is a fine Saxon cross in the churchyard.

Crich National Tramway Museum ②
This unique museum is in an unused quarry. Visitors can take rides on old trolleys from all over the world, along reconstructed Victorian streets.

Cromford ①
Arkwright's Mill *(see p322)* was the first water-powered cotton mill in England. It stands next to the Cromford Canal, part of which can be toured by horse-drawn narrowboats in the summer.

HIGH RAKE
▲
391 m
1,283 ft

CHESTERFIELD

Bakewell

Matlock

Cromford

MANSFIELD

Crich

DERBY

HARBORO ROCKS
▲
379 m
1,243 ft

Carsington Water

0 kilometers 3

0 miles 2

Ashbourne

DERBY

Street-by-Street: Lincoln ❼

Carving in Angel Choir

SURROUNDED BY the flat landscape of the Fens, Lincoln rises dramatically on a cliff above the River Witham, the three towers of its massive cathedral visible from afar. The Romans *(see pp44–5)* founded the first settlement here in AD 48. By the time of the Norman Conquest *(see p47)*, Lincoln was the fourth most important city in England (after London, Winchester and York). The city's wealth was due to its strategic importance for the export of wool from the Lincolnshire Wolds to Europe. Lincoln has managed to retain much of its historic character. Many remarkable medieval buildings have survived, most of which are along the aptly named Steep Hill, leading to the cathedral.

Humber Bridge ↑

2nd-century Newport Arch

Museum of Lincolnshire Life

WESTGATE

BAILGATE

CASTLE HILL

STEEP HILL

DRURY LANE

MICHAELGATE

House of Aaron the Jew

★ **Lincoln Castle**
The early Norman castle, rebuilt at intervals, acted as the city prison from 1787–1878. The chapel's coffinlike pews served to remind felons of their fate.

KEY

– – – Suggested route

Jew's House
Lincoln had a large medieval Jewish community. This fine early 12th-century stone house, one of the oldest of its kind in existence, was owned by a Jewish family.

15th-century Stonebow Gate and railroad station

0 meters	100
0 yards	100

STAR SIGHTS

★ **Lincoln Castle**

★ **Lincoln Cathedral**

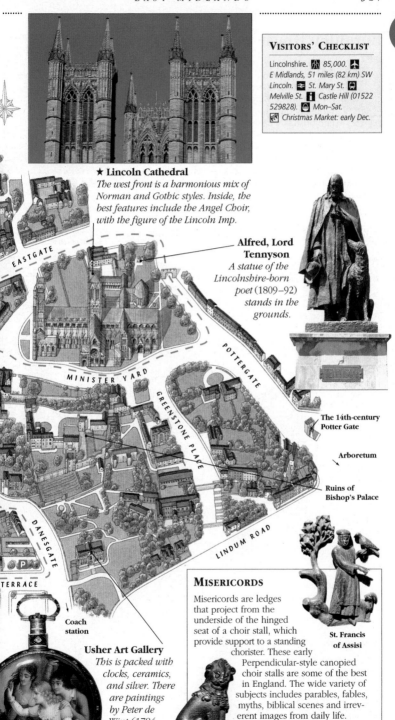

★ Lincoln Cathedral
*The west front is a harmonious mix of
Norman and Gothic styles. Inside, the
best features include the Angel Choir,
with the figure of the Lincoln Imp.*

**Alfred, Lord
Tennyson**
*A statue of the
Lincolnshire-born
poet (1809–92)
stands in the
grounds.*

EASTGATE

MINISTER YARD

POTTERGATE

GREENSTONE PLACE

**The 14th-century
Potter Gate**

Arboretum

**Ruins of
Bishop's Palace**

DANESGATE

LINDUM ROAD

TERRACE

**Coach
station**

Usher Art Gallery
*This is packed with
clocks, ceramics,
and silver. There
are paintings
by Peter de
Wint (1784–
1849) and
J.M.W. Turner
(see p93).*

MISERICORDS

Misericords are ledges
that project from the
underside of the hinged
seat of a choir stall, which
provide support to a standing
chorister. These early
Perpendicular-style canopied
choir stalls are some of the best
in England. The wide variety of
subjects includes parables, fables,
myths, biblical scenes and irrev-
erent images from daily life.

**St. Francis
of Assisi**

One of a pair of lions

Burghley House ❽

Portrait of Sir Isaac Newton, Billiard Room

WILLIAM CECIL, 1ST LORD BURGHLEY (1520–98) was Queen Elizabeth I's adviser and confidant for 40 years. He built the wonderfully dramatic Burghley House in 1560–87, probably designing it himself. The roof line bristles with stone pyramids, chimneys disguised as Classical columns and towers shaped like pepper pots. The busy skyline only resolves itself into a symmetrical pattern when viewed from the west, where a lime tree stands, one of many planted by Capability Brown *(see p23)* when the surrounding deer park was landscaped in 1760. Burghley's interior is lavishly decorated with Italian paintings of Greek gods enacting their dramas across the walls and ceiling.

★ Old Kitchen
Gleaming copper pans hang from the walls of the fan-vaulted kitchen, little altered since the Tudor period.

North Gate
Intricate examples of 19th-century wrought-iron work adorn the principal entrances.

The Billiard Room
has many fine portraits inset in oak paneling.

Cupolas were very fashionable details, inspired by European Renaissance architecture.

A chimney has been disguised as a Classical column.

Mullioned windows were added in 1683 when glass became less expensive.

The Gatehouse, with its side turrets, is a typical feature of the "prodigy" houses of the Tudor era *(see p288)*.

West Front
Featuring the Burghley crest, the West Front was finished in 1577 and formed the original main entrance.

STAR SIGHTS
★ Old Kitchen
★ Heaven Room
★ Hell Staircase

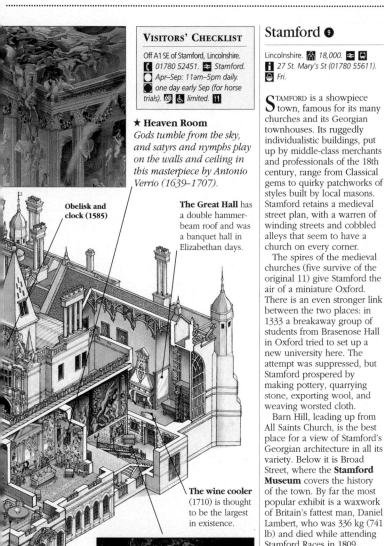

★ **Heaven Room**
*Gods tumble from the sky,
and satyrs and nymphs play
on the walls and ceiling in
this masterpiece by Antonio
Verrio (1639–1707).*

**Obelisk and
clock (1585)**

The Great Hall has
a double hammer-
beam roof and was
a banquet hall in
Elizabethan days.

The wine cooler
(1710) is thought
to be the largest
in existence.

**The Fourth George
Room**, one of a
suite, is paneled in
oak stained with ale.

★ **Hell Staircase**
*Verrio painted the
ceiling to show Hell
as the mouth of a
cat crammed with
tormented sinners.
The staircase, of
local stone, was
installed in 1786.*

Stamford ❾

Lincolnshire. *👥* 18,000. *≈* *▢*
ℹ 27 St. Mary's St (01780 55611).
▢ Fri.

STAMFORD is a showpiece
town, famous for its many
churches and its Georgian
townhouses. Its ruggedly
individualistic buildings, put
up by middle-class merchants
and professionals of the 18th
century, range from Classical
gems to quirky patchworks of
styles built by local masons.
Stamford retains a medieval
street plan, with a warren of
winding streets and cobbled
alleys that seem to have a
church on every corner.

The spires of the medieval
churches (five survive of the
original 11) give Stamford the
air of a miniature Oxford.
There is an even stronger link
between the two places: in
1333 a breakaway group of
students from Brasenose Hall
in Oxford tried to set up a
new university here. The
attempt was suppressed, but
Stamford prospered by
making pottery, quarrying
stone, exporting wool, and
weaving worsted cloth.

Barn Hill, leading up from
All Saints Church, is the best
place for a view of Stamford's
Georgian architecture in all its
variety. Below it is Broad
Street, where the **Stamford
Museum** covers the history
of the town. By far the most
popular exhibit is a waxwork
of Britain's fattest man, Daniel
Lambert, who was 336 kg (741
lb) and died while attending
Stamford Races in 1809.

The old **Assembly Room**
of 1725 and the **Old Theatre**
of 1768, both in Maiden Lane,
have been combined to form
an Arts Centre. Nearby is **St.
Martin's Church**, where
Daniel Lambert was buried. It
has two interesting tombs:
one commemorates William
Cecil, Lord Treasurer under
Elizabeth I; the other his
patrician descendant, the 5th
Earl of Exeter (1648–1700).

THE NORTH
COUNTRY

The North Country at a Glance

R UGGED COASTLINES, spectacular walks and
climbs, magnificent stately homes and
breathtaking cathedrals all have their place in
the north of England, with its dramatic history
of Roman rule, Saxon invasion, Viking attacks
and border skirmishes. Reminders of the
industrial revolution are found in cities such
as Halifax, Liverpool and Manchester, and
peace and inspiration in the dramatic
scenery of the Lake District, with its awe-
inspiring mountains and waters.

Hadrian's Wall (see
pp408–9), built about
120 to protect Roman
Britain from the Picts to
the north, cuts through
rugged Northumberland
National Park scenery.

NORTHUMBRI
(see pp400–41)

Northumberla

The Lake District (see pp340–57)
is a combination of superb peaks,
tumbling rivers and falls and
shimmering lakes such as Wast Water.

Durha

Cumbria

**Yorkshire Dales
National Park**
(see pp370–72) creates
a delightful environ-
ment for walking and
touring the farming
landscape, scattered with
attractive villages such as
Thwaite, in Swaledale.

Lancashire

**LANCASHIRE
AND THE LAKES**
(see pp340–366)

Greater Manchester

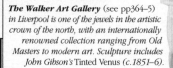

The Walker Art Gallery (see pp364–5)
in Liverpool is one of the jewels in the artistic
crown of the north, with an internationally
renowned collection ranging from Old
Masters to modern art. Sculpture includes
John Gibson's Tinted Venus (c.1851–6).

Merseyside

◁ **The 11th-century Alnwick Castle, Alnwick, Northumberland, from across the River Aln**

Durham Cathedral (see pp414–5), *a striking Norman structure with an innovative southern choir aisle and fine stained glass, has towered over the city of Durham since 995.*

Fountains Abbey (see pp376–7), *one of the finest religious buildings in the north, was founded in the 12th century by monks who desired simplicity and austerity. Later the abbey became extremely wealthy.*

Castle Howard (see pp384–5), *a triumph of Baroque architecture, offers many magnificent settings, including this Museum Room (1805–10), designed by C.H. Tatham.*

Cleveland

North Yorkshire

*ne
nd
ear*

ORKSHIRE
AND
MBERSIDE
(pp366–399)

West Yorkshire

South Yorkshire

Humberside

York (see pp390–95) *is a city of historical treasures, ranging from the medieval to Georgian. Its magnificent minster has a large collection of stained-glass and the medieval city walls are well preserved. Other sites include churches, narrow alleyways and notable museums.*

0 kilometers 25

0 miles 25

The Industrial Revolution in the North

THE FACE OF NORTHERN ENGLAND in the 19th century was dramatically altered by the development of the coal mining, textile and shipbuilding industries. Lancashire, Northumberland and the West Riding *(see p367)* of Yorkshire all experienced population growth and migration to cities. The hardships of urban life were partly relieved by the actions of several wealthy industrial philanthropists, but many people lived in extremely deprived conditions. Although most traditional industries have now declined sharply or disappeared as demand has moved elsewhere, a growing tourist industry has developed in many of the former industrial centers.

Back-to-backs *or colliers' rows, such as these houses at Easington, were provided by colliery owners from the 1800s onward. They comprised two small rooms for cooking and sleeping, and an outside toilet.*

1815 Sir Humphrey Davy invented a safety oil lamp for miners. Light shone through a cylindrical gauze sheet, which prevented the heat of the flame igniting methane gas in the mine. Thousands of miners benefited from this device.

Coal mining *was a family industry in the North of England with women and children working alongside the men.*

1750	1800
PRE-STEAM AGE	**STEAM AGE**
1750	1800

1781 Leeds–Liverpool Canal opened. The building of canals facilitated the movement of raw materials and finished products, and aided the process of mechanization immeasurably.

1830 Liverpool a **Manchester** railr opened, connecting the biggest cities outs London. Within a month railway carried 1 passeng

Halifax's Piece Hall (see pp398–9), *restored in 1976, is the most impressive surviving example of industrial architecture in northern England. It is the only complete 18th-century cloth market building in Yorkshire. Merchants sold measures of cloth known as "pieces" from rooms lining the cloisters inside.*

Hebden Bridge (see p398), *a typical West Riding textile mill town jammed into the narrow Calder Valley, typifies a pattern of workers' houses surrounding a central mill. The town benefited from its position when the Rochdale Canal (1804) and then the railroad (1841) took advantage of this relatively low, level route over the Pennines.*

Saltaire (see p397) *was a model village built by the wealthy cloth merchant and mill-owner Sir Titus Salt (1803–76), for the benefit of his workers. Seen here in the 1870s, it included houses and facilities such as shops, gardens and fields, with poorhouses, a hospital, school and chapel. A disciplinarian, he banned alcohol and pubs from Saltaire.*

George Hudson *(1800–71) built the first railroad station in York (see p394) in 1840–42). In the 1840s he owned more than a quarter of the railroads in Britain and was known as the "railway king."*

1842 Coal Mines Act prevented women and children from working in harsh conditions in the mines.

Port Sunlight *(see p365) was founded by William Hesketh Lever (1851–1925) to provide housing for workers at his Sunlight soap factory. Between 1889 and 1914 he built 800 cottages. Amenities included a pool.*

Strikes to improve working conditions were common. Violence flared in July 1893 when colliery owners locked miners out of their pits and stopped their pay after the Miners' Federation resisted a 25 percent wage cut. Over 300,000 men struggled without pay until November, when work resumed at the old rate.

1850	1900
FULL MECHANIZATION	
1850	1900

Power loom weaving *transformed the textile industry while creating unemployment among skilled hand loom weavers. By the 1850s, the West Riding had 30,000 power looms, used in cotton and woollen mills. Of 79,000 workers, over half were to be found in Bradford alone.*

Furness dry dock *was built in the 1890s when the shipbuilding industry moved north, in search of cheap labour and materials. Barrow-in-Furness, Glasgow (see pp502–5) and Tyne and Wear (see p410) were the new centers.*

Joseph Rowntree *(1836–1925) founded his chocolate factory in York in 1892, having formerly worked with George Cadbury. As Quakers, the Rowntrees believed in the social welfare of their workers (establishing a model village in 1904), and, with Terry's confectionery (1767), they made a vast contribution to York's prosperity. Today, Nestlé Rowntree is the world's largest chocolate factory and York is Britain's chocolate capital.*

North Country Abbeys

NORTHERN ENGLAND has some of the finest and best-preserved religious houses in Europe. Centers of prayer, learning and power in the Middle Ages, the larger of these were designated abbeys and were governed by an abbot. Most were located in rural areas, considered appropriate for a spiritual and contemplative life. Viking raiders had destroyed many Anglo-Saxon religious houses in the 8th and 9th centuries *(see pp46–7)* and it was not until William the Conqueror founded the Benedictine Selby Abbey in 1069 that monastic life revived in the north. New orders, Augustinians in particular, arrived from the Continent and by 1500, Yorkshire had 83 monasteries.

Cistercian monk

Ruins of St. Mary's Abbey today

The Liberty of St. Mary was the name given to the land around the abbey, almost a city within a city. Here, the abbot had his own market, fair, prison and gallows – all exempt from the city authorities.

ST. MARY'S ABBEY

Founded in York in 1086, this Benedictine abbey was one of the wealthiest in Britain. Its involvement in the wool trade in York, and the granting of royal and papal privileges and land, led to a relaxing of standards by the early 12th century. The abbot was even allowed to dress in the same style as a bishop, and was raised by the pope to the status of a "mitered abbot." As a result, 13 monks left in 1132, to found Fountains Abbey *(see pp376–7)*.

Gatehouse and
St. Olave's church

Interval
tower

Water tower

Hospitium or
guest house

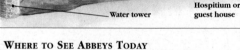

MONASTERIES AND LOCAL LIFE

As one of the wealthiest landowning sections of society, the monasteries played a vital role in the local economy. They provided employment, particularly in agriculture, and dominated the wool trade, England's largest export during the Middle Ages. By 1387 two-thirds of all wool exported from England passed through St. Mary's Abbey, the largest wool trader in York.

Cistercian monks tilling their land

WHERE TO SEE ABBEYS TODAY

Fountains Abbey *(see pp376–7)*, founded by Benedictine monks and later taken over by Cistercians, is the most famous of the numerous abbeys in the region. Rievaulx *(see p379)*, Byland *(see p378)* and Furness *(see p356)* were all founded by the Cistercians, and Furness became the second wealthiest Cistercian house in England after Fountains. Whitby Abbey *(see p382)*, sacked by the Vikings, was later rebuilt by the Benedictine order. Northumberland is famous for its early Anglo-Saxon monasteries, such as Ripon, Lastingham and Lindisfarne *(see pp404–5)*.

Mount Grace Priory (see p380), *founded in 1398, is the best-preserved Carthusian house in England. The former individual gardens and cells of each monk are still clearly visible.*

The Dissolution of the Monasteries (1536–40)

By the early 16th century, the monasteries owned one-sixth of all English land and their annual income was four times that of the Crown. Henry VIII ordered the closure of all religious houses in 1536, acquiring their wealth in the process. His attempt at dissolution provoked a large uprising of Catholic northerners led by Robert Aske later that year. The rebellion failed and Aske and others were executed for conspiracy. The dissolution continued under Thomas Cromwell, who became known as "the hammer of the monks."

Thomas Cromwell (c.1485–1549)

The large Abbot's House testified to the grand lifestyle that late medieval abbots adopted.

The Chapter House, an assembly room, was the most important building after the church.

Lavatory

The Warming House was the only room in the monastery, apart from the kitchen, which had a fire.

Kitchen

Refectory   **The Abbey Wall** had battlements added in 1318 to protect it against raids by Scottish armies.

Common parlor   **Cloister**

Kirkham Priory, an Augustinian foundation of the 1120s, enjoys a tranquil setting on the banks of the River Derwent, near Malton. The finest feature of the ruined site is the 13th-century gatehouse, which leads into the priory complex.

Kirkstall Abbey was founded in 1152 by monks from Fountains Abbey. The well-preserved ruins of this Cistercian house near Leeds include the church, the late-Norman chapter house and the abbot's lodging. This evening view was painted by Thomas Girtin (1775–1802).

Easby Abbey lies beside the River Swale, outside the pretty market town of Richmond. Among the remains of this Premonstratensian house, founded in 1155, are the 13th-century refectory and sleeping quarters and 14th-century gatehouse.

The Geology of the Lake District

Piece of Lake District slate

THE LAKE DISTRICT contains some of England's most spectacular scenery. Concentrated in just 900 sq miles (231 sq km) are the highest peaks, deepest valleys and longest lakes in the country. Today's landscape has changed little since the end of the Ice Age 10,000 years ago, the last major event in Britain's geological history. But the glaciated hills revealed by the retreating ice were once part of a vast mountain chain whose remains can be seen as the Appalachian Mountains. The mountains were first raised by the gradual fusion of two landmasses that, for millions of years, formed a single continent. Eventually the continent broke into two, forming Europe and America, separated by the widening Atlantic Ocean.

Honister Pass, with its distinctive U-shape, is an example of a glaciated valley, once completely filled with ice.

GEOLOGICAL HISTORY

The oldest rock formed as sediment under an ocean called Iapetus. Some 450 million years ago, Earth's internal movements made two continents collide, and the ocean disappear.

1 *The collision buckled the former sea bed into a mountain range. Magma rose from Earth's mantle, altered the sediments and cooled into volcanic rock.*

2 *In the Ice Age, glaciers slowly excavated huge rock basins in the mountainsides, dragging debris to the valley floor. Frost sculpted the summits.*

3 *The glaciers retreated 10,000 years ago, their meltwaters forming lakes in valleys dammed by debris. As the climate improved, plants colonized the fells.*

RADIATING LAKES

The diversity of lakeland scenery owes much to its geology: hard volcanic rocks in the central lakes give rise to rugged hills, while soft slates to the north produce a more rounded topography. The lakes form a radial pattern, spreading out from a central volcanic rock zone.

Scafell Pike is the highest peak in England. One of the three Scafell Pikes, its two neighbors are Broad Crag and Ill Crag.

▲ **Great Gable**

▲ **Old Man of Coniston**

Coniston Water

Wast Water *is the deepest of the lakes. Its southeastern cliffs are streaked with granite scree – the debris formed each year as rock shattered by the winter frost tumbles down during the spring thaw.*

MAN ON THE MOUNTAIN

The sheltered valley floors with their benign climate and fertile soils are ideal for settlement. Farmhouses, drystone walls, pasture and sheep pens are an integral part of the landscape. Higher up, the absence of trees and bracken are the result of wind and a cooler climate. Old mine workings and tracks are the relics of once-flourishing industries.

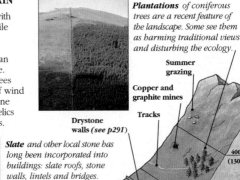

Plantations *of coniferous trees are a recent feature of the landscape. Some see them as harming traditional views and disturbing the ecology.*

Summer grazing

Copper and graphite mines

Tracks

Drystone walls *(see p291)*

400–500 m (130–170 ft)

Slate *and other local stone has long been incorporated into buildings: slate roofs, stone walls, lintels and bridges.*

Hedges

300–400 m (100–130 ft)

Sheep pens for winter grazing

▲ Blencathra

iwaite

nt Water

▲ Helvellyn

Ullswater

▲ High Street

Windermere

Skiddaw *is composed of slate, formed when the muddy sediment of the ancient ocean floor was altered by extreme pressure.*

Striding Edge *is a long, twisting ridge that leads to the summit of Helvellyn. It was sharpened by the widening of the valleys on either side caused by the buildup of glaciers.*

The Langdale Pikes *are remnants of the volcanic activity which once erupted in the area. They are made of hard igneous rocks, known as Borrowdale Volcanics. Unlike the Skiddaw Slates, they have not eroded smoothly, so they leave a craggy skyline.*

MERSEYSIDE
MARITIME
MUSEUM

LANCASHIRE AND THE LAKES

CUMBRIA · LANCASHIRE · GREATER MANCHESTER · MERSEYSIDE

THE LANDSCAPE PAINTER *John Constable (1776–1837) declared that the Lake District, now visited by 18 million people annually, had "the finest scenery that ever was." The Normans built many religious houses here, and William II created estates for English barons. Today, the National Trust is its most important landowner.*

Within the 30 mile (45 km) radius of the Lake District lies an astonishing number of fells and lakes. Today, all looks peaceful, but from the Roman occupation to the Middle Ages, the northwest was a turbulent area, as successive kings and rulers fought over the territory. Historians can revel in the various Celtic monuments, Roman remains, stately homes and monastic ruins. Although the scenery is paramount, there are many outdoor activities as well as spectator sports, such as Cumbrian wrestling, and wildlife to observe.

Lancashire's portfolio of tourist attractions includes the fine county town of Lancaster, bright Blackpool with its autumn illuminations and fairground attractions, and the peaceful seaside beaches to the south. Inland, the most appealing regions are the Forest of Bowland, a sparse expanse of heathery grouse moor, and the picturesque Ribble Valley. Farther south still are the industrial conurbations of Manchester and Merseyside, where the attractions are more urban.

There are many fine Victorian buildings in Manchester, where the industrial quarter of Castlefield has been revitalized. Liverpool, with its restored Albert Dock, is best known as the seaport city of the Beatles. It has a lively club scene and is increasingly used as a film location. Both cities have good art galleries and museums.

Jetty at Grasmere, one of the most popular regions of the Lake District

◁ Restored Albert Dock, lining the River Mersey in Liverpool

Exploring Lancashire and the Lakes

THE LAKE DISTRICT'S natural scenery outweighs any of its man-made attractions. Its natural features are the result of geological upheavals over millennia *(see pp338–9)*, and four of its peaks are higher than 1,000 m (3,300 ft). Human influences have left their mark too; the main activities are quarrying, mining, farming and tourism.

The Lakes are most crowded in summer when activities include lake trips and hiking. The best bases are Keswick and Ambleside, but there are also good hotels on the shores of Windermere and Ullswater and in the Cartmel area.

Lancashire's Forest of Bowland is an attractive place to explore on foot, with picturesque villages. Farther south, Manchester and Liverpool have excellent museums and galleries.

Canoeing, a popular sporting pastime, at Derwent Water in the Northern Fells and Lakes area

GETTING AROUND

For many, the first glimpse of the Lake District is from the M6 near Shap Fell, but the A6 is a more dramatic route. You can reach Windermere by train, but you need to change at Oxenholme, on the main InterCity route from Euston to Carlisle. Penrith also has rail services and bus links into the Lakes. L'al Ratty, the miniature railroad up Eskdale, and the Lakeside & Haverthwaite railroad, which connects with the steamers on Windermere,

make for enjoyable outings. Regular buses link all the main centers where excursions are organized. One of the most enterprising is the Mountain Goat minibus, in Windermere and Keswick.

Lancaster, Liverpool and Manchester are on the main rail and bus routes and also have airports. For Blackpool, you need to change trains in Preston. Wherever you go in the area, one of the best means of getting around is on foot.

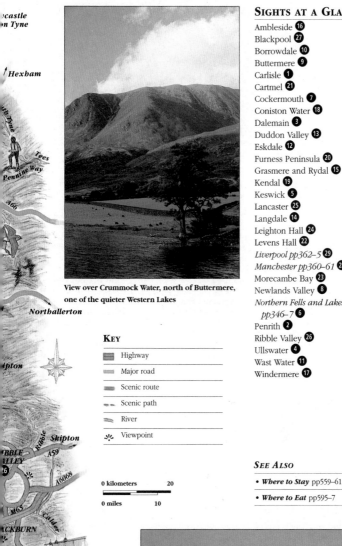

View over Crummock Water, north of Buttermere, one of the quieter Western Lakes

Northallerton

KEY

▬▬	Highway
▬▬	Major road
▬▬	Scenic route
▬ ▬	Scenic path
≈	River
☀	Viewpoint

0 kilometers 20

0 miles 10

Leeds

MANCHESTER 28

Sheffield

ingham

Birmingham

SIGHTS AT A GLANCE

SEE ALSO

Preserved docks and Liver Building, Liverpool

Carlisle ❶

Cumbria. 🏘 *105,000.* ✈ ☒ 🚌
🛈 *The Old Town Hall, Green Market (01228 512444).*

DUE TO ITS proximity to the Scottish border, this city has long been a defensive site. Known as Luguvalium by the Romans, it was an outpost of Hadrian's Wall *(see pp408–9).* Carlisle was sacked and pillaged repeatedly by the Danes, the Normans and border raiders, and suffered damage as a Royalist stronghold under Cromwell *(see p52).* Today, Carlisle is the capital of Cumbria. In its center are the timber-framed Guildhall and market cross, and fortifications still exist around its West Walls, drum-towered gates and its Norman **castle**. The castle tower has a small museum devoted to the King's Own Border Regiment. The cathedral, originally an Augustinian priory, dates from 1133. One of its best features is a decorative east window. Carlisle's **Tullie House Museum** imaginatively recreates the city's past with sections on Roman history, border disputes

Façade of Hutton-in-the-Forest with medieval tower on the right

and Cumbrian wildlife. Nearby lie the evocative sandstone ruins of **Lanercost Priory** (c.1166) surrounded by placid cattle meadows.

⚜ Carlisle Castle
Castle Way. 📞 *01228 591922.* ◯ *daily.* ● *Dec 25.* 🏛 🗎 *limited.*

🏛 Tullie House Museum
Castle St. 📞 *01228 34781.* ◯ *daily.* ● *Dec 25.* 🏛 🗎

⛪ Lanercost Priory
Nr Brampton. 📞 *016977 3030.* ◯ *Apr–Sep: daily.* 🏛 🗎 *limited.*

Penrith ❷

Cumbria. 🏘 *13,000.* 🛈 *Robinson's School, Middlegate (01768 867466).* 🚌 *Tue, Sat.*

TIMEWARP SHOPFRONTS on the market square and a 14th-century **castle** of sandstone are Penrith's main attractions. There are some strange hog-back stones in St. Andrew's churchyard, allegedly a giant's

grave, and the 285 m (937 ft) Beacon provides stunning views of distant fells.

ENVIRONS: Just north of Penrith at Little Salkeld is one of the area's most notable ancient monuments, a Bronze Age circle (with about 70 tall stones) known as **Long Meg and her Daughters** *(see pp42–3).* Six miles (9 km) northwest of Penrith lies **Hutton-in-the-Forest**. The oldest part of this house is the 13th-century tower, built to withstand Scots raiders. Inside is a magnificent Italianate staircase, a sumptuously paneled 17th-century Long Gallery, a delicately stuccoed Cupid Room dating from the 1740s, and several Victorian rooms. Outside, you can walk around the walled garden and topiary terraces or explore the woods.

⚜ Penrith Castle
Ullswater Rd. ◯ *daily.* 🗎 *in grounds.*

🏚 Hutton-in-the-Forest
Off B5305. 📞 *017684 84449.* **House** ◯ *May–Sep: Thu, Fri, Sun & public hols (pm); Aug: Wed–Fri, Sun & public hols (pm).* **Grounds** ◯ *Sun–Fri.* ● *Dec 25.* 🏛 🗎 *limited.*

Dalemain ❸

Penrith, Cumbria. 📞 *017684 86450.* 🚌 🚉 *Penrith then taxi.* ◯ *Apr–mid-Oct: Sun–Thu.* 🏛 🗎 *limited.*

A SEEMINGLY GEORGIAN façade gives this fine house near Ullswater the impression of architectural unity, but hides a greatly altered medieval and Elizabethan structure with a maze of rambling passages. Public rooms include a superb Chinese drawing room with hand-painted wallpaper, and

Saxon iron sword in the Tullie House Museum

TRADITIONAL CUMBRIAN SPORTS

Cumberland wrestling is one of the most interesting sports to watch in the summer months. The combatants, clad in long-johns and embroidered velvet pants, clasp one another in an armlock and attempt to topple each other over. Technique and good balance outweigh physical force. Other traditional Lakeland sports include fell-racing, a grueling test of speed and stamina up and down local peaks at ankle-breaking speed. Hound-trailing is also a popular sport in which specially bred hounds follow an aniseed trail over the hills. Sheep-dog trials, flower shows and gymkhanas take place in summer. The Egremont Crab Fair in September holds lighthearted events such as greased-pole climbing.

Cumberland wrestlers

Sheep resting at Glenridding, on the southwest shore of Ullswater

a paneled 17th-century drawing room. Several small museums occupy various outbuildings, and the gardens contain a fine collection of fragrant shrub roses and a huge silver fir.

Sumptuous Chinese drawing room at Dalemain

Ullswater ❹

Cumbria. 🚉 Penrith. ℹ️ Main car park, Glenridding, Penrith (017684 82414).

OFTEN CONSIDERED the most beautiful of all Cumbria's lakes, Ullswater stretches from gentle farmland near Penrith to dramatic hills and crags at its southern end. The main western shore road can be very busy. In summer, two restored Victorian steamers ply regularly from Pooley Bridge to Glenridding. One of the best walks crosses the eastern shore from Glenridding to Hallin Fell and the moorland of Martindale. The western side passes Gowbarrow, where Wordsworth's immortalized "host of golden daffodils" bloom in spring *(see p352)*.

Keswick ❺

Cumbria. 🏔️ 5,000. ℹ️ Moot Hall, Market Sq (017687 72645).

POPULAR SINCE Victorian times, Keswick has guest houses, a summer repertory theater, outdoor equipment stores and a serious parking problem in tourist season. Its most striking central building is the **Moot Hall**, dating from 1813, now used as the tourist office. The town first prospered on wool and leather, then in Tudor times deposits of graphite were discovered that made Keswick an important center for pencil manufacturing. In World War II, hollow pencils were made to hide espionage maps on thin paper. The old factory is now the **Pencil Museum** with good audio-visual shows. Among the many interesting exhibits at the **Keswick Museum and Art Gallery** are the manuscripts of Lakeland writers such as Robert Southey (1774–1843) and William Wordsworth *(see p352)*. In the new shopping center is a multimedia presentation on **Beatrix Potter's Lake District** *(see p353)*, and her role in the National Trust.

🏛️ **Pencil Museum**
Carding Mill Lane. 📞 017687 73626.
⬜ daily. ⬤ Dec 25, 26, Jan 1. 🎫 ♿
🏛️ **Keswick Museum and Art Gallery**
Fitz Park, Station Rd. 📞 017687 73263. ⬜ Easter–Oct: daily. 🎫 ♿
🏛️ **Beatrix Potter's Lake District**
Packhorse Court. 📞 017687 75173. ⬜ Apr–Oct: daily; Nov–Mar: Sat & Sun. ⬤ Dec 25, 26, Jan 1. 🎫 ♿

Outdoor equipment shop in Keswick

Northern Fells and Lakes ❻

The rare red squirrel, native to the area

Mᴀɴʏ ᴠɪsɪᴛᴏʀs praise this northern area of the Lake District National Park for its scenery and geological interest *(see pp338–9)*. It is ideal walking country, and nearby Derwent Water, Thirlmere and Bassenthwaite provide endless scenic views, rambles and opportunities for watersports. Large areas surrounding the regional center of Keswick *(see p345)* are accessible only on foot, particularly the huge mass of hills known as Back of Skiddaw – located between Skiddaw and Caldbeck – or the Helvellyn range, east of Thirlmere.

The Whinlatter Pass is an easy route from Keswick to the forested Lorton Vale. You have a good view of Bassenthwaite Lake and a glimpse of Grisedale Pike.

Bassenthwaite is best viewed from the east shore. The road passes through Dodd Wood at the foot of Skiddaw.

CARLISLE
B5291
BASSENTHWAITE LAKE
A591
Derwent
WORKINGTON
A66
High Lorton
LORTON VALE
WHINLATTER PASS
B5292
Braithwaite
B5289
LOWESWATER
Newlands Beck
DERWENT
Grange
BUTTERMERE

Lorton Vale
The lush, green farmland south of Cockermouth creates a marked con-trast with the more rugged mountain landscapes of the central Lake District. In the village of Low Lorton is the private manor house of Lorton Hall, dating from the 15th century.

Derwent Water
Surrounded by woodland slopes and fells, this attractive oval lake is dotted with tiny islands. One of these was inhabited by St. Herbert, a disciple of St. Cuthbert (see p405), who lived there as a hermit until 687. A boat from Keswick provides a lake excursion.

Tʜᴇ Mᴀᴊᴏʀ Pᴇᴀᴋs

The Lake District hills are the highest in England. Although they seem small by Alpine or world standards, the scale of the surrounding terrain makes them look extremely large. Some of the most important peaks are shown on the following pages. Each peak is regarded as having its own personality. This section shows the Skiddaw fells, which are north of Keswick.

① ▲ Blencathra
▲ Skiddaw
② ▲ Grisedale Pike
③ ▲ Grasmoor
▲ Knott Rigg
▲ Helvellyn
▲ Grasmoor
▲ Great Gable
▲ High Street
Wast Water ▲
Scafell ▲
▲ Hard Knott
▲ The Old Man of Coniston
Screes
④
⑤
⑥

Kᴇʏ

— From ① Blencathra to ② Cockermouth *(see opposite)*

— From ③ Grisedale Pike to ④ the Old Man of Coniston *(see pp348–9)*

— From ⑤ the Old Man of Coniston to ⑥ Windermere and Tarn Crag *(see pp350–51)*

— National Park boundary

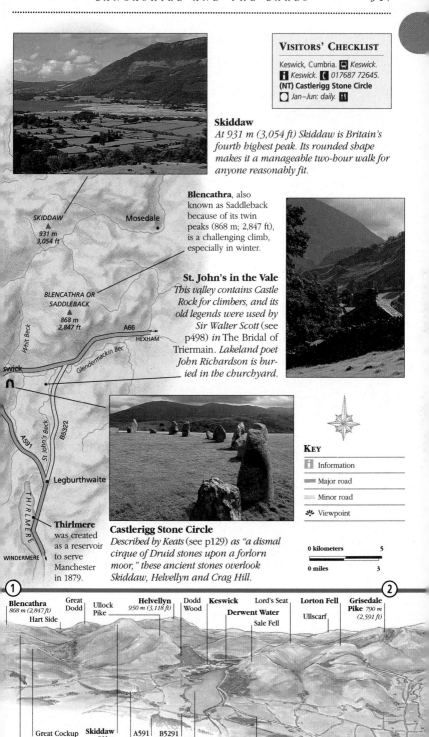

Skiddaw

At 931 m (3,054 ft) Skiddaw is Britain's fourth highest peak. Its rounded shape makes it a manageable two-hour walk for anyone reasonably fit.

Blencathra, also known as Saddleback because of its twin peaks (868 m; 2,847 ft), is a challenging climb, especially in winter.

St. John's in the Vale

This valley contains Castle Rock for climbers, and its old legends were used by Sir Walter Scott (see p498) *in* The Bridal of Triermain. *Lakeland poet John Richardson is buried in the churchyard.*

SKIDDAW
931 m
3,054 ft

Mosedale

BLENCATHRA OR
SADDLEBACK
868 m
2,847 ft

A66
HEXHAM

Whit Beck

Glendermackin Bec

swick

A591

St. John's Beck

B5322

● Legburthwaite

T H I R L M E R E

Thirlmere was created as a reservoir to serve Manchester in 1879.

WINDERMERE

KEY

ℹ️ Information

▬▬ Major road

▬▬ Minor road

☀ Viewpoint

Castlerigg Stone Circle

Described by Keats (see p129) *as "a dismal cirque of Druid stones upon a forlorn moor," these ancient stones overlook Skiddaw, Helvellyn and Crag Hill.*

0 kilometers   5

0 miles   3

① Blencathra
868 m (2,847 ft)
Hart Side

Great
Dodd

Ullock
Pike

Helvellyn
950 m (3,118 ft)

Dodd
Wood

Keswick

Derwent Water

Lord's Seat

Sale Fell

Lorton Fell

Ullscarf

Grisedale
Pike 790 m
(2,591 ft) ②

Great Cockup
Great Calva

Skiddaw
931 m
(3,054 ft)

A591

B5291

Bassenthwaite
Lake

A66 to
Cockermouth

Bassenthwaite Village

Crummock Water, one of the quieter "western lakes"

Cockermouth **7**

Cumbria. 🏠 7,000. 🚆 Workington.
🚌 ℹ Town Hall, Market St (01900
822634). 🛒 Mon.

COLORWASHED TERRACES and
restored workers' cottages
beside the river are especially
attractive in the busy market
town of Cockermouth, which
dates from the 12th century.
The place not to miss is the
handsome **Wordsworth
House**, on the main street,
where the poet was born *(see
p352)*. This fine Georgian
building still contains a few
of the family's possessions,
and is furnished in the style
of the late 18th century.
Wordsworth mentions the
attractive terraced garden,
which overlooks the River
Derwent, in his *Prelude*. The
local parish church contains a
Wordsworth memorial window.

Cockermouth **castle** is partly
ruined but still inhabited and
not open to the public. The
town also has small museums
of printing, toys and a mineral
collection, and an art gallery.
The **Jennings Brewery**,
founded in 1828, invites
visitors for tours and tastings.

🏛 **Wordsworth House**
(NT) Main St. 📞 01900 824805.
⬤ Apr–Jun, Sep, Oct: Mon–Fri, Sat,
public hols; Jul, Aug: Mon–Sat.
🍴 ♿ gardens.
🍺 **Jennings Brewery**
Castle Brewery. 📞 01900 823214.
⬤ Mar–Oct: daily.

Newlands Valley **8**

Cumbria. 🚆 Workington then bus. 🚌
Cockermouth. ℹ Town Hall, Market
St, Cockermouth (01900 822634).

FROM THE gently wooded
shores of Derwent Water,
the Newlands Valley runs
through a scattering of farms
toward rugged heights of 335
m (1,100 ft) at the top
of the pass, where steps lead
to the waterfall, Moss Force.
Grisedale Pike, Grasmoor
and Knott Rigg all provide
excellent fell walks, passing
through bracken-covered
land grazed by hardy sheep.
Local mineral deposits of
copper, graphite, lead and
even small amounts of gold
and silver were extensively
mined here from Elizabethan
times onward. **Little Town**
was used as a setting by
Beatrix Potter *(see p353)* in
The Tale of Mrs. Tiggywinkle.

Kitchen, with an old range and tiled floor, at Wordsworth House

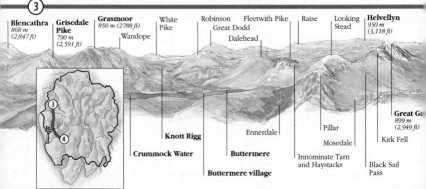

| Blencathra 868 m (2,847 ft) | Grisedale Pike 790 m (2,591 ft) | Grasmoor 850 m (2788 ft) Wandope | White Pike | Robinson Great Dodd Dalehead | Fleetwith Pike | Raise | Looking Stead | Helvellyn 950 m (3,118 ft) |

Knott Rigg

Crummock Water

Ennerdale

Buttermere

Buttermere village

Innominate Tarn and Haystacks

Pillar

Mosedale

Great Ga 899 m (2,949 ft)

Kirk Fell

Black Sail Pass

Buttermere 9

Cumbria. ⊵ *Workington then bus.* 🏠 *Cockermouth.* 🚹 *Town Hall, Market St, Cockermouth (01900 822634).*

INTERLINKING WITH Crummock Water and Loweswater, Buttermere and its surroundings contain some of the most appealing countryside in the region. Often known as the "western lakes," the three are remote enough not to become too crowded. Buttermere is a jewel amid grand fells: High Stile, Red Pike and Haystacks. Here the ashes of A.W. Wainwright, the celebrated hill-walker and author of fell-walking books, are scattered.

The village of Buttermere, with its handful of houses and a couple of inns, is a popular starting point for walks around all three lakes. Loweswater is hardest to reach and therefore the quietest, surrounded by woods and gentle hills. Nearby Scale Force is the highest waterfall in the Lake District, plunging 36 m (120 ft).

Verdant valley of Borrowdale, a favorite with artists

Borrowdale 10

Cumbria. ⊵ *Workington.* 🏠 *Cockermouth.* 🚹 *Town Hall, Market St, Cockermouth (01900 822634).*

THIS ROMANTIC VALLEY, subject of a myriad sketches and watercolors before photography stole the scene, lies beside the densely wooded shores of Derwent Water under towering crags. It is a popular trip from Keswick and a great variety of walks are possible along the valley.

The tiny hamlet of **Grange** is one of the prettiest spots, where the valley narrows dramatically to form the "Jaws of Borrowdale." Nearby Castle Crag has superb views.

From Grange you can complete the circuit of Derwent Water along the western shore, or move southward to the more open farmland around Seatoller. As you head south by road, look for a National Trust sign *(see p25)* to the **Bowder Stone**, a delicately poised block weighing nearly 2,000 tons, which may have fallen from the crags above or been deposited by a glacier millions of years ago.

Two attractive hamlets in Borrowdale are **Rosthwaite** and **Stonethwaite**. Also worth a detour, preferably on foot, is Watendlath village, off a side road near the famous beauty spot of **Ashness Bridge**.

WALKING IN THE LAKE DISTRICT

Typical Lake District stile over drystone wall

Two long-distance footpaths pass through the Lake District's most spectacular scenery. The 70 mile (110 km) Cumbrian Way runs from Carlisle to Ulverston via Keswick and Coniston. The western section of the Coast-to-Coast Walk *(see p33)* passes through this area. There are hundreds of shorter walks along lake shores, nature trails or following more challenging uphill routes. Walkers should stick to paths to avoid erosion, and check weather conditions at National Park information centers.

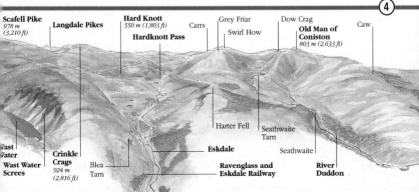

Scafell Pike
978 m
(3,210 ft)

Langdale Pikes

Hard Knott
550 m (1,803 ft)

Hardknott Pass

Carrs

Grey Friar

Swirl How

Dow Crag

Old Man of Coniston
803 m (2,633 ft)

Caw

Harter Fell

Seathwaite Tarn

Vast Water

Wast Water Screes

Crinkle Crags
924 m
(2,816 ft)

Blea Tarn

Eskdale

Ravenglass and Eskdale Railway

Seathwaite

River Duddon

Convivial Wasdale Head Inn *(see p561)* at Wasdale Head

Wast Water ⓫

Cumbria. ⌖ *Seascale.* ℹ *12 Main St, Egremont (01946 820693).*

A SILENT REFLECTION of truly awesome surroundings, black, brooding **Wast Water** is a mysterious, evocative lake. The road from Nether Wasdale continues along its northwest side. Along its eastern flank loom walls of sheer scree over 600 m (2,000 ft) high. Beneath them the water looks inky black, whatever the weather, plunging an icy 80 m (260 ft) from the waterline to the bottom to form England's deepest lake. You can walk along the screes, but it is an uncomfortable and dangerous scramble. Boating on the lake is banned for conservation reasons, but fishing permits are available from the nearby National Trust camp site.

At **Wasdale Head** lies one of Britain's finest views: the austere pyramid of **Great Gable**, centerpiece of a fine mountain composition, with the huge forms of Scafell and **Scafell Pike**. The scenery is utterly unspoiled, and the only buildings lie at the far end of the lake: an inn and a tiny church commemorating fallen climbers. Here the road ends, and you must turn back or start hiking, following signs for Black Sail Pass and Ennerdale, or walk up the great fells ahead. Wasdale's irresistible backdrop was the inspiration of the first serious British mountaineers, who flocked here during the 19th century, insouciantly clad in tweed jackets, carrying little more than a length of rope slung over their shoulders.

Eskdale ⓬

Cumbria. ⌖ *Ravenglass then narrow-gauge railway to Eskdale (Easter–Oct: daily; Nov–Easter: Sat, Sun).* ℹ *12 Main St, Egremont (01946 820693).*

THE PASTORAL DELIGHTS of Eskdale are best encountered over the grueling **Hardknott Pass**, which is the most taxing drive in the Lake District, with steep gradients. You can pause at the summit (393 m; 1,291 ft) to explore the Roman **Hardknott Fort**, where there is a lovely view of the valley below. As you descend into Eskdale, rhododendrons and pines flourish in a landscape of small hamlets, narrow lanes and gentle farmland. The main settlements below are the attractive villages of Boot and coastal Ravenglass, both with old **grain mills**.

Just south of Ravenglass is the impressive **Muncaster Castle**, the richly furnished home of the Pennington family. Another way to enjoy the spectacular scenery is to take a trip on the miniature railroad (La'l Ratty) that runs from Ravenglass to Dalegarth.

🏭 **Eskdale Mill**
Boot. 📞 *019467 233335.* ◯ *Apr–Sep: Tue–Sun, public hols.* ♿
🏭 **Muncaster Mill**
Ravenglass. 📞 *01229 717232.* ◯ *Apr–Oct: daily.* ♿
🏰 **Muncaster Castle**
Ravenglass. 📞 *01229 717614.* ◯ *Apr–Oct: Tue–Sun; public hols (Mon).* ♿ ♿ *ground floor only.*

Remains of the Roman Hardknott Fort, Eskdale

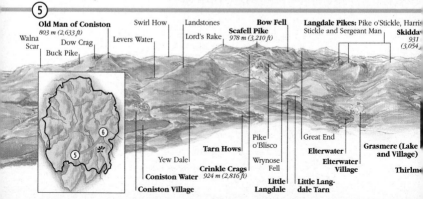

⑤

Old Man of Coniston 803 m (2,633 ft) | Swirl How | Landstones | **Bow Fell** | **Langdale Pikes:** Pike o'Stickle, Harris Stickle and Sergeant Man | **Skidda** 931 (3,054

Walna Scar | Dow Crag | Levers Water | Lord's Rake | **Scafell Pike** 978 m (3,210 ft)

Buck Pike

Pike o'Blisco | Great End

Tarn Hows | Elterwater | **Grasmere (Lake and Village)**

Yew Dale | Wrynose Fell | Elterwater Village

Crinkle Crags 924 m (2,816 ft) | **Thirlme**

Coniston Water | **Little Langdale** | **Little Langdale Tarn**

Coniston Village

Autumnal view of Seathwaite, in the Duddon Valley, a popular center for walkers and climbers

Duddon Valley ⑬

Cumbria. 🚃 *Ulverston.* 🛈 *Ruskin Ave, Coniston (015394 41533).*

ALSO KNOWN as Dunnerdale, this picturesque tract of countryside inspired 35 of Wordsworth's sonnets *(see p352)*. The prettiest stretch lies between Ulpha and Cockley Beck. In autumn the colors of heather moors and a light sprinkling of birch trees are particularly beautiful. Stepping stones and bridges span the river at intervals, the most charming being Birk's Bridge, near Seathwaite. At the southern end of the valley, where the River Duddon meets the sea at Duddon Sands, is

Broughton-in-Furness, a pretty village of 18th-century houses, with an 11th-century church. Note the old stocks, and the stone slabs used for fish on market day in the main square.

Langdale ⑭

Cumbria. 🚃 *Windermere.* 🛈 *The Old Courthouse, Church St, Ambleside (015394 32582).*

STRETCHING FROM Skelwith Bridge, where the Brathay surges powerfully over waterfalls, to the summits of Great Langdale is the two-pronged Langdale Valley. Walkers and climbers throng here to take on **Pavey Ark, Pike o'Stickle,**

Crinkle Crags and **Bow Fell**. The local mountain rescue teams are the busiest in Britain.

Great Langdale is the more spectacular valley and it is often crowded, but quieter **Little Langdale** has many attractions too. It is worth completing the circuit back to Ambleside via the southern route, stopping at Blea Tarn. Reedy **Elterwater** is a picturesque spot, once a site of the gunpowder industry. Wrynose Pass, west of Little Langdale, climbs to 390 m (1,281 ft), a warm-up for Hardknott Pass farther on. At its top is Three Shires Stone, marking the former boundary of the old counties of Cumberland, Westmorland and Lancashire.

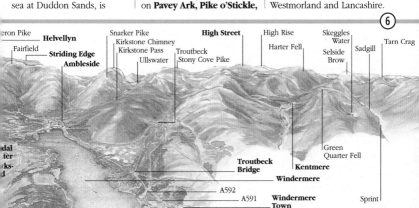

Rydal Water, one of the major attractions of the Lake District

Ambleside ⑯

Cumbria. 🏃 3,400. 🚉 🚌 *The Old Courthouse, Church St (015394 32582).* 🚃 *Wed.*

A MBLESIDE has good road connections to all parts of the Lakes and is an attractive base, especially for walkers and climbers. Victorian in character, it has dignified architecture and a good range of outdoor clothing, crafts and specialty food stores. An enterprising little movie house and a classical music festival, held in the summer months, give it additional life in the evenings. Sights in town are small-scale: the remnants of the Roman fort of Galava, AD 79, the Stock Ghyll Force waterfall and the tiny **Bridge House** over Stock Beck, now an information center.

ENVIRONS: Within easy reach are the wooded Rothay valley, the **Kirkstone Galleries** at Skelwith Bridge, with their unusual souvenirs, and the bleak Kirkstone Pass. At nearby Troutbeck you can visit

The Old Bridge House over Stock Beck in Ambleside

Grasmere and Rydal ⑮

Cumbria. **Grasmere** 🏃 700. **Rydal** 🏃 100. 🚉 *Grasmere.* 🚌 *Redbank Rd, Grasmere (015394 35245).*

T HE POET William Wordsworth lived in both these pretty villages on the shores of two sparkling lakes. Fairfield, Hart Crag and Loughrigg Fell rise steeply above their reedy shores and offer good opportunities for walking. Grasmere is now a sizable settlement of cottages, shops and restaurants. The famous Grasmere sports *(see p344)*, held here every August, attract large crowds.

The Wordsworth family is buried in St. Oswald's Church, and crowds flock to the annual ceremony of strewing the church's earth floor with fresh rushes. Most visitors head for **Dove Cottage**, where the poet spent his most creative years. The museum in the barn behind includes such artifacts as the great man's socks. The Wordsworths moved to a

larger house, **Rydal Mount**, in Rydal in 1813 and lived here until 1850. The grounds have waterfalls and a summerhouse where the poet often sat. Dora's Field nearby is a blaze of daffodils in spring and Fairfield Horseshoe offers an energetic, challenging walk.

🏛 **Dove Cottage and the Wordsworth Museum**
Off A591 nr Grasmere. 📞 *015394 35544.* 🕐 *daily.* ⬤ *Dec 24–26, mid-Jan–mid-Feb.* 🎫 ♿

🏛 **Rydal Mount**
Rydal. 📞 *015394 33002.* 🕐 *Mar–Oct: daily; Nov–Feb: Wed–Mon.* 🎫

BEATRIX POTTER AND THE LAKE DISTRICT

Although best known for her children's stories with characters such as Peter Rabbit and Jemima Puddleduck, which she also illustrated, Beatrix Potter (1866–1943) became a champion of conservation in the Lake District after moving there in 1906. She married William Helis, devoted herself to farming, and was an expert on Herdwick sheep. To conserve her beloved countryside, she donated land to the National Trust.

Cover illustration of *Jemima Puddleduck* (1908)

the restored farmhouse of **Townend**, dating from 1626, whose interior gives an insight into Lakeland domestic life.

🏛 **Kirkstone Galleries**
Skelwith Bridge. 📞 *015394 34002.*
◻ *daily.* ◑ *Dec 24–26.*
🏛 **Townend**
Troutbeck. 📞 *015394 32628.*
◻ *Apr–Oct: Tue–Fri & public hols.* 🏷

Windermere ⑰

Cumbria. 🚉 *Station Rd.* 🚌 *Victoria St.* 🛈 *Victoria St (015394 46499) or Glebe Rd, Bowness-on-Windermere (015394 42895).*

AT OVER 10 miles (16 km) long, this dramatic watery expanse is England's largest mere. Industrial magnates built mansions around its shores long before the railroad arrived. Stately **Brockhole**, now a national park visitor center, was one such grand estate. When the railroad reached Windermere in 1847, it enabled crowds of workers to visit the area on day trips.

Today, a year-round car ferry service connects the lake's east and west shores (it runs between Ferry Nab and Ferry House), and summer steamers link Lakeside, Bowness and Ambleside on the north-south axis. Belle Isle, an intriguing wooded island on which a unique round house stands, is one of the lake's most attractive features, but landing is not allowed there. The best place for swimming is **Fell Foot Park** at the south end of the lake, and there are good lakeshore walks on the northwest side. One of the most stunning viewpoints is Orrest Head 238 m (784 ft), northeast of Windermere village.

ENVIRONS: Bowness-on-Windermere, on the east shore, is a hugely popular center. Many of its buildings display Victorian details, and St. Martin's Church dates back to the 15th century. The **Windermere Steamboat Museum** recalls the Victorian age in a collection of superbly restored craft, and one of these vessels, *Osprey*, makes regular lake trips. The **World of Beatrix Potter** recreates her characters in an exhibition, and a film tells her life story.

Beatrix Potter wrote many of her books at **Hill Top**, the 17th-century farmhouse at Near Sawrey, northwest of Windermere. The house is so popular that it is advisable to avoid visits at peak times. Hill Top is furnished with many of Potter's possessions, left as they were in her lifetime. The **Beatrix Potter Gallery** in Hawkshead has a permanent exhibition of her manuscripts.

🛈 **Brockhole Visitor Centre**
On A591. 📞 *015394 46601.*
◻ *Apr–Oct: daily.* 🏷 ♿
♣ **Fell Foot Park**
(NT) Newby Bridge. 📞 *015395 31273.* ◻ *Apr–Oct: daily.* ♿
🏛 **Windermere Steamboat Museum**
Rayrigg Rd, Windermere. 📞 *015394 45555.* ◻ *Apr–Oct: daily.* 🏷 ♿
🏛 **World of Beatrix Potter**
The Old Laundry, Crag Brow.
📞 *015394 88444.* ◻ *daily.* 🏷 ♿
⛪ **Hill Top**
(NT) The Square, Hawkshead. 📞 *015394 36269.* ◻ *Apr–Oct: Sat–Wed.*
🏛 **Beatrix Potter Gallery**
(NT) The Square, Hawkshead.
📞 *015394 36355.* ◻ *Apr–Oct: Sun–Thu.* 🏷

Boats moored along the shore at Ambleside, the north end of Windermere

Peaceful Coniston Water, the setting of Arthur Ransome's novel, *Swallows and Amazons* (1930)

Coniston Water ⑱

Cumbria. 🚆 *Windermere then bus.*
🚌 *Ambleside then bus.* ℹ️ *Coniston car park (015394 41533).*

FOR THE FINEST VIEW of this stretch of water just outside the Lake District, you need to climb. The 19th-century art critic, writer and philosopher John Ruskin, had a fine view from his house, **Brantwood**, where his paintings and memorabilia can be seen today. The Ruskin and Gandhi exhibition explores Ruskin's influence on India's legendary statesman, Mahatma Gandhi (1869–1948).

An enjoyable excursion is the summer lake trip from Coniston Pier on the National Trust steam yacht, *Gondola*, stopping at Brantwood and Park-a-Moor. Coniston was also the scene of Donald Campbell's fatal attempt on the world water speed record in 1967. The green-slate village of Coniston, once a center for copper mining, now caters to local walkers.

Also interesting is the traffic-free village of **Hawkshead** to the northwest, with its quaint alleyways and timber-framed houses. To the south is the vast Grizedale Forest, dotted with woodland sculptures.

Just north of Coniston Water is the man-made **Tarn Hows**, a landscaped pool surrounded by woods. There is a pleasant climb up the 803 m (2,635 ft) Old Man of Coniston.

🏛 Brantwood
Off B5285, nr Hawkshead Hill. 📞
015394 41396. ⭕ *mid-Mar–mid-Nov: daily; mid-Nov–mid-Mar: Wed–Sun.*
⬛ *Dec 25, 26.* 💷 ♿ *limited.*

Kendal ⑲

Cumbria. 🏘 *26,000.* 🚆 ℹ️ *Town Hall, Highgate (01539 725758).*
🛒 *Wed, Sat.*

A BUSY MARKET TOWN, Kendal is the administrative center of the region and the southern gateway to the Lake District. Built in gray limestone, it has an enterprising arts center, the **Brewery**, and a central area, that is best enjoyed on foot.

Kendal mint cake, the famous lakeland energy-booster for walkers

The **Abbot Hall** (1759) art collection has paintings by Turner and Romney as well as Gillows furniture *(see p358)*. In Abbot Hall's stable block you can visit the **Museum of Lakeland Life and Industry**, with lively workshops demonstrating local crafts and trades. There are dioramas of geology and wildlife in the **Museum of Natural History and Archaeology**. About 3 miles

(5 km) south of the town is 14th-century **Sizergh Castle**, with a fortified tower, carved fireplaces and a lovely garden.

🏛 Abbot Hall Art Gallery and Museum of Lakeland Life and Industry
Kirkland. 📞 *01539 722464.* ⭕ *mid-Feb–Dec 22: daily.* 💷 ♿ *gallery.*
🏛 Kendal Museum of Natural History and Archaeology
Station Rd. 📞 *01539 721374.*
⭕ *mid-Feb–Dec 22: daily.* ⬛ *Dec 23–mid-Feb.* 💷 ♿ *limited.*
⚜ Sizergh Castle
(NT) off A591& A590. 📞 *015395 60070.* ⭕ *Easter–Oct: Sun–Thu.*
💷 ♿ *grounds only.*

Furness Peninsula ⑳

Cumbria. 🚆 🚌 *Barrow-in-Furness.*
ℹ️ *28 Duke St, Barrow-in-Furness (01229 870156).*

B ARROW-IN-FURNESS, now a lesser shipbuilding center *(see p335)*, is the peninsula's main town. Its **Dock Museum**, cleverly built over a Victorian dock where ships were repaired, traces the history of Barrow using lively displays, including an old schooner, *Emily Barratt*. Ruins of the red sandstone walls of **Furness Abbey** remain in the wooded Vale of Deadly Nightshade, with a small exhibition of monastic life. The historic town of Ulverston received its charter

◁ **The attractive woodland of Thirlmere, under the shadow of Helvellyn**

in 1280. **Ulverston Heritage Center** charts its growth from market town to port. Stan Laurel, the thin comedian of Laurel and Hardy fame, was born here in 1890. The **museum** has a movie theater.

🏛 Dock Museum
North Rd, Barrow-in-Furness. [01229 870871. ◯ Apr–Oct: Wed–Sun; Nov–Mar: Wed–Sun (Sat, Sun: pm); public hols. ● Dec 25, Jan 1. &

🏰 Furness Abbey
Vale of Deadly Nightshade. [01229 823420. ◯ Easter–Oct: daily; Nov–Easter: Wed–Sun. ● Dec 25. ▨ &

🏛 Ulverston Heritage Centre
Lower Brook St. [01229 580820. ◯ Apr–Jan: Mon–Sat; Jan–Mar: Mon, Tue, Thu–Sat. ● Dec 25, 26, Jan 1. ▨ & limited.

🏛 Laurel and Hardy Museum
Upper Brook St, Ulverston. [01229 582292. ◯ daily. ● Dec 25. ▨ &

Staircase at Holker Hall

Cartmel ㉑

Cumbria. 🅰 700. 🛈 Victoria Hall, Main St (015395 34026).

THE HIGHLIGHT of this pretty village is its 12th-century **priory**, one of the finest Lake District churches. Little remains of the original priory except the pretty gatehouse in the village center, owned by the National Trust *(see p25)* and leased as an art gallery. The restored church has an attractive east window, a stone-carved 14th-century tomb, and beautiful misericords.

Cartmel also boasts a small racecourse. The village has given its name to its surroundings, a hilly district of green farmland with variegated woods and limestone scars.

One of the main local attractions is **Holker Hall**, former residence of the Dukes of Devonshire. Inside are lavishly furnished rooms, with fine marble fireplaces, and a superb oak staircase. Outside are the award-winning formal gardens and a deer park.

🏰 Holker Hall
Cark-in-Cartmel. [015395 58328. ◯ Apr–Oct: Sun–Fri. ▨ & limited.

Levens Hall ㉒

Nr Kendal, Cumbria. [015395 60321. 🚌 from Kendal or Lancaster. ◯ Apr–Sep: Sun–Thu. ▨ ⓟ & gardens only.

THE OUTSTANDING attraction of this Elizabethan mansion is its famous topiary, but the house itself has much to offer. Built around a 13th-century fortified tower, it contains a fine collection of Jacobean furniture and watercolors by Peter de Wint (1784–1849). Also of note are the ornate plaster ceilings, carved Charles II dining chairs, the earliest example of English patchwork and the gilded hearts on the drainpipes.

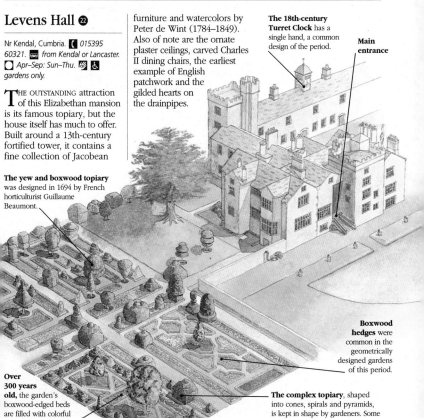

The 18th-century Turret Clock has a single hand, a common design of the period.

Main entrance

The yew and boxwood topiary was designed in 1694 by French horticulturist Guillaume Beaumont.

Over 300 years old, the garden's boxwood-edged beds are filled with colorful herbaceous displays.

Boxwood hedges were common in the geometrically designed gardens of this period.

The complex topiary, shaped into cones, spirals and pyramids, is kept in shape by gardeners. Some specimens are 6 m (20 ft) high.

Morecambe Bay, looking northwest toward Barrow-in-Furness

Morecambe Bay ㉓

Lancashire. ⊠ Morecambe.
⊞ Heysham (to Isle of Man). ⓘ
Central Promenade (01524 582808).

THE BEST WAY to explore
Morecambe Bay is by train
from Ulverston to Arnside. The
track follows a series of low
viaducts across an expanse of
glistening tidal flats where
thousands of wading birds
feed and breed. The bay is
one of the most important
bird reserves in Britain. On
the Cumbrian side, retirement
homes have expanded the
sedate Victorian resort of
Grange-over-Sands, which
grew up after the arrival of
the railroad in 1857. Its best
feature is its natural setting.
Nearby, **Hampsfield Fell**
and **Humphrey Head Point**
give fine views along the bay.

Leighton Hall ㉔

Carnforth, Lancashire. ☏ 01524
734474. ⊞ to Yealand Conyers (from
Lancaster). ◯ May–Jul, Sep: Tue–Fri &
Sun (pm); Aug: Tue–Fri & Sun. ◑
occasional special events. ◪ ⓑ

LEIGHTON HALL'S estate dates
back to the 13th century,
but most of the present building is 19th century, including
its pale Neo-Gothic façade. It
is owned by the Gillow family,
founders of the Lancastrian
furniture business, whose
exquisite products are now
highly prized antiques. Some
excellent pieces can be seen
here, including a ladies' work-
box inlaid with biblical scenes.

There is also a large collection
of birds of prey, and in the
afternoon the eagles and falcons put on an air show.

Lancaster ㉕

Lancashire. ⩑ 45,000.
⊠ ⓐ ⓘ Castle Hill
(01524 32878).
⊜ Mon–Sat.

THIS COUNTY TOWN
of Lancashire is
tiny compared to
Liverpool or
Manchester
(now counties
in their own
right), but it
has a long history. The Romans
named it after their camp over
the River Lune. Originally a
defensive site, it developed

**Tawny eagle at
Leighton Hall**

into a prosperous port largely
on the proceeds of the slave
trade. Today, its university and
cultural life still thrive. The
Norman **Lancaster Castle** was
expanded in the 14th and 16th
centuries. It has been a crown
court and a prison since the
18th century. The Shire Hall is
decorated with 600 heraldic
shields. Some fragments from
Adrian's Tower (which has a
collection of torture instruments) are 2,000 years old.
   The nearby priory church
of **St. Mary** is on Castle Hill.
Its main features include a
Saxon doorway and carved
14th-century choir stalls. There
is an outstanding museum of
furniture in the 17th-century
Judge's Lodgings, while the
Maritime Museum, in the
Georgian custom house
on St. George's Quay,
contains displays on the
port's history. The **City
Museum**, based in the
old town hall, concen-
trates on Lancaster's
shore-based aspects.
The splendid **Lune
Aqueduct** carries the
canal over the
River Lune on
five wide arches.
Other attractions
are found in
**Williamson
Park**, site of
the 1907 Ashton Memorial.
This folly was built by the
local linoleum magnate and
politician, Lord Ashton.

CROSSING THE SANDS

Morecambe Bay sands are very dangerous. Travelers used to
cut across the bay at low tide to shorten the long trail around
the Kent estuary. Many perished as the rising water turned
the beach to quicksand, and sea fogs hid the paths. Locals
who knew the bay became guides, and today you can travel
with a guide from Kents Bank to Hest Bank near Arnside.

The High Sheriff of Lancaster Crossing Morecambe Sands (anon)

There are fine views from the top of this 67 m (220 ft) domed structure. Opposite is the tropical butterfly house, and the pavilion café.

Façade of Lancaster's Judge's Lodgings, now a museum

♠ **Lancaster Castle**
Castle Parade. 📞 01524 64998. ◻ Easter–Oct: daily. ● when court is in session. 🎦 ♿ limited.

🏛 **Judge's Lodgings**
Church St. 📞 01524 32808. ◻ Easter–Jun, Oct: Mon–Sat (pm); Jul–Sep: daily. 🎦

🏛 **Maritime Museum**
Custom House, St George's Quay. 📞 01524 64637. ◻ daily (Easter–Nov: pm). ● Dec 24–27, Jan 1, 2. 🎦 ♿

🏛 **City Museum**
Market Sq. 📞 01524 64637. ◻ Mon–Sat. ● Dec 24–Jan 2. ♿ limited.

♣ **Williamson Park**
Quernmore Rd. 📞 01524 33318. ◻ daily. ● Dec 25–26, Jan 1. 🎦 limited.

Ribble Valley ㉖

Lancashire. 🚆 Clitheroe. 🛈 Market Place, Clitheroe 01200 25566.

CLITHEROE, A SMALL market town with a hilltop castle, is a good center for exploring the pretty Ribble Valley landscape with its wide rivers and old villages, such as Slaidburn and Waddington. Ribchester has the remains of a **Roman fort** and museum, and there is a ruined **Cistercian abbey** at Whalley. East is Pendle Hill (560 m; 1,830 ft) with a Bronze Age burial mound at its peak. West is the Forest of Bowland.

THE WITCHES OF PENDLE

In 1612, ten women were convicted of witchcraft at Lancaster Castle. The evidence against them was mostly based on the revelations of a small child who implicated them in satanic rituals. Many of the accused came from two peasant families, reduced to penury by a feud, who roamed the countryside begging and cursing those who refused to oblige. Several of the women confessed to their crimes, but whether they were coerced, deranged or had indeed dabbled in the "black arts" is impossible to assess.

Mother Chattox, a Pendle "witch"

🏛 **Ribchester Roman fort**
Ribchester. 📞 01254 878261. ◻ daily. ● Dec 24, 25. 🎦 ♿

🏛 **Whalley Abbey**
Whalley. 📞 01254 822268. **Grounds** ◻ daily. **Exhibition Centre** ◻ Easter–Oct: daily. 🎦 ♿

Blackpool ㉗

Lancashire. 👥 150,000. ✈ 🚆 🚌 🛈 Clifton St (01253 21623).

BRITISH VACATION patterns have changed in the past few decades, and Blackpool is no longer the apogee of seaside entertainment it once was.

A seamless wall of amusement arcades, piers, bingo halls and fast-food stands stretch behind the sands. Nostalgic trolleys run along the promenade. At night, entertainers strut their stuff under the bright lights. The town attracts thousands of visitors during September and October when spectacular colored lights outline the skeleton of the 158 m (518 ft) Blackpool Tower. Blackpool's resort life dates back to the 18th century, but it burst into prominence when the railroad first arrived in 1840, bringing Lancastrian workers to this vacation resort.

Blackpool Tower, painted gold for its centenary in 1994

Manchester 🄮

Sign for the John Rylands Library

MANCHESTER'S HISTORY dates back to Roman times, when, in AD 79, Agricola's legions set up a base camp called Mancunium on the site of the present city. It rose to prominence in the late 18th century, when Richard Arkwright's steam-powered spinning machines introduced the brave new world of cotton processing. By 1830, the first railroad linked Manchester and Liverpool; in 1894 the Manchester Ship Canal opened, allowing cargo vessels 36 miles (55 km) inland. Confident civic buildings sprang up from the proceeds of cotton wealth, but these were in stark contrast to the overcrowded slums of the millworkers. Social discontent led writers, politicians and reformers to espouse liberal or radical causes. One result was the foundation in 1821 of the forthright local newspaper, the *Manchester Guardian,* now an important national daily. The city was the first to introduce massive slum clearance and smokeless zones during the 1950s.

Exploring Manchester

Manchester is a fine, compact city with much to see in its central areas. The imaginative restoration of the trolley system has helped to ease the pressures of urban travel. The mills and docks have left a huge architectural heritage. Among the fine 19th-century buildings are the Neo-Gothic cathedral, the **John Rylands Library**, now part of the university, the **Town Hall**, the **Royal Exchange**, now a theater and restaurant, and the **Free Trade Hall**, home of the famous Hallé concerts. Night owls can enjoy the city's lively club scene, and its many ethnic restaurants.

The G-Mex Exhibition and Event Centre, once the central railroad station

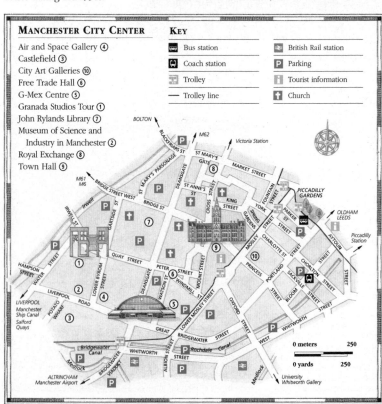

MANCHESTER CITY CENTER

Air and Space Gallery ④
Castlefield ③
City Art Galleries ⑩
Free Trade Hall ⑥
G-Mex Centre ⑤
Granada Studios Tour ①
John Rylands Library ⑦
Museum of Science and Industry in Manchester ②
Royal Exchange ⑧
Town Hall ⑨

KEY

🚌 Bus station
🚏 Coach station
🚋 Trolley
— Trolley line

🚢 British Rail station
P Parking
ℹ Tourist information
✝ Church

0 meters 250
0 yards 250

Trafford Road Bridge on the Manchester Ship Canal

VISITORS' CHECKLIST

Greater Manchester. 2.5 million. Off M56 11 miles (18 km) S Manchester. Oxford Road, Victoria, Piccadilly. Chorlton St. Lloyd St (0161 234 3157). daily. Manchester Festival: Sep.

🏛 Museum of Science and Industry in Manchester
Liverpool Rd. 0161 832 2244. daily. Dec 24–26.
Part of the Castlefield Urban Heritage Park, this museum captures the spirit of scientific enterprise and industrial might that characterized Manchester in its heyday. Among the best sections are the Power Hall, a collection of working steam engines, the Electricity Gallery, which traces the history of domestic power, and an exhibition on the Liverpool and Manchester Railway. There are hot-air balloons and space suits in the Air and Space Gallery across the street.

🎬 Granada Studios Tour
Water St. 0161 832 9090. Apr–Sep: Tue–Sun; Oct–Mar: Wed–Sun; Jan: Fri–Sun, public & school hols. week before Christmas.
Just around the corner are the Granada Studios, where visitors can take a **tour** through the backlots of popular television shows. Most famous is the set of *Coronation Street*, Britain's longest running soap opera.
   Close by, in **Castlefield**, you can see the rebuilt "castle in the field" (the ruined Roman fort), and the restored wharves of the Bridgewater Canal.

🏛 City Art Galleries
Mosley St. 0161 236 5244. daily (Sun: pm). Dec 25, 26, Jan 1, Good Fri.
The porticoed building that Sir Charles Barry (1795–1860) designed in 1824, contains an excellent collection of British art, notably Pre-Raphaelites

such as Holman Hunt and Dante Gabriel Rossetti. Early Italian, Flemish and French Schools are also represented. It has a fine collection of silver, ceramics and glass.

🏛 G-Mex Centre
Windmill St. 0161 834 2700. Mon–Sat. Dec 25.
The former central railroad station, closed in 1969, is now a huge exhibition center. It has more than 9,290 sq m (100,000 sq ft) of pillarless floor space in which to host major concerts and shows. It looks particularly dramatic when lit up at night.

Jacob Epstein's *Genesis* (1930–1) in Whitworth Art Gallery

🏞 Manchester Ship Canal
This magnificent engineering feat was inaugurated by Queen Victoria in May 1894. It was designed to bring deep sea shipping from Eastham on the Mersey into the heart of the city, at Salford Quays, 36 miles (58 km) inland. Three thousand ships still use the canal every year, and the docks at the head of the canal are being restored.

🏛 Whitworth Art Gallery
University of Manchester, Oxford Rd. 0161 273 4865. Mon–Sat. Dec 23–Jan 2, Good Fri.
   This fine redbrick building, named after the Manchester machine tool manufacturer and engineer, Sir Joseph Whitworth, houses a superb collection of contemporary art, textiles and prints. Jacob Epstein's *Genesis* nude occupies the entrance, but the Turner *(see p93)* watercolors are more universally appreciated. Japanese woodcuts and some examples of one of Manchester's little-known industries, wallpaper-making, are an extra bonus.

THE PETERLOO MASSACRE

In 1819, the working conditions of Manchester's factory workers were so bad that social tensions reached the breaking point. On August 16, 50,000 people assembled in St. Peter's Field to protest at the oppressive Corn Laws. Initially peaceful, the mood darkened and the poorly

trained mounted troops panicked and charged the crowd. Eleven were killed and many wounded. The incident was called Peterloo (the Battle of Waterloo had taken place in 1815). Reforms such as the Factory Act came in that year.

G. Cruikshank's *Peterloo Massacre* cartoon

Liverpool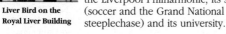

TRACES OF SETTLEMENT on Merseyside date back to the 1st century. In 1207 "Livpul," a fishing village, was granted a charter by King John. The population was only 1,000 in Stuart times, but during the 17th and 18th centuries Liverpool's westerly seaboard gave it a leading edge in the lucrative Caribbean slave trade. The first docks opened in 1715 and eventually stretched 7 miles (11 km) along the Mersey. Liverpool's first ocean steamer set out from here in 1840, and would-be emigrants to the New World poured into the city from Europe, including a flood of Irish refugees from the potato famine. Many settled permanently in Liverpool and a large, mixed community developed. Today, the port still handles similar volumes of cargoes as in the 1950s and 1960s, but container ships use Bootle docks. Despite economic and social problems, the irrepressible "Scouse" or Liverpudlian spirit re-emerged in the Swinging Sixties, when four local lads stormed the pop scene. Many people still visit Liverpool to pay homage to the Beatles, but the city is also known for its orchestra, the Liverpool Philharmonic, its sports (soccer and the Grand National steeplechase) and its university.

Liver Bird on the Royal Liver Building

Victorian ironwork, restored and polished, at Albert Dock

Exploring Liverpool
Liverpool's waterfront by the Pier Head, guarded by the legendary Liver Birds (a pair of cormorants with seaweed in their beaks) on the Royal Liver Building, is one of the most easily recognized in Britain. Nearby are the famous ferry terminal across the River Mersey and the revitalized

LIVERPOOL CITY CENTER

Beatles Story ⑤	Royal Liver Building ⑨
Cavern Quarter ①	Tate Gallery Liverpool ⑥
Liverpool Museum ②	Town Hall ⑩
Maritime Museum ⑦	*Walker Art Gallery pp364–5* ③
Metropolitan Cathedral ④	
Museum of Liverpool Life ⑧	

KEY

- 🚌 Bus station
- 🚉 British Rail station
- ⛴ Ferry terminal
- 🅿 Parking
- ℹ Tourist information
- ✝ Church

docklands. Other attractions include top-class museums and fine galleries, such as the Walker Art Gallery (see pp364–5). Its wealth of interesting architecture includes some of Britain's finest Neo-Classical buildings in the city center, and two cathedrals.

Albert Dock

Wapping. [0151 708 8854. ☐ daily. ● Dec 25. ☒ some attractions. &

The five warehouses surrounding Albert Dock were designed by Jesse Hartley in 1846. By the early 1900s the docks had become less important and had closed by 1972. After a decade of dereliction, these Grade I listed buildings (see p617) were restored in a development that includes TV studios, museums, stores, restaurants and businesses.

Albert Dock quay beside the River Mersey

🏛 Maritime Museum

Albert Dock. [0151 207 0001. ☐ daily. ● Dec 24–26, Jan 1, Good Fri. ☒ & not Piermaster's House or basement.

Ship's bell in the Maritime Museum

Devoted to the history of the Port of Liverpool, this large complex has good sections on shipbuilding and the Cunard and White Star liners as well as a new Transatlantic Slavery gallery. The area on the Battle of the Atlantic in World War II includes models and charts. Another gallery deals with emigration to the New World. The Customs and Excise section reveals the world of smuggling in all its modern forms, with sniffer dogs and swallowed heroin packages. Across the quayside is the rebuilt Piermaster's House and the Cooperage.

🏛 Museum of Liverpool Life

Mann Island. [0151 207 0001. ☐ daily. ● Dec 24–26, Jan 1, Good Fri. ☒ &

Many aspects of Liverpool culture converge here. Exhibits range from the oldest Trade Union banner in Britain to a recreated Co-op shop, and from the first Ford Anglia built at nearby Halewood, to a traditional print shop. There is a mock-up of Becher's Brook, the famous Grand National water jump at Aintree. One of the city's soccer teams, Everton, is also represented.

🏛 Beatles Story

Britannia Pavilion. [0151 709 1963. ☐ daily. ● Dec 25, 26. ☒ &

In a walk-through exhibition, this museum records the history of The Beatles' meteoric rise to fame, from their first record, *Love Me Do*, through Beatlemania to their last live appearance together in 1969, and their eventual break-up. The hits that mesmerized a generation can be heard.

🏛 Tate Gallery Liverpool

Albert Dock. [0151 709 3223. ☐ Tue–Sun, public hols. ● Mon; Dec 25. &

The northern Tate houses one of the best selections of contemporary art outside London. Marked by bright blue and orange panels, the gallery was converted from its warehouse setting by contemporary architect James Stirling. It opened in 1988 as the London Tate's first branch. Three spacious floors provide an ideal setting for the changing exhibitions of painting and sculpture housed here.

THE BEATLES

Liverpool has produced many good bands and a host of singers, comedians and entertainers before and since the 1960s. But the Beatles – John Lennon, Paul McCartney, George Harrison and Ringo Starr – were the most sensational, and locations associated with the band, however tenuous, are revered as shrines in Liverpool. Bus and walking tours trace the hallowed ground of *Strawberry Fields*, a Salvation Army home, *Penny Lane* (both outside the city center), and the boys' old homes. The most visited site is Mathew Street, near Central Station, where the Cavern Club first throbbed to the authentic Mersey Beat. The original site is now a shopping arcade, but the bricks have been used to create a replica. Nearby stand statues of the Beatles and *Eleanor Rigby*.

Liverpool: Walker Art Gallery

FOUNDED IN 1873 by Sir Andrew Barclay Walker, a local brewer and Mayor of Liverpool, this gallery houses one of the finest art collections in the North. Paintings range from early Italian and Flemish works to Rubens, Rembrandt, Poussin, and French Impressionists such as Degas's *Woman Ironing* (c.1890). Among the strong collection of British artists from the 18th century on are works by Millais and Turner and Gainsborough's famed *Countess of Sefton* (1769). There is 20th-century art by Hockney and Sickert, and the sculpture collection includes works by Henry Moore.

Italian dish (c.1500)

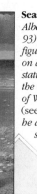

Seashells *(1870) Albert Moore (1841–93) painted female figures based on antique statues. Under the influence of Whistler (see p505), he adopted subtle shades.*

Bowring gallery

Interior at Paddington
(1951) Lucian Freud's friend Harry Diamond posed for six months for this picture, intended by the artist to "make the human being uncomfortable."

First floor

6 7 5 8 9 2 1

12 11 10 4

Ground floor

Façade was designed by H.H. Vale and Cornelius Sherlock.

Main entrance

GALLERY GUIDE
All the art galleries are on the first floor. The Cole and Bowring galleries house medieval and Renaissance paintings; the Wavertree and Audley have 17th-century Dutch, French, Italian and Spanish art. British 18th- and 19th-century works are in Rooms 1–9. Modern art is in Rooms 10 and 12, and Room 11 has Impressionists and Post-Impressionists.

Sleeping Shepherd *(1835) The greatest British Neo-Classical sculptor of the mid-19th century, John Gibson (1790–1866), used traditional colors to give his statuary a smooth appearance.*

VISITORS' CHECKLIST

William Brown St, Liverpool.
📞 0151 207 0001. 🚋 Lime St.
🚌 to Empire Theatre or Lime St.
🕐 10am–5pm Mon–Sat; noon–
5pm Sun. ● Dec 24–26,
Jan 1, Good Fri.

Cole gallery

Wavertree gallery

Audley gallery

The 7th-century Kingston Brooch in Liverpool Museum

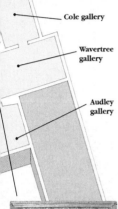

Christ Discovered in the Temple *(1342)*
Framed by a typically jewel-like Gothic setting, Simone Martini's Holy Family conveys emotional tension using graceful but highly expressive body language.

KEY

☐	13th–17th-century European
☐	18th–19th-century British, Pre-Raphaelites and Victorian
☐	19th-century British and temporary exhibitions
☐	Impressionist/Post-Impressionist
☐	20th-century British
☐	Sculpture gallery
☐	Nonexhibition space

🏛 Liverpool Museum

William St. 📞 0151 207 0001.
🕐 daily. ● Dec 24–26, Jan 1, Good
Fri. 💷 for some exhibitions. 🚻
Five floors of exhibits in this excellent museum include a fine collection of Nigerian Benin bronzes, a section on Egyptian Greek and Roman antiquities and some natural history galleries. It also has a fine ceramics collection, a planetarium, and a number of temporary exhibitions.

⛪ Anglican Cathedral

St. James' Mount. 📞 0151 709
6271. 🕐 daily (Sun: pm). 🚻
Although Gothic in style, this building was only completed in 1978. The largest Anglican cathedral in the world is a fine red sandstone edifice designed by Sir Giles Gilbert Scott. The foundation stone was laid in 1904 by Edward VII, but dogged by two world wars, building work dragged on to modified designs. The aisles are built as tunnels through the walls. Note the stained glass, high altar and sumptuous embroidery collection.

⛪ Metropolitan Cathedral of Christ the King

Mount Pleasant. 📞 0151 709 9222.
🕐 daily. **Donation**. 🚻
Liverpool's Roman Catholic cathedral rejected traditional forms in favor of a striking modern design. Early plans drawn up by Pugin and later by Lutyens *(see p25)* in the 1930s proved too expensive. The final version, brainchild of Sir Frederick Gibberd and built from 1962–7, is a circular building surmounted by a stylized crown of thorns 88 m (290 ft) high. It is irreverently known as "Paddy's Wigwam" by non-Catholics (a reference to Liverpool's large Irish population). The stained-glass lantern, designed by John Piper and Patrick Reyntiens, floods the circular nave with diffused bluish light. A tour around the inner walls reveals many sculptures and a fine bronze of Christ by Elisabeth Frink (1930–94) on the altar.

ENVIRONS: A spectacular richly timbered building dating from 1490, **Speke Hall** lies 6 miles (10 km) east of Liverpool's center surrounded by lovely grounds. The oldest parts of the hall enclose a cobbled courtyard dominated by two yew trees, Adam and Eve. The 16th-century hiding places for persecuted priests still remain.

Birkenhead on the Wirral peninsula has been linked to Liverpool by ferry for more than 800 years. Now, road and rail tunnels supplement access. The Norman Priory is still in use on Sundays, and stately Hamilton Square was designed from 1825–44 by J. Gillespie Graham, one of the architects of Edinburgh's New Town.

On the Wirral side of the Mersey is **Port Sunlight Heritage Centre** *(see p335)*, a Victorian garden village built by successful and enlightened soap manufacturer William Hesketh Lever for the benefit of his factory workers.

🏛 Speke Hall

(NT) The Walk, Speke. 📞 0151 427
7231. 🕐 Apr–Oct: Tue–Sun & public
hols (pm); Nov–Dec: Sat & Sun (pm).
💷 🚻 limited.

🏛 Port Sunlight Heritage Centre

95 Greendale Rd, Port Sunlight, Wirral.
📞 0151 644 6466. 🕐 Apr–Oct:
daily; Nov–Mar: Mon–Fri & public hols.
● Dec 23–Jan 3. 💷 🚻 limited.

Entrance to the half-timbered manor house of Speke Hall

YORKSHIRE AND HUMBERSIDE

NORTH YORKSHIRE · WEST YORKSHIRE · HUMBERSIDE

*W*ITH THE HISTORIC CITY *of York at its heart, this is an area of great scenic beauty, dramatic moorland, green valleys and picturesque villages. To the north lie the Yorkshire Dales and the North York Moors; eastward, a coastline with beaches and birdlife; and southward, a landscape of lush meadows.*

Yorkshire was originally made up of three separate counties, formerly known as "Ridings." Today, in combination with Humberside, it covers 5,950 sq miles (15,400 sq km). The northeast section has dramatic limestone scenery that was carved by glaciers in the Ice Age. Farming was the original livelihood, and the dry-stone walls weaving up precipitous scars and fells were used to divide the land. Imposed on this were the industries of the 19th century; blackened mill chimneys and crumbling viaducts are as much a part of the landscape as the grand houses of those who profited from them.

Humberside is very different, dominated historically by the now flagging fishing industry, and geographically by sprawling meadows. Its coastline is exceptional, and farther north are the attractions of sandy beaches and bustling harbor towns. Yet it is the contrasting landscapes that make the area so appealing, ranging from the bleak moorland of the Brontë novels to the ragged cliff coast around Whitby, and the flat expanse of Humberside's Sunk Island.

The city of York, where Roman and Viking relics exist side by side, is second only to London in the number of visitors that tread its streets. Indeed the historical center of York is Yorkshire and Humberside's foremost attraction. Those in search of a real taste of the region, however, should head for the countryside. In addition to excellent touring routes, a network of rewarding walking paths range from mellow ambles along the Cleveland Way to rocky scrambles over the Pennine Way at Pen-y-Ghent.

Lobster pots on the quayside at the picturesque fishing port of Whitby

◁ **The peaceful valley of Rosedale, North York Moors**

Exploring Yorkshire and Humberside

YORKSHIRE COVERS A WIDE AREA, once made up of three counties or "Ridings." Until the arrival of railroads, mining and the wool industry in the 19th century, the county was a farming area. Drystone walls dividing fields still pepper the northern part of the county, alongside 19th-century mill chimneys and country houses. Among the many abbeys are Rievaulx and the magnificent Fountains. The medieval city of York is a major attraction, as are Yorkshire's beaches. Humberside is characterized by the softer, rolling countryside of the Wolds, and its nature preserves attract large quantities of birds.

Rosedale village in the North York Moors

SIGHTS AT A GLANCE

Darlington

RICHMOND

Kendal

YORKSHIRE DALES NATIONAL PARK

FOUNTAINS ABBEY

MARKENFIELD HALL

RIPON

MALHAM WALK

SKIPTON

Clitheroe

HAREWOOD HOUSE

HAWORTH

BRADFORD

HEBDEN BRIDGE

HALIFAX

YORKSHIRE MINING MUSEUM

HUDDERSFIELD

Manchester

YORKSHIRE SCULPTURE PARK

Manchester

Swale

Ure

Nidd

Wharfe

Aire

Ribble

Calder

SEE ALSO

• *Where to Stay* pp562–3
• *Where to Eat* pp597–9

**Section of Lendal Bridge (1863)
crossing the Ouse in York**

Middlesbrough

MOUNT
GRACE
PRIORY
15

Cleveland Way

84

NORTH YORK
MOORS
NATIONAL PARK

Esk

WHITBY 19

ROBIN
HOOD'S
BAY
20

A171

NORTH YORK
MOORS TOUR 17

18 NORTH YORK
MOORS RAILWAY

Derwent

HUTTON-LE-
HOLE 16

Seven

A170

21 SCARBOROUGH

IEVAULX ABBEY 14

13 HELMSLEY

TTON
BANK 9

10 BYLAND
ABBEY

COXWOLD 11

12 NUNNINGTON HALL

CASTLE
HOWARD

Rye

A170

Hertford

A64

BEMPTON &
FLAMBOROUGH HEAD
26

22

23 EDEN CAMP

Derwent

A165

WHARRAM PERCY 24

BURTON AGNES 25

A166

A166

A64

N
O
R
T
H

S
E
A

RESBOROUGH

A19

Ouse

A59

Nidd

A64

32 YORK

A1079

A164

A165

BEVERLEY 27

Hull

28 BURTON CONSTABLE

A1

A63

Aire

M62

A63

B1238

KINGSTON UPON HULL 29

A63

SUNK
ISLAND

M62

Dow

Trent

A15

Humber

A180

A15

HOLDERNESS
& SPURN
HEAD
30

M18

M180

GRIMSBY 31

DONCASTER ●

A1(M)

A15

A16

M18

Newark-on-
Trent

M1

Nottingham

0 kilometers   15

0 miles   10

GETTING AROUND

The area is served by the A1, the M1,
the M62 and the A59. InterCity trains
run to major cities such as York and
Leeds, and there are train or bus links
between many towns and hamlets. The
Yorkshire Dales and North York Moors
national parks are good for walkers
and cyclists can enjoy rides around
Humberside and York.

KEY

	Highway
	Major road
	Minor road
	Scenic route
	Scenic path
	River
	Viewpoint

Yorkshire Dales National Park ❶

T HE YORKSHIRE DALES is a farming landscape, formed
from three principle dales, Swaledale, Wharfedale
and Wensleydale, and a number of small ones, such as
Deepdale. Glaciation in the Ice Age helped carve out
these steep-sided valleys, and this scenery contrasts with
the high moorlands. However, 12 centuries of settlement
have altered the landscape in the form of cottages, castles
and villages, which create a delightful environment for
walking. A national park since 1954, the area provides
recreation while serving local community needs.

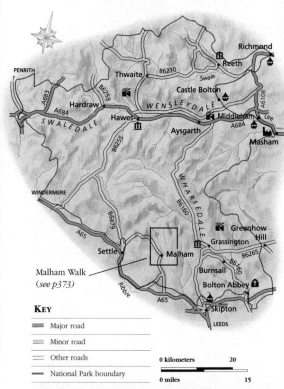

KEY

▨	Major road
▨	Minor road
═	Other roads
▬	National Park boundary

Malham Walk
(see p373)

0 kilometers 20

0 miles 15

**Monk's Wynd – one of Richmond's
narrow, winding streets**

Exploring Swaledale
Swaledale's prosperity was
founded largely on wool, and
it is famous for its herd of
sheep that graze on the wild
higher slopes in the harshest
weather. The fast-moving river
Swale that gives the northern-
most dale its name travels from
bleak moorland down magnificent waterfalls into the richly
wooded lower slopes, passing
through the villages of Reeth,
Thwaite and Richmond.

♜ Richmond Castle
Tower Street. 〖 01748 822493.
◯ daily. ◉ Dec 24–26, Jan 1. 〖 ⚹
Swaledale's main point of entry
is the medieval market town
of Richmond, which has the
largest cobbled marketplace in
England. Alan Rufus, the
Norman 1st Earl of Richmond,
began building the castle in
1071, and some of the masonry
on the curtain walls probably
dates from that time. It has a
fine Norman keep, 30 m (100
ft) high with walls 3.3 m (11
ft) thick. An 11th-century arch
leads into a courtyard containing Scolland's Hall (1080), one
of England's oldest buildings.
   Richmond's marketplace was
once the castle's outer bailey.
Its quaint, narrow streets gave
rise to the song, *The Lass of
Richmond Hill* (1787), written
by Leonard McNally for his
wife, Frances L'Anson, who
was brought up in Hill House,
on Richmond Hill. Turner (see

The green, rolling landscape of Deepdale, near Dent

p93) depicted the town many times. The Georgian Theatre (1788), which was restored in 1962, is the only one of its age still surviving.

🏛 Swaledale Folk Museum
Reeth Green. [01748 884373.
☐ *Easter–Oct: daily.*
Reeth, a town that became known as the center of the lead mining industry and helped bring prosperity to the region, houses this museum in a former Methodist Sunday school (1830). Included in it are mining and woolmaking artifacts (wool from the hardy Swaledale sheep was another mainstay of the economy) and brass band memorabilia.

🥾 Buttertubs
Near Thwaite, on the B6270 Hawes road, are a series of potholes that streams empty into. These were known as Buttertubs, since farmers going to market lowered their butter into the holes to keep it cool.

Buttertubs, near Thwaite

Exploring Wensleydale
The largest of the Yorkshire dales, Wensleydale is famous for its cheese and more recently for James Herriot's books and the television series, *All Creatures Great and Small*. It is easy walking country for anyone seeking an alternative to major moorland hikes.

🏛 Dales Countryside Museum
Station Yard, Hawes. [01969 667450. ☐ *Easter–Oct daily.*
In a former railway goods warehouse in Hawes, capital of Upper Wensleydale, is a

Barrels at the Theakston Brewery

fascinating museum, filled with items from life and industry in the 18th- and 19th-century Upper Dales. This includes cheese- and buttermaking equipment. Wensleydale cheese was created by monks at nearby Jervaulx Abbey. There is also a ropemaking works a short walk away.

Hawes itself is the highest market town in England, at 259 m (850 ft) above sea level. It is a thriving center where thousands of sheep and cattle are auctioned each summer.

🥾 Hardraw Force
At the tiny village of Hardraw, nearby, is England's tallest single-drop waterfall, with no outcrops to interrupt its 29 m (96 ft) fall. It became famous in Victorian times when the daredevil Blondin walked across it on a tightrope. Today, you can walk right under this fine waterfall, against the rock face, and look through the stream without getting wet.

🥾 Aysgarth Waterfalls
An old packhorse bridge gives a clear view of the point at which the previously placid River Ure suddenly begins to plunge in foaming torrents over wide limestone shelves. Turner painted the impressive lower falls in 1817.

🏛 Theakston Brewery
Masham. [01765 689057.
☐ *Apr–Oct: Wed–Mon; Nov–mid-Dec: Wed, Sat, Sun; Mar: Wed, Sat.*
🦽 🔥 *limited.*
The pretty village of Masham is the home of Theakston brewery, creator of the potent ale Old Peculier. The history of this local family brewery from its origin in 1827 is

displayed in the visitors' center. Masham village has an attractive square once used for sheep fairs, surrounded by 17th- and 18th-century houses. There is also a medieval church.

♟ Bolton Castle
Castle Bolton, nr Leyburn. [01969 23981. ☐ *Mar–Oct: daily.*
Located in the village of Castle Bolton, this castle was built in 1379 by the 1st Lord Scrope, Chancellor of England, for use as comfortable living quarters. It was used as a fortress from 1568 to 1569 when Mary, Queen of Scots *(see p497)* was held prisoner here by Elizabeth I *(see pp50–51),* who feared rebellion. Three of the castle's four towers remain at their original height of 30 m (100 ft).

♟ Middleham Castle
Middleham, nr Leyburn. [01969 23899. ☐ *Apr–Oct: daily; Nov–Mar: Wed–Sun.* ⬤ *Dec 24–26, Jan 1.* 🦽 🔥
Owned by Richard Neville, Earl of Warwick, it was built in 1170. The castle is better known as home to Richard III *(see p49)* when he was made Lord of the North. It was one of the strongest fortresses in the north but during the 15th century, many of its stones were then used for nearby buildings. The keep provides a fine view of the landscape.

Remains of Middleham Castle, once residence of Richard III

Extensive ruins of Bolton Priory, dating from 1154

Exploring Wharfedale

This dale is characterized by gritstone moorland, contrasting with quiet market towns along meandering sections of river. Many consider Grassington a central point for exploring Wharfedale, but the showpiece villages of Burnsall, overlooked by a 506 m (1,661 ft) fell, and Buckden, near Buckden Pike (701 m; 2,302 ft), also make excellent bases.

The area contains the Three Peaks of Whernside (736 m; 2,416 ft), Ingleborough (724 m; 2,376 ft) and Pen-y-Ghent (694 m; 2,278 ft). They are known for their potholes and tough terrain, but this does not deter walkers from attempting to climb them all in one day. If you sign in at the Pen-y-Ghent café at Horton-in-Ribblesdale, and complete the 20-mile (32-km) course, reaching the summit of all three peaks in less than 12 hours, you can qualify for membership in the Three Peaks of Yorkshire Club.

🏠 Burnsall

St. Wilfrid's, Burnsall. **C** 01756 720232. ☐ daily. ♿
Preserved in St. Wilfrid's church graveyard are the original village stocks, gravestones from Viking times and a headstone carved in memory of the Dawson family by sculptor Eric Gill (1882–1940). The village, centered around a century-old five-arched bridge, also hosts Britain's oldest fell race every August.

🏛 Upper Wharfedale Museum

The Square, Grassington. **C** 01756 752800. ☐ Apr–Sep: daily; Oct–Mar: Sat & Sun (pm). 🎫 ♿ limited.
This folk museum is set in two 18th-century lead-miners' cottages. Its exhibits illustrate the domestic and working history of the area, including farming and lead mining.

🏠 Bolton Priory

Bolton Abbey, nr Skipton. **C** 01756 710238. ☐ daily. ♿
One of the most beautiful areas of Wharfedale is around the village of Bolton Abbey, set in an estate owned by the Dukes of Devonshire. While preserving its astounding beauty, its managers have incorporated over 30 miles (46 km) of footpaths, many suitable for the disabled and young families.

The ruins of Bolton Priory, established by Augustinian canons in 1154 on the site of a Saxon manor, are extensive. They include a church, chapter house, cloister and prior's lodging. These all demonstrate the wealth accumulated by the canons from the sale of wool from their flocks of sheep. The priory nave is still used as a parish church. Another attraction of the estate is the "Strid," a point where the River Wharfe surges spectacularly through a gorge, foaming yellow and gouging holes out of the rocks.

🗻 Stump Cross Caverns

Greenhow, Pateley Bridge. **C** 01756 752780. ☐ Easter–Oct: daily; Nov–Easter: Sat, Sun; winter school hols: daily. ● Dec 25. 🎫
These caves were formed over a period of half a million years: trickles of underground water formed intertwining passages and carved them into fantastic shapes and sizes. Sealed off in the last Ice Age, the caves were only discovered in the 1850s when lead miners sank a mine shaft into the caverns.

♣ Skipton Castle

High St. **C** 01756 792442. ☐ daily. ● Dec 25. 🎫
Situated outside the national park boundary, the market town of Skipton is still one of the largest auctioning and stockraising centers in the north. Its 11th-century castle was almost entirely rebuilt by Robert de Clifford in the 14th century. Beautiful Conduit Court was added by Henry, Lord Clifford in Henry VIII's reign. Even more striking is the central yew tree, which Lady Anne Clifford planted in 1659 to mark restoration work to the castle after Civil War damage.

Conduit Court (1495) and yew tree at Skipton Castle

Malham Walk ❷

THE MALHAM AREA, shaped by glacial erosion 10,000 years ago, has one of Great Britain's most dramatic limestone landscapes. The walk from Malham village can take over four hours if you pause to enjoy the viewpoints and take a detour to Gordale Scar. Those who are short of time tend to go only as far as Malham Cove. This vast natural amphitheater, formed by a huge geological tear, is like a giant heel mark in the landscape. Above lie the deep crevices of Malham Lings, where rare flora such as hart's-tongue flourishes. Unusual plants grow in the lime-rich Malham Tarn, said to have provided inspiration for Charles Kingsley's *The Water Babies* (1863). Coot and mallard visit the tarn in summer, and tufted duck in winter.

Sandpiper at Malham Tarn

Where the path meets the road ⑤
From here, you can catch a bus back to Malham village.

🚻 Malham Tarn House

P MALHAM

④

Malham Tarn ④
Yorkshire's second-largest lake lies 305 m (1,000 ft) above sea level in a designated nature preserve.

Malham Lings ③
This fine limestone pavement was formed when Ice Age meltwater seeped into cracks in the rock, then froze and expanded.

SETTLE

③

Gordale Scar ⑥
Guarded by steep limestone cliffs, this deep gorge was created by meltwater from Ice Age glaciers.

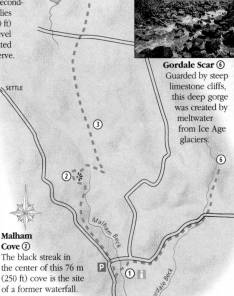

⑥

②

Malham Cove ②
The black streak in the center of this 76 m (250 ft) cove is the site of a former waterfall.

Malham Beck

Gordale Beck

P i ①

SKIPTON

KEY

▪ ▪	Walk route
—	Minor road
☀	Viewpoint
P	Parking
i	Tourist information
🚻	Toilets

Malham ①
An attractive riverside village, it has an information center with details of drives and walks.

0 kilometers   1

0 miles   ½

TIPS FOR WALKERS

Starting point: Malham.
Getting there: Leave M65 at Junction 14 and take A56 to Skipton, then follow signs to Malham which is off A65.
Length: 7 miles (11 km).
Difficulty: Malham Cove is steep but the Tarn area is flatter.

A 1920s poster advertising the spa town of Harrogate

Harrogate ❸

North Yorkshire. 🚶 69,000. 🚈 🅿
🛈 Assembly Rooms, Crescent Rd
(01423 525666). 🛒 Mon–Sat.

Between 1880 and World War I, Harrogate was the north's leading spa town, with nearly 90 medicinal springs. It was ideal for aristocrats who, after a tiring London season, were able to stop for a health cure before journeying on to grouse-shooting in Scotland.

Today, Harrogate's main attractions are its spa town atmosphere, fine architecture, public gardens and its convenience as a center for visiting North Yorkshire and the Dales.

The naturally welling spa waters may not currently be in use, but you can still go for a Turkish bath in one of the country's most attractive steam rooms. The entrance at the side of the Royal Assembly Rooms (1897) is unassuming,

but once inside, the century-old **Turkish Sauna Suite** is a visual feast of tiled Victoriana.

The town's spa history is recorded in the **Royal Pump Room Museum**. At the turn of the century, the waters were thought to be rich in iron early in the day. So, between 7am and 9am, the 1842 octagonal building would have been filled with rich and fashionable people drinking glasses of water as part of their rest cure. Poorer people could take water from the pump outside, which still works. Today you can sample the waters and enjoy the museum's exhibits, which include an 1874 Penny Farthing bicycle.

Harrogate is also known for the rainbow-colored flower-beds in **The Stray**, a common space to the south of the town center, and for the ornamental **Harlow Car Gardens**, owned by the Northern Horticultural Society. In spring and autumn,

(see p64) it holds two spectacular flower festivals. Visitors can enjoy the delicious cakes and genteel atmosphere of **Betty's Café Tea Rooms** (see p598).

🏛 **Turkish Sauna Suite**
Assembly Rooms, Crescent Rd. ☎ 01423 562498. ⬤ **Men**: Mon, Wed & Fri: (pm); Tue: (am); Sat. **Women**: Tue & Thu: (pm); Fri (am); Sun. ● public hols. ♿

🏛 **Royal Pump Room Museum**
Crown Pl. ☎ 01423 503340. ⬤ Apr–Oct: daily. ♿ ♿

🏛 **Betty's Café Tea Rooms**
1 Parliament St. ☎ 01423 502746. ⬤ daily. ● Dec 25.

🌿 **Harlow Car Gardens**
Crag Lane. ☎ 01423 565418. ⬤ daily. ♿ ♿

Knaresborough ❹

North Yorkshire. 🚶 14,000. 🚌 from Harrogate. 🛈 35 Market Place (01423 866886). 🛒 Wed.

Perched precipitously above the River Nidd is one of England's oldest towns and is mentioned in the Domesday Book of 1086 (see p48). Its historic streets – which link the church, John of Gaunt's ruined castle, and the market place with the river – are now lined with fine 18th-century houses.

Nearby is **Mother Shipton's Cave**, reputedly England's oldest tourist attraction. It first opened to the public in 1630 as the birthplace of Ursula Sontheil, a local prophetess. Today, people can view the effect the well near her cave

Mother Shipton's cave, where objects are encased in limestone

Tudor gatehouse and moat at Markenfield Hall

has on objects hung under the dripping, smooth surface. Almost any item, from gloves or umbrellas to soft toys, will become encased in limestone within a few weeks.

🕯 Mother Shipton's Cave
Prophesy House, High Bridge.
☎ 01423 864600. ⬜ daily.
● Dec 25. 🎫 🚹 limited.

Ripley ❺

North Yorkshire. 🏠 150. 🚌 from Harrogate or Ripon.

SINCE THE 1320s, when the first generation of the Ingilby family lived in an early incarnation of **Ripley Castle**, the village has been made up almost exclusively of castle employees. The influence of one 19th-century Ingilby had the most visual impact. In the 1820s, Sir William Amcotts Ingilby was so entranced by a village in Alsace Lorraine that he created a similar one in French Gothic style, complete with an *Hotel de Ville*. Present-day Ripley has a cobbled market square, and quaint cottages line the streets. The church-yard has a medieval cross with niches for kneeling at the base.

Ripley Castle, with its 15th-century gatehouse, was where Oliver Cromwell *(see p52)* stayed following the Battle of Marston Moor. The 28th generation of Ingilbys live here, and it is open for tours. The attractive grounds contain two lakes and a deer park, as well as more formal gardens.

⚜ Ripley Castle
Ripley. ☎ 01423 770152. ⬜ Apr–May, Oct: Sat, Sun; Jul–Aug: daily; Jun, Sep: Thu–Sun. ● public hols.
🎫 🚹

Markenfield Hall ❻

Nr Markenfield, North Yorkshire.
ℹ 01765 604625. 🚌 from Harrogate or Ripon. ⬜ Apr–Oct: Mon. 🎫
🚹 limited.

A MOATED MANOR house dating from the 14th century, Markenfield Hall is unmarked and open only in the summer. To find it you need to drive 5 km (3 miles) south of Ripon, and turn up a farm track marked with a bridleway sign (Hell Wath Lane). On one side of the drawbridge, between the moat and the manor walls, is the farmer's vegetable patch. Once inside the L-shaped house, note the great banqueting hall, chapel and kitchen fireplace.

The Markenfields were one of the major northern families to oppose Henry VIII and the Dissolution of the Monasteries *(see p50)*. It was from their manor that an army set off in 1569 to attempt to remove Elizabeth I from the throne and replace her with the Catholic Mary, Queen of Scots.

Fountains Abbey ❼

See pp376–7.

Ripon ❽

North Yorkshire. 🏠 14,000. 🚌 from Harrogate. ℹ Minster Rd (01765 604625). ⬜ Thu.

R IPON, A CHARMING small city, is best known for the cathedral and "the watch," which has been announced since the Middle Ages by the Wakeman. In return for protecting Ripon citizens, he would charge an annual toll of two pence per household. Today, a man still blows a horn in the Market Square each evening at 9pm, and every Thursday a handbell is rung to open the market.

The **Cathedral of St. Peter and St. Wilfrid** is built above a 7th-century Saxon crypt. At less than 3 m (10 ft) high and just over 2 m (7 ft) wide, it is held to be the oldest complete crypt in England. The cathedral is known for its collection of misericords *(see p327)*, and the cathedral contains both pagan and Old Testament examples. The architectural historian Sir Nikolaus Pevsner (1902–83) considered the cathedral's West Front the finest in England.

Ripon's **Prison and Police Museum**, housed in the 1686 "House of Correction," has exhibits relating to the history of the police. Conditions in Victorian prisons are shown in the first floor cells.

🏛 Prison and Police Museum
St. Marygate. ☎ 01765 690799.
⬜ Apr–Oct: daily. 🎫 🚹 limited.

Ripon's Wakeman, who blows his horn nightly in the Market Square

Fountains Abbey ●

NESTLING in the wooded valley of the River Skell are the extensive sandstone ruins of Fountains Abbey and the outstanding water garden of Studley Royal. Fountains Abbey was founded by Benedictine monks in 1132 and taken over by Cistercians three years later. By the mid-12th century it had become the wealthiest abbey in Britain, though it fell into ruin during the Dissolution *(see p50)*. In 1720, John Aislabie, the MP for Ripon and Chancellor of the Exchequer, developed the land and forest of the abbey ruins. He began work, continued by his son William, on the famous water garden, the statuary and Classical temples in the grounds. This makes a dramatic contrast to the simplicity of the abbey.

Fountains Hall
Built by Sir Stephen Proctor about 1611, with stones from the abbey ruins, its design is attributed to architect Robert Smythson. It included a great hall with a minstrels' gallery and an entrance flanked by Classical columns.

THE ABBEY

The abbey buildings were designed to reflect the Cistercians' desire for simplicity and austerity. The abbey frequently dispensed charity to the poor and the sick, as well as travelers.

The Chapel of Nine Altars *at the east end of the church was built from 1203 to 1247. It is ornate, compared to the rest of the abbey, with an 18 m (60 ft) high window complemented by another at the western end of the nave.*

Chapter house
Abbot's house
Cloister
Cellarium (storehouse)
Kitchen
Monks' infirmary hall
Refectory
Lay brothers' infirmary
Lay brothers' refectory

The undercroft*, supported by 19 pillars, with vaulting 90 m (300 ft) long, was used for storing fleeces, which the abbey monks sold to Venetian and Florentine merchants.*

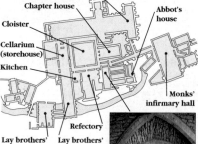

To Visitor Centre and parking lot

River Skell

Paths leading to the estate park

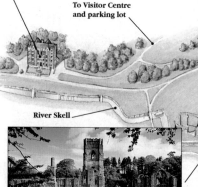

★ **Abbey**
This was built by using stones taken from the Skell valley.

STAR SIGHTS
★ Abbey
★ Temple of Piety

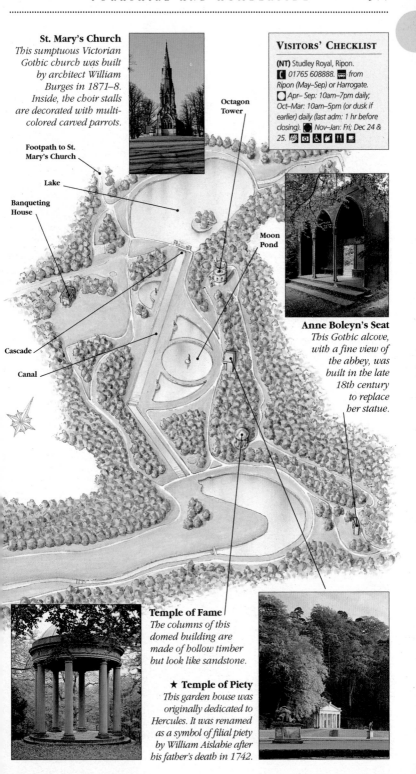

St. Mary's Church
This sumptuous Victorian Gothic church was built by architect William Burges in 1871–8. Inside, the choir stalls are decorated with multi-colored carved parrots.

Octagon Tower

Footpath to St. Mary's Church

Lake

Banqueting House

Moon Pond

Cascade

Canal

Anne Boleyn's Seat
This Gothic alcove, with a fine view of the abbey, was built in the late 18th century to replace her statue.

Temple of Fame
The columns of this domed building are made of hollow timber but look like sandstone.

★ Temple of Piety
This garden house was originally dedicated to Hercules. It was renamed as a symbol of filial piety by William Aislabie after his father's death in 1742.

The 19th-century white horse, seen on one of the walks around Sutton Bank

Sutton Bank ❾

North Yorkshire. ⊷ *Thirsk.* ℹ *Sutton Bank (01845 597426).*

NOTORIOUS AMONG motorists for its 1 in 4 gradient, which climbs for about 107 m (350 ft), Sutton Bank itself is well known for its panoramic views. On a clear day you can see from the Vale of York to the Peak District *(see pp324–5)*. William and his sister Dorothy Wordsworth stopped here to admire the vista in 1802, on their way to visit his future wife, Mary Hutchinson, at Brompton. Apart from Sutton Bank, where you can walk around the white horse, the area is less wild than the coastal side, and suitable for children.

Byland Abbey ❿

Coxwold, York. ☎ *01347 868614.*
🚌 *from York or Helmsley.* ⊷ *Thirsk.*
◯ *Apr–Oct: daily; Nov–Mar: Wed–Sun.* ⬤ *Dec 25, 26, Jan 1.* 🎫 ♿

THIS CISTERCIAN monastery was founded in 1177 by monks from Furness Abbey in Cumbria. It featured what was then the largest church in Britain, 100 m (328 ft) long and 41 m (135 ft) wide across the transepts. The layout of the entire monastery, including extensive cloisters and the west front of the church, is still visible today, as is the green and yellow glazed tile floor. Fine workmanship is shown in carved stone details and in the carvings of the capitals, kept in the small museum.

In 1322 the Battle of Byland was fought nearby, and King Edward II *(see p40)* narrowly escaped capture when the invading Scottish army learned that he was dining with the Abbot. In his hurry to escape, the king had to leave many treasures behind, which were looted by the invading soldiers.

Coxwold ⓫

North Yorkshire. 🏠 *160.*
ℹ *Kirkgate, Thirsk (01845 522755).*

SITUATED JUST inside the bounds of the North York Moors National Park *(see p381)*, this charming village nestles at the foot of the Howardian Hills. Its pretty houses are built from local stone, and the 15th-century church has some fine Georgian box pews and an impressive

Shandy Hall, home of author Laurence Sterne, now a museum

octagonal tower. But Coxwold is best known as the home of the author Laurence Sterne (1713–68), whose writings include *Tristram Shandy* and *A Sentimental Journey*.

Sterne came to Coxwold in 1760 as the church curate. He rented a rambling house that he named **Shandy Hall** after a Yorkshire expression, which means eccentric. Originally built as a timber-framed, open-halled house during the 15th century, it was modernized in the 17th century and Sterne later added a façade. His grave is situated beside the porch at Coxwold's church.

Shandy Hall

Coxwold. 01347 868465. Jun–Sep: Wed & Sun (pm). limited. **Gardens** Jun–Sep: Sun–Fri.

Nunnington Hall ⓬

(NT) Nunnington, York. 01439 748283. Malton, then bus or taxi. Apr–Jun, Sep–Oct: Tue–Thu, Sat, Sun; Jul–Aug: Tue–Sun, public hols (pm). ground floor.

SET IN ALLURING surroundings, this 17th-century manor house is a combination of architectural styles, including features from the Elizabethan and Stuart periods. Both inside and outside, a notable architectural feature is the use of the broken pediment (the upper arch is left unjoined).

Nunnington Hall was a family home until 1952, when Mrs. Ronald Fife donated it to the National Trust. A striking

The miniature Queen Anne drawing room at Nunnington Hall

feature is the paneling in the Oak Hall. Formerly painted, it extends over the three-arched screen to the Great Staircase. Nunnington's collection of 22 miniature furnished period rooms is popular with visitors.

A mid-16th-century tenant Dr. Robert Huickes, physician to Henry VIII *(see p50–51)*, is best known for advising Elizabeth I that she should not, at the age of 32, consider having any children.

Helmsley ⓭

North Yorkshire. 2,000. from Malton. Town Hall, Market Place (01439 770173). Fri.

THIS PRETTY MARKET TOWN is noted for its **castle**, now an imposing ruin. Built from 1186 to 1227, its main function and supreme strength as a fortress is illustrated by the remaining keep, tower and curtain walls. The original D-shaped keep had one part blasted away in the Civil War *(see p52)*, but remains the dominant feature. The castle

was so impregnable that there were few attempts to force entry. However, in 1644, after holding out for a three-month seige against Sir Thomas Fairfax, the Parliamentary general, the castle was finally taken and dismantled.

Helmsley church tower

Rievaulx Abbey ⓮

Nr Helmsley, North Yorkshire. 01439 798228. Thirsk, then bus or taxi. daily. Dec 24–26, Jan 1. limited.

RIEVAULX IS PERHAPS the finest abbey in the area, partly due to its dramatic setting in the steep wooded valley of the River Rye and partly to its extensive remains. It is almost entirely surrounded by steep banks that form natural barriers to the outside world. Monks of the French Cistercian order from Clairvaux founded this, their first major monastery in Britain, in 1132. The main buildings, which include the Cistercian nave, were finished before 1200. The layout of the chapel, kitchens and infirmary give an idea of monastic life.

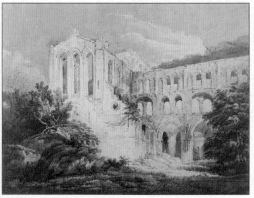
Rievaulx Abbey, painted by Thomas Girtin (1775–1802)

Mount Grace Priory ruins, with farm and mansion in foreground

Mount Grace Priory ⑮

(NT) Northallerton, North Yorkshire.
📞 01609 883494. 🚆 Northallerton
then bus. ◯ Apr–Oct: daily.
⬤ Dec 24–26, Jan 1. 🏤 ♿ grounds
& shop only.

FOUNDED BY Thomas Holland,
Duke of Surrey, and in use
from 1398 until 1539, this is
the best-preserved Carthusian
or charterhouse monastery *(see
pp336–7)* in England. The
monks, just 20 of them at the
beginning, took a vow of
silence and lived in solitary
cells, each with his own garden and an angled
hatch so that he would
not even see the per-
son serving his food.
They only met at
matins, vespers and
feast-day services.
Attempts at escape by
those who could not
endure the rigor of the
rules were punished
by imprisonment.
   The ruins of the
priory include the for-
mer prison, gatehouse
and outer court, barns,
guesthouses, cells and
the church. The 14th-
century church is
particularly small,
since it was only rarely
used by the monastic
community. A monk's
cell has been recon-
structed to give an
impression of
everyday life.

Hutton-le-Hole ⑯

North Yorkshire. 🏠 400.
🚆 Malton then bus. ℹ️ Eastgate
Car Park (01751 473791).

THIS PICTURESQUE VILLAGE is
characterized by a spacious
green, grazed by roaming
sheep and surrounded by
well-maintained houses, an
inn and shops. Lengths of
white wood, replacing stone
bridges, span the moorland
stream. Its cottages, some
announcing their age on date
panels over the doors, are
made from limestone, with
red pantiled roofs. In the
village center is the **Ryedale**

Wheelwright's workshop at Ryedale Folk Museum

Folk Museum, which records
the lifestyle of an agricultural
community by means of
Romano-British artifacts and
reconstructed buildings.

🏛 **Ryedale Folk Museum**
Hutton-le-Hole. 📞 01751 417367.
◯ Mar–Oct: daily. 🏤 ♿

North York Moors Tour ⑰

See p381.

North York Moors Railway ⑱

Pickering, North Yorkshire. 📞 01947
895359. ◯ Apr–Oct: daily; some
weekends in Dec. 🏤 ♿

DESIGNED in 1831 by George
Stephenson as a route
along the Esk Valley linking
Pickering and Whitby *(see
p382)*, this railroad was considered an engineering miracle.
Due to budget constraints,
Stephenson was not able to
build a tunnel, but had to lay
the route down the mile-long
(1.5 km) incline between
Beck Hole and Goathland.
The area around Fen Bog had
to be stabilized using timber,
heather, brushwood and wool
so that a causeway could be
built over it. A horse was
used to pull a coach
along the track at 10
miles (16 km) per
hour. After horse-
power came steam,
and for almost 130
years the railroad
linked Whitby to the
rest of the country. In
the early 1960s, the
line was declared
impractical and closed.
But in 1967, a group
of locals began a
campaign to relaunch
the line, and in 1973 it
was officially reopened
by the Duchess of
Kent. Today, the 18-
mile (29-km) line runs
from Pickering via
Levisham, Newtondale
Halt and Goathland
before stopping at
Grosmont, through the
scenic heart of the
North York Moors.

North York Moors Tour ⑰

THIS TOUR PASSES THROUGH part of the area between Cleveland, the Vale of York and the Vale of Pickering known as the North York Moors National Park. The landscape consists of bleakly beautiful moors interspersed with lush green valleys. Farming is the main source of income, and until the advent of coal, the communities' local source of fuel was turf. In the 19th century, the geology of the area created extractive industries that included ironstone, lime, coal and building stone.

Mallyan Spout ⑦
A footpath leads to this waterfall from Goathland.

Goathland ⑧
A center for forest and moorland walks, it has 19th-century houses and good accommodations.

Farndale ③
During springtime, this area is famous for the beauty and profusion of its daffodils.

"Fat Betty" White Cross ④
In medieval times, coins would have been left under this cross for poor travelers.

DANBY MOORS CENTRE

Egton Bridge

LEALHOLM

Wheeldale Gill

West Beck

WHITBY

Thorgill

Seven

Hartoft Beck

Ruimoor Beck

Blawath Beck

Rosedale ⑤
After the discovery of ironstone in 1856, this pretty valley became a busy mining center. Remains of the iron kilns can still be seen.

Hutton-le-Hole ②
This lovely village has an excellent museum with displays on local crafts and customs.

Dove

Spaunton

Wade's Causeway ⑥
This road was built by the Roman army about AD 80, from sandstone slabs laid over a ridge of gravel and sand. It is said that a giant called Wade built the road as a footpath for his wife.

TIPS FOR DRIVERS

Tour length: 28 miles (45 km).
Stopping-off points: The Forge Tea Shop at Hutton-le-Hole is open daily from Mar–Oct and at weekends during Nov–Feb. The Mallyan Spout inn (see p610) at Goathland is popular with walkers. (See also pp636–7.)

Lastingham ①
Lastingham's church, dating from 1078, has a Norman crypt with ancient stone carving. Under the crypt lies St. Cedd, founder of the original Saxon monastery in 654.

KEY

▬▬ Tour route

═══ Other roads

☀ Viewpoint

0 kilometers 2

0 miles 2

Whitby ⑲

WHITBY'S KNOWN HISTORY dates back to the 7th century, when a Saxon monastery was founded on the site of today's famous 13th-century abbey ruins. In the 18th and early 19th centuries it became an industrial port and shipbuilding town, as well as a whaling center. In the Victorian era, the red-roofed cottages at the foot of the east cliff were filled with work-shops crafting jet into jewelry and ornaments. Today, the tourist shops that have replaced them sell antique-crafted examples of the distinctive black gem.

Jet comb (c.1870)

VISITORS' CHECKLIST

North Yorkshire. 🚷 13,500.
✈ Teeside, 50 miles (80 km)
NW Whitby. 🚆 Station Sq.
ℹ Langborne Rd (01947
602674). 🚌 Tue, Sat.
🎪 Whitby Festival: Jun; Angling
Festival: Jul; Lifeboat Day: Jul 29;
Whitby Regatta: Aug; Captain
Cook Festival: Oct.

Exploring Whitby

Whitby is divided into two by the estuary of the River Esk. The Old Town, with its pretty cobbled streets and pastel-hued houses, huddles round the harbor. High above it is St. Mary's Church with a wood interior reputedly fitted by ships' carpenters. The ruins of the 13th-century Whitby Abbey nearby are still used as a landmark by mariners. From them you get a fine view over the still-busy harbor, strewn with colorful nets.

A pleasant place for a stroll, the harbor is overlooked by an imposing bronze clifftop statue of the explorer Captain James Cook (1728–79), who was apprenticed as a teenager to a Whitby shipping firm.

Lobster pots lining the quayside of Whitby's quaint harbor

Medieval arches above the nave of Whitby Abbey

⚐ Whitby Abbey

Green Lane. 📞 01947 603568.
◯ daily. ● Dec 24–26, Jan 1. 🎟
The monastery that Abbess Hilda founded in 657 for men and women was sacked by Vikings in 870. At the end of the 11th century it was rebuilt as a Benedictine Abbey. The present ruins date mainly from 13th-century rebuilding.

⛪ St. Mary's Parish Church

East Cliff. 📞 01947 603421. ◯ daily.
Stuart and Georgian alterations to this Norman church have left a mixture of twisted wood columns and mazelike 18th-century box pews. The 1778 triple-decker pulpit is hung with ear-trumpets used by a Victorian rector's deaf wife.

🏛 Captain Cook Memorial Museum

Grape Lane. 📞 01947 601900.
◯ Apr–Oct: daily. 🎟
The young James Cook slept in the attic of this 17th-century harborside house when apprenticed. The museum has period furniture in the style described in Cook's inventories and watercolors by artists who traveled on his voyages.

🏛 Whitby Museum and Pannett Art Gallery

Pannett Park. 📞 01947 602908.
◯ May–Sep: daily (Sun: pm); Oct–Apr: Mon & Tue (am), Wed–Sat: daily, Sun (pm). ● Dec 24–Jan 2. 🎟
museum. ♿ limited.
The Pannett park grounds, museum and gallery were a gift of Whitby lawyer, Robert Pannett (1834–1920), to house his art collection. Among the museum's treasures are fine collections of objects illustrating local history, such as jet jewelry, fossils, model ships and Captain Cook artifacts.

🏛 Museum of Victorian Whitby

Sandgate. 📞 01947 606393.
◯ Mar–Dec: daily; Jan–Feb: Thu–Sun. ● Dec 25. 🎟
Among the exhibits on Victorian life in Whitby are the animated wheel-house of a whaling ship and a unique collection of miniature room settings.

⚐ Caedmon's Cross

East Cliff. 📞 01947 603421.
On the path side of the abbey's clifftop graveyard is the cross of Caedmon, an illiterate laborer who worked at the abbey in the 7th century. He had a vision that inspired him to compose cantos of Anglo-Saxon religious verse still sung today.

Cross of Caedmon (1898)

Robin Hood's Bay ⑳

North Yorkshire. 🏘 *1,400.* 🚆 🚌
Whitby. ℹ️ *Langbourne Rd, Whitby
(01947 602674).*

L EGEND HAS IT that Robin
Hood *(see p322)* kept his
boats here in case he needed
to make a quick getaway. The
village has a history as a smugglers' haven, and many houses
have ingenious hiding places
for contraband beneath the
floor and behind the walls. The
cobbled main street is so steep
that visitors need to leave
their cars in the parking lot.
In the village center, attractive
narrow streets full of color-
washed stone cottages huddle
around a quaint quay. There
is a rocky beach with rock
pools for children to play in.
At low tide, the pleasant walk
south to Boggle Hole takes
15 minutes, but you need to
keep an eye on the tides.

**Cobbled alley in the Bay Town
area of Robin Hood's Bay**

The fishing port and town of Scarborough nestling round the harbor

Scarborough ㉑

North Yorkshire. 🏘 *54,000.* 🚆 🚌
ℹ️ *St. Nicholas Cliff (01723 373333).*
🛒 *Mon–Sat.*

T HE HISTORY of Scarborough
as a resort can be traced
back to 1626, when it became
known as a spa. In the Industrial Revolution *(see pp334–5)*
it was nicknamed "the Queen
of the Watering Places," but
the post-World War II trend
for vacations abroad has meant
fewer visitors. The town has
two separate beaches, and
the South Bay amusement
arcades contrast with the
quieter atmosphere of North

Bay. The playwright Alan
Ayckbourn premiers his work
at the Joseph Rowntree theater,
and Anne Brontë *(see p398)* is
buried in St. Mary's Church.
    Bronze and Iron Age relics
have been found on the site
of **Scarborough Castle**, and
Wood End Museum, former
home of the eccentric Sitwells,
exhibits local geology and
history. The **Rotunda** (1828–9)
was one of Britain's first built-
to-order museums. Works by
local Victorian artist Atkinson
Grimshaw (1836–93) hang in
Scarborough Art Gallery.
The **Sea-Life Centre** includes
baby seahorses and **Peasholm
Park** holds summer concerts.

♣ **Scarborough Castle**
Castle Rd. 📞 *01723 372451.* 🕐
daily. ● *Dec 24–26, Jan 1.* 🕐 ♿
🏛 **Wood End Museum**
The Crescent. 📞 *01723 367326.* 🕐
*Apr–Sep: Tue–Sun; Oct–May: Fri–Sun
& public hols.* ● *Dec 25, 26, Jan 1.*
🏛 **Rotunda Museum**
Vernon Rd. 📞 *01723 374839.* 🕐
*Apr–Sep: Tue–Sun; Oct–May: Fri–Sun
& public hols.* ● *Dec 25, 26, Jan 1.*
🏛 **Scarborough Art Gallery**
The Crescent. 📞 *01723 374753.* 🕐
*Apr–Sep: Tue–Sun; Oct–May: Fri–Sun
& public hols.* ● *Dec 25, 26, Jan 1.*
🐟 **Sea-Life Centre**
Scalby Mills Rd. 📞 *01723 376125.*
🕐 *daily.* ● *Dec 25.* 🕐 ♿
🌸 **Peasholm Park**
Columbus Ravine. 📞 *01723 373333.*
🕐 *daily.* 🕐 ♿

THE GROWING POPULARITY OF SWIMMING

During the 18th century, swimming came to be regarded
as a healthy pastime, and from 1735 onward men and
women, on separate stretches of the
coast, could be wheeled out into the
sea in bathing huts, or "machines."
In the 18th century, swimming
was segregated but nudity was
permitted. The Victorians brought
in fully clothed bathing, and
19th-century workers from
Britain's industrial heartlands
used the new steam trains to
visit the coast for their vacations. At this time, British
seaside resorts such as
Blackpool *(see p359)* and
Scarborough expanded to
meet the new demand.

A Victorian bathing hut on wheels

Castle Howard ㉒

Pillar detail in the Great Hall, carved by Samuel Carpenter

Still owned and lived in by the Howard family, Castle Howard was created by Charles, 3rd Earl of Carlisle. When he came to his title in 1692, he commissioned Sir John Vanbrugh, a man of dramatic ideas but with no previous architectural experience, to design a palace for him. Vanbrugh's grand designs of 1699 were put into practice by architect Nicholas Hawksmoor (see p24) and the main body of the house was completed by 1712. The West Wing was built in 1753–9, using a design by Thomas Robinson, son-in-law of the 3rd Earl. Castle Howard was used as the location for the television version of Evelyn Waugh's novel *Brideshead Revisited* (1945).

Temple of the Four Winds
Vanbrugh's last work, designed in 1724, has a dome and four Ionic porticoes. Situated in the grounds at the end of the terrace, it is typical of an 18th-century "landscape building."

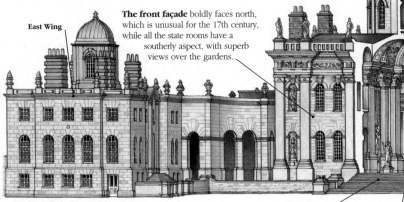

The front façade boldly faces north, which is unusual for the 17th century, while all the state rooms have a southerly aspect, with superb views over the gardens.

East Wing

North Front

★ Great Hall
Rising 20 m (66 ft) from its 515 sq m (5,500 sq ft) floor to the dome, the Great Hall has columns by Samuel Carpenter (1660–1713), wall paintings by Pellegrini and a circular gallery.

SIR JOHN VANBRUGH

Vanbrugh (1664–1726) trained as a soldier, but became better known as a playwright, architect and member of the Whig nobility. He collaborated with Hawksmoor over the design of Blenheim Palace, but his bold architectural vision, later greatly admired, was mocked by the establishment. He died while working on the garden buildings and grounds of Castle Howard.

Chapel Stained Glass
Admiral Edward Howard, Lord Lanerton, altered the chapel in 1870–75. The windows were designed by Edward Burne-Jones and William Morris.

VISITORS' CHECKLIST

A64 from York, Yorkshire.
☎ 01653 648444. 🚉 York then bus or Malton then taxi.
House ◯ Mar–Oct: 11am–4:30pm daily. **Grounds** ◯ 10am–4:30pm. ♿ ⛲ 🖼 🍴 🎁

Bust of the 7th Earl
JH Foley sculpted this head and shoulders portrait, which stands at the top of the Grand Staircase in the West Wing, in 1870.

★ Long Gallery
The Howard lineage is illustrated here by a large number of portraits, including works by Lely, Holbein and Van Dyck.

West Wing

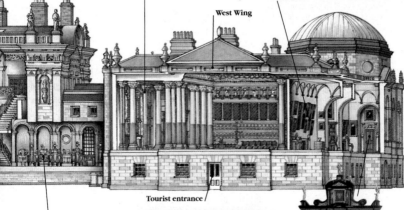

Tourist entrance

Antique Passage
Antiquities collected in the 18th and 19th centuries by the various earls of Carlisle are on display here. The plethora of mythical figures and gods reflects contemporary interest in Classical civilizations.

STAR SIGHTS

★ Great Hall

★ Long Gallery

Museum Room
Furniture here includes Regency chairs, Persian rugs and this 17th-century cabinet.

Eden Camp 23

Malton, North Yorkshire. 01653 697777. Malton then taxi. mid-Jan–mid Feb: Mon–Fri; mid-Feb–Dec: daily. Dec 24–mid-Jan.

THIS IS AN UNUSUAL, award-winning theme museum that pays tribute to the British people during World War II. Italian and German prisoners of war were kept at Eden Camp between 1939 and 1948. Today, some original huts built by Italian prisoners in 1942 are used as a museum, with period tableaux and a soundtrack. Each hut adopts a theme to take the visitor through civilian life in wartime, from Churchill's radio announcement of the outbreak of hostilities to the coming of peace. Visitors, including schoolchildren and nostalgic veterans, can see the Doodle-bug V-1 bomb that crashed outside the Officers' Mess, have tea in the canteen or experience a night in the Blitz. A tour can last for several hours.

British and American flags by the sign for Eden Camp

Wharram Percy 24

North Yorkshire. 0191 2611585 (English Heritage). Malton, then taxi. daily.

THIS IS ONE OF England's most important medieval village sites. Recent excavations have unearthed evidence of a 30-household community, with two manors, and the remains of a medieval church. There is also a millpond that has beautiful wild flowers in late spring. Wharram Percy is set in a pretty valley, well-marked off the B1248 from Burdale, in the heart of the green, rolling Wolds. It is about a 20-minute walk from the parking lot, and makes an ideal picnic stop.

Alabaster carving on the chimney piece at Burton Agnes

Burton Agnes 25

Nr Driffield, East Yorkshire. 01262 490324. Driffield, then bus. Apr–Oct: daily. limited in house.

OF ALL THE GRAND HOUSES in the triangle between Hull, York and Scarborough, Burton Agnes Hall is a firm favorite. This is partly because the attractive redbrick Elizabethan mansion has such a homey atmosphere. One of the first portraits you see in the Small Hall is of Anne Griffith, whose father, Sir Henry, built the house. There is a monument to him in the local church.

Burton Agnes has remained in the hands of the original family and has changed little since it was built – between 1598 and 1610. You enter it by the turreted gatehouse, and the entrance hall has a fine Elizabethan alabaster chimney piece. The massive oak staircase is an impressive example of Elizabethan woodcarving.

In the library is a collection of Impressionist and Post-Impressionist art, pleasantly out of character with the rest of the house, including works by André Derain, Renoir and Augustus John. The extensive grounds include a play area specially built for children.

Bempton and Flamborough Head 26

East Yorkshire. 4,300. Bempton. Bridlington. Prince St, Bridlington (01262 673474).

BEMPTON, WHICH CONSISTS OF 5 miles (8 km) of steep chalk cliffs between Speeton and Flamborough Head, is the largest seabird-breeding colony in England, and is famous for its puffins. The weathered ledges and fissures provide ideal nest-sites for more than 100,000 pairs of

Nesting gannet on the chalk cliffs at Bempton

birds. Today, eight different species, including skinny black shags and kittiwakes, thrive on the Grade 1 listed *(see p617)* Bempton cliffs. Bempton is the only mainland site for goose-sized gannets, well known for their dramatic fishing techniques. May, June and July are the best bird-watching months.

The spectacular cliffs are best seen from the north side of the Flamborough Head peninsula, which offers attractive walks.

Beverley ㉗

Humberside. 🏘 *26,000.* ℹ *The Guildhall, Register Sq (01482 867430).* 🖹 *Sat.*

THE HISTORY of Beverley dates back to the 8th century, when Old Beverley served as a retreat for John, later Bishop of York, who was canonized for his healing powers. Over the centuries Beverley grew as a medieval sanctuary town. Like York, it is an attractive combination of medieval and Georgian buildings.

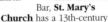

The best way to enter Beverley is through the last of five town gates, the castellated North Bar that allowed the medieval inhabitants in and out of the town's surrounding walls. It was rebuilt in 1409–10.

The skyline is dominated by the twin towers of the magnificent **minster**. This was co-founded in 937 by Athelstan, King of Wessex, in place of the church that John of Beverley had chosen as his final resting place in 721. The decorated nave is the earliest surviving building work that dates back to the early 1300s. It is particularly famous for its 16th-century choir stalls and 68 misericords *(see p327).*

The minster contains many early detailed stone carvings, including a set of four from about 1308, which illustrate figures with ailments such as toothache and lumbago. On the north side of the altar is the richly carved 14th-century Gothic Percy tomb, thought to be that of Lady Idoine Percy, who died in 1365. Also on the north side is the Fridstol, or Peace Chair, said to date from 924–39, the time of Athelstan. Anyone who sat on it would then be granted 30 days sanctuary. Within the North Bar, **St. Mary's Church** has a 13th-century chancel and houses the largest number of medieval stone

Famous pilgrim rabbit in St. Mary's Church, Beverley

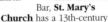

Minstrel Pillar in St. Mary's Church

carvings of musical instruments in Britain. The brightly painted 16th-century Minstrel Pillar is particularly notable. Painted on the paneled chancel ceiling are the portraits of English monarchs after 1445. On the richly sculpted doorway of St. Michael's Chapel is the grinning pilgrim rabbit said to have inspired Lewis Carroll's White Rabbit in *Alice in Wonderland.*

Southeast of the minster, the **Museum of Army Transport** contains over 100 exhibits of army vehicles. The Saturday market has existed here ever since the Middle Ages.

🏛 Museum of Army Transport

Flemingate. 📞 *01482 860445.* ◯ *daily.* ⬤ *Dec 24–26.* 📷 ♿

Beverley Minster, one of Europe's finest examples of Gothic architecture

Burton Constable ❷

Nr Hull, North Humberside. ☎ *01964 562400.* 🚆 *Hull then taxi.* ⏰ *Easter–Jun, Sep: Sun–Thu; Jul–Aug: Sat–Thu.* 🖼 ♿

THE CONSTABLE FAMILY have been leading landowners since the 13th century, and have lived at Burton Constable since work began on it in 1570. It is an Elizabethan house, altered in the 18th century by Thomas Lightholer, Thomas Atkinson and James Wyatt. Today, its 30 rooms include, Georgian and Victorian interiors. Burton Constable has a fine collection of Chippendale furniture and family portraits dating from the 16th century. Most of the collections of prints, textiles and drawings belong to Leeds City Art Galleries. The family still lives in the south wing.

Painting of Burton Constable (c.1690) by an anonymous artist

The Princes' Dock in Kingston upon Hull's restored docks area

Kingston upon Hull ❷

Humberside. 🏠 *270,000.* 🚆 ✈ 🚢 ℹ *Carr Lane (01482 223559).* 🛒 *Tue, Fri, Sat.*

THERE IS A LOT MORE to Hull than the heritage of a thriving fishing industry. The restored town center docks are attractive, and Hull's Old Town, laid out in medieval times, is all cobbled, winding streets and quaintly askew redbrick houses. You can follow the Fish Trail, a path of inlaid metal fishes on the city's sidewalks that illustrates the many different varieties that have been landed in Hull, from anchovy to shark. In Victoria Square is the **Town**

Docks Museum. Built in 1871 as the offices of the Hull Dock Company, it traces the city's maritime history. Among its exhibits are an ornate whalebone and vertebrae bench and a display of complicated rope knots such as the Eye Splice and the Midshipman's Hitch.

An imposing Elizabethan building, the **Old Grammar School**, explores Hull's story through a collection of some of its families' artifacts.

In the heart of the Old Town, on a street that often reeks of salty sea air, is the **William Wilberforce House**, one of the surviving examples of the High Street's brick merchants' dwellings. Its first-floor oak-paneled rooms date from the 17th century, but most of the house is dedicated to the Wilberforce family, whose

connection began in 1732 with the grandfather of the abolitionist. Among the more gruesome museum exhibits are iron ankle fetters for slaves. A fine Victorian doll collection strikes a lighter note.

Nearby is the **Streetlife Transport Museum,** Hull's newest and noisiest museum, popular with children. It includes a mailboy's boot from the 18th century, toughened to protect him against horses' hooves, and a re-creation of a bicycle repair workshop.

🏛 **Town Docks Museum**
Queen Victoria Sq. ☎ *01482 593902.* ⏰ *daily.* ● *Dec 25–27, Jan 1, Good Fri.* ♿
🏛 **Old Grammar School**
South Churchside. ☎ *01482 593952.* ⏰ *daily.* ● *Dec 25–27, Jan 1, Good Fri.* ♿

WILLIAM WILBERFORCE (1758–1833)

William Wilberforce, born in Hull to a merchant family, was a natural orator. After studying Classics at Cambridge, he entered politics and in 1784 gave one of his first public addresses in York. The audience was captivated, and Wilberforce realized the potential of his powers of persuasion. From 1785 onward, adopted by the Pitt government as spokesman for the abolition of slavery, he conducted a determined and conscientious campaign. But his speeches won him enemies, and in 1792, threats from a slave importer meant that he needed a constant armed guard. In 1807 his bill to abolish the lucrative slave trade became law.

A 19th-century engraving of Wilberforce by J. Jenkins

🏛 **William Wilberforce House**
South Churchside. ☎ 01482 593902. ⬜ daily. ● Dec 25–27, Jan 1, Good Fri. ♿

🏛 **Streetlife Transport Museum**
South Churchside. ☎ 01482 593902. ⬜ daily. ● Dec 25–27, Jan 1, Good Fri. ♿

Holderness and Spurn Head ⑳

North Humberside. 🚆 Hull (Paragon St) then bus. 🛈 Newbegin, Hornsea (01964 536404).

THIS CURIOUS FLAT AREA east of Hull, with straight roads and delicately waving fields of oats and barley, in many ways resembles Holland, except that its mills are derelict. Beaches stretch for 30 miles (46 km) along the coastline. The main resort towns are **Withernsea** whose lighthouse is now a museum and **Hornsea**, well known for its pottery.

The Holderness landscape only exists because of erosion higher up the coast. The sea continues to wash down tiny bits of rock that accumulate. About 1560 they began to form a sandbank. By 1669 the sandbank was large enough to be colonized as Sonke Sand. The last bits of silting mud and debris joined the island to the mainland as recently as the 1830s. Today, you can drive through the eerie, lush wilderness of Sunk Island on the way west to Spurn Head. This is located at the tip of the Spurn Peninsula, a 3.5 mile (6 km) spit of land that has also built up as the result of coastal erosion elsewhere. Flora, fauna and bird-life have been protected here by the Yorkshire Naturalists' Trust since 1960. Walking gives the eerie feeling that the land could be eroded from under your feet at any time. A surprise discovery at the end of Spurn Head is a tiny community of pilots and lifeboat crew, constantly on call to guide ships into Hull harbor, or help cope with disasters.

Fishing boat at Grimsby's National Fishing Heritage Centre

Grimsby ㉛

South Humberside. 👥 92,000. 🚆 🚌 🛈 Heritage Sq (01472 342422). 🛒 Tue, Thu, Sat.

PERCHED AT THE mouth of the River Humber, Grimsby was founded in the Middle Ages by a Danish fisherman by the name of Grim, and rose to prominence in the 19th century as one of the world's largest fishing ports. Its first dock was opened in 1800 and, with the arrival of the railroads, the town secured the means of transporting its catch all over the country. Even though the traditional fishing industry had declined by the 1970s, dock area redevelopment has made sure that Grimsby's unique heritage is retained.

This is best demonstrated by the award-winning **National Fishing Heritage Centre**, a museum that recreates the industry in its 1950s heyday, capturing the atmosphere of the period. Visitors sign on as crew members on a trawler and, by means of a variety of vivid interactive displays, travel from the back streets of Grimsby to the Arctic fishing grounds. On the way, they can experience the roll of the ship, the smell of the fish and the heat of the engine. The tour can be finished off with a guided tour of the restored 1950s trawler, the *Ross Tiger*.

Other attractions in Grimsby include an International Jazz Festival every July, a restored Victorian shopping street called Abbeygate, a market, a wide selection of restaurants, and the nearby seaside resorts of Cleethorpes, Mablethorpe and Skegness.

🏛 **National Fishing Heritage Centre**
Heritage Sq, Alexandra Dock. ☎ 01472 344868. ⬜ daily. ● Dec 25, 26, Jan 1. 🎫 ♿

Isolated lighthouse at Spurn Head, at the tip of Spurn Peninsula

Street-by-Street: York ☻

Monk Bar coat of arms

THE CITY OF YORK has retained so much of its medieval structure that walking into its center is like entering a living museum. Many of the ancient timbered houses, perched on narrow, winding streets, such as the Shambles, are protected by a conservation order. Cars are banned from the center, so there are always student bikes bouncing over cobbled streets. Its strategic position led to its development as a railroad center in the 19th century.

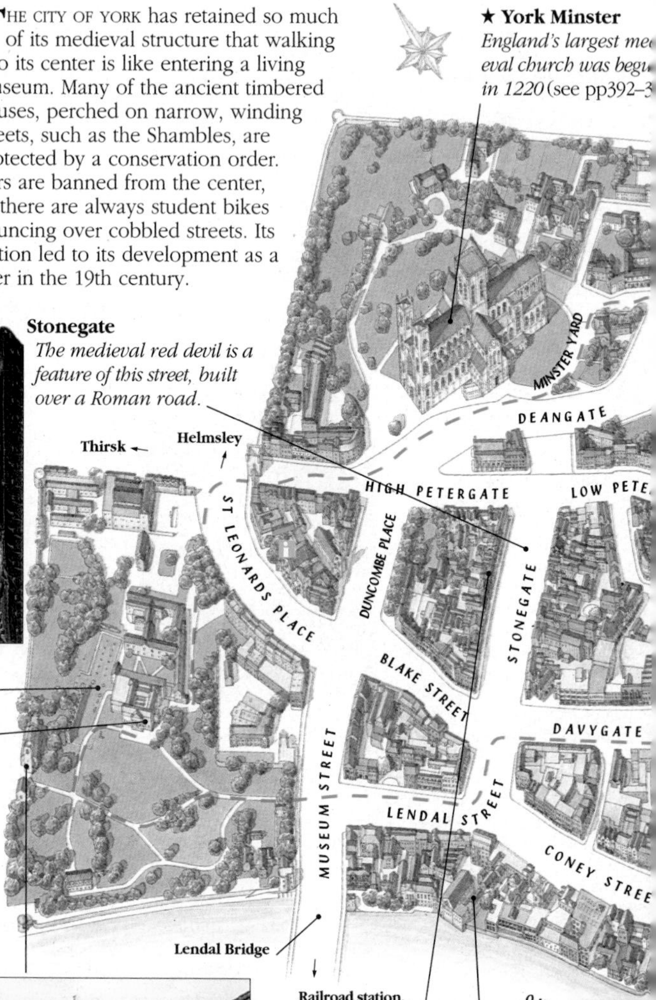

★ York Minster
England's largest medieval church was begun in 1220 (see pp392–3).

Stonegate
The medieval red devil is a feature of this street, built over a Roman road.

St. Mary's Abbey

Yorkshire Museum contains a fine collection of fossils, discovered at Whitby in the 19th century.

Thirsk ← Helmsley ↑

DEANGATE

HIGH PETERGATE   LOW PETE.

ST LEONARDS PLACE

DUNCOMBE PLACE

STONEGATE

BLAKE STREET

DAVYGATE

MUSEUM STREET

LENDAL STREET

CONEY STREE

Lendal Bridge

Railroad station, coach station, National Railway Museum, and Leeds

OUSE

Ye Old Starre Inne is one of the oldest pubs in York.

St. Olave's Church
The 11th-century church, next to the gatehouse of St. Mary's Abbey (see p392), was founded by the Earl of Northumbria in memory of St. Olaf, King of Norway. To the left is the Chapel of St. Mary on the Walls.

Guildhall
This two-headed medieval roof boss is on the 15th-century Guildhall, situated beside the River Ouse and restored after bomb damage during World War II.

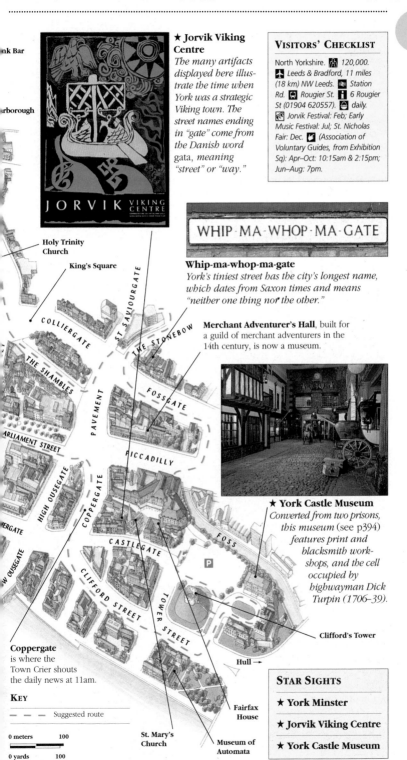

★ Jorvik Viking Centre

The many artifacts displayed here illustrate the time when York was a strategic Viking town. The street names ending in "gate" come from the Danish word gata, *meaning "street" or "way."*

VISITORS' CHECKLIST

North Yorkshire. 120,000.
Leeds & Bradford, 11 miles
(18 km) NW Leeds. Station
Rd. Rougier St. 6 Rougier
St (01904 620557). daily.
Jorvik Festival: Feb; Early
Music Festival: Jul; St. Nicholas
Fair: Dec. (Association of
Voluntary Guides, from Exhibition
Sq): Apr–Oct: 10:15am & 2:15pm;
Jun–Aug: 7pm.

WHIP·MA·WHOP·MA·GATE

Whip-ma-whop-ma-gate
York's tiniest street has the city's longest name, which dates from Saxon times and means "neither one thing nor the other."

Merchant Adventurer's Hall, built for a guild of merchant adventurers in the 14th century, is now a museum.

Holy Trinity Church

King's Square

COLLIERGATE

ST SAVIOURGATE

THE STONEBOW

THE SHAMBLES

PAVEMENT

FOSSGATE

ARLIAMENT STREET

PICCADILLY

HIGH OUSEGATE

COPPERGATE

ERGATE

CASTLEGATE

FOSS

W OUSEGATE

CLIFFORD STREET

TOWER STREET

P

★ York Castle Museum
Converted from two prisons, this museum (see p394) features print and blacksmith workshops, and the cell occupied by highwayman Dick Turpin (1706–39).

Clifford's Tower

Hull →

Coppergate
is where the Town Crier shouts the daily news at 11am.

KEY

– – – Suggested route

0 meters   100

0 yards   100

St. Mary's Church

Fairfax House

Museum of Automata

STAR SIGHTS

★ York Minster

★ Jorvik Viking Centre

★ York Castle Museum

York Minster

Central sunflower in rose window

THE LARGEST Gothic church north of the Alps, York Minster is 163 m (534 ft) long and 76 m (249 ft) wide and houses the largest collection of medieval stained glass in Britain (*see p395*). The word "minster" means a church served by monks, but priests always served at York. The minster probably began as a wooden chapel used to baptize King Edwin of Northumbria in 627. There have been several cathedrals on the site, including an 11th-century Norman structure. The present minster was begun in 1220 and completed 250 years later. In 1984, the south transept roof was destroyed by fire. Restoration cost over $3 million.

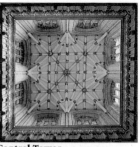

Central Tower
Reconstructed in 1420–65 (after partial collapse in 1407), from a design by the master stonemason William Colchester, its geometrical roof design has a central lantern.

Lady Chapel

The Choir has a vaulted entrance with a 12th-century boss of the Assumption of the Virgin.

Exit in south transept

The 16th-century rose window

★ **Choir Screen**
Placed between the choir and the nave, this 15th-century stone screen depicts kings of England from William I to Henry VI, and has a canopy of angels.

The Nave, built in 1291, was severely damaged by fire in 1840. Rebuilding costs were heavy, but it was reopened with a new peal of bells in 1844.

★ **Chapter House**
A Latin inscription near the entrance of the wooden-vaulted Chapter House (1260–85) reads: "As the rose is the flower of flowers, so this is the house of houses."

Timbered interior of the Merchant Adventurers' Hall

The western towers, with their
15th-century decorative paneling
and elaborate pinnacles, contrast
with the simpler design of the
north transept. The southwest
tower is the minster belfry.

Great west door

Great west window
(see p395)

🏰 Monk Bar

This is one of York's finest original medieval gates, situated
at the end of Goodramgate. It
is vaulted on three floors, and
the portcullis still works. In
the Middle Ages, the rooms
above it were rented out, and
it was a prison in the 16th
century. Its decorative details
include men holding stones
ready to drop on intruders.

🏛 Museum of Automata

9 Tower St. (01904 655550.
◯ daily. ● Dec 25. 🖼 &
The history of mechanically
moving objects, from simple
articulated figurines of ancient
civilizations to 20th-century
artworks, is charted in this
museum. Automata too fragile
for frequent operation,
such as the acrobats and
clowns in the French
Gallery, which date
from the 1820s, are
brought to life on
a video wall.

**One of the mechanical toys at the
Museum of Automata**

🏰 Clifford's Tower

Clifford's St. (01904 646940.
◯ daily. ● Dec 25, 26. 🖼
Sited on top of a mound that
William the Conqueror built
for his original wooden castle,
destroyed by fire during anti-
Jewish riots in 1190, Clifford's
Tower dates from the 13th
century. Built by Henry III,
it commemorates Roger de
Clifford who was hanged in
1322 after being captured at
the Battle of Boroughbridge.

🏛 ARC

St. Saviourgate. (01904 654324.
◯ Mon–Sat. ● Good Fri, Dec 18–31.
🖼 &
Housed in a restored medieval
church off the Shambles, the
ARC is a center for exploring
archaeology. Visitors are
allowed to handle ancient
finds and experiment with
traditional crafts and computers. Archaeologists show
how to identify exhibits such
as pottery by age and type.

🏰 Merchant
Adventurers' Hall

Fossgate. (01904 654818. ◯ mid-
Mar–mid-Nov: daily; mid-Nov–mid-Mar:
Mon–Sat. ● Dec 23–Jan 2. 🖼 &
Built by the York Merchants'
Guild, which controlled the
northern cloth trade in the
15th–17th centuries, this building has fine timberwork. The
Great Hall is probably the
best example of its kind in
Europe. Among its paintings
is an unattributed 17th-
century copy of Van Dyck's
portrait of Charles I's queen,
Henrietta Maria. Below the
Great Hall is the hospital,
used by the guild until 1900,
and a private chapel.

Exploring York

THE APPEAL OF YORK is its many layers of history. A medieval city constructed on top of a Roman one, it was first built in AD 71, when it became capital of the northern province and was known as Eboracum. It was here that Constantine the Great was made emperor in 306, and reorganized Britain into four provinces. A hundred years later, the Roman army had withdrawn. Eboracum was renamed Eoforwic, under the Saxons, and then became a Christian stronghold. The Danish street names are the reminder that it was a Viking center from 867, and one of Europe's chief trading bases. Between 1100 and 1500 it was England's second city. The glory of York is the minster *(see pp392–3)*. The city also boasts 18 medieval churches, 3 mile long (4.8 km) medieval city walls, elegant Jacobean and Georgian architecture and fine museums.

The Middleham Jewel, York-shire Museum

Grand staircase and fine plaster ceiling at Fairfax House

🏛 York Castle Museum

The Eye of York. **(** *01904 653611.*
🔘 *daily.* ● *Dec 25, 26, Jan 1.* 🦽 ground floor only.

Housed in two 18th-century prisons, the museum has a fine folk collection, started by Dr. John Kirk of the market town of Pickering. Opened in 1938, its period displays include a Jacobean dining room, a moorland cottage, and a 1950s front room. It also contains a large collection of early 20th-century household gadgets.

The most famous exhibits include the reconstructed Victorian street of Kirkgate, complete with storefronts and model carriage horse, and the Anglo Saxon York Helmet, the finest example of only three ever found, discovered in 1982.

🏛 York Minster

See pp392–3.

🏛 Jorvik Viking Centre

Coppergate. **(** *01904 643211.*
🔘 *daily.* ● *Dec 25.* 🦽

This popular center is built on the site of the original Viking settlement that archaeologists uncovered at Coppergate. It is most famous for re-creating the smells of Viking York. A "time car" travels through a model Viking street, and provides a commentary on its history. An exhibition illustrates how the best-preserved Viking village in Britain was discovered.

🏛 Yorkshire Museum and St Mary's Abbey

Museum Gardens. **(** *01904 629745.*
🔘 *daily.* ● *Dec 25, 26, Jan 1.* 🦽
Yorkshire Museum was in the news when it purchased the 15th-century Middleham Jewel for £2.5 million, one of the finest pieces of English Gothic jewelry found this century. Other exhibits include 2nd-century Roman mosaics and an Anglo-Saxon silver gilt bowl.

St. Mary's Abbey *(see p336)* in the riverside grounds is where the medieval York Mystery Plays are set every three years.

🏛 Fairfax House

Castlegate. **(** *01904 655543.*
🔘 *mid-Feb–Jan 6: Sat–Thu.* ● *Dec 25, 26.* 🦽 🦽 limited.
From 1755 to 1762 Viscount Fairfax built this fine Georgian town house for his daughter, Anne. The house was designed by John Carr *(see p24)*, and restored in the 1980s. Between 1920 and 1965 it was a cinema and dancehall. Today, visitors can see the bedroom of Anne Fairfax (1725–93), and a fine collection of 18th-century furniture, porcelain and clocks.

🏛 National Railway Museum

Leeman Rd. **(** *01904 621261.*
🔘 *daily.* ● *Dec 24–26, Jan 1.* 🦽 🦽
Set in a former steam engine maintenance shed, the world's largest railroad museum covers nearly 200 years of history using paintings, photographs and visual aids. Visitors can try wheel-tapping and shunting in the interactive gallery, or find out what made Stephenson's *Rocket* so successful. Exhibits include uniforms, rolling stock from 1797 onward and Queen Victoria's carriage from the Royal Train, as well as the very latest in techno-logical innovations.

Reproduction of an engine and 1830s first-class carriage (left) in York's National Railway Museum

The Stained Glass of York Minster

Y ORK MINSTER houses the largest collection of medieval stained glass in Britain, some of it dating from the late 12th century. The glass was generally colored during production, using metal oxides to produce the desired color, then worked on by craftsmen on site. When a design had been produced, the glass was first cut, then trimmed to shape. Details

were painted on, using iron oxide-based paint that was fused to the glass by firing in a kiln. Individual pieces were then leaded together to form the finished window.

Part of the fascination of the minster glass is its variety of subject matter. Some windows were paid for by lay donors who specified a particular subject, others reflect ecclesiastical patronage.

Window detail

Miracle of St. Nicholas *(late 12th century) was put in the nave over 100 years after it was made. It shows a Jew's conversion.*

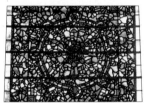

The Five Sisters *in the north transept are the largest examples of grisaille glass in Britain. This popular 13th-century technique involved creating fine patterning on clear glass and decorating it with black enamel.*

St. John the Evangelist, *in part of the Great West Window (c.1338), is holding an eagle, itself an example of stickwork, where paint is scraped off to reveal clear glass.*

Noah's Ark *with its distinct boatlike shape is easily identified in the Great East Window.*

Edward III *is a fine example of the 14th-century "soft" style of painting, achieved by stippling the paint.*

The Great East Window *(1405-8), the size of a tennis court, is the largest area of medieval painted glass in the world. The Dean and Chapter paid master glazier John Thornton four shillings a week for this celebration of the Creation.*

Walter Skirlaw, *whose bishopric was revoked in favor of Richard Scrope, donated this window on its completion in 1408.*

Harewood House ㉝

Harewood, Yorkshire. 0113 2886331. Leeds then bus.
Mar–Oct: daily.

DESIGNED BY John Carr in 1759, Harewood House is the Yorkshire home of the Earl and Countess of Harewood.

The grand Palladian exterior is impressive, with interiors created by Robert Adam and an unrivaled collection of 18th-century furniture made specifically for Harewood by Yorkshire-born Thomas Chippendale (1711–79). Harewood has a fine collection of paintings by Italian and English artists, including Reynolds and Gainsborough, and two new watercolor rooms. The grounds, developed by Capability Brown (*see p23*) include the **Harewood Bird Garden**, which has exotic and native species on show and a breeding program of certain endangered varieties.

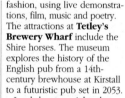

Bali starling, one of Harewood's rare birds

Leeds ㉞

Yorkshire. 700,000.
Leeds City Station (0113 2478301).
Mon–Sun.

THE THIRD LARGEST of Britain's provincial cities, Leeds was at its most prosperous during the Victorian period. The most impressive legacy from this era is a series of ornate, covered shopping arcades. Also of note is the **Town Hall**, designed by Cuthbert Brodrick and opened by Queen Victoria in 1858.

Today, although Leeds is primarily an industrial city, it also offers a thriving cultural scene. Productions at **The Grand** by Opera North, one of Britain's top operatic companies, are of a high quality.

The **City Art Gallery** has an impressive collection of British 20th-century art and fine examples of Victorian paintings including works by local artist Atkinson Grimshaw (1836–93). Among the late 19th-century

French art are works by Signac, Courbet and Sisley. The Henry Moore Institute, added in 1993, is devoted to the research, study and display of sculpture of all periods. It comprises a reading room, study center, library and video gallery, as well as galleries and an archive of material on and by Moore and other sculptural pioneers.

The **Armley Mills Museum**, in a 19th-century woollen mill, explores the industrial heritage of Leeds. Filled with original equipment, recorded sounds and models in 19th-century workers' clothes, it traces the history of the ready-to-wear industry.

A striking waterfront development by the River Aire has attracted two museums. Due to open in 1996 is the **Royal Armouries Museum**, from the Tower of London. It tells the story of arms and armor around the world in battle, sports, self-defense and fashion, using live demonstrations, film, music and poetry. The attractions at **Tetley's Brewery Wharf** include the Shire horses. The museum explores the history of the English pub from a 14th-century brewhouse at Kirstall to a futuristic pub set in 2053.

Leeds has two sights that are especially suitable for children. **Tropical World**

The County Arcade, one of Leeds' restored shopping arcades

features crystal pools, a rainforest house, butterflies and tropical fish. There is also a farm and a Rare Breeds center in the grounds of the Tudor-Jacobean **Temple Newsam House**, with a fine collection of Chippendale furniture.

City Art Gallery
The Headrow. 0113 2478248.
Mon–Sat. public hols.
Armley Mills Museum
Canal Rd, Armley. 0113 2637861.
Tue–Sun, public hols. Dec 24–26, Jan 1.
Royal Armouries
Waterloo Hse. 0113 2444332.
spring 1996.
Tetley's Brewery Wharf
The Waterfront. 0113 2420666.
Apr–Sep: daily; Oct–Mar: Wed–Sun. Dec 24–26, Jan 1.
Tropical World
Canal Gdns, Princes Ave. 0113 2661850. daily. Dec 25.
Temple Newsam House
Off A63. 0113 2647321.
Tue–Sun, public hols. Dec 25, 26, Jan 1. limited in house.

Working loom at the Armley Mills Museum in Leeds

The Other Side (1990–93) by David Hockney at Bradford's 1853 Gallery in Saltaire

Bradford ㉟

West Yorkshire. 🏠 *475,000.* 🚉
🚆 🚌 ℹ️ *National Museum of Photography, Film & Television, Pictureville (01274 753678).* 🛒 *Mon–Sat.*

IN THE 16TH CENTURY, Bradford was a thriving market town, and the opening of its canal in 1774 boosted trade. By 1850, it was the world's capital for worsted (fabric made from closely twisted wool). Many of the city's well-preserved civic and industrial buildings date from this period, such as the Wool Exchange on Market Street. In the 1800s a number of German textile manufacturers settled in what is now called Little Germany. Their houses are characterized by decorative stone carvings that illustrated the wealth and standing of the occupants.

The **National Museum of Photography, Film and Television**, founded in 1983, explores the technology and art of these media. There is a television section called TV Heaven, where visitors can ask to watch their favorite program. They are also encouraged to see themselves read the news on TV. The giant IMAX screen uses the world's largest film format. Film subjects include journeys

Daguerreotype camera by Giroux (1839)

into space, Yellowstone Park in the US and the original Rolling Stones band.

The **Colour Museum** traces dyeing and textile printing from ancient Egypt to the present day. Hands-on elements include taking charge of computerized technology to test the color of a material. **Bradford Industrial Museum** is housed in an original spinning mill. As well as seeing and hearing all the mill machinery, you can try riding on a horse-drawn trolley. Saltaire, one of Britain's Victorian planned industrial villages *(see p335)*, is on the outskirts of the city. Built by Sir Titus Salt for his Salts Mill workers, it was completed in 1873. The **1853 Gallery** in the main mill has works by David Hockney, born in Bradford in 1937.

🏛️ **National Museum of Photography, Film and Television**
Pictureville. ☎ *01274 727488.*
🕐 *Tue–Sun, public hols.* 🔴 *Dec 24–26, Jan 1.* ♿

🏛️ **Colour Museum**
82 Grattan Rd. ☎ *01274 390955.* 🕐
Tue–Sat. 🔴 *Dec 24–26, Jan 1.* 📷 ♿

🏛️ **Bradford Industrial Museum**
Moorside Mills, Moorside Rd. ☎
01274 631756. 🕐 *Tue–Sun, public hols.* 🔴 *Dec 25, 26.* ♿ *limited.*

🏛️ **1853 Gallery**
Salts Mill, Victoria Rd. ☎ *01274 531163.* 🕐 *daily.* 🔴 *Dec 24–26, Jan 1.* ♿ *limited.*

BRADFORD'S INDIAN COMMUNITY

Immigrants from the Indian subcontinent originally came to Bradford in the 1950s to work in the mills, but with the decline of the textile industry many began small businesses. By the mid-1970s there were 1,400 such enterprises in the area. Almost one-fifth were in the food sector, born out of simple cafés catering for mill-workers whose families were far away. As Indian food became more popular, these restaurants thrived, and today there are over 200 serving the highly spiced dishes of the Indian subcontinent.

Balti in a Bradford restaurant

Haworth Parsonage, home to the Brontë family, now a museum

Haworth ③⑥

West Yorkshire. 👥 *5,000.*
🚉 *Keighley.* 🛈 *2–4 West Lane
(01535 642329).*

THE SETTING OF HAWORTH, in
bleak Pennine moorland
dotted with farmsteads, has
changed little since it was
home to the Brontë family. The
town boomed in the 1840s,
when there were more than
1,200 hand-looms in operation,
but is more famous today for
the Brontë connection.

You can visit the **Brontë
Parsonage Museum**, home
from 1820–61 to novelists
Charlotte, Emily and Anne,
their brother Branwell and
their father, the
Reverend Patrick
Brontë. Built in
1778–9, the house
remains decorated
as it was during
the 1850s. Eleven
rooms, including
the kitchen,
children's study
and Charlotte's room,
display letters to friends,
manuscripts, books, furniture
and personal treasures.

Also evocative of the Brontë
sisters' novels are the local
walks, for which sturdy boots
are advised. They include the
Brontë Falls and **Brontë
Bridge**. Nearby is the **Brontë
Seat**, a chair-shaped stone.

In summer, the nostalgic
Victorian **Keighley and Worth
Valley Railway** runs through
Haworth. It stops at Oakworth

**Charlotte Brontë's
childhood story book,
for her sister, Anne**

station, where parts of *The
Railway Children* were filmed.
At the end of the line is the
Railway Museum at Oxenhope.

🏛 Brontë Parsonage
Museum
Church Lane. 📞 *01535 642323.* ◯
daily. ◯ *Dec 24–27, Jan 9–Feb 3.* 🎟

Hebden Bridge ③⑦

West Yorkshire. 👥 *4,500.* 🚉 🛈 *1
Bridgegate (01422 843831).* 🛒 *Thu.*

HEBDEN BRIDGE is a delightful
West Riding mill town,
surrounded by steep hills and
former 19th-century mills, and
is home to
Britain's last
clog mill.
The houses
seem to
defy gravity
as they
cling to
the valley
sides. Due
to the
gradient,
one house
is made
from two
bottom floors and the top two
floors form another unit. To
separate legal ownership of
these "flying freeholds," an Act
of Parliament was devised.

There is a superb view of
Hebden Bridge from nearby
Heptonstall, where the cult
poet Sylvia Plath (1932–63)
is buried. The village contains
a Wesleyan chapel (1764).

Halifax ③⑧

West Yorkshire. 👥 *88,000.* 🚉 🛈
🛈 *Piece Hall (01422 368725).*
🛒 *Thu–Sat.*

HALIFAX'S HISTORY has been
influenced by textiles
since the Middle Ages, but
today's visual reminders date
mainly from the 19th century.
The town inspired William
Blake's vision of "dark Satanic
mills" in his poem *Jerusalem*
(1820). The wool trade helped
to make the Pennines into
Britain's industrial backbone.

Until the mid-15th century
cloth production was modest,
but vital enough to inspire
the 11th-century Gibbet Law,
that stated that anyone caught
stealing cloth could be
hanged. There is a replica of
the gibbet used for hanging at
the bottom of Gibbet Street.
Many of Halifax's 18th- and

CHARLOTTE BRONTË

During a harsh, motherless
childhood, Charlotte (1816-
55) and her sisters, Emily
and Anne, retreated into
fictional worlds of their
own, writing poems and
stories. As adults, they had
to work as governesses or
teachers, but still published
a poetry collection in 1846.
Only two copies were sold,
but in the following year
Charlotte had great success
with *Jane Eyre*, which
became a best seller. After
the deaths of her siblings
in 1848–9 Charlotte turned
to the solitude of writing
and published her last
novel, *Villette*, in 1852. She
married the Reverend
Arthur Bell Nicholls, her
father's curate, in 1854, but
she died shortly afterward.

Children playing on the Giant Mouth at Halifax's Eureka! museum

19th-century buildings owe their existence to wealthy cloth traders. Sir Charles Barry (1795–1860), architect of the Houses of Parliament, was commissioned by the Crossley family to design the Town Hall. They also paid for the landscaping of the People's Park by the creator of the Crystal Palace, Sir Joseph Paxton (1801–65). Thomas Bradley's 18th-century **Piece Hall** *(see p398)*, where wool merchants once sold their pieces of cloth, trading in one of the hall's 315 "Merchants' Rooms." It has a massive Italianate courtyard built by the town's wool merchants and now beautifully restored. Today, Halifax's market takes place here.

Adjoining Piece Hall is **Calderdale Industrial Museum**, which charts the area's industrial past. Among over 20 industries illustrated are clock-making and candy manufacturing. It has working displays of textile machinery.

Eureka! is a museum designed for children under 12, who are promised "learning adventures" on exhibits such as the Giant Mouth Machine and the Wall of Water. **Shibden Hall Museum** is a fine period house, parts of which date back to the 15th century. It reflects the prosperous home life of a 17th–18th-century manufacturer. Its 17th-century Pennine barn is filled with horse-drawn vehicles. In the cobbled courtyard, 19th-century workshops include a saddler and a blacksmith.

🏛 Calderdale Industrial Museum
Central Works, Square Rd. 【 01422 358087. ◯ Tue–Sun (pm), public hols. ● Dec 25, 26, Jan 1. 🖾 &
🏛 Eureka!
Discovery Rd. 【 01426 983191. ◯ daily. ● Dec 24–26. 🖾 &
🏛 Shibden Hall Museum
Listers Rd. 【 01422 352246. ◯ Mar–Nov: daily; Feb: Sun. 🖾 & very limited.

Yorkshire Mining Museum ㊴

Wakefield, West Yorkshire. 【 01924 848806. � Wakefield then bus. ◯ daily. ● Dec 24–26, Jan 1. 🖾 &

HOUSED IN THE old Caphouse Colliery, this museum gives visitors the chance to go into a real mine shaft, so warm clothing is advised. A tour takes you, equipped with a hat and a miner's lamp, 137 m (450 ft) underground. You can enter some of the narrow seams and see exhibits such as life-size working models. Other displays depict mining methods and conditions from 1820 to the present day.

Yorkshire Sculpture Park ㊵

Wakefield, West Yorkshire. 【 01924 830302. ⊡ Wakefield then bus. ◯ daily. ● Dec 25, Jan 1. &

THIS IS ONE of Europe's leading open-air galleries situated in 45 ha (110 acres) of beautiful 18th-century parkland. Each year a program of large temporary exhibitions of sculpture by international artists is organized alongside the existing collection, which includes work by Barbara Hepworth, Sol LeWitt and Mimmo Paladino. Henry Moore (1898-1986), the Park's first patron, believed that daylight and sun were necessary to appreciate sculpture. Bretton Country Park features his largest European collection.

Large Two Forms (1966–9) by Henry Moore in Bretton Country Park

NORTHUMBRIA

NORTHUMBERLAND · DURHAM · TYNE & WEAR · CLEVELAND

ENGLAND'S NORTHEAST *extremity is a tapestry of moorland, ruins, castles, cathedrals and huddled villages. With Northumberland National Park and Kielder Water reservoir to the north, a rugged eastern coastline, and the cities of Newcastle and Durham to the south, the area combines a dramatic history with abundant natural beauty.*

The empty peaceful hills, elusive wildlife and panoramic vistas of Northumberland National Park belie the area's turbulent past. Warring Scots and English, skirmishing tribes, cattle drovers and whisky smugglers have all left traces on ancient routes through the Cheviot Hills. Slicing through the southern edge of the park is the famous reminder of the Romans' 400-year occupation of Britain, Hadrian's Wall, the northern boundary of their Empire.

Conflict between Scots and English continued for 1,000 years after the Romans departed, and even after the 1603 union between the two crowns. A chain of huge, crenellated medieval castles punctuates the coastline, while other forts that once defended England's northern flank along the River Tweed lie mostly in ruins. Seventh-century Northumbria was the cradle of Christianity under St. Aidan, but this was sharply countered by Viking violence from 793 onward, as the Scandinavian invaders raided the monasteries. But a reverence for Northumbrian saints is in the local psyche, and St. Cuthbert and the Venerable Bede are both buried in Durham Cathedral.

The influence of the Industrial Revolution, concentrated around the mouths of the rivers Tyne, Wear and Tees, made Newcastle upon Tyne the north's main center for coal mining and shipbuilding. Today, the city is famous for its "industrial heritage" attractions and urban renewal plans.

Section of Hadrian's Wall, built by the Romans in about 120, looking east from Cawfields

◁ **The towers of Durham Cathedral, rising above the River Wear**

Eyemout

Exploring Northumbria

BERWICK-UPON-T

HISTORIC SITES ARE PLENTIFUL along Northumbria's coast.
South of Berwick-upon-Tweed, a causeway leads to
the ruined priory and castle on Lindisfarne, and there are
major castles at Bamburgh, Alnwick and Warkworth. The
hinterland is a region of wide open spaces, with wilderness
in the Northumberland National Park, and fascinating Roman
remains of Hadrian's wall at Housesteads and elsewhere.
The glorious city of Durham is dominated by its castle and
cathedral, and Newcastle upon Tyne has a lively nightlife.

SIGHTS AT A GLANCE

Alnwick Castle **5**
Bamburgh **4**
Barnard Castle **17**
Beamish Open Air Museum **13**
Berwick-upon-Tweed **1**
Cheviot Hills **8**
Corbridge **10**
Durham pp414–15 **14**
Farne Islands **3**
Hadrian's Wall pp408–409 **11**
Hexham **9**
Kielder Water **7**
Lindisfarne **2**
Middleton-in-Teesdale **16**
Newcastle upon Tyne **12**
Warkworth Castle **6**

Walks and Tours
North Pennines Tour **15**

SEE ALSO

The wilderness of Upper Coquetdale in the sparsely
populated Cheviot Hills

0 kilometers   10

0 miles   10

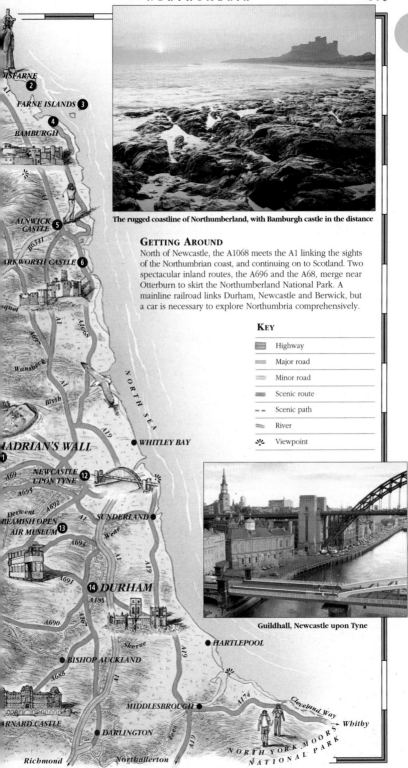

ISFARNE ❷

FARNE ISLANDS ❸

❹

BAMBURGH

ALNWICK CASTLE ❺

ARKWORTH CASTLE ❻

Wansbeck

Blyth

NORTH SEA

HADRIAN'S WALL ❶

NEWCASTLE UPON TYNE ⓬

Derwent

BEAMISH OPEN AIR MUSEUM ⓭

SUNDERLAND

Wear

⓮ **DURHAM**

WHITLEY BAY

Skerne

HARTLEPOOL

BISHOP AUCKLAND

MIDDLESBROUGH

Tees

ARNARD CASTLE

DARLINGTON

Richmond   *Northallerton*

Cleveland Way

→ *Whitby*

NORTH YORK MOORS NATIONAL PARK

The rugged coastline of Northumberland, with Bamburgh castle in the distance

GETTING AROUND

North of Newcastle, the A1068 meets the A1 linking the sights of the Northumbrian coast, and continuing on to Scotland. Two spectacular inland routes, the A696 and the A68, merge near Otterburn to skirt the Northumberland National Park. A mainline railroad links Durham, Newcastle and Berwick, but a car is necessary to explore Northumbria comprehensively.

KEY

▬▬	Highway
▬▬	Major road
▬▬	Minor road
▬▬	Scenic route
--	Scenic path
≋	River
☀	Viewpoint

Guildhall, Newcastle upon Tyne

View over Berwick-upon-Tweed's three bridges

Berwick-upon-Tweed ❶

Northumberland. 🏛 *13,000.*
🚉 🚌 🛈 *Castlegate car park
(01289 330733).* 🚩 *Wed, Sat.*

Between the 12th and 15th centuries Berwick-upon-Tweed changed hands 14 times in the wars between the Scots and English. Its location, at the mouth of the river that divides the two nations, made the town strategically vital.

The English finally gained permanent control in 1482 and maintained Berwick as a massively fortified garrison. Ramparts dating from 1555, 1.5 miles (2.5 km) long and 7 m (23 ft) thick, offer superb views over the Tweed. Within the same 18th-century barracks are the **King's Own Scottish Borderers Regimental Museum**, the town **museum**

and **art gallery**, and **By Beat of Drum**, which charts the history of British infantrymen.

🏛 King's Own Scottish Borderers Regimental Museum

The Barracks. 🕿 *01289 307427.*
🕐 *Mon–Sat.* ⬤ *Dec 23–Jan 3, public hols.* 🖼

Lindisfarne ❷

Northumberland. 🚉 🚌 *Berwick-upon-Tweed then bus.* 🛈 *Castlegate car park (01289 330733).*

Twice daily a long, narrow neck of land sinks under the North Sea tide for five hours, separating Lindisfarne, or Holy Island, from the coast. At low tide, visitors stream over the causeway to the island made famous by St. Aidan, St. Cuthbert and the Lindisfarne gospels. Nothing remains of

the Celtic monks' monastery, finally abandoned in 875 after successive Viking attacks, but the magnificent arches of the 11th-century **Lindisfarne Priory** are still visible, and they soar above the grass.

After 1540, stones from the priory were used to build **Lindisfarne Castle**, which was restored and made into a private home by Sir Edwin Lutyens *(see p25)* in 1903. It includes an attractive walled garden created by Gertrude Jekyll *(see p23).*

⛪ Lindisfarne Castle

(NT) Holy Island. 🕿 *01289 389244.*
🕐 *Apr–Oct: Sat–Thu & Good Fri (pm).* 🖼

Farne Islands ❸

(NT) Northumberland. 🛥 *from Seahouses.* 🛈 *Castlegate car park (01289 330733).*

There are between 15 and 28 Farne Islands off Bamburgh, some 10 miles (16 km) south of Lindisfarne, some of them periodically covered by the sea. The highest is 31 m (100 ft) above sea level. Wildlife wardens and lighthouse keepers share them with seals, puffins and other seabirds.

Boat tours depart from **Seahouses** harbor and can only land on Staple and Inner Farne, site of St. Cuthbert's 14th-century chapel.

Lindisfarne Castle (1540), the main landmark on the island of Lindisfarne

Celtic Christianity

St. Cuthbert on a sea voyage

THE IRISH MONK St. Aidan arrived in Northumbria in 635 from the island of Iona, off western Scotland, to evangelize the north of England. He founded the monastery on the island of Lindisfarne, and it became one of the most important centers for Christianity in England. This and other monastic communities thrived in Northumbria, becoming rich in scholarship, although the monks lived simply. It also emerged as a place of pilgrimage after miracles were reported at the shrine of St. Cuthbert, Lindisfarne's most famous bishop. But the monks' pacifism made them defenseless against 9th-century Viking raids.

St. Aidan's Monastery *was added to over the centuries to become Lindisfarne Priory. This 8th-century relic with interlaced animal decorations is from a cross at the site.*

The Venerable Bede *(673–735), the most brilliant early medieval scholar, was a monk at the monastery of St. Paul in Jarrow. He wrote* The Ecclesiastical History of the English People *in 731.*

St. Aidan *(600–651), an Irish missionary, founded a monastery at Lindisfarne and became Bishop of Northumbria in 635. This 1960 sculpture of him, by Kathleen Parbury, is in Lindisfarne Priory grounds.*

St. Cuthbert *(635–87) was the monk and miracle worker most revered of all. He lived as a hermit on Inner Farne (a chapel was built there in his memory) and later became Bishop of Lindisfarne.*

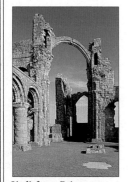

Lindisfarne Priory *was built by Benedictines in the 11th century, on the site of St. Aidan's earlier monastery.*

THE LINDISFARNE GOSPELS

This book of richly illustrated portrayals of Gospel stories is one of the masterpieces of the "Northumbrian Renaissance" that left a permanent mark on Christian art and history. The work was carried out by monks at Lindisfarne under the direction of Bishop Eadfrith, around 700. Monks saved the book *(see p109)* and carried it with them when they fled from Lindisfarne in 875 after suffering repeated Viking raids. Many other treasures were plundered.

Elaborately decorated initial to the *Gospel of St. Matthew* (c.725)

Illustration of Grace Darling from the 1881 edition of *Sunday at Home*

Bamburgh ❹

Northumberland. 🏛 1,100.
🚋 Berwick. 🛈 Castlegate Car Pk
(01289 330733).

Due to Northumbria's history of hostility against the Scots, there are more strongholds and castles here than in any other part of England. Most were built from the 11th to the 15th centuries by local warlords, and Bamburgh's red sandstone **castle** is one such great coastal fortress. Its position on an outcrop had been fortified since prehistoric times, but the first major stronghold was built in 550 by a Saxon chieftain, Ida the Flamebearer.

In its heyday between 1095 and 1464, Bamburgh was the royal castle that was used by the Northumbrian kings for coronations. By the end of the Middle Ages it had fallen into obscurity, but in 1894 it was bought by Newcastle arms tycoon Lord Armstrong, who restored it. Works of art are exhibited in the cavernous Great Hall, and there are suits of armor and medieval artifacts in the basement.

Bamburgh's other main attraction is the tiny **Grace Darling Museum** that celebrates the bravery of the 23-year-old, who, in 1838, rowed through tempestuous seas with her father, the keeper of the Longstone lighthouse, to rescue nine people from the wrecked *Forfarshire* steamboat.

🏰 **Bamburgh Castle**
Bamburgh. 📞 01668 214208.
🕐 Easter–Oct: daily. 🅿 ♿
🏛 **Grace Darling Museum**
Radcliffe Rd. 📞 01665 214465.
🕐 Good Fri–Sep: daily. ♿

Alnwick Castle ❺

Alnwick, Northumberland. 📞 01665 510777. 🚋 Alnmouth. 🕐 Easter–mid-Oct: daily. 🅿 ♿ limited.

Dominating the market town on the River Aln, is another great fortress, Alnwick Castle. Described by the Victorians as the "Windsor of the north," it is the main seat of the Duke of Northumberland, whose family, the Percys, have lived here since 1309. This border stronghold has survived many battles, but now peacefully dominates the pretty market town of Alnwick, overlooking landscape designed by Capability Brown. The stern medieval exterior belies the fine treasure house within, furnished in palatial Renaissance style with an exquisite collection of Meissen china and paintings by Titian, Van Dyck and Canaletto. The Postern Tower contains a collection of early British and Roman relics. The **Regimental Museum of Royal Northumberland Fusiliers** is in the Abbot's Tower. Among other attractions are the Percy state coach, the dungeon, the gun terrace and superb countryside views.

Carrara marble fireplace (1840) at Alnwick Castle

Warkworth Castle ❻

Nr Amble. 📞 01665 711423.
🕐 daily. ● Jan 1, Dec 24–26. 🅿
♿ limited.

Warkworth castle sits on a green hill overlooking the River Coquet. It was the Percy family home at a time when Alnwick Castle lay derelict. Shakespeare's *Henry V* features the castle in scenes between the Earl of Northumberland and his son, Harry Hotspur. Much of the present-day castle remains date from the 14th century. The unusual turreted, cross-shaped keep, which was added in the 15th century, is a central feature of the castle tour.

Warkworth Castle reflected in the River Coquet

Kielder Water ❼

Yarrow Moor, Falstone, Hexham.
📞 01434 240398. 🕐 daily. ● Dec 24, 25, Jan 1, 2. ♿

One of the top attractions of Northumberland, Kielder Water lies close to the Scottish border, surrounded by spectacular scenery. With a perimeter of 27 miles (44 km), it is Europe's largest man-made lake, and offers facilities for sailing, windsurfing, canoeing, water-skiing and fishing. In summer, the cruiser *Osprey* departs from Leaplish on trips around the lake. The Kielder Water Exhibition, next to the Tower Knowe Visitor Centre, depicts the history of the valley from the Ice Age to the present day.

Cheviot Hills ⓼

THESE BARE, LONELY MOORS, smoothed into rounded humps by Ice Age glaciers, form a natural border with Scotland. Walkers and outdoor enthusiasts find a near-wilderness unmatched anywhere else in England. This most remote part of the Northumberland National Park nevertheless has a long and vivid history. Roman legions, warring Scots and English border raiders, cattle drovers and whisky smugglers have all left traces along the ancient routes and tracks they carved out here.

VISITORS' CHECKLIST

Northumberland. 🚆 Berwick-upon-Tweed. 🛈 Eastburn, South Park, Hexham. 📞 01434 605555.

The Cheviots' isolated burns and streams are among the last habitats in England for the shy, elusive otter.

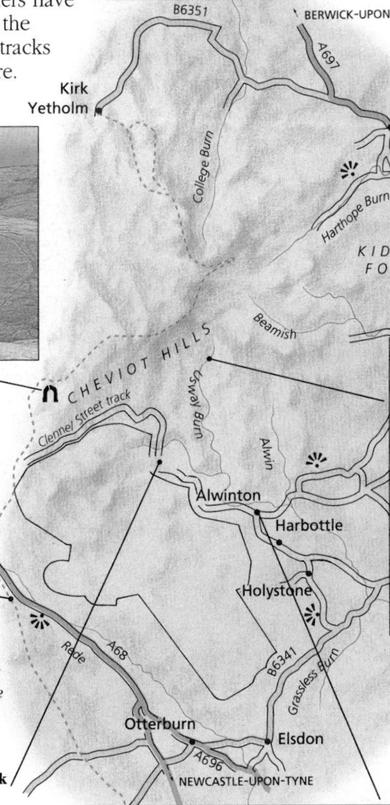

Chew Green Camp, which to the Romans was ad fines, or, "toward the last place," has fine views from the remaining fortified earthworks.

The Pennine Way starts in Derbyshire and ends at Kirk Yetholm in Scotland. The final stage (shown here) goes past Byrness, crosses the Cheviots and traces the Scottish border.

Uswayford Farm track

Uswayford Farm, is perhaps the most remote farm in England, and one of the hardest to reach. It is set in deserted moorland.

KEY

▭▭▭ A roads

▭▭▭ B roads

▭▭▭ Minor roads

--- Pennine Way

☀ Viewpoint

0 kilometers 5

0 miles 5

Alwinton, a tiny village built mainly from gray stone, is situated beside the River Coquet. It is an access point for many fine walks in the area, and the wild landscape is deserted except for sheep.

Hexham 9

Northumberland. 🏃 10,000. 🚋 🚌
ℹ The Manor Office, Hallgate (01434 605225). 🏠 Tue.

THE BUSY MARKET TOWN of Hexham was established in the 7th century, growing up around the church and monastery built by St. Wilfrid, but the Vikings sacked and looted it in 876. In 1114, Augustinians began work on a priory and abbey, building on the original church ruins to create

Hexham Abbey, which still towers over the market square today. The atmospheric Saxon crypt, built partly with stones from the former Roman fort at Corbridge, is all that remains

Ancient stone carvings at Hexham Abbey

of St. Wilfrid's Church. The south transept of the abbey has a 12th-century night stair: stone steps leading from the dormitory. In the chancel is the Frith Stool, a Saxon throne in the center of a circle which gave protection to fugitives. Narrow medieval streets and alleys, many with Georgian and Victorian shopfronts, spread out from the market square, The 15th-century Moot Hall was once a council chamber, and the old jail contains a **museum** charting border history.

Hadrian's Wall 10

ON THE ORDERS of Emperor Hadrian, work began in 120 on a 73 mile (117 km) wall to be erected across northern England, to mark and defend the northern limits of the British province and the northwest boundary of the Roman Empire. Troops were stationed at milecastles spaced along the wall, and large turrets, later forts, were built at 5 mile (8 km) intervals. The wall, now owned by the National Trust, was abandoned in 383 as the Roman Empire crumbled, but much of it remains.

Location of Hadrian's Wall

Vindolanda is the site of several forts. The first timber fort dated from AD 90 and a stone fort was not built until the 2nd century. The museum has a collection of Roman writing tablets providing details of food, clothes and work.

Carvoran Fort is probably pre-Hadrianic. Little of the fort survives, but the Roman Army museum nearby covers the wall's history.

Great Chesters Fort was built facing east to guard Caw Gap, but there are few remains today. To the south and east of the fort are traces of a civil settlement and a bathhouse.

Housesteads Settlement includes the remains of terraced shops or taverns.

Emperor Hadrian (76–138) came to Britain in 120 to order a stronger defense system. Coins were often cast to record emperors' visits, such as this bronze sestertius. Until 1971, the penny was abbreviated to d, short for denarius, a Roman coin.

Cawfields, 2 miles (3 km) north of Haltwhistle, is the access point to one of the highest and most rugged sections of the wall. To the east, the remains of a milecastle sit on Whin Sill crag.

🏛 **Hexham Abbey**
Market Sq. ☎ 01434 602031.
🕐 daily. ♿
🏛 **Border History Museum**
Old Jail, nr Market Place. ☎ 01434
652349. 🕐 Easter–Oct: daily; Nov,
Feb–Easter: Sat–Tue. 🗺

Corbridge ⑩

Northumberland. 🏘 3,500. 🚆
ℹ Hill St (01434 632815).

THIS QUIET TOWN conceals a
few historic buildings
constructed with stones from
the Roman garrison town of

**The parson's 14th-century forti-
fied tower house at Corbridge**

nearby Corstopitum. Among
these are the thickset Saxon
tower of St. Andrew's Church
and the 14th-century fortified
tower house built to protect
the local clergyman. Excavations of Corstopitum, now
known as **Corbridge Roman
Site and Museum**, have
exposed earlier forts, a well-
preserved granary, temples,
fountains and an aqueduct.

🏛 **Corbridge Roman Site
and Museum**
☎ 01434 632349. 🕐 Apr–Sep:
daily; Oct–Mar: Wed–Sun. ● Dec
25, 26, Jan 1. 🗺 ♿ limited.

THE WALL COAST-TO-COAST

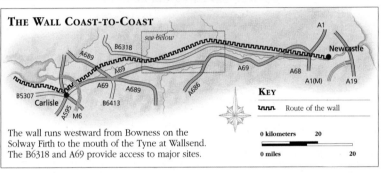

see below

Newcastle

KEY

〰〰 Route of the wall

0 kilometers   20

0 miles   20

The wall runs westward from Bowness on the
Solway Firth to the mouth of the Tyne at Wallsend.
The B6318 and A69 provide access to major sites.

Carrawburgh Fort, a 500-man
garrison, guarded the Newbrough
Burn and North Tyndale approaches.

Limestone Corner Milecastle is
sited at the northernmost part of
the wall and has magnificent views
of the Cheviot Hills *(see p407)*.

Sewingshields Milecastle, *with
magnificent views west to Housesteads,
is one of the best places for walking.
This reconstruction shows the layout
of a Roman milecastle on the wall.*

Chesters Fort was a
bridgehead over the
North Tyne. In the
museum are altars, sculp-
tures and inscriptions.

Chesters Bridge crossed the
Tyne. The original Hadrianic
bridge was rebuilt in 207. The
remains of this second bridge
abutment can still be seen.

Housesteads Fort *is the best-
preserved site on the wall, with
fine views over the countryside.
The excavated remains include
the commanding officer's house
and a Roman hospital.*

0 meters   500

0 yards   500

Newcastle upon Tyne ⑫

Tyne & Wear. 🏛 273,000. ✈ 🚆
🅿 🚢 ℹ *Central Library, Princess Sq (0191 2610610).* 🚌 *Sun.*

NEWCASTLE OWES ITS NAME to its Norman **castle** which was founded in 1080 by Robert Curthose, the eldest son of William the Conqueror *(see p47).* The Romans had bridged the Tyne and built a fort on the site 1,000 years earlier. During the Middle Ages it was still a fortress town guarding the mouth of the river and was used as a base for English campaigns against the Scots. From the Middle Ages on, the city flourished as a coal mining and exporting center. It was known in the 19th century for

engineering, steel production and later as the world's foremost shipyard. The city's industrial base has declined in recent years, but "Geordies," as inhabitants of the city are known, have refocused their civic pride on the ultramodern Metro Centre shopping mall

Bridges crossing the Tyne at Newcastle

at Gateshead, some 4 miles (6 km) southwest of the city, and Newcastle United soccer team. The city's lively night scene includes clubs, pubs, theaters and ethnic restaurants. The visible trappings of its past are reflected in the magnificent Tyne Bridge and in Benjamin Green's monument commemorating Earl Grey. The grand façades of city center thoroughfares, such as Grey Street, also reflect this former prosperity. Despite some derelict areas, many buildings on the quayside are being restored.

🏰 **The Castle**
St. Nicholas St. ☏ *0191 2327938.* ⏰ *Tue–Sun & public hols.* ● *Dec 25, 26, Jan 1, Good Fri.* 🎫
Curthose's original wooden "new castle" was rebuilt in stone in

Beamish Open Air Museum ⑬

Tram symbol

THIS GIANT OPEN AIR MUSEUM, spread over 120 ha (300 acres) of County Durham, re-creates an authentic picture of family, working and community life in the northeast before World War I. It has a typical High Street, a colliery village, abandoned mine, a school, chapel and farm, all with guides in period costume. A restored trolleyline serves the different parts of the museum, which carefully avoids romanticizing the past.

The station has locomotives, coaches, freight trucks, a platform, a signal box and a wrought-iron footbridge. Working locomotives are often found in station and colliery areas.

Home Farm *re-creates the atmosphere of an old-fashioned farmyard. Rare breeds of cattle and sheep, more common before the advent of mass breeding, can be seen.*

School

Miners' houses were tiny, oil-lit dwellings, backing onto vegetable plots and owned by the colliery.

Chapel

the 12th century. Only the thickset, crenellated keep remains intact with two suites of royal apartments. A series of staircases spiral up to the renovated battlements, from where there are fine views over the city and the Tyne. The castle also has a restored Norman chapel (c.1168–78), Great Hall and garrison room.

�︎ St. Nicholas Cathedral
St. Nicholas Sq. 📞 *0191 2321939.* ◯ *daily.* ♿
This is one of Britain's tiniest cathedrals. There are remnants inside of the original 11th-century Norman church on which the present 14th- and 15th-century structure was founded. Its most striking feature is its ornate "lantern tower" – half tower, half spire – of which there are only three others in Britain. First built in 1448, it was rebuilt in 1608, then repaired during the 18th and 19th centuries.

Reredos of the Northumbrian saints in St. Nicholas Cathedral

🏛 Bessie Surtees' House
41–44 Sandhill. 📞 *0191 2611585.* ◯ *Mon–Fri.* ● *Dec 25, 26, Jan 1, public hols.*
The story of beautiful, wealthy Bessie, who lived here before eloping with penniless John Scott, later Lord Chancellor of

England, is the romantic tale behind these half-timbered 16th- and 17th-century houses. The window through which Bessie escaped now has a blue glass pane. These buildings also throw light on mercantile life in the quayside district.

🏛 Tyne Bridge
Newcastle–Gateshead. 📞 *0191 2328520.* ◯ *daily.* ♿
Opened by King George V in 1928, this two-pin steel arch was the longest of its type in Britain with a span of 162 m (531 ft). Designed by Mott, Hay and Anderson, it soon became the city's most potent symbol.

🏛 Earl Grey's Monument
Grey St. 📞 *0191 2328520.* ◯ *Easter 1996.* 📷
Benjamin Green created this memorial to the 2nd Earl Grey, Liberal Prime Minister from 1830 to 1834 and responsible for the Great Reform Bill. The statue is by Edward H. Baily.

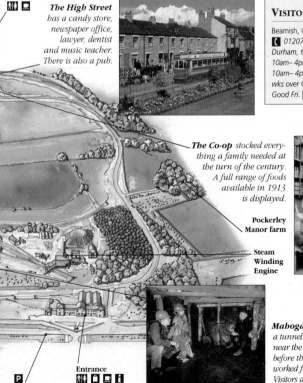

🚶 🖼 *The High Street has a candy store, newspaper office, lawyer, dentist and music teacher. There is also a pub.*

The Co-op stocked everything a family needed at the turn of the century. A full range of foods available in 1913 is displayed.

Pockerley Manor farm

Steam Winding Engine

Entrance
🚶 📷 🖼 �︎

P

Mahogany Drift mine, a tunnel driven into coal seams near the surface, was here long before the museum and was worked from the 1850s to 1958. Visitors are given guided tours to underground pits.

Houses built by the London Lead Company in Middleton-in-Teesdale

Durham ⑭

See pp414–5.

North Pennines Tour ⑮

See p413.

Cotherstone cheese, a specialty of the Middleton-in-Teesdale area

Middleton-in-Teesdale ⑯

County Durham. 🏠 *1,100.* 🚃 *Darlington.* ℹ️ *1C Chapel Row.*

CLINGING TO A HILLSIDE amid wild Pennine scenery on the River Tees is the old lead mining town of Middleton-in-Teesdale. Many of its rows of gray stone cottages were built by the London Lead Company, a paternalistic, Quaker-run organization whose influence spread to every corner of its employees' daily lives.

The company began mining in 1753, and soon it virtually owned the town. Workers were expected to observe strict temperance, send their children to Sunday school and conform to the many company maxims. Today, mining has all but ceased in Teesdale, with Middleton standing as a monument to the 18th-century idea of the "company town." The offices of the London Lead Company can still be seen, as well as Nonconformist chapels from the era and a memorial fountain made of iron.

The crumbly Cotherstone sheep's cheese, a specialty of the surrounding dales, is widely available in the shops.

Barnard Castle ⑰

County Durham. 🏠 *5,000.* 🚃 *Darlington.* ℹ️ *43 Galgate (01833 690909).* 🛒 *Wed.*

BARNARD CASTLE, known in the area as "Barney," is a little town full of character, with old storefronts and a cobbled market overlooked by the ruins of the Norman castle from which it takes its name. The original Barnard Castle was built around 1125–40 by Bernard Balliol, ancestor of the founder of Balliol College, Oxford *(see p211)*, to guard a river crossing point. Later, the market town grew up around the fortification.

Today, Barnard Castle is known for the extraordinary French-style château to the east of the town, surrounded by acres of formal gardens. Started in 1860 by the local aristocrat John Bowes and his French wife Josephine, an artist and actress, it was never a private residence, but always intended to be a museum and public monument. The château finally opened in 1892, by which time the Bowes's were dead. Nevertheless, the **Bowes Museum** stands as a monument to his wealth and her extravagance.

The museum houses a strong collection of Spanish art that includes El Greco's *The Tears of St. Peter*, dating from the 1580s, and Goya's *Don Juan Meléndez Váldez*, painted in 1797. Clocks, porcelain, furniture, musical instruments, toys and tapestries are among its treasures, with a mechanical silver swan as a showpiece.

🏛 **Bowes Museum**
Barnard Castle. 📞 *01833 690606.* ⭕ *daily (Sun: pm).* ● *Dec 19–26, Jan 1.* 🔲 🚻

The Bowes Museum, a French-style château near Barnard Castle

North Pennines Tour ⑮

STARTING JUST TO THE SOUTH of Hadrian's Wall, this tour explores the South Tyne Valley, and Upper Weardale. It crosses one of England's wildest and most remote tracts of moorland, then heads north again. The high ground is mainly blanketed with heather, dotted with sheep or crisscrossed with drystone

Sheep grazing on the moors

walls, a feature of this region. Harriers and other birds hover above, and streams tumble into valleys of tightly huddled villages.

Celts, Romans and other settlers have left imprints on the North Pennines. The wealth of the area was based on lead mining and stone quarrying, which has long coexisted with farming.

Haltwhistle ①
In the Church of the Holy Cross is the tomb of John Ridley, brother of Anglican martyr Nicholas Ridley *(see p211)*.

Haydon Bridge ③
There are some delightful walks near this spa town where the painter John Martin was born in 1789. Nearby Langley Castle is worth a visit.

Hexham ④
A picturesque old town *(see p409)*, Hexham has a fine abbey.

Blanchland ⑤
Some houses in this 17th-century lead-mining village, are built on the site of a 12th-century abbey, using pieces of the original stone.

Bardon Mill ②
To the north is the Roman fort and civilian settlement of Vindolanda *(see p408)*.

Allendale ⑦
With its capital at Allendale Town, this is an area of spectacular scenery, with many trout-fishing and walking opportunities.

Stanhope ⑥
An 18th-century castle overlooks the market square. The giant stump of a fossilized tree, said to be 250 million years old, guards the graveyard.

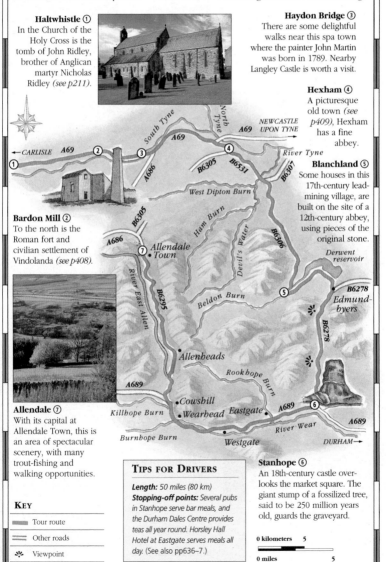

KEY

▬▬ Tour route

═══ Other roads

☆ Viewpoint

TIPS FOR DRIVERS

Length: 50 miles (80 km)
Stopping-off points: Several pubs in Stanhope serve bar meals, and the Durham Dales Centre provides teas all year round. Horsley Hall Hotel at Eastgate serves meals all day. (See also pp636–7.)

0 kilometers   5

0 miles   5

Durham ⑭

Cathedral Sanctuary knocker

THE CITY OF DURHAM was built on Island Hill or "Dunholm" in 995. This rocky peninsula, which defies the course of the River Wear's route to the sea, was chosen as the last resting place for the remains of Saint Cuthbert. The relics of the Venerable Bede were brought to the site 27 years later, adding to its attraction for pilgrims. Durham Cathedral was treated by architects as an experiment for geometric patterning, while the Castle served as the Episcopal Palace until 1832, when Bishop William van Mildert gave it up and surrendered part of his income to found Britain's third university. The 23 ha (57 acre) peninsula has many foot-paths, views and fine buildings.

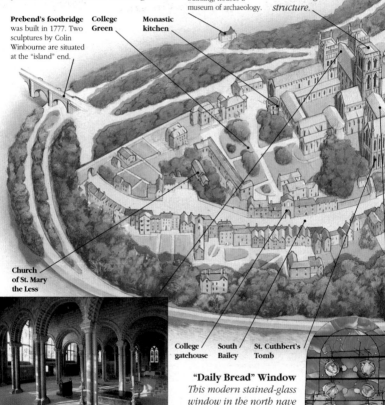

Old Fulling Mill, a largely 18th-century building, houses a museum of archaeology.

★ Cathedral
Built from 1093 to 1274, it is a striking Norman structure.

Prebend's footbridge was built in 1777. Two sculptures by Colin Winbourne are situated at the "island" end.

College Green

Monastic kitchen

Church of St. Mary the Less

College gatehouse

South Bailey

St. Cuthbert's Tomb

"Daily Bread" Window
This modern stained-glass window in the north nave aisle was donated in 1984 by a local department store.

Galilee Chapel
Architects began work on the exotic Galilee Chapel in 1170, drawing inspiration from the Great Mosque of Cordoba in Andalucia. It was altered by Bishop Langley (d.1437) whose tomb is by the west door.

STAR SIGHTS

★ **Cathedral**

★ **Castle**

★ Castle

Begun in 1072, the castle is a fine Norman fortress. The keep, built on a mound, is now part of the university.

Town Hall (1851)

St. Nicholas' Church (1857)

alace
Green

VISITORS' CHECKLIST

County Durham. 🚋 Station Approach. 🚌 North Rd. ℹ️ Market Pl (0191 384 3720). 🏛️ Sat. **Cathedral** ◯ May–Sep: 7:15am–8pm; Oct–Apr: 7:15am– 6pm. ✝️ 10:15am Sun. 📷 ♿ **Castle** ☎ 0191 374 3800. ◯ *univ hols: daily; term: Mon, Wed, Sat (pm).* 📷 🍴 ♿ 🚻

Tunstal's Chapel

Situated at the end of the Tunstal's Gallery, the castle chapel was built c.1542. Its fine woodwork includes this unicorn misericord (see p327).

University buildings were built by Bishop John Cosin in the 17th century.

Castle Gatehouse

Traces of Norman stone-work can be seen in the outer arch, while the sturdy walls and upper floors are 18th-century, rebuilt in a style dubbed "gothick" by detractors.

urch of St.
ary le Bow

**Kingsgate
ootbridge,**
built from
62–3, leads
to North
Bailey.

CATHEDRAL ARCHITECTURE

The vast dimensions of the 900-year-old columns, piers and vaults, and the inventive giant lozenge and chevron, trellis and dogtooth patterns carved into the stone columns are the main innovative features of Durham cathedral. It is believed that 11th- and 12th-century architects such as Bishop Ranulph Flambard tried to unify all parts of the structure. This can be seen in the south aisle of the nave below.

Ribbed vaults, growing logically out from the walls, are now common in church ceilings. One of the major achievements of Gothic architecture, they were first built at Durham.

The lozenge shape is a pattern from prehistoric carving, but never before seen in a cathedral.

Chevron patterns on some of the piers in the nave are evidence of Moorish influence.

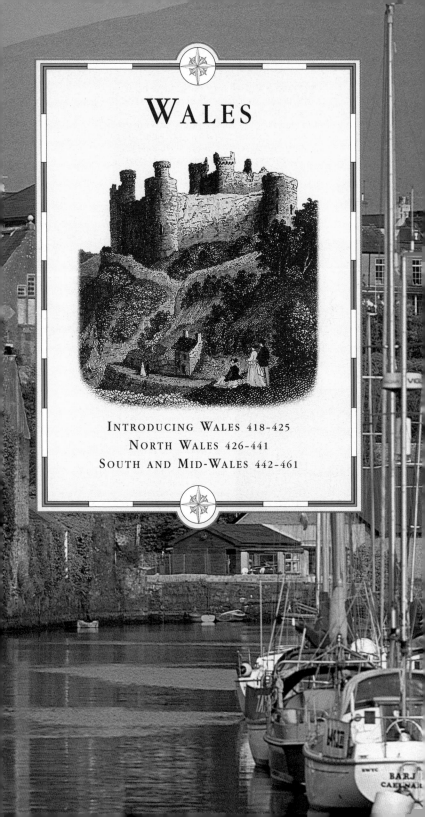

WALES

Wales at a Glance

WALES IS A COUNTRY OF outstanding natural beauty with varied landscapes. Visitors come to climb dramatic mountain peaks, go walking in the forests, fish in the broad rivers and enjoy the miles of unspoiled coastline. The country's many seaside resorts have long been popular with English vacationers. As well as outdoor pursuits there is the vibrancy of Welsh culture, with its strong Celtic roots, to be experienced. Finally, there are many fine castles, ruined abbeys, mansions and cities full of magnificent architecture.

Anglesey

Caernarfonshire & Merionethshire

Beaumaris Castle *was intended to be a key part of Edward I's "iron ring" to contain the rebellious Welsh (see p422). Begun in 1295 but never completed, the castle (see p424) has a sophisticated defense structure that is unparalleled in Wales.*

Portmeirion (see pp440–41) *is a private village whose astonishing buildings seem rather incongruous in the Welsh landscape. The village was created by the architect Sir Clough Williams-Ellis to fulfill a personal ambition. Some of the buildings are assembled from pieces of architecture taken from sites around the country.*

Cardig

Carmarthenshi

Pembrokeshire

St. David's *is the smallest city in Britain. The cathedral (see pp450–51) is the largest in Wales, and its nave is noted for its carved oak roof and beautiful rood screen. Next to the cathedral is the medieval Bishop's Palace, now a ruin.*

◁ **Caernarfon's colorful quayside marina**

Llanberis and Snowdon
(see p437) *is an area famous for dangerous, high peaks, long popular with climbers. Mount Snowdon's summit is most easily reached from Llanberis. Its Welsh name,* Yr Wyddfa Fawr, *means "great tomb" and is the legendary burial place of a giant slain by King Arthur (see p269).*

Flintshire

erconwy
Colwyn
Denbighshire

NORTH WALES
(see pp426–41)

Wrexham

Conwy Castle *guards one of the best-preserved medieval fortified towns in Britain (see pp432–3). Built by Edward I, the castle was, besieged and came close to surrender in 1294. It was taken by Owain Glyndŵr's supporters in 1401.*

Powys

SOUTH AND MID-WALES
(see pp442–61)

The Brecon Beacons *(see pp454–5) is a national park, a lovely area of mountains, forest and moorland in South Wales, which is a favorite with walkers and naturalists. Pen-y-Fan is one of the principal summits.*

Monmouthshire

ardiff, Swansea & Environs

Cardiff Castle's *(see pp458–9), Clock Tower is just one of many 19th-century additions by the eccentric but gifted architect William Burges. His flamboyant style still delights and amazes visitors.*

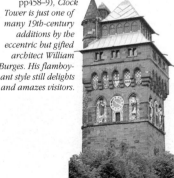

0 kilometers   25

0 miles   25

A PORTRAIT OF WALES

ONG POPULAR WITH BRITISH VACATIONERS, *the many charms of Wales are now becoming better known internationally. They include spectacular scenery and a vibrant culture specializing in male-voice choirs, poetry and a passionate love of team sports. Despite having been governed from Westminster since 1536, Wales is very much a country with its own distinct Celtic identity.*

Much of the Welsh landmass is covered by the Cambrian Mountain range, which effectively acts as a barrier from England. Wales is warmed by the Gulf Stream and has a mild climate, with more rain than most of Britain. The land is unsuitable for arable farming, but sheep and cattle thrive; the drove roads, along which sheep used to be driven across the hills to England, are now popular walking trails. It is partly because of the rugged terrain that the Welsh have managed to maintain their separate identity and their ancient language.

One of Wales's splendid National Parks

Welsh is an expansive, musical language, spoken by only one-fifth of the 2.7 million inhabitants, but in parts of North Wales it is still the main language of conversation. There is an official bilingual policy: road signs are in Welsh and English, even in areas where Welsh is little spoken. Welsh

Mountain sheep – a familiar sight in rural Wales

place names intrigue visitors, being made up of native words that describe features of the landscape or ancient buildings. Examples include *Aber* (river mouth), *Afon* (river), *Fach* (little), *Llan* (church), *Llyn* (lake) and *Nant* (valley).

The Romans conquered Wales, but the Saxons did not. The land and the people therefore retained their Celtic patterns of settlement and husbandry for six centuries before the Norman Conquest in 1066. This allowed time for the development of a distinctive Welsh nation whose homogeneity continues to this day.

The early Norman kings subjugated the Welsh by appointing "Marcher Lords" to control the areas that bordered England. A string of huge castles provides evidence of the turbulent years when Welsh insurrection was a constant threat. It was not until 1535 that Wales formally became part of Britain, and today it is governed from Westminster, with a cabinet minister responsible for its affairs.

Rugby, the popular Welsh sport

Religious nonconformism and radical politics are deeply rooted in Welsh consciousness. Saint David converted the country to Christianity in the 6th century. Methodism, chapel and teetotalism became firmly entrenched in

A *gorsedd* (assembly) of bards at the eisteddfod

of music derives from the ancient bards: minstrels and poets, who may have been associated with the Druids. Bardic tales of quasihistorical figures and magic were part of the oral tradition of the Dark Ages. They were first written down in the 14th century as the *Mabinogion,* which has inspired Welsh poets up to the 20th century's Dylan Thomas. The male-voice choirs found in many towns, villages and factories, particularly in the industrial south, express the Welsh musical heritage. Choirs compete in *eisteddfods:* festivals that celebrate Welsh culture.

the Welsh psyche during the 19th century. Even today some pubs stay closed on Sundays (alcohol is not sold at all in the Llŷn Peninsula). A longstanding oral tradition in Wales has produced many outstanding public speakers, politicians and actors. Welsh labor leaders have played important roles in the British trade union movement and the development of socialism.

Welsh heritage is steeped in song, music, poetry and legend rather than handicrafts, although one notable exception is the carved Welsh lovespoon – a craft recently revived. The well-known Welsh love

Welsh lovespoon

In the 19th century, the opening of the South Wales coalfield in Mid-Glamorgan – for a time the biggest in the world – led to an industrial boom, with mass migration from the countryside to the iron- and steelworks. This prosperity was not to last: apart from a brief respite in World War II, the coal industry has been in terminal decline for decades, causing severe economic hardship. Today tourism is being promoted in the hope that the wealth generated, by outdoor activities in particular, will be able to take "King Coal's" place.

Conwy's picturesque, medieval walled town, fronted by a colorful harbor

The History of Wales

WALES HAS BEEN SETTLED since prehistoric times, its history shaped by many factors, from invasion to industrialization. The Romans set up bases in the mountainous terrain, but it was effectively a separate Celtic nation when Offa's Dike was built as the border with England in 770. Centuries of cross-border raids and military campaigns followed before England and Wales were formally united by the Act of Union in 1535. The rugged northwest, the former stronghold of the Welsh princes, remains the heartland of Welsh language and culture.

St. David, patron saint of Wales

Owain Glyndŵr, heroic leader of Welsh opposition to English rule

THE CELTIC NATION

Ornamental Iron Age bronze plaque from Anglesey

WALES WAS SETTLED by waves of migrants in prehistoric times. By the Iron Age *(see p42)*, Celtic farmers had established hillforts and their religion, Druidism. From the 1st century AD until the legions withdrew around 400, the Romans built fortresses and roads and mined lead, silver and gold. During the next 200 years, Wales was converted to Christianity by missionaries from Europe. St. David *(see pp450–51)*, the Welsh patron saint, is said to have turned the leek into a national symbol. He persuaded soldiers to wear leeks in their hats to distinguish themselves from Saxons during a 6th-century skirmish.

The Saxons *(see pp46–7)* failed to conquer Wales, and in 770 the Saxon King Offa built a defensive earthwork along the unconquered territory *(see p447)*. Beyond Offa's Dike the people called themselves *Y Cymry* (fellow countrymen) and the land *Cymru*. The Saxons called the land "Wales" from the Old English *wealas*, meaning foreigners. It was divided into kingdoms of which the main ones were Gwynedd in the north, Powys in the center and Dyfed in the south. There were strong trade, cultural and linguistic links between each.

MARCHER LORDS

THE NORMAN INVASION of 1066 *(see p47)* did not reach Wales, but the border territory ("the Marches") was given by William the Conqueror to three powerful barons based at Shrewsbury, Hereford and Chester. These Marcher Lords made many incursions into Wales and controlled most of the lowlands. But the Welsh

Edward I designating his son Prince of Wales in 1301

princes held the mountainous northwest and exploited English weaknesses. Under Llywelyn the Great (d.1240), North Wales was almost completely independent; in 1267 his grandson, Llywelyn the Last, was acknowledged as Prince of Wales by Henry III.

In 1272 Edward I came to the English throne. He built fortresses and embarked on a military campaign to conquer Wales. In 1282 Llywelyn was killed in a skirmish, a shattering blow for the Welsh. Edward introduced English law and proclaimed his son Prince of Wales *(see p430)*.

OWAIN GLYNDŴR'S REBELLION

WELSH RESENTMENT against the Marcher Lords led to rebellion. In 1400 Owain Glyndŵr (c.1350–1416), a descendant of the Welsh princes, laid waste to English-dominated towns and castles. Declaring himself Prince of Wales, he found Celtic allies in Scotland, Ireland, France and Northumbria. In 1404 Glyndŵr captured Harlech and Cardiff, and formed a parliament in Machynlleth *(see p448)*. In 1408 the French made a truce with the English king, Henry IV. The rebellion then failed and Glyndŵr went into hiding until his death.

UNION WITH ENGLAND

WALES SUFFERED greatly during the Wars of the Roses *(see p49)* as Yorkists and Lancastrians tried to gain control of the strategically important Welsh castles. The wars ended in 1485, and the Welshman Henry Tudor, born in Pembroke, became Henry VII. The Act of Union in 1535 and other laws abolished the Marcher Lordships, giving Wales parliamentary representation in London instead. English practices replaced inheritance customs, and English became the language of the courts and administration. The Welsh language survived, partly helped by the church and by Dr. William Morgan's translation of the Bible in 1588.

Miners from South Wales pictured in 1910

Vernacular Bible, which helped to keep the Welsh language alive

INDUSTRY AND RADICAL POLITICS

THE INDUSTRIALIZATION of south and east Wales began with the development of open-cast coal mining near Wrexham and Merthyr Tydfil in the 1760s. Convenient ports and the arrival of the railroads helped the process. By the second half of the 19th century open-cast mines had been superseded by deep pits in the Rhondda Valley.

Living and working conditions were poor for industrial and agricultural workers. A series of "Rebecca Riots" in South Wales between 1839 and 1843, involving tenant farmers (dressed as women) protesting about tithes and rents, was forcibly suppressed. The Chartists, trade unions and the Liberal Party had much Welsh support.

The rise of Methodism *(see p265)* roughly paralleled the growth of industry: 80 percent of the population was Methodist by 1851. The Welsh language persisted, despite attempts by the British government to discourage its use, which included punishing children caught speaking it.

WALES TODAY

IN THE 20TH CENTURY the Welsh, for the first time, became a power in British politics. David Lloyd George, although not born in Wales, grew up there and was the first British Prime Minister to come from a Welsh family. Aneurin Bevan, a miner's son who became a Labour Cabinet Minister, helped create the National Health Service *(see p58)*.

Welsh nationalism continued to grow: in 1926 Plaid Cymru, the Welsh Nationalist Party, was formed. In 1955 Cardiff was recognized as the capital of Wales *(see p456)* and four years later the ancient symbol of the red dragon became the emblem on Wales' new flag. Plaid Cymru won two parliamentary seats at Westminster in 1974, but in a 1979 referendum the Welsh rejected limited home rule.

The Welsh language has declined: half the population could speak it in 1901, but the figure was down to 21 percent 70 years later. The 1967 Welsh Language Act gave it protection by making Welsh compulsory in schools, and the television channel S4C (Sianel 4 Cymru), formed in 1982, broadcasts many programs in Welsh.

After the 1960s the steel and coal industries declined, creating mass unemployment. This has been only partly alleviated by the emergence of new, high-tech industries and by the recent growth in tourism and higher education.

The logo of S4C, Wales's own television station

Castles of Wales

A French 15th-century painting of Conwy Castle

WALES IS RICH in romantic medieval castles. Soon after the Battle of Hastings in 1066 *(see p47)*, the Normans turned their attentions to Wales. They built earth and timber fortifications, later replaced by stone castles, initiating a building program that was pursued by the Welsh princes and invading forces. Construction reached its peak during the reign of Edward I *(see p422)*. As the need for security lessened in the later Middle Ages, some castles became stately homes.

The north gatehouse was planned to be 18 m (60 ft) high, providing lavish royal accommodation, but its top story was never built.

The inner ward was lined with a hall, granary, kitchens and stables.

Rounded towers, with fewer blind spots than square ones, gave better protection.

Arrow slit

BEAUMARIS CASTLE

The last of Edward I's Welsh castles *(see p430)*, this perfectly symmetrical, concentric design was intended to combine impregnable defense with comfort. Invaders would face many obstacles before reaching the inner ward.

Moat

Curtain wall

WHERE TO SEE WELSH CASTLES

In addition to Beaumaris, in North Wales there are medieval forts at Caernarfon *(see p430)*, Conwy *(see p432)* and Harlech *(see p440)*. Edward I also built Denbigh, Flint (near Chester) and Rhuddlan (near Rhyll). In South and mid-Wales, Caerphilly (near Cardiff), Kidwelly (near Carmarthen) and Pembroke were built between the 11th and 13th centuries. Spectacular sites are occupied by Cilgerran (near Cardigan), Criccieth (near Porthmadog) and Carreg Cennen *(see p454)*. Chirk Castle, near Llangollen, is a good example of a fortress that has since become a stately home.

Caerphilly, 6 miles (10 km) north of Cardiff, is a huge castle with concentric stone and water defenses that cover 12 ha (30 acres).

Harlech Castle (see p440) *is noted for its massive gatehouse, twin towers and the fortified stairway to the sea. It was the headquarters of the Welsh resistance leader Owain Glyndŵr (see p422) from 1404–8.*

CASTELL-Ŷ-BERE

This native Welsh castle at the foot of Cader Idris *(see p440)* was founded by Llywelyn the Great in 1221 *(see p422)*, to secure internal borders rather than to resist the English.

Entrance

The D-shaped, elongated tower is a typical feature of Welsh castles.

The castle's construction follows the shape of the rock. The curtain walls are too low and insubstantial to be of much practical use.

Drawbridge

he Chapel Tower has a eautiful medieval chapel.

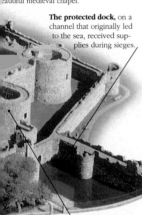

The protected dock, on a channel that originally led to the sea, received supplies during sieges.

e inner wall, with an er passage, was higher n the curtain wall to mit simultaneous firing.

Twin-towered gatehouse

Edward I (see p422) *was the warrior king whose castles played a key role in the subjugation of the Welsh people.*

EDWARD I AND MASTER JAMES OF ST. GEORGE

In 1278 Edward I brought over from Savoy a master stonemason who became a great military architect, James of St. George. Responsible for planning and building at least 12 of Edward's fine Welsh castles, James was paid well and liberally pensioned off, indicating the esteem in which he was held by the king.

A plan of Caernarfon Castle illustrates how its position, on a promontory surrounded by water, has determined the building's shape and defense.

Caernarfon Castle (see p430), *birthplace of the ill-fated Edward II* (see p315), *was intended to be the official royal residence in North Wales, and has palatial private apartments.*

Castell Coch was restored in Neo-Gothic style by Lord Bute and William Burges (see p458). Mock-castles were built by many Victorian industrialists.

Conwy Castle (see p433), *like many other castles, required forced labor on a massive scale for its construction.*

NORTH WALES

ABERCONWY & COLWYN · ANGLESEY · CAERNARFONSHIRE &
MERIONETHSHIRE · DENBIGHSHIRE · FLINTSHIRE · WREXHAM

THE NORTH WALES LANDSCAPE *has a dramatic quality reflected in its history. In prehistoric times, Anglesey was a stronghold of the religious elite known as the Druids. Roman and Norman invasions concentrated on the coast, leaving the mountains to the Welsh. These wild areas are the center of Welsh language and culture.*

Defense and conquest have been constant themes in Welsh history. North Wales was the scene of ferocious battles between the Welsh princes and Anglo-Norman monarchs determined to establish English rule. The string of formidable castles that still stand in North Wales are as much a testament to Welsh resistance as to the wealth and strength of the invaders. Several massive fortresses, including Beaumaris, Caernarfon and Harlech, almost surround the rugged high country of Snowdonia, an area that even today maintains an untamed quality.

Sheep and cattle farming are the basis of the rural economy here, though there are also large areas of forestry. Along the coast, tourism is a major activity. Llandudno, a specially built Victorian resort, popularized the sandy northern coastline in the 19th century. The area continues to attract large numbers of visitors, although major development is confined to the narrow coastal strip that lies between Prestatyn and Llandudno, leaving the island of Anglesey and the remote Llŷn Peninsula largely untouched.

The Llŷn Peninsula remains one of the strongholds of the Welsh language, along with rather isolated inland communities, such as Dolgellau and Bala.

No part of North Wales can truly be called industrial, although there are still remnants of the once-prosperous slate industry in Snowdonia, where the stark, gray quarries provide a striking contrast to the natural beauty of the surrounding mountains. At the foot of Snowdon (the highest mountain in Wales), the villages of Beddgelert, Betws-y-Coed and Llanberis are popular bases for walkers who come to enjoy the spectacular views and striking beauty of this remote region.

Caernarfon Castle, one of the forbidding fortresses built by Edward I

◁ The River Dee at Llangollen, still an area of unspoiled natural beauty

Exploring North Wales

THE DOMINANT FEATURE of North Wales is Snowdon, the highest mountain in Wales. Snowdonia National Park extends dramatically from the Snowdon massif south beyond Dolgellau, with thickly wooded valleys, mountain lakes, moors and estuaries. To the east are the softer Clwydian Hills, and unspoiled coastlines can be enjoyed on Anglesey and the beautiful Llŷn Peninsula.

A lighthouse perched on the sea cliffs of Anglesey

KEY

▭	Major road
▭	Minor road
▭	Scenic route
--	Scenic path
▭	River
⚹	Viewpoint

HOLYHEAD

ANGLESEY

A5025

B5111

A5025

A5

A4080

BEAUMARIS

2

LLANDUD

CONW

A55

A5

A487

CAERNARFON 1

LLANBERIS & SNOWDON 10

SNOWDON

A4086

NATIONAL P

A498

A470

BLAEN FFEST 9

BEDDGELERT 11

A487

PORTHMADOG

13 PORTMEIRIC

A499

A497

PWLLHELI

LLŶN PENINSULA

B4417

B4417

12

B4413

A499

ABERSOCH

14 HARLECH

A496

DOLGELLAU

A493

A493

Aberyst

ABERDYFI 16

The peaks and moorland of Snowdonia

GETTING AROUND

The main route into North Wales from the northwest of England is the A55, a good two-lane highway that bypasses several places that used to be traffic bottlenecks, including Conwy. The other main route through the region is the A5 Shrewsbury to Holyhead road, which follows a trail through the mountains pioneered by the 19th-century engineer Thomas Telford *(see p433)*. Rail services run along the coast to Holyhead, connecting with ferries across the Irish Sea to Dublin and Dun Laoghaire. Scenic branch lines travel from Llandudno Junction to Blaenau Ffestiniog (via Betws-y-Coed) and along the southern Llŷn Peninsula.

SIGHTS AT A GLANCE

Aberdyfi **16**
Bala **7**
Beaumaris **2**
Beddgelert **11**
Betws-y-Coed **8**
Blaenau Ffestiniog **9**
Caernarfon **1**
Conwy pp432–3 **3**
Dolgellau **15**
Harlech **14**
Llanberis and Snowdon **10**
LLandudno **4**
LLangollen **6**
Llŷn Peninsula **12**
Portmeirion pp440–41 **13**
Ruthin **5**

RHYL

COLWYN BAY
A55

A525

A548

A55

Offa's Dyke Path

Clwyd

A544

A543

DENBIGH

A525

A543

A494

A55

Liverpool

Chester

A483

5 RUTHIN

S-Y-COED

A5

A494

A525

Dee

WREXHAM

Dee

A525

A4212

A494

A5

6 LLANGOLLEN

7 BALA

0 kilometers   10

0 miles   10

A458   ← Shrewsbury

SEE ALSO

• *Where to Stay* pp564–565

• *Where to Eat* pp601–602

The imposing castle built at Conwy by Edward I in the 13th century

Caernarfon Castle, built by Edward I as a symbol of his power over the conquered Welsh

Caernarfon ❶

Caernarfonshire & Merionethshire
(Gwynedd). 🚶 10,000. 🚌
🛈 Castle St (01286 672232). 🚆 Sat.

ONE OF THE MOST FAMOUS
castles in Wales looms
over this busy town. Both
were created after Edward I's
defeat of the last native Welsh
prince, Llywelyn ap Gruffydd,
in 1283 *(see p422)*. The town
walls merge with shopping
streets that spread beyond the
medieval center and open
into a market square.

Overlooking the town and
its harbor, **Caernarfon
Castle** *(see p425)*, with its

THE INVESTITURE

In 1301 the future Edward
II became the first English
Prince of Wales *(see p422)*,
a title since held by the
British monarch's eldest
son. In 1969 the invest-
iture in Caernarfon Castle
of Prince Charles *(above)*
as Prince of Wales drew
500 million TV viewers.

polygonal towers, was built
as a seat of government for
North Wales. Caernarfon was
a thriving port in the 19th
century, and during this
period the castle ruins were
restored by the architect
Anthony Salvin. The castle
now contains several interesting displays, including the
Royal Welch Fusiliers Museum,
and exhibitions tracing the
history of the Princes of Wales
and exploring the theme
"Chieftains and Princes."

On the hill above the town
are the ruins of **Segontium**,
a Roman fort built in about
AD 78. According to a rather
unlikely local legend, the first
Christian Emperor of Rome,
Constantine the Great, was
born here in 280.

♣ **Caernarfon Castle**
Y Maes. 📞 01286 677617. 🕐 daily.
⬤ Dec 24, 25, Jan 1. 🎟 🚻 limited.
⋔ **Segontium**
Beddgelert Rd. 📞 01286 675625.
🕐 daily. ⬤ Dec 24–26, Jan 1. 🎟
🚻 limited.

Beaumaris ❷

Anglesey (Gwynedd). 🚶 2,000. 🚌
🛈 Llanfair PG, Station Site, Holyhead
Rd, Anglesey (01248 713177).

HANDSOME GEORGIAN and
Victorian architecture
gives Beaumaris the air of a
resort on England's southern
coast. The buildings reflect
this sailing center's past role
as Anglesey's chief port, before
the island was linked to the
mainland by the road and
railway bridges built across

the Menai Strait in the 19th
century. This was the site of
Edward I's last, and possibly
greatest, **castle** *(see p424)*,
which was built to command
this important ferrying point
to the mainland of Wales.

Ye Olde Bull's Head inn,
on Castle Street, was built in
1617. Its celebrated literary
patrons have included Dr.
Samuel Johnson (1709–84)
and Victorian novelist Charles
Dickens *(see p173)*.

The town's **Courthouse**,
built in 1614, is still in use,
and the restored 1829 **jail**
preserves its soundproofed
punishment room and a huge
treadmill for prisoners. Two
public hangings took place
here. Richard Rowlands, the
last victim, protested his inno-
cence of murder and cursed
the church clock as he was
being led to the gallows,
declaring that its four faces
would never show the same
times again. The clock failed
to show consistent times until
it had an overhaul in 1980.

Beaumaris's award-winning
Museum of Childhood
contains a nostalgic collection
of toys and games from the
19th and 20th centuries.

♣ **Beaumaris Castle**
Castle St. 📞 01248 810361.
🕐 daily. ⬤ Dec 24–26, Jan 1. 🎟
🏛 **Courthouse**
High St. 📞 01286 679098. 🕐 Jun–
Sep: daily. 🎟 🚻 limited.
🏛 **Jail**
Bunkers Hill. 📞 01286 679098.
🕐 Jun–Sep: daily. 🎟
🏛 **Museum of Childhood**
Castle St. 📞 01248 712498.
🕐 mid-Mar–Oct: daily. 🎟

ALICE IN WONDERLAND

The Gogarth Abbey Hotel, Llandudno, was the summer home of the Liddells. Their friend, Charles Dodgson (1832–98), would entertain young Alice Liddell with stories of characters such as the White Rabbit and the Mad Hatter. As Lewis Carroll, Dodgson wrote his magical tales in *Alice's Adventures in Wonderland* (1865) and *Through the Looking-Glass* (1871).

Arthur Rackham's illustration (1907) of *Alice in Wonderland*

Conwy ❸

See pp432–3.

Llandudno ❹

Aberconwy & Colwyn (Gwynedd).
🚶 19,000. 🚆 🚌 🛈 1–2 Chapel St (0492 876413). 🛒 Mon–Sat.

Llandudno's crescent-shaped bay

LLANDUDNO retains much of the holiday spirit of the 19th century, when the new railways brought crowds to the coast. Its **pier**, more than 700 m (2,295 ft) long, and its canopied walkways recall the heyday of seaside holidays. The town is proud of its association with the author Lewis Carroll. **The Rabbit Hole** is a grotto decorated with life-sized scenes from his children's books.

Llandudno's cheerful and informal seaside atmosphere owes much to a strong sense of its Victorian roots – unlike many other British seaside towns, which have embraced the flashing lights and noisy rides of the 20th century. To take advantage of its wide

beach, Llandudno was laid out between its two headlands, Great Orme's Head and Little Orme's Head.

Great Orme's Head, now a Country Park and Nature Reserve, rises to a height of 207 m (680 ft) and has a long history of human settlement. In the Bronze Age copper was mined here; the **copper mines** and their excavations are open to the public. The **church** on the headland was first built from timber in the 6th century by missionary St. Tudno, rebuilt in stone in the 13th century, restored in 1855 and is still in use today. Great Orme's Head's history and wildlife can be traced in an information center which is on the summit.

There are two effortless ways to reach the summit: on the **Great Orme Tramway**, one of only three cable-hauled street tramways in the world (the others are in San

Francisco and Lisbon), or by the **Llandudno Cable Car**. Both operate only in summer.

🏛 **The Rabbit Hole**
Trinity Sq. 📞 01492 860082.
🕐 Easter–Oct: daily; Nov–Easter: Mon–Sat. ⬤ Dec 25. 🅿 ♿
⛏ **Great Orme Copper Mines**
Off A55. 📞 01492 870447.
🕐 Feb–Nov: daily. 🅿 ♿ limited.

Ruthin ❺

Denbighshire (Clwyd). 🚶 5,000. 🚌
🛈 Craft Centre, Park Rd (01824 703992). 🛒 1st Tue every month.

RUTHIN'S LONG-STANDING prosperity as a market town is reflected in its fine half-timbered medieval buildings. These include the National Westminster and Barclays banks in St. Peter's Square. The former was a 15th-century courthouse and prison, the latter the home of Thomas Exmewe, Lord Mayor of London in 1517–18. **Maen Huail** ("Huail's stone"), a boulder outside Barclays, is said to be where King Arthur *(see p271)* beheaded Huail, his rival in a love affair.

St. Peter's Church, on the edge of St. Peter's Square, was founded in 1310 and has a beautiful Tudor oak roof in the north aisle, with 500 carved panels. Next to the Castle Hotel is the 17th-century **Myddleton Arms** pub, whose seven unusual, Dutch-style, dormer windows are known locally as the "eyes of Ruthin."

The "eyes of Ruthin," an unusual feature in Welsh architecture

Street-by-Street: Conwy ❸

Conwy is one of Britain's most underrated historic towns. Until the early 1990s it was famous as a traffic bottleneck, but thanks to a town bypass, its concentration of architectural riches – unparalleled in Wales – can now be appreciated. The castle dominates: a brooding, intimidating monument built by Edward I *(see p422)*. But Conwy is set apart from other medieval towns by its amazingly well-preserved town walls. Fortified with 21 towers and three gateways, the walls form an almost unbroken shield around the old town.

Smallest House
This fisherman's cottage on the quayside, just over 3 m (10 ft) high, is said to be the smallest house in Britain.

Plas Mawr, the "Great Mansion," was built by a nobleman, Robert Wynne, in 1576.

St. Mary's Church
This medieval church, on the site of a 12th-century Cistercian abbey, is set in peaceful grounds.

Bangor

BERRY STREET

CHAPEL STREET

HIGH STREET

LANCASTER SQUARE

CHURCH STREET

UPPER GATE STREET

ROSEMARY LANE

Upper Gate

Llywelyn's Statue
Llywelyn the Great (see p422) was arguably Wales's most successful medieval leader.

Aberconwy House
This restored 14th-century house was once the home of a wealthy merchant.

THOMAS TELFORD

Thomas Telford (1757–1834) was the gifted Scottish engineer responsible for many of Britain's roads, bridges and canals. The Menai Bridge *(see p430)*, the Pontcysyllte Aqueduct *(see p436)* and Conwy Bridge are his outstanding works in Wales. Telford's graceful bridge at Conwy has esthetic as well as practical qualities. Completed in 1826 across the mouth of the Conwy estuary, it was designed in a castellated style to blend with the castle. Before the bridge's construction the estuary could only be crossed by ferry.

VISITORS' CHECKLIST

Aberconwy & Colwyn (Gwynedd).
8,000. Conwy. 01492 592248. Conwy Festival: Jul.
Aberconwy House, Castle St.
01492 592246. Wed–Mon.
Conwy Castle, Castle Square.
01492 592358. daily.
Smallest House, Lower Gate St.
01492 593484. daily.

★ Town Walls
These remarkably well-preserved medieval walls are 1,280 m (4,200 ft) long and over 9 m (30 ft) high.

Chester

NEW BRIDGE

CASTLE STREET

CASTLE SQUARE

STREET

Telford's bridge

Railroad bridge

0 meters 50
0 yards 50

Entrance to castle

KEY
— — Suggested route

STAR SIGHTS
★ Town Walls
★ Conwy Castle

★ Conwy Castle
This atmospheric watercolor, Conwy Castle *(c.1770), is by the Nottingham artist Paul Sandby .*

Pontcysyllte Aqueduct, built in 1795–1805, carrying the Llangollen Canal

Llangollen ➏

Denbighshire (Clwyd). 🚶 *5,000.*
🚉 ℹ️ *Town Hall, Castle St (01978
860828).* 🚌 *Tue.*

BEST KNOWN for its annual
eisteddfod (festival), this
pretty town sits on the River
Dee, which is spanned by a
14th-century bridge. The town
became notorious in the 18th
century, when two eccentric
Irishwomen, Lady Eleanor
Butler and Sarah Ponsonby,
the "Ladies of Llangollen," set
up house together in the half-
timbered **Plas Newydd**. Their
unconventional dress and
literary enthusiasms attracted
such celebrities as the Duke
of Wellington *(see p148)* and
William Wordsworth *(see
p352)*. The ruins of a 13th-
century castle, **Castell Dinas
Brân**, occupy the summit of
a hill overlooking the house.

ENVIRONS: Boats on the
Llangollen Canal sail from
Wharf Hill in summer and
cross the spectacular 300 m
(1,000 ft) long Pontcysyllte
Aqueduct, built by Thomas
Telford *(see p433)*.

🏛 Plas Newydd
Hill St. 📞 *01978 861314.*
⭕ *Apr–Oct: daily.* 🅿️ 🚹 *limited.*

Bala ➐

Caernarfonshire & Merionethshire
(Gwynedd). 🚶 *2,000.* 🚌 *from
Llangollen.* ℹ️ *Pensarn Rd (01678
521021).*

BALA LAKE, Wales's largest
natural lake, lies between
the Aran and Arenig mountains

at the fringes of Snowdonia
National Park. It is popular
for water-sports and boasts a
unique fish called a *gwyniad*,
which is related to the salmon.
    The little gray-stone town
of Bala is a Welsh-speaking
community, strung along a
single street at the lake's east
end. Thomas Charles (1755–
1814), a Methodist church
leader, once lived here. A
plaque on his former home
recalls Mary Jones who, in
1800, walked 25 miles (40 km)
barefoot from Abergynolwyn
to buy a bible. This prompted
Charles to establish the Bible
Society, to provide inexpensive
bibles to the working class.
    The narrow-gauge **Bala
Lake Railway** follows the
lake shore from Llanuwchllyn,
4 miles (6 km) southwest.

Betws-y-Coed ➑

Aberconwy & Colwyn (Gwynedd).
🚶 *600.* 🚆 ℹ️ *Royal Oak Stables
(01690 710426).*

THIS VILLAGE near the peaks
of Snowdonia has been a
hiking center since the 19th

WORLD CULTURES
IN LLANGOLLEN

Llangollen's International
Eisteddfod *(see p63)* in
the first week of July
draws musicians, singers
and dancers from around
the world. First held in
1947 as a gesture of postwar international unity, it
now attracts over 12,000
performers from nearly 50
countries to the six-day-
long competition-cum-fair.

Choristers at the eisteddfod,
a popular Welsh festival

century. To the west are the
Swallow Falls, where the
River Llugwy flows through a
wooded glen. The bizarre **Tŷ
Hyll** ("Ugly House"), is a *tŷ
unnos* ("one-night house");
traditionally, houses erected
between dusk and dawn on
common land were entitled
to freehold rights, and the
owner could enclose land as
far as he could throw an ax
from the door. To the east is
Waterloo Bridge, built by
Thomas Telford to mark
victory against Napoleon.

🏛 Tŷ Hyll
Capel Curig. 📞 *01690 4287.*
⭕ *May–Oct: daily; Nov–Apr: Mon–Fri.*
⭕ *Dec 25, 26, Jan 1.* 🅿️ 🚹 *limited.*

The ornate Waterloo Bridge, built in 1815 after the famous battle

◁ **The picturesque village of Beddgelert in Snowdonia National Park**

A view of the Snowdonia countryside from Llanberis Pass, the most popular route to Snowdon's peak

Blaenau Ffestiniog ❾

Caernarfonshire & Merionethshire (Gwynedd). 5,500. Betws-y-Coed (01690 710426). Tue (Jun–Sep).

BLAENAU FFESTINIOG, once the slate capital of North Wales, sits among mountains riddled with quarries. The **Llechwedd Slate Caverns**, overlooking Blaenau, opened to visitors in the early 1970s, marking a new role for the declining industrial town. The electric Miners' Tramway takes passengers on a tour into the original caverns.

On the Deep Mine tour, visitors descend on Britain's steepest passenger inclined railroad to the underground chambers, while sound effects recreate the atmosphere of a working quarry. The dangers included landfalls and floods, as well as the more gradual threat of slate dust breathed into the lungs.

There are slate-splitting demonstrations on the surface and a row of reconstructed quarrymen's cottages, each one furnished to illustrate the cramped and basic living conditions endured by workers between the 1880s and 1945. The narrow-gauge **Ffestiniog Railway** *(see pp438–9)* runs from Blaenau to Porthmadog.

Llechwedd Slate Caverns
Crimea Pass. 01766 830306. *daily.* *Dec 25, 26, Jan 1.* *except the Deep Mine.*

Llanberis and Snowdon ❿

Caernarfonshire & Merionethshire (Gwynedd). 2,100. *High St, Llanberis (01286 870765).*

SNOWDON, which at 1,085 m (3,560 ft) is the highest peak in Wales, is the main focus of the vast Snowdonia National Park, whose scenery ranges from this rugged mountain country to moors and beaches. The easiest route to Snowdon's summit begins in Llanberis: the 5 mile (8 km) **Llanberis Track**. From Llanberis Pass, the Miners' Track (once used by copper miners) and the Pyg Track are alternative paths. Hikers should beware of sudden weather changes. The narrow-gauge **Snowdon Mountain Railway**, opened in 1896, is an easier option.

Llanberis was a major 19th-century slate town, with gray terraces hewn into the hills. Other attractions are the 13th-century shell of **Dolbadarn Castle**, on a bluff between lakes Padarn and Peris, and, above Lake Peris, the **Power of Wales Museum**, which arranges tours of the biggest hydroelectric pumped storage station in Europe.

Dolbadarn Castle
Off A4086 nr Llanberis. 01286 870765. *daily.* *Dec 24–26, Jan 1.*

Power of Wales Museum
Llanberis. 01286 870636. *Mar–Oct: daily; Nov–Feb: Tue–Thu, Sat.*

Britain's Center of Slate

Welsh slates provided roofing material for Britain's new towns in the 19th century. In 1898, the slate industry employed nearly 17,000 men, a quarter of whom worked at Blaenau Ffestiniog. Foreign competition and new materials later took their toll. Quarries such as Gloddfa Ganol and Llechwedd in Blaenau Ffestiniog now survive on the tourist trade.

The dying art of slate-splitting

The village of Beddgelert, set among the mountains of Snowdonia

Beddgelert ⓫

Caernarfonshire & Merionethshire
(Gwynedd). 🚉 *500.* 🚌 *High St,
Porthmadog (01766 512981).*

BEDDGELERT enjoys a spectacular location among some of Snowdonia's most dramatic landscapes. The village sits on the confluence of the Glaslyn and Colwyn rivers at the approach to two mountain passes: the beautiful Nant Gwynant Pass, which leads to Snowdonia's highest reaches,

and the Aberglaslyn Pass, a narrow wooded gorge that acts as a gateway to the sea.

Business was given a boost by Dafydd Pritchard, the landlord of the Royal Goat Hotel, who in the early 19th century adapted an old Welsh legend to associate it with Beddgelert. Llywelyn the Great *(see p422)* is said to have left his faithful hound Gelert to guard his infant son while he went hunting. He returned to find the cradle overturned and Gelert covered in blood. Thinking

the dog had savaged his son, Llywellyn slaughtered Gelert, but then discovered the boy, unharmed, under the cradle. Nearby was the corpse of a wolf, which Gelert had killed to protect the child. To support the tale, Pritchard created **Gelert's Grave** (*bedd Gelert* in Welsh) by the River Glaslyn, a mound of stones a short walk south of the village.

ENVIRONS: There are many fine walks in the area: one leads south to the Aberglaslyn Pass and along an unused part of the Welsh Highland Railroad. The **Sygun Copper Mine**, 1 mile (1.5 km) northeast of Beddgelert, offers fascinating guided tours of illuminated caverns and levels cut into the mountain, re-creating the life of Victorian miners.

🏭 Sygun Copper Mine
On A498. 📞 *01766 890595.*
⭕ *daily.* ⬤ *Dec 24, 25.* 🎫 ♿

Ffestiniog Railway

THE FFESTINIOG narrow-gauge railway takes a scenic 14-mile (22-km) route from Porthmadog Harbour to the mountains and the slate town of Blaenau Ffestiniog *(see p437).* Designed to carry slate from the quarries to the quay, the railroad

Engine plaque

replaced a horse-drawn tramway constructed in 1836, operating on a 60 cm (2 ft) gauge. After it closed in 1946, it was maintained by volunteers and re-opened in sections after 1955.

Steam traction *trains were first used on the Ffestiniog Railway in 1863. There are some diesel engines but most trains are still steam-powered.*

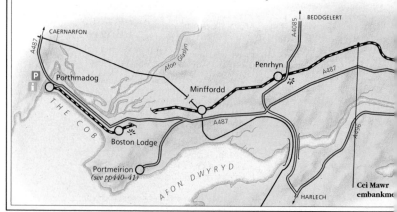

Llŷn Peninsula ⑫

Caernarfonshire & Merionethshire
(Gwynedd). 🚆 🚌 *Pwllheli.*
🚢 *from Pwllheli & Aberdaron to
Bardsey Island.* 🛈 *Min-y-don,
Station Sq, Pwllheli (01758 613000).*

THIS 24-MILE (38-km) finger of land points southwest from Snowdonia into the Irish Sea. Although it has many popular beaches, notably at Pwllheli, Criccieth, Abersoch and Nefyn, the overriding feature of this coast is its untamed beauty. Views are at their most dramatic in the far west and along the mountain-backed northern shores.

The windy headland of **Braich-y-Pwll**, to the west of Aberdaron, looks out toward Bardsey Island, the "Isle of 20,000 Saints." This became a place of pilgrimage in the 6th century, when a monastery was founded here. Some saints are said to be buried in the churchyard of the ruined 13th-century **St. Mary's Abbey**. Nearby, the small bay of **Porth Oer** is known as "Whistling Sands" due to the sound of its sand underfoot.

East of Aberdaron is the 4 mile (6.5 km) bay of **Porth Neigwl**, known in English as Hell's Mouth, the scene of many shipwrecks due to the bay's treacherous currents. Hidden in sheltered grounds above Porth Neigwl bay, 1 mile (1.5 km) northeast of Aberdaron, is **Plas-yn-Rhiw**, a small, medieval manor house with Tudor and Georgian additions and lovely gardens.

The former quarrying village and "ghost town" of **Llithfaen**, tucked away below the sheer cliffs of the mountainous north coast, is now a center for Welsh language studies.

🏛 **Plas-yn-Rhiw**
(NT) off B4413. 📞 *01758 780219.*
⭕ *Apr–Sep: Sun–Fri; Oct: Sun.* 🈶 ♿

Llithfaen village, now a language center, on the Llŷn Peninsula

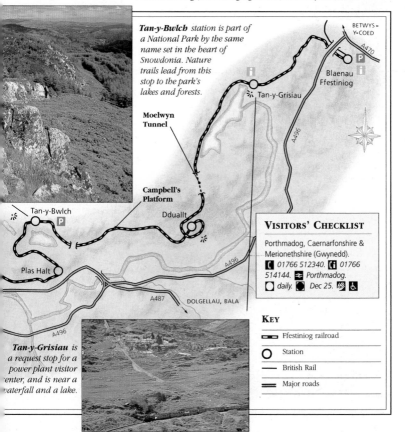

Tan-y-Bwlch station is part of a National Park by the same name set in the heart of Snowdonia. Nature trails lead from this stop to the park's lakes and forests.

BETWYS-Y-COED

A470

Blaenau Ffestiniog

Tan-y-Grisiau

A496

Moelwyn Tunnel

Campbell's Platform

Dduallt

Tan-y-Bwlch

Plas Halt

A487 DOLGELLAU, BALA

A496

Tan-y-Grisiau is a request stop for a power plant visitor center, and is near a waterfall and a lake.

VISITORS' CHECKLIST

Porthmadog, Caernarfonshire & Merionethshire (Gwynedd).
📞 *01766 512340.* 🚍 *01766 514144.* 🚆 *Porthmadog.*
⭕ *daily.* ⭕ *Dec 25.* 🈶 ♿

KEY

▬▬	Ffestiniog railroad
O	Station
—	British Rail
═	Major roads

Portmeirion ⑬

Caernarfonshire & Merionethshire
(Gwynedd). **C** 01766 770228.
Z Minffordd. **◯** daily. **●** Dec 25.
⟨⟩ **&**

THIS BIZARRE ITALIANATE village
on a private peninsula at
the top of Cardigan Bay was
created by Welsh architect Sir
Clough Williams-Ellis (1883–
1978). He fulfilled a childhood
dream by building a village
"to my own fancy on my own
chosen site." About 50 buildings surround a central
piazza, in styles from
Oriental to Gothic.
Visitors can stay
at the luxurious
hotel or in one
of the charming
village cottages.
Portmeirion has
been an atmo-
spheric location
for many films
and television
programs, in-
cluding the
popular 1960s
television series
The Prisoner.

**Sir Clough
Williams-Ellis at
Portmeirion**

*Hercules is a life-sized 19th-
century copper statue near
the Town Hall, where a 17th-
century ceiling, rescued from
a demolished mansion,
depicts his legend.*

Fountain Cottage is
where Noel Coward
(1899–1973) wrote
Blithe Spirit.

The **Amis
Reunis** is a
stone replica
of a boat that
sank in the bay

**Swimming
pool**

*The Portmeirion Hotel
has many exotic interiors: the
furniture in the Jaipur Bar
comes from Rajasthan, India.*

Harlech ⑭

Caernarfonshire & Merionethshire
(Gwynedd). **♦** 1,300. **Z** **i** High
St (01766 780658). **▲** Sun (summer).

THIS SMALL TOWN with fine
beaches is dominated by
Harlech Castle, a medieval
fortress *(see p424)* built by
Edward I between 1283 and
1289. The castle sits on a precipitous crag, with superb
views of Tremadog Bay and
the Llŷn Peninsula to the west,
and Snowdonia to the north.
When the castle was built, the
sea reached a fortified stairway
cut into the cliff, so that supplies could arrive by ship, but
now the sea has receded. A
towering gatehouse protects
the inner ward, enclosed by
walls and four round towers.

Despite its defenses, Harlech
Castle fell to Owain Glyndŵr
(see p422) in 1404 and served
as his court until its recapture
four years later. The song *Men
of Harlech* is thought to have
been inspired by the castle's
heroic resistance during an
eight-year siege in the Wars
of the Roses *(see p49)*.

♣ Harlech Castle
Castle Sq. **C** 01766 780552.
◯ daily. **●** Dec 24–26. **⟨⟩**

Dolgellau ⑮

Caernarfonshire & Merionethshire
(Gwynedd). **♦** 2,650. **i** Eldon Sq
(01341 422888). **▲** Fri (livestock).

THE DARK LOCAL STONE gives
a stern, solid look to this
market town, where the Welsh
language and customs are still
very strong. It lies in the long
shadow of the 892-m (2,927-ft)
mountain of Cader Idris, where,
according to legend, anyone
who spends a night on its
summit will awake a poet or
a madman – or not at all.

Dolgellau was gripped by
gold fever in the 19th century,
when high-quality gold was

Harlech Castle's strategic site overlooking mountains and sea

The Triumphal Arch is the main entrance to Portmeirion village.

Central Piazza

Lodge

Campanile

Royal Dolphin Cottage

Bristol Colonnade

Viewing platform

The Ship Shop sells Portmeirion's famous flowered pottery.

The Pantheon was built in 1958, but lack of funds meant that the dome was originally made from plywood instead of copper and painted green. The Pantheon's unusual façade is formed by the upper half of a music room fireplace by Norman Shaw (see p25).

Dolgellau's gray-stone buildings, dwarfed by the mountain scenery

discovered in the Mawddach Valley nearby. To the north of Dolgellau, at the **Gwynfynydd Gold Centre and Mine**, visitors can pan for gold dust and keep what they find.

Dolgellau is a fine center for walking, set in beautiful countryside, with river valleys and dramatic mountain views. The lovely **Cregennen lakes** are high in the hills above the wooded **Mawddach Estuary** to the northwest; north are the **Rhinog moors**, one of Wales's last true wildernesses.

Gwynfynydd Gold Centre and Mine

Marian Mawr. ☎ 01341 423332. ◯ Apr–Sep: daily. **Centre:** ◯ Oct–Mar: Mon–Fri. ◯ Dec 25, Jan 1.

Aberdyfi ⑯

Caernarfonshire & Merionethshire (Gwynedd). ♘ 900. ☲ ⬛ Wharf Gardens (01654 767321).

PERCHED ON THE MOUTH of the Dyfi Estuary, this little harbor resort and sailing center makes the most of its splendid but rather confined location, its houses occupying every yard of a narrow strip of land between mountain and sea. In the 19th century, local slate was exported from here, and between the 1830s and the 1860s about 100 ships were built in the port. *The Bells of Aberdovey*, a song by Charles Dibdin for his opera *Liberty Hall* (1785), tells the legend of Cantref-y-Gwaelod, thought to have been located here, which was protected from the sea by dikes. One stormy night, the sluice gates were left open by Prince Seithenyn when he was drunk, and the land was lost beneath the waves. The submerged church bells are said to peal under the water to this day.

Neat Georgian houses by the sea, Aberdyfi

SOUTH AND MID-WALES

···

CARDIFF, SWANSEA & ENVIRONS · CARDIGANSHIRE
CARMARTHENSHIRE · MONMOUTHSHIRE · POWYS · PEMBROKESHIRE

*S*OUTH AND MID-WALES *are less homogeneous regions than North Wales. Most of the population lives in the southeast corner. To the west is Pembrokeshire, the loveliest stretch of Welsh coastline. To the north the industrial valleys give way to the wide hills of the Brecon Beacons and the rural heartlands of central Wales.*

South Wales's coastal strip has been settled for many centuries. There are prehistoric sites in the Vale of Glamorgan and Pembrokeshire. The Romans established a major base at Caerleon, and the Normans built castles all the way from Chepstow to Pembroke. In the 18th and 19th centuries, coal mines and ironworks opened in the valleys of South Wales, attracting immigrants from all over Europe. Close communities developed here, focused on the coal trade, which turned Cardiff from a sleepy coastal town into the world's busiest coal-exporting port.

The declining coal industry has again changed the face of this area: slag heaps have become green hills, and the valley towns struggle to find alternative forms of employment. Coal mines such as Blaenafon's Big Pit are now tourist attractions; today, many of the tour guides taking visitors underground are ex-miners, who can offer a first-hand glimpse of the hard life found in mining communities before the pits closed.

The southern boundary of the Brecon Beacons National Park marks the beginning of rural Wales. With a population sparser than anywhere in England, this is an area of small country towns, hill-sheep farms, forestry plantations and spectacular man-made lakes.

The number of Welsh-speakers increases and the sense of Welsh culture becomes stronger as you travel farther from the border with England, with the exception of an English enclave in south Pembrokeshire.

The changing face of the coal industry: former miners take visitors down the Big Pit in Blaenafon

◁ **Magnificent coastal scenery near St. David's, Pembrokeshire**

Exploring South and Mid-Wales

MAGNIFICENT COASTAL SCENERY marks the Pembrokeshire Coast National Park and cliff-backed Gower Peninsula, while Cardigan Bay and Carmarthen Bay offer quieter beaches. Walkers can enjoy grassy uplands in the Brecon Beacons and gentler country in the leafy Wye Valley. Urban life is concentrated in the southeast of Wales, where old mining towns line the valleys north of Cardiff, the capital.

MACHYNLLI

GETTING AROUND

The M4 motorway is the major route into Wales from the south of England, and there are good road links west of Swansea running to the coast. To mid-Wales, take the A483 and A488 from the Midlands. Frequent rail services connect London with Cardiff, Swansea and the ferry port of Fishguard.

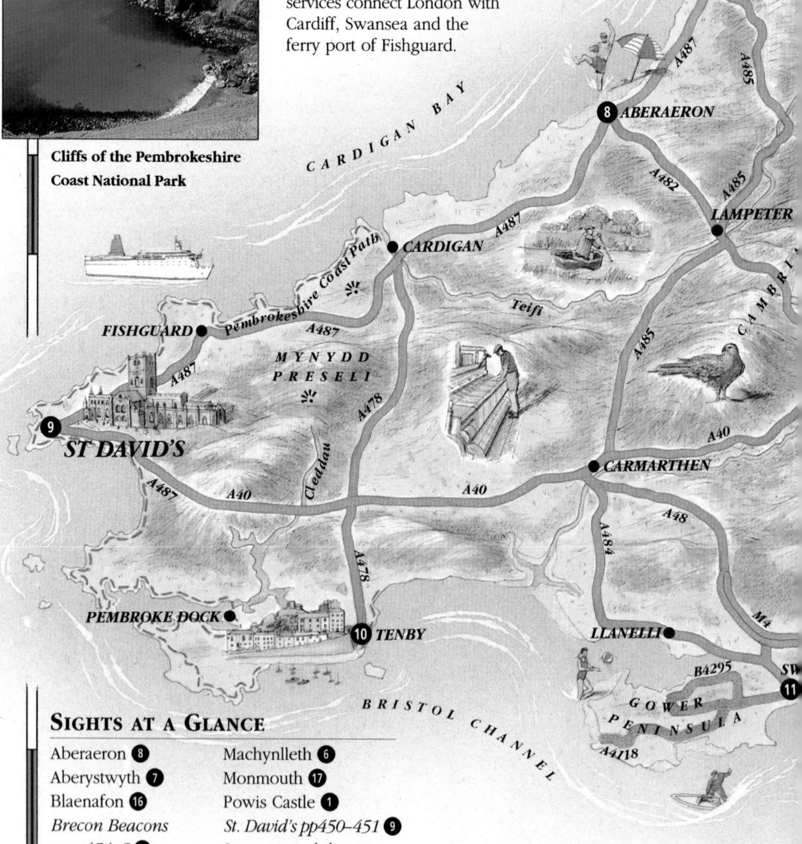

Cliffs of the Pembrokeshire Coast National Park

CARDIGAN BAY

ABERYSTWYTH **7**   *Rheidol*

8 *ABERAERON*

LAMPETER

● *CARDIGAN*

Teifi

FISHGUARD ●

MYNYDD PRESELI

Pembrokeshire Coast Path

9
ST DAVID'S

Cleddau

CARMARTHEN ●

PEMBROKE DOCK ●

10 *TENBY*

LLANELLI ●

BRISTOL CHANNEL

GOWER PENINSULA

11

SIGHTS AT A GLANCE

SEE ALSO

- *Where to Stay* pp 565–8
- *Where to Eat* pp602–4

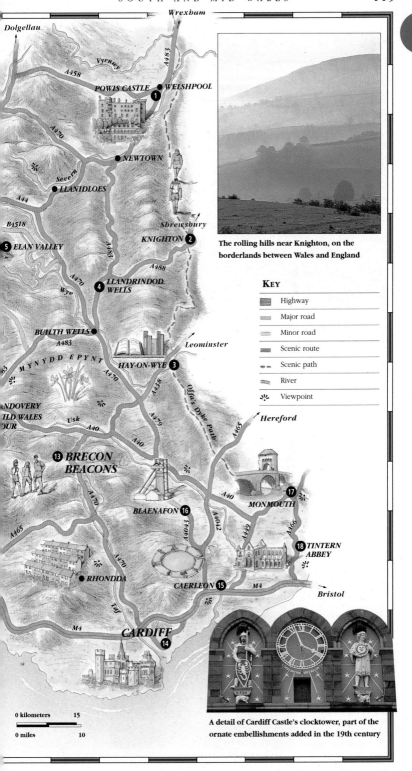

Dolgellau

Wrexham

Vyrnwy

A483

A458

POWIS CASTLE ● **WELSHPOOL**
1

A470

● **NEWTOWN**

Severn
● **LLANIDLOES**

A44

Shrewsbury

B4518

A483

5 ELAN VALLEY

KNIGHTON 2

A488

A470

LLANDRINDOD
4 WELLS

Wye

BUILTH WELLS ●

A483

Leominster ↗

M Y N Y D D   E P Y N T

HAY-ON-WYE 3

A470

A438

Olfta's Dyke Path

A479

NDOVERY
ILD WALES
OUR

Usk   A40

Hereford →

A465

13 BRECON
BEACONS

A40

A40

17 MONMOUTH

A465

A470

BLAENAFON 16

A4042

A449

A466

18 TINTERN
ABBEY

A4043

A4058

● **RHONDDA**

CAERLEON 15

M4

Bristol →

Taff

M4

CARDIFF
14

The rolling hills near Knighton, on the
borderlands between Wales and England

KEY

	Highway
	Major road
	Minor road
	Scenic route
	Scenic path
	River
☼	Viewpoint

0 kilometers   15

0 miles   10

A detail of Cardiff Castle's clocktower, part of the
ornate embellishments added in the 19th century

The Italianate terraces and formal gardens of Powis Castle add a Mediterranean air to the Welsh borderlands

Powis Castle ❶

(NT) Welshpool, Powys. ☎ 01938 554336. ☒ Welshpool then bus. ☐ Apr–Oct: Wed–Sun & public hols. (Jul–Aug: Tue–Sun). 🅿 🅺 limited.

Powis castle – the spelling is an archaic version of "Powys" – has outgrown its military roots. Despite its sham battlements and dominant site, 1.6 km (1 mile) to the southwest of the border town of Welshpool, this splendid red-stone building has served as a country mansion for centuries. Yet it began life in the 13th century as a fortress, built by the princes of Powys to control the border with England.

The castle is entered through one of few surviving medieval features: a gateway, built in 1283 by Owain de la Pole. The gate is flanked by two round towers with arrow slits and portcullis slots.

The castle's lavish interiors soon banish all thoughts of war. A **Dining Room**, decorated with fine 17th-century paneling and family portraits, was originally designed as the castle's Great

Hall. The **Great Staircase**, added in the late 17th century and elaborately decorated with carved fruit and flowers, leads to the main apartments: an early 19th-century library, the paneled **Oak Drawing Room** and the Elizabethan **Long Gallery**, where ornate plasterwork on the fireplace and ceiling dates from the 1590s. In the **Blue Drawing Room** there are three 18th-century Brussels tapestries.

The Herbert family bought the property in 1587 and were proud of their Royalist connections; the paneling in

The richly carved 17th-century Great Staircase

the **State Bedroom** bears the royal monogram. Powis castle was defended for Charles I in the Civil War *(see pp52–3)*, but fell to Parliament in 1644. The 3rd Baron Powis, a supporter of James II, had to flee the country when William and Mary took the throne in 1688 *(see pp52–3)*.

The castle's **Clive Museum** has an exhibition concerning "Clive of India" (1725–74), the general and statesman who helped strengthen British control in India in the mid-18th century. The family's link with Powis Castle was established by the 2nd Lord Clive, who married into the Herbert family and became the Earl of Powis in 1804.

The gardens at Powis are among the best known in Britain, with their series of elegant Italianate terraces, adorned with statues, niches, balustrades, and hanging gardens, all stepped into the steep hillside beneath the castle walls. Created between 1688 and 1722, these are the only formal gardens of this period in Britain that are still kept in their original form *(see pp22–3)*.

Knighton ②

Powys. 🏘 2,800. 🚂 🚌 West St (01547 528753). 🚌 Thu.

KNIGHTON'S WELSH NAME, Tref y Clawdd ("The Town on the Dyke"), reflects its status as the only original settlement on **Offa's Dyke**. In the 8th century, King Offa of Mercia (central and southern England) constructed a ditch and bank to mark out his territory, and to enable the enforcement of a Saxon law: "Neither shall a Welshman cross into English land without the appointed man from the other side, who should meet him at the bank and bring him back again without any offense being committed." Some of the best-preserved sections of the 6 m (20 ft) high earthwork lie in the hills around Knighton.

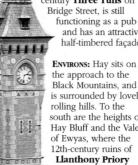

Knighton's clock

The Offa's Dyke Footpath runs for 285 km (177 miles) along the border between England and Wales.

Knighton is set on a steep hill, sloping upward from **St. Edward's Church** (1877) with its medieval tower, to the summit, where a castle once stood. The main street leads via the market square, marked by a 19th-century clock tower, along **The Narrows**, a Tudor street crowded with little shops. **The Old House**, on Broad Street, is a medieval "cruck" house (a style that uses pairs of curved timbers to form a frame to support the roof), and has a hole in the ceiling instead of a chimney.

Hay-on-Wye ③

Powys. 🏘 1,300. 🚌 Oxford Rd (01497 820144). 🚌 Thu.

BOOK LOVERS from all over the world come to this quiet border town in the Black Mountains. Hay-on-Wye has over 25 second-hand bookstores stocking millions of titles, and in early summer hosts a prestigious Festival of Literature. The town's love affair with books began when a bookstore was opened in the 1960s by Richard Booth, who claims the (fictitious) title of King of Independent Hay and lives in **Hay Castle**, a 17th-century mansion in the grounds of the original 13th-century castle. Hay's oldest inn, the 16th-century **Three Tuns** on Bridge Street, is still functioning as a pub and has an attractive half-timbered façade.

ENVIRONS: Hay sits on the approach to the Black Mountains, and is surrounded by lovely rolling hills. To the south are the heights of Hay Bluff and the Vale of Ewyas, where the 12th-century ruins of **Llanthony Priory** *(see p455)* retain fine stonework and pointed arches.

🔱 **Hay Castle**
Castle Sq. 🕻 01497 820503. ◻ daily. ● Dec 25. 🎫 gardens only.

Llandrindod Wells ④

Powys. 🏘 5,000. 🚂 🚌 Memorial Gardens (01597 822600). 🚌 Fri.

LANDRINDOD is a perfect example of a Victorian town, with canopied streets, delicate wrought ironwork, gabled villas, and ornamental parklands. This planned spa town became Wales's premier inland resort of the 19th

One of Hay-on-Wye's bookstores

century. Its sulfur and magnesium spring waters were taken to treat skin complaints, kidney diseases, and a range of other ailments.

The town now makes every effort to preserve its Victorian character, with a boating lake and the well-tended **Rock Park Gardens**. The restored 19th-century **Pump Room** in the **Spa Centre** serves tea, and is the focus of the summer Victorian Festival, when residents don period costume and all cars are banned from the town center.

The **Radnorshire Museum** traces the town's past as one of a string of 19th-century Welsh spas that included Builth (now a farming town), Llangammarch (a sleepy hamlet), and **Llanwrtyd** (now a pony trekking center).

🏛 **Spa Centre**
Rock Park Gardens. 🕻 01597 822997. ◻ daily. ● Dec 25, 26, Jan 1. 🔾

🏛 **Radnorshire Museum**
Memorial Gardens. 🕻 01597 824513. ◻ Mon, Tue, Thu–Sat (am). ● 2 wks in Dec. 🔾 limited.

Victorian architecture on Spa Road, Llandrindod Wells

Craig Goch, one of the original chain of Elan Valley reservoirs

Elan Valley ❺

Powys. ⬛ *Llandrindod.*
ℹ *Rhayader (01597 810898).*

A STRING OF SPECTACULAR
reservoirs, the first of the
country's man-made lakes,
has made this one of Wales's
most famous valleys. **Caban
Coch**, **Garreg Ddu**, **Pen-y-
Garreg** and **Craig Goch**,
were created between 1892
and 1903 to supply water to
Birmingham, 73 miles (117
km) away. They form a chain
of lakes about 9 miles (14 km)
long, holding 50 billion liters
(13 billion gallons) of water.
Victorian engineers selected
these high moorlands on the
Cambrian Mountains, for their
high annual rainfall of 1,780
mm (70 inches). The choice
created bitter controversy
and resentment: more than a
thousand people had to move
from the valley that was
flooded in order to create
Caban Coch.

Unlike their more utilitarian
modern counterparts, these
dams were built during an era
when decoration was seen as
an integral part of any design.
Finished in dressed stone,
they have an air of grandeur,
which is lacking in the huge
Claerwen reservoir, a stark
addition built during the early
1950s to double the lakes' cap-
acity. Contained by a 355 m
(1,165 ft) dam, it lies 4 miles
(6 km) along the B4518 that
runs through Elan Valley and
offers magnificent views.

The remote moorlands and
woodlands surrounding the
lakes are an important habitat

for wildlife; the rare red kite
can often be seen here. The
Elan Valley Visitors' Centre,
beside the Caban Coch dam,
describes the construction of
the lakes, as well as the
valley's own natural
history. **Elan Village**,
set beside the center,
is an unusual ex-
ample of a model
workers' village, built
during the 1900s to
house the water-
works staff. Outside
the centre is a statue
of the poet Percy
Bysshe Shelley
(see p208), who
stayed in the valley at
the mansion of
Nantgwyllt in 1810
with his wife, Harriet. The
house now lies underneath
the waters of Caban Coch,
along with the rest of the old
village. Among the buildings
submerged were the village
school and a church.

**The trail from Machynlleth to
Devil's Bridge, near Aberystwyth**

Machynlleth ❻

Powys. 👥 *2,200.* ⬛ ℹ *Canolfan
Owain Glyndŵr (01654 702401).*
🅐 *Wed.*

HALF-TIMBERED BUILDINGS
and Georgian façades
appear among the gray-stone
houses in Machynlleth. It was
here that Owain Glyndŵr,
Wales's last native leader *(see
p422)*, held a parliament in
1404. The restored **Parliament
House** has displays on his life
and a brass-rubbing center.

The ornate **Clock Tower**,
in the middle of Maengwyn
Street, was erected in 1874 by
the Marquess of Londonderry
to mark the coming of age of
his heir, Lord Castlereagh.
The Marquess lived in **Plas
Machynlleth**, a 17th-century
house in parkland off the main
street, which is now
a center of Celtic
heritage and culture.

ENVIRONS: In an old
slate quarry 2.5 miles
(4 km) to the north,
a "village of the
future" is run by the
**Centre for Alter-
native Technology**.
A water-balanced
cliff railroad takes
visitors to view low-
energy houses and
organic gardens, to
see how to make the best of
Earth's resources.

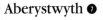

**Parliament House
sign, Machynlleth**

🏛 **Parliament House**
Maengwyn St. 📞 *01654 702827.*
🅞 *Easter–Sep: daily.* ♿
🏛 **Centre for Alternative
Technology**
On A487. 📞 *01654 702400.*
🅞 *daily.* ⬤ *end Dec–mid-Jan.* 🈂

Aberystwyth ❼

Cardiganshire (Dyfed). 👥 *11,000.*
⬛ 🅟 ℹ *Terrace Rd (01970 612125).*

THIS SEASIDE AND UNIVERSITY
town claims to be the
capital of mid-Wales. By the
standards of this rural area,
"Aber" is a big place, its
population increased for
much of the year by students.

To Victorian travelers,
Aberystwyth was the "Biarritz
of Wales." There have been

no great changes along the promenade, with its gabled hotels, since the 19th century. **Constitution Hill**, a steep outcrop at the northern end, can be scaled in summer on the electric **Cliff Railway**, built in 1896. At the top, in a *camera obscura*, a lens projects views of the town. The

Music on Aberystwyth's seafront

ruined **Aberystwyth Castle** (1277) is south of the promenade. In the town center, the **Ceredigion Museum**, in an old music hall, traces the town's past. To the northeast of the town, **The National Library of Wales**, next to the university, has a valuable collection of ancient Welsh manuscripts.

ENVIRONS: During the summer the narrow-gauge Vale of Rheidol Railway runs 12 miles

(19 km) to **Devil's Bridge**, where a dramatic series of waterfalls plunges through a wooded ravine and a steep trail leads to the valley floor.

🏛 Ceredigion Museum
Terrace Rd. 📞 01970 634212. ⬜ Mon–Sat. ● Dec 25–Jan 3, Good Fri. ♿

Aberaeron ❽

Cardiganshire (Dyfed). 👥 1,500. 🚌 Aberystwyth. 🛈 The Quay (01545 570602).

ABERAERON'S HARBOR, lined with Georgian houses, became a trading port and shipbuilding center in the early 19th century. Its orderly streets were laid out in pre-railway days, when the ports along Cardigan Bay enjoyed considerable wealth. The last boat was built in 1994 and its harbor is now full of holiday sailors. It can be crossed in summer on the **Aeron Ferry**, a precarious-looking replica of the original 1885 hand-operated gondola. On the quayside, the **Honey Bee Exhibition** makes use of observation hives to show honey bees at work.

🏛 Honey Bee Exhibition
Cadwgan Pl. 📞 01545 570445. ⬜ Whitsun–mid-Sep: daily. 📷

Rows of brightly painted Georgian houses line the harbor at Aberaeron

St. David's ❾

ST. DAVID, the patron saint of Wales, founded a monastic settlement in this remote corner of southwest Wales in about 550, which became one of the most important Christian shrines. The present cathedral, built in the 12th century, and the Bishop's Palace, added a century later, are set in a grassy hollow below St. David's town, officially Britain's smallest city. The date of St. David's death, March 1, is commemorated throughout Wales.

Icon of Elijah, south transept

St. David's Cathedral, the largest in Wales

★ Great Hall
The open arcade and decorated parapet were added by Bishop Gower (1328–47) to unify the different sections of the palace.

The Private Chapel
was a late 14th-century addition, built, like the rest of the palace, over a series of vaults.

Entrance

BISHOP'S PALACE
The bishop's residence, built between 1280–1350 and now in ruins, had lavish private apartments.

Palace latrines

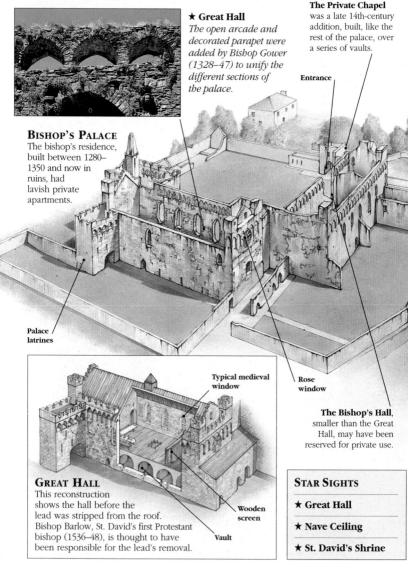

Typical medieval window

Rose window

The Bishop's Hall, smaller than the Great Hall, may have been reserved for private use.

GREAT HALL
This reconstruction shows the hall before the lead was stripped from the roof. Bishop Barlow, St. David's first Protestant bishop (1536–48), is thought to have been responsible for the lead's removal.

Wooden screen

Vault

STAR SIGHTS

★ **Great Hall**

★ **Nave Ceiling**

★ **St. David's Shrine**

★ Nave Ceiling
The roof of the nave is lowered and hidden by an early 16th-century oak ceiling. A beautiful 14th-century rood screen divides the nave from the choir.

VISITORS' CHECKLIST

Cathedral Close, St. David's, Pembrokeshire (Dyfed). 01437 720202. Haverfordwest then bus. 7am–7pm daily 7:30am, 8am, 6pm, Mon–Sat; 9:30am, 11am, 6pm Sun.

CATHEDRAL
St. David was one of the founders of the Celtic Christian church, so this became an important site of pilgrimage. Three visits here were equal to one to Jerusalem.

Stained-Glass Window
In the nave's west end, eight panels, produced in the 1950s, radiate from a central window showing the dove of peace.

Bishop Vaughan's Chapel has a fine early Tudor roof with fan-tracery.

St. Mary's College Chapel

Entrance

Tower Lantern Ceiling
The medieval roof was decorated with episcopal insignia when restored in the 1870s by Sir George Gilbert Scott (see p302).

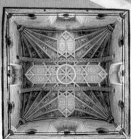

Sixteenth-Century Choir Stalls
The royal coat of arms on one of the carved choir stalls shows that the sovereign is a member of St. David's Chapter. There are some interesting misericords (see p327) in these stalls.

★ St. David's Shrine
The original was stolen in 1089 and this 1275 shrine was stripped of jewels in the Dissolution (see pp50–51). In 1866 relics of St. David were found underneath the floor.

Tenby ❿

Pembrokeshire (Dyfed). 👥 5,000.
🚇 🚌 🏢 ℹ The Croft (01834
842402).

Tenby has successfully trodden the fine line between overcommercialization and popularity, refusing to submit its historic character to the garish excesses of some seaside towns. Georgian houses overlook its handsome harbor, which is backed by a well-preserved medieval clifftop town of narrow streets and passages. The old town was defended by a headland fortress, now ruined, flanked by two wide beaches and a ring of 13th-century walls. These survive to their full height in places, along with a fortified gateway, the **Five Arches**.

The three-storied **Tudor Merchant's House** is a 15th-century relic of Tenby's highly prosperous seafaring days, with original fireplaces and chimneys. From the picturesque harbor there are regular boat trips to **Caldey Island**, 3 miles (5 km) offshore, home of a monastic community that makes perfume from local wild flowers.

🏛 **Tudor Merchant's House**
(NT) Quay Hill. ☎ 01834 842279.
⭘ Apr–Oct: Mon–Fri, Sun: by appt.

A partly medieval restaurant next to the Tudor Merchant's House

Swansea and the Gower Peninsula ⓫

Swansea (West Glamorgan). 👥
190,000. 🚇 🚌 🏢 ℹ Singleton St
(01792 468321). 🏪 Mon–Sat.

Swansea, Wales's second city, is set along a wide, curving bay. The city center was rebuilt after heavy bombing in World War II but despite the modern buildings, a traditional Welsh atmosphere prevails. This is particularly noticeable in the excellent food market, full of Welsh delicacies such as laverbread *(see p36)* and locally caught cockles.

The award-winning **Maritime Quarter** redevelopment has transformed the old docklands. In an old warehouse on the waterfront, the **Maritime and Industrial Museum** has displays on the city's copper- and tinplate industries, and on the first passenger-carrying railroad in the world, the horse-drawn Mumbles Railway, opened in 1807.

A statue of copper magnate John Henry Vivian (1779–1855) overlooks the marina. The Vivians, a leading Swansea family, founded the **Glynn Vivian Art Gallery**, which has exquisite Swansea pottery and porcelain. Archaeology and Welsh history feature at the **Swansea Museum**, established in 1838 and is the oldest museum in Wales.

The poet Dylan Thomas (1914–53), whose statue overlooks the Maritime Quarter, spent his childhood in the hilly suburbs west of the city center. **Cwmdonkin Park** was the scene of one of his early poems, *The Hunchback in the Park*, and its water garden has a memorial stone quoting from one of his most popular works, *Fern Hill*.

Swansea's austere **Guildhall** (1934) has a surprisingly rich interior. The huge panels, by

Swansea's most celebrated son, the poet Dylan Thomas

Picturesque fishermen's cottages at the Mumbles seaside resort

Sir Frank Brangwyn (1867–1956), on the theme of the British Empire, were originally painted for the House of Lords, but were considered too incongruous and colorful.

Swansea Bay leads to the **Mumbles**, a popular watersports center at the gateway to the 18-mile-long (29-km) Gower Peninsula, which in 1956 was the first part of Britain to be declared an Area of Outstanding Natural Beauty. A string of sheltered, southfacing bays leads to Oxwich and Port-Eynon beaches, once the haunt of smugglers.

From Port-Eynon a curtain of limestone cliffs ends dramatically at Rhossili and the spectacular promontory of Worm's Head, accessible by a low-tide causeway. Rhossili's enormous beach leads to north Gower and a coastline of lowlying burrows, salt marshlands and cockle beds. The peninsula is littered with ancient sites such as **Parc Le Breose**, a prehistoric burial chamber.

🏛 **Maritime and Industrial Museum**
Museum Sq. ☎ 01792 650351.
⭘ Tue–Sun & public hols. ⭘ Dec 25,
26, Jan 1. ♿
🏛 **Glynn Vivian Art Gallery**
Alexandra Rd. ☎ 01792 655006.
⭘ Tue–Sun & public hols. ⭘ Dec
25, 26, Jan 1. ♿
🏛 **Swansea Museum**
Victoria Rd. ☎ 01792 653763.
⭘ Tue–Sun & public hols. ⭘ Dec 25,
26, Jan 1.
🏛 **Guildhall**
Brangwyn. ☎ 01792 302489. ⭘
Mon–Fri. ⭘ public hols. ♿ limited.

Wild Wales Tour ⑫

THIS TOUR WEAVES ACROSS the Cambrian Mountains' windswept moors, green hills and high deserted plateaus. New roads have been laid to the massive Llyn Brianne Reservoir, north of Llandovery, and the old drover's road across to Tregaron has a tarmac surface. But the area is still essentially a "wild Wales" of hidden hamlets, isolated farmsteads, brooding highlands and traditional, quiet market towns.

Llanidloes ⑥
The town was a center of religious and social unrest in the 17th and 18th centuries *(see p423)*. There is a rare example of a free-standing Tudor market hall. The medieval church was restored in the late 19th century.

Devil's Bridge ④
This is a popular, romantic beauty spot with waterfalls, rocks, wooded glades and an ancient stone bridge – built by the Devil, according to legend.

Strata Florida ③
This famous ruined abbey was an important political, religious and educational center during the Middle Ages.

Elan Valley ⑤
This is an area of lakes and important wildlife habitats *(see p448)*.

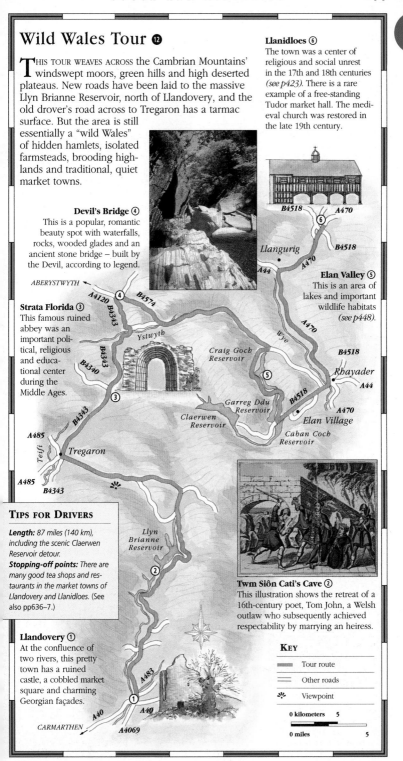

TIPS FOR DRIVERS

Length: *87 miles (140 km), including the scenic Claerwen Reservoir detour.*
Stopping-off points: *There are many good tea shops and restaurants in the market towns of Llandovery and Llanidloes. (See also pp636–7.)*

Twm Siôn Cati's Cave ②
This illustration shows the retreat of a 16th-century poet, Tom John, a Welsh outlaw who subsequently achieved respectability by marrying an heiress.

Llandovery ①
At the confluence of two rivers, this pretty town has a ruined castle, a cobbled market square and charming Georgian façades.

KEY

▬▬▬ Tour route

═══ Other roads

☼ Viewpoint

0 kilometers   5

0 miles   5

Brecon Beacons ®

THE BRECON BEACONS National Park covers 519 sq miles (1,345 sq km) from the Wales–England border almost all the way to Swansea. There are four mountain ranges within the park: the Black Mountain (to the west), Fforest Fawr, the Brecon Beacons and the Black Mountains (to the east). Much of the area consists of high, open country with smooth, grassy slopes on a bedrock of red sandstone. The park's southern rim has limestone crags, wooded gorges, waterfalls and caves. Visitors can enjoy many outdoor pursuits, from fishing in the numerous reservoirs to pony trekking, spelunking and walking.

Trekking in the Beacons

Llyn y Fan Fach
This remote, myth-laden glacial lake is a 4 mile (6.5 km) walk from Llanddeusant.

The Black Mountain, a largely unexplored wilderness of knife-edged ridges and high, empty moorland, fills the western corner of the National Park.

BUILTH WELLS

LAMPETER

Llandovery

A40

USK RESERVOIR

Sennybridge

Usk

Crai

A4067

A40

Senni

A421

L

CARMARTHEN

Tywi

Llanddeusant

Llandeilo

Trapp

B L A C K   M O U N T A I N

A4069

Twrch

Gred

A4067

YSTRADFELLT RESERVOI

FFOREST FAWR

Melte

Llandybie

A47

Tawe

Hepste

LLANELLI

A483

Ammanford

A4068

A4221

A4109

A4059

SWANSEA

Ystradgynlais

A465

NEATH

Hirwaun

0 kilometers   10

0 miles   5

Fforest Fawr ("Great Forest") is named after an area that was a medieval royal hunting ground.

Dan-yr-Ogof Caves
A labyrinth of caves runs through the Brecon Beacons. Guided tours of two large caves are offered here.

Carreg Cennen Castle
Spectacularly sited, the ruined medieval fortress of Carreg Cennen (see p424) stands on a sheer limestone cliff near the village of Trapp.

KEY

▭▭▭	A road
▭▭▭	B road
═══	Minor road
– –	Footpath
☆	Viewpoint

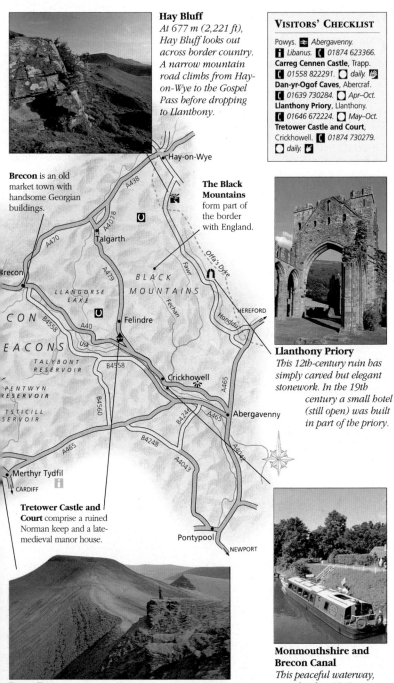

Hay Bluff
*At 677 m (2,221 ft),
Hay Bluff looks out
across border country.
A narrow mountain
road climbs from Hay-
on-Wye to the Gospel
Pass before dropping
to Llanthony.*

Brecon is an old
market town with
handsome Georgian
buildings.

**The Black
Mountains**
form part of
the border
with England.

Llanthony Priory
*This 12th-century ruin has
simply carved but elegant
stonework. In the 19th
century a small hotel
(still open) was built
in part of the priory.*

**Tretower Castle and
Court** comprise a ruined
Norman keep and a late-
medieval manor house.

Pen y Fan
*At 886 m (2,907 ft), Pen y Fan is the highest point in
South Wales. Its distinctive, flat-topped summit, once
a Bronze Age burial ground (see p42), can be reached
by foot paths from Storey Arms on the A470.*

**Monmouthshire and
Brecon Canal**
*This peaceful waterway,
completed in 1812, was
once used to transport raw
materials between Brecon
and Newport. It is now
popular with leisure boats.*

Cardiff ⓮

CARDIFF WAS FIRST OCCUPIED by the Romans, who built a fort here in AD 75 *(see pp44–5)*. Little is known of its subsequent history until Robert FitzHamon *(see p458)*, a knight in the service of William the Conqueror, was given land here in 1093. By the 13th century, the settlement was substantial enough to be granted a royal charter, but it remained a quiet country town until the 1830s when the Bute family, who inherited land in the area, began to develop it as a port. By 1913 Cardiff was the world's busiest coal-exporting port, profiting from rail links with the South Wales mines. Its wealth paid for grandiose architecture, while the docklands became a raucous boomtown. Cardiff was confirmed as the Welsh capital in 1955, when demand for coal was falling and the docks were in decline. The city is now dedicated to commerce and administration, and is being transformed by urban renewal programs.

Fireplace detail in the Banqueting Hall, Cardiff Castle *(see pp458–9)*

City Hall's dome, adorned with a dragon, the emblem of Wales

Exploring Cardiff

Cardiff is a city with two focal points. The center, laid out with Victorian and Edwardian streets and gardens, is the first of these. There is a Neo-Gothic castle and Neo-Classical civic buildings, as well as indoor shopping malls and a 19th-century **covered market**. Canopied arcades, lined with stores, lead off the main streets, the oldest being the **Royal Arcade** of 1856.

To the south of the center, the docklands are now being transformed into the second focal point by the creation of a marina and waterfront. A new Cardiff is taking shape, especially around the Inner Harbour area. The **Pier Head Building**, constructed on Cardiff Bay in 1896 for the Cardiff Railway Company, is a reminder of the city's heyday. Its intricate decoration and terra-cotta detail was partly influenced by the red Mogul

buildings of India. Other attractions are **National Techniquest**, a hands-on science museum, and the **Welsh Industrial Maritime Museum**, where exhibits such as a re-created ship's bridge illustrate the historical links between transportation and industry in Wales.

The wooden **Norwegian Church** on Waterfront Park was first erected in 1868 for Norwegian sailors bringing wooden props for use in the coal pits of the South Wales valleys. Once surrounded by warehouses, it was taken apart and rebuilt during the dockland development. It now houses a cultural center

and the **Cardiff Bay Visitor Centre**, which has displays on the building projects that are uniting the civic center with the maritime district.

♠ Cardiff Castle
See pp458–9.

🏛 City Hall and Civic Centre

Cathays Park. 📞 *01222 822075.* ⭕ *Mon–Fri.* ⬤ *public hols.* ♿
Cardiff's civic center of Neo-Classical buildings in white Portland stone is set among parks and avenues around Alexandra Gardens. City Hall (1905), one of its first buildings, is dominated by its 60 m (200 ft) dome and clock tower. Members of the public can visit the first floor Marble Hall, which is furnished with Siena marble columns and statues of Welsh heroes, among them St. David, Wales's patron saint *(see pp450–51).* The Crown Building, at the northern end of the complex,

The Pier Head Building overlooking the redeveloped area of Cardiff Bay now houses the Welsh Office, which is responsible for all Welsh government affairs.

⛪ National Museum of Wales

Cathays Park. 📞 01222 397951. 🕐 Tue–Sun & public hols. 🔴 Dec 25, 26, Jan 1. 🎫 ♿

Opened in 1927, the museum occupies an impressive civic building with a colonnaded portico, guarded by a statue of David Lloyd George *(see p423).*

Displays include a magnificent collection of Impressionist art by Renoir, Monet and Van Gogh, donated after World War II by two local sisters Gwendoline and Margaret Davies.

⛪ Old Library

Trinity St. 📞 01222 222584. 🕐 Mon–Sat. 🔴 public hols. 🎫 ♿

Until 1988, the main library was housed in this 1882 building of white Portland, Bath, and yellow Ham Hill

Statue of Welsh politician David Lloyd George

stone. The interior includes a corridor of Arts and Crafts tiles. An 1896 extension has a bust of Athene, the Goddess of Wisdom, and the Welsh aphorism: *"Ny bydd ddoeth ny ddarlleno"* ("He will not be wise who does not read"). The building now houses a crafts center and a Museum of Magical Machines that features displays of kinetic sculptures by local artist Charles Byrd.

ENVIRONS: Established during the 1940s at St. Fagans, on the western edge of the city, the open-air **Museum of Welsh Life** was one of the first of its kind. Buildings from all over Wales, including workers' terraced cottages, farmhouses, a tollhouse, a row of stores, a chapel and an old schoolhouse have been carefully reconstructed within the 40 ha (100 acre) parklands, along with a re-created Celtic village. There

VISITORS' CHECKLIST

Cardiff (South Glamorgan). 🏠 285,000. ✈ Rhoose. ⬛ Central Sq. 🚌 Wood St. ℹ Central Sq (01222 227281). 🚌 Sun. 🎡 Cardiff Festival: Aug.

is also a Tudor mansion which can be visited, with beautiful gardens on the grounds.

Llandaff Cathedral lies in a deep, grassy hollow beside the River Taf at Llandaff – a pretty "village suburb," which is 2 miles (3 km) northwest of the city center. The cathedral was first a medieval building, occupying the site of a 6th-century monastic community. Restored after suffering severe bomb damage during World War II, it reopened in 1957 with the addition of Sir Jacob Epstein's huge, stark statue, *Christus*, which is mounted on a concrete arch.

⛪ Museum of Welsh Life

St Fagans. 📞 01222 569441. 🕐 Apr–Oct: daily; Nov–Mar: Mon–Sat. 🔴 Dec 25, 26, Jan 1. 🎫 ♿

CARDIFF CITY CENTER

Cardiff Castle pp458–9 ③
City Hall & Civic Centre ②
Covered Market ④
National Museum of
  Wales ①
National Techniquest ⑥
Norwegian Church &
  Visitor Centre ⑨
Old Library ⑤
Pier Head Building ⑧
Welsh Industrial Maritime
  Museum ⑦

0 meters 500
0 yards 500

KEY

🚌 Coach station
⬛ Train station
🅿 Parking
ℹ Tourist information
✝ Church

Cardiff Castle

Cardiff castle began life as a Roman fort, whose remains are separated from later work by a band of red stone. A keep was built within the Roman ruins in the 12th century. Over the following 700 years, the castle passed to several powerful families and eventually to John Stuart, the Earl of Bute, in 1766. His great-grandson, the 3rd Marquess of Bute, employed the "eccentric genius," architect William Burges, who created an ornate mansion between 1867 and 1875, rich in medieval images and romantic detail.

Arab Room
The gilded ceiling, with Islamic marble and lapis lazuli decorations, was produced by Arab craftsmen in 1881.

Animal Wall
A lion and other creatures guard the wall to the south of the castle. They were added between 1880 and 1920.

Herbert Tower

★ **Summer Smoking Room**
This was part of a complete bachelor suite in the Clock Tower, which also included a Winter Smoking Room.

Clock Tower

Main entrance to apartments

TIMELINE

AD 75 Roman fort constructed	**1107** Castle inherited by Mabel Fitzhamon, whose husband is made Lord of Glamorgan	**1422–45** Beauchamp family adds the Octagon Tower and Great Hall ceiling	**1867** 3rd Marquess of Bute begins reconstruction
	1183 Castle damaged during Welsh uprising	**1445–1776** Castle passes in turn to Nevilles, Tudors and Herberts	

1000	1200	1400	1600	1800

1093 First Norman fort built by Robert Fitzhamon of Gloucester	**1308–1414** Despenser family holds castle		**1766** Bute family acquires the castle
			1948 The castle is given in trust to the city of Cardiff

Banqueting Hall wall detail

★ Banqueting Hall
The design and decoration of this 15th-century room depicts the castle's history, making ingenious use of the murals and castellated fireplace.

The Octagon Tower, also called the Beauchamp Tower, is the setting for Burges's Chaucer Room, decorated with themes from the *Canterbury Tales (see p172).*

★ Roof Garden
Using tiles, shrubs and a central fountain, Burges aimed to create a Mediterranean feel in this indoor garden, turning it into the crowning glory of the castle's apartments.

The Bute Tower had a suite of private rooms added in 1873, including a dining room, bedroom and sitting room.

★ Library
Carved figures representing ancient characters of Greek, Assyrian, Hebrew and Egyptian alphabets decorate the library's chimneypiece.

STAR SIGHTS

★ Banqueting Hall

★ Library

★ Summer Smoking Room

★ Roof Garden

Remains of Caerleon's amphitheater, built in the 2nd century

Caerleon **⑮**

Newport (Gwent). 🏘 *11,000.*
ℹ️ *Ffwrwm Art & Craft Centre, High St (01633 430777).*

TOGETHER WITH YORK *(see pp390–91)* and Chester *(see pp296–7)*, Caerleon was one of only three fortress settlements in Britain built for the Romans' elite legionary troops. From AD 74 Caerleon (*Isca* to the Romans, after the River Usk that flows beside the town) was home to the 2nd Augustan Legion, which had been sent to Wales to crush the native Silures tribe. The remains of their base now lie between the modern town and the river.

An altar at Caerleon's Legionary Museum

The excavations at Caerleon are of great social and military significance. The Romans built not only a fortress for their crack 5,500-strong infantry division but a complete town, equipped with a stone amphitheater. Judging by the results of the excavation work carried out since the archaeologist Sir Mortimer Wheeler unearthed the amphitheater in 1926, Caerleon is one of the largest and most important Roman military sites in Europe. The defenses enclosed an area of 20 ha (50 acres), with 64 rows of barracks, arranged in pairs, a hospital, and a bathhouse complex.

Outside the settlement, the amphitheater's large stone foundations have survived in an excellent state of preservation. Six thousand spectators could sit here and enjoy the violence of blood sports and gladiators' combat.

More impressive still is the fortress baths complex, which opened to the public in the mid-1980s. The baths were designed on a lavish scale to bring all the home comforts to an army posted to barbaric Britain. The Roman troops could take a dip in the open-air swimming pool, play sports in the exercise yard or covered hall, or enjoy a series of hot, warm and cold baths.

Nearby are the foundations of the only legionary barracks on view in Europe. The many artifacts that have been excavated on the site, including a remarkable collection of engraved gemstones, are now displayed at the **Legionary Museum**.

🏛 **Legionary Museum**
High St. 🅲 *01633 423134.* ☐ *daily.*
⬤ *Dec 24–26, Jan 1.* 📷 🚻

Big Pit Mining Museum, reminder of a vanished industrial society

Blaenafon **⑯**

Torfaen (Gwent). 🏘 *9,500.*
ℹ️ *94 Broad St (01495 792477).*

COMMERCIAL COAL MINING has now all but ceased in the South Wales valleys – an area that only 100 years ago was gripped by the search for its "black gold." Though coal is no longer produced at **Big Pit** in Blaenafon, the **Mining Museum** provides a vivid reminder of this tough industry. The Big Pit closed as a working mine in 1980, opened three years later as a museum. Visitors follow a marked-out route around the mine's surface workings to the miners' baths, the blacksmith's forge, the workshops and the engine house. There is also a replica of an underground gallery on the surface, where mining methods are explained. But the climax of any visit to Big Pit is beneath the ground. Equipped with miners' helmets, lamps and safety batteries, visitors are lowered by cage 90 m (300 ft) down the mineshaft and then guided by ex-miners on a tour of the underground workings and pit ponies' stables.

Blaenafon also has remains of the iron-smelting industry. Across the valley from Big Pit stand the 18th-century smelting furnaces and workers' cottages, that were once part of the **Blaenafon Ironworks**, and which are now open as an industrial museum.

🏛 **Big Pit Mining Museum**
Pit Rd. 🅲 *01495 790311.* ☐ *Mar–Nov: daily.* 📷 🚻 *phone first.*
🏛 **Blaenafon Ironworks**
North St. 🅲 *01495 792615.*
☐ *May–Sep: daily.* 📷 🚻

Monmouth **⑰**

Monmouthshire (Gwent). 🏘 *8,500.*
🚌 ℹ️ *Shire Hall (01600 713899).*
🚌 *Fri, Sat.*

THIS MARKET TOWN, which sits at the confluence of the Wye and Monnow rivers, has many historical associations. The 11th-century castle, behind Agincourt Square, is in ruins but the **Regimental Museum**,

Monnow Bridge in Monmouth, once a watchtower and jail

beside it, remains open to the public. The castle was the birthplace of Henry V *(see p49)* in 1387. A statue of Henry stands in the square, along with that of Charles Stewart Rolls (born at nearby Hendre), co-founder of the Rolls-Royce car manufacturers, who died in a plane crash in 1910.

Lord Horatio Nelson *(see p54)*, the famous admiral, visited Monmouth in 1802. An excellent collection of Nelson memorabilia, gathered by Lady Llangattock, mother of Charles Rolls, is displayed at the **Monmouth Museum**.

Monmouth was the county town of the old Monmouthshire. The wealth of elegant Georgian buildings, including the elaborate **Shire Hall**, which dominates Agincourt Square, reflect its former status. The most famous architectural feature in Monmouth is **Monnow Bridge**, a narrow 13th-century gateway on its western approach, thought to be the only surviving fortified bridge gate in Britain.

For a view of the town's borderland setting, climb the Kymin, a 256 m (840 ft) hill crowned by a **Naval Temple** built in 1801, when Britain's navy "ruled the waves."

♙ Monmouth Castle and Regimental Museum
The Castle. 📞 *01600 772175.*
◯ *Apr–Oct: daily (pm).* ♿
🏛 Monmouth Museum
Priory St. 📞 *01600 713519.*
◯ *daily.* ● *Dec 25, 26, Jan 1.* 🎟

Tintern Abbey ⑱

Monmouthshire (Gwent). 📞 *01291 689251.* 🚆 *Chepstow then bus.* ◯ *daily.* ● *Dec 24–26, Jan 1.* 🎟 ♿

EVER SINCE THE 18th century, travelers have been enchanted by Tintern's setting in the steep and wooded Wye Valley and by the majestic ruins of its abbey. Poets were often inspired by the scene. Wordsworth's sonnet, *Lines composed a few miles above Tintern Abbey*, embodied his romantic view of landscape:

> *once again*
> *Do I behold these steep and*
> *lofty cliffs,*
> *That on a wild, secluded*
> *scene impress*
> *Thoughts of more deep*
> *seclusion*

The abbey was founded in 1131 by Cistercian monks, who cultivated the surrounding lands (now forest), and developed it as an influential religious center. By the 14th century this was the richest abbey in Wales, but along with other monasteries it was dissolved in 1536 by Henry VIII *(see p50)*. Its skeletal ruins are now roofless and exposed, the soaring arches and windows giving them a poignant grace and beauty.

Tintern Abbey in the Wye Valley, in the past a thriving center of religion and learning, now a romantic ruin

SCOTLAND

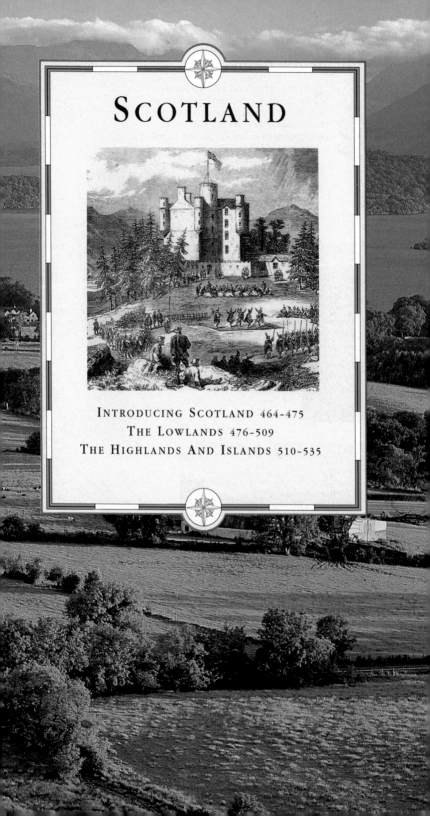

Scotland at a Glance

STRETCHING from the rich farmlands of the Borders to a chain of isles only a few degrees south of the Arctic Circle, the Scottish landscape has a diversity without parallel in Britain. As you travel northwest from Edinburgh, the land becomes more mountainous and its archaeological treasures more numerous. In the far northwest, Scotland's earliest relics stand upon the oldest rock on Earth.

Western Isles

THE HIGHLANDS AND ISLANDS (see pp510–35)

Skye (see pp520–21), *renowned for its dramatic scenery, has one of Scotland's most striking coastlines. On the east coast, a stream plunges over Kilt Rock, a cliff of hexagonal basalt columns named after its likeness to an item of Scottish national dress.*

Strathclyde

The Trossachs (see pp480–81) are a beautiful range of hills straddling the border between the Highlands and the Lowlands. At their heart, the forested slopes of Ben Venue rise above the still waters of Loch Achray.

Culzean Castle (see pp508–9) stands on a cliff's edge on the Firth of Clyde, amid an extensive country park. One of the jewels of the Lowlands, Culzean is a magnificent showcase of work by the Scottish-born architect, Robert Adam (see p24).

◁ Loch Lomond, the Lowlands

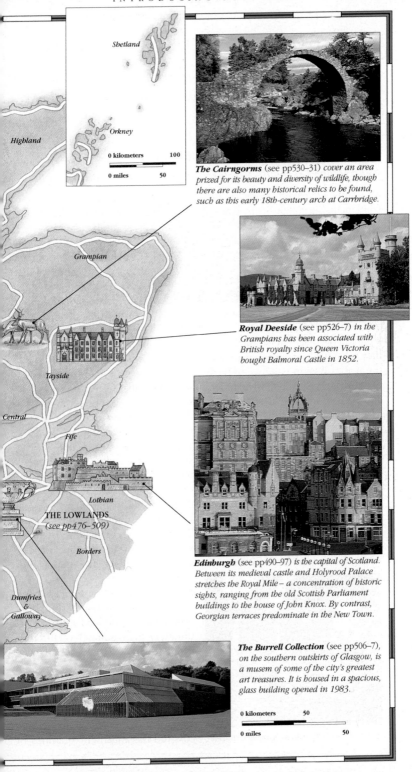

Shetland

Highland

Orkney

0 kilometers   100

0 miles   50

The Cairngorms (see pp530–31) *cover an area prized for its beauty and diversity of wildlife, though there are also many historical relics to be found, such as this early 18th-century arch at Carrbridge.*

Grampian

Royal Deeside (see pp526–7) *in the Grampians has been associated with British royalty since Queen Victoria bought Balmoral Castle in 1852.*

Tayside

Central

Fife

THE LOWLANDS
(see pp476–509)

Lothian

Borders

Dumfries & Galloway

Edinburgh (see pp490–97) *is the capital of Scotland. Between its medieval castle and Holyrood Palace stretches the Royal Mile – a concentration of historic sights, ranging from the old Scottish Parliament buildings to the house of John Knox. By contrast, Georgian terraces predominate in the New Town.*

The Burrell Collection (see pp506–7), *on the southern outskirts of Glasgow, is a musem of some of the city's greatest art treasures. It is housed in a spacious, glass building opened in 1983.*

0 kilometers   50

0 miles   50

A PORTRAIT OF SCOTLAND

FROM THE GRASSY HILLS *of the Borders to the desolate Cuillin Ridge of Skye, the landscape of Scotland is breathtaking in its variety. Lonely glens, sparkling lochs and everchanging skies give the land a challenging character, which is reflected in the qualities of the Scottish people. Tough and self-reliant, they have produced some of Britain's finest soldiers, its boldest explorers and most astute industrialists.*

Although governed from London, the six million Scots are proud of their separate identity and their own systems of law, education and local administration. That they accepted the union with England in 1707 was due in part to the fact that it was effected under a Scottish king. But despite their national pride, they are not a homogeneous people, the main division is between traditionally Gaelic-speaking Highlanders, and the Lowlanders who spoke Scots, a form of Middle English, now extinct. Today, though Gaelic survives (chiefly in the Western Isles), most people speak richly accented English or regional dialects. Many Scottish surnames derive from Gaelic: the prefix "mac" means "son of." A Norse heritage can be found in the far north, where Shetlanders welcome the annual return of the sun during the Viking fire festival, Up Helly Aa.

A hammer-thrower at the Braemar Games

In the 16th century, a suspicion of authority and dislike of excessive flamboyance attracted many Scots to the Presbyterian church with its absence of bishops and its stress on simple worship. The Presbyterian Church of Scotland was established in 1689, although a substantial Catholic minority remained, which today predominates in the crofting (small-scale farming) communities of the Western Isles. Now sparsely populated, the Isles preserve a rural culture that once dominated the Highlands, a region that is the source of much that is distinctively Scottish. The clan system originated there, along with the tartans, the bagpipes and such unique sports as tossing the caber – a large tree trunk. Highland sports, along with traditional dances, are still performed at annual games *(see p64).*

Edinburgh bagpiper

Resourcefulness has always been a prominent Scottish virtue, and Scotland has produced a disproportionately high number of Britain's geniuses. James Watt designed the first effective steam engine to power the Industrial Revolution, while Adam Smith became the 18th century's most influential economist. In the 19th century, James Simpson discovered the anesthetic qualities of

The Viking festival, Up Helly Aa, in Lerwick, Shetland

A traditional stone croft on the Isle of Lewis

With some of the harshest weather conditions in Europe it is perhaps less surprising that Scotland has bred numerous great explorers, the most famous being Robert Scott (of the Antarctic) and African missionary David Livingstone. There is also a strong intellectual and literary tradition, from the 18th-century philosopher David Hume, through novelists Sir Walter Scott and Robert Louis Stevenson, to the poetry of Robert Burns. Today Scotland hosts a variety of arts festivals, such as Edinburgh's.

chloroform, James Young developed the world's first oil refinery and Alexander Bell revolutionized communications by inventing the telephone. The 20th century saw one of the greatest advances in medicine with the discovery of penicillin by Alexander Fleming.

The Scots are also known for being shrewd businessmen, and have always been prominent in finance: both the Bank of England and the Royal Bank of France were founded by Scots, while Andrew Carnegie created one of 19th century-America's biggest business empires.

Detail of Edinburgh's Festival Fringe office

With a population density only one-fifth of England and Wales, Scotland has vast tracts of untenanted land that offer numerous outdoor pleasures.

It is richly stocked with game, and the opening of the grouse season on 12 August is a highlight on the social calendar. Fishing and hill-walking are popular and in winter thousands flock to the Cairngorms and Glencoe for skiing. Though the weather may be harsher than elsewhere, the Scots will claim that the air is purer – and that their enjoyment of rugged conditions is what distinguishes them from their soft southern neighbors.

The blue waters of Loch Achray in the heart of the Trossachs, north of Glasgow

The History of Scotland

Bonnie Prince Charlie, by G. Dupré

SINCE THE ROMAN INVASION of Britain, Scotland's history has been characterized by its resistance to foreign domination. The Romans never conquered the area, and when the Scots extended their kingdom to its present boundary in 1018, a long era of conflict began with England. After many wars, the Scots accepted union with the "auld enemy": first with the union of crowns, and then with the Union of Parliament in 1707. The partnership has been fruitful for both countries, but Scottish self-rule is still a political issue.

An elaborately carved Pictish stone at Aberlemno, Angus

EARLY HISTORY

THERE IS MUCH EVIDENCE in Scotland of important prehistoric population centers, particularly in the Western Isles, which were peopled mostly by Picts who originally came from the Continent. By the time Roman Governor Julius Agricola invaded in AD 81, there were at least 17 independent tribes, including the Britons in the southwest, for him to contend with.

The Romans reached north to the Forth and Clyde valleys, but the Highlands deterred them from going farther. By AD 120, they had retreated to the line where the Emperor Hadrian had built his wall to keep the Picts at bay (not far from today's border). By 163 the Romans had retreated south for the last time. The Celtic influence began when

"Scots" arrived from Ireland in the 6th century, bringing the Gaelic language with them.

The Picts and Scots united under Kenneth McAlpin in 843, but the Britons remained separate until 1018, when they became part of the Scottish kingdom.

THE ENGLISH CLAIM

THE NORMAN KINGS regarded Scotland as part of their territory but seldom pursued the claim. William the Lion of Scotland recognized English sovereignty by the Treaty of Falaise (1174), though English control never spread to the northwest. In 1296 William Wallace, supported by the French (the start of the Auld Alliance, which lasted two centuries), began the long war of independence. During this bitter conflict, Edward I seized the sacred Stone of Destiny from Scone *(see p484)*, and took it to Westminister Abbey. The war lasted for more than 100 years, its great hero was Robert the Bruce, who defeated the English in 1314 at Bannockburn. The English held the upper hand after that, even though the Scots would not accept their rule.

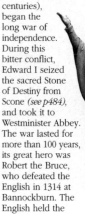

John Knox statue in Edinburgh

THE ROAD TO UNION

THE SEEDS OF UNION between the crowns were sown in 1503 when James IV of Scotland married Margaret Tudor, daughter of Henry VII. When her brother, Henry VIII, came to the throne, James sought to assert independence but was defeated and killed at Flodden Field in 1513. His granddaughter, Mary, Queen of Scots *(see p497)*, married the French Dauphin in order to cement the Auld Alliance and gain assistance in her claim

***Bruce in Single Combat at Bannockburn* (1906) by John Hassall**

to the throne of her English cousin, Elizabeth I. She had support from the Catholics wanting to see an end to Protestantism in England and Scotland. However, fiery preacher John Knox won support for the Protestants and established the Presbyterian Church in 1560. Mary's Catholicism led to the loss of her Scottish throne in 1568, and her subsequent flight to England, following defeat at Langside. Finally, after nearly 20 years of imprisonment she was executed for treason by Elizabeth in 1587.

The factories on Clydeside, once creators of the world's greatest ships

UNION AND REBELLION

O N ELIZABETH I's death in 1603, Mary's son, James VI of Scotland, succeeded to the English throne and became James I, king of both countries. Thus the crowns were united, though it was 100 years before the formal Union of Parliaments in 1707. During that time, religious differences within the country

Articles of Union between England and Scotland, 1707

reached the boiling point. There were riots when the Catholic-influenced Charles I restored bishops to the Church of Scotland and authorized the printing of a new prayer book. This culminated in the signing of the National Covenant (1638), a document that condemned all Catholic doctrines. Although the Covenanters were suppressed, the Protestant William of Orange took over the English throne in 1688 and the crown passed out of Scottish hands.

In 1745, Bonnie Prince Charlie *(see p521)*, descended from the Stuart kings, tried to seize the throne from the Hanoverian George II. He marched far into England, but was driven back and defeated at Culloden field *(see p523)* in 1746.

INDUSTRIALIZATION AND SOCIAL CHANGE

I N THE LATE 18TH AND 19th centuries, technological progress transformed Scotland from a nation of crofters to an industrial powerhouse. In the notorious Highland Clearances *(see p517)*, from the 1780s on, landowners ejected tenants from their smallholdings and gave the land over to sheep and other livestock. The first ironworks was established in 1760 and was soon followed by coal mining, steel production and shipbuilding on the Clyde. Canals were cut, railroads and bridges built.

A strong socialist movement developed as workers sought to improve their conditions. Keir Hardie, an Ayrshire coal miner, in 1892 became the first socialist elected to parliament, and in 1893 founded the Independent Labour Party. The most enduring symbol of this time is the spectacular Forth rail bridge *(see p488)*.

SCOTLAND TODAY

A LTHOUGH THE STATUS of the country appeared to have been settled in 1707, a strong nationalist sentiment remained and was heightened by the Depression of the 1920s and 30s, which had severe effects on the heavily industrialized Clydeside. This was when the Scottish National Party formed, advocating self-rule. The Nationalists asserted themselves in 1950 by stealing the Stone of Scone from Westminster Abbey.

The discovery of North Sea oil in 1970 encouraged a nationalist revival and, in 1979, the Government promised to establish a separate assembly if 40 per cent of the electorate endorsed the plan in a referendum. The figure was not reached, but of the votes cast, more were in favor than against. The issue is still hotly debated.

A North Sea oil rig, helping to provide prosperity in the 1970s

Clans and Tartans

THE CLAN SYSTEM, by which Highland society was divided into tribal groups led by autocratic chiefs, can be traced to the 12th century, when clans were already known to wear the checkered wool cloth later called tartan. All members of the clan bore the name of their chief, but not all were related by blood. Although they had noble codes of hospitality, the clansmen had to be warriors to protect their herds, as can be seen from their mottoes. After the Battle of Culloden *(see p523)*, all the clan lands were forfeited to the Crown, and the wearing of tartan was banned for nearly 100 years.

The Mackays, *also known as the Clan Morgan, won lasting fame during the Thirty Years War.*

The MacLeods *are of Norse heritage. The clan chief still lives in Dunvegan Castle, Skye (see p520).*

The Mackenzies *received much of the lands of Kintail (see p516) from David II in 1362.*

The MacDonalds *were the most power- ful of all the clans, holding the title of Lords of the Isles.*

CLAN CHIEF

The chief was the clan's patriarch, judge and leader in war, commanding absolute loyalty from his clansmen who gave mili- tary service in return for his protection. The chief sum- moned his clan to do battle by sending a run- ner across his land bearing a burning cross.

Bonnet with eagle feathers, clan crest and plant badge.

Dirk

Sporran, or pouch, made of badger's skin.

Feileadh- mor, or "great plaid," (the early kilt) wrap- ped around waist and shoulder.

Basket- hilted sword

The Campbells *were a widely feared clan who fought the Jacobites in 1746 (see p523).*

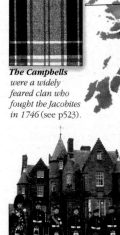

The Black Watch, *raised in 1729 to keep peace in the Highlands, was one of the Highland regiments in which the wearing of tartan sur- vived. For civilians, after 1746, wearing tartan was punishable by exile for up to seven years.*

The Sinclairs came from France in the 11th century and became Earls of Caithness in 1455.

The Frazers came to Britain from France with William the Conqueror's troops in 1066.

George IV, dressed as a Highlander, visited Edinburgh in 1822, the year of the tartan revival. Many tartan "setts" (patterns) date from this time, as the original ones were lost.

The Gordons were famously good soldiers; the clan motto is "by courage, not by craft."

The Stuarts were Scotland's royal dynasty. Their motto was "no one harms me with impunity."

CLAN TERRITORIES

The territories of 10 prominent clans are marked here with their clan crests. Clans with very colorful dress tartans wore darker ones just for hunting.

The Douglas clan were prominent in Scottish history, though their origin is unknown.

PLANT BADGES

Each clan had a plant associated with its territory. It was worn on the bonnet, especially on the day of battle.

Scots pine was worn by the MacGregors of Argyll.

Rowan berries were worn by the Clan Malcolm.

Ivy was worn by the Clan Gordon of Aberdeenshire.

Spear thistle, now a national symbol, was a Stuart badge.

Cotton grass was worn by the Clan Henderson.

HIGHLAND CLANS TODAY

Once the daily dress of the clansmen, the kilt is now largely reserved for formal occasions. The one-piece *feileadh-mor* has been replaced by the *feileadh-beag*, or "small plaid," made from approximately 7 m (23 ft) of material with a double apron fastened at the front with a silver pin. Though they exist now only in name, the clans are still a strong source of pride for Scots, and many still live in areas traditionally belonging to their clans. Many visitors to Britain can trace their Scots ancestry (see p27) to the Highlands.

Modern Highland formal dress

Evolution of the Scottish Castle

THERE ARE FEW more romantic sights in the British Isles than a Scottish castle on an island or at a lochside. These formidable retreats, often in remote settings, were essential all over the Highlands, where incursions and strife between the clans were common. From the earliest Pictish *brochs (see p42)* and Norman-influenced motte and bailey castles, the distinctively Scottish tower house evolved, first appearing in the 14th century. By the mid-17th century fashion had become more important than defense, and there followed a period in which numerous huge Scottish palaces were built.

Detail of the Baroque façade, Drumlanrig

MOTTE AND BAILEY

These castles first appeared in the 12th century. They stood atop two adjacent mounds enclosed by a wall, or palisade, and defensive ditches. The higher mound, or motte, was the most strongly defended as it held the keep and chief's house. The lower bailey was where the people lived. Of these castles little more than earthworks remain today.

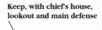

Keep, with chief's house, lookout and main defense

All that remains today of Duffus Castle, Morayshire

Duffus Castle, (c.1150), was atypically made of stone rather than wood. Its fine defensive position dominates the surrounding flatlands north of Elgin.

Motte of earth or rock, sometimes partially man-made

Bailey enclosing dwellings and storehouses

EARLY TOWER HOUSE

Designed to deter local attacks rather than a major assault, the first tower houses appeared in the 13th century, though their design lived on for 400 years. They were built initially on a rectangular plan, with a single tower divided into three or four floors. The walls were unadorned, with few windows. Defensive structures were on top, and extra space was made by building adjoining towers. Extensions were made as vertically as possible, to minimize the area open to attack.

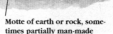

Crenellated parapet for sentries

Featureless, straight walls with arrow slits for windows

Claypotts Castle (c.1570) with uniquely projecting garrets above its towers

Braemar Castle (c.1630), a conglomeration of extended towers

Neidpath Castle, standing upon a steep rocky crag above the River Tweed, is an L-shaped tower house dating from the late 14th century. Once a stronghold for Charles II, its walls still bear damage from a siege conducted by Oliver Cromwell (see p52).

Small, inconspicuous doorway

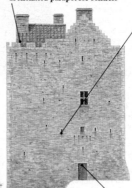

LATER TOWER HOUSE

Though the requirements of defense were being replaced by those of comfort, the style of the early tower house remained popular. By the 17th century, wings for accommodation were being added around the original tower (often creating a courtyard). The battlements and turrets were kept more for decorative than defensive reasons.

Drum Castle *(see p527)*, a 13th-century keep with a mansion house extension from 1619

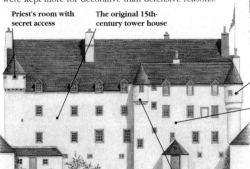

Priest's room with secret access

The original 15th-century tower house

Round angle tower, containing stairway

A 16th-century horizontal extension

Traquair House (see p488), *by the Tweed, is reputedly the oldest continuously inhabited house in Scotland. The largely unadorned, roughcast exterior dates to the 16th century, when a series of extensions were built around the original 15th-century tower house.*

Decorative, corbelled turret

Blair Castle *(see p529)*, incorporating a medieval tower

CLASSICAL PALACE

By the 18th century, the defensive imperative had passed and castles were built in the manner of country houses, rejecting the vertical tower house in favor of a horizontal plan (though the building of imitation fortified buildings continued into the 19th century with the mock-Baronial trend). Outside influences came from all over Europe, including Renaissance and Gothic revivals, and echoes of French châteaux.

Dunrobin Castle (c.1840), Perthshire

Larger windows due to a lesser need for defense

Decorative cupola

Balustrades instead of battlements

Drumlanrig Castle (see p500) *was built in the 17th century. There are many traditional Scots aspects as well as such Renaissance features as the decorated stairway and façade.*

Renaissance-style colonnade

Baroque horseshoe stairway

Scottish Food and Drink

THE SCOTTISH LARDER is generous in meat and fish, which are usually served simply, without heavy sauces. Grouse and deer range the hills, Aberdeen Angus beef is world famous, and the rivers are renowned for their salmon and trout. With Scotland's cold, wet climate and shallow soil, wheat was grown less than oats, which are still present in traditional Scottish foods, such as oatmeal and oatcakes (rather than bread) and, of course, haggis.

Oatmeal is a breakfast of oats, boiled in water and milk, with salt or sugar.

Kippers, eaten at breakfast, are fresh herring split down the back, salted and cured by smoking over a fire.

Poached salmon tastes best when cooked whole in a bouillon of water, wine and vegetables, during which its deep red flesh turns a delicate pink. Salmon are caught in Scotland's east coast rivers.

Scotch broth is a light, thin soup based on neck of mutton or beef, to which pearl barley and vegetables are added.

Venison is allowed to hang for ten days before being seasoned with mixed spices, wine and vinegar, and then roasted.

Haggis, served boiled with rutabagas and potatoes, is spiced sheep's innards, here mixed with oatmeal.

MARMALADE

Marmalade was created in Dundee *(see p485)* in the 1700s after a rash purchase left grocer James Keiller with a large cargo of bitter Seville oranges. He was unable to resell them, so his wife Janet added them to a preserve. Word soon spread about her delicious creation, which now appears on breakfast tables throughout the world.

Traditional orange   **Grapefruit and ginger**

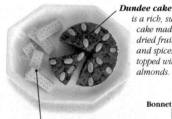

Dundee cake is a rich, sweet cake made of dried fruits and spices topped with almonds.

Bonnet

Shortbread   **Bonchester**

Scottish oatcakes are flat cookies of fine oatmeal that accompany sweets or canapés. Hard Bonnet and soft Bonchester are popular among the Scottish cheeses.

How Whisky is Made

Traditionally made from just barley, yeast and stream water, Scottish whisky (from the Gaelic *usquebaugh*, or the "water of life") takes a little over three weeks to produce, although it must be given at least three years to mature. Maturation usually takes place in oak casks, often in barrels previously used for sherry. The art of blending was pioneered in Edinburgh in the 1860s.

Barley grass

1 Malting is the first stage. Barley grain is soaked in water and spread on the malting floor. With regular turning the grain germinates, producing a "green malt." Germination stimulates the production of enzymes that turn the starches into fermentable sugars.

2 Drying of the barley stops germination after 12 days of malting. This is done over a peat fire in a pagoda-shaped malt-kiln. The peat-smoke gives flavor to the malt and eventually to the mature whisky. The malt is gleaned of germinated roots and then milled.

3 Mashing of the ground malt, or "grist," occurs in a large vat, or "mash tun," which holds a vast quantity of hot water. The malt is soaked and begins to dissolve, producing a sugary solution called "wort," which is then extracted for fermentation.

4 Fermentation occurs when yeast is added to the cooled wort in wooden vats, or "wash-backs." The mixture is stirred for hours as the yeast turns the sugar into alcohol, producing a clear liquid called "wash."

5 Distillation involves boiling the wash twice so that the alcohol vaporizes and condenses. In copper "pot stills," the wash is distilled – first in the "wash still," then in the "spirit still." Now purified, with an alcohol content of 57 percent, the result is young whisky.

6 Maturation is the final process. The whisky mellows in oak casks for a legal minimum of three years. Premium brands give the whisky a 10- to 15-year maturation, although some are given up to 50 years.

Traditional drinking vessels, or *quaichs*, made of silver

Blended whiskies are made from a mixture of up to 50 different single malts.

Single malts vary according to regional differences in the peat and stream water used.

THE LOWLANDS

STRATHCLYDE · CENTRAL · TAYSIDE · FIFE
LOTHIANS · DUMFRIES AND GALLOWAY · BORDERS

OUTHEAST *of the Highland boundary fault line lies a part of Scotland very different in character from its northern neighbor. If the Highlands embody the romance of Scotland, the Lowlands have traditionally been her powerhouse. Lowlanders have always prospered in agriculture and, more recently, in industry and commerce.*

Being the region of Scotland closest to the English border, the Lowlands inevitably became the crucible of Scottish history. For centuries after the Romans built the Antonine Wall (*see p44*) across the Forth–Clyde isthmus, the area was engulfed in conflict. The Borders are scattered with the castles of a territory in uneasy proximity to rapacious neighbors, and the ramparts of Stirling Castle overlook no fewer than seven different battlefields fought over in the cause of independence.

The ruins of medieval abbeys, such as Melrose, also bear witness to the dangers of living on the invasion route from England, though the woolen trade founded by their monks still flourishes in Peebles and Hawick.

North of the Borders lies Edinburgh, the cultural and administrative capital of Scotland. With its Georgian squares dominated by a medieval castle, it is one of Europe's most elegant cities. While the 18th and 19th centuries saw a great flowering of the arts in Edinburgh, the city of Glasgow became a merchant city second only to London. Fueled by James Watt's development of the steam engine in the 1840s, Glasgow became the cradle of Scotland's Industrial Revolution, which created a prosperous cotton industry and launched the world's greatest ships.

Both cities retain this dynamism today: Edinburgh annually hosts the world's largest arts festival, and Glasgow is acclaimed as a model of industrial renaissance.

A juggler performing at the annual arts extravaganza, the Edinburgh Festival

◁ **Glamis Castle, 12 miles (19 km) north of Dundee, with its typically Scottish turreted exterior**

Exploring the Lowlands

THE LOWLANDS are traditionally all
the land south of the fault line
stretching northeast from Loch Lomond
to Stonehaven. Confusingly, they include plenty of wild upland country.
The region illustrates best the diversity of Scotland's magnificent scenery.
The wooded valleys and winding rivers
of the border country give way to the
stern moorland hills of the Cheviots and
Lammermuirs. Lively little fishing
villages cling to the rocky east coast,
while the Clyde coast and its islands
are dotted with vacation towns. Inland
lie the Trossachs; these romantic
mountains surrounding Loch Lomond
are a magnet for walkers *(see pp32–3)*
and are well within reach of Glasgow.

**Loch Lomond seen from the summit of
Ben A'an, the Trossachs**

SEE ALSO

- **Where to Stay** pp568-70

- **Where to Eat** pp604-6

SIGHTS AT A GLANCE

Walks and Tours

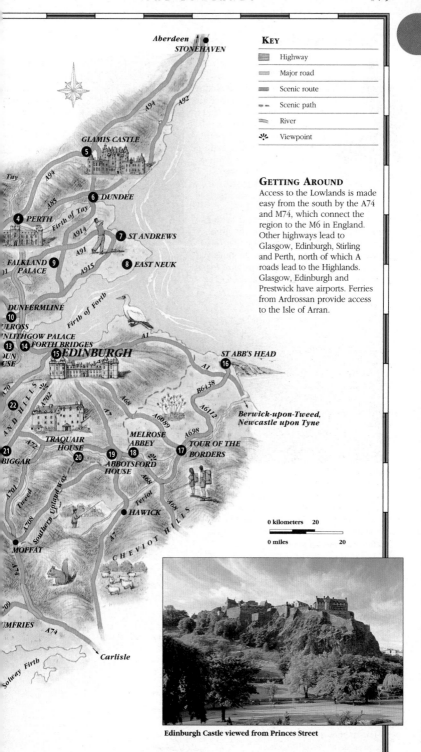

Aberdeen
STONEHAVEN

A94   A92

A94

Tay

A85

GLAMIS CASTLE
5

6 **DUNDEE**

4 **PERTH**

Firth of Tay

A914   **7** **ST ANDREWS**

A91

FALKLAND **9**
PALACE

A915   **8** **EAST NEUK**

DUNFERMLINE
10

Firth of Forth

ULROSS

NLITHGOW PALACE

13 **14** **FORTH BRIDGES**

15 **EDINBURGH**

A1

ST ABB'S HEAD
16

A1

B6438

A6112

*Berwick-upon-Tweed,
Newcastle upon Tyne*

A70

A702

22

D HILLS

A7

A68

A6089

A698

**MELROSE
ABBEY**
18

17 **TOUR OF THE
BORDERS**

21

**TRAQUAIR
HOUSE**
A72

20

19 **ABBOTSFORD
HOUSE**

A68

BIGGAR

A701

Tweed

Southern Upland Way

A708

Teviot

A7   **HAWICK**

CHEVIOT HILLS

A68

MOFFAT

UMFRIES   A74

Solway Firth

Carlisle

KEY

▨	Highway
▨	Major road
▨	Scenic route
--	Scenic path
≈	River
☆	Viewpoint

GETTING AROUND

Access to the Lowlands is made
easy from the south by the A74
and M74, which connect the
region to the M6 in England.
Other highways lead to
Glasgow, Edinburgh, Stirling
and Perth, north of which A
roads lead to the Highlands.
Glasgow, Edinburgh and
Prestwick have airports. Ferries
from Ardrossan provide access
to the Isle of Arran.

0 kilometers   20

0 miles   20

Edinburgh Castle viewed from Princes Street

The Trossachs ❶

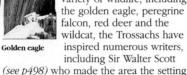
Golden eagle

COMBINING THE RUGGEDNESS of the Grampians with the pastoral tranquillity of the Borders, this beautiful region of craggy hills and sparkling lochs is the colorful meeting place of the Lowlands and Highlands. Home to a wide variety of wildlife, including the golden eagle, peregrine falcon, red deer and the wildcat, the Trossachs have inspired numerous writers, including Sir Walter Scott *(see p498)* who made the area the setting for several of his novels. It was the home of Scotland's folk hero, Rob Roy, who was so well known that, in his own lifetime, he was fictionalized in *The Highland Rogue* (1723), a novel attributed to Daniel Defoe.

Loch Katrine
The setting of Sir Walter Scott's Lac of the Lake (181(this freshwater loch can be explored on the Victorian steame Sir Walter Scott, which cruises fro the Trossachs Pier

Loch Lomond
Britain's largest freshwater lake was immortalized in a ballad composed by a local Jacobite soldier, dying far from home. He laments that although he will return home before his companions who travel on the high road, he will be doing so on the low road (of death).

Luss
With its exceptionally picturesque cottages, Luss is one of the prettiest villages in the Lowlands. Surrounded by grassy hills, it occupies one of the most scenic parts of Loch Lomond's eastern shore.

The West Highland Way provides a good footpath through the area.

FORT WILLIAM

Inveruglas

LOCH ARKLET

Tarbet

BEN LOMOND
▲
974 m
3,196 ft

Kinloch

BEN UIRD
▲
596 m
1,955 ft

Luss

Balma

L O C H
L O M O N D

Balloch

GLASGOW

KEY

🛈	Tourist information
▬▬	A road
▬	B road
═	Minor road
- -	Footpath
⁂	Viewpoint

0 kilometers   5

0 miles   5

Inchmahome Priory

Mary, Queen of Scots (see p497) was hidden on this island priory to escape the armies of Henry VIII (see p498).

VISITORS' CHECKLIST

Central. ⊞ *Stirling.* 🚌 *Callander.*
🛈 Rob Roy & Trossachs Centre,
Ancaster Sq, Callander (01877
330342). **Inchmahome Priory**,
off A81, nr Aberfoyle
📞 0131 2443101. ⬜ Apr–Sep:
daily. 🖼 🔥 limited.
ss Sir Walter Scott: phone
Visitor Centre for details.

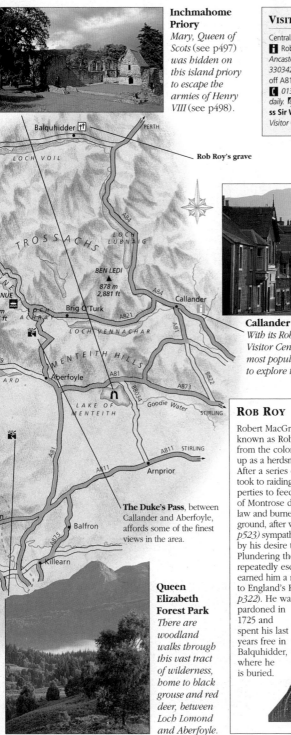

Rob Roy's grave

Callander

With its Rob Roy and Trossachs Visitor Centre, Callander is the most popular town from which to explore the Trossachs.

ROB ROY

Robert MacGregor (1671–1734), known as Rob Roy (Red Robert) from the color of his hair, grew up as a herdsman near Loch Arklet. After a series of harsh winters, he took to raiding richer Lowland properties to feed his clan. The Duke of Montrose declared him an outlaw and burned Rob's house to the ground, after which his Jacobite *(see p523)* sympathies became inflamed by his desire to avenge the crime. Plundering the duke's lands and repeatedly escaping from prison earned him a reputation similar to England's Robin Hood *(see p322)*. He was pardoned in 1725 and spent his last years free in Balquhidder, where he is buried.

The Duke's Pass, between Callander and Aberfoyle, affords some of the finest views in the area.

Queen Elizabeth Forest Park

There are woodland walks through this vast tract of wilderness, home to black grouse and red deer, between Loch Lomond and Aberfoyle.

The 17th-century town house of the Dukes of Argyll, Stirling

Stirling ❷

Central. 🏛 28,000. ⊒ ▣
ℹ️ Dunbarton Rd (01786 475019).

LOCATED BETWEEN the Ochil Hills and the Campsie Fells, the town of Stirling developed around its castle, historically one of Scotland's most important fortresses. Below the castle the Old Town is still protected by the original walls, built in the 16th century to keep Mary, Queen of Scots *(see p497)* safe from Henry VIII. The medieval **Church of the Holy Rude**, on Castle Wynd, where the infant James VI was crowned in 1567, has one of Scotland's few surviving hammerbeam oak roofs. In front of the church, the ornate façade of **Mar's Wark** is all that remains of a grand palace, which, though never completed, was commissioned in 1570 by the 1st Earl of Mar. It was destroyed by the Jacobites *(see p523)* in 1746. Opposite stands the beautiful 17th-century town house of the Dukes of Argyll.

ENVIRONS: Two miles (3 km) south, the **Bannockburn Heritage Centre** stands by the field where Robert the Bruce defeated the English *(see p468)*. After the battle, he dismantled the castle so it would not fall back into English hands. A bronze equestrian statue commemorates the man who became an icon of Scottish independence.

🏛 **Bannockburn Heritage Centre**
(NTS) Glasgow Rd. 📞 01786 812664. ⬜ Mar–Dec 23: daily. ⬛ Dec 24–Feb. 🅿️ 🚻

Stirling Castle

RISING HIGH on a rocky crag, this magnificent castle, which dominated Scottish history for centuries, now remains one of the finest examples of Renaissance architecture in Scotland. Legend says that King Arthur *(see p269)* wrested the original castle from the Saxons, but there is no evidence of a castle before 1124. The present building dates from the 15th and 16th centuries and was last defended, against the Jacobites *(see p523)*, in 1746. From 1881 to 1964 the castle was a depot for recruits into the Argyll and Sutherland Highlanders, but now it serves no military function.

Gargoyle on castle wall

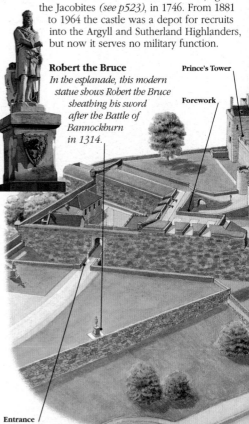

Robert the Bruce
In the esplanade, this modern statue shows Robert the Bruce sheathing his sword after the Battle of Bannockburn in 1314.

Prince's Tower

Forework

Entrance

***Stirling Castle in the Time of the Stuarts**, painted by Johannes Vorsterman (1643–99)*

★ Palace
The otherwise sparse interiors of the royal apartments contain the Stirling Heads. These Renaissance roundels depict 38 figures, thought to be contemporary members of the royal court.

The King's Old Building houses the Regimental Museum of the Argyll and Sutherland Highlanders.

★ Chapel Royal
Seventeenth-century frescoes by Valentine Jenkins adorn the chapel, reconstructed in 1594.

Nether Bailey

The Great Hall, built in 1500, has a roof similar to that of Edinburgh Castle *(see pp492–3).*

STAR SIGHTS

★ Palace

★ Chapel Royal

The Elphinstone Tower was made into a gun platform in 1714.

Grand Battery
Seven guns stand on this parapet, built in 1708 during a strengthening of defenses following the revolution of 1688 (see p53).

STIRLING BATTLES

At the highest navigable point of the Forth and holding the pass to the Highlands, Stirling occupied a key position in Scotland's struggles for independence. Seven battlefields can be seen from the castle; the 67 m (220 ft) Wallace Monument at Abbey Craig recalls William Wallace's defeat of the English at Stirling Bridge in 1297, foreshadowing Bruce's victory in 1314 *(see p468).*

The Victorian Wallace Monument

Perth seen from the east across the Tay

Doune Castle ❸

Doune, Central. **[** 01786 841742.
⇄ 🚌 Stirling then bus. ☐ Apr–Sep:
daily; Oct–Mar: Sat–Thu. ● Dec 25,
26, Jan 1–3. 🏚 ⚹

BUILT AS THE residence of
Robert, Duke of Albany,
in the 14th century, **Doune
Castle** was a Stuart stronghold
until it fell into ruin in the 18th
century. Now fully restored,
Doune is one of the most
beautifully complete castles of
its time and offers a unique
view into the life of the
medieval royal household.

The Gatehouse, once a self-
sufficient residence with its
own water supply, leads
through to the central courtyard from which the Great
Hall can be entered. Complete
with its reconstructed open-
timber roof, minstrels' gallery
and central fireplace, the
Hall adjoins the Lord's Hall
and Private Room with its
original privy and well-hatch.

A number of private stairs and
narrow passages illustrate how
the royal family tried to protect
itself during times of danger.

Perth ❹

Tayside. 🏚 42,000. ⇄ 🚌 🚹 45
High St (01738 38353). 🛒 Sun.

ONCE THE CAPITAL of medieval Scotland, Perth's rich
heritage is reflected in many of
its buildings. It was in the
Church of Saint John,
founded in 1126, that John
Knox (see p469) delivered the
fiery sermons that led to the
destruction of many local monasteries. The Victorianized **Fair
Maid's House**, on North Port,
is one of the oldest houses in
town (c.1600) and was the
fictional home of the heroine
of Sir Walter Scott's (see p498)
The Fair Maid of Perth (1828).

In **Balhousie Castle**, the
Museum of the Black Watch
commemorates the first

Highland regiment, while the
Art Gallery and Museum has
displays on local industry and
exhibitions of Scottish painting.

ENVIRONS: Two miles (3 km)
north of Perth, the Gothic
mansion of **Scone Palace**
stands on the site of an abbey
destroyed by John Knox's followers in 1559. Between the
9th and 13th centuries, Scone
guarded the sacred Stone of
Destiny (see pp468–9), now
kept in Westminister Abbey
(see pp94-5), on which the
Scottish kings were crowned.
Mary, Queen of Scots' (see
p497) embroideries are among
the priceless displays here.

♣ **Balhousie Castle**
RHQ Black Watch, Hay St.
[01738 621281. ☐ Apr–Sep:
Mon–Sat; Oct–Apr: Mon–Fri.
● Dec 23–Jan 3.
🏛 **Art Gallery and Museum**
78 George St. **[** 01738 632488.
☐ daily. ● Dec 24–Jan 4. ⚹
♣ **Scone Palace**
A93 to Braemar. **[** 01738 552300.
☐ Good Fri–mid-Oct: daily. 🏚 ⚹

Glamis Castle ❺

Forfar, Tayside. **[** 01307 840242.
⇄ 🚌 Dundee then bus. ☐ Apr–Oct:
daily. 🏚 ⚹ grounds.

WITH THE pinnacled fairy-
tale outline of a Loire
chateau, the imposing medieval tower-house of **Glamis
Castle** began as a royal

Glamis Castle with statues of James VI (left) and Charles I (right)

hunting lodge in the 11th-century but underwent extensive reconstruction in the 17th century. It was the childhood home of Queen Elizabeth the Queen Mother, and her former bedroom can be seen with a youthful portrait by Henri de Laszlo (1878-1956).

Behind the castle's gray-pink walls, many rooms are open to the public, including Duncan's Hall, the oldest in the castle and Shakespeare's setting for the king's murder in *Macbeth*. Together, the rooms present an array of china, paintings, tapestries and furniture spanning five centuries. In the grounds stand a pair of wrought-iron gates made for the Queen Mother on her 80th birthday in 1980.

View of St. Andrews over the ruins of the cathedral

Dundee ❻

Tayside. 🏠 180,000. ✈ ⇌ 🚌 ℹ 4 City Square (01382 227723). 🛒 Tue, Fri–Sun.

FAMOUS FOR ITS cake, marmalade and the D.C. Thompson publishing empire (creators of children's magazines *Beano* and *Dandy*), **Dundee** was also a major shipbuilding center in the 18th and 19th centuries, a period atmospherically recreated by a trip to the Victoria Docks.

HMS Unicorn, built in 1824, is the oldest British-built warship still afloat and is still fitted as it was on its last voyage. Anchored at Craig Pier is the royal research ship **Discovery**. Built here in 1901 for the first of Captain Scott's

voyages to the Antarctic, the *Discovery* was one of the last sailing ships to be made in Britain. Housed in a Victorian Gothic building, the **McManus Galleries** provide a glimpse of Dundee's industrial heritage, as well as exhibitions covering archaeology and Victorian art. The eerie **Howff Burial Ground**, northwest of City Square, contains a number of intriguing inscriptions carved on its Victorian tombstones.

🏛 **HMS Unicorn**
Victoria Docks. 📞 01382 200900. ◯ daily. ● Dec 25, Jan 1. 📷 & limited.

🏛 **Discovery**
Discovery Point. 📞 01382 201245. ◯ daily. ● Dec 25, Jan 1, 2. 📷 &

🏛 **McManus Gallery**
Albert Sq. 📞 01382 432020. ◯ daily. ● Dec 25–27, Jan 2–4. &

St. Mary's College insignia, St. Andrews University

St. Andrews ❼

Fife. 🏠 14,000. ⇌ Leuchars. 🚌 Dundee. ℹ 70 Market St (01334 472021).

SCOTLAND'S OLDEST UNIVERSITY town and one-time ecclesiastical capital, **St. Andrews** is now a shrine to golfers from all over the world *(see below)*. Its three main streets and numerous cobbled alleys, full of crooked housefronts, dignified university buildings and medieval churches, converge on the venerable ruins of the 12th-century **cathedral**. Once the largest in Scotland, the cathedral was later pillaged for stones to build the town. **St. Andrew's Castle** was built for the bishops of the town in 1200. The dungeon in which many religious Reformers were held can still be seen. The city's golf courses occupy the land to the north and each is open for a modest fee. The **British Golf Museum**, which tells how the city's Royal and Ancient Golf Club became the ruling arbiter of the game, will delight golf enthusiasts.

♣ **St. Andrew's Castle**
South St. 📞 01334 477196. ◯ daily. ● Dec 25, 26, Jan 1–3. 📷 &

🏛 **British Golf Museum**
Bruce Embankment. 📞 01334 478880. ◯ May–Oct: daily; Nov–Apr: Thu–Mon.

THE ANCIENT GAME OF GOLF

Scotland's national game was pioneered on the sandy links around St. Andrews. The earliest record dates from 1457, when golf was banned by James II on the grounds that it was interfering with his subjects' archery practice.

Mary, Queen of Scots *(see p497)* enjoyed the game and was berated in 1568 for playing immediately after the murder of her husband Darnley.

Mary, Queen of Scots at St. Andrews in 1563

The central courtyard of Falkland Palace, bordered by rose bushes

East Neuk ⑧

Fife. ⭐ 🚌 *Glenrothes.*
ℹ️ *St. Andrews (01334 472021).*

A STRING of pretty fishing villages scatters the shoreline of the **East Neuk** (the eastern "corner") of Fife, stretching from Earlsferry to Fife Ness. Much of Scotland's medieval trade with Europe passed through these ports, a connection reflected in the Flemish-inspired crow-stepped gables of many of the cottages. Although the herring industry has declined and the area is now a peaceful vacation center, fishing boats still bob against the quays and the sea still dominates village life. Fishing boats are built and repaired at St. Monans, a charming town of narrow twisting streets, while Pittenweem is the base for the East Neuk fishing fleet.

The town is also known for **St. Fillan's Cave**, the retreat of a 9th-century hermit whose relic was used to bless the army of Robert the Bruce *(see p468)* before the Battle of Bannockburn. A church stands among the cobbled lanes and colorful cottages of Crail; the stone by the church gate is said to have been hurled to the mainland from the Isle of May by the Devil.

A number of 16th- to 19th-century buildings in the village of Anstruther contain the **Scottish Fisheries Museum**, which tells the area's history with the aid of cottage interiors, boats and displays on whaling. From the village you can also embark for the nature reserve on the **Isle of May**, which teems with seabirds and a colony of gray seals. The statue of Alexander Selkirk in Lower Largo recalls the local boy whose seafaring adventures inspired Daniel Defoe's novel *Robinson Crusoe* (1719). After disagreeing with his captain, he was dumped on a desert island where he survived for five years.

🏛 Scottish Fisheries Museum
Harbour Head, St. Ayles, Anstruther.
📞 *01333 310628.* ⏰ *daily.* 🈺 ♿

THE PALACE KEEPER

Due to the size of the royal household and the necessity for the king to be itinerant, the office of Keeper was created by the medieval kings who required custodians to maintain and replenish the resources of their many palaces while they were away. Now redundant, it was a hereditary title and gave the custodian permanent and often luxurious lodgings.

James VI's bed in the Keeper's Bedroom, Falkland Palace

Falkland Palace ⑨

(NTS) Falkland, Fife. 📞 *01337 857397.* ⭐ 🚌 *Ladybank, Kirkcaldy, then bus.* ⏰ *Apr–Oct: daily.* 🈺

T HIS STUNNING Renaissance palace was designed as a hunting lodge of the Stuart kings. Although its construction was begun by James IV in 1500, most of the work was carried out by his son, James V *(see p496)*, in the 1530s. Under the influence of his two French wives, he employed French workmen to redecorate the façade of the East Range with dormers, buttresses and medallions, and to build the beautifully proportioned South Range. The palace fell into ruin during the years of the Commonwealth *(see p52)* and was occupied briefly by Rob Roy *(see p481)* in 1715.

After buying the estates in 1887, the 3rd Marquess of Bute became the Palace Keeper and restored it to the form we see today. The richly paneled interiors are filled with superb furniture and contemporary portraits of the Stuart monarchs. The royal tennis court in the garden was built in 1539 for James V, and is the oldest in Britain.

Dunfermline ⑩

Fife. 🏠 *45,000.* ⭐ 🚌 ℹ️ *13–15 Maygate (01383 720999).*

S COTLAND'S CAPITAL until 1603, Dunfermline is dominated by the ruins of the 12th-century abbey and palace, which recall its royal past. The city first came to prominence in the 11th century as the seat of King Malcolm III, who founded a priory on the present site of the **Abbey Church**. With its Norman nave and 19th-century choir, the church contains the tombs of 22 Scottish kings and queens, including Robert the Bruce *(see p468)*.

The ruins of the **palace**, where Malcolm married his queen, Margaret, soar over the beautiful gardens of Pittencrieff Park. Dunfermline's most famous resident, philanthropist Andrew Carnegie (1835–1919), had been forbidden entrance

The 12th-century Norman nave of Dunfermline Abbey Church

to the park as a boy, though after making his fortune he bought the entire Pittencrieff estate and gave it to the people of Dunfermline. He was born in the city, though moved with his family to Pennsylvania in his teens. There, he made a vast fortune in the iron and steel industry, becoming one of the wealthiest men in the world, and donating some $350 million for the benefit of mankind. The **Carnegie Birthplace Museum** is still furnished as it was when he lived there, and tells the story of his meteoric career and many charitable donations.

⛪ Carnegie Birthplace Museum
Moodie St. **C** 01383 724302. ◯ daily. ● Dec 24–26, 31, Jan 1. 🏛 ♿

Culross ⓫

Fife. 🚶 350. 🚌 � ⓘ National Trust Visitors' Centre, The Square (01383 880359). ◯ Apr–Sep: daily. 🏛 ♿

AN IMPORTANT religious center in the 6th century, the town of Culross is said to have been the birthplace of St. Mungo in 514. Now a beautifully preserved 17th- and 18th-century village, Culross prospered in the 16th century with the growth of its coal and salt industries, most notably under the genius of Sir George Bruce. Descended from the family of Robert the Bruce (see p468), Sir George took charge of the Culross colliery in 1575 and created a drainage system called the "Egyptian Wheel," which cleared a mile-long (1.5 km) mine beneath the River Forth.

During its subsequent decline Culross stood unchanged for over 150 years. The National Trust for Scotland began restoring the town in 1932 and now provides a guided tour. This starts at the **Visitors' Centre**, housed in the one-time village prison.

Built in 1577, Bruce's **palace** has the crow-stepped gables, decorated windows and red pantiles typical of the period. The interior retains its original early 17th-century painted ceilings, which are among the finest in Scotland. Crossing the Square, past the **Oldest**

House, dating from 1577, head for the **Town House** to the west. Behind it, a cobbled street known as the Back Causeway (with its raised section for nobility) leads to the turretted **Study**, built in 1610 as a house for the Bishop of Dunblane. The main room is open to visitors and should be seen for its original Norwegian ceiling. Continuing northward to the ruined abbey, fine church and Abbey House, don't miss the Dutch-gabled **House with the Evil Eyes**.

The 17th-century Study, with its decorated ceiling, Culross

Linlithgow Palace ⓬

Linlithgow, Lothian. **C** 01506 842 896. 🚌 🚶 ◯ daily. ● Dec 25, 26, Jan 1–3. 🏛 ♿ limited.

STANDING ON THE EDGE of Linlithgow Loch, the former royal palace of **Linlithgow** is now one of the country's most visited ruins. Today's remains are mostly of the building commissioned by James V in 1425, though some sections date from the 14th century. The scale of the building is demonstrated by the 28 m (94 ft) long Great Hall, with its huge fireplace and windows. The restored fountain in the courtyard was a wedding present in 1538 from James V to his wife, Mary of Guise. His daughter, Mary, Queen of Scots (see p497), was born here in 1542.

The adjacent **Church of St. Michael** is Scotland's largest pre-Reformation church and a fine example of the Scottish Decorated style.

The 16th-century palace of industrialist George Bruce, Culross

Hopetoun House ⑬

Lothian. 📞 *0131 331 2451.*
🚇 *Dalmeny then taxi.* ⏱ *mid-Apr–Sep: daily.* 🚫 ♿ *limited.*

A<small>N EXTENSIVE PARKLAND</small> by the Firth of Forth, designed in the style of Versailles, is the setting for one of Scotland's finest stately homes. The original house (of which only the central block remains) was built by 1707; it was later absorbed into William Adam's grand extension. The dignified, horseshoe-shaped plan and lavish interior plasterwork represent Neo-Classical 18th-century architecture at its finest. Of the state apartments, the red and yellow drawing rooms, with their Rococo plasterwork and highly ornate mantelpieces, are particularly impressive. The Marquess of Linlithgow, whose family still occupies part of the house, is a descendant of the 1st Earl of Hopetoun, for whom the house was built.

A wooden panel above the main stair, depicting Hopetoun House

Forth Bridges ⑭

Lothian. 🚇 🚌 *Dalmeny, Inverkeithing.*

T<small>HE SMALL TOWN</small> of South Queensferry is dominated by the two great bridges that span the mile (1.6 km) across the River Forth to the town of Inverkeithing. The spectacular rail bridge, the first major steel-built bridge in the world, was opened in 1890 and remains one of the greatest engineering achievements of the late

The shattered crags and cliffs of St. Abb's Head

Victorian era. Its massive cantilevered sections are held together by more than 8 million rivets, and the painted area adds up to some 55 ha (135 acres). The saying "it's like painting the Forth Bridge" has become a byword for nonstop, repetitive endeavor. It was the rail bridge that inspired the book *The Bridge* (1986) by the popular Scottish writer Iain Banks.

The neighboring road bridge was the largest suspension bridge outside the US when it was opened in 1964, a distinction now held by the Humber Bridge in England. The two bridges make an impressive contrast, best seen from South Queensferry promenade. The town received its name from the 11th-century Queen Margaret *(see p493),* who used the ferry here on her journeys between Edinburgh and the royal palace at Dunfermline *(see p487).*

Edinburgh ⑮

See pp490–97.

St. Abb's Head ⑯

Borders. 🚇 *Berwick-upon-Tweed.*
🚌 *Edinburgh.*

T<small>HE JAGGED CLIFFS</small> of St. Abb's Head, rising 91 m (300 ft) from the North Sea near the southeastern tip of Scotland, offer a spectacular view of thousands of seabirds wheeling and diving below. This 80 ha (200 acre) nature preserve is an important site for cliff-nesting sea birds and becomes, during the May to June breeding season, the home of more than 50,000 birds, including fulmars, guillemots, kittiwakes and puffins that throng the headland near the fishing village of St. Abbs. The village has one of the few unspoiled working harbors on Britain's east coast. A clifftop trail begins at the **Visitors' Centre**, where displays include identification boards and a touch table where young visitors can come to grips with wings and feathers.

🛈 **Visitors' Centre**
St. Abb's Head. 📞 *018907 71443.*
⏱ *Easter–mid-Nov: daily.*

The huge, cantilevered Forth Rail Bridge, seen from South Queensferry

A Tour of the Borders ⑰

BECAUSE OF THEIR PROXIMITY to England, the Scottish Borders are scattered with the ruins of many ancient buildings destroyed in the conflicts between the two nations. Most poignant of all are the Border abbeys, whose magnificent architecture bears witness to their former spiritual and political power. Founded during the 12th-century reign of David I, the abbeys were destroyed by Henry VIII *(see p498)*.

Kelso Abbey ①
The largest of the Border Abbeys, Kelso was once the most powerful ecclesiastical establishment in Scotland.

Melrose Abbey ⑥
Once one of the richest abbeys in Scotland, it is here that Robert the Bruce's heart is said to be buried *(see p498).*

Floors Castle ②
Open in summer, the Duke of Roxburghe's ancestral home was built in the 18th century by William Adam.

BERWICK-UPON-TWEED

Scott's View ⑤
This was Sir Walter Scott's favorite view of the Borders. During his funeral, the hearse stopped here briefly as Scott had done so often in life.

KEY

▬▬▬	Tour route
═══	Other roads
✳	Viewpoint

Dryburgh Abbey ④
Set on the banks of the Tweed, Dryburgh is considered the most evocative monastic ruin in Scotland. Sir Walter Scott is buried here.

TIPS FOR DRIVERS

Length: 32 miles (50 km).
Stopping-off points: Leave the car in Kelso and take the Cobby Riverside Walk for lunch at the restaurant in Floors Castle. (See also pp636–7.)

0 kilometers	5
0 miles	3

Jedburgh Abbey ③
Though established in 1138, fragments of 9th-century Celtic stonework survive from an earlier structure. A Visitors' Centre illustrates the lives of the Augustinian monks who once lived here.

Edinburgh ⑮

Royal Scots soldiers from the castle

WITH ITS STRIKING medieval and Georgian districts, overlooked by the volcanic sill of Arthur's Seat to the south and Calton Hill to the north, Edinburgh is widely regarded as one of Europe's loveliest capitals. The city is famous for the arts (it was once known as "the Athens of the North"), a preeminence reflected in its hosting every year of Britain's largest arts extravaganza, the Edinburgh Festival *(see p495)*. Its museums and galleries display the riches of many cultures.

Exploring Edinburgh

Edinburgh falls into two main sightseeing areas, divided by Princes Street, the city's busiest thoroughfare and commercial center. The Old Town straddles the volcanic ridge between the castle and the Palace of Holyrood, with most of the city's medieval history clustered in the alleys of the Grassmarket and Royal Mile areas. The New Town, to the north, evolved after 1767 when wealthy merchants expanded the city beyond its medieval walls. This district contains Britain's finest concentration of Georgian architecture.

🏛 National Gallery of Scotland

The Mound. 📞 0131 556 8921.
⬜ daily. ⬤ Dec 25, 26, Jan 1, 2, May Day. ♿
One of Scotland's finest art galleries, the National Gallery of Scotland is worth visiting for its 15th- to 19th-century British and European paintings alone, though plenty more can be found to delight the art-lover.

Crowded ranks of paintings hang on deep red walls behind a profusion of statues and other works of art. Highlights among the Scottish works on exhibition include society portraits by Allan Ramsay and Henry Raeburn, such as his *Reverend Robert Walker Skating on Duddingston Loch* (c.1800). The Early German collection includes Gerard David's almost comic-strip treatment of the *Three Legends of Saint Nicholas* (c.1500). Works by Raphael, Titian and Tintoretto accompany southern European paintings such as Velazquez's *An Old Woman Cooking Eggs* (1620) and the entire room devoted to *The Seven Sacraments* (c.1640) by Nicholas Poussin. Flemish painters represented include Rembrandt, Van Dyck and Rubens while, among the British, important works by Reynolds, Ramsay and Gainsborough can be seen.

Raeburn's *Rev. Robert Walker Skating on Duddingston Loch*

The doorway of the Georgian House, 7 Charlotte Square

♿ Georgian House

7 Charlotte Sq. 📞 0131 225 2160.
⬜ Apr–Oct: daily. 📷 ♿ limited.
In the heart of the New Town, Charlotte Square is a superb example of Georgian architecture, its north side, built in the 1790s, being a masterwork by the architect Robert Adam *(see pp24–25)*. The Georgian House at No. 7 has been furnished and repainted in its original 18th-century colors, which provide a memorable introduction to the elegance of wealthy New Town life. The dining room table is arranged with Sheffield plate, Wedgwood china and mid-18th-century glasses, while the chairs are mainly Edinburgh "brander backs." The drawing room, arranged with chairs around the perimeter, is in stately contrast to the intimacy of the parlor with its Staffordshire and Spode china services.

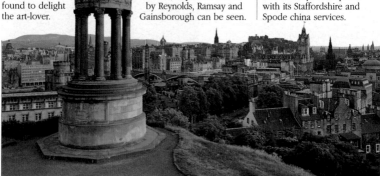

The view from Duncan's Monument on Calton Hill, looking west toward the castle

m National Gallery of Modern Art

Belford Rd. **(** 0131 556 8921. ◯ daily. ● Dec 25, 26, Jan 1, 2. &

Medieval ivory chessmen, Museum of Antiquities

Situated amid extensive grounds, a classical 19th-century school is home to the National Gallery of Modern Art. Most of the European and American 20th-century greats are represented here, ranging from Vuillard and Picasso, to Magritte and Lichtenstein. Work by John Bellany can be found among the Scottish painters, while sculpture by Henry Moore and Eduardo Paolozzi is on display in the garden.

Lichtenstein's *In the Car*, National Gallery of Modern Art

m Museum of Antiquities

Queen St. **(** 0131 225 7534. ◯ daily. ● Dec 25, 26, Jan 1, 2. &

Viking silver from Orkney *(see p514)* and a hoard of treasures from St. Ninian's Isle in Shetland *(see p514)* are among the eclectic variety of Scottish antiquities to be found in this fascinating museum. The ground floor collection of Dark Age sculpture includes the stone-carved 8th-century Birsay Warriors of Orkney, and a set of 12th-century walrus-ivory chessmen found on the Isle of Lewis *(see p515)*. The Roman occupation of Scotland is the subject of the top floor, with cooking pots, weapons, craftsmen's tools and other artifacts illustrating the lives of the Romans along the Antonine Wall *(see p468)*.

VISITORS' CHECKLIST

Lothian ⚑ 420,000. ✈ Islington, 8 miles (13 km) W Edinburgh. ⚐ North Bridge (Waverley Station). ⚏ St. Andrew St. ⓘ 3 Princes St (0131 557 1700). ⚐ Edinburgh International: Aug; Military Tattoo: Aug; Edinburgh Fringe: Aug.

m Scottish National Portrait Gallery

Queen St. **(** 0131 556 8921. ◯ daily. ● Dec 25, 26, 31, Jan 1, 2, May Day. &

The National Portrait Gallery contains a rich and informative exhibition on the royal house of Stuart, explaining the turbulent history of 12 generations of Scottish monarchs from Robert the Bruce *(see p468)* to Queen Anne. Memorabilia from many reigns include Mary, Queen of Scots' *(see p497)* jewelry and a silver traveling canteen abandoned by Bonnie Prince Charlie *(see p521)* at Culloden *(see p523)*. The upper gallery has a number of portraits of famous Scots, including a picture of Robert Burns *(see p501)* by Alexander Nasmyth.

EDINBURGH CITY CENTER

Edinburgh Castle pp492–3 ②
Georgian House ①
Gladstone's Land ⑤
Greyfriars Bobby ⑥
Holyrood Palace ⑪
Museum of Antiquities & Scottish National Portrait Gallery ③

Museum of Childhood ⑩
National Gallery of Scotland ④
Parliament House ⑧
Royal Museum of Scotland ⑨
St. Giles Cathedral ⑦

KEY

🚌 Bus station
🚉 Railroad station
🅿 Parking
ⓘ Tourist information
✝ Church

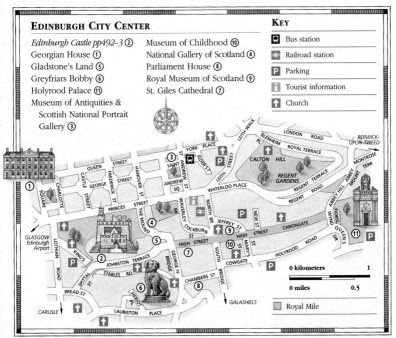

Edinburgh Castle

STANDING UPON the granite core of an extinct volcano, Edinburgh Castle is an assemblage of buildings dating from the 12th to the 20th century, reflecting its changing role as fortress, royal palace, military garrison and state prison. Though there is evidence of Bronze Age occupation of the site, the original fortress was built by the 6th-century Northumbrian King Edwin, from whom the city takes its name. The castle was a favorite royal residence until the Union of Crowns *(see p469)* in 1603, after which the king resided in England. After the Union of Parliaments in 1707, the Scottish regalia were walled up in the Palace for over a hundred years. Now the permanent head-quarters of the Royal Scots regiment, the castle was last defended in 1745 against an ineffective Jacobite assault *(see p523)*.

Beam support in the Great Hall

Scottish Crown
Now on display in the palace, the Crown was restyled by James V of Scotland in 1540.

Military Prison

Governor's House
Complete with Flemish-style crow-stepped gables, this building was con-structed for the governor in 1742 and now serves as the Officers' Mess for the castle garrison.

Old Back Parade

MONS MEG

Now kept in the castle vaults, the siege gun (or *bombard*) Mons Meg was made in Belgium in 1449 for the Duke of Burgundy, who gave it to his nephew, James II of Scotland. It was used by James against the Douglas family in their stronghold of Threave Castle *(see p501)* in 1455, and later by James IV against Norham Castle in England. After exploding during a salute to the Duke of York in 1682, it was kept in the Tower of London. It was returned to Edinburgh in 1829, at Sir Walter Scott's request.

Vaults
This French graffiti, dating from 1780, recalls the many prisoners who were held in the vaults during the wars with France in the 18th and 19th centuries.

STAR SIGHTS
★ Great Hall
★ Palace

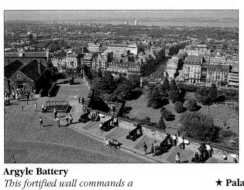

VISITORS' CHECKLIST

Castle Hill. 0131 225 9846.
Apr–Sep: 9:30am–6pm daily;
Oct–Mar: 9:30am–5pm daily (last
adm: 45 mins before closing).
Dec 25, 26, Jan 1, 2.

Argyle Battery
*This fortified wall commands a
spectacular northern view of the
city's New Town.*

★ Palace
*Mary, Queen of
Scots (see p497)
gave birth to James
VI in this 15th-
century palace,
where the Scottish
regalia are on
display.*

Entrance

Royal
Mile

The Esplanade is the
location of the Military
Tattoo *(see p495)*.

**The Half Moon
Battery** was built in
the 1570s as a platform
for the artillery defen-
ding the northeastern
wing of the castle.

St. Margaret's Chapel
*This stained-glass
window depicts Malcolm
III's saintly queen, to
whom the chapel is
dedicated. Probably built
by her son, David I, in
the early 12th century,
the chapel is the castle's
oldest existing building.*

★ Great Hall
*With its restored open-timber
roof, the Hall dates from the
15th century and was the
meeting place of the Scottish
parliament until 1639.*

Exploring the Royal Mile: Castle Hill to High Street

Eagle sign outside Gladstone's Land

THE ROYAL MILE is a stretch of four ancient streets (from Castle Hill to Canongate) that formed the main thoroughfare of medieval Edinburgh, linking the castle to Holyrood Palace. Confined by the city wall, the "Old Town" grew upward, with some tenements rising to 20 stories. It is still possible, among the 66 alleys and closes off the main street, to sense the city's medieval past.

Locator map

Gladstone's Land is a preserved 17th-century merchant's house.

The Scotch Whisky Centre introduces visitors to Scotland's national drink.

The Outlook Tower contains an observatory from which to view the city.

Edinburgh Castle ←

CASTLE HILL

LAWNMARKET

The Tollbooth Kirk (c.1840) has the city's highest spire.

Lady Stair's House
This 17th-century house is now a museum of the lives and works of Burns, Scott (see p498) and Stevenson.

🏛 Gladstone's Land

(NTS) 477B Lawnmarket. ☎ 0131 2265856. ◯ Apr–Oct: daily. 🏷

This 17th-century merchant's house, recently restored, provides a window on life in a typical Old Town house before

The bedroom of Gladstone's Land

overcrowding drove the rich northwest to the expanding Georgian New Town. "Lands," as they were known, were tall, narrow buildings erected over the Royal Mile tenements or on small plots of land. The six-story Gladstone's Land was named after Thomas Gledstanes, the merchant who built it in 1617. The house still has the original arcade booths on the street front and a painted ceiling with fine Scandinavian floral designs. Though extravagantly furnished, it also contains items that are reminders of the less salubrious side of the old city, such as wooden overshoes that had to be worn in the dirty streets. A chest in the beautiful

Painted Chamber is said to have been given by a Dutch sea captain to a Scottish merchant who saved him from a shipwreck. A similar house, Morocco Land, can be found on Canongate *(see p497)*.

🏛 Parliament House

Parliament Sq, High St. ☎ 0131 2252595. ◯ Mon–Fri. 🌑 public hols. ♿

This majestic, Italianate building was constructed in the 1630s for the Scottish parliament. Parliament House has been home to the Court of Session and the High Court since the Union of Parliaments *(see p469)* in 1707. It is well worth seeing, as much for the spectacle of its many gowned and wigged advocates as for the stained-glass window in its Great Hall, commemorating the inauguration of the Court of Session by James V, in 1532.

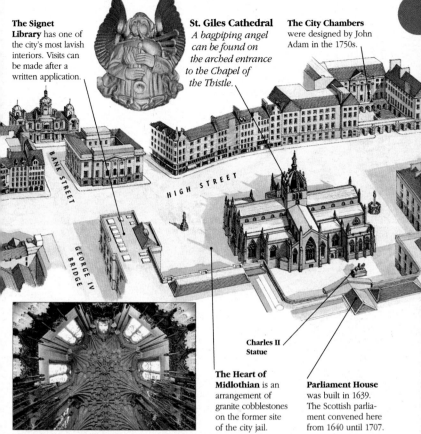

The Signet Library has one of the city's most lavish interiors. Visits can be made after a written application.

St. Giles Cathedral
A bagpiping angel can be found on the arched entrance to the Chapel of the Thistle.

The City Chambers were designed by John Adam in the 1750s.

BANK STREET

HIGH STREET

GEORGE IV BRIDGE

Charles II Statue

The Heart of Midlothian is an arrangement of granite cobblestones on the former site of the city jail.

Parliament House was built in 1639. The Scottish parliament convened here from 1640 until 1707.

Rib-vaulting in St. Giles Cathedral

🏛 St. Giles Cathedral

High St. ☎ 0131 2259442.
☐ daily. ◯ Dec 25, 26, 27, Jan 1.
Properly known as the High Kirk (church) of Edinburgh, it is ironic that St. Giles is popularly known as a cathedral. Though it was twice the seat of a bishop in the 17th century, it was from here that John Knox *(see p469)* directed the Scottish Reformation with its emphasis on individual worship freed from the authority of bishops. A tablet marks the place where Jenny Geddes, a stallholder from a local market, scored a victory for the Covenanters *(see p469)* by hurling her stool at a preacher reading from an English prayer book in 1637.

The Gothic exterior is dominated by a 15th-century tower, the only part to escape heavy renovation in the 19th century. Inside, the impressive Thistle Chapel can be seen, with its elaborate rib-vaulted roof and carved heraldic canopies. The chapel honors the knights, past and present, of the Most Ancient and Most Noble Order of the Thistle. The carved royal pew in the Preston Aisle is used by the Queen when she stays in Edinburgh.

EDINBURGH FESTIVAL

Every year, for three weeks in late summer *(see p63)*, Edinburgh hosts one of the world's most important arts festivals, with every available space (from theaters to street corners) overflowing with international artists and performers. It has been held in Edinburgh since 1947 and brings together the best in contemporary theater, music, dance and opera. The alternative Festival Fringe, with some 600 companies involved, balances the classic productions with a host of innovative performances. The most popular event is the Edinburgh Tattoo, held on the Castle Esplanade – a spectacle of Scottish infantry battalions marching to pipe bands from all over the world.

Street performer from the Edinburgh Festival Fringe

Exploring the Royal Mile: High Street to Canongate

THE SECOND SECTION of the Royal Mile passes two monuments to the Reformation: John Knox's house and the Tron Kirk. The latter is named after a medieval *tron* (weighing beam) that stood nearby. The Canongate was once an independent district, owned by the canons of the Abbey of Holyrood, and sections of its south side have been excellently restored. Beyond Morocco's Land, the road stretches for the final half-mile (800 m) to Holyrood Palace.

Locator map

HIGH STREET

SOUTH BRIDGE STREET

Royal Museum of Scotland,
↓ **Greyfriars Bobby**

The Mercat Cross marks the city center. It was here that Bonnie Prince Charlie *(see p521)* was proclaimed king in 1745.

The Tron Kirk was built in 1630 for the Presbyterians who left St. Giles Cathedral when it came under the Bishop of Edinburgh's control.

🏛 Museum of Childhood

42 High St. 📞 0131 529 4142.
◻ Mon–Sat. ● Dec 25–27, Jan 1.
♿ limited.

This lovely museum is not merely a toy collection but a magical insight into childhood, with all its joys and trials. Founded in 1955 by a city councillor, Patrick Murray (who claimed to enjoy eating children for breakfast), it was the first museum in the world to be devoted to the history and theme of childhood. The collection includes medicines, school books and prams as well as galleries full of old-fashioned toys. With its nickel-odeon, antique slot machines

An 1880 automaton of the Man on the Moon, Museum of Childhood

The entrance to Holyrood Palace, seen from the west

and the general enthusiasm of visitors, this has been called the world's noisiest museum.

👑 Holyrood Palace

East end of Royal Mile. 📞 0131 556 1096. ◻ daily. ● Dec 25–27, Jan 1, 2. ♿ 🚫 ♿ 🅿

Now the Queen's official Scottish residence, Holyrood Palace is named after the "rood," or cross, which King David I is said to have seen between the antlers of a stag he was hunting when in 1128. The present palace was built in 1529 to accommodate James V *(see p487)* and his French wife, Mary of Guise, though it was remodeled in the 1670s for Charles II. The

Royal Apartments (including the Throne Room and Royal Dining Room) are used for investitures and banquets whenever the Queen visits the palace, but they are otherwise open to the public. A chamber in the James V tower is associated with the unhappy reign of Mary, Queen of Scots. It was here, in 1566, that she saw the murder of her trusted Italian secretary, David Rizzio, by her jealous husband, Lord Darnley. She had married Darnley a year earlier in Holyrood chapel.

Bonnie Prince Charlie held court at Holyrood Palace in 1745 in the early stages of the Jacobite *(see p523)* risings.

John Knox's House
Built in 1490, the oldest house in the city was the home of John Knox (see p469) in the 1560s. He is said to have died in an upstairs room. Open daily, it contains relics of his life.

Morocco Land is a reproduction of a 17th-century tenement house. It takes its name from the statue of a Moor that adorns the entrance.

CANONGATE

→ **Holyrood Palace**

Moubray House was to be the signing place of the Treaty of Union in 1707 *(see p469)*, until a mob forced the authorities to retreat to another place.

Museum of Childhood

MUSEUM OF CHILDHOOD

Though created as a museum for adults by a city councillor who was thought to dislike children, this lively museum now attracts flocks of young visitors.

🏛 Royal Museum of Scotland
Chamber St. 📞 *0131 225 7534.*
🕐 *daily.* 🔴 *Dec 25, 26, Jan 1, 2.* ♿
With its soaring glass and iron interior, this elegant museum, specially built in 1861, is a showcase for international collections of the decorative arts and the sciences. In the Main Hall a fine collection of Asian sculpture includes a beautiful 13th-century statue of the Hindu goddess Parvati. European Art from 1200 to 1800, including furniture and displays of tapestry, can be found on the first floor, while the second floor exhibits rare scientific instruments. Among these is the world's

Parvati, at the Royal Museum of Scotland

oldest astrolabe. Eastern decorative arts are on the top floor, alongside a collection of geological specimens.

🐕 Greyfriars Bobby
On an old drinking fountain near the gateway to Greyfriars Church stands the statue of a little Skye terrier. This commemorates the dog who, for 14 years, guarded the grave of his master, John Gray, who died in 1858. The people of Edinburgh fed him until his death in 1872. He was also granted citizenship to prevent him being destroyed as a stray.

MARY, QUEEN OF SCOTS (1542–87)

Born only days before the death of her father, James V, the young Queen Mary spent her childhood in France, after escaping Henry VIII's invasion of Scotland *(see p498)*. A devout Catholic, she married the French Dauphin, and made claims on the English throne. This alarmed Protestants throughout England and Scotland, and when she returned as an 18-year-old widow to Holyrood, she was harangued for her faith by John Knox *(see p469)*. In 1567 she was accused of murdering her second husband, Lord Darnley. Two months later, when she married the Earl of Bothwell (also implicated in the murder), rebellion ensued. She lost her crown. She fled to England where she was held prisoner for 20 years, before being charged with treason and beheaded at Fotheringhay.

The ruins of Melrose Abbey, viewed from the southwest

Melrose Abbey ⑱

Melrose, Borders. 📞 01896 822562.
🚌 from Melrose. ◯ daily. ⬤ Dec
25, 26, Jan 1–3. 📷 ♿ limited.

THE ROSE-PINK RUINS of one
of the most beautiful of
the border abbeys *(see p489)*
bear testimony to the hazards
of standing in the path of successive English invasions.
Built by David I in 1136 for
Cistercian monks from Yorkshire, and also to replace a
7th-century monastery, Melrose
was repeatedly ransacked by
English armies, notably in 1322
and 1385. The final blow, from
which none of the abbeys
recovered, came in 1545 during Henry VIII's destructive
Scottish policy known as the

"Rough Wooing." This resulted
from the failure of the Scots to
ratify a marriage treaty between
Henry VIII's son and the infant
Mary, Queen of Scots *(see
p497)*. What remains of the
abbey are the outlines of cloisters, the kitchen and other
monastic buildings and the
shell of the abbey church with
its soaring east window and
profusion of medieval carvings. The rich decorations of
the south exterior wall include
a gargoyle shaped like a pig
playing the bagpipes, and a
number of animated figures,
including a cook with his
ladle. An embalmed heart,
found here in 1920, is probably
that of Robert the Bruce *(see
p468)*, the abbey's chief benefactor, who had decreed that

his heart be taken on a crusade to the Holy Land. It was
returned to Melrose after its
bearer, Sir James Douglas *(see
p501)*, was killed in Spain.

Abbotsford House ⑲

Galashiels, Borders. 📞 01896 752043.
🚌 from Galashiels. ◯ Apr–Oct:
daily (Sun: pm). 📷 ♿ limited.

FEW HOUSES bear the stamp
of their creator so intimately
as Abbotsford House, the
home of Sir Walter Scott for
the last 20 years of his life.
He bought a farm here in 1811,
known as Clarteyhole ("dirty
hole" in Lowland Scots),
though he soon renamed it
Abbotsford, in memory of the
monks of Melrose Abbey who
used to cross the River Tweed
nearby. He later demolished
the house to make way for
the turreted building we see
today, its construction funded
by the sales of his enormously
popular novels.

Scott's library contains more
than 9,000 rare books and his
collections of historic relics
reflect his passion for the
heroic past. The walls bristle
with an extensive collection of
arms and armor, including
Rob Roy's broadsword *(see
p481)*. Stuart mementos include a crucifix that belonged
to Mary, Queen of Scots and
a lock of Bonnie Prince
Charlie's *(see p521)* hair. The
small study where Scott wrote
his *Waverley* novels can be
visited, as can the room that
overlooks the river, in which
he died in 1832.

SIR WALTER SCOTT

Sir Walter Scott (1771–1832)
was born in Edinburgh and
trained as a lawyer. He is best
remembered as a major champion and literary figure of
Scotland, whose poems and
novels (most famously his
Waverley series) created
enduring images of a heroic
wilderness filled with the
romance of the clans. His
orchestration, in 1822, of the
state visit of George IV to
Edinburgh *(see p471)* was an
extravaganza of Highland culture that helped establish
tartan as the national dress of Scotland. He served as Clerk of
the Court in Edinburgh's Parliament House *(see p494)* and for
30 years was Sheriff of Selkirk. He loved the Scottish Border
country, putting the Trossachs *(see pp480–81)* firmly on the
map with the publication of the *Lady of the Lake* (1810). His
final years were spent writing to pay off a £114,000 debt following the failure of his publisher in 1827. He died with his
debts paid, and was buried at Dryburgh Abbey *(see p489)*.

**The Great Hall at Abbotsford,
adorned with arms and armor**

Traquair House ⓴

Peebles, Borders. 📞 *01896 830323.*
🚍 *from Peebles.* ⭕ *Apr–Oct: daily.*
💺 ♿ *limited.*

AS SCOTLAND'S OLDEST continuously inhabited house,
Traquair has deep roots in
Scottish religious and political
history, stretching back over
900 years. Evolving from a
fortified tower to a stout-walled
17th-century mansion *(see
p473)*, the house was a
Catholic Stuart strong-
hold for 500 years.
Mary, Queen of
Scots *(see p497)*
was among the many
monarchs to have
stayed here and her
bed is covered by a
bedspread that she
made. Family letters and
a collection of engraved
Jacobite *(see p523)*
drinking glasses are
among relics recall-
ing the period of the
Highland rebellions.
After a vow made
by the 5th Earl,
Traquair's Bear
Gates (the "Steekit
Yetts"), which closed after
Bonnie Prince Charlie's *(see
p521)* visit in 1745, will not
reopen until a Stuart reas-
cends the throne. A secret
stairway leads to the Priest's
Room, which, with its clerical

**Mary, Queen of
Scots' crucifix,
Traquair House**

vestments that could be disguised as bedspreads, attests to
the problems faced by Catholic
families until Catholicism was
legalized in 1829. Traquair
House Ale is still produced in
the 18th-century brewery.

Biggar ㉑

Strathclyde. 🏠 *2,000.* 🛈 *High St
(01899 21066).*

THIS TYPICAL Lowland mar-
ket town has a number of
museums worth visiting.
The **Gladstone Court
Museum** boasts a recon-
structed Victorian street
complete with a milliner's,
printer's and a village library,
while the grimy days of the
town's industrial past are
recalled at the **Gasworks
Museum**, with its collection
of engines, gaslights and
appliances. Established in
1839 and preserved after
the advent of North Sea
gas in the 1970s, the
Biggar Gasworks is the
only remaining rural
gasworks in Scotland.

🏛 **Gladstone Court
Museum**
Northback Rd. 📞 *01899 21050.* ⭕
Apr–Oct: daily (Sun: pm). 💺 ♿
🏛 **Gasworks Museum**
Gasworks Rd. 📞 *0131225 7534.*
⭕ *Jun–Sep: daily (pm).* ♿

Pentland Hills ㉒

Lothian. 🚆 *Edinburgh.*
🛈 *Regional Park Headquarters,
Biggar Rd, Edinburgh (0131 4453383).*

THE LOW-LYING Pentland Hills,
stretching for 16 miles (26
km) southwest of Edinburgh,
offer some of the best hill-
walking country in the Lowlands. Leisurely walkers can
saunter along the many
footpaths, while the more
adventurous can take the
chairlift at the Hillend dry ski
slope to reach the higher
ground leading to the 493-m
(1,617-ft) hill of Allermuir. Even
more ambitious is the classic
scenic route along the ridge
from Caerketton to West Kip.
To the east of the A703,
in the lee of the Pentlands,
stands the exquisite and
ornate 15th-century **Roslin
Chapel**. It was originally
intended as a church, but
after the death of its founder,
William Sinclair, it was used
as a burial ground for his
descendants. The delicately
wreathed Apprentice Pillar
recalls the legend of the
apprentice carver who was
killed by the master stonemason in a fit of jealousy at
his pupil's superior skill.

🔒 **Roslin Chapel**
Roslin. 📞 *0131 4402159.*
⭕ *Apr–Oct: daily.* 💺 ♿ *limited.*

Details of the decorated vaulting in Roslin Chapel

The Classical 18th-century tenements of New Lanark on the banks of the Clyde

New Lanark ㉓

Strathclyde. 👥 *150.* 🚆
ℹ️ *Ladyacre Rd (01555 661661).*
🚌 *Mon.*

S ITUATED BY THE beautiful
falls of the River Clyde, the
village of New Lanark was
founded in 1785 by the industrial entrepreneur David Dale.
Ideally located for the working

DAVID LIVINGSTONE

Scotland's great missionary
doctor and explorer was
born in Blantyre, where
he began working life as a
mill boy at the age of ten.
Livingstone (1813–73)
made three epic journeys
across Africa, from 1840,
promoting "commerce and
Christianity." He became
the first European to see
Victoria Falls and died in
1873 while searching for
the source of the Nile. He
is buried in Westminster
Abbey *(see pp94–5).*

of its water-driven mills, the
village had become Britain's
largest cotton producer by
1800. Dale and his successor,
Robert Owen, were philan-
thropists whose reforms
demonstrated that commercial
success need not undermine
the well-being of the work-
force. Now preserved as a
museum, New Lanark is a window on to working life in the
early 19th century. The **Annie
McLeod Experience** provides
a special-effects ride into the
past, illustrating the life of a
10-year-old mill girl in 1820.

ENVIRONS: 24 km (15 miles)
north, the town of Blantyre
has a memorial to the Clyde
Valley's most famous son, the
explorer David Livingstone.

🏛 **Annie McLeod Experience**
New Lanark Visitor Centre. 📞 *01555
661345.* 🔵 *daily.* 🔴 *Dec 25, Jan 1, 2.*
🌀 ♿

Glasgow ㉔

See pp502–7.

Sanquhar ㉕

Dumfries & Galloway. 👥 *2,500.* 🚆
🚌 ℹ️ *The Tolbooth, High St. (01659
50185).*

N OW OF CHIEFLY historic
interest, the town of
Sanquhar was famous in the
history of the Covenanters

(see p469). In the 1680s, two
declarations opposing the rule
of bishops were pinned to the
Mercat Cross, the site of which
is now marked by a granite
obelisk. The first protest was
led by a local teacher, Richard
Cameron, whose followers
became the Cameronian regiment. The Georgian **Tolbooth**
was designed by William
Adam *(see p534)* in 1735 and
houses a local interest museum
and tourist center. The Post
Office, opened in 1763, is the
oldest in Britain, predating
the mail coach service.

Drumlanrig Castle ㉖

Thornhill, Dumfries & Galloway.
📞 *01848 331682.* 🚆 🚌 *Dumfries,
then bus.* 🔵 *May– Aug: Fri–Wed.* 🌀

R ISING SQUARELY from a
grassy platform, the
massive fortress-palace of
Drumlanrig *(see p473)* was
built from pink sandstone
between 1679 and 1691 on the
site of a 15th-century Douglas
stronghold. A formidable

**The Baroque front steps and
doorway of Drumlanrig Castle**

multiturreted exterior contains a priceless collection of art treasures as well as such Jacobite relics as Bonnie Prince Charlie's camp kettle, sash and money box. Hanging within oak-paneled rooms are paintings by Leonardo da Vinci, Holbein and Rembrandt. The emblem of a crowned and winged heart recalls Sir James, the "Black Douglas," who lived here. He bore Robert the Bruce's *(see p468)* heart while on crusade to fulfill a vow made by the former king. After being mortally wounded he threw the heart at his enemies with the words "Forward, brave heart!"

The sturdy island fortress of Threave Castle on the Dee

Threave Castle ㉗

(NTS) Castle Douglas, Dumfries & Galloway. ☎ 01556 502611. ☒ Dumfries. ☐ Apr–Sep: daily. ☒

THIS MENACING GIANT of a tower, a 14th-century Black Douglas *(see above)* stronghold standing on an island on the Dee, commands the most complete medieval riverside harbor in Scotland. Douglas's struggles against the early Stewart kings culminated in his surrender here after a two-month siege in 1455 – but only after James II had brought the cannon Mons Meg *(see p492)* to batter the castle. Threave was finally dismantled after an army of Protestant Covenanters *(see p469)* defeated its Catholic defenders in 1640. Inside the tower, only the shell of the

kitchen, great hall and domestic levels remains. Projecting over the 15th-century doorway is the "gallows knob," a reminder of grim times when the owners are said to have boasted that it never lacked its noose. Access to the castle is made by rowing boat.

Whithorn ㉘

Dumfries & Galloway. ☒ 1,000. ☒ Stranraer. ☒ ☒ Dashwood Sq, Newton Stewart (01671 402431).

THE EARLIEST SITE of continuous Christian worship in Scotland, Whithorn (meaning white house) takes its name from the white chapel built here by St. Ninian in 397. Though nothing remains of his chapel, a guided tour of the archaeological dig reveals evidence of Northumbrian, Viking and Scottish settlements ranging from the 5th to the 19th centuries. A visitors' center, **Whithorn: Cradle of Christianity**, provides audiovisual information on the excavations and contains a fine collection of carved stones. One of the stones (dedicated to Latinus) dates to 450, making it Scotland's earliest Christian monument.

🏛 Whithorn: Cradle of Christianity

The Whithorn Trust, 45–47 George St. ☎ 01988 500508. ☐ Apr–Oct daily. ☒

Culzean Castle ㉙

See pp508–9.

Robert Burns surrounded by his creations, by an unknown artist

Burns Cottage ㉚

Alloway, Dumfries & Galloway. ☎ 01292 441215. ☒ Ayr, then bus. ☐ May–Oct: daily; Nov–Apr: Mon–Sat. ☒ Dec 25, 26, Jan 1, 2. ☒ ☒

ROBERT BURNS (1759–96), Scotland's favorite poet, was born and spent his first seven years in this small thatched cottage in Alloway. Built by his father, the cottage still contains much of its original furniture, and among the memorabilia in the museum next door, many of Burns's manuscripts can be found alongside early editions of his works. Much of his poem *Tam o' Shanter* (1774) is set in Alloway, which remembers him with a huge monument on the outskirts of the village.

Burns became a celebrity following the publication in 1786 of the Kilmarnock Edition of his poems. He died at the age of 37 from heart disease. Scots, home and abroad, gather to celebrate Burns Night *(see p65)* on his birthday, January 25.

SCOTTISH TEXTILES

Weaving in the Scottish Borders goes back to the Middle Ages, when monks from Flanders established a thriving woolen trade with the Continent. Cotton became an important source of wealth in the Clyde Valley during the 19th century, when handloom weaving was overtaken by power-driven mills. The popular Paisley patterns were based on Indian designs.

A colorful pattern from Paisley

Glasgow ㉔

The coat of arms of Glasgow city

Though its Celtic name, *Glas cu*, meant "dear green place," Glasgow is more often associated with its industrial past, which once earned it the title of Second City of the Empire (after London). The city's architectural standing as Scotland's finest Victorian city reflects its era of great prosperity, when ironworks, cotton mills and shipbuilding were fueled by Lanarkshire coal seams. Voted the 1990 European City of Culture, Glasgow now rivals Edinburgh *(see pp490–97)* in the arts, with notable galleries such as the Kelvingrove and the Burrell Collection *(see pp506–7)*.

Glasgow's medieval cathedral viewed from the southwest

Exploring Glasgow

With its grimy industrial past and glossy new image, modern Glasgow is a city of contrasts. The deprived area of the East End, with its busy weekend market, "the Barras," stands by the restored 18th-century Merchant City and Victorian George Square. The more affluent West End prospered in the 19th century as a retreat for wealthy merchants escaping the heavily industrialized Clydeside, and it is here that Glasgow's premier galleries and museums can be found.

South of the river, the Govan and Gorbals districts give way to the Pollok Country Park, site of the Burrell Collection. An underground network provides easy travel around the city.

🏠 Glasgow Cathedral

Castle St. 🔲 *0141 5526891*
🔘 *daily.* **Donation.** 🔲
As one of the only cathedrals to escape destruction during the Scottish Reformation *(see pp468–9)* – by adapting itself to Protestant worship – this is a rare example of an almost complete 13th-century church.

It was built on the site of a chapel founded by the city's patron saint, St. Mungo, a 6th-century bishop of Strathclyde. According to legend, Mungo placed the body of a holy man named Fergus on a cart yoked to two wild bulls, telling them to take it to the place ordained by God. In the "dear green place" at which the bulls stopped he built his church. Because of its sloping site, the cathedral is on two levels. The crypt contains the tomb of St. Mungo, surrounded by

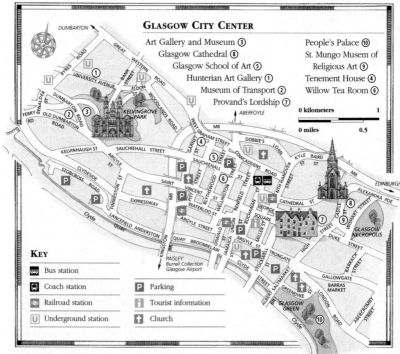

0 kilometers   1

0 miles   0.5

KEY

🚌 Bus station

🚍 Coach station

🚆 Railroad station

Ⓤ Underground station

🅿 Parking

ℹ Tourist information

✝ Church

Dali's *Christ of St. John of the Cross* at the St. Mungo Museum of Religious Life and Art

in the world. The main exhibition illustrates its religious themes with superb artifacts from all over the world, including a 19th-century dancing Shiva and an Islamic painting entitled the *Attributes of Divine Perfection* (1986) by Ahmed Moustafa. An exhibition on religion in Glasgow throws light on the life of the missionary David Livingstone *(see p500)*. Recently moved from the Kelvingrove Art Gallery and Museum *(see p505)*, Salvador Dali's powerful work *Christ of St. John of the Cross* (1951) is now here. Outside you can visit Britain's only permanent Zen Buddhist garden.

VISITORS' CHECKLIST

Strathclyde. 735,000.
Argyle St (Glasgow Central).
Buchanan St. 35 St.
Vincent Place (0141 204 4400).
Sat, Sun. Mayfest : May;
Jazz Festival: July.

The preserved Edwardian kitchen of the Tenement House

an intricate forest of columns springing up to end in delicately carved rib-vaulting. The Blacader Aisle, reputed to have been built over a cemetery blessed by St. Ninian *(see p501)*, has a ceiling thick with decorative bosses.

☖ St. Mungo Museum of Religious Life and Art

2 Castle St. 0141 5532557.
daily. Dec 25, 26, Jan 1.
Situated appropriately in the cathedral precinct, this new museum is the first of its kind

☗ Tenement House

(NTS) 145 Buccleuch St.
0141 3330183. *Mar–Oct: daily (pm).*
Less a museum than a time capsule, the Tenement House is an almost undisturbed record of life in a modest Glasgow apartment in a tenement during the early 20th century. Glasgow owed much of its vitality and neighborliness to tenement life, although many of these Victorian and Edwardian apartments were home to poverty and over-

crowding, and many have now been torn down. The Tenement House was first owned by Miss Agnes Toward who lived here from 1911 until 1965. It remained largely unaltered and, since Agnes threw very little away, it is now a treasure-trove of social history. The parlor, previously used only on formal occasions, has afternoon tea laid out on a white lace cloth. The kitchen, with its coal-fired stove and box bed, is filled with the tools of a vanished era such as a goffering iron for crisping waffles, a washboard and a stone hot-water bottle.

Agnes's medicines and lavender water are still arranged in the bathroom, much as if she had stepped out for a minute 70 years ago and had forgotten to return.

The Kelvingrove Art Gallery and the Glasgow University buildings, viewed from the south

Glasgow's medieval house, Provand's Lordship

🏛 Museum of Transport

1 Bunhouse Rd. [0141 2219600.
○ daily. ● Dec 25, 26, Jan 1, 2. &
Housed in Kelvin Hall, this large, imaginative museum conveys much of the optimism and vigor of the city's industrial heyday. Model ships in the Clyde Room, and gleaming Scottish-built steam trains, cars and motorcycles recall the 19th and early 20th centuries, when Glasgow's supremacy in shipbuilding, trade and manufacturing made her the "second city" of the British Empire. Old Glasgow can be seen in fascinating footage of the town in a movie and through a dramatic reconstruction of a 1938 street, complete with Art Deco store fronts, theater and Underground station.

The Museum of Transport's reconstructed 1938 street, with Underground station

🏛 Provand's Lordship

3 Castle St. [0141 5528819.
○ daily. ● Dec 25, 26, Jan 1, 2.
🎞 & very limited.
Now a museum, Provand's Lordship was built as a canon's house in 1471, and is the city's oldest surviving house. Its low ceilings and austere wooden furnishings create a vivid impression of life in a wealthy 15th-century household. Mary, Queen of Scots *(see p497)* may have stayed here when she visited Glasgow in 1566 to see her cousin and husband, Lord Darnley.

🏛 Willow Tea Room

217 Sauchiehall St. [0141 332
0521. ○ Mon–Sat. ● public
hols, Jan 2.
This is the sole survivor of a series of delightfully frivolous tea-rooms created by Charles Rennie Mackintosh at the turn of the century for the celebrated restaurateur Miss Kate Cranston. Everything from the high-backed chairs to the tables and cutlery was of his own design. In particular, the 1904 Room de Luxe sparkles with eccentricity: striking mauve and silver furniture, colored glass and a flamboyant leaded door create a remarkable spot in which to enjoy afternoon tea.

Mackintosh's interior of the Willow Tea Room

⌂ Glasgow Necropolis

Cathedral Sq. [0141 3057561.
○ daily. &
Behind the cathedral, the reformer John Knox *(see p469)* surveys the city from his Doric pillar overlooking a Victorian cemetery. It is filled with crumbling monuments to the dead of Glasgow's wealthy merchant families.

CHARLES RENNIE MACKINTOSH

Glasgow's most celebrated designer, Charles Rennie Mackintosh (1868–1928), entered Glasgow School of Art at 16. After his first big break with the Willow Tea Room, he became a leading figure in the Art Nouveau movement, developing a unique style that borrowed from Gothic and Scottish Baronial designs. He believed a building should be a fully integrated work of art, creating furniture and fittings that complemented the overall construction. Nowhere is this total design better seen than in the Glasgow School of Art, which he designed in 1896. Unrecognized in his lifetime, Mackintosh's work is now widely imitated. Its characteristic straight lines and flowing detail are the hallmark of early 20th-century Glasgow style, in all fields of design from textiles to architecture.

A Mackintosh floral design

🏛 People's Palace

Glasgow Green. 📞 *0141 5540223.*
⭕ *daily.* 🌑 *Dec 25, 26, Jan 1, 2.* ♿

This Victorian sandstone structure was specially designed in 1898 as a cultural museum for the people of Glasgow's East End. It houses everything from temperance tracts to trade-union banners, suffragette posters to comedian Billy Connolly's banana-shaped boots, providing a social history of the city from the 12th to the 20th century. A superb conservatory at the back contains an exotic winter garden with tropical plants and birds.

🏛 Glasgow School of Art

167 Renfrew St. 📞 *0141 3534526.*
⭕ *Mon–Sat (tours only).* 🌑 *Dec 23–Jan 3.* 🖼 🎟 ♿

Widely considered to be Charles Rennie Mackintosh's greatest architectural work, the Glasgow School of Art was built between 1897 and 1909 to a design he submitted in a competition. It was built in two periods due to financial reasons. The later, western wing displays a softer design than the more severe eastern half, built only a few years earlier and compared by a contemporary critic to a prison.

A student guide takes you through the building to the Furniture Gallery, Board Room and the Library, the latter a masterpiece of spatial composition. Each room is an exercise in contrasts between height, light and shade, with innovative details echoing the architectural themes of the structure. How much of the school can be viewed depends on the students' curricular requirements.

🏛 Hunterian Art Gallery

82 Hillhead St. 📞 *0141 3305431.*
⭕ *Mon–Sat.* 🌑 *Dec 24–Jan 5, public hols.* ♿

Built to house a number of paintings bequeathed to Glasgow University by ex-student and physician Dr. William Hunter (1718–83), the Hunterian Art Gallery contains Scotland's largest print collection and works by major European artists stretching back to the 16th century. A collection of work by Charles Mackintosh is supplemented

George Henry's *Japanese Lady with a Fan* (1894), Art Gallery and Museum

by a complete reconstruction of No. 6 Florentine Terrace, where he lived from 1906 to 1914. A major collection of 19th- and 20th-century Scottish art includes work by William McTaggart (1835–1910), but by far the gallery's most famous collection is of work by the Paris-trained American painter, James McNeill Whistler (1834–1903).

Whistler's *Sketch for Annabel Lee* (c.1869), Hunterian Art Gallery

🏛 Art Gallery and Museum

Dunbarton Rd, Kelvingrove. 📞 *0141 2219600.* ⭕ *Mon–Sat.* 🌑 *Dec 25, 26, Jan 1.* ♿

An imposing red sandstone building, Scotland's most popular gallery houses a magnificent art collection. Best known for its 17th-century Dutch and 19th-century French paintings, the collection began as the gift of a Glasgow coach-builder who died in 1854, leaving works by Botticelli, Giorgione and Rembrandt. Prominent among Continental artists are Degas, Millet and Monet, while in the Scottish Gallery, the famous *Massacre of Glencoe (see p529)* by James Hamilton (1853–94) can be seen alongside works by the Glasgow Boys.

Other exhibitions cover an extraordinary number of subjects, including ceramics, silver, European arms and armor, and the geology of Scotland. The archaeological display includes a reconstruction of the Antonine Wall *(see p44).*

The Georgian Pollok House, viewed from the south

🏛 Pollok House

2060 Pollokshaws Rd. 🄲 0141 6320274. ⭘ daily. ⬤ Dec 25, 26, Jan 1, 2. 🚻

Pollok House, Glasgow's finest 18th-century domestic building, contains one of Britain's best collections of Spanish paintings. The Neo-Classical central block was finished in 1750, the somberness of its exterior contrasting with the exuberant plasterwork within. The Maxwells have lived at Pollok since the mid-13th century, but the male line ended with Sir John Maxwell, who added the grand entrance hall in the 1890s. An avid plant collector, he also designed most of the terraced gardens and parkland beyond.

Hanging above the family silver, porcelain, hand-painted Chinese wallpaper and Jacobean glass, the Stirling Pollok paintings are strong on British and Dutch schools, and include William Blake's *Sir Geoffrey Chaucer and the Nine and Twenty Pilgrims* (1745) as well as William Hogarth's portrait of James Thomson, the author of the words to *Rule Britannia*.

The Spanish 16th- to 19th-century art collection predominates: El Greco's aristocratic *Lady in a Fur Wrap* (1541) hangs in the library, while the drawing room contains works by Francisco Goya and Esteban Murillo. In 1966 Mrs. Anne Maxwell Macdonald gave the house and 146 ha (361 acres) of parkland to the City of Glasgow. The extensive park provided a site for the city's Burrell Collection.

Glasgow: The Burrell Collection

GIVEN TO THE CITY in 1944 by Sir William Burrell (1861–1958), a wealthy shipping agent, this acclaimed collection is the star of Glasgow's renaissance, with objects of major importance in many fields of interest. The building was specially designed in 1983. In the sun, the stained glass blazes with color, while the shaded tapestries seem a part of the surrounding woodland.

Bull's Head
Dating from the 7th century BC, this bronze head from Turkey was once part of a cauldron handle.

Hutton Castle Dining Room
This is a reconstruction of the Dining Room at Burrell's own home – the 16th-century Hutton Castle, near Berwick-upon-Tweed. The Hall and Drawing Rooms can also be seen nearby.

Hornby Portal
This 14th-century arch, with its heraldic display, comes from Hornby Castle in Yorkshire.

Main entrance

B

A

9

5

14

11

STAR SIGHTS

★ **Stained Glass**

★ **Tapestries**

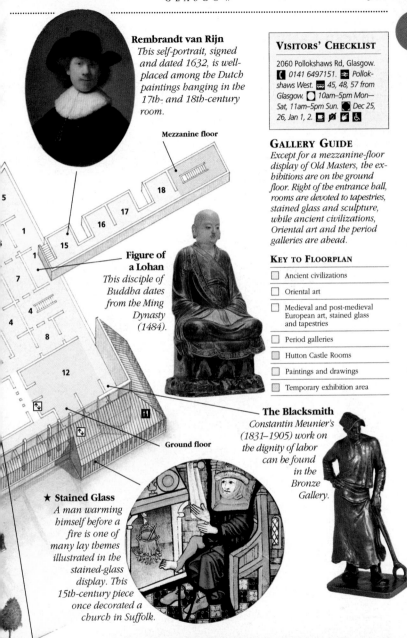

Rembrandt van Rijn
This self-portrait, signed and dated 1632, is well-placed among the Dutch paintings hanging in the 17th- and 18th-century room.

Mezzanine floor

Figure of a Lohan
This disciple of Buddha dates from the Ming Dynasty (1484).

Ground floor

★ Stained Glass
A man warming himself before a fire is one of many lay themes illustrated in the stained-glass display. This 15th-century piece once decorated a church in Suffolk.

The Blacksmith
Constantin Meunier's (1831–1905) work on the dignity of labor can be found in the Bronze Gallery.

VISITORS' CHECKLIST

2060 Pollokshaws Rd, Glasgow.
0141 6497151. Pollokshaws West. 45, 48, 57 from Glasgow. 10am–5pm Mon–Sat, 11am–5pm Sun. Dec 25, 26, Jan 1, 2.

GALLERY GUIDE
Except for a mezzanine-floor display of Old Masters, the exhibitions are on the ground floor. Right of the entrance hall, rooms are devoted to tapestries, stained glass and sculpture, while ancient civilizations, Oriental art and the period galleries are ahead.

KEY TO FLOORPLAN

- [ ] Ancient civilizations
- [ ] Oriental art
- [ ] Medieval and post-medieval European art, stained glass and tapestries
- [ ] Period galleries
- [ ] Hutton Castle Rooms
- [ ] Paintings and drawings
- [ ] Temporary exhibition area

★ Tapestries
A detail from the Swiss work in wool, Scenes from the Life of Christ and of the Virgin (c.1450), is one of many tapestries displayed.

Culzean Castle ㉙

Robert Adam by **George Willison**

STANDING ON A CLIFF'S EDGE in an extensive parkland estate, the 16th-century keep of Culzean (pronounced Cullayn), home of the Earls of Cassillis, was remodeled between 1777 and 1792 by the Neo-Classical architect Robert Adam *(see p24)*. Restored in the 1970s, it is now a major showcase of his later work. The grounds became Scotland's first public country park in 1969; with farming flourishing alongside ornamental gardens, they reflect both the leisure and everyday activities of a great country estate.

View of Culzean Castle (c.1815), by Nasmyth

Lord Cassillis's Rooms contain typical mid-18th-century furnishings, including a gentleman's wardrobe of the 1740s.

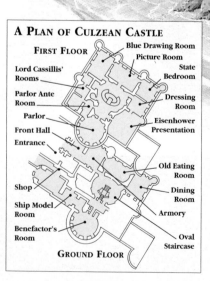

A PLAN OF CULZEAN CASTLE

FIRST FLOOR

Blue Drawing Room
Picture Room
State Bedroom
Lord Cassillis' Rooms
Parlor Ante Room
Parlor
Dressing Room
Front Hall
Eisenhower Presentation
Entrance
Shop
Old Eating Room
Ship Model Room
Dining Room
Benefactor's Room
Armory
Oval Staircase

GROUND FLOOR

The clock tower, fronted by the circular carriageway, was originally the family coach house and stables. The clock was added in the 19th century, and today the buildings are used for residential and educational purposes.

STAR SIGHTS

★ **Parlor**

★ **Oval Staircase**

Armory
On the walls are the bayonet blades and flintlock pistols issued to the West Lowland Fencible Regiment when Napoleon threatened to invade in the early 1800s.

VISITORS' CHECKLIST

(NTS) 4 miles (6 km) W Maybole.
☎ 01655 760 269. 🚌 Ayr, then bus. **Castle** ○ Apr–Oct: daily 10:30am– 5:30pm (last adm: 5pm). **Grounds** ○ dawn until dusk daily. 🖼 🅰 📷 🍴 🛍

Fountain Court
This sunken garden is a good place to begin a tour of the grounds to the east.

The Eisenhower Presentation
honors the general who was given the top floor of Culzean in gratitude for his role in World War II.

Carriageway

★ Parlor
With its restored 18th-century color scheme and Louis XVI chairs, this elegant parlor perches on the cliff's edge 46 m (150 ft) above the Firth of Clyde. The carpet is a copy of the one designed by Adam.

★ Oval Staircase
Illuminated by an overarching skylight, the staircase, with its Ionic and Corinthian pillars, is considered one of Adam's finest achievements.

THE HIGHLANDS AND ISLANDS

SHETLAND · ORKNEY · WESTERN ISLES
HIGHLAND · GRAMPIAN · STRATHCLYDE · TAYSIDE

M OST OF THE STOCK IMAGES *of Scottishness – clans and tartans, whisky and porridge, bagpipes and heather – originate in the Highlands and enrich the popular picture of Scotland as a whole. But for many centuries the Gaelic-speaking, cattle-raising Highlanders had little in common with their southern neighbors.*

Clues to the non-Celtic ancestors of the Highlanders lie scattered across the Highlands and Islands in the form of stone circles, brochs and cairns spanning over 5,000 years. By the end of the 6th century, the Gaelic-speaking Celts had arrived from Ireland, along with St. Columba who introduced Christianity. Its fusion with Viking culture in the 8th and 9th centuries produced St. Magnus Cathedral in the Orkney Isles.

For over 1,000 years, Celtic Highland society was founded on a clan system, built on family ties to create loyal groups dependent on a feudal chief.

However, the clans were systematically broken up by England after 1746, following the defeat of the Jacobite attempt on the British crown, led by Bonnie Prince Charlie (*see p521*). A more romantic vision of the Highlands started in the early 19th century. Its creation was largely due to Sir Walter Scott, whose novels and poetry depicted the majesty and grandeur of a country previously considered merely poverty-stricken and barbaric. Another great popularizer was Queen Victoria, whose passion for Balmoral helped to establish the trend for acquiring Highland sporting estates. But behind the sentimentality lay harsh economic realities that drove generations of farmers to seek a new life overseas.

Today, over half the inhabitants of the Highlands and Islands still live in communities of less than 1,000. However fishing, oil, handicrafts and whisky are now thriving businesses and population figures are rising.

A wintry dawn over the Cairngorms, the home of Britain's only herd of reindeer

◁ The lonely castle of Eilean Donan, Loch Duich in Glen Shiel

Exploring the Highlands and Islands

To the north and west of Stirling (the historic gateway to the Highlands) lie the magnificent mountains and glens, fretted coastlines and lonely isles that are the epitome of Scottish scenery. Inverness, the Highland capital, makes a good starting point for exploring Loch Ness and the Cairngorms, while Fort William holds the key to Ben Nevis. Inland from Aberdeen lie Royal Deeside and the Spey Valley whisky heartland. The romantic Hebrides are only a short ferry-ride from Oban or Ullapool.

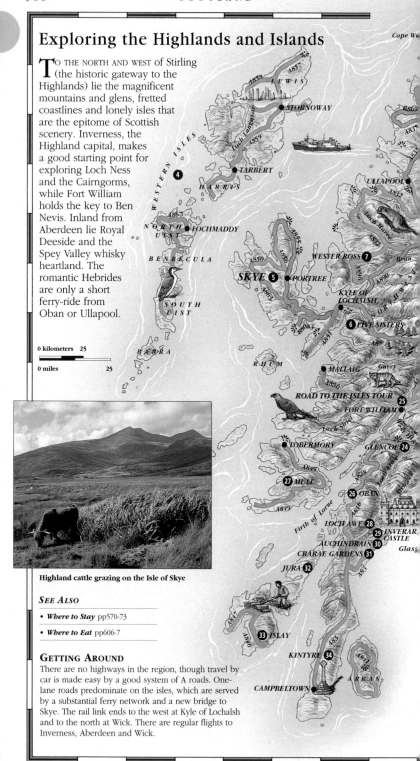

0 kilometers   25

0 miles   25

Highland cattle grazing on the Isle of Skye

SEE ALSO

- *Where to Stay* pp570-73

- *Where to Eat* pp606-7

GETTING AROUND

There are no highways in the region, though travel by car is made easy by a good system of A roads. One-lane roads predominate on the isles, which are served by a substantial ferry network and a new bridge to Skye. The rail link ends to the west at Kyle of Lochalsh and to the north at Wick. There are regular flights to Inverness, Aberdeen and Wick.

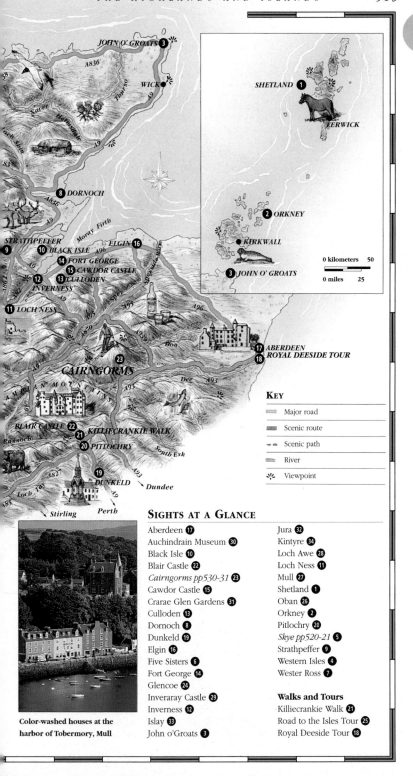

JOHN O' GROATS **3**

WICK

SHETLAND **1**

A836

LERWICK

8 DORNOCH

Natar

Moray Firth

2 ORKNEY

STRATHPEFFER **9**

10 BLACK ISLE *A96* ELGIN **16**

14 FORT GEORGE

15 CAWDOR CASTLE

12 INVERNESS **13** CULLODEN

11 LOCH NESS

KIRKWALL

3 JOHN O' GROATS

0 kilometers 50

0 miles 25

CAIRNGORMS

23

Dee *A93*

17 ABERDEEN
18 ROYAL DEESIDE TOUR

BLAIR CASTLE **22** KILLIECRANKIE WALK

21

20 PITLOCHRY

South Esk

19 DUNKELD → *Dundee*

Loch Tay *A9*

Stirling *Perth*

KEY

▬ Major road

▬ Scenic route

– – Scenic path

▬ River

☼ Viewpoint

**Color-washed houses at the
harbor of Tobermory, Mull**

Shetland ❶

Shetland. 🏃 *21,500*. ✈ 🚢 *from Aberdeen & John o'Groats.* 🛈 *Lerwick (01595 693434).*

LYING SIX DEGREES SOUTH of the Arctic Circle, the rugged Shetland islands are Britain's most northerly region and were, with Orkney, part of the kingdom of Norway until 1469. In the main town of Lerwick, this Norse heritage is remembered during the ancient midwinter festival Up Helly Aa *(see p466)*, in which costumed revelers set fire to an imitation Viking longship. Also in the town, the **Shetland Museum** tells the story of a people dependent on the sea, right up to modern times with the discovery of North Sea oil and gas in the 1970s.

One of Shetland's greatest treasures is the Iron Age tower, **Mousa Broch**, which can be visited on the isle by boat from Sandwick. There is more ancient history at Jarlshof where a museum explains the sprawling sea-front ruins that span 3,000 years.

A boat from Lerwick sails to the isle of Noss where gray seals bask beneath sandstone cliffs crowded with Shetland's seabirds – a spectacle best seen between May and June.

🏛 Shetland Museum
The Hillhead, Lerwick. 📞 *01595 695057.* ⏰ *Mon–Sat.* ⬤ *Dec 24–26, Jan 1, 2.* ♿

Orkney ❷

Orkney. 🏃 *19,600*. ✈ 🚢 *from John o'Groats, Aberdeen, Scrabster.* 🛈 *Broad St, Kirkwall (01856 872856).*

THE FERTILE ISLES of Orkney are remarkable for the wealth of prehistoric monuments that place them among Europe's most treasured archaeological sites. In the town of Kirkwall, the sandstone **St. Magnus Cathedral** stands amid a charming core of narrow streets. Its many interesting tombs include that of its 12th-century patron saint. Nearby, the early 17th-century **Earl's Palace** is widely held

to be one of Scotland's finest Renaissance buildings. To the west of Kirkwall lies Britain's most impressive chambered tomb, the cairn of **Maes Howe**. Dating from 2000 BC, the tomb has runic graffiti on its walls believed to have been left by Norsemen returning from the crusades in 1150.

Nearby, the magnificent **Standing Stones of Stenness** may have been associated with Maes Howe rituals, though details of these remain a mystery. Farther west, on a bleak heath, stands the Bronze Age **Ring of Brodgar**.

Another archaeological treasure can be found in the Bay of Skail – the complete Stone Age village of **Skara Brae**. It was unearthed by a storm in 1850, after lying buried for 4,500 years. Farther south, the town of Stromness was a vital

center of Scotland's herring industry in the 18th century. Its story is told in the local museum, while the **Pier Arts Centre** displays work by British artists and holds regular exhibitions of international art.

👑 Earl's Palace
Palace Rd, Kirkwall. 📞 *01856 87546.* ⏰ *Apr–Sep: daily (Sun: pm).* 📷 ♿

🏛 Pier Arts Centre
Victoria St, Stromness. 📞 *01856 850209.* ⏰ *Tue–Sat.* ⬤ *Dec 24–Jan 10.* ♿ *limited.*

John o'Groats ❸

Caithness. 🏃 *500*. ✈ 🚢 🚌 *Wick* 🚢 *May–Sep: John o'Groats to Burwick, Orkney.* 🛈 *Whitechapel Rd, Wick (01955 602596).*

SOME 876 miles (1,409 km) north from Land's End, Britain's most northeasterly village faces Orkney, 8 miles (13 km) across the turbulent Pentland Firth. The village takes its name from a 15th-century Dutchman John de Groot, who, to avoid accusations of favoritism, is said to have built an octagonal house here with one door for each of his eight heirs. The spectacular cliffs and rock stacks of Duncansby Head lie a few miles farther east.

Puffin

Great Skua

Fulmar

Black Guillemot

Herring Gull

Razorbills

The Norman façade of the St. Magnus Cathedral, Orkney

Western Isles ❹

WESTERN SCOTLAND ENDS with this remote chain of islands, made of some of the oldest rock on Earth. Almost treeless landscapes are divided by countless waterways, the western, windward coasts edged by miles of white sandy beaches. For centuries, the eastern shores, composed largely of peat bogs, have provided the islanders with fuel. Man has been here for 6,000 years, living off the sea and the thin turf, although such monuments as an abandoned Norwegian whaling station on Harris attest to the difficulties in commercializing the islanders' traditional skills. Gaelic, part of an enduring culture, is still widely spoken.

The Black House Museum, a traditional croft on Lewis

The monumental Standing Stones of Callanish in northern Lewis

Lewis and Harris

Western Isles. ✈ Stornoway.
🚹 22,000. ⛴ Uig (Skye), Ullapool,
Kyle of Lochalsh. 🅸 26 Cromwell St,
Stornoway, Lewis (01851 703088).
Black House Museum ☎ 01851
710395. 🔿 Apr–Oct: Mon–Sat;
Nov–Mar: Mon–Thu, Sat. ● pub hols.

Forming the largest landmass of the Western Isles, Lewis and Harris are a single island, though Gaelic dialects differ between the two areas. From the administrative center of **Stornoway**, with its bustling harbor and colorful house fronts, the ancient **Standing Stones of Callanish** are only 16 miles (26 km) to the east. Just off the road on the way to Callanish are the ruins of **Carloway Broch**, a Pictish *(see p468)* tower over 2,000 years old. The more recent past can be explored at Arnol's **Black House Museum** – a showcase of crofting life as it was until only 50 years ago.

South of the rolling peat moors of Lewis, a range of mountains marks the border with Harris, which one enters as one passes Aline Lodge at the head of Loch Seaforth. Only a little less spectacular than the "Munros" (peaks over 914 m or 3,000 ft) of the

mainland and the Isle of Skye *(see pp520–21)*, the mountains of Harris are a paradise for the hiker and, from their summits on a clear day, the distant Isle of St. Kilda can be seen 50 miles (80 km) to the west.

The ferry port of Tarbert stands on a slim isthmus separating North and South Harris. The tourist office provides addresses for local weavers of the tough Harris Tweed. Some still use indigenous plants to make their dyes.

From the port of Leverburgh, on the southern tip of Harris, a passenger ferry can be taken to the isles of Berenay and North Uist.

The Uists, Benbecula and Barra

Western Isles. 🚹 7,200. ✈ Barra,
Benbecula. ⛴ From Uig (Skye), Oban
& Mallaig. 🚌 🚊 Oban, Mallaig,
Kyle of Lochalsh. 🅸 26 Cromwell St,
Stornoway, Lewis (01851 703088).

After the dramatic scenery of Harris, the lower-lying, largely waterlogged southern isles may seem an anticlimax, although they nurture secrets well worth discovering. Long, white sandy beaches fringe the Atlantic coast, edged with one of Scotland's natural treasures: the lime-rich soil known as *machair*. During the summer months, the soil is covered with wild flowers, the unique fragrance of which can be smelled far out to sea.

From **Lochmaddy**, North Uist's main village, the A867 crosses 3 miles (5 km) of causeway to Benbecula, the isle from which the brave Flora MacDonald smuggled Bonnie Prince Charlie *(see p521)* to Skye. Another causeway leads to South Uist, part of a National Scenic Area renowned for its golden beaches. From Lochboisdale, a ferry sails to the tiny isle of Barra. The ferry docks in Castlebay, affording an unforgettable view of **Kisimul Castle**, ancestral stronghold of the clan Macneil.

The remote and sandy shores of South Uist

The eastern side of the Five Sisters of Kintail, seen from Glen Shiel

Isle of Skye ❺

See pp520–1.

Five Sisters ❻

Skye & Lochalsh. ⬇ *Kyle of Lochalsh.* ⬇ *Glen Shiel.* ℹ *Meall House, Portree (01478 612137).*

DOMINATING ONE of Scotland's most haunting regions, the awesome summits of the Five Sisters of Kintail rear into view at the northern end of Loch Cluanie as the A87 enters Glen Shiel. The **Visitor Centre** at Morvich offers ranger-led excursions in the summer. Farther west, the road passes the romantic castle of **Eilean Donan**, standing on an island in Loch Duich and connected to the shore by a causeway. Once a Jacobite *(see p523)* stronghold, it was destroyed in 1719 by English warships. Now rebuilt, the castle contains relics of the Jacobite cause.

♣ **Eilean Donan Castle**
Off A87 nr Dornie. 📞 *01599 555202.* ⬜ *Apr–Oct: daily.*

Wester Ross ❼

Ross & Cromarty. ⬇ *Achnasheen, Strathcarron.* ℹ *Gairloch (01445 712130).*

LEAVING LOCH CARRON to the south, the A890 suddenly enters the Northern Highlands and the great wilderness of Wester Ross. The Torridon Estate, sprawling on either side of Glen Torridon, includes some of the oldest mountains on Earth (Torridonian rock is over 600 million years old) and is home to red deer, wildcats and wild goats. Peregrine falcons and golden eagles nest in the towering sandstone mass of Beinn Eighe, above the village of Torridon with its breathtaking views over the region of Applecross to Skye. The **Torridon Countryside Centre** provides guided walks in season and essential information on the natural history of the region. Traveling north, the A832 cuts through the Beinn Eighe National Nature Reserve where remnants of the ancient Caledonian pine forest still stand on the banks and isles of Loch Maree. Along the coast, a surprising series of exotic gardens thrive in the warming currents of the Gulf Stream, the most impressive being the **Inverewe Garden**, created in 1862 by Osgood Mackenzie (1842–1922). May

Typical Torridonian mountain scenery in the Wester Ross

and June are the months to see the display of rhododendrons and azaleas; July and August for the herbaceous borders and walled gardens.

🏛 **Torridon Countryside Centre**
(NTS) Torridon. 📞 *01445 791221.* ⬜ *May–Sep: daily.* 🏞 ♿
♣ **Inverewe Garden**
(NTS) Off A832 nr Poolewe. 📞 *01445 781200.* ⬜ *daily.* 🏞 ♿

Dornoch ❽

Sutherland. 🏘 *2,200.* ⬇ *Golspie, Tain.* ℹ *The Square, Dornoch (01862 810400).*

WITH ITS FIRST-CLASS golf course and extensive sandy beaches, Dornoch is a popular vacation resort, although it has retained its peaceful atmosphere. Now the parish church, the medieval cathedral was all but destroyed in a clan dispute in 1570; it was restored in the 1920s for its 700th anniversary. A stone at the beach end of River Street marks the place where Janet Horne, the last woman to be tried in Scotland for witchcraft, was executed in 1722.

ENVIRONS: Twelve miles (19 km) northeast of Dornoch is the stately Victorianized bulk of **Dunrobin Castle**, magnificently situated in a great park with formal gardens overlooking the sea. Since the 13th century, this has been the seat of the Earls of Sutherland.

Many of its rooms are open to visitors. A steam-powered fire engine is among the miscellany of objects on display.

To the south stands the peaceful town of **Tain**. Though once patronized by medieval kings as a place of pilgrimage, the town became an administrative center of the Highland Clearances, during which the tollbooth was used as a jail. All is explained in the heritage center, **Tain Through Time**.

⚜ Dunrobin Castle
Nr Golspie. ☎ *01408 633177.*
🕐 *May–mid-Oct: daily.* ♿
🏛 Tain Through Time
Tower St. ☎ *01862 894089*
🕐 *Apr–Sep: daily; Nov–Mar: daily (pm).* ⬤ *Dec 25, 26, Jan 1, 2, 15–30.* 📷 ♿

The serene cathedral precinct in the town of Dornoch

Strathpeffer ⑨

Ross & Cromarty. 👥 *1,400.*
ℹ *North Kessock (01463 731505).*

STANDING 5 MILES (8 km) east of the Falls of Rogie, the popular vacation center of Strathpeffer still has the refined charm for which it was well known in Victorian times, when it flourished as a spa and health resort. The town's huge hotels and gracious layout recall the days when European royalty and lesser mortals flocked to the chalybeate- and sulfur-laden springs, believed to provide a cure for tuberculosis. The water can still be sampled at the unmanned **Water Tasting Pavilion** in the town square.

🚰 Water Tasting Pavilion
The Square. 🕐 *Easter–Oct: daily.*

The shores of the Black Isle in the Moray Firth

Black Isle ⑩

Ross & Cromarty. 🚆 🚌 *Inverness.*
ℹ *North Kessock (01463 731505).*

THOUGH THE DRILLING platforms in the Cromarty Firth are reminders of how oil has changed the local economy, the broad peninsula of the Black Isle is still largely composed of lush farmland and charming fishing villages. The town of **Cromarty** was an important port in the 18th century, with thriving rope and lace industries. Many of its merchant houses still stand; the award-winning museum in the **Cromarty Courthouse** provides heritage tours of the town. The thatched **Hugh Miller's Cottage** is a museum to the theologian and geologist Hugh Miller (1802–56), who was born here.

Fortrose boasts a ruined 14th-century cathedral, while a stone on Chanonry Point commemorates the Brahan Seer, a 17th-century prophet. He was burned alive in a barrel of tar by the Countess of Seaforth after foreseeing her husband's infidelity. For local archaeology, the **Groam House Museum**, in the town of Rosemarkie, is worth a visit.

🏛 Cromarty Courthouse
Church St, Cromarty. ☎ *01381 600418.* 🕐 *Apr–Oct: daily; Nov–Mar: daily (pm).* ⬤ *Dec 25, 26, Jan 1, 2, 15–30.* 📷
🚰 Hugh Miller's Cottage
(NTS) Church St, Cromarty. ☎ *01381 600245.* 🕐 *May–Sep: daily.* 📷
🏛 Groam House Museum
High St, Rosemarkie. ☎ *01381 620961.* 🕐 *Easter week, May–Sep: daily (Sun: pm); Oct–Apr: Sat & Sun (pm).* 📷 ♿ *ground floor only.*

HIGHLAND CLEARANCES

During the heyday of the clan system *(see p470)*, tenants paid their landholding chieftains rent in the form of military service. However, with the destruction of the clan system after the Battle of Culloden *(see p523)*, landowners began to demand a financial rent which their tenants were unable to afford, and the land was gradually bought up by Lowland and English farmers. In what became known as "the year of the sheep" (1792), thousands of tenants were evicted (often forcibly) to make way for livestock. Many families emigrated to Australia and America. The ruins of their crofts can still be seen, mainly in Sutherland and the Wester Ross.

The Last of the Clan (1865) by Thomas Faed

Isle of Skye ❺

Otter in the haven by the coast at Kylerhea

THE LARGEST of the Inner Hebrides, Skye can be reached by the bridge linking Kyleakin and the Kyle of Lochalsh. A turbulent geological history has given the island some of Britain's most varied and dramatic scenery. From the rugged volcanic plateau of northern Skye to the ice-sculpted peaks of the Cuillins, the island is divided by numerous sea-lochs, leaving the traveler never more than 5 miles (8 km) from the sea. Limestone grasslands predominate in the south, where the hillsides, now the home of sheep and cattle, are scattered with the ruins of crofts abandoned during the Clearances (see p517). Historically, Skye is best known for its association with Bonnie Prince Charlie.

Skeabost has the ruins of a chapel associated with St. Columba (see p511). Medieval tombstones can be found in the graveyard.

Grave of Flora MacDonald

Dunvegan Castle
The seat of the chiefs of the Clan MacLeod since the 11th century, Dunvegan contains the Fairy Flag, a fabled piece of magical silk treasured by the clan for its protection.

The Talisker distillery produces one of the best Highland malts, often described as "the lava of the Cuillins."

Cuillins
Britain's finest mountain range is within three hours' walk from Sligachan, and in the summer a boat sails from Elgol to the desolate inner sanctuary of Loch Coruisk. As he fled across the surrounding moorland, Bonnie Prince Charlie is said to have claimed: "even the Devil shall not follow me here!"

KEY

🛈	Tourist information
▬▬	A road
▭▭	B road
—	Minor road
❊	Viewpoint

◁ **Dawn over the desolate tablelands of northern Skye, viewed from the Quiraing**

Quiraing
A series of landslides has exposed the roots of this volcanic plateau, revealing a fantastic terrain of spikes and towers. They are easily explored off the Uig–Staffin road.

Storr
The erosion of this basalt plateau has created the Old Man of Storr, a monolith rising to 55 m (180 ft) by the Portree road.

Luib has a beautiful thatched cottage, preserved as it was 100 years ago.

Loch Coruisk

Bridge to mainland

Portree
With its colorful harbor, Portree (meaning "port of the king") is Skye's metropolis. It received its name after a visit by James V in 1540.

Otters can be seen at the haven in Kylerhea.

Armadale Castle houses the Clan Donald Visitor Centre.

Kilchrist Church
This ruined pre-Reformation church once served Skye's most populated areas, though the surrounding moors are now deserted. Its last service was held in 1843, after a new church was built in Broadford.

BONNIE PRINCE CHARLIE

The last of the Stuart claimants to the Crown, Charles Edward Stuart (1720–88), came to Scotland from France in 1745 to win the throne. After marching as far as Derby, his army was driven back to Culloden (*see p523*) where it was defeated. Hounded for five months through the Highlands, he escaped to Skye, disguised as the maidservant of a woman from Uist, Flora MacDonald. From the mainland he sailed to France in September 1746 (*see p532*), and died in Rome. Flora was buried in 1790 at Kilmuir, on Skye, wrapped in a sheet from the bed of the "bonnie" (handsome) prince.

The prince, disguised as a maidservant

The ruins of Urquhart Castle on the western shore of Loch Ness

Loch Ness ⓫

Inverness. 🚉 🚌 Inverness.
🈺 Castle Wynd, Inverness (01463 234353).

A T 24 MILES (39 km) long, one mile (1.5 km) at its widest and up to 305 m (1,000 ft) deep, **Loch Ness** fills the northern half of the Great Glen fault that divides the Highlands from Fort William to Inverness. It is joined to lochs Oich and Lochy by the

THE LOCH NESS MONSTER

First sighted by St. Columba in the 6th century, "Nessie" has attracted increasing attention since ambiguous photographs were taken in the 1930s. Though serious investigation is often undermined by hoaxers, sonar techniques continue to yield enigmatic results: plesiosaurs, giant eels and too much whisky are the most popular explanations. Nessie appears to have a close relative in the waters of Loch Morar (*see p532*).

22 mile (35 km) Caledonian Canal, designed by the Scottish engineer Thomas Telford (*see p433*). On the western shore, the A82 passes the ruins of the 16th-century **Urquhart Castle**, which was blown up by government supporters in 1692 to prevent it falling into Jacobite hands. A short distance to the west, the **Loch Ness Monster Exhibition Centre** provides a wealth of audio-visual information on the loch's oldest and most famous resident.

Kiltmaker with royal Stuart tartan

🔼 **Urquhart Castle**
Nr Drumnadrochit. 📞 01456 450551. ◻ daily. ● Dec 25, 26, Jan 1, 2. 🈺
🏛 **Loch Ness Monster Exhibition Centre**
Drumnadrochit. 📞 01456 450573. ◻ daily. ● Dec 25. 🈺 ♿

Inverness ⓬

Highland. 🔼 42,000. 🚉 🚌
🈺 Castle Wynd. (01463 234353).

A S THE HIGHLAND capital, Inverness makes an ideal base from which to explore the surrounding countryside. The Victorian castle dominates the town center, the oldest buildings of which are found in nearby Church Street. Today the castle is used as law courts.

The **Inverness Museum and Art Gallery** provides a good introduction to the history of the Highlands with exhibits including a lock of Bonnie Prince Charlie's (*see p521*) hair and a fine collection of Inverness silver. **Balnain House** is an excellent showcase of Highland music and musical instruments, while those in search of tartans and knitwear need go no further than the **James Pringle Weavers of Inverness**. Moored in Muirtown Basin, to the northwest, is the 1885 **Amazon Museum Ship**. It is the sole survivor of the wooden steam yachts of its type and, with its original fitments, is a time capsule of Victorian life afloat.

🏛 **Museum and Art Gallery**
Castle Wynd. 📞 01463 237114. ◻ Mon–Sat. ● Good Fri, Dec 24–26, Jan 1, 2. ♿
🈺 **James Pringle Weavers of Inverness**
Holm Woollen Mill, Dores Rd. 📞 01463 223311. ◻ daily. ● Dec 25, Jan 1. ♿
🏛 **Balnain House**
40 Huntly St. 📞 01463 715757. ◻ Jul–Aug: daily; Sep–Jun: Tue–Sun. ● Dec 25, 26, Jan 1, 2. 🈺 ♿ limited.
🏛 **Amazon Museum Ship**
On A862. 📞 01463 242154. ◻ Apr–Sep: daily; Oct–Dec 24: Mon–Fri (am). ● Dec 25–Mar. 🈺

Culloden ⓭

(NTS) Inverness. 🚇 🚌 Inverness.

A DESOLATE STRETCH of moorland, Culloden looks much as it did on April 16, 1746, the date of the last battle to be fought on British soil *(see p469)*. Here the Jacobite cause, with Bonnie Prince Charlie's *(see p521)* leadership, finally perished under the onslaught of nearly 9,000 Hanoverian troops led by the Duke of Cumberland. All is explained, with audio-visual displays, in the excellent **NTS Visitor Centre** on the site.

ENVIRONS: Watch for signs a mile (1.5 km) or so east for the outstanding Neolithic burial sites, the **Clava Cairns**.

🛈 NTS Visitor Centre
On the B9006 east of Inverness.
📞 01463 790607. ◯ daily.
⬤ Dec 25, 26, Jan–Feb. 🎟 ♿

Fort George ⓮

Inverness. 📞 01667 462777.
🚇 🚌 Inverness, Nairn. ◯ daily.
⬤ Dec 25, 26, Jan 1, 2. 🎟 ♿

O NE OF THE FINEST works of European military architecture, Fort George stands on a windswept promontory jutting into the Moray Firth, ideally located to suppress the Highlanders. Completed in 1769, the fort was built after the Jacobite risings to discourage further rebellion in the Highlanders and has remained a military garrison ever since. The Fort houses the **Regimental Museum** of

THE JACOBITE MOVEMENT

The first Jacobites (mainly Catholic Highlanders) were the supporters of James II of England (James VII of Scotland) who was deposed by the "Glorious Revolution" of 1688 *(see p53)*. With the Protestant William of Orange on the throne, the Jacobites' desire to restore the Stuart monarchy led to the uprisings of 1715 and 1745. The first, in support of James VIII, the "Old Pretender," ended at the Battle of Sherrifmuir (1715). The failure of the second uprising,

James II, by Samuel Cooper (1609–72)

with the defeat at Culloden, saw the end of Jacobite hopes and led to the end of the clan system and the suppression of Highland culture for over a century *(see p471)*.

The drawbridge on the eastern side of Cawdor Castle

the Queen's Own Highlanders, and some of its barrack rooms have been designed to reconstruct the conditions of the common soldiers stationed here more than 200 years ago. The **Grand Magazine** contains an outstanding collection of arms and military equipment. Fort George's extensive battlements also make an excellent place from which to watch dolphins tumbling in the Moray Firth.

Cawdor Castle ⓯

On B9090 (off A96). 📞 01667 404615. 🚇 Nairn, then bus or taxi. ◯ May–Oct: daily. 🎟 ♿ gardens only.

W ITH ITS TURRETED central tower, moat and drawbridge, Cawdor Castle is one of the most romantic stately homes in the Highlands. Although the castle is famed for being the 11th-century home of Shakespeare's *(see p310)* Macbeth and the scene of his murder of King Duncan, it is historically unproven that either came here.

An ancient holly tree preserved in the vaults is said to be the one under which, in 1372, Thane William's donkey, laden with gold, stopped for a rest during its master's search for a place to build a fortress. According to legend, this was how the site for the castle was chosen. Now, after 600 years of continuous occupation (it is still the home of the Thanes of Cawdor), the house is a treasury of family history, containing a number of rare tapestries and portraits by the 18th-century painters Joshua Reynolds (1723–92) and George Romney (1734–1802). Furniture in the Pink Bedroom and Woodcock Room includes work by the 18th-century designers Chippendale and Sheraton. In the Old Kitchen, the huge Victorian cooking range stands as a shrine to below-stairs drudgery. The castle's extensive grounds provide beautiful nature trails as well as a nine-hole golf course.

A contemporary picture, *The Battle of Culloden* (1746), by D. Campbell

Elgin ⑯

Grampian. 🏘 25,000. 🚆 🚌
ℹ️ High St, Moray (01343 542666).

W ITH ITS COBBLED market-
place and crooked lanes,
the popular vacation center of
Elgin still retains much of its
medieval layout. The 13th-
century **cathedral** ruins next
to King Street are all that
remain of one of Scotland's
architectural triumphs, the
design of its tiered windows
reminiscent of the interior at
St. Andrews *(see p485)*. Once
known as the Lantern of the
North, the cathedral was
severely damaged in 1390 by
the Wolf of Badenoch (the son
of Robert II) in revenge for
his excommunication by the
Bishop of Moray. Even worse
damage came in 1576 when
the Regent of Moray ordered
the stripping of its lead roofing,
which left the interior open to
the elements. Among its outstanding remains is a Pictish

**Details of the central tower of
Elgin Cathedral**

cross-slab in the nave, and a
basin in a corner where one of
Elgin's benefactors, Andrew
Anderson, was kept as a baby
by his homeless mother. As
well as local history, the **Elgin
Museum** has anthropological
and geological displays, while
the **Moray Motor Museum**
has over 40 cars and motorbikes dating from 1904.

🏛 **Elgin Museum**
High St. 📞 01343 543675.
⭕ Apr–Oct: daily. 📷 ♿
🏛 **Moray Motor Museum**
Bridge St, Bishopsmill. 📞 01343
544933. ⭕ Easter–Oct: daily. 📷 ♿

Aberdeen ⑰

S COTLAND'S THIRD LARGEST CITY and Europe's offshore
oil capital, Aberdeen has prospered since the discovery of petroleum in the North Sea in 1972. The seabed
has now yielded 50 oil fields. Known as the Granite
City, its forbidding and rugged outlines are softened by
sumptuous year-round floral displays in its public parks
and gardens, the Duthie Park Winter Gardens, the
largest in Europe. The city harbor, one of Britain's most
important fishing ports, is at its best early in the morning during the auctions at Scotland's largest fish market.

The spires of Aberdeen, rising behind the city harbor

Exploring Aberdeen
The city center flanks the mile-
long (1.5 km) Union Street
ending to the east at the Mercat
Cross. The cross stands by
Castlegate, the one-time site
of the city castle, now only a
marketplace. From here the
cobbled Shiprow winds southwest and passes Provost Ross's
House *(see p526)* on its way to
the harbor with its fish market. A bus can be taken a mile
(1.5 km) north of the center to
Old Aberdeen, which, with its
medieval streets and wynds,
has the peaceful character of
a separate village. Driving is
restricted on some streets.

👑 **King's College**
High St. 📞 01224 273702. ⭕ daily.
⭕ Dec 24–Jan 3. ♿
Founded in 1495 as the city's
first university, the college
now has a Visitor Centre that
provides details of its history.
The interdenominational
chapel, consecutively Catholic
and Protestant in the past, has
a distinctive lantern tower
rebuilt after a storm in 1633.
Douglas Strachan's stained-
glass windows add a contemporary touch to the interior,
which contains a 1540 pulpit,
later carved with heads of
Stuart monarchs.

🔒 **St. Andrew's Cathedral**
King St. 📞 01224 640290.
⭕ mid-May–mid-Sep: daily. ♿
The Mother Church of the
Episcopal Communion in
America, St. Andrew's has a
memorial to Samuel Seabury,
the first Episcopalian bishop
in the United States, who was
consecrated in Aberdeen in
1784. A series of coats of arms
adorns the ceiling above the
north and south aisles, contrasting colorfully with the
white walls and pillars. They
represent the American States
and the Jacobite *(see p523)*
families of Aberdeenshire.

**The elegant lantern tower of the
chapel at King's College**

PROVOST SKENE'S HOUSE

Guestrow. 01224 641086. Mon–Sat. Dec 25, 26, Jan 1, 2.
Once the home of Sir George Skene, a 17th-century provost
(mayor) of Aberdeen, the house was built in 1545 and remains
one of the oldest houses in the city. Inside, period rooms span
200 years of design. The Duke of Cumberland stayed here
during the weeks preceding the Battle of Culloden (see p523).

VISITORS' CHECKLIST

Grampian. 220,000.
8 miles (13 km) NE Aberdeen.
Guild St. Broad St
(01224 632727). Thu, Fri, Sat.

The 18th-century Parlor,
with its walnut harpsichord and
covered chairs by the fireplace,
was the informal room where
the family would have tea.

The Regency Room typifies
early 19th-century elegance. A
harp dating from 1820 stands
by a Grecian-style sofa and a
French writing table.

The Painted Gallery has
one of Scotland's most important cycles of religious art. The
panels are early 17th century,
though the artist is unknown.

The 17th-century Great Hall
contains heavy oak dining
furniture. Provost Skene's
wood-carved coat of arms
hangs above the fireplace.

The Georgian Dining Room,
with its Classical design, was
the main formal room in the
16th century and still has its
original flagstone floor.

Entrance

ABERDEEN CITY CENTER

Aberdeen Art Gallery ①
St. Andrew's Cathedral ⑤
Fish Market ⑧
Marischal College ④
Maritime Museum ⑦
Mercat Cross ⑥
St. Nicholas Church ②
Provost Skene's
House ③

KEY

Coach station
Railroad station
Ferry service
Parking
Tourist information
Church

0 meters 200
0 yards 200

🏛 Art Gallery

Schoolhill. 📞 01224 646333 ◯ daily.
⬤ Dec 25, 26, Jan 1, 2. ♿
Housed in a Neo-Classical building, built to order in 1884, the Art Gallery has a wide range of exhibitions, with emphasis on contemporary work. A fine collection of Aberdonian silver can be found among the decorative arts on the ground floor, and is the subject of a video presentation.

A permanent collection of 18th–20th-century fine art features such names as Toulouse-Lautrec, Raeburn, Reynolds, and Zoffany. Several of the works were bequeathed in 1900 by a local granite merchant, Alex Macdonald. He commissioned many of the paintings in the Macdonald Room, which displays 92 self-portraits by

Aberdonian silver in the Art Gallery

British artists. There are occasional poetry readings, music recitals and films, which add to the rich variety of cultural experiences on offer.

⛪ Church of St. Nicholas

George St. ◯ May–Sep: daily; Oct–Apr: Mon–Fri (am). ♿
Founded in the 12th century, St. Nicholas is Scotland's largest parish church. Though the present structure dates from 1752, many relics of earlier times can be seen inside.

After being damaged during the Reformation, the interior was divided in two. A chapel in the East Church contains iron rings used to secure witches in the 17th century. The West Church chapel has some embroidered panels attributed to one Mary Jameson (1597–1644).

🏛 Aberdeen Maritime Museum

Shiprow. 📞 01224 585788.
◯ Mon–Sat. ⬤ Dec 25, 26, Jan 1, 2.
Overlooking the harbor is the Provost Ross's House (1593), one the oldest residential buildings in town. This museum traces Aberdeen's long seafaring history. Exhibitions cover numerous topics from shipwrecks, rescues and shipbuilding to the workings of the many oil installations off Scotland's east coast.

⛪ St. Machar's Cathedral

The Chanonry. ◯ daily. ♿
Dominating Old Aberdeen, the 15th-century edifice of St. Machar's is the oldest granite building in the city. The stonework of one arch dates back to the 14th century. The nave now serves as a parish church and its magnificent oak ceiling is adorned with the coats of arms of 48 popes, emperors and princes of Christendom.

Royal Deeside Tour ⑱

S INCE QUEEN VICTORIA'S purchase of Balmoral Castle in 1852, Deeside has been best known as the summer home of the British Royal Family, although it has been associated with royalty since the time of Robert the Bruce *(see p468)*. The route follows the Dee, one of the world's most prolific salmon rivers, through some magnificent Grampian scenery.

Muir of Dinnet Nature Reserve ④
An information center on the A97 provides an excellent place from which to explore this beautiful mixed woodland area, formed by the retreating glaciers of the last Ice Age.

BRAEMAR, PERTH

A939 Gairn A93 Dee ⑤ B976 Muick ④ B9119 A97 Tanar B9094 •*Aboyne* B976

⑥ ⑤

Balmoral ⑥
Bought by Queen Victoria for 30,000 guineas in 1852, after its owner choked to death on a fishbone, the castle was rebuilt in the Scottish Baronial style at Prince Albert's request.

Ballater ⑤
The old railroad town of Ballater has royal warrants on many of its store fronts. It grew as a 19th-century spa town, its waters reputedly providing a cure for tuberculosis.

Dunkeld ⑲

Tayside. 🏘 *2,200.* ⬆ 🚌
🛈 *The Cross (01350 727688).*

Sᴵᴛᴜᴀᴛᴇᴅ ʙʏ the River Tay, this ancient and charming village was all but destroyed in the Battle of Dunkeld, a Jacobite *(see p523)* defeat, in 1689. The **Little Houses** lining Cathedral Street were the first to be rebuilt, and remain fine examples of imaginative restoration. The sad ruins of the 14th-century **cathedral** enjoy an idyllic setting on shady lawns beside the Tay, against a backdrop of steep and wooded hills. The choir is used as the parish church and its north wall contains a Leper's Squint: a little hole through which lepers could see the altar during mass. It was while on holiday in the Dunkeld countryside that Beatrix Potter *(see p353)* found the location for her Peter Rabbit stories.

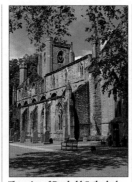
The ruins of Dunkeld Cathedral

Pitlochry ⑳

Tayside. 🏘 *2,500.* ⬆ 🚌
🛈 *22 Atholl Rd (01796 472215).*

Sᴜʀʀᴏᴜɴᴅᴇᴅ ʙʏ the pine-forested hills of the Central Highlands, Pitlochry became famous after Queen Victoria *(see p56)* described it as one of the finest resorts in Europe. In early summer, wild salmon leap high up the salmon ladder built into the the Power Station Dam, on their way to spawning grounds upriver. The **Power Station Visitor Center** outlines the hydroelectric scheme that harnesses the waters of Loch Faskally. The home of Bell's whisky can be found at the **Blair Atholl Distillery,** which has produced it since 1798. Open to the public, the distillery gives visitors an insight into whisky-making *(see p475)*. One of Scotland's most famous stages, the **Festival Theater**, is best seen in the summer, when the program changes every day.

🛈 **Power Station Visitor Center**
Port-na-Craig. 📞 *01796 473152.*
🕐 *Apr–Oct: daily.* ♿ *limited.*
🎭 **Festival Theater**
Port-na-Craig. 📞 *01796 472680.*
🕐 *May–Oct: Mon–Sat.* 📷 ♿
🏭 **Blair Atholl Distillery**
Perth Rd. 📞 *01796 472234.*
🕐 *Apr–Sep: daily.* 📷 ♿ *limited.*

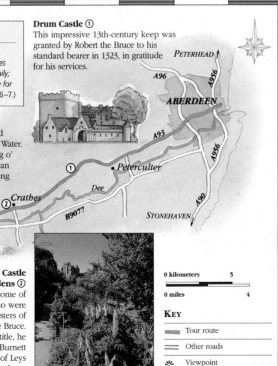

Tɪᴘs ꜰᴏʀ Dʀɪᴠᴇʀs

Length: 69 miles (111 km).
Stopping-off points: Crathes Castle cafe. 🕐 *May–Sep: daily;* Tor-na-Collie Hotel, Banchory for Scottish meals. (See also pp636–7.)

Drum Castle ①
This impressive 13th-century keep was granted by Robert the Bruce to his standard bearer in 1323, in gratitude for his services.

Banchory ③
Lavender is grown here and distilled into Dee Lavender Water. From the 18th-century Brig o' Feugh, salmon can be seen leaping upstream.

Crathes Castle and Gardens ②
This is the family home of the Burnetts, who were made Royal Foresters of Drum by Robert the Bruce. Along with the title, he gave Alexander Burnett the ivory Horn of Leys which is still on show.

PETERHEAD ↑
A96
A956
ABERDEEN
A93
A956
① • Peterculter
Dee
② Crathes
A93
A980
A93
③
B974
B9077
STONEHAVEN
A90

0 kilometers 5
0 miles 4

Kᴇʏ

▬▬ Tour route
═══ Other roads
🌿 Viewpoint

Killiecrankie Walk ㉑

I N AN AREA famous for its scenery and historical connections, this circular walk offers typical Highland views. The route is fairly flat, though ringed by mountains, and meanders through a wooded gorge, passing the Soldier's Leap and a Victorian viaduct. There are several ideal picnic spots along the way. On reaching Loch Faskally, panoramic views open up over Blair Atholl. Returning along the River Tummel, the walk crosses one of Queen Victoria's favorite Highland areas, before doubling back to complete the circuit.

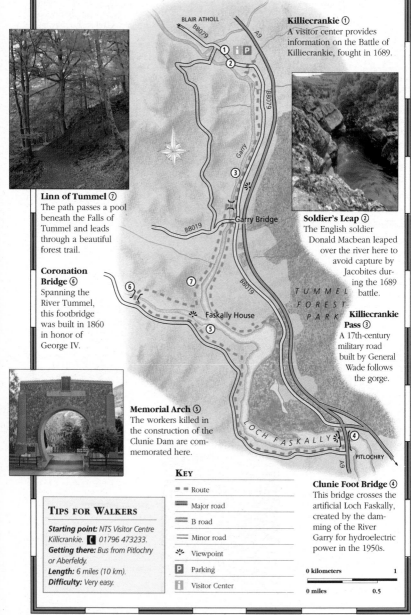

Killiecrankie ①
A visitor center provides information on the Battle of Killiecrankie, fought in 1689.

Soldier's Leap ②
The English soldier Donald Macbean leaped over the river here to avoid capture by Jacobites during the 1689 battle.

Killiecrankie Pass ③
A 17th-century military road built by General Wade follows the gorge.

Linn of Tummel ⑦
The path passes a pool beneath the Falls of Tummel and leads through a beautiful forest trail.

Coronation Bridge ⑥
Spanning the River Tummel, this footbridge was built in 1860 in honor of George IV.

Memorial Arch ⑤
The workers killed in the construction of the Clunie Dam are commemorated here.

Clunie Foot Bridge ④
This bridge crosses the artificial Loch Faskally, created by the damming of the River Garry for hydroelectric power in the 1950s.

KEY

- ▬ ▬ Route
- ▭ Major road
- ▭ B road
- ▭ Minor road
- ✤ Viewpoint
- 🅿 Parking
- ℹ Visitor Center

TIPS FOR WALKERS

Starting point: NTS Visitor Centre Killiecrankie. 📞 01796 473233.
Getting there: Bus from Pitlochry or Aberfeldy.
Length: 6 miles (10 km).
Difficulty: Very easy.

0 kilometers 1
0 miles 0.5

The ridge of Aonach Eagach, Glencoe, in late autumn

Blair Castle ②

Blair Atholl, Tayside. ☎ 01796
481207. ☒ Blair Atholl, then bus.
◯ Apr–Oct: daily. 🎫 ♿ limited.

THIS RAMBLING, turreted castle
has been altered and extended so often in its 700-year history that it now provides a unique insight into the history of Highland aristocratic life. The elegantly plastered 18th-century wing, with its drafty Victorian passages hung with antlers, has a display containing the gloves and pipe of Bonnie Prince Charlie (see p521), who spent two days here gathering Jacobite (see p523) support. Family portraits cover 300 years and include paintings by such masters as Johann Zoffany and Sir Peter Lely. Sir Edwin Landseer's priceless *Death of a Stag in Glen Tilt* (1850) was painted nearby. In 1844 Queen Victoria visited the castle and conferred on its owners, the Dukes of Atholl, the distinction of being allowed to maintain a private army. The Atholl Highlanders still flourish.

The Cairngorms ㉓

See pp530–31.

Glencoe ㉔

Lochaber. ☒ Fort William.
🚌 Glencoe. ℹ Cameron Sq, Fort William (01397 703781).

RENOWNED for its awesome scenery and savage history, Glencoe was compared by Dickens to "a burial ground of a race of giants." The precipitous cliffs of Buachaille Etive Mor and the knife-edged ridge of Aonach Eagach (both over 900 m; 3,000 ft) present a formidable challenge even to experienced mountaineers.

Against a dark backdrop of craggy peaks and the tumbling River Coe, the Glen offers superb hill walking in the summer. Sturdy footwear, waterproof clothing and attention to safety warnings are essential. Details on routes, ranging from the easy half-hour between the **NTS Visitor Centre** and Signal Rock (where the signal was given to start the massacre) to a stiff 6 mile (10 km) haul up the Devil's Staircase, can be obtained from the Visitor Centre. Guided walks are offered in summer by the NTS Ranger service.

ℹ **NTS Visitor Centre**
Ballachulish. ☎ 01855 811307.
◯ Apr–Oct: daily. 🎫 ♿

THE MASSACRE OF GLENCOE

In 1692, the chief of the Glencoe MacDonalds was five days late in registering an oath of submission to William III, giving the government an excuse to root out a nest of Jacobite (p523) supporters. For ten days 130 soldiers, captained by Robert Campbell, were hospitably entertained by the unsuspecting MacDonalds. At dawn on February 13, in a terrible breach of trust, the soldiers fell on their hosts, killing some 38 MacDonalds. Many more died in their wintry mountain hideouts. The massacre, unsurprisingly, became a political scandal, though there were to be no official reprimands for three years.

Detail of *The Massacre of Glencoe* by James Hamilton

The Cairngorms ㉓

RISING TO A HEIGHT of 1,309 m (4,296 ft), the Cairngorm mountains form the highest land mass in Britain. Now Britain's premier ski resort, a chairlift can be taken to the summit of Cairn Gorm where a weather station provides regular reports, essential in an area known for sudden changes of weather. Now a popular tourist destination and one of Scotland's great whisky regions, only a short time ago the Spey Valley depended on farming, and many of today's estates have centers that introduce the visitor to Highland land use.

Wild goat

Strathspey Steam Railway
This track between Aviemore and Boat of Garten dates from 1863.

Aviemore, the commercial center of the Cairngorms, provides buses to the ski area 8 miles (11 km) away.

Kincraig Highland Wildlife Park
Driving through the Kincraig Highland Wildlife Park, the visitor can see bison alongside bears, wolves and wild boar. They were all once native to the Spey Valley.

INVERNESS

Carrbridge

Boat of Garten

Aviemore

Coylumb

Kincraig

LOCH AN EILEIN

LOCH INSH

Spey

Feshie

Kingussie

NEWTONMORE

PERTH

B970

Tolvah

BRAERIACH
▲
1,295 m
4,248 ft

LOCH EINICH

0 kilometers　　5

0 miles

The Cairngorms, from Aviemore

Rothiemurchus Estate
Highland cattle can be seen among many other creatures at Rothiemurchus. A Visitors' Centre provides guided walks and illustrates life on a Highland estate.

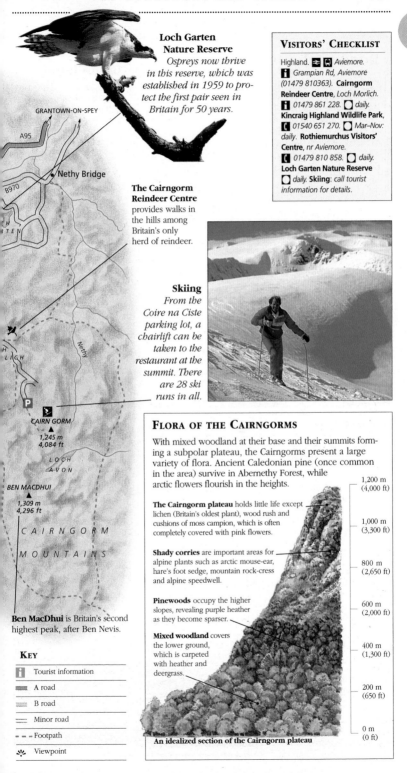

Loch Garten Nature Reserve

Ospreys now thrive in this reserve, which was established in 1959 to protect the first pair seen in Britain for 50 years.

GRANTOWN-ON-SPEY

A95

Nethy Bridge

B970

The Cairngorm Reindeer Centre provides walks in the hills among Britain's only herd of reindeer.

VISITORS' CHECKLIST

Highland. ⚡ 🚆 Aviemore.
ℹ Grampian Rd, Aviemore
(01479 810363). **Cairngorm
Reindeer Centre**, Loch Morlich.
ℹ 01479 861 228. ☐ daily.
Kincraig Highland Wildlife Park,
📞 01540 651 270. ☐ Mar–Nov:
daily. **Rothiemurchus Visitors'
Centre**, nr Aviemore.
📞 01479 810 858. ☐ daily.
Loch Garten Nature Reserve
☐ daily. **Skiing**: call tourist
information for details.

Skiing

From the Coire na Ciste parking lot, a chairlift can be taken to the restaurant at the summit. There are 28 ski runs in all.

P

CAIRN GORM
▲
1,245 m
4,084 ft

LOCH
AVON

BEN MACDHUI
▲
1,309 m
4,296 ft

CAIRNGORM

MOUNTAINS

Ben MacDhui is Britain's second highest peak, after Ben Nevis.

FLORA OF THE CAIRNGORMS

With mixed woodland at their base and their summits forming a subpolar plateau, the Cairngorms present a large variety of flora. Ancient Caledonian pine (once common in the area) survive in Abernethy Forest, while arctic flowers flourish in the heights.

The Cairngorm plateau holds little life except lichen (Britain's oldest plant), wood rush and cushions of moss campion, which is often completely covered with pink flowers.

Shady corries are important areas for alpine plants such as arctic mouse-ear, hare's foot sedge, mountain rock-cress and alpine speedwell.

Pinewoods occupy the higher slopes, revealing purple heather as they become sparser.

Mixed woodland covers the lower ground, which is carpeted with heather and deergrass.

1,200 m (4,000 ft)
1,000 m (3,300 ft)
800 m (2,650 ft)
600 m (2,000 ft)
400 m (1,300 ft)
200 m (650 ft)
0 m (0 ft)

An idealized section of the Cairngorm plateau

KEY

ℹ	Tourist information
▬▬▬	A road
▬▬▬	B road
═══	Minor road
- - -	Footpath
☼	Viewpoint

Road to the Isles Tour ㉕

THIS SCENIC ROUTE goes past vast mountain corridors, breathtaking beaches of white sand and tiny villages, to the town of Mallaig, one of the ferry ports for the isles of Skye, Rhum and Eigg. As well as the stunning scenery, the area is steeped in Jacobite history *(see p523)*.

TIPS FOR DRIVERS

Tour length: 45 miles (72 km).
Stopping-off points: Glenfinnan NTS Visitors' Centre (01397 722 250) explains the Jacobite risings and serves refreshments; the Arisaig House Hotel has excellent Scottish food. (See also pp636–7.)

Mallaig ⑦
The Road to the Isles ends just north of Mallaig, an active little fishing port with a very good harbor and one of the main ferry links to Skye *(see pp520-21)*.

Morar ⑥
The road continues through Morar, an area renowned for its white sands and rumored to be the home of a 12 m (40 ft) monster known as Morag.

Prince's Cairn ⑤
Crossing the Ardnish Peninsula to Loch Nan Uamh, a cairn marks the spot from which Bonnie Prince Charlie finally left Scotland for France in 1746.

Oban ㉖

Argyll. 8,000. Boswell Hse, Argyll Sq (01631 63122). Fri.

LOCATED ON the Firth of Lorne and commanding a magnificent view of the Argyll coast, the bustling port of Oban is a popular destination for travelers on their way to Mull and the Western Isles *(see p515)*.

Dominating the skyline is McCaig's Tower, an unfinished Victorian in imitation of the Colosseum in Rome. It is worth the 10-minute climb from the town center for the sea views alone. Attractions in the town include working centers for glass, pottery and whisky; the Oban distillery produces one of the country's finest malt whiskies *(see p475)*. A remarkable collection of dolls' houses can be found in **A World in Miniature**, including interiors designed by Charles Rennie Mackintosh *(see p504)*. A busy harbor shelters numerous car ferries leaving for distant Barra and South Uist, Mull, Tiree and Colonsay.

⊞ A World in Miniature
North Pier. 01852 316272. Apr–Oct: daily (Sun: pm).

Mull ㉗

Argyll. 2,800. from Oban. Tobermory (01688 302182).

MOST ROADS on this easily accessible Hebridean island follow the sharply indented rocky coastline, affording wonderful sea views. From Craignure, the Mull and West Highland Railway serves the baronial **Torosay Castle**. A pathway through its gardens is lined with statues, while inside, 19th-century furniture and paintings can be found. On a promontory a short drive to the east lies **Duart Castle**, home of the chief of Clan Maclean. Visitors can see the Banqueting Hall and State Rooms in the 13th-century keep. Its dungeons once held prisoners from a Spanish Armada galleon sunk, while docked, by one Donald Maclean in 1588.

Looking out to sea across Tobermory Bay, Mull

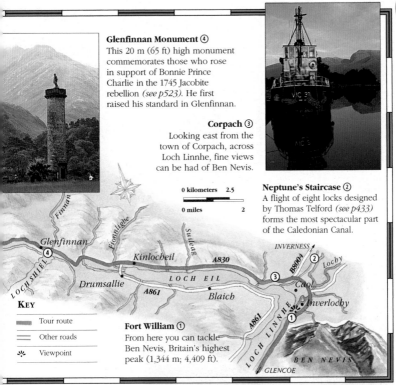

Glenfinnan Monument ④
This 20 m (65 ft) high monument commemorates those who rose in support of Bonnie Prince Charlie in the 1745 Jacobite rebellion *(see p523)*. He first raised his standard in Glenfinnan.

Corpach ③
Looking east from the town of Corpach, across Loch Linnhe, fine views can be had of Ben Nevis.

0 kilometers 2.5
0 miles 2

Neptune's Staircase ②
A flight of eight locks designed by Thomas Telford *(see p433)* forms the most spectacular part of the Caledonian Canal.

INVERNESS
Lochy
Glenfinnan ④
Kinlocheil A830
LOCH SHIEL
Drumsallie LOCH EIL ③ *Caol*
A861 *Blaich* *Inverlochy*

KEY
▬▬▬ Tour route
═══ Other roads
⚹ Viewpoint

Fort William ①
From here you can tackle Ben Nevis, Britain's highest peak (1,344 m; 4,409 ft).

BEN NEVIS
GLENCOE

ENVIRONS: From Fionnphort, a ferry can be taken to **Iona**, with its abbey ruins. This is where the Irish missionary St. Columba *(see p511)* began his mission in Scotland in 563. North of Iona, the Isle of Staffa should be visited for its magnificent **Fingal's Cave**.

♠ **Torosay Castle**
Off A849, nr Craignure. ☎ 01680 812421. **Castle** ⬜ Apr– Sep: daily. **Gardens** ⬜ daily. 🖼
♠ **Duart Castle**
Off A849, nr Craignure. ☎ 01680 821309. ⬜ Apr–mid-Oct: daily. 🖼

Loch Awe ㉘

Argyll. 🚂 🚌 Dalmally. 🛈 Front St, Inveraray (01499 312063).

ONE of the longest of Scotland's freshwater lochs, Loch Awe fills a 25-mile (40-km) glen in the south-western Highlands. A short drive north of the town of Lochawe leads to the lochside remains of **Kilchurn Castle**,

The ruins of Kilchurn Castle on the shore of Loch Awe

which was abandoned after being struck by lightning in the 18th century. Dwarfing the castle is the huge bulk of Ben Cruachan, whose summit can be reached by the narrow Pass of Brander, in which Robert the Bruce *(see p468)* fought the Clan MacDougal in 1308. From the A85, a tunnel leads to the cavernous Cruachan Power Station in the very heart of the mountain.

Near the village of Taynuilt the preserved Lorn Furnace at Bonawe is a reminder of the iron-smelting industry that caused the destruction of much of the area's woodland in the 18th and 19th centuries.

Marked prehistoric cairns are found off the A816 between Kilmartin and Dunadd. The latter boasts a 6th-century hill fort from which the Stone of Destiny *(see p468)* originated.

Inveraray Castle ㉙

Inveraray, Strathclyde. 🚂 *Arrochar, then bus.* 📞 01499 302203. 🚪 *Apr–Jun, Sep–Oct: Thu–Sat: Jul–Aug; daily.* 🅿️ ♿ *limited.*

T HIS MULTITURRETED mock Gothic palace is the family home of the powerful Clan Campbell who have been the Dukes of Argyll since 1701. Built in 1745 by architects Roger Morris and William Adam on the site and ruins of a 15th century castle, the conical towers were added later, after a fire in 1877. Magnificent interiors, designed by Robert Mylne in the 1770s, form a backdrop to such treasures as a huge collection of Oriental and European porcelain and Regency furniture and portraits by Ramsay, Gainsborough and Raeburn. One of the most impressive displays is the Armoury Hall; the Campbells collected early weaponry to fight the Jacobites *(see p523)*. In the stables, the Combined Operations Museum commemorates the 250,000 allied troops who trained here during World War II.

Auchindrain Museum ㉚

Inveraray, Strathclyde. 📞 01499 500235. 🚌 *Inveraray, then bus.* 🚪 *Apr: Sun–Fri; May–Sep: daily.* 🅿️ ♿ *limited.*

T HE FIRST OPEN-AIR museum in Scotland, the Auchindrain illuminates the working lives of the kind of farming community typical of the Highlands until the late 19th century. Constituting a township of some 20 thatched cottages, the site was communally farmed by its tenants until the last one retired in 1962. Visitors can wander through the houses, most of which combine

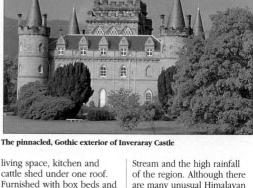

The pinnacled, Gothic exterior of Inveraray Castle

living space, kitchen and cattle shed under one roof. Furnished with box beds and rush lamps, and surrounded by herb gardens, the homes of Auchindrain are a memorial to the time before the transition from subsistence to commercial farming.

A traditional crofter's plow at the Auchindrain Museum

Crarae Garden ㉛

Crarae, Strathclyde. 📞 01546 86614. 🚌 *Inveraray, then bus.* 🚪 *daily.* 🅿️ ♿

W IDELY CONSIDERED the most beguiling of the many spectacular gardens of the West Highlands, the **Crarae Garden** was created in the 1920s by Lady Grace Campbell. She was the aunt of explorer Reginald Farrer, whose specimens from Tibet were the beginnings of a collection of exotic plants. Now more like a Himalayan ravine, the garden is nourished by the warmth of the Gulf

Stream and the high rainfall of the region. Although there are many unusual Himalayan rhododendrons flourishing here, the garden is also home to exotic plants from Tasmania, New Zealand and the United States. Great plant collectors still contribute to the garden, which is best seen in spring and early summer, against the blue waters of Loch Fyne.

Jura ㉜

Strathclyde. 🚶 300. ⛴ *from Kennacraig.* ℹ️ *The Square, Bowmore (0149 6810254).*

B ARREN, MOUNTAINOUS and overrun by red deer, the isle of Jura has only one road that connects the single village of Craighouse to the Islay ferry. Though walking is restricted during the stalking (deer hunting) season between August and October, the island offers superb hiking, especially on the slopes of the three main peaks, known as the Paps of Jura. The tallest of these is Beinn An Oir at 784 m (2571 ft). Beyond the northern tip of the isle the notorious whirlpools of Corryvreckan can be seen. The novelist George Orwell (who came to the island to write his final novel, *1984*) nearly lost his life here in 1946 when he fell into the water. A legend tells

Lagavulin distillery, producer of one Scotland's finest malts, on Islay

Mist crowning the Paps of Jura, seen at sunset across Loch Tarbert

of Prince Breackan who, to win the hand of a princess, tried to keep his boat anchored in the whirlpool for three days, held by ropes made of hemp, wool and maidens' hair. The Prince drowned when a single rope, containing the hair of a girl who had been untrue, finally broke.

Islay ㉝

Argyll & Bute. 5,000. from Kennacraig. The Square, Bowmore (01496 810254).

THE MOST SOUTHERLY of the Western Isles, Islay (pronounced 'Eyeluh') is the home of such respected Highland single malt whiskies as Lagavulin and Laphroaig. Most of the island's eight distilleries produce heavily peated malts with a distinctive tang of the sea. The Georgian village of Bowmore has the island's oldest distillery and a circular church designed to minimize the Devil's possible lurking-places. The **Museum of Islay Life** in Port Charlotte contains a wealth of information concerning the island's social and natural history. Seven miles (11 km) east of Port Ellen stands the Kildalton Cross. A block of local green stone adorned with Old Testament scenes, it is one of the finest 8th-century Celtic

crosses in Britain. Worth a visit for its archaeological interest is the medieval stronghold of the Lords of the Isles, **Finlaggan**, which is under excavation. Islay's superb beaches support a variety of bird life, some of which can be observed at the RSPB reserve at Gruinart.

🏛 **Museum of Islay Life**
Port Charlotte. 01496 850358. Easter–Oct: daily; Nov–Apr: Sun (pm). limited.

Kintyre ㉞

Argyll & Bute. Oban. Campbeltown. Portavadie, Lochranza. MacKinnon House, The Pier, Campbeltown (01586 552056).

A LONG, NARROW PENINSULA stretching far south of Glasgow, Kintyre has superb views across to the islands of Gigha, Islay and Jura. The 9-mile (14 km) Crinan Canal,

opened in 1801, is a delightful inland waterway, its 15 locks bustling with pleasure craft in the summer. The town of Tarbert (meaning "isthmus" in Gaelic) takes its name from the neck on which it stands, which is narrow enough to drag a boat across between Loch Fyne and West Loch Tarbert. This feat was first achieved by the Viking King Magnus Barfud who, in 1198, was granted by treaty as much land as he could sail around. Traveling south past Campbeltown, the B842 ends at the headland known as the Mull of Kintyre, which was made famous when former Beatle Paul McCartney commercialized a traditional pipe tune of the same name. Westward lies the isle of Rathlin, where Robert the Bruce *(see p468)* learned patience in his struggles against the English by watching a spider weaving a web in a cave.

Fishing boats moored at Tarbert harbor, Kintyre

TRAVELERS' NEEDS

WHERE TO STAY

THE RANGE OF HOTELS and accommodations available in Britain is extensive, and whatever your budget you should find something to suit you. Various types of accommodations are described over the next four pages, and the hotel listings section *(see pp542–573)* includes over 350 of the best places to stay, from luxurious country-house hotels to cozy bed-and-breakfasts. This selection has been made on the basis that it represents excellence and a good value.

Hilton doorman, London

The confusing rating systems for hotel classification operated by the various tourist authorities in Great Britain is also demystified. Information is included on vacation apartments, which are becoming increasingly popular, particularly for those on a shoestring budget, with young children, or both. We have also added some introductory information on Britain's many campsites and trailer parks that can provide an adventurous, reasonably priced alternative to bricks and mortar.

COUNTRY-HOUSE HOTELS

THE PECULIARLY BRITISH concept of the countryhouse hotel has grown stronger over the last 15 years. The term has been somewhat liberally used by unscrupulous hoteliers where some cursory redecoration, gas-log fires and reproduction furniture justified the words "country house" being added to the new hotel brochure. However, the genuine article is not hard to spot: the buildings are invariably of some architectural value, and filled with antiques and fine furnishings. Often they are situated on extensive grounds. Comfort and luxury are guaranteed – as well as a high price tag. Some countryhouses are run by resident owner-proprietors such as Chedington Court *(see p551)*, while others may be owned by hotel chains such as Historic House Hotels.

CORPORATE HOTELS AND HOTEL CHAINS

OFTEN AT THE TOP END of the market are the large corporate hotels, such as the Sheraton group, which provide every imaginable comfort and facility, nearly always including excellent restaurants, swimming pool and a leisure and fitness center. Though they tend to lack individuality and atmosphere, they make up for this in creature comforts.

Major hotel chains such as Forte Crest are to be found in all the larger cities. Prices can be high, but are often quoted for the room rather than per person. They do not always include breakfast, so check before you book. Sometimes chain hotels will offer special weekend rates for tourists who book in advance, although weekdays are often full with business travelers and conference delegates.

Atholl Palace Hotel *(see p572)*

CLASSIC HOTELS AND COACHING INNS

IN THE MIDDLE PRICE range there are traditional hotels. They are often family-run and rely on a regular clientele; sometimes they can be a little uninspiring but usually offer reasonable comfort and decor. In towns you may also find small, privately run modern hotels offering bargains.

"Coaching inns," such as the Swan in Suffolk *(see p548)* can be found all over England and Wales. They used to be staging points for people journeying by horse and carriage, where horses would be rested, and travelers refreshed and given lodging. They are generally attractive historic buildings. Often they are the town's focal point, usually decorated traditionally, with a reliable restaurant and a friendly atmosphere.

Buckland Manor *(see p555)*, Worcestershire

◁ **The 11th-century ruins of Corfe Castle, Dorset**

The Swan, Suffolk *(see p548)*, a converted coaching inn

BED-AND-BREAKFASTS AND GUEST HOUSES

BED-AND-BREAKFAST hotels, or B&Bs as they are more commonly known, dominate the lower price range, and these guesthouses and farmhouses can be found all over Britain. They are often family-owned and offer basic, no-frills accommodation, usually with a choice of English or Continental breakfast included in the price of the room.

B&Bs don't normally accept traveler's checks, personal checks or credit cards.

They prefer that you pay them in cash. Many tourist boards publish a *Bed & Breakfast Touring Map,* which gives details of places they have inspected.

WOLSEY LODGES

WOLSEY LODGES are a group of privately owned, very comfortable houses, mostly in the country, which offer hospitality. They are named after Cardinal Wolsey who traveled around the country in the 16th century expecting the highest standards from his hosts.

Food is an important feature of your stay, and dinner is often along the lines of a dinner party; everyone eats around one table, along with the host and hostess. You feel

as though you are staying in a familiar home rather than an impersonal hotel.

The aim is to make visitors feel like welcome guests rather than paying clients. Prices vary from £20 to £45 per person for a double room with bathroom and a full breakfast. Brochures can be obtained from local tourist offices or the Wolsey Lodge office *(see Directory p541).*

HOTEL CLASSIFICATIONS

ONE USEFUL GUIDE to follow when making your hotel selection is the British Tourist Authority's crown classification system. Over 17,000 hotels, guesthouses, motels, inns, B&Bs and farmhouses take

part in the system. The classification gradings range from "listed" (the lowest category) to "five crowns."

An annual inspection is carried out by the local tourist board to make sure standards are maintained. The number of crowns given relates to the range of facilities and services offered, but a lower classification does not imply lower standards. This is where the BTA's "quality gradings" system comes in. These grade places, but on criteria such as warmth of welcome and comfort of furnishings. The four levels of ratings are termed "approved," "commended," "highly commended" and "de luxe." Thus you may come across a de luxe B&B that has only one crown – this means that while its facilities are limited they are nevertheless of a very high standard.

HIDDEN EXTRAS

TIPPING is not usually expected in Britain, and is becoming rare except in the most exclusive hotels, or on occasions when you have been particularly impressed with the quality of service.

One of the most expensive extras on all hotel bills can be the telephone. Hotels will usually charge a higher price for calls made from your room – check the rate before you launch into lengthy conversations – it may well be worth buying a phonecard and using the telephone in the hotel lobby instead.

Hintlesham Hall, Suffolk *(see p548)*

PRICES AND BOOKING

HOTEL RATES are normally quoted per room and are inclusive of VAT and service charge; if single rooms are not available the supplement charged on a double room is generally quite substantial. Top-of-the range hotels could cost you over £200 for a nights stay and may not even include breakfast.

An average hotel in London will cost about £70 to £150 for two persons including bathroom and breakfast. Outside London expect to pay from £50 to £90 for facilities that will be of a similar standard.

Bed-and-breakfast accommodation (out of London) depends on the time of year and ranges from about £12.50 to £30 per person, per night.

The elegant hallway of the Gore Hotel in London *(see p542)*

A guest house (also outside London) would start at about £20 per person for one night. Farmhouse lodgings nearly always include a substantial dinner, so for full board you are likely to pay between £19 to £30 per person per night.

Some hotels ask for a deposit in advance when a written or telephone booking is made. This can sometimes be as a request for your credit card number – the amount will be charged to you regardless of whether you show up or not. Acceptance of a booking by telephone, in writing or by fax constitutes a legally binding contract in Britain, but if you cancel any reservation as early as possible, you may not necessarily have to pay the full amount.

The folly of Doyden Castle, Cornwall, now a National Trust vacation cottage

APARTMENTS

FOR THOSE WHO prefer to stay in one place and be independent, or have young children and a limited budget, furnished apartments are an excellent option. There are many places all around the country, and of all types, from luxury apartments and log cabins to beautifully converted barns or mills. Local tourist offices have the most comprehensive and up-to-date lists (they can also provide a booking service).

The **British Tourist Authority** classifies apartment accommodation in a system similar to its hotel ratings. Those that have been inspected are given a "key rating." One to five keys are awarded, dependent on the range of facilities and equipment on offer, and similar to the hotel system *(see p539)*, they can be

Roadside signboard for bed-and-breakfast

further rated on four gradings of commendation and quality.

In Scotland, the classification uses crowns and follows the same criteria as the quality gradings in England.

Unlike Scotland and England, the Welsh authorities combine their classifications into one: dragons reflect the quality of the accommodations, the number of facilities and also their standard.

The **Landmark Trust** is an organization that has saved many historic or unusual buildings, and then made them available to the public to rent on a weekend or weekly basis. Book ahead.

The **National Trust** *(see p25)* also has a section that offers interesting historic buildings or houses for rent.

CAMPING AND MOTOR HOMES

THERE IS A good choice of camp sites and trailer parks throughout Britain, normally open from Easter to October. During the peak summer months, parks fill up quickly, so book in advance. In England, the tourist offices listed can be contacted during the summer to check on availability. International trailer and camping signs indicate many park locations on the main roads. The BTA publishes a fairly comprehensive list called *Camping and Caravan Parks in Britain*. Two clubs – the **Caravan Club**, and the **Camping and Caravanning Club** – publish guides listing their parks, and it may be worthwhile to join. Both clubs operate their own grading system. A typical camping or trailer site will cost approximately £6 to £10 per night.

An alternative to a tent or trailer is to rent a motor home, which gives you great freedom to explore at your own pace and to stay almost anywhere. They are usually comfortable and very well equipped. The BTA guide *Britain: Vehicle Hire* provides full details of motor home rental. Expect to pay between £500 and £800 per week for a luxury six-berth vehicle, which can even include a generator, microwave and television. Motor home companies can arrange for you to pick up your vehicle direct from the airport or ferry terminal. Most camping and trailer sites in Britain welcome motor home drivers.

Campsite, Ogwen Valley, Snowdonia

Disabled Travelers

DISABLED TRAVELERS should look for the "Tourism for All" symbol, which indicates properties that have satisfied specific accessibility requirements. **RADAR**, the Royal Association for Disability and Rehabilitation, publishes *Holidays in the British Isles: A Guide for Disabled People* annually and it is available by mail order from their offices or from major UK travel bookstores. Contact RADAR for any advice on traveling in Britain. We have indicated in our hotel listings *(see pp538–573)* those that have facilities for the disabled.

The facilities provided for disabled campers are generally of a better standard on the newer, more modern sites. Both the Camping and Caravanning Club and the Caravan Club can give you details of all their sites that are accessible to wheelchairs and have washing and toilet facilities for the disabled.

The **Scottish Tourist Board** has access information included in all its major accommodation and sightseeing guides. The **Disability Scotland Information Service** is another invaluable source of information, who produce a free directory for visitors to north of the border.

The **Holiday Care Service** has information on all aspects of accommodation and travel for visitors with disabilities.

Choosing a Hotel

THE HOTELS in this guide have been selected across a wide price range for their excellent facilities and locations. Many also have a recommended restaurant. The chart lists the hotels by region, starting with London; color-coded thumb tabs indicate the regions covered on each page. For restaurant listings, see pp574–607.

	CREDIT CARDS	RESTAURANT	CHILDREN WELCOME	GARDEN/TERRACE	NUMBER OF ROOMS

LONDON

WEST END & WESTMINSTER: *Hazlitt's.* **Map 4 D5.** ££££
6 Frith St, W1V 5TZ. ¶ 0171-434 1771. FAX 0171-439 1524.
Set in three 18th-century houses. Although not luxurious, it is civilized.
Bedrooms are restfully plain, with interesting antiques. ● Dec 24–26. ☎

| AE DC MC V | | | | 23 |

WEST END & WESTMINSTER: *Goring.* **Map 5 C3.** ££££
Beeston Pl, Grosvenor Gardens, SW1W 0JW. ¶ 0171-396 9000. FAX 0171-834 4393.
Edwardian building that is grand and family-run. The third-generation
Gorings keep immaculate standards; superb restaurant. ☎ 24 P &

| AE DC MC V | ■ | | | 80 |

WEST END & WESTMINSTER: *22 Jermyn St.* **Map 5 D1.** ££££
22 Jermyn St, SW1Y 6HL. ¶ 0171-734 2353. FAX 0171-734 0750.
A warren of luxurious suites and studios for the business visitor. They
are lavishly decorated and beautifully maintained. ☎ 24 ✂ &

| AE DC MC V | | ● | | 18 |

WEST END & WESTMINSTER: *Waldorf.* **Map 4 F5.** ££££
Aldwych, WC2B 4DD. ¶ 0171-836 2400. FAX 0171-836 7244.
Still stylish, this superior hotel is no longer quite the exclusive haunt
of its heyday. Some bedrooms are being refurbished. ☎ 24 ✂ &

| AE DC MC V | ■ | ● | | 292 |

WEST END & WESTMINSTER: *Claridge's.* **Map 3 C5.** £££££
Brook St, W1A 2JQ. ¶ 0171-629 8860. FAX 0171-499 2210.
Claridge's favors tradition – yet the ambience is surprisingly unstarchy.
Art Deco blends with marble mosaic Classical grandeur. ☎ 24 ✂

| AE DC MC V | ■ | ● | | 190 |

WEST END & WESTMINSTER: *Connaught.* **Map 3 B5.** £££££
Carlos Pl, W1Y 6AL. ¶ 0171-499 7070. FAX 0171-495 3262.
So self-confident is this famous hotel that it offers neither brochure
nor prices. To book, don't call – write, well in advance. ☎ 24 &

| MC V | ■ | | | 90 |

WEST END & WESTMINSTER: *Ritz.* **Map 6 D1.** £££££
Piccadilly, W1V 9DG. ¶ 0171-493 8181. FAX 0171-493 2687.
Undeniably grand marbled, Frenchified rooms – in the restaurant
gilded chandeliers hang from a fresco of clouds. ☎ 24 &

| AE DC MC V | ■ | ● | ■ | 129 |

WEST END & WESTMINSTER: *Savoy.* **Map 4 F5.** £££££
Strand, WC2R 0EU. ¶ 0171-836 4343. FAX 0171-240 6040.
"Standardization is not part of hotel-keeping," says the managing director.
Certainly few hotels share this distinctive Art Deco elegance. ☎ 24 ✂ P

| AE DC MC V | ■ | ● | | 200 |

SOUTH KENSINGTON & HYDE PARK: *Knightsbridge Green.* **Map 5 A2.** ££
159 Knightsbridge, SW1X 7PD. ¶ 0171-584 6274. FAX 0171-225 1635.
Long-established, upscale bed-and-breakfast popular with women.
Tea and coffee available all day in the Club Room. ● Dec 24–27. ☎ &

| AE DC MC V | | ● | | 24 |

SOUTH KENSINGTON & HYDE PARK: *Beaufort.* **Map 5 A3.** £££
33 Beaufort Gardens, SW3 1PP. ¶ 0171-584 5252. FAX 0171-589 2834.
Sheer elegance partially excuses the high prices of this classy little place
near Harrods. Personal service and pampering are what you pay for. ☎

| AE DC MC V | | ● | | 28 |

SOUTH KENSINGTON & HYDE PARK: *Gore.* **Map 2 D5.** £££
189 Queen's Gate, SW7 5EX. ¶ 0171-584 6601. FAX 0171-589 8127.
This idiosyncratic Victorian hotel is over a pair of chic restaurants.
Bedrooms vary from tiny singles to Tudor fantasies with their own
minstrels' galleries. Charming service. Prices vary greatly. ☎

| AE DC MC V | ■ | | | 54 |

SOUTH KENSINGTON & HYDE PARK: *Basil Street.* **Map 5 A3.** ££££
Basil St, SW3 1AH. ¶ 0171-581 3311. FAX 0171-581 3693.
Old-fashioned hotel with an unpretentious Edwardian air and enduring
popularity. Its brasserie-wine bar is superb, and excellent value for the
area. Many of the regular "Basilites" are women. ☎ 24 &

| AE DC MC V | ■ | ● | | 96 |

<table>
<tr><td colspan="2">

Price categories for a standard double room per night, inclusive of breakfast, service charges and any additional taxes such as VAT:
£ under £50
££ £50–£100
£££ £100–£150
££££ £150–£200
£££££ £200 plus.

</td></tr>
</table>

RESTAURANT
Hotel restaurant or dining room usually open to non-residents unless otherwise stated.

CHILDREN WELCOME
Cribs and a baby-sitting service available. Some hotel restaurants have children's portions and high chairs.

GARDEN/TERRACE
Hotels with a garden, courtyard or terrace, often providing tables for eating outside.

CREDIT CARDS
Indicates which credit cards are accepted: *AE* American Express; *DC* Diners Club; *MC* Master Card/Access; *V* Visa.

	Credit Cards	Restaurant	Children Welcome	Garden/Terrace	Number of Rooms
REGENT'S PARK & BLOOMSBURY: *Academy.* Map 4 D3. **££** 17–21 Gower St, WC1E 6HG. 0171-631 4115. FAX 0171-636 3442. Three Georgian town houses near the heart of London University. Inside the ambience is sophisticated without excess.	AE DC MC V	■	●	■	33
REGENT'S PARK & BLOOMSBURY: *Blandford.* Map 3 B4. **££** 80 Chiltern Street, W1M 1PS. 0171-486 3103. FAX 0171-487 2786. A welcoming and inexpensive bed-and-breakfast. It is a family-run establishment giving simple, unassuming, and practical accommodations and serving a lavish, hearty English breakfast.	AE DC MC V				33
REGENT'S PARK & BLOOMSBURY: *Durrants.* Map 3 A4. **£££** George St, W1H 6BJ. 0171-935 8131. FAX 0171-487 3510. Georgian hotel that still has the feel of the old coaching inn it once was. The look is of old leather and wood. Bedrooms are unfussy.	AE DC MC V	■	●		96
REGENT'S PARK & BLOOMSBURY: *Russell.* Map 4 E3. **£££** Russell Sq, WC1B 5BE. 0171-837 6470. FAX 0171-837 2857. One of the most impressive buildings in Russell Square. Inside wood paneling, leather chesterfields and chandeliers give this hotel a suitably literary feel. The best rooms overlook the square.	AE DC MC V	■	●	■	328
REGENT'S PARK & BLOOMSBURY: *Langham Hilton.* Map 3 C4. **£££££** 1 Portland Pl, W1N 3AA. 0171-636 1000. FAX 0171-323 2340. The Langham has lavishly recreated its former Victorian splendor, in addition to all the conveniences you could possibly wish for.	AE DC MC V	■	●	■	380
FARTHER AFIELD: *Abbey House, Kensington.* Map 1 C3. **£** 11 Vicarage Gate, W8 4AG. 0171-727 2594. Once a Victorian family home, now a no-frills bed and breakfast. Rooms are spacious but simply furnished without *en suite* bathrooms.					13
FARTHER AFIELD: *Collin House, Victoria.* Map 5 B4 **£** 104 Ebury St, SW1W 9QD. 0171-730 8031. Small guesthouse amid many, but set apart by the welcome. Decor is hardly fashionable, but rooms fresh and clean. ● Dec 23–Jan 2.		■	●		13
FARTHER AFIELD: *Edward Lear, Marble Arch.* Map 3 5A **£** 28–30 Seymour St, W1H 5WD. 0171-402 5401. FAX 0171-706 3766. Clean, simple bed-and-breakfast, once the home of the author Edward Lear. Single travelers and families are made very welcome.			●		31
FARTHER AFIELD: *Hotel 167, South Kensington.* **£** 167 Old Brompton Rd, SW5 0AN. 0171-373 3221. FAX 0171-373 3360. This little gem gives a unique brand of bed-and-breakfast. Bedrooms are stylishly practical, with pleasant furnishings and bathrooms.	AE DC MC V				19
FARTHER AFIELD: *Windermere, Pimlico.* Map 5 C4 **£** 142–144 Warwick Way, SW1V 4JE. 0171-834 5163. FAX 0171-630 8831. Inexpensive, friendly hotel, just ten minutes walk from Victoria Station. Inside it is as neat as a pin, with a lovely breakfast room that doubles as a dining room. Light, clean bedrooms. Helpful service.	AE MC V	■			23
FARTHER AFIELD: *Aster House, South Kensington.* **££** 3 Sumner Pl, SW7 3EE. 0171-581 5888. FAX 0171-584 4925. Several houses in this elegant terrace are discreet, upscale hotels, but few have such reasonable prices. Bedrooms are all nonsmoking.	AE DC MC V		●	■	12
FARTHER AFIELD: *Bryanston Court, Marble Arch.* Map 3 5A **££** 56–60 Great Cumberland Pl, W1H 7FD. 0171-262 3141. FAX 0171-262 7248. The atmosphere is civilized and old-fashioned, but with a personal touch – lacking in many West End hotels. Rooms are simple, and although fairly small, functional and pleasant.	AE DC MC V				56

For key to symbols see back flap

Price categories for a standard double room per night, inclusive of breakfast, service charges and any additional taxes such as VAT: **£** under £50 **££** £50–£100 **£££** £100–£150 **££££** £150–£200 **£££££** £200 plus.	**RESTAURANT** Hotel restaurant or dining room usually open to non-residents unless otherwise stated. **CHILDREN WELCOME** Cribs and a baby-sitting service available. Some hotel restaurants have children's portions and high chairs. **GARDEN/TERRACE** Hotels with a garden, courtyard or terrace, often providing tables for eating outside. **CREDIT CARDS** Indicates which credit cards are accepted: *AE* American Express; *DC* Diners Club; *MC* Master Card/Access; *V* Visa.			

	CREDIT CARDS	**RESTAURANT**	**CHILDREN WELCOME**	**GARDEN/TERRACE**	**NUMBER OF ROOMS**
FARTHER AFIELD: *Byron, Bayswater.* **Map 2 D2.** **££** 36–38 Queensborough Terrace, W2 3SH. **(** *0171-243 0987.* **FAX** *0171-792 1957.* Decor ranges from country-house style in the cozy lounge to unfussy neutrality in the bedrooms. A friendly, unpretentious hotel.	AE DC MC V		●		42
FARTHER AFIELD: *Ebury Court, Victoria.* **Map 5 B4.** **££** 28 Ebury St, SW1W 0LU. **(** *0171-730 8147.* **FAX** *0171-823 5966.* Several adjacent town houses make up this classy hotel. Family heirlooms deck cozy public rooms. Most bedrooms small and plain.	AE DC MC V	■			42
FARTHER AFIELD: *Five Sumner Place, South Kensington.* **££** 5 Sumner Pl, SW7 3EE. **(** *0171-584 7586.* **FAX** *0171-823 9962.* This Victorian terraced town house is elegant and stylish, and provides a quiet haven from the bustle and noise of central London.	AE DC MC V			■	13
FARTHER AFIELD: *Mornington, Bayswater.* **Map 2 E2.** **££** 12 Lancaster Gate, W2 3LG. **(** *0171-262 7361.* **FAX** *0171-706 1028.* The clubby intimacy of the book-lined library-lounge provides a good contrast to the Scandinavian austerity of the bedrooms.	AE DC MC V		●		68
FARTHER AFIELD: *Portobello, Notting Hill.* **Map 1 A2.** **££** 22 Stanley Gardens, W11 2NG. **(** *0171-727 2777.* **FAX** *0171-792 9641.* Eccentric place that has a darkish and sophisticated decor – a mix of Victorian and Edwardian periods. Rooms range from tiny to lavish.	AE DC MC V	■			25
FARTHER AFIELD: *Abbey Court, Notting Hill.* **Map 1 C2.** **£££** 20 Pembridge Gardens, W2 4DU. **(** *0171-221 7518.* **FAX** *0171-727 8166.* Lavishly decorated town house that provides luxury bed and breakfast. Bedrooms vary, but all have handsome Victorian-style antiques. A good number of single rooms for the solo traveler.	AE DC MC V		●		22
FARTHER AFIELD: *Cannizaro House, Wimbledon.* **£££** West Side, Wimbledon Common, SW19 4UF. **(** *0181-879 1464.* **FAX** *0181-879 7338.* Originally dating from 1705, this Georgian hotel has ostentatious style. Splendid secluded gardens give it a country-house feel.	AE DC MC V	■		■	46
FARTHER AFIELD: *Dorset Square, Marylebone.* **Map 3 A3.** **£££** 39–40 Dorset Sq, NW1 6QN. **(** *0171-723 7874.* **FAX** *0171-724 3328.* Beautifully restored Regency building with antiques, bold fabrics, *objets d'art* and interesting paintings, overlooking a fine 18th-century square. Rooms have distinct characters, service is friendly.	AE DC MC V	■	●		37
FARTHER AFIELD: *Sydney House, Chelsea.* **£££** 9–11 Sydney St, SW3 6PU. **(** *0171-376 7711.* **FAX** *0171-376 4233.* Marvel at palazzo-wall treatments, Bugatti furniture, and chandeliers in the foyer. Each room is a self-contained world. An extremely reasonable price for an altogether stylish and urbane hotel.	AE DC MC V	■			21
FARTHER AFIELD: *Pembridge Court, Notting Hill.* **£££** 34 Pembridge Gardens, W2 4DX. **(** *0171-229 9977.* **FAX** *0171-727 4982.* This elegant town house is comfortable and civilized, with displays of costume accessories: gloves, fans and purses in the rooms.	AE DC MC V	■	●		21
FARTHER AFIELD: *La Reserve, Chelsea.* **£££** 422–428 Fulham Rd, SW6 1DU. **(** *0171-385 8561.* **FAX** *0171-385 7662.* Although the frontage is Classical, the hotel is very different inside. The minimalist and ultramodern rooms have good bathrooms.	AE DC MC V	■	●	■	37
FARTHER AFIELD: *Draycott, Chelsea.* **Map 5 A4.** **££££** 24–26 Cadogan Gardens, SW3 2RP. **(** *0171-730 6466.* **FAX** *0171-730 0236.* Knightsbridge mansion that is more like a residential club than a hotel. Plants, antiques, prints and marble baths furnish the rooms. A place that exudes London sophistication and *savoir faire*.	AE DC MC V	■		■	40

FARTHER AFIELD: *Fenja, Chelsea.* **Map 5 A4.** ⓔⓔⓔ
69 Cadogan Gardens, SW3 2RB. **(** 0171-589 7333. **FAX** 0171-581 4958.
This quietly grand bed-and-breakfast has the air of a private home.
Many of the building's original Victorian features remain. 🔲 24

| | | | | 13 |

FARTHER AFIELD: *Sheraton Skyline, Heathrow Airport* ⓔⓔⓔⓔ
Bath Rd, Hayes, Middlesex, UB3 5BP. **(** 0181-759 2535. **FAX** 0181-750 9150.
One of the main attractions (apart from a useful location) is an indoor
pool amid a jungle of foliage – a nice setting for lunch. 🔲 24 ⚡ 🅿 ♿

| | | | 354 |

FARTHER AFIELD: *Blakes, South Kensington.* ⓔⓔⓔⓔⓔ
33 Roland Gardens, SW7 3PF. **(** 0171-370 6701. **FAX** 0171-373 0442.
The green façade distinguishes it instantly, and a glimpse at the exotic
interior declares this is no ordinary hotel. Bedrooms are unique. 🔲 24

| | | | 52 |

FARTHER AFIELD: *Halkin, Belgravia.* ⓔⓔⓔⓔⓔ
5 Halkin St, SW1X 7DJ. **(** 0171-333 1000. **FAX** 0171-333 1100.
For those weary of artificial period charm, the minimalism of the
Halkin is a breath of fresh air. Utterly contemporary. 🔲 24 ♿

| | | | 41 |

FARTHER AFIELD: *Lowndes, Knightsbridge.* **Map 5 B3.** ⓔⓔⓔⓔⓔ
Lowndes St, SW1X 9ES. **(** 0171-823 1234. **FAX** 0171-235 1154.
A hotel with a pleasant, small-scale feel, and guests can use the related
Hyatt Carlton Tower's excellent facilities at no extra cost. 🔲 24 ⚡

| | | | 78 |

THE DOWNS AND CHANNEL COAST

BATTLE: *Powdermills* ⓔⓔ
Powermill Lane, Battle, E Sussex TN33 0SP. **(** 01424 775511. **FAX** 01424 774540.
Surrounded by parkland that includes a fishing lake, this hotel has
very comfortable rooms and an attractive restaurant. 🔲 TV 🅿 ≋

| | | | | 23 |

BONCHURCH: *Winterbourne* ⓔⓔⓔ
Bonchurch, nr Ventnor, Isle of Wight PO38 1RQ.
(01983 852535. **FAX** 01983 853056.
Reserve a room overlooking the sea – the views are wonderful over the
well-kept gardens. A bit old-fashioned in places but price does include
breakfast and an evening meal. 🔲 TV 🅿 ≋

| | | | | 17 |

BOUGHTON LEES: *Eastwell Manor* ⓔⓔⓔⓔ
Eastwell Park, Boughton Lees, Ashford TN25 4HR.
(01233 635751. **FAX** 01233 635530.
The present house is modern but the manor's history goes back to 1069.
Comfortable bedrooms. Excellent restaurant. *(See also p582.)* 🔲 TV 🔲 🅿

| | | | | 23 |

BOUGHTON MONCHELSEA: *Tanyard* ⓔⓔⓔ
Wierton Hill, Boughton Monchelsea, Maidstone, Kent ME17 4JT.
(01622 744705. **FAX** 01622 741998.
Great views across the Weald of Kent from a particularly well-restored
medieval house. Comfortable public rooms with roaring fires. 🔲 TV 🅿

| | | | 6 |

BRIGHTON: *Dove* ⓔⓔ
18 Regency Square, Brighton, E Sussex BN1 2FG.
(01273 779222. **FAX** 01273 746912.
Only a few minutes walk to the sea, this family-run Regency house has
modern pristine bedrooms. Service is efficient and friendly. Evening
meals can be arranged. 🔲 TV 🅿

| | | | 10 |

BRIGHTON: *Topps* ⓔⓔ
17 Regency Square, Brighton, E Sussex BN1 2FG.
(01273 729334. **FAX** 01273 203679.
This stylish hotel is a pair of beautifully furnished Regency town houses.
Most bedrooms have gas-coal fires and large bathrooms. 🔲 TV 🔲 🅿

| | | | | 15 |

CANTERBURY: *Thanington* ⓔⓔ
140 Wincheap, Canterbury, Kent CT1 3RY. **(** 01227 453227. **FAX** 01227 453225.
Only minutes from the town center, this stylish Georgian house offering
bed and breakfast is immaculately kept throughout. An indoor heated
swimming pool is an unusual added bonus. 🔲 TV 🅿

| | | | 10 |

CHARTHAM: *Thruxted Oast* ⓔⓔ
Mystole, Chartham, Canterbury, Kent CT4 7BX. **(** 01227 730080.
In the heart of the village, this restored oast house (hops kiln) *(see p147)*
offers B&B only. Quite expensive but a comfortable place to stay. 🔲 TV 🅿

| | | | 3 |

Price categories for a standard double room per night, inclusive of breakfast, service charges and any additional taxes such as VAT:
£ under £50
££ £50–£100
£££ £100–£150
££££ £150–£200
£££££ £200 plus.

RESTAURANT
Hotel restaurant or dining room usually open to non-residents unless otherwise stated.

CHILDREN WELCOME
Cribs and a baby-sitting service available. Some hotel restaurants have children's portions and high chairs.

GARDEN/TERRACE
Hotels with a garden, courtyard or terrace, often providing tables for eating outside.

CREDIT CARDS
Indicates which credit cards are accepted: AE American Express; DC Diners Club; MC Master Card/Access; V Visa.

		CREDIT CARDS	RESTAURANT	CHILDREN WELCOME	GARDEN/TERRACE	NUMBER OF ROOMS
CUCKFIELD: *Ockenden Manor* £££ Ockenden Lane, Cuckfield, W Sussex RH17 5LD. 01444 416111. FAX 01444 415549. A 16th-century manor with lovely gardens and views of the South Downs. Extremely comfortable with a good restaurant.		AE DC MC V	■	●	■	22
DOVER: *Number One Guesthouse* £ 1 Castle St, Dover, Kent CT16 1QH. 01304 202007. Immaculate B&B overlooked by Dover Castle, only minutes to the Channel Tunnel and ferry. Breakfast served in your room.				●	■	6
HAYLING ISLAND: *Cockle Warren Cottage* ££ 36 Seafront, Hayling Island, Hants PO11 9HL. 01705 464961. Across the road from the sea, this modern hotel has a conservatory restaurant. Bedrooms are small but pleasant.		AE MC V	■	●	■	5
HORDLE: *Gordleton Mill* £££ Silver St, Hordle, Lymington, Hants SO41 6DJ. 01590 6882219. FAX 01590 683073. Attractive 17th-century mill house on the River Avon with large garden. Luxurious bedrooms and a highly recommended restaurant.		AE MC	■	●	■	7
MIDHURST: *Angel* £££ North St, Midhurst, W Sussex GU29 9DN. 01730 812421. FAX 01730 815928. Stylishly modernized 16th-century coaching inn, in the center of this historic village. Both restaurant and brasserie are excellent.		AE DC MC V	■	●	■	25
RINGWOOD: *Moortown Lodge* ££ 244 Christchurch Rd, Ringwood, Hants BH24 3AS. 01425 471404. FAX 01425 476052. Simple but attractive hotel with comfortable rooms. Traffic noise no problem even though it's on a main road. Good-value restaurant.		AE MC V	■	●	■	6
RYE: *Old Vicarage* £ 66 Church Square, Rye, E Sussex TN31 7HF. 01797 222119. FAX 01797 227466. Very attractive pink 18th-century house in the heart of historic Rye. Comfortable, pretty rooms and delicious breakfasts.		AE			■	6
RYE: *Jeake's House* ££ Mermaid St, Rye, E Sussex TN31 7ET. 01797 222828. FAX 01797 222623. A 17th-century house on one of the prettiest cobbled streets in Rye. Comfortable well-decorated rooms. Lots of choice at breakfast.		MC V		●	■	12
RYE: *Little Orchard House* ££ West St, Rye, E Sussex TN31 7ES. 01797 223831. Close to the old district of town, this 18th-century town house offers comfortable B&B. Lovely decoration and hearty breakfasts.		MC V				5
ST. MARGARET'S-AT-CLIFFE: *Wallett's Court* ££ West Cliffe, St. Margaret's at Cliffe, Dover, Kent CT15 6EW. 01304 852424. FAX 01304 853430. Well-positioned for Dover, this family-run 17th-century manor house is comfortably old-fashioned with a good restaurant.		MC V	■	●	■	10
SEAVIEW: *Seaview* ££ High St, Seaview, Isle of Wight PO34 5EX. 01983 612711. FAX 01983 613729. The hotel has great views of the sea from some of the bedrooms and the sitting room. A choice of two bars to unwind in.		AE DC MC V	■	●	■	17
SMARDEN: *Bell* £ Bell Lane, Smarden, Kent TN27 8PW. 01233 770283. Friendly pub dating back to the 16th century, with wooden and stone floors, open fires and bar food. Bedrooms are simple with shared bathrooms. Good home cooking.		AE MC V			■	4

UCKFIELD: *Hooke Hall* £££ 250 High St, Uckfield, E Sussex TN22 1EN. [01825 761578. FAX 01825 768025. Right in the center of town, this Queen Anne house offers a very high standard of comfort. Restaurant specializes in Italian cooking. 🛏 TV P	AE MC V	▦	●	▦		9
WICKHAM: *Old House* ££ The Square, Wickham, Hants PO17 5JG. [01329 833049. FAX 01329 833672. All the buildings in the Square are listed, and this hotel dates from the 18th century. Simple yet stylish decor and excellent food. 🛏 TV P	AE DC MC V					12
WINCHESTER: *Wykeham Arms* ££ 75 Kingsgate St, Winchester, Hants SO23 9PE. [01962 853834. FAX 01962 854411. One of the oldest pubs in the town with its original charm intact. The bars are lit by low lights and log fires. Cozy bedrooms. 🛏 TV P	AE MC V	▦	●	▦		7

EAST ANGLIA

ALDEBURGH: *Austins* ££ 243 High St, Aldeburgh IP15 5DN. [01728 453932. FAX 01728 453668. A small, sophisticated hotel, close to the beach, furnished with antiques. The bedrooms are light and tastefully decorated. 🛏 TV P	MC V	▦				7
BLAKENEY: *White Horse* ££ 4 High St, Blakeney, Holt, Norf NR25 7AL. [01263 740574. A friendly pub in the center of this attractive coastal village. Restaurant in a converted coach house. Pleasant bedrooms. 🛏 TV P	AE DC MC V	▦	●	▦		9
BROXTED: *Whitehall* £££ Broxted, nr Stansted Airport, Essex CM6 2BZ. [01279 850603. FAX 01279 850385. Useful for the airport, this Elizabethan manor, modern extension and converted barn has large bedrooms. Excellent restaurant. 🛏 TV P ≋	AE DC MC V	▦	●	▦		25
BURNHAM MARKET: *Hoste Arms* ££ The Green, Burnham Market, Kings Lynn, Norf PE31 8HD. [01328 738257. FAX 01328 730103. A popular inn facing the green, with bars and a choice of restaurants. Decor throughout is attractive. Good-sized bedrooms. 🛏 TV P	MC V	▦	●	▦		15
BURY ST EDMUNDS: *Ounce House* ££ Northgate St, Bury St Edmunds, Suff IP33 1HP. [01284 761779. FAX 01284 768315. A few minutes walk from the market place, this is a well-presented small hotel, furnished with antiques. 🛏 TV P	DC MC V		●	▦		4
CAMPSEA ASHE: *Old Rectory* ££ Campsea Ashe, nr Woodbridge, Suff IP13 OPU. [01728 746524. A part-Georgian, part-Tudor creeper-clad rectory. In summer, dinner is in the conservatory overlooking the lovely gardens. 🛏 P	AE DC MC V	▦		▦		9
CLEY-NEXT-THE-SEA: *Cley Mill* ££ Cley-next-the-sea, Holt, Norf NR25 7NN. [01263 740209. Converted 18th-century windmill makes for an unusual hotel. Charming rooms with views across the marshes. Evening meal on request. 🛏 P				▦		6
DEDHAM: *Dedham Hall* ££ Brook St, Dedham, Essex CO7 6AD. [01206 323027. A 15th-century cottage with an annex of bedrooms. Comfy sitting rooms with log fires and games. Good home cooking. 🛏 TV P	AE DC MC V	▦	●	▦		16
DEDHAM: *Maison Talbooth* £££ Stratford Rd, Dedham, Essex CO7 6HN. [01206 322367. FAX 01206 322752. This grandiose Edwardian house is an extremely upscale B&B. Very civilized with a fine drawing room and huge bedrooms. Run by the owners of the nearby Le Talbooth restaurant *(see p585)*. 🛏 TV P	AE DC MC V		●	▦		10
DISS: *Salisbury House* ££ 84 Victoria Rd, Diss, Norf IP22 3JG. [01379 644738. Decor downstairs is Victorian, in keeping with the house. Bedrooms are large and comfortable. Excellent restaurant. 🛏 TV P	MC V	▦	●	▦		4
GREAT DUNMOW: *Starr* ££ Market Place, Great Dunmow, Essex CM6 1AX. [01371 874321. FAX 01371 876337. Originally a pub, the 500-year-old Starr is now a restaurant-with-rooms. Lots of beams and low lighting make it cozy. Excellent home cooking and pleasant bedrooms make it warm and welcoming. 🛏 TV P	AE MC V	▦	●	▦		8

<table>
<tr><td>

Price categories for a standard double room per night, inclusive of breakfast, service charges and any additional taxes such as VAT:
£ under £50
££ £50–£100
£££ £100–£150
££££ £150–£200
£££££ £200 plus.

</td><td>

RESTAURANT
Hotel restaurant or dining room usually open to non-residents unless otherwise stated.
CHILDREN WELCOME
Cribs and a baby-sitting service available. Some hotel restaurants have children's portions and high chairs.
GARDEN/TERRACE
Hotels with a garden, courtyard or terrace, often providing tables for eating outside.
CREDIT CARDS
Indicates which credit cards are accepted: *AE* American Express; *DC* Diners Club; *MC* Master Card/Access; *V* Visa.

</td></tr>
</table>

	CREDIT CARDS	RESTAURANT	CHILDREN WELCOME	GARDEN/TERRACE	NUMBER OF ROOMS
GREAT SNORING: *Old Rectory* **££** Barsham Rd, Great Snoring, Fakenham, Norf NR21 0HP. 📞 01328 820597. FAX 01328 820048. Close to Walsingham, this coastal hotel makes a perfect base for exploring this part of Norfolk. Homey comfort in a peaceful setting. 🔲 📺 🅿	AE DC	■		■	6
GRIMSTON: *Congham Hall* **£££** Grimston, Kings Lynn, Norf PE32 1AH. 📞 01485 600250. FAX 01485 601191. A fine Georgian house with a restaurant that uses herbs and vegetables from their garden. Guests expected to change for dinner. 🔲 📺 🅿 🏊	AE DC MC V	■		■	14
HINTLESHAM: *Hintlesham Hall* **£££** George St, Hintlesham, nr Ipswich, Suff IP8 3NS. . 📞 01473 652334. FAX 01473 652463. With a fine symmetrical Georgian frontage, this hotel is sophisticated but not stuffy. A range of restaurants and room styles to suit a variety of tastes and budgets. *(See also p585.)* 🔲 📺 🅿 🏊	AE DC MC V	■	●	■	33
HORDON-ON-THE-HILL: *Hill House* **££** Hordon-on-the-Hill, Essex SS17 8LD. 📞 01375 673154. FAX 01375 361611. Bedrooms are well decorated with good bathrooms. Guests can eat at the Bell, a few yards down the road. Excellent value. 🔲 📺 🅿	AE MC V	■	●		11
LAVENHAM: *Angel* **££** Market Pl, Lavenham, Suff CO10 9QZ. 📞 01787 247388. FAX 01787 247057. Friendly, unpretentious 600-year-old inn. Great atmosphere with a rustic feel. Lots of beams. Bedrooms are clean and cheerful. 🔲 📺 🅿	MC V	■	●		8
LAVENHAM: *Great House* **££** Market Pl, Lavenham, Suff CO10 9QZ. 📞 01787 247431. FAX 01787 248080. Huge bedrooms upstairs and a large French restaurant downstairs. Accommodations are impressive and the food is delicious. 🔲 📺 🅿	AE MC V	■			4
LAVENHAM: *Swan* **£££** High St, Lavenham, Sudbury, Suff CO10 GQA. 📞 01787 247477. FAX 01787 248286. In this historical village, the Swan dates back to the 14th century: full of cozy corners. Well-decorated paneled bedrooms. 🔲 📺 🔳 🅿	AE DC MC V	■	●	■	47
LONG MELFORD: *Black Lion* **££** The Green, Long Melford, Sudbury CO10 9DN. 📞 01787 312356. FAX 01787 374557. Very popular, friendly place overlooking the green. Unpretentious and bright with lots of books, games and childrens' toys. Good food. 🔲 📺 🅿	MC V	■			9
LONG MELFORD: *Bull* **££** Hall St, Long Melford, Suff CO10 9JG. 📞 01787 378494. FAX 01787 880307. The centrally located Bull is a reliable base for the area. The pretty village of Long Melford is famous for antique shops. 🔲 📺 🅿	AE DC MC V	■	●		25
MORSTON: *Morston Hall* **£££** Morston, Holt, Norf NR25 7AA. 📞 01263 741041. FAX 01263 741041. Comfort and delicious food on this isolated but beautiful stretch of the north Norfolk coast. Price includes four-course dinner. 🔲 📺 🅿	AE MC V	■	●	■	5
ROCHFORD: *Renouf* **££** Bradley Way, Rochford, Essex. 📞 01702 541334. FAX 01702 549563. A modern, efficiently run, comfortable hotel. Extremely good French restaurant. Excellent value and high standards. 🔲 📺 🅿	AE DC MC V	■	●		24
SOUTHWOLD: *Crown* **££** High St, Southwold, Suff IP18 6DP. 📞 01502 722275. FAX 01502 724805. Friendly atmosphere with wooden floors, benches and armchairs in the bars. Food is excellent. Old-fashioned bedrooms, but good value. 🔲 📺 🅿	AE DC MC V	■			12

SOUTHWOLD: *Swan*   **£££** | AE DC MC V | 45
Market Pl, Southwold, Suff IP18 6EG. [01502 722186. FAX 01502 724800.
A stylish family hotel. The dinner menu is traditionally English. Bedrooms
are decorated to a high standard with all the trimmings. 🛏 TV P

STOKE-BY-NAYLAND: *Angel*   **££** | AE DC MC V | 6
Stoke-by-Nayland, nr Colchester, Essex CO6 4SA.
[01206 263245. FAX 01206 337324.
In the heart of the village, the Angel is immediately welcoming. Homey
rooms and excellent food. Low-ceiling bars buzz with activity.

SWAFFHAM: *Strattons*   **££** | AE MC V | 7
4 Ash Close, Swaffham PE37 7NH. [01760 723845. FAX 01760 720458.
Elegance and panache evident in this small but special hotel. Bedrooms
are luxurious but the atmosphere is relaxed and informal. 🛏 TV P

THORNHAM: *LifeBoat*   **££** | DC MC V | 13
Ship Lane, Thornham, Norf PE36 6LT. [01485 512236. FAX 01485 512323.
Attractive pub overlooking the marshes. Rooms of a high standard.
The pub is traditional, but the restaurant sophisticated. 🛏 TV P

THAMES VALLEY

AYLESBURY: *Hartwell House*   **££££** | AE DC MC V | 47
Oxford Rd, Aylesbury, Bucks HP17 8NL. [01296 747444. FAX 01296 747450.
A Grade I listed (*p617*) house. Immense care has been taken to enhance
all the house's features. Superb comfort, cuisine and service. 🛏 TV 🐾 P 🏊 &

BURFORD: *Andrews*   **££** | MC V | 8
High St, Burford, Oxon OX18 4QA. [01993 823151. FAX 01993 823240.
In a touristy village, this 15th-century house offers B&B and high teas.
Residents escape to their own lounge and luxurious bedrooms. 🛏 TV

CHADLINGTON: *Chadlington House*   **££** | AE DC | 10
Chadlington, Oxon OX7 3LZ. [01608 676437. FAX 01608 676503.
An unpretentious, long-established hotel with many regular guests.
A mixture of old-fashioned and modern furnishings. 🛏 TV P

CLANFIELD: *Plough*   **££** | AE DC MC V | 6
Bourton Rd, Clanfield, Oxford OX18 2RB. [0136 781222. FAX 0136 781596.
Very attractive Cotswold-stone village inn. Popular throughout the year,
with a great atmosphere in the bar. Comfortable bedrooms. 🛏 TV P

GREAT MILTON: *Le Manoir aux Quat'Saisons*   **££££** | AE DC MC V | 19
Great Milton, Oxford OX44 7PD. [01844 278881. FAX 01844 278847.
One of the most exclusive hotel-restaurants in the UK. Sophisticated,
luxurious bedrooms and superb food. (*See also p586.*) 🛏 TV P 🏊 &

HENLEY-ON-THAMES: *Red Lion*   **££** | AE MC V | 26
Hart St, Henley-on-Thames, Oxon RG9 2AR. [01491 572161. FAX 01491 410039.
A 16th-century coaching inn on the river. A major refurbishing program
nearing completion. Pristine but lacks some atmosphere. 🛏 TV P

HUNGERFORD: *Marshgate Cottage*   **£** | AE MC V | 9
Marsh Lane, Hungerford, Berks RG17 0QX. [01488 682307. FAX 01488 685475.
Small family hotel about a mile from the center of Hungerford. The
dining room serves good food with a Danish emphasis. 🛏 TV P &

HURLEY: *Ye Olde Bell*   **££££** | AE DC MC V | 36
High St, Hurley, Berks SL6 5LX. [01628 825881. FAX 01628 825939.
Dating back to the 12th century and said to be England's oldest inn.
Bedrooms and the public rooms retain the house's character. 🛏 TV P

MARLOW BOTTOM: *Holly Tree House*   **££** | AE MC V | 5
Burford Close, Marlow Bottom, Bucks SL7 3NF.
[01628 891110. FAX 01628 481278.
An efficient, modern B&B with plenty of facilities and good breakfasts.
Near the center of Marlow but in a rural setting. 🛏 TV P 🏊

MOULSFORD ON THAMES: *Beetle and Wedge*   **££** | AE DC MC V | 10
Ferry Lane, Moulsford on Thames, Oxon OX10 9JF.
[0149 651381. FAX 0149 651376.
An exceptionally appealing hotel on the banks of the Thames. Friendly
and efficient service, excellent food and pleasant bedrooms. 🛏 TV P

For key to symbols see back flap

	CREDIT CARDS	RESTAURANT	CHILDREN WELCOME	GARDEN/TERRACE	NUMBER OF ROOMS

Price categories for a standard double room per night, inclusive of breakfast, service charges and any additional taxes such as VAT:
£ under £50
££ £50–£100
£££ £100–£150
££££ £150–£200
£££££ £200 plus.

RESTAURANT
Hotel restaurant or dining room usually open to non-residents unless otherwise stated.
CHILDREN WELCOME
Cribs and a baby-sitting service available. Some hotel restaurants have children's portions and high chairs.
GARDEN/TERRACE
Hotels with a garden, courtyard or terrace, often providing tables for eating outside.
CREDIT CARDS
Indicates which credit cards are accepted: *AE* American Express; *DC* Diners Club; *MC* Master Card/Access; *V* Visa.

		CREDIT CARDS	RESTAURANT	CHILDREN WELCOME	GARDEN/TERRACE	NUMBER OF ROOMS
NORTH NEWINGTON: *La Madonette Country Guest House* **£** North Newington, Banbury, Oxon OX15 6AA. 📞 01295 730212. 🆗 01295 730363. A former mill-house, this is a very attractive B&B. In a rural setting, yet close to Banbury. A good-value base for exploring the area. 🛏️ 📺 🅿️ 🏊		MC V		●	■	5
OXFORD: *Cotswold House* **££** 363 Banbury Rd, Oxford OX2 7PL. 📞 01865 310558. 🆗 01865 310558. A small, friendly guesthouse 2 miles (3 km) from the city center on a main residential road. Built in a traditional style, the house is modern and clean with contemporary furnishings. 🛏️ 📺 🅿️					■	7
OXFORD: *Old Parsonage* **£££** 1 Banbury Rd, Oxford OX2 6NN. 📞 01865 310210. 🆗 01865 311262. Very comfortable, civilized hotel. Relaxed atmosphere in an excellent spot for sightseeing of the city and the outlying countryside. 🛏️ 📺 🅿️		AE DC MC V	■		■	30
OXFORD: *Randolph* **£££** Beaumont St, Oxford OX1 2LN. 📞 01865 247481. 🆗 01865 791678. A grand Victorian hotel in the city center. Traditional and luxurious. High ceilings and panelled rooms. 🛏️ 📺 🐕 🅿️ ♿		AE DC MC V	■	●		109
SHIPTON-UNDER-WYCHWOOD: *Shaven Crown* **££** Shipton-under-Wychwood, Oxon OX7 6BA. 📞 01993 830330. 🆗 01993 830330. Beautiful old inn with a history dating back to 1350, built around a medieval courtyard. Magnificent residents' lounge. 🛏️ 📺 🅿️		MC V	■	●	■	9
TOWERSEY: *Upper Green Farm* **£** Manor Rd, Towersey, nr Thame, Oxon OX9 3QR. 📞 01844 212496. 🆗 01844 260399. Very pretty B&B in a picturesque thatched cottage. Charming bedrooms in the house and converted barn. One of their delicious breakfasts is a great way to start a day's sightseeing. 🛏️ 📺 🅿️					■	8
UFFINGTON: *Craven* **£** Uffington, Oxon SN7 7RD. 📞 013678 20449. Attractive 17th-century B&B in a thatched cottage with some rooms in an annex. Dinner around the kitchen table by prior arrangement. 🛏️ 🅿️				●	■	7
WARE: *Hanbury Manor* **£££** Ware, Herts SG12 0SD. 📞 01920 487722. 🆗 01920 487692. Luxury hotel and leisure center with golf course, health club and swimming pool. Ideal place to relax and unwind. Great comfort coupled with excellent restaurants. 🛏️ 📺 🐕 🅿️ 🏊		AE DC MC V	■	●	■	96
WELWYN GARDEN CITY: *Tewin Bury Farmhouse* **££** Tewin, nr Welwyn Garden City, Herts AL6 0JB. 📞 01438 717793. 🆗 01438 840440. Efficient, friendly operation set in farmland. Most bedrooms and the rustic-style restaurant are in converted outbuildings. 🛏️ 📺 🅿️		AE MC V	■	●	■	18
WOODSTOCK: *Feathers* **£££** Market St, Woodstock, Oxon OX20 1SX. 📞 01993 312291. 🆗 01993 813158. Stylish hotel within walking distance of Blenheim Palace. Lunch in the hotel bar or the excellent restaurant. *(See also p587.)* 🛏️ 📺 🅿️		AE DC MC V	■	●	■	17

WESSEX

		CREDIT CARDS	RESTAURANT	CHILDREN WELCOME	GARDEN/TERRACE	NUMBER OF ROOMS
ASHTON KEYNES: *Two Cove House* **£** Ashton Keynes, Wilts SN6 6SN. 📞 01285 861221. Delightful family home – most bedrooms come complete with slightly old-fashioned *en suite* bathrooms. Twenty-four hours notice is required for dinner, eaten with the owners. 🛏️ 🅿️				●	■	4

BARWICK: *Little Barwick House* £££
Barwick Village, nr Yeovil, Somer BA22 9TD. 📞 01935 23902. 📠 01935 20908.
Attractive restaurant-with-rooms near the center of Barwick. Extremely
friendly, relaxed atmosphere. Cozy bedrooms and good food. 🛏 📺 P

| | AE MC V | ■ | ● | | 6 |

BATH: *Cheriton House* £
9 Upper Oldfield Park, Bath, Avon BA2 3JX. 📞 01225 429862. 📠 01225 428403.
Reasonably priced B&B about ten minutes walk from the town center.
Simple, unfussy decor in the sitting room and bedrooms. 🛏 📺 P

| | MC V | | | ■ | 9 |

BATH: *Paradise House* ££
86–88 Holloway, Bath, Avon BA2 4PX. 📞 01225 317723. 📠 01225 482005.
An attractive Georgian house within easy walking distance of Bath's
center. Extremely well-decorated with a relaxed atmosphere. 🛏 📺 P

| | AE MC V | | ● | ■ | 9 |

BATH: *Sydney Gardens* ££
Sydney Rd, Bath, Avon BA2 6NT. 📞 01225 464818.
Italianate Victorian villa just outside Bath offering B&B. A delight to
stay in. Welcoming, with high standards of comfort and service. 🛏 📺 P

| | AE MC V | | | ■ | 6 |

BATH: *Queensberry* £££
Russell Street, Bath, Avon BA1 2QF. 📞 01225 447928. 📠 01225 446065.
Three 18th-century terraced houses form a stylish hotel in the heart of
Bath. Fine, high-ceilinged rooms decorated with style. 🛏 📺 🛁 24

| | AE MC V | ■ | ● | ■ | 22 |

BATH: *Royal Crescent* ££££
15–16 Royal Crescent, Bath, Avon BA1 2LS. 📞 01225 319090. 📠 01225 339401.
Part of one of the most beautiful Regency crescents in Europe, this hotel
offers the highest standards of luxury and comfort. The hotel restaurant
also serves excellent cuisine. 🛏 📺 🛁 24 P 🏊 ㅎ

| | AE DC MC V | ■ | ● | ■ | 42 |

BATHFORD: *Eagle House* £
Church St, Bathford, Bath BA17RS. 📞 01225 859946. 📠 01225 859069.
Beautiful Georgian house situated in this village only 3 miles (5 km) from
Bath. Large, light and airy rooms. 🛏 📺 P

| | MC V | | ● | ■ | 8 |

BRADFORD-ON-AVON: *Bradford Old Windmill* ££
4 Masons Lane, Bradford on Avon, Wilts BA15 1QN.
📞 01225 866842. 📠 01225 866648.
This converted windmill is unique. The cozy circular rooms make this
a memorable place to stay. Efficient service with a smile. 🛏 📺 P

| | AE MC V | | | ■ | 4 |

BRADFORD-ON-AVON: *Priory Steps* ££
Newtown, Bradford on Avon, Wilts BA15 1NQ.
📞 01225 862230. 📠 01225 866248.
A fine lodge where guests are treated like family. Dinner is eaten round
the communal table and must be ordered in advance. 🛏 📺 P

| | MC V | | ● | ■ | 5 |

CASTLE COMBE: *Manor House* £££
Castle Combe, Chippenham, Wilts SN14 7HR.
📞 01249 782206. 📠 01249 783100.
A grand formal place in the village center. Set in stunning
gardens. Elegant public rooms and attentive service. 🛏 📺 24 P 🏊

| | AE DC MC V | ■ | | ■ | 36 |

CHEDINGTON: *Chedington Court* ££
Chedington, nr Beaminster, Dorset. 📞 01935 891265. 📠 01935 891442.
A mock-Jacobean manor house where you can enjoy the true country-
house experience. Beautiful gardens and elegant rooms. 🛏 📺 P

| | AE MC V | ■ | ● | ■ | 10 |

CRUDWELL: *Crudwell Court House* ££
Crudwell, nr Malmesbury, Wilts SN16 9EP. 📞 01666 577194. 📠 01666 577853.
This 17th-century former rectory is now a beautiful restaurant-with-
rooms, with a relaxed atmosphere and excellent food. 🛏 📺 P 🏊

| | DC MC V | ■ | ● | ■ | 15 |

EVERSHOT: *Summer Lodge* £££
Evershot, Dorset DT2 0JR. 📞 01935 83424.
One of the country's most attractive hotels. The building was designed
by the author Thomas Hardy. Always full of beautiful flowers. Pretty
bedrooms. Extensive wine list in the restaurant. 🛏 📺 P 🏊

| | AE DC MC V | ■ | ● | ■ | 17 |

HAWKRIDGE: *Tarr Steps* ££
Hawkridge, Dulverton, Somer TA22 9PY. 📞 0164 385 293. 📠 0164 385 218.
A genuine country home – boots and hunting trophies in the hall – in
a peaceful location above Tarr Steps. Friendly, welcoming owners. 🛏 P

| | MC V | ■ | ● | | 13 |

Price categories for a standard double room per night, inclusive of breakfast, service charges and any additional taxes such as VAT: **£** under £50 **££** £50–£100 **£££** £100–£150 **££££** £150–£200 **£££££** £200 plus.	**RESTAURANT** Hotel restaurant or dining room usually open to non-residents unless otherwise stated. **CHILDREN WELCOME** Cribs and a baby-sitting service available. Some hotel restaurants have children's portions and high chairs. **GARDEN/TERRACE** Hotels with a garden, courtyard or terrace, often providing tables for eating outside. **CREDIT CARDS** Indicates which credit cards are accepted: *AE* American Express; *DC* Diners Club; *MC* Master Card/Access; *V* Visa.	**CREDIT CARDS**	**RESTAURANT**	**CHILDREN WELCOME**	**GARDEN/TERRACE**	**NUMBER OF ROOMS**
HINTON CHARTERHOUSE: *Homewood Park* **££** Hinton Charterhouse, Bath BA3 6BB. **☎** 01225 723731. **FAX** 01225 723820. A stylish Georgian house in large well-kept gardens. An attractive alternative to staying in Bath. Very good restaurant. 🔗 📺 **P**	AE DC MC V	■	●	■	15
HORTON: *Northill House* **££** Horton, Wimborne, Dorset BH21 7HL. **☎** 01258 840407. Large Victorian farmhouse in a peaceful setting. Light, airy bedrooms are split between the main house and the converted stables. 🔗 📺 **P**	AE MC V	■		■	9
KILVE: *Meadow House* **££** Sea Lane, Kilve, Bridgwater, Somer TA5 1EG. **☎** 01278 741546 **FAX** 01278 741663. Set in the Quantock Hills, five minutes from the sea, this mainly Georgian house has great views from most bedrooms. Spacious and light. 🔗 📺 **P**	AE MC V	■	●	■	10
NETTLETON: *Fosse Farmhouse* **££** Nettleton Shrub, Nettleton, nr Chippenham, Wilts SN14 7NJ. **☎** 01249 782286. **FAX** 01249 783066. Charming small country hotel built of Cotswold stone. There's also a tea-room and antique shop. A hotel with lots of originality. 🔗 📺 **P**	AE MC V	■	●	■	6
SHIPHAM: *Daneswood House* **££** Cuck Hill, Shipham, nr Winscombe, Somer BS25 1RD. **☎** 01934 843145. **FAX** 01934 843824. Imposing Edwardian hotel with hospitable owners. The main house has rooms with immense character. Modern styling in the new wing. 🔗 📺 **P**	AE DC MC V	■	●	■	123
SIMONSBATH: *Simonsbath House* **££** Simonsbath, Exmoor, Somer TA24 7SH. **☎** 0164 383 259. A 300-year-old family-run hotel in the heart of Exmoor. Cozy and welcoming. Creaky floors make the place atmospheric. 🔗 📺 **P**	AE DC MC V	■		■	7
SOMERTON: *Lynch Country House* **£** Somerton, Somer TA11 7PD. **☎** 01458 272316. **FAX** 01458 272590. Bright friendly Georgian house with comfortable bedrooms. Eat breakfast watching the antics of their exotic ducks. 🔗 📺 **P**	AE DC MC V		●		5
STON EASTON: *Ston Easton Park* **££££** Ston Easton, Bath, Avon BA3 4DF. **☎** 01761 241631. **FAX** 01761 241377. Superbly restored Georgian house in beautiful grounds. Elegant rooms. Jacket and tie required at dinner. *(See also p589.)* 🔗 📺 **P**	AE DC MC V	■	●	■	21
TAUNTON: *Castle* **£££** Castle Green, Taunton, Somer TA1 1NF. **☎** 01823 272671. **FAX** 01823 336066. Magnificent castle clad in wisteria: a local landmark. The building dates back to Norman times but the standards are definitely 20th century. Very good cooking. *(See also p589.)* 🔗 📺 **24** **P**	AE DC MC V		●	■	35
TROWBRIDGE: *Old Manor* **££** Trowle, Trowbridge, Wilts BA14 9BL. **☎** 01225 777393. **FAX** 01225 765443. Most rooms are in the converted buildings across the courtyard. The homey sitting rooms are in the manor farmhouse. 🔗 📺 **24** **P**	AE DC MC V	■	●	■	14
VELLOW: *Curdon Mill* **££** Vellow, Williton, Somer TA4 4LS. **☎** 01984 656522. **FAX** 01984 656197. This converted water mill offers neat bedrooms and a sitting room. You can also enjoy a delicious dinner by the old millshaft. 🔗 📺 **P** ♒	MC V	■		■	6
WEST BEXINGTON: *Manor* **££** West Bexington, Dorchester, Dorset DT2 9DE. **☎** 01308 897616. **FAX** 01308 897035. A warm welcome is assured at the Manor, only minutes from Chesil Beach. Inviting residents' lounge with views of the sea. 🔗 📺 **P** **24**	AE DC MC V	■	●		13

DEVON AND CORNWALL

	Price	Cards				No.
ASHBURTON: *Holne Chase* 2 Bridges Rd, Ashburton, Devon TQ13 7NS. 📞 *01364 613471.* FAX *01364 613453.* Comfortable, informal country-style hotel in a peaceful position. Large grounds, including a stretch of the River Dart for fishing guests. 🛏 📺 🅿	££	AE DC MC V	■	●	■	14
BARNSTAPLE: *Lynwood House* Bishops Tawton Rd, Barnstaple, Devon EX32 9DZ. 📞 *01271 43695.* FAX *01271 79340.* Adequate, well-planned bedrooms have everything you need, although Lynwood's emphasis is on its excellent restaurant. 🛏 📺 24 🅿	££	AE DC MC V	■		■	5
BISHOPS TAWTON: *Downrew House* Bishops Tawton, nr Barnstaple, Devon EX32 ODY. 📞 *0127 46673.* FAX *0127 23947.* A tranquil hotel surrounded by meadows and gardens. Comfort and personal service rather than style. Plenty of sports offered. 🛏 📺 🅿 ≋	££	MC V	■	●	■	12
BISHOPS TAWTON: *Halmpstone Manor* Bishops Tawton, Barnstaple, Devon EX32 OEA. 📞 *01271 830321.* FAX *01271 830826.* Converted farmhouse in a peaceful setting, run with great style. Lovely paneled dining room and huge bedrooms. 🛏 📺 🅿	££	AE DC MC V	■		■	5
BOTALLACK: *Manor Farm* Botallack, St. Just, nr Penzance, Corn TR19 7QG. 📞 *01736 788525.* This comfortable 300-year-old house offers B&B only, but there's good pub food to be found in the village. Substantial breakfasts. 🛏 📺 🅿	£				■	3
BOVEY TRACEY: *Edgemoor* Haytor Rd, Bovey Tracey, South Devon TQ13 9LE. 📞 *01626 832466.* FAX *01626 834760.* A 19th-century creeper-clad hotel close to Dartmoor National Park. Neat and efficiently run with attractive public rooms and bedrooms. 🛏 📺 🅿	££	AE DC MC V	■	●	■	16
BRANSCOMBE: *Bulstone* Higher Bulstone, Branscombe, nr Seaton, Devon EX12 3BL. 📞 *0129 7680 446.* Hotel with excellent facilities for children. Suites with parents' and children's rooms, baby-sitting, a playroom and outdoor play area. 🛏 🅿	£		■	●	■	13
BRANSCOMBE: *Look Out* Branscombe, Seaton, Devon. 📞 *0129 780 262.* FAX *0129 780 272.* Two former coastguard cottages form this attractive, relaxed hotel in a stunning position on the cliff-top. Efficient service. 🛏 📺 🅿	££		■		■	9
CALSTOCK: *Danescombe Valley* Lower Kelly, Calstock, Corn PL18 9RY. 📞 *01822 832414.* FAX *01822 832414.* Welcoming hotel in a superb position with a very romantic atmosphere. Mouthwatering food. *(See also p589.)* ● *Nov–Mar.* 🛏 🅿	£££	AE DC MC V	■		■	5
CHAGFORD: *Mill End* Sandy Park, Chagford, Devon TQ13 8JN. 📞 *01647 432282.* FAX *01647 433106.* Well-run, converted flour mill in a lovely setting in the Teign valley. Cozy sitting rooms and a restaurant offering exceptionally good food. 🛏 📺 🅿	££	AE DC MC V	■	●	■	16
CHAGFORD: *Gidleigh Park* Chagford, Devon TQ13 8HH. 📞 *01647 432367.* FAX *01647 432574.* One of the country's leading hotels, set in beautiful gardens. Everything of the highest standard, including the views. *(See also p590.)* 🛏 📺 🅿	£££££	AE DC MC V	■	●	■	15
CULLOMPTON: *Manor House* Fore St, Cullompton, Devon. 📞 *01884 32281.* FAX *01884 38344.* Pristine town hotel only minutes from the A5. Built in the 17th century and faithfully restored, it has elegance and charm. 🛏 📺 🅿	£	DC MC V	■	●	■	10
DARTMOUTH: *Royal Castle* 11 The Quay, Dartmouth, Devon TQ6 9PS. 📞 *01803 833033.* FAX *01803 835445.* Popular, 300-year-old coaching inn on the Quay. Bar food with a more chic restaurant upstairs. Great views from some bedrooms. 🛏 📺 24	££	MC V	■			25
DITTISHAM: *Old Coombe Manor* Dittisham, Dartmouth TQ6 OJA. 📞 *01803 722398.* FAX *01803 722401.* Highly individual hotel mixing a warm welcome with informality and comfort. Charming both inside and out. 🛏 🅿 ≋	££	AE DC MC V	■		■	9

Price categories for a standard double room per night, inclusive of breakfast, service charges and any additional taxes such as VAT: **£** under £50 **££** £50–£100 **£££** £100–£150 **££££** £150–£200 **£££££** £200 plus.	**RESTAURANT** Hotel restaurant or dining room usually open to non-residents unless otherwise stated. **CHILDREN WELCOME** Cribs and a baby-sitting service available. Some hotel restaurants have children's portions and high chairs. **GARDEN/TERRACE** Hotels with a garden, courtyard or terrace, often providing tables for eating outside. **CREDIT CARDS** Indicates which credit cards are accepted: *AE* American Express; *DC* Diners Club; *MC* Master Card/Access; *V* Visa.				

	CREDIT CARDS	RESTAURANT	CHILDREN WELCOME	GARDEN/TERRACE	NUMBER OF ROOMS
DODDISCOMBLEIGH: *Nobody Inn* **££** Doddiscombsleigh, nr Exeter EX6 7PS. 【 *01647 252394.* FAX *01647 252394.* A 16th-century inn, close to Dartmoor National Park. Extremely popular; additional bedrooms located in a nearby house. 🛏 TV P	AE MC V	■		■	7
DREWSTEIGNTON: *Hunts Tor* **£** Drewsteignton, Devon EX6 6QW. 【 *01647 281228.* Interesting 17th- and 18th-century building with a turn of the century interior. Extremely good set dinner is served at 7:30pm. 🛏 TV		■			4
EAST PORTLEMOUTH: *Gara Rock* **£** East Portlemouth, nr Salcombe, Devon TQ8 8PH. 【 *01548 842342.* FAX *01548 843033.* Ex-Admiralty coastguard station in a wonderful setting on the cliff-top. Lacking style, but good facilities. A hotel for all the family. 🛏 TV P ▨	MC V	■	●	■	33
FOWEY: *Marina* **££** The Esplanade, Fowey, Corn PL23 1HY. 【 *01726 833315.* FAX *01726 832 779.* Compact, neat hotel with efficient service overlooking the Fowey Estuary. A good base for exploring East Cornwall's fishing villages. 🛏 TV 24	AE MC V	■		■	11
LYDFORD: *Castle Inn* **£** Lydford, Okehampton, Devon EX20 4BU. 【 *0182 282 242.* FAX *0182 282 454.* Very appealing pink-washed inn. Jolly, convivial atmosphere in the bar and restaurant. Food imaginative and delicious. 🛏 TV 24 P	AE DC MC V	■	●	■	8
MITHIAN: *Rose-in-Vale Country House* **££** Mithina, St. Agnes, Corn TR5 0QD. 【 *01872 552202.* FAX *01872 552700.* Once the home of a tin-mine owner, this Georgian house is now run as a country-house hotel with dedication and efficiency. 🛏 TV P ▨	AE DC MC V	■	●	■	17
NORTH BOVEY: *Blackaller* **££** North Bovey, Devon TQ13 8QY. 【 *01647 40322.* Delightful and individual converted woollen mill. Full of interesting antiques and curios, it is an extremely relaxing, comfortable place to stay and a good base for the area. 🛏 TV P		■	●	■	5
PADSTOW: *St. Petroc's House* **££** Riverside, Padstow PL28 8BY. 【 *01841 532485.* FAX *01841 533344.* St. Petroc's is just round the corner from the Seafood Restaurant *(see p590)* and has simple, charming rooms. Bedrooms above the restaurant are extremely chic, stylish and comfortable. 🛏 TV P	AE MC V	■	●		19
PENZANCE: *Abbey* **££** Abbey St, Penzance, Corn TR18 4AR. 【 *01736 66906.* FAX *01736 51163.* A blue-painted, Gothic exterior and an original interior give this comfortable hotel a Bohemian feel. An exceptional place. 🛏 TV P	AE MC V			■	7
ST. IVES: *Garrack* **££** Burthallan Lane, St. Ives, Corn TR26 3AA. 【 *01736 796199.* FAX *01736 798955.* A family-run hotel above St. Ives, within easy reach of the center. The standard of decor in the bedrooms varies considerably. 🛏 TV P ▨	AE DC MC V	■	●	■	18
ST. KEYNE: *Well House* **££** St. Keyne, Liskeard, Corn PL14 4RN. 【 *01579 342001.* FAX *01579 343891.* Stylish, small hotel in an attractive Victorian building with a well-kept garden. The food is flawless as are the comfort and service. 🛏 TV P ▨	MC V	■	●	■	7
SIDMOUTH: *Riviera* **£££** The Esplanade, Sidmouth, Devon EX10 8AY. 【 *01395 515201.* FAX *01395 577775.* Stylish, efficient hotel, part of a fine Regency terrace on the sea front in this pretty seaside town. Strongly co-ordinated decor in public rooms and bedrooms. Helpful staff. 🛏 TV 🔊 24 P	AE DC MC V	■	●	■	27

TRURO: *Alverton Manor* ££££ | AE DC MC V | 34
Tregolls Rd, Truro, Corn TR1 1XQ. 01872 76633. FAX 01872 222989.
The exterior betrays the fact that this was once a religious establishment.
The interior is stylish. Atmosphere a little formal.

VERYAN: *Nare Head* £££ | MC V | 36
Carne Beach, Veryan, Truro, Corn TR2 5PF.
01872 501279. FAX 01872 501856.
A modern hotel, with a Victorian-style interior. Most rooms have
exceptional views looking straight out to sea.

WIDEGATES: *Coombe Farm* £ | | 9
Widegates, nr Looe, Corn PL13 1QN. 01503 240223.
Comfortable, friendly place in a peaceful spot. Lovely views down
the valley to the sea. Nov–Feb.

THE HEART OF ENGLAND

BIBURY: *Bibury Court* ££ | AE DC V MC | 20
Bibury, nr Cirencester, Glos GL7 5NT. 01285 740337. FAX 01285 740660.
Jacobean country-house. Old-fashioned in parts, but a very relaxing,
friendly place to stay. Tranquil setting.

BIBURY: *Swan* £££ | AE MC V | 18
Bibury, Glos GL7 5NW. 01285 740695. FAX 01285 740473.
Smart operation, combining hotel, bar and brasserie. Public rooms
ranging from grand to cozy, and beautiful bedrooms.

BIRMINGHAM: *Copperfield House* ££ | AE MC V | 17
60 Upland Rd, Selly Park, Birmingham B29 7JS.
0121 472 8344. FAX 0121 472 8344.
Town-house hotel just over 2 miles (3 km) from city center. Rooms
vary in standard and size, some have been refurbished. Small attractive
restaurant serving good food.

BOTTOMHOUSES: *Pethills Bank Cottage* £ | | 3
Bottomhouses, nr Leek, Staffs ST13 7PF. 01538 304 277. FAX 01538 304575.
Just outside the the Peak District National Park, this 18th-century cottage
has been extensively modernized. Convivial atmosphere and well-
equipped rooms make this an agreeable choice.

BROAD CAMPDEN: *Malt House* ££ | MC V | 5
Broad Campden, Glos GL55 6UU. 01386 840295. FAX 01386 841334.
Pretty 17th-century cottage with a lovely garden, a charming place
furnished with antiques throughout. Very good food.

BUCKLAND: *Buckland Manor* ££££ | AE MC V | 13
Buckland, nr Broadway, H & W WR12 7LY. 01386 852626. FAX 01386 853557.
Lovely old manor house built of Cotswold stone, dating back to the
13th century. A luxury hotel that has managed to keep its original
charm intact and provide high standards.

CHIPPING CAMPDEN: *Cotswold House* £££ | AE MC V | 15
Chipping Campden, Glos GL55 6AN. 01386 840330. FAX 01386 840310.
A 17th-century house that is an extremely smart, stylish hotel.
Exceptional bedrooms and a choice of restaurants.

CORSE LAWN: *Corse Lawn House* ££ | AE DC MC | 19
Corse Lawn, Glos GL19 4LZ. 01452 780771. FAX 01452 780840.
Elegant Queen Anne house on the edge of the village. Outstanding
bedrooms, formal dining room and a lower-priced bistro.

EDGBASTON: *Asquith House* ££ | AE MC V | 10
19 Portland Rd, Edgbaston, Birmingham B16 9HN.
0121 454 5282. FAX 0121 456 4668.
Close to the center of Birmingham, this ivy-clad Victorian house
is immaculate; decor in keeping with the period.

EVESHAM: *Evesham* ££ | AE DC MC V | 40
Coopers Lane, off Waterside, Evesham, H & W WR11 6DA.
01386 765566. FAX 01386 765443.
Highly original family hotel that will appeal especially to parents and
children. Everything has been thought of to keep all ages amused.
Excellent restaurant, with an unusual wine list.

Price categories for a standard double room per night, inclusive of breakfast, service charges and any additional taxes such as VAT: **£** under £50 **££** £50–£100 **£££** £100–£150 **££££** £150–£200 **£££££** £200 plus.	**RESTAURANT** Hotel restaurant or dining room usually open to non-residents unless otherwise stated. **CHILDREN WELCOME** Cribs and a baby-sitting service available. Some hotel restaurants have children's portions and high chairs. **GARDEN/TERRACE** Hotels with a garden, courtyard or terrace, often providing tables for eating outside. **CREDIT CARDS** Indicates which credit cards are accepted: *AE* American Express; *DC* Diners Club; *MC* Master Card/Access; *V* Visa.	**CREDIT CARDS**	**RESTAURANT**	**CHILDREN WELCOME**	**GARDEN/TERRACE**	**NUMBER OF ROOMS**

	Credit Cards	Restaurant	Children Welcome	Garden/Terrace	Number of Rooms
EYTON: *Marsh Country* **£££** Eyton, Leominster, H & W HR6 0AG. **[** 01568 613952. This 14th-century beamed building is an extremely relaxing place to stay. Set in a wonderfully peaceful spot and surrounded by gardens.	AE DC MC V	■	●		5
GREAT RISSINGTON: *Lamb Inn* **£** Great Rissington, Cheltenham, Glos GL54 2LP. **[** 01451 820388. **FAX** 01451 820724. A most attractive village tavern in this quintessentially English spa town. Food served in the bar and the rustic-style restaurant.	AE MC V	■	●	■	13
HANWOOD: *White House* **£** Hanwood, Shrewsbury, Shrops SY5 8LP. **[** 01743 860414. Attractive hotel just south of Shrewsbury. A well-restored 16th-century building with beautiful antique furniture. Good value.		■		■	6
HARDWICKE: *Haven* **£** Hardwicke, Hay-on-Wye, H & W HR3 5TA. **[** 01497 831254. Victorian vicarage in a quiet rural setting. Delicious dinners (for residents only) made from local produce.	AE		●		6
HARVINGTON: *Mill at Harvington* **££** Anchor Lane, Harvington, Evesham, H & W WR11 5NR. **[** 01386 870688. **FAX** 01386 870688. Appealing hotel consisting of a Georgian house and a converted mill alongside it. The River Avon passes through the grounds. Excellent restaurant with efficient staff.	AE DC MC V	■	●	■	15
IRONBRIDGE: *Severn Lodge* **£** New Rd, Ironbridge, Shrops TF8 7AS. **[** 01952 432148. **FAX** 01952 432148. Comfortable, upscale B&B in a quiet spot but only a few minutes walk from the center of Ironbridge. Delicious breakfasts.				■	3
KENILWORTH: *Castle Laurels* **£** 22 Castle Rd, Kenilworth, Warw CVP 1NG. **[** 01926 56179. **FAX** 01926 54954. Victorian house on main road opposite the ruins of Kenilworth Castle, minutes from town center. Well-kept. No smoking allowed.	MC V	■			12
LUDLOW: *Number Eleven* **££** Dinham, Ludlow, Shrops SY8 1EJ. **[** 01584 878584. In a stylish terrace of 18th-century houses, looking on to Ludlow Castle, this B&B is well decorated and furnished. A civilized place to stay.		■		■	4
MARKET DRAYTON: *Goldstone Hall* **££** Market Drayton, Shrops TF9 2NA. **[** 01630 661202. **FAX** 01630 661585. Reliable country-house hotel, in a rural setting. Open fires in the public rooms in winter and well-appointed bedrooms.	AE DC MC V	■	●	■	8
MOLLINGTON: *Crabwall Manor* **££££** Mollington, Chester, Ches CH1 6NE. **[** 01244 851666. **FAX** 01244 851400. Original, charming turreted manor house that is a stylish, luxury hotel in large grounds. Very good restaurant. *(See also p593.)*	AE DC MC	■	●	■	48
OAKMERE: *Nunsmere Hall* **£££** Tarporley Rd, Oakmere, nr Northwich, Ches CW8 2ES. **[** 01606 889100 **FAX** 01606 889055. Huge Edwardian house with vast lake. Stylish and unstuffy. Delicious food in the excellent restaurant.	AE DC MC V	■	●	■	32
PAINSWICK: *Painswick* **££** Kemps Lane, Painswick, Glos GL6 6YB. **[** 01452 812160. **FAX** 01452 814059. A hotel in the heart of the Cotswolds off a main road. Set in peaceful grounds. Civilized and stylish throughout with a good bar.	AE DC V	■	●	■	19

PETERSTOW: *Peterstow Country House* Peterstow, Ross-on-Wye, H & W HR9 6LB. **℡** *01989 562826.* **FAX** *01989 567264.* Spacious, beautifully restored rectory in lovely grounds. Well-decorated throughout. Formal dining room but a relaxed atmosphere. 🛏 📺 24 ℗	££	AE DC MC V	▦		▦		9
SHREWSBURY: *Manse* 16 Swan Hill, Shrewsbury, Shrops SY1 1NL. **℡** *01743 242659.* Only two bedrooms in this centrally located Georgian house. You may have to share a bathroom but it is a charming place to stay. 🛏 📺 ℗	£						2
STANSHOPE: *Stanshope Hall* Stanshope, nr Ashbourne, Staffs DE6 2AD. **℡** *01335 310278.* **FAX** *01335 310470.* Historic building on a hill with good views. Highly original with snug public rooms and bedrooms painted by local artists. 🛏 📺 ℗	£			●	▦		3
STOW-ON-THE-WOLD: *Wyck Hill House* Burford Rd, Stow-on-the-Wold, Glos GL54 1HY. **℡** *01451 831936.* **FAX** *01451 832243.* Manor house with superb views over Windrush Valley. Cheaper rooms in the courtyard. Good food in the formal restaurant. 🛏 📺 ♨ 24 ℗ ♿	£££	AE DC MC V		●	▦		31
STRATFORD-UPON-AVON: *Caterham House* 58–59 Rother St, Stratford-upon-Avon, Warw CV37 6LT. **℡** *01789 267309.* **FAX** *01789 414836.* Centrally placed hotel made from two Georgian houses. Very attractive inside and out. Comfortable, stylish and well run. Superb restaurant. ℗	££	MC V	▦	●	▦		13
TUTBURY: *Mill House* Corn Mill Lane, Tutbury, Burton-on-Trent, Staffs DE13 9HA. **℡** *01283 813300.* Immaculately neat B&B in a charming spot by an old mill. Light, spacious bedrooms attractively decorated and furnished. 🛏 📺 ℗	£				▦		3
ULLINGSWICK: *Steppes Country House* Ullingswick, nr Hereford HR1 3JG. **℡** *01432 820424.* **FAX** *01432 820042.* Restored 400-year-old former farmhouse that is elegant and charming. A good comfortable base from which to explore the area. 🛏 📺 ℗	££	AE MC V	▦		▦		6
WATERHOUSES: *Old Beams* Waterhouses, Staffs ST10 3HW. **℡** *01538 308254.* **FAX** *01538 308157.* Stylish restaurant-with-rooms in a low-beamed building. Double-glazing blocks the noise from the nearby A523. 🛏 📺 ℗ ♿	££	AE DC MC V	▦		▦		5
WELLAND: *Holdfast Cottage* Marlbank Rd, Welland, Little Malvern, H & W WR13 6NA. **℡** *01684 310288.* **FAX** *01684 311117.* Small, wisteria-covered hotel, originally 17th century with Victorian additions. Public rooms and bedrooms are well-decorated. 🛏 📺 ℗	££	MC V	▦	●	▦		8
WESTON-UNDER-REDCASTLE: *Citadel* Weston-under-Redcastle, nr Shrewsbury, Shrops SY4 5JY. **℡** *01939 685204.* Unusual castellated house built in the early 19th century. Its position is peaceful with great views from most of the rooms. 🛏 📺 24 ℗	££			▦			3
WILLERSEY: *Old Rectory* Church St, Willersey, nr Broadway, H & W WR12 7PN. **℡** *01386 853729.* A very welcoming B&B hotel in a charming Cotswold village. No restaurant but plenty of places for dinner nearby. 🛏 📺 24 ℗	££	MC V			▦		8
WILMCOTE: *Pear Tree Cottage* Church Rd, Wilmcote, Stratford-upon-Avon, Warw CV37 9UX. **℡** *01789 205889.* **FAX** *01789 262862.* Charming part-Elizabethan cottage, brilliantly positioned for touring Shakespeare Country. Furnished with antiques. 🛏 📺 ℗	£			●	▦		7
WOOLSTASTON: *Rectory Farm* Woolstaston, Leebotwood, nr Church Stretton, Shrops SY6 6NN. **℡** *01694 751306.* Convivial atmosphere in attractive, half-timbered farmhouse with garden and fields. Cozy sitting rooms and large bedrooms with *en suite* bathrooms. A good base for discovering the area. 🛏 📺 24 ℗	£				▦		3
WORFIELD: *Old Vicarage* Worfield, Bridgnorth, Shrops WV15 5JZ. **℡** *01746 716497.* **FAX** *01746 716552.* Imposing Edwardian vicarage with friendly owners. Pristine decoration. Comfortable rooms with views of the garden and meadows. 🛏 📺 ℗ ♿	££	AE DC MC V	▦	●	▦		14

For key to symbols see back flap

Price categories for a standard double room per night, inclusive of breakfast, service charges and any additional taxes such as VAT:
£ under £50
££ £50–£100
£££ £100–£150
££££ £150–£200
£££££ £200 plus.

RESTAURANT
Hotel restaurant or dining room usually open to non-residents unless otherwise stated.

CHILDREN WELCOME
Cribs and a baby-sitting service available. Some hotel restaurants have children's portions and high chairs.

GARDEN/TERRACE
Hotels with a garden, courtyard or terrace, often providing tables for eating outside.

CREDIT CARDS
Indicates which credit cards are accepted: *AE* American Express; *DC* Diners Club; *MC* Master Card/Access; *V* Visa.

EAST MIDLANDS

		CREDIT CARDS	RESTAURANT	CHILDREN WELCOME	GARDEN/TERRACE	NUMBER OF ROOMS
ALDWINCLE: *Maltings*	£	MC V			■	3
Main St, Aldwincle, Oundle, Northants NN14 3EP. [01832 720233. FAX 01832 720326. Delicious breakfasts served in the house. The two main bedrooms are in the converted granary next door. 🔜 P						
BASLOW: *Cavendish*	£££	AE DC MC V	■	●	■	24
Baslow, Derby DE45 1SP. [01246 582311. FAX 01246 582312. Very attractive roadside hotel surrounded by the Chatsworth estate. Well-appointed, civilized, and decorated to a high standard. Superb food served in the restaurant. 🔜 TV P 🔽						
BOURNE: *Bourne Eau House*	££		■	●	■	3
South St, Bourne, Lincoln PE10 9LY. [01778 423621. Friendly and welcoming, where guests are part of the family. Nearby is a ruined castle – the whole area is full of history. 🔜 TV 24 P						
CASTLE ASHBY: *Falcon*	££	AE MC V	■		■	14
Castle Ashby, Northampton NN7 1LF. [01604 696200. FAX 01604 696673. Attractive 16th-century stone inn with a warm atmosphere and friendly owners. Good quality furnishings in the comfortable rooms. 🔜 TV P						
CASTLE DONINGTON: *Donington Thistle*	£££	AE DC MC V	■	●	■	100
East Midlands International Airport, Castle Donington, Derby DE74 2SH. [01332 850700. FAX 01332 850823. Huge hotel conveniently located for the nearby airport; mainly catering for conferences and business travelers. Good facilities. 🔜 TV 24 P 🏊 🔽						
EAST BARKWORTH: *Grange*	£				■	3
Torrington Lane, East Barkworth, Lincoln LN3 5RY. [01673 858249. Lovely Georgian house full of interesting antiques. Large, bright rooms are tasteful and very pleasant. Dinner can be served by arrangement with the management. 🔜 TV P						
GLOSSOP: *Wind in the Willows*	££	AE DC MC V	■		■	12
Derbyshire Level, Glossop, Derby SK13 9PT. [01457 868001. FAX 01457 853354. Victorian house overlooking the Peak District National Park, efficiently run by mother-and-son team. Ideally situated as a base for exploring this part of the country. Golf course nearby. 🔜 TV P						
HAMBLETON: *Hambleton Hall*	£££	AE DC MC V	■	●	■	15
Hambleton, Oakham, Rutland, Leic LE15 8TH. [01572 756991. FAX 01572 724721. One of the top country-house hotels in Britain. Well-decorated, under-stated luxury that is comfortable yet relaxing. A wide range of facilities provided. Excellent restaurant. *(See also p594.)* 🔜 TV 🔽 P 🏊 🔽						
HATHERSAGE: *Highlow Hall*	£		■	●	■	6
Highlow, Hathersage, Derby S30 1AX. [01433 650393. Imposing 16th-century hall in the heart of the Peak District. Inside it is comfy and unpretentious. Friendly management. P						
ISLEY WALTON: *Park Farmhouse*	££	AE DC MC V	■	●	■	9
Melbourne Rd, Isley Walton, nr Castle Donington, Leic DE74 2RN. [01332 862409. FAX 01332 862364. Easy-going atmosphere and great hospitality in this 17th-century farm-house. Cozy lounge and bar and neat bedrooms. 🔜 TV P 🔽						
LANGAR: *Langar Hall*	££	AE MC V	■	●	■	10
Langar, nr Nottingham NG13 9HG. [01949 60559. FAX 01949 61045. Attractive 19th-century country house built of pale stone. Inside it is full of antiques. Charming hostess and welcoming atmosphere. 🔜 TV P						

LINCOLN: *D'Isney Place* £££
Eastgate, Lincoln LN2 4AA. 01522 538881. FAX 01522 511321.
Smart, elegant B&B in the heart of Lincoln, close to the cathedral. No lounge, but the bedrooms more than compensate. 🛏 TV 24 P &
AE DC MC V — 17

LINCOLN: *White Hart* £££
Bailgate, Lincoln, Lincs LN1 3AR. 01522 526222. FAX 01522 531798.
Lovely coaching inn that has been receiving guests for over 600 years. Next to the castle walls, this is a chic, well-run hotel. 🛏 TV 24 P
AE DC MC V — 48

MATLOCK BATH: *Hodgkinson's* ££
150 South Parade, Matlock Bath, Derby DE4 3NR. 01629 582170.
Unique hotel-restaurant, lovingly restored. Individually decorated and furnished bedrooms. Delicious food served in restaurant. 🛏 TV P
AE MC V — 7

PRESTBURY: *White House Manor* £££
Hew Rd, Prestbury, Ches SK10 4DG. 01625 829376. FAX 01625 828627.
Very comfy hotel – breakfasts served in the bedrooms. Jacket and tie required for dinner served in the nearby restaurant. 🛏 TV P
AE DC MC V — 9

REDMILE: *Peacock Farm Guest House* £
Redmile, Vale of Belvoir, Leic NG13 0GQ. 01949 842475. FAX 01949 843127.
Warm welcome in a rambling, extended farmhouse. Good atmosphere and reasonable comfort. Children made welcome. 🛏 TV P ≋ &
AE MC V — 10

STAPLEFORD: *Stapleford Park* ££££
Stapleford, Leic LE14 2EF. 01572 787 522. FAX 01572 787651.
Huge Jacobean and Neo-Classical country-house hotel. A wonderful, easy-going place to stay and very luxurious. 🛏 TV 24 P &
AE DC MC V — 42

UPPINGHAM: *Lake Isle* ££
16 High St East, Uppingham LE15 9PZ. 01572 822951. FAX 01572 822951.
Individually decorated bedrooms in a French-style restaurant-with-rooms. Excellent cooking and a relaxed, convivial atmosphere. 🛏 TV P
AE DC MC V — 12

WHAPLODE: *Guy Wells* £
Eastgate, Whaplode, Spalding, Lincs PE12 6TZ. 01406 422239.
An 18th-century Queen Anne farmhouse in a lovely, peaceful spot. An ideal base for touring the Fens. Friendly welcome to nonsmokers. 🛏 P
— 3

WINSTER: *Dower House* £
Main St, Winster, Derby DE4 2DH. 01629 650213. FAX 01629 650894.
Delightful bed-and-breakfast hotel in a perfect position for touring the Peak District. Simple but attractive decor and charming owners. 🛏 TV P
— 3

LANCASHIRE AND THE LAKES

AMBLESIDE: *Chapel House* £
Kirkstone Rd, Ambleside, Cumbria LA22 9DZ. 015394 33143.
A few minutes steep walk up from the main street to this friendly guesthouse. Small, cottagey bedrooms, some with *en suite* bathrooms at a slightly higher price. Delicious dinners. P
— 10

AMBLESIDE: *Wateredge* ££
Waterhead, Ambleside, Cumbria LA22 OEP. 015394 32332. FAX 015394 32332.
On the shores of Windermere, with panoramic views from the sitting room. A bit staid, but relaxing. New suites in the annex. 🛏 TV 24 P
AE MC V — 23

AMBLESIDE: *Rothay Manor* £££
Rothay Bridge, Ambleside, Cumbria LA22 0EH. 015394 33605. FAX 015394 33607.
Elegant and civilized Regency hotel. Lovely bedrooms and a highly regarded restaurant serving a varied menu. 🛏 TV P &
AE DC MC V — 15

BASSENTHWAITE: *Ravenstone Lodge* ££
Bassenthwaite, Keswick, Cumbria CA12 4QG. 017687 76629. FAX 017687 76629.
This attractive B&B has wonderful views across the fields to Bassenthwaite Lake. Charming owners make guests feel very welcome. 🛏 P
— 9

BASSENTHWAITE LAKE: *Pheasant Inn* ££
Bassenthwaite Lake, Cockermouth, Cumbria CA13 9YE.
017687 76234. FAX 017687 76002.
A lovely old country inn next to the lakeside that has lots of regular customers both in the bar and staying in the rooms. A choice of cozy sitting rooms. Unfussy bedrooms with modern bathrooms. 🛏 P &
MC V — 20

Price categories for a standard double room per night, inclusive of breakfast, service charges and any additional taxes such as VAT: **£** under £50 **££** £50–£100 **£££** £100–£150 **££££** £150–£200 **£££££** £200 plus.	**RESTAURANT** Hotel restaurant or dining room usually open to non-residents unless otherwise stated. **CHILDREN WELCOME** Cribs and a baby-sitting service available. Some hotel restaurants have children's portions and high chairs. **GARDEN/TERRACE** Hotels with a garden, courtyard or terrace, often providing tables for eating outside. **CREDIT CARDS** Indicates which credit cards are accepted: *AE* American Express; *DC* Diners Club; *MC* Master Card/Access; *V* Visa.	**CREDIT CARDS**	**RESTAURANT**	**CHILDREN WELCOME**	**GARDEN/TERRACE**	**NUMBER OF ROOMS**
BOLTON-BY-BOWLAND: *Harrop Fold* **££** Bolton-by-Bowland, Clitheroe, Lancs BB7 4PJ. 📞 01200 447600. This farmhouse hotel is in a secluded place surrounded by moorland. Hospitable owners see to guests' every need. 🛏 📺 🅿	*MC* *V*	■	●	■	8
BOWNESS-ON-WINDERMERE: *Linthwaite House* **££** Crook Rd, Bowness-on-Windermere, Cumbria LA23 3JA. 📞 015394 88600. **FAX** 015394 88601. Very stylish and comfortable Edwardian hotel in a stunning location overlooking the lake. Outside breakfast terrace; good food. 🛏 📺 🅿 ♿	*AE* *MC* *V*	■	●	■	20
BRACKENTHWAITE: *Pickett Howe* **££** Brackenthwaite, Buttermere Valley, Cumbria CA13 9UY. 📞 01900 85444. Style and comfort in this attractive 17th-century farmhouse in a peaceful setting. Beautifully renovated and furnished. Good food. 🛏 🅿	*MC* *V*	■		■	4
BRAMPTON: *Farlam Hall* **££** Brampton, Cumbria CA8 2NG. 📞 016977 46234. **FAX** 016977 46683. Part 17th- and part 19th-century ivy-clad house set in lovely grounds. Fairly formal – gentlemen are required to wear a jacket and tie for the excellent dinners. Pleasant sitting rooms. 🛏 📺 🅿	*AE* *MC* *V*	■		■	12
CARLISLE: *Beeches* **£** Wood St, Carlisle CA1 2SF. 📞 01228 511962. Pretty, pink-washed Georgian cottage with typical English garden. Bedrooms attractively decorated. Excellent base for Carlisle. 📺 🅿			●	■	3
CARTMEL: *Aynsome Manor* **££** Cartmel, nr Grange-over-Sands, Cumbria LA11 6HH. 📞 015395 36653. **FAX** 015395 36016. Traditional country-house hotel – cozy and welcoming. There are great views from most rooms over the peaceful vale of Cartmel. 🛏 📺 🅿	*AE* *MC* *V*	■	●	■	12
CARTMEL FEN: *Lightwood* **£** Cartmel Fell, nr Bowland Bridge, Cumbria LA11 6NP. 📞 015395 31454. A 17th-century farmhouse in a peaceful location. Some pretty, cottage-style bedrooms in converted outbuildings. B&B only. 🛏 🅿	*MC* *V*		●	■	9
CLAPPERSGATE: *Nanny Brow* **££** Clappersgate, Ambleside, Cumbria LA22 9NF. 📞 015394 32036. **FAX** 015394 32450. Well-run, comfortable hotel close to Ambleside, set in lovely grounds. Lots of facilities and an excellent restaurant. 🛏 📺 🅿 ♿	*AE* *DC* *MC* *V*	■	●	■	18
GRANGE-IN-BORROWDALE: *Borrowdale Gates* **£** Grange-in-Borrowdale, Keswick, Cumbria CA12 5UQ. 📞 017687 77204. **FAX** 017687 77254. Traditionally furnished, comfortable hotel, well off the beaten track. Great views from the huge picture windows. 🛏 📺 🅿 ♿	*MC* *V*	■	●	■	23
GRASMERE: *White Moss House* **£££** Rydal Water, Grasmere, Cumbria LA22 9SE. 📞 015394 35295. This 18th-century, creeper-covered house has an outstanding reputation for its food, but is also a civilized, comfortable place to stay. 🛏 📺 24 🅿	*MC* *V*	■		■	6
LITTLE SINGLETON: *Mains Hall* **££** Little Singleton, Blackpool, Lancs FY6 7LE. 📞 01253 885130. **FAX** 01253 894132. George IV stayed in this historic house, which has lovely grounds and good views over the River Wyre. 🛏 📺 24 🅿 ♿	*AE* *DC* *MC* *V*	■	●	■	9
MANOR BROW: *Grange Country House* **££** Manor Brow, Keswick CA12 4BA. 📞 017687 72500. Stone house in an excellent hilly vantage point on the edge of town. Unexceptional decor but a reliable base for this area. 🛏 📺 🅿	*MC* *V*	■		■	10

MUNGRISDALE: *Mill*
Mungrisdale, Penrith, Cumbria CA11 0XR. ⚫ *017687 79659.*
Lovely setting for this former mill cottage. Simple, immaculate bedrooms
and cozy public rooms. Exceptional food. ⚫ *Dec–Feb.* 🛏 📺 🅿
££ | | ▣ | | | 9

SEATOLLER: *Seatoller House*
Seatoller, Borrowdale, Keswick, Cumbria CA12 5XN. ⚫ *017687 77218.*
Charming guesthouse with friendly, relaxed hosts. It is an ideal walking
base and very good value. Excellent set dinners eaten at 7pm. 🛏 🅿
£ | | ▣ | | | 9

SLAIDBURN: *Parrock Head*
Slaidburn, nr Clitheroe, Lancs BB7 3AH. ⚫ *01200 446614.* 📠 *01200 446313.*
Beautifully sited 17th-century farmhouse. Good quality cottage-style
furnishings give this hotel a welcoming atmosphere. 🛏 📺 🅿 ♿
££ | AE MC V | ▣ | ● | ▣ | | 9

SPARK BRIDGE: *Bridgefield House*
Spark Bridge, nr Ulverston, Cumbria LA12 8DA.
⚫ *0122985 239.* 📠 *0122985 379.*
A 19th-century house with convivial owners. Exceptionally good food
makes dinner a very special, memorable occasion. 🛏 🅿
££ | MC V | ▣ | ● | ▣ | | 5

TROUTBECK: *Mortal Man*
Troutbeck, Windermere, Cumbria LA23 1PL. ⚫ *015394 33193.* 📠 *015394 31261.*
There are wonderful views down the valley to Windermere from this
300-year-old inn. A mixture of beamed rooms and Victoriana. 🛏 📺 🅿
££ | | ▣ | | | 12

ULLSWATER: *Sharrow Bay*
Lake Ullswater, Penrith, Cumbria CA10 2LZ. ⚫ *017684 86301.* 📠 *017684 86349.*
The first "country-house hotel" in Britain and still considered one of the
best. Impeccable service. Excellent restaurant. *(See also p597.)* 🛏 📺 🅿
£££££ | | ▣ | | ▣ | 28

WASDALE HEAD: *Wasdale Head Inn*
Wasdale Head, Gosforth, Cumbria CA20 1EX.
⚫ *019467 26229.* 📠 *019467 26334.*
Archetypal walkers' pub. Largely Victorian, serving traditional beers and
wholesome food. Simple, unadorned bedrooms. 🛏 🅿
££ | MC V | ▣ | ● | ▣ | | 6

WATERMILLOCK: *Old Church*
Watermillock, Penrith, Cumbria CA11 0JN. ⚫ *017684 86204.* 📠 *017684 86368.*
On the shores of Ullswater, this imaginatively decorated country-house
hotel is one of the best in the area. Stylish and comfortable. 🛏 📺 24 🅿
££ | MC V | ▣ | ● | ▣ | | 10

WATER YEAT: *Water Yeat Country Guest House*
Water Yeat, nr Ulverston, Cumbria LA12 8JD. ⚫ *01229 885306.*
Charming 17th-century farmhouse in a lovely setting, run with great
style and flair. Very attractive bedrooms and imaginative cooking. 📺 🅿
£ | | ▣ | | ▣ | 7

WHITEWELL: *Inn at Whitewell*
Whitewell, Forest of Bowland, Clitheroe, Lancs BB7 3AT.
⚫ *01200 448222.* 📠 *01200 448298.*
Special pub with style, sophistication and a relaxed atmosphere. Great
bar and a relaxing, comfortable residents' lounge along with excellent
well-appointed bedrooms. 🛏 📺 24 🅿
££ | AE DC MC V | ▣ | ● | ▣ | | 10

WINDERMERE: *Holbeck Ghyll*
Holbeck Lane, Windermere, Cumbria LA23 1LU.
⚫ *015394 32375.* 📠 *015394 34743.*
Imposing Victorian house in a superb position with views over the lake
to the mountains. Comfortable, with an easy-going atmosphere. Very
attentive courteous service. 🛏 📺 24 🅿
£££ | AE DC MC | ▣ | ● | | | 14

WINDERMERE: *Miller Howe*
Rayrigg Road, Windermere, Cumbria LA23 1EY.
⚫ *015394 42536.* 📠 *015394 45664.*
Very well-known restaurant and hotel. Set in superb countryside and
flamboyantly decorated. Outstanding and highly original food. Very
comfortable with tastefully furnished rooms. 🛏 📺 🅿
££££ | AE V | ▣ | | ▣ | 13

WITHERSLACK: *Old Vicarage*
Witherslack, nr Grange-over-Sands, Cumbria LA11 6RS.
⚫ *015395 52381.* 📠 *015395 52373.*
Informal country-house style hotel situated at the end of a leafy country
lane. Quite hard to find, but very tranquil. A perfect place to escape the
crowds on the tourist trail. Very good restaurant. 🛏 📺 🅿
£££ | MC V | ▣ | ● | ▣ | | 15

For key to symbols see back flap

Price categories for a standard double room per night, inclusive of breakfast, service charges and any additional taxes such as VAT:
£ under £50
££ £50–£100
£££ £100–£150
££££ £150–£200
£££££ £200 plus.

RESTAURANT
Hotel restaurant or dining room usually open to non-residents unless otherwise stated.
CHILDREN WELCOME
Cribs and a baby-sitting service available. Some hotel restaurants have children's portions and high chairs.
GARDEN/TERRACE
Hotels with a garden, courtyard or terrace, often providing tables for eating outside.
CREDIT CARDS
Indicates which credit cards are accepted: *AE* American Express; *DC* Diners Club; *MC* Master Card/Access; *V* Visa.

	CREDIT CARDS	RESTAURANT	CHILDREN WELCOME	GARDEN/TERRACE	NUMBER OF ROOMS
YORKSHIRE AND HUMBERSIDE					
ASKRIGG: *Kings Arms* ££ Askrigg, Wensleydale, N Yorks DL8 3HQ. 📞 *01969 650258.* 📠 *01969 650635.* This has been an inn since 1810. A popular place with comfortable bedrooms and a choice of two restaurants. 🛏 📺 🅿	AE MC V	■	●		11
HARROGATE: *White House* ££ 10 Park Parade, Harrogate, N Yorks HG1 5AH. 📞 *01423 5011388.* 📠 *01423 527973.* A larger-than-life Victorian exterior belies a wonderful interior. An original, very agreeable hotel that offers many extras. 🛏 📺 🅿	AC DC MC V	■	●	■	10
HAWORTH: *Weavers* ££ 15 West Lane, Haworth, W Yorks BD22 8DU. 📞 *01535 643822.* Three traditional cottages make up this agreeable restaurant-with-rooms in the village where the Brontë sisters grew up. Delicious, wholesome northern food and large, comfortable bedrooms. 🛏 📺 🅿	AE DC MC V	■		■	4
HOLDSWORTH: *Holdsworth House* ££ Holdsworth, Halifax, W Yorks HX2 9TG. 📞 *01422 240024.* 📠 *01422 245174.* Extremely pretty, Jacobean house near Halifax, with most of the decor in keeping with the period. Excellent food. 🛏 📺 🅿 ♿	AC DC MC V	■	●	■	40
HUDDERSFIELD: *Lodge* ££ 48 Birkby Lodge Rd, Birkby, Huddersfield HD2 2BG. 📞 *01484 431001.* 📠 *01484 421590.* On the outskirts of Huddersfield in a residential street, this is an agreeable, well-maintained hotel. Very good restaurant. 🛏 📺 🅿 ♿	AC MC V	■	●	■	11
HUDDERSFIELD: *Wellfield House* ££ 33 New Hey Rd, Marsh, Huddersfield HD3 4AL. 📞 *01484 425776.* 📠 *01484 532122.* Well-run Victorian-style house in a residential terrace. Pleasant rooms, individually decorated and furnished. 🛏 📺 🅿	AE MC V	■		■	5
HUNMANBY: *Wrangham House* ££ 10 Stonegate, Hunmanby, nr Filey, N Yorks YO14 0NS. 📞 *01723 891333.* Former vicarage with 17th-century origins. Tastefully decorated, with a relaxed, hospitable atmosphere. 🛏 📺 🅿 ♿	AE DC MC V	■		■	13
ILKLEY: *Rombalds* ££ West View, Wells Rd, Ilkley, W Yorks LS29 9JG. 📞 *01943 603201.* 📠 *01943 816586.* Family-run hotel that maintains consistently good standards. Overlooking both the town and beautiful Ilkley Moor. The views are outstanding. Extremely good restaurant. 🛏 📺 24 🅿	AE DC MC	■	●	■	15
LASTINGHAM: *Lastingham Grange* ££ Lastingham, York YO6 6TH. 📞 *01751 417345.* Family-run hotel for the last 40 years with a traditional, homey feel. Well-situated for exploring the historic city of York and the county of Yorkshire. Quiet and peaceful and set in large grounds. 🛏 📺 🅿		■	●	■	12
LEEDS: *42 The Calls* ££ 42 The Calls, Leeds, W Yorks LS2 7EW. 📞 *01132 440099.* 📠 *01132 344100.* Very chic, stylish city hotel with a quiet, informal atmosphere. Good brasserie and smart, well-equipped bedrooms. 🛏 📺 🖥 24 🅿 ♿	AE DC MC V	■		■	41
MARKINGTON: *Hob Green* ££ Markington, Harrogate, N Yorks HG3 3PJ. 📞 *01423 770031.* 📠 *01423 771589.* Family-run hotel just outside Markington. Lovely grounds including a croquet lawn. Relaxing public rooms. 🛏 📺 🅿	AE DC MC V	■	●	■	12

MASHAM: *King's Head*
£ | AC DC MC V | | | 10
Market Place, Masham, N Yorks HGG4 4EF. 📞 *01765 689295.*
Friendly and traditional inn situated in the brewery town of Masham.
An excellent selection of local beers in the bar. 🛏 📺 P

MIDDLEHAM: *Miller's House*
££ | MC V | | | 7
Middleham, Wensleydale, N Yorks DL8 4NR. 📞 *01969 622630.* FAX *01969 623570.*
Just off the market place in this attractive village – an excellent base for
exploring the area. Immaculate throughout with cozy rooms. 🛏 📺 24 P

ROSEDALE ABBEY: *White Horse Farm*
££ | AC DC MC V | | | 15
Rosedale Abbey, nr Pickering, N Yorks YO18 8SE.
📞 *01751 417239.* FAX *01751 417781.*
Unpretentious hotel overlooking the village – an inn since 1702. Full
of charm and character. A warm welcome is assured. 🛏 📺 P

SEDBUSK: *Stonehouse*
££ | MC V | | | 18
Sedbusk, nr Hawes, Wensleydale, N Yorks DL8 3PT.
📞 *01969 667571.* FAX *01969 667720.*
Attractive stone house built in 1908 and surrounded by old-fashioned
English gardens. Family-run, with a relaxed atmosphere. 🛏 📺 P ♿

STOKESLEY: *Chapters*
££ | AE DC MC | | | 13
27 High St, Stokesley, Middlesbrough, Cleveland T59 5AD.
📞 *01642 711888.* FAX *01642 713387.*
Restored 18th-century coaching inn in the town center with an excellent
restaurant and comfortable, individually decorated bedrooms. 🛏 📺 P

WALKINGTON: *Manor House*
££ | MC V | | | 7
Northlands, Walkington, nr Beverley, Humbs HU17 8RT.
📞 *01482 881645.* FAX *01482 866501.*
Civilized and comfortable hotel in a lovely location in the heart of
the Wolds. Lovely, light rooms and delicious food. 🛏 📺 P

WINTERINGHAM: *Winteringham Fields*
££ | AE MC V | | | 7
Winteringham, Scunthorpe, Humbs DN15 9PF.
📞 *01724 733096.* FAX *01724 733898.*
A 400-year-old farmhouse, now a popular restaurant-with-rooms *(see
also p599).* Good food and comfortable bedrooms. 🛏 📺 24 P ♿

YORK: *Holmwood House*
££ | AE MC V | | | 12
114 Holgate Rd, York YO2 4BB. 📞 *01904 626183.* FAX *01904 670899.*
Exceptional B&B about 15 minutes' walk from the center of the city. Very
comfortable. Delicious breakfasts and charming owners. 🛏 📺 P

YORK: *Middlethorpe Hall*
££££ | AE DC MC V | | | 30
Bishopthorpe Rd, York YO2 1QB. 📞 *01904 641241.* FAX *01904 620176.*
Superbly restored and beautifully furnished manor just outside York.
Top class standards and service. 🛏 📺 🐾 P

NORTHUMBRIA

BELLINGHAM: *Wesfield Guest House*
£ | MC V | | | 5
Bellingham, Northum NE48 2DP. 📞 *01434 220340.*
Cozy and welcoming guesthouse in a very attractive rural position. Peace
and quiet is assured in simple rooms. Dinner on request. P

BERWICK-UPON-TWEED: *Old Vicarage*
£ | | | | 7
Church Rd, Tweedmouth, Berwick upon Tweed TD15 2AN. 📞 *01289 306909.*
A few minutes' walk from this 19th-century former vicarage and you
will find yourself right in the center of town. Coziness, comfort
and hospitable management. 🛏 📺 P

BLANCHLAND: *Lord Crewe Arms*
£££ | AE DC MC V | | | 18
Blanchland, nr Consett, Co Durham DH8 9SP.
📞 *01434 675251.* FAX *01434 675337.*
This historic coaching inn at the center of the village has a convivial
atmosphere, and is very popular both with locals and visitors. 🛏 📺 24 P

CORBRIDGE: *Low Barns*
£ | MC V | | | 3
Thornbrough, Corbridge, Northum NE45 5LX. 📞 *01434 632408.*
Just east of Corbridge and only a few miles from Hexham, this attractive
stone farmhouse makes an excellent base to explore the area. Friendly
and comfortable with good breakfasts. 🛏 📺 P

	Price categories for a standard double room per night, inclusive of breakfast, service charges and any additional taxes such as VAT: £ under £50 ££ £50–£100 £££ £100–£150 ££££ £150–£200 £££££ £200 plus.	**RESTAURANT** Hotel restaurant or dining room usually open to non-residents unless otherwise stated. **CHILDREN WELCOME** Cribs and a baby-sitting service available. Some hotel restaurants have children's portions and high chairs. **GARDEN/TERRACE** Hotels with a garden, courtyard or terrace, often providing tables for eating outside. **CREDIT CARDS** Indicates which credit cards are accepted: *AE* American Express; *DC* Diners Club; *MC* Master Card/Access; *V* Visa.	CREDIT CARDS	RESTAURANT	CHILDREN WELCOME	GARDEN/TERRACE	NUMBER OF ROOMS
DURHAM: *Georgian Town House* £ 10 Crossgate, Durham DH1 4PS. 【 0191 3868070. Lovely Georgian house in the heart of the city, decorated with great flair and imagination. Bright bedrooms and good breakfasts. 🛏 TV						■	6
DURHAM: *Royal County* £££ Old Elvet, Durham DH1 3JN. 【 0191 3866821. FAX 0191 3860704. In a great position beside the river, this hotel has many different types of facilities including its own health club. 🛏 TV 🛁 24 P ≈ ♿			AE DC MC V	■	●	■	150
HEXHAM: *Middlemarch* £ Hencotes, Hexham, Northum NE46 2EB. 【 01434 605003. Attractive Georgian town house, very much the owner's home. The delicious breakfasts are served around the kitchen table. TV P						■	3
HIGH BUSTON: *High Buston Hall* ££ High Buston, Alnmouth, Alnwick, Northum NE66 3QH. 【 01665 830341. Wonderful views out to the North Sea from this Georgian house. Plain bedrooms and a residents' lounge. Dinner by arrangement. 🛏 TV P					●	■	3
LONGHORSLEY: *Linden Hall* £££ Longhorsley, Morpeth, Newcastle upon Tyne, Northum NE65 8XF. 【 01670 516611. FAX 01670 788544. Surrounded by 160 ha (400 acres) of parkland, this fine Georgian house has become a grand hotel and health spa. 🛏 TV 🛁 24 P ≈ ♿			AE DC MC V	■		■	50
NEWCASTLE: *Waterside* ££ 48–52 Sandhill, Quayside, Newcastle NE1 3JF. 【 0191 2300111. FAX 0191 2301615. Stylish hotel on the city's Quayside. Neat and new, it has well-furnished bedrooms and a good Italian restaurant. 🛏 TV 🛁 24 P			AE MC	■		■	20
POWBURN: *Breamish Country House* ££ Powburn, nr Alnwick, Northum NE66 4LL. 【 01665 578266. FAX 01665 578500. Attractive house dating from 17th century with lovely grounds. Lots of personal touches give the place charm. Excellent restaurant. 🛏 TV P			MC V	■		■	11
ROMALDKIRK: *Rose and Crown* ££ Romaldkirk, Teesdale DL12 9EB. 【 01833 650213. FAX 01833 650828. Popular inn on the village green. Well-equipped bedrooms, and a choice of bar food or meals in the wood-paneled restaurant. 🛏 TV P ♿			MC V	■	●	■	12
NORTH WALES							
ABERDYFI: *Penhelig Arms* ££ Aberdyfi, C & M LL35 0LT. 【 01654 767215. FAX 01654 767690. All but one of the bedrooms in this whitewashed inn have a sea view. It has been recently refurbished and is stylish and comfortable. 🛏 TV P			MC V	■	●	■	10
ABERSOCH: *Porth Tocyn* ££ Abersoch, Pwllheli, C & M LL53 7BU. 【 01758 713303. FAX 01758 713538. Very cozy hotel. Children are particularly welcome but there's room for adults to find peace and quiet. *(See also p601.)* 🛏 TV P ≈ ♿			MC V	■	●	■	17
BEDDGELERT: *Sygun Fawr Country House* £ Beddgelert, C & M LL55 4NE. 【 01766 890258. Old hotel with its original beams but with light, pretty bedrooms. Very well-placed for climbing and walking in Snowdonia. 🛏 P				■	●	■	7
BENLLECH: *Bryn Meirion* ££ Amlwch Rd, Benllech, C & M LL74 8SR. 【 01248 853118. Superb views over Conwy Bay from this modern guesthouse. The public rooms, some of the bedrooms, bathrooms and garden have been adapted with disabled visitors in mind. 🛏 TV P ♿				■	●	■	8

CAPEL GARMON: *Tan-y-Foel* £££
Capel Garmon, Betws-y-Coed, A & C LL26 0RE.
01690 710507. FAX 01690 710681.
Converted farmhouse with guest sitting rooms, and individual bedrooms.
Situated in a beautifully secluded spot near Snowdonia.
AE DC MC V — 7

CRICCIETH: *Mynydd Ednyfed* ££
Caernarfon Rd, Criccieth, C & M LL52 0PH. 01766 523269.
Over 400 years old, this hotel has charm and character, together with
all the modern conveniences. Lovely views to the sea.
AE MC V — 9

LLANDRILLO: *Tyddyn Llan* ££
Llandrillo, nr Corwen, Denbigh LL21 0ST. 01490 440264. FAX 01490 440414.
Relaxed place to stay. Stylish with lovely decor and furnishings; each
bedroom individually decorated. *(See also p602.)*
MC V — 10

LLANDUDNO: *St. Tudno* ££
Promenade, Llandudno, A & C LL30 2LP. 01492 874411. FAX 01492 860407.
Regulars return time and again to this Victorian house on the seafront.
Charming and friendly. Bedrooms vary in size.
AE DC MC V — 20

LLANDUDNO: *Bodysgallen Hall* ££££
Llandudno, A & C LL30 1RS. 01492 584466. FAX 01492 582519.
One of the most attractive hotels in the country. A beautiful house,
expertly restored. Lovely garden.
AE DC MC V — 29

LLANGOLLEN: *Gales* £
18 Bridge St, Llangollen, Denbigh LL20 8PF. 01978 860089. FAX 01978 861313.
Variety of sizes and styles of rooms. Relaxed atmosphere in the wine bar
Especially lively during the International Eisteddfodd *(see p436).*
MC V — 14

LLECHWEDD: *Berthlwyd Hall* ££
Llechwedd, Conwy, C & M LL32 8DQ. 01492 592409. FAX 01492 572290.
Victorian mansion that has many of its original features. Residents' lounge
in keeping with the period. Very good French cooking.
DC MC V — 9

NANTGWYNANT: *Pen-y-Gwryd* £
Nantgwynant, C & M. 01286 870211.
Spartan accommodation and simple food in a bleak, remote spot in
Snowdonia that is nevertheless beautiful. Generous hospitality.
— 20

PENMAENPOOL: *Penmaenuchaf Hall* £££
Penmaenpool, Dolgellau, C & M LL40 1YB. 01341 422129. FAX 01341 422129.
Luxury hotel in a very peaceful spot with glorious views. Lovingly
decorated, and highly recommended food.
AE DC MC — 14

PORTMEIRION: *Portmeirion* ££££
Portmeirion, Penrhyndeudraeth, C & M LL48 6ER.
01766 770228. FAX 01766 771331.
It is a unique experience staying in this Mediterranean-style village. The
hotel itself is no disappointment. *(See also p602.)*
AE DC MC V — 35

PWLLHELI: *Plas Bodegroes* £££
Nefyn Rd, Pwllheli, C & M LL53 5TH. 01758 612363. FAX 01758 701247.
Outstandingly pretty, small Georgian manor house in a lovely setting.
Good bedrooms and top-class food. *(See also p602.)*
AE MC V — 8

TALSARNAU: *Maes-Y-Neuadd* £££
Talsarnau, nr Harlech, C & M LL47 6YA. 01766 780200. FAX 01766 780211.
Part of this gray-stone house dates back to the 14th century. Beautifully
restored affording great comfort. Good food.
AE DC MC V — 16

TALYLLYN: *Minffordd* £
Talyllyn, Twyn, C & M LL36 9AJ. 01654 761665. FAX 01654 761517.
This simple whitewashed building is a marvelous place to stay. A dramatic
location, looking across the valley to the mountains beyond.
MC V — 6

SOUTH AND MID-WALES

ABERYSTWYTH: *Conrah Country House* ££
Chancery, Aberystwyth, Cardigan SY23 4DF. 01970 617941. FAX 01970 624546.
Comfortable if quite formal country-house hotel set in over 9 ha (22 acres)
of grounds with lovely views from public rooms and bedrooms.
Very good food.
AE DC MC V — 20

For key to symbols see back flap

Price categories for a standard double room per night, inclusive of breakfast, service charges and any additional taxes such as VAT:
£ under £50
££ £50–£100
£££ £100–£150
££££ £150–£200
£££££ £200 plus.

RESTAURANT
Hotel restaurant or dining room usually open to non-residents unless otherwise stated.
CHILDREN WELCOME
Cribs and a baby-sitting service available. Some hotel restaurants have children's portions and high chairs.
GARDEN/TERRACE
Hotels with a garden, courtyard or terrace, often providing tables for eating outside.
CREDIT CARDS
Indicates which credit cards are accepted: *AE* American Express; *DC* Diners Club; *MC* Master Card/Access; *V* Visa.

		CREDIT CARDS	RESTAURANT	CHILDREN WELCOME	GARDEN/TERRACE	NUMBER OF ROOMS
BERRIEW: *Lion* Berriew, nr Welshpool, Powys SY21 8PQ. (01686 640452. FAX 01686 640604. Friendly pub in the center of the village. Great atmosphere and imaginative food. The bedrooms are quite grand. ▣ TV P	££	AE DC MC V	■		■	7
DRUIDSTONE HAVEN: *Druidstone* Druidstone Haven, nr Haverfordwest, Pembroke SA62 3NE. (01437 781221. Hotel with an artistic touch – drama and musical evenings sometimes staged. An ideal spot for families, with a beach nearby and large grounds for the children to explore. P ≥	£	AE MC V	■	●	■	13
EGLWYSFACH: *Ynyshir Hall* Eglwysfach, Machynlleth, Powys SY20 8TA. (01654 781209. FAX 01654 781366. An elegant part-Georgian country house that is run with style and panache by its management. Each room is individually styled and the cuisine is second to none. ▣ TV P	£££	AE DC MC V	■		■	8
FISHGUARD: *Manor House* Main St, Fishguard, Pembroke SA65 9HG. (01348 873260. Good value, friendly, family-run hotel overlooking the harbor. An attractive Georgian house with a pleasant restaurant. ▣ TV	£	MC V	■	●	■	6
FISHGUARD: *Three Main Street* 3 Main St, Fishguard, Pembroke SA65 9HG. (01348 874275. Informal but stylishly decorated restaurant, coffee shop and guesthouse. It has great charm, pristine bedrooms and delicious food. ▣ TV P	£		■			3
FORDEN: *Edderton Hall* Forden, Welshpool, Powys SY21 8RZ. (01938 580339. FAX 01938 580452. Attractive but slightly rundown exterior to this Georgian house. Friendly, but with an air of faded grandeur. Spacious bedrooms.	££	AE DC MC V	■		■	8
GLYNARTHEN: *Penbontbren Farm* Glynarthen, Cardigan SA44 6PE. (01239 810248. FAX 01239 811129. Part working farm, part hotel, this is a taste of rural Wales. The stone outbuildings have been converted into bedrooms. ▣ TV 24 P ≥	£	AE MC V	■	●	■	10
GOVILON: *Llanwenarth House* Govilon, Abergavenny, Cardigan NP7 9SF. (01873 830289. FAX 01873 832199. A historic country-house hotel that has an intimate atmosphere. There is a strong emphasis on personal service. ▣ TV P	££		■		■	10
GWAUN VALLEY: *Tregynon Country Farmhouse* Gwaun Valley, nr Fishguard, Pembroke SA65 9TU. (01239 820531. FAX 01239 820808. Exceptionally well-renovated, 16th-century farmhouse with many of the original beams. Pretty surroundings. ▣ TV P ≣	£	MC V	■	●	■	8
HAVERFORDWEST: *Foxdale* Glebe Lane, Marloes, Haverfordwest, Pembroke SA62 3AY. (01646 636243. Family-run, good value guest house on the cliff path, close to the island of Skomer, famous for its puffins. A must for any ornithologist. P ≣	£			●	■	4
JEFFRESTON: *Jeffreston Farmhouse* Jeffreston, nr Kilgetty, Pembroke SA68 ORE. (01646 651291. FAX 01646 651291. Converted farmhouse that is now a restaurant-with-rooms. This hotel represents good value accommodation and serves traditional, hearty fare. ▣ TV P	£	MC V	■		■	3
LLANDEGLEY: *Ffaldau Country House* Llandegley, Llandrindod Wells, Powys LD1 5UD. (01597 851421. Very attractive, comfortable, mullion-windowed guesthouse in this picturesque part of Wales. Hospitable owners. ▣ P	£	MC V	■		■	4

LLANGAMMARCH WELLS: *Lake Country House* £££
Llangammarch Wells, Powys LD4 4BS. (01591 620202. FAX 01591 620457.
An impressive Edwardian country house, stylishly decorated with elegant
public rooms and luxurious bedrooms. 🛏 TV P
AE DC MC V — 19

LLANSANFFRAID GLAN CONWY: *Old Rectory* ££
Llanddwyn Glan Conwy, Colwyn Bay, A & C LL28 5LF. (01591 610248.
Stunning views over the Conwy Estuary and an intimate atmosphere.
Tastefully decorated rooms and superb cuisine. 🛏 TV P
AE DC MC V — 6

LLANWDDYN: *Lake Vyrnwy* ££
Llanwddyn, Powys SY10 0LY. (01691 870692. FAX 01691 870259.
Ex-hunting lodge on the edge of Lake Vyrnwy – the location is stunning.
Panoramic views across the water from the restaurant. 🛏 TV P
AE DC MC — 37

LLANWRTYD WELLS: *Carlton House* £
Llanwrtyd Wells, Powys LD5 4SN. (01591 610248.
Very well run, good-value guesthouse with well-furnished rooms through-
out. Beautifully prepared, well-presented dinners. 🛏 TV
AE MC V — 6

LLANWRTYD WELLS: *Cwmirfon Lodge* £
Llanwrtyd Wells, Powys LD5 4TN. (01591 610217.
Stylish, tastefully decorated Victorian house, with an excellent standard
of personal service. Very hospitable owners. 🛏 TV P
MC V — 3

LLYSWEN: *Llangoed Hall* £££
Llyswen, Brecon, Powys LD3 0YP. (01874 754525. FAX 01874 754545.
Magnificent Edwardian country house, beautifully furnished and expertly
decorated by the family of Laura Ashley. A wide range of beautifully
cooked dishes served in the restaurant. 🛏 TV 24 P
AE MC V — 23

MILEBROOK: *Milebrook House* ££
Milebrook, Knighton, Powys LD7 1LT. (01547 528632. FAX 01547 520509.
A relaxed atmosphere in this attractively decorated house in the Teme
Valley. Bedrooms are spacious and the food is delicious. 🛏 TV
MC V — 6

PORTHKERRY: *Egerton Grey Country House* ££
Porthkerry, nr Cardiff, V of Glam CF62 3BZ. (01446 711666. FAX 01446 711690.
Part-Victorian, part-Edwardian house close to Cardiff airport, although its
size and location make it seem a million miles away. It combines both
comfort and sophistication. Excellent food. 🛏 TV P
AE DC MC V — 10

REYNOLDSTON: *Fairyhill Country House* ££
Reynoldston, Gower, Swansea SA3 1BS.
(01792 390139. FAX 01792 391358.
Stylish and civilized country-house hotel surrounded by woodland
on the Gower Peninsula. Restful and relaxing. 🛏 TV P
AE MC V — 11

ST. BRIDES WENTLOOG: *West Usk Lighthouse* £
Lighthouse Rd, St. Brides Wentloog, Newport NP1 9SF.
(01633 810126. FAX 01633 815582.
This former lighthouse is a unique and original place to stay. Pleasant
owners and an easygoing atmosphere. 🛏 TV P
AE MC V — 5

SEION LLANDDEINIOLEN: *Tyn Ross Country House* ££
Seion Llanddeiniolen, Caernarfon, C & M LL55 3AE. (01248 670489. FAX 01248 670079.
Stylishly decorated hotel with a civilized air. Good food in the
restaurant. Excellent hospitality. 🛏 TV P
AE MC V — 11

THREE COCKS: *Three Cocks* ££
Three Cocks, nr Brecon, Powys LD3 0SL. (01497 847215.
Small and friendly roadside coaching inn offering very good food.
Unfussy decor and furnishings with light, airy bedrooms. 🛏 TV P
MC V — 7

TINTERN: *Parva Farmhouse* ££
Tintern, Monmouth NP6 6SQ. (01291 689411. FAX 01291 689557.
Converted farmhouse on the banks of the Wye, immaculately neat both
inside and out. Only minutes from the ruins of Tintern Abbey. 🛏 TV P
MC V — 9

WELSH HOOK: *Stone Hall* ££
Welsh Hook, Haverfordwest, Pembroke SA62 5NS.
(013481 840212. FAX 013481 840815.
Part-14th century and set in lovely grounds, this is a welcoming hotel
with comfy rooms and very good French cooking. 🛏 TV P
AE MC V — 5

<table>
<tr><td colspan="2">

Price categories for a standard double room per night, inclusive of breakfast, service charges and any additional taxes such as VAT:
£ under £50
££ £50–£100
£££ £100–£150
££££ £150–£200
£££££ £200 plus.

RESTAURANT
Hotel restaurant or dining room usually open to non-residents unless otherwise stated.
CHILDREN WELCOME
Cribs and a baby-sitting service available. Some hotel restaurants have children's portions and high chairs.
GARDEN/TERRACE
Hotels with a garden, courtyard or terrace, often providing tables for eating outside.
CREDIT CARDS
Indicates which credit cards are accepted: *AE* American Express; *DC* Diners Club; *MC* Master Card/Access; *V* Visa.

</td></tr>
</table>

		Price	CREDIT CARDS	RESTAURANT	CHILDREN WELCOME	GARDEN/TERRACE	NUMBER OF ROOMS
WHITEBROOK: *Crown*	££		AE DC MC V	■	●		12

Whitebrook, Monmouth 0NP5 4TX. **(** 01600 860254. **FAX** 01600 860607.
Set just back from the road up in the wooded hills above the Wye valley, this is a fairly informal restaurant-with-rooms. High quality French cooking and reasonable bedrooms. 🛏 📺 24 **P**

THE LOWLANDS

AUCHENCAIRN: *Balcary Bay*	££		MC	■	●	■	17

Auchencairn, Castle Douglas, D & G D67 1Q2. **(** 01556 640217. **FAX** 01556 640272.
Family-run hotel in an excellent location on the shores of Balcary Bay. Quality of service is is shown by the fact that many visitors return here year after year. Friendly and traditional. 🛏 📺 **P**

AUCHENCAIRN: *Collin House*	££		MC V	■		■	6

Auchencairn, Castle Douglas, D&G DG7 1QN. **(** 01556 640292. **FAX** 01556 640276.
Pretty Georgian house overlooking Balcary Bay. Delightfully decorated throughout. Stylish, with excellent food. 🛏 📺 **P**

AUCHTERARDER: *Auchterarder House*	£££		AE DC MC V	■		■	15

Auchterarder PH3 1DZ. **(** 01764 663646. **FAX** 01764 662939.
A fine Victorian Baronial style house, the rooms have royal proportions but the ambience is relaxed and cozy. Very good food. 🛏 📺 24 **P** &

AUCHTERARDER: *Gleneagles*	££££		AE DC MC V	■	●	■	243

Auchterarder PH3 1NF. **(** 01764 662231. **FAX** 01764 662134.
Originally built by the Caledonian Railway Company in 1924, this hotel is nationally renowned. Huge, luxurious, brilliantly run with some of the best facilities in the country. 🛏 📺 🏊 24 **P** 🏊 &

BALQUHIDDER: *Monachyle Manor Farmhouse*	£		V	■		■	8

Balquhidder, Lochearnhead, Perth & Kinross FK19 8PQ.
(01877 384622. **FAX** 01877 384 305.
Set in extensive grounds overlooking Loch Voil, this hotel combines friendliness and high standards. Excellent restaurant and cozy bar. The area has some outstanding walks and views. 🛏 **P**

BLAIRGOWRIE: *Kinloch House*	££		AE DC MC V	■	●	■	21

Nr Blairgowrie, Perth & Kinross, Tays PH10 6SG. **(** 01250 884237. **FAX** 01250 884333.
A handsome Baronial house, this hotel's emphasis is on country pursuits. Wonderful, relaxed surroundings. Recommended restaurant. 🛏 📺 **P** &

CALLANDER: *Roman Camp*	££		AE DC MC V	■	●	■	14

Callander FK17 8BG. **(** 01877 330003. **FAX** 01877 331533.
Set in extensive gardens, but in the center of town, this is a peaceful, charming retreat with a unique atmosphere. 🛏 📺 **P**

DUNOON: *Enmore*	££		MC V	■	●	■	10

Marine Parade, Dunoon, Argyll & Bute, Strath PA23 8HH.
(01369 2230. **FAX** 01369 2148.
Very well-kept family hotel on the seafront. Cheerful and friendly, with very obliging, courteous service. 🛏 📺 **P**

EDINBURGH: *Drummond House*	££		MC V	■			3

17 Drummond Pl, Edinburgh EH3 6PL. **(** 0131 557 9189. **FAX** 0131 557 9189.
Attractive Georgian house close to the center of Edinburgh with elegant decor and furnishings. Guests dine with the owners. 🛏 **P**

EDINBURGH: *Sibbet House*	££		MC V	■	●		3

26 Northumberland St, Edinburgh EH3 6LS. **(** 0131 556 1078. **FAX** 0131 557 9445.
Friendly guesthouse in an attractive Georgian building tastefully decorated and furnished with antiques. Breakfasts are especially noteworthy. 🛏 📺 **P**

EDINBURGH: *Channings* £££ | AE DC MC V | | 48
South Learmonth Gardens, Edinburgh EH4 1EZ.
C *0131 315 2226.* **FAX** *0131 332 9631.*
Close to the city center, this hotel consists of five converted Edwardian houses. Stylish and very well kept but still homey. 🔒 📺 24 P

EDINBURGH: *Howard* ££££ | AE DC MC V | | 16
32–36 Great King St, Edinburgh EH3 6QH. **C** *0131 557 3500.* **FAX** *0131 557 6515.*
Stylish and urbane small hotel, converted from three adjoining Georgian houses. Superb facilities and exemplary service. 🔒 📺 🔖 P &

EDINBURGH: *Caledonian* £££££ | AE DC MC V | | 239
Princes St, Edinburgh EH1 2AB. **C** *0131 225 2433.* **FAX** *0131 225 6632.*
This hotel is an institution in Edinburgh. Centrally located, and a popular meeting place. Very good facilities. 🔒 📺 🔖 24 P &

GLASGOW: *Babbity Bowster* ££ | AE MC V | | 6
16–18 Blackfriars St, Glasgow G1 1PE. **C** *0141 552 5055.* **FAX** *0141 552 5215.*
Unusual hotel with immense character. Behind the finely restored Adam façade are a few simple, neat bedrooms and a relaxed, fashionable pub and restaurant. 🔒 P

GLASGOW: *Town House* ££ | MC V | | 10
4 Hughenden Terrace, Glasgow G12 9XR. **C** *0141 357 0862.* **FAX** *0141 339 9605.*
Expertly restored Victorian house, where you are assured a friendly welcome. Bedrooms have grand proportions. 🔒 📺 P

GLASGOW: *Town House* ££ | AE DC MC V | | 34
54 West George St, Glasgow G2 1NG. **C** *0141 332 3320.* **FAX** *0141 332 9756.*
Fine Edwardian building that is now a comfortable, well-run hotel in the center of Glasgow. Formerly the Royal Scottish Academy of Music, the old recital room is now the restaurant. 🔒 📺 24

GLASGOW: *Hilton* £££ | AE DC MC V | | 319
1 William St, Glasgow G1 8HT. **C** *0141 204 5555.* **FAX** *0141 204 5004.*
Large city-center hotel that is both smart and stylish. Predominantly catering for the business market, it has a very comprehensive range of facilities. 🔒 📺 🔖 24 P ≋ &

GLASGOW: *One Devonshire Gardens* ££££ | AE DC MC V | | 27
1 Devonshire Gardens, Glasgow G12 OUX. **C** *0141 339 2001.* **FAX** *0141 337 1663.*
The ultimate stylish town-hotel. Lavish furnishings and stylish decor. First class service. Excellent restaurant. *(See also p605.)* 🔒 📺 24 P

HAWKCRAIG POINT: *Hawkcraig House* £ | | | 2
Hawkcraig Point, Aberdour, Fife KY3 0TZ. **C** *01383 860335.*
Staying in this small, whitewashed, old ferryman's house is a very pleasant experience. Lovely setting and very friendly owners. 🔒 📺 P

JEDBURGH: *Hundalee House* £ | | | 5
Jedburgh, Roxburgh, Border TD8 6PA. **C** *01835 863011.*
Well-presented B&B in an attractive 18th-century house. Set in large gardens; guests are assured privacy and seclusion. 🔒 📺 P

KIRKCUDBRIGHT: *Gladstone House* ££ | MC V | | 3
48 High St, Kirkcudbright, D & G DG6 4JX. **C** *01557 331734.*
Exceptional bed-and-breakfast hotel in this appealing town. Decorated with taste, it is an attractive and civilized place to stay. 🔒 📺

MARKINCH: *Balbirnie House* £££ | AE DC MC V | | 30
Balbirnie Park, Markinch, Fife KY7 6NE. **C** *01592 610066.* **FAX** *01592 610529.*
Surrounded by extensive parkland, the setting for this Georgian mansion is outstanding. It is unashamedly luxurious, yet informal and unstuffy. 🔒 📺 24 P &

MOFFAT: *Beechwood Country House* ££ | AE MC V | | 7
Harthorpe Pl, Moffat, D & G DG10 9RS. **C** *01683 20210.* **FAX** *01683 20889.*
Family-run hotel that is friendly and efficient. Perched on a hill and surrounded by trees. Simple decor and carefree atmosphere. 🔒 📺 P

MUIRFIELD: *Greywalls* ££££ | AE DC MC V | | 22
Muirfield, Gullane, E Lothn EH31 2EG. **C** *01620 842144.* **FAX** *01620 842241.*
This place is a delight. Lovely rooms, great vistas and extreme comfort. Excellent Scottish hospitality. 🔒 📺 24 P &

For key to symbols see back flap

Price categories for a standard double room per night, inclusive of breakfast, service charges and any additional taxes such as VAT: **£** under £50 **££** £50–£100 **£££** £100–£150 **££££** £150–£200 **£££££** £200 plus.	**RESTAURANT** Hotel restaurant or dining room usually open to non-residents unless otherwise stated. **CHILDREN WELCOME** Cribs and a baby-sitting service available. Some hotel restaurants have children's portions and high chairs. **GARDEN/TERRACE** Hotels with a garden, courtyard or terrace, often providing tables for eating outside. **CREDIT CARDS** Indicates which credit cards are accepted: *AE* American Express; *DC* Diners Club; *MC* Master Card/Access; *V* Visa.	**CREDIT CARDS**	**RESTAURANT**	**CHILDREN WELCOME**	**GARDEN/TERRACE**	**NUMBER OF ROOMS**

	CREDIT CARDS	RESTAURANT	CHILDREN WELCOME	GARDEN/TERRACE	NUMBER OF ROOMS
PEEBLES: *Cringletie House* **££** Peebles, Borders EH45 8PL. **(** 01721 730233. **FAX** 01721 730244. Comfortable, reliable hotel set in large grounds that has been run successfully by the same family for years. 🚡 TV P	MC V	■	●		13
PORTPATRICK: *Crown* **££** North Crescent, Portpatrick, Stranraer DG9 8SX. **(** 01776 810261. **FAX** 01776 810551. Popular pub-hotel overlooking the harbor. Bedrooms spotless, bright and neat. Food served in the traditional-style bar and the stylish conservatory restaurant. 🚡 TV P	MC V	■	●		12
QUOTHQUAN: *Shieldhill House* **££** Quothquan, nr Biggar, Clydesdale, Strath ML12 6NA. **(** 01899 20035. **FAX** 01899 21092. Delightful hotel in a building whose origins go back to the 12th century. Elegant public rooms and spacious bedrooms. 🚡 TV P	AE DC MC V	■		■	11
ST. ANDREWS: *St. Andrews Old Course* **£££££** St. Andrews KY16 9SP. **(** 01334 474371. **FAX** 01334 477668. Not a very beautiful hotel outside but no expense has been spared inside – the result is tasteful luxury. 🚡 TV 24 P 🏊 ♿	AE DC MC	■	●		125
STEWARTON: *Chapeltoun House* **£££** Irving Rd, Stewarton, Kilmarnock & Loudoun, Strath KA3 3ED. **(** 01560 482696. **FAX** 01560 485100. Country-house hotel decorated with understated elegance. Friendly and hospitable and in peaceful surroundings. 🚡 TV P	AE MC V	■		■	8
STRACHUR: *Creggans Inn* **££** Strachur, Argyll & Bute, Strath PA27 8BX. **(** 0136 986 279. **FAX** 0136 986 637. Convivial inn in a superb spot overlooking Loch Fyne. Pretty bedrooms. Excellent food in the formal restaurant or at the bar. 🚡 TV P ♿	AE DC MC	■	●	■	21
TURNBERRY: *Turnberry* **£££££** Turnberry, Kilmarnock & Loudoun, Strath KA26 9LT. **(** 01655 331000. **FAX** 01655 331706. Huge Edwardian hotel and health spa refurbished to luxurious standards. What it lacks in atmosphere it makes up in comfort. 🚡 TV 24 P 🏊 ♿	AE DC MC V	■	●		132
WALKERBURN: *Tweed Valley* **££** Walkerburn, nr Peebles, Tweeddale, Border EH43 6AA. **(** 01896 870636. **FAX** 01896 870639. Family hotel with an emphasis on relaxation and comfort, close to the village and River Tweed. A lovely location. 🚡 TV P	MC V	■	●	■	16

THE HIGHLANDS AND ISLANDS

	CREDIT CARDS	RESTAURANT	CHILDREN WELCOME	GARDEN/TERRACE	NUMBER OF ROOMS
ACHILTIBUIE: *Summer Isles* **££** Achiltibuie, nr Ullapool, Ross & Cromarty, Highl IV26 2YG. **(** 01854 622282. **FAX** 01854 622251. Special hotel that meets all expectations. Well-appointed rooms and superb restaurant. Breathtaking views to the Summer Isles. 🚡 P		■		■	12
ARISAIG: *Arisaig House* **£££** Beasdale, nr Arisaig, Inverness, Highl PH39 4NR. **(** 01687 450622. **FAX** 01687 450626. Dour exterior but a bright, cheerful interior. Smart, stylish public rooms and pleasant bedrooms. Pretty gardens and good restaurant. 🚡 TV P	AE MC V	■		■	14
BALLATER: *Tullich Lodge* **£££** Ballater, Angus, Grampn AB35 5SB. **(** 013397 55406. **FAX** 013397 55397. A highly unusual hotel specializing in delicious food. The individually decorated rooms are very appealing. 🚡 TV P	AE DC MC V	■		■	10

BALLINDALLOCH: *Delnashaugh Inn* €€€ | MC V | 9
Ballindalloch, Banff & Buchan, Grampn AB37 9AS.
(01807 500255. **FAX** 01807 500389.
Overlooking the River Avon in the Spey valley, this hotel makes a perfect base for exploring the area. Good food. 🖼 TV P &

BRAE: *Busta House* €€ | AE DC MC V | 20
Busta, Brae, Shetld ZE2 9QN. **(** 01806 522506. **FAX** 01806 522588.
Very civilized, family-run hotel. Beside its own little harbor, this early 18th-century house offers a relaxed and comfortable stay. 🖼 TV P

BUNESSAN: *Ardfenaig House* €€€ | MC V | 5
Nr Bunessan, Isle of Mull, Strath PA67 6DX. **(** 01681 700210. **FAX** 01681 700210.
In a superb position at the head of Loch Caol in the southwest of the island. Comfortable rooms with great views. Many different types of sports can be enjoyed here. 🖼 P

CRINAN: *Crinan Hotel* €€€ | AE MC V | 20
Crinan, Strath PA31 8SR. **(** 01546 83 261. **FAX** 01546 83 209.
Hotel in a superb position on the harbor where the Firth of Cromarty meets the Atlantic Ocean. An ideal spot to watch boats come and go is from the rooftop restaurant. 🖼 TV 🔼 P

CROMARTY: *Royal* €€ | AE MC V | 10
Marine Terrace, Cromarty, Ross & Cromarty, Highl IV11 8YN. **(** 01381 600217.
Overlooking the Firth of Cromarty, this friendly, unpretentious hotel has a traditional feel. Well-decorated bedrooms. 🖼 TV P

DERVAIG: **DRUIMNACROISH COUNTRY HOUSE** €€€ | AE DC MC V | 6
Druimnacroish, Dervaig, Isle of Mull, Strath PA75 6QW.
(016884 274. **FAX** 016884 311.
Relax in this converted farmhouse in a peaceful and beautiful spot on the historic Isle of Mull. Spacious rooms. 🖼 TV 24 P

DUNKELD: *Kinnaird* €€€€ | AE MC V | 99
Kinnaird Estate, nr Dunkeld, Tays PH8 OLB.
(01796 482440. **FAX** 01796 482289.
Surrounded by a vast, beautiful country estate, this 18th-century house has recently been converted into a luxury hotel where no expense has been spared. Sumptuous. *(See also p606.)* 🖼 TV 🔼

DUNVEGAN: *Harlosh House* €€ | MC V | 6
Nr Dunvegan, Isle of Skye, Highl IV55 8ZG. **(** 01470 521367. **FAX** 01470 521367.
This small hotel provides a friendly, peaceful base for exploring the island of Skye. Very good food. Situated in a superb location on the shores of Loch Bracadale. 🖼 P

ELGIN: *Mansion House And Country Club* €€€ | AE DC MC V | 22
The Haugh, Elgin, Moray, Grampn IV30 1AW.
(01343 548811. **FAX** 01343 547916.
Imposing Victorian mansion which also has a leisure and country club. Welcoming and unpretentious. 🖼 TV 24 P 🏊

GRANTOWN-ON-SPEY: *Culdearn House* €€ | DC MC V | 9
Woodlands Terrace, Grantown-on-Spey, Moray, Grampn PH26 3JU.
(01479 872106. **FAX** 01479 873641.
Traditionally decorated Victorian villa with friendly, welcoming owners. Highland dancing displays are put on regularly. 🖼 TV P

INVERNESS: *Dunain Park* €€€ | AE DC MC | 14
Inverness IV3 6JN. **(** 01463 230512. **FAX** 01463 224532.
Surrounded by a large garden and close to Inverness, this hotel is a convenient and peaceful base for the area. Pleasant staff and comfortable standards. 🖼 TV P 🏊 &

ISLE OF IONA: *Argyll* €€ | MC V | 17
Isle of Iona, Strath PA76 6SJ. **(** 01681 700334. **FAX** 01681 700334.
Unpretentious, friendly hotel on this very special island. Simple, unfussy style throughout. Ask for a bedroom facing the sea. 🖼 P

ISLE OF ORNSAY: *Eilean Iarmain* €€ | AE MC V | 12
Sleat, Isle of Skye, Highl IV43 8QR. **(** 0147833 332. **FAX** 0147833 275.
Traditional 19th-century seaside inn with a Gaelic feel. Wonderful views from the comfy bedrooms and public rooms. 🖼 P

<table>
<tr><td colspan="2">

Price categories for a standard double room per night, inclusive of breakfast, service charges and any additional taxes such as VAT:
£ under £50
££ £50–£100
£££ £100–£150
££££ £150–£200
£££££ £200 plus.

</td><td>

RESTAURANT
Hotel restaurant or dining room usually open to non-residents unless otherwise stated.
CHILDREN WELCOME
Cribs and a baby-sitting service available. Some hotel restaurants have children's portions and high chairs.
GARDEN/TERRACE
Hotels with a garden, courtyard or terrace, often providing tables for eating outside.
CREDIT CARDS
Indicates which credit cards are accepted: *AE* American Express; *DC* Diners Club; *MC* Master Card/Access; *V* Visa.

</td></tr>
</table>

	CREDIT CARDS	RESTAURANT	CHILDREN WELCOME	GARDEN/TERRACE	NUMBER OF ROOMS
KENTALLEN OF APPIN: *Ardsheal House* **££** Kentallen of Appin, Argyll & Bute, Strath PA38 4BX. 📞 01631 740227. **FAX** 01631 740342. Set above the shores of Loch Linnhe, with stunning views. Very hospitable. Both bedrooms and public rooms are well furnished. 🏠 **P**	AE MC V	■	●		13
KILDRUMMY: *Kildrummy Castle* **£££** Kildrummy, nr Alford, Gordon, Grampn AB33 8RA. 📞 019755 71288. **FAX** 019755 71345. Large, rather stately Victorian castellated building. Set in lovely gardens overlooking a 13th-century castle ruin. Elegant decor. 🏠 TV **P**	AE MC V	■	●		16
KILMORE: *Glenfeochan House* **£££** Kilmore, nr Oban, Argyll & Bute, Strath PA34 4QR. 📞 01631 770273. **FAX** 01631 770624. Painstakingly restored turreted Victorian building with beautiful garden. Guests are made to feel very welcome. 🏠 TV 24 **P**	MC V	■		■	3
KIRKWALL: *Foveran* **££** St. Ola, Kirkwall, Orkney KW15 1SF. 📞 01856 872389. **FAX** 01856 876430. Modern hotel with great views over Scapa Flow and the South Isles. Small but comfortable rooms and a good restaurant. 🏠 TV 24 **P** 🚻	MC V	■	●		8
LARGS: *Brisbane House* **££** 14 Greenock Rd, Esplanade, Largs, Strath KA30 8NF. 📞 01475 6867200. **FAX** 01475 676295. Attractive 18th-century house completely modernized to make it chic and stylish. Some of the rooms look over the Firth of Clyde. 🏠 TV 24 **P**	AE DC MC V			■	23
LEDAIG: *Isle of Eriska* **££££** Ledaig, nr Oban, Argyll & Bute, Strath PA37 1SD. 📞 01631 720 371. **FAX** 01631 720 531. Situated on its very own island, this grand, 19th-century Baronial hall has charming rooms. Service in the dining room is formal in the evenings and guests are expected to change for dinner. 🏠 TV 24 **P** 🏊 🚻	MC V	■	●	■	17
MARNOCH: *Old Manse of Marnoch* **££** Bridge Of Marnoch, nr Huntly, Gordon, Grampn AB54 5RS. 📞 01466 780873. **FAX** 01466 780873. Very attractive part-Georgian, part-Edwardian house, decorated with flair and style. Bedrooms are very comfortable. 🏠 TV 24 **P**	MC V	■		■	5
MUIR OF ORD: *Dower House* **££** Highfield, Muir of Or, Inverness, Highl IV6 7XN. 📞 01463 870090. **FAX** 01463 870090. Extremely agreeable small hotel that is attractively decorated. Pleasing bedrooms and a first-rate restaurant. 🏠 TV **P**	MC V	■	●	■	5
NAIRN: *Clifton House* **££** Nairn, Highl IV12 4HW. 📞 01667 453119. **FAX** 01667 452836. Individual town-hotel, decorated and furnished with style and flair. The restaurant comes highly recommended. 🏠 **P**	AE DC MC V	■		■	12
OBAN: *Knipoch* **£££** Kilninver, nr Oban, Argyll PA34 4QT 📞 01852 316251. **FAX** 01852 316249. Panoramic views across Loch Feochan from this expertly restored 16th-century house. Pristine bedrooms and charming service. 🏠 TV **P**	AE DC MC V	■	●	■	17
PITLOCHRY: *Atholl Palace* **££** Pitlochry, Perth & Kinross, Tays PH16 5LY. 📞 01796 472400. **FAX** 01796 473036. Huge and grandiose hotel, though somewhat overbearing, that is an excellent example of Scottish Baronial architecture. Vast rooms with various styles of decor and furnishings. 🏠 TV **P** 🏊 🚻	AE DC MC V	■	●	■	79

PORT APPIN: *Airds* £££ AE MC V 12
Port Appin, Appin, Argyll & Bute, Strath PA38 4DF.
(01631 730236. FAX 01631 7302535.
A former ferry inn with a modest whitewashed exterior. Inside it is stylish and comfortable. Very good restaurant. (See also p607.) 🔒 TV P

PORTREE: *Viewfield House* £ MC V 11
Portree, Isle of Skye, Highl IV51 9EU. (01478 612217. FAX 01478 613517.
200-year-old family house. Guests are made very welcome in this rambling building where everyone dines together. 🔒 P

SCARISTA: *Scarista House* ££ 8
Isle of Harris, Highl PA85 3HX. (01859 550238. FAX 01859 550277.
A Georgian manse provides an extremely agreeable retreat. Set in a wonderfully remote spot overlooking a beach. Delicious food. 🔒 P

SCONE: *Murrayshall House And Golf Course* £££ AE DC MC V 19
Scone, Perth & Kinross, Tays PH2 7PH. (01738 551171. FAX 01738 552595.
Turreted, Baronial hall set in its own golf course. Formal, starchy rooms but luxuriously comfortable. Excellent food served in the restaurant. 🔒 TV 24 P

SHIELDAIG: *Tigh-Eilean* ££ MC V 11
Shieldaig, nr Strathcarron, Ross & Cromarty, Highl IV54 8XN.
(01520 755251. FAX 01520 755321.
On the banks of Loch Shieldaig, this is one of the best small hotels in Scotland. Very comfortable, with charming owners and a high standard of both food and service. 🔒 P

THURSO: *Forss House* ££ AE MC V 7
Thurso, Caithness, Highl KW14 7XY. (01847 861 201. FAX 01847 861 301.
Welcoming hotel in the wilds of the northern coast. Imposing on the outside, but inside it is comfortable and cheerful. 🔒 TV 24 P

TIMSGARRY: *Baile Na Cille* £ MC V 14
Timsgarry, Isle of Lewis, Highl PA86 9JD. (01851 672 242. FAX 01851 672 241.
Very easy-going, friendly hotel in an amazing location at the end of a long beach. A perfect place to get away from it all. 🔒 P

TORLUNDY: *Inverlochy Castle* £££££ AE MC V 17
Torlundy, Fort William, Inverness, Highl PH33 6SN.
(01397 702177. FAX 01397 702953.
Superbly run country-house hotel. Fine, elegant rooms with beautiful furniture and high ceilings. Huge luxurious bedrooms. 🔒 TV 24 P

TUMMEL BRIDGE: *Kynachan Lodge* ££ MC V 6
Tummel Bridge, Pitlochry, Perth & Kinross, Tays PH16 5SB.
(01882 634214. FAX 01882 634316.
Former sporting lodge now a peaceful, very well-kept hotel. Surrounded by landscaped grounds, with a loch and the hills beyond. 🔒 TV P

ULLAPOOL: *Altnaharrie Inn* ££ MC V 8
Ullapool, Ross & Cromarty, Highl IV26 2SS. (01854 633230.
Reached by boat from Ullapool, this hotel will guarantee you tranquil panoramic views. Staying here is a special experience. Good food. No smoking allowed. (See also p607.) 🔒 P

ULLAPOOL: *Ceilidh Place* ££ AE DC MC V 13
14 West Argyle St, Ullapool, Ross & Cromarty, Highl LV26 2TY.
(01854 612103. FAX 01854 612886.
Lots going on here – musical evenings and exhibitions. There is also a café and bookstore. Residents can escape the hurly-burly to their own peaceful sitting room. 🔒 P

WALLS: *Burrastow House* ££ 5
Walls, Shetl ZE2 9PB. (0159571 307. FAX 0159571 213.
Hotel in a very remote part of western Shetland. This is a wonderful place to escape to absolute calm and tranquility. Comfort is not sacrificed here, and the food is delicious. 🔒 P

WHITEBRIDGE: *Knockie Lodge* ££ DC MC V 10
Whitebridge, Inverness, Highl IV1 2UP. (01456 486276. FAX 01456 486389.
Outstanding setting for this former hunting lodge above Loch Nan Lann. Nothing for miles – you can enjoy the good food undisturbed. 🔒 P

For key to symbols see back flap

WHERE TO EAT

BRITISH FOOD need strike no terrors to the visiting gourmet's heart; the UK's restaurant scene has moved far from its once dismal reputation. This is partly due to an influx of foreign chefs and cooking styles; you can now sample a wide range of international cuisine throughout Britain, with the greatest choice in London and the other major cities. Home-grown restaurateurs have risen to the challenge of redeeming British food too, and the indigenous cooking (once thought to consist only of fish and chips, overcooked vegetables, meat pies and

Michelin Man at Bibendum, London

lumpy custard) has improved out of all recognition in the last decade. You can now also eat extremely well in Britain whatever your budget – and at most times of day in the towns. Much less elaborate, but well-prepared, affordable food is making a mark in all types of brasseries, restaurants and cafés throughout the country; more modern approaches combine fresh produce and dietary common sense with influences from around the world. The restaurant listings *(see pp578–607)* feature some of the very best places as well as those with a steady track record.

WHAT'S ON THE MENU?

THE CHOICE seems endless in large cities, particularly London. Cuisines from all over the world are represented, as well as their infinite variations – Thai and Tex-Mex, Turkish and Tuscan, Tandoori, Bhel Poori and Balti. There are many more unusual styles of cooking such as Hungarian, Polish, Caribbean and Pacific Rim. French and Italian restaurants are still highly regarded, offering everything from pastries and espresso coffee to the highest standards of *haute cuisine*. Outside the major cities the food scene is more limited, but most towns will have at least a couple of Italian,

Indian and Chinese restaurants. The vague term "modern-international cuisine" adopted by many restaurants disguises a conglomeration of styles. The spectrum ranges from French to Asian recipes, loosely characterized by the imaginative use of fresh, high-quality ingredients, which are cooked simply with imaginative seasonings.

Nostalgic yearnings for British food have produced a revival of hearty traditional dishes such as steak and kidney pie and treacle pudding *(see p37)*, although "Modern British" cooking adopts a lighter, more innovative approach to old-fashioned stodge. The distinctions between this and Modern

International food are starting to blur, which is mostly a change for the better as young chefs apply oriental and Mediterranean flavors to homegrown ingredients.

BREAKFAST

IT USED TO BE SAID that the best way to enjoy British food was to eat breakfast three times a day. Traditional British breakfast starts with cereal and milk followed by bacon, eggs and tomato, perhaps with fried black pudding *(see p37)* in the North and Scotland. It is finished off with toast and marmalade washed down with tea. Or you can just have black coffee and fruit juice, with a croissant or two (known as continental breakfast in hotels). The price of breakfast is often included in hotel bills in Britain.

LUNCH

MANY RESTAURANTS offer light lunches at fixed prices, often only two courses (choose either an appetizer or dessert). The most popular lunchtime foods are sandwiches, salads, baked potatoes with fillings and plowman's lunches, the latter found mainly in pubs. A traditional Sunday lunch of roast chicken, lamb or beef is served in some pubs and restaurants.

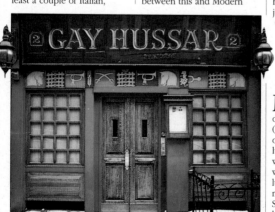

The Gay Hussar, London, a top Hungarian restaurant *(see p578)*

AFTERNOON TEA

No visitor should miss the experience of a proper English afternoon tea, which rivals breakfast as the most enjoyable meal of the day *(see p34)*. Some of the most palatial teas are offered by country houses and top London hotels such as the Ritz or Browns. The area that is best known for its classic "cream teas" is the West Country *(see p271)*; these always include scones, spread with clotted cream, butter and jam. Wales, Scotland, Yorkshire and the Lake District also offer tasty teas with regional variations; in the North Country a slice of apple pie or fruit cake is served hot with a piece of North Yorkshire Wensleydale cheese on top.

An afternoon tea including sandwiches, cakes and scones

DINNER

At dinner time, the better restaurants and hotels offer elaborately staged meals, sometimes billed as five or six courses (though one may be simply a sorbet, or coffee with *petits fours*). Dessert is often followed by cheese and crackers. Confusingly, in the North of England and Scotland "lunch" can be called "dinner" and "dinner" may be called "tea."

Generally, you can choose to take your dinner before 6pm or after 9pm only in larger towns, where there is a broad choice of ethnic restaurants, bars and all-day brasseries, which often stay open late.

Leith Docks in Edinburgh, a center of good pubs, bars and restaurants

PLACES TO EAT

Eating places are extremely varied, with brasseries, bistros, wine bars, tearooms, *tapas* bars and theater cafés now competing with the more conventional cafés and restaurants. Many pubs also now serve excellent bar food at reasonable prices *(see pp608–11)*.

BRASSERIES, BISTROS AND CAFÉS

French-style café-brasseries are now popular in Britain. Sometimes they stay open all day, serving coffee, snacks and fairly simple dishes along with a selection of beers and wines. Alcoholic drinks, however, may only be available at certain times of day. The atmosphere is usually young and urbane, with decor to match. Drinks such as imported bottled beers, exotic spirits or cocktails may be fairly expensive.

The interior of the Tate Gallery café, St. Ives, Cornwall *(see p591)*

Wine bars are similar to brasseries, but with a better selection of wines, that may include English varieties *(see pp146–47)*. Some bars have a good range of ciders and real ales as well *(see p34)*. Bistros are another French import, serving full meals at lunch and dinner time with less formality and more moderate prices than you would expect at a restaurant. Expect to pay anything from £12 to £30 ($18 to $47) for a standard three-course meal in a bistro.

RESTAURANTS-WITH-ROOMS AND HOTELS

Restaurants-with-rooms are a new breed of small establishments with a handful of bedrooms and usually excellent food. They tend to be expensive and are usually in rural locations.

Many hotel restaurants happily serve nonresidents. They are often expensive, but the best can be unparalleled. Hotels serving a high standard of food are included in the hotel listings.

RESTAURANT ETIQUETTE

As a rule of thumb, the more expensive the restaurant, the more formal the dress code – though few restaurants today will expect men to wear a coat and tie. If you are not sure, call first.

Some establishments do not allow smoking at all, while others now have separate sections or tables for people who wish to smoke.

Raymond Blanc's Le Manoir Aux Quat'Saisons *(see p586)*, one of Britain's most acclaimed restaurants-with-rooms

ALCOHOL

Britain's laws concerning the sale of alcohol, the "licensing laws," were once among the most restrictive in Europe. Now they are more relaxed, but some establishments may still only serve alcohol at set times with food. Some unlicensed restaurants operate a "Bring Your Own" policy. A corkage fee is often charged. The Scottish laws are different from the rest of Britain, most apparent in the later closing times of pubs.

VEGETARIAN FOOD

Britain is ahead of many of its European counterparts in providing vegetarian alternatives to meat dishes. A few of our selections serve only vegetarian meals, but most cater to carnivores as well. Vegetarians who want a wider choice should seek out South Indian, Chinese and other ethnic restaurants, which have a tradition of vegetarian cuisine.

FAST FOOD

Fast food comes much cheaper, usually well under £10. Apart from the numerous individually owned fish and chip shops, there are many fast food chains in Britain, such as McDonald's, Burger King, Pizza Hut and KFC.

Sandwich bars are very popular, and are often good value; some also have seating. Budget cafés, nicknamed "greasy spoons," serve simple, inexpensive food, often in the form of endless variations of the fried breakfast *(see p36)*.

Betty's Café in Harrogate *(see p598)*

BOOKING AHEAD

It is always safer to book a table first before making a special trip to a restaurant; city restaurants can be very busy and some of the more renowned establishments can be fully booked a month in advance. If you cannot keep a reservation, you should call up and cancel. A lot of restaurants operate on knife-edge profit margins, and customers not turning up can threaten their livelihood.

CHECKING THE BILL

All restaurants are required by law to display their current prices outside the door. These amounts include Value Added Tax (VAT), currently at 17.5 percent. Service and cover charges (if any) are also specified, so you should have a rough idea of what a meal may cost beforehand.

Wine is always pricey in Britain, and extras like coffee or bottled water can be disproportionately expensive.

Service charges (usually between 10 percent and 15 percent) are sometimes automatically added to your bill. If you feel that the service has been poor, you are entitled to subtract this service charge. If no service charge has been added, you are expected to add 10 to 15 percent to the bill, but it is your decision.

Some restaurants may leave the "total" box of credit card slips blank, hoping customers will add something extra to the service charge. Another growing trend is for smart restaurants to boost their sagging profit margins with a "cover charge" for flowers, bread and butter, etc. Live entertainment may also be costed. The majority of restaurants accept credit cards, or travelers' checks with an I.D. card, but pubs and cafés expect cash – do not rely on plastic.

MEALTIMES

BREAKFAST IS A MOVABLE feast. It may be as early as 6:30am in a city business hotel (most hoteliers will make special arrangements if you have a plane to catch or some other reason for checking out early) or as late as 10:30am in relaxed country house establishments. Few hoteliers relish cooking bacon and eggs that late, however, and some insist you are up and about by 9:00 sharp if you want anything to eat. But you can find breakfast all day long in some urban restaurants. The American concept of Sunday "brunch" (a leisurely halfway house between breakfast and lunch) is becoming increasingly popular in some hotels, restaurants and cafés.

Lunch in pubs and restaurants is usually served between 12:30pm and 2:30pm. Try to arrive in time to order the main course before 1:30pm, or you may find choice restricted and service peremptory. Most tourist areas have plenty of cafés, fast-food diners and coffee bars where you can have a snack at any time of day. During peak hours there may be a minimum charge.

If you are lucky enough to be in one of the places where you can get a traditional afternoon tea, it is usually served between 3pm and 5pm.

Dinner is usually served from 7pm until 10pm; some places, especially ethnic restaurants, stay open later. In guest houses or small hotels, dinner may be served at a specific time (sometimes uncomfortably early).

CHILDREN

THE CONTINENTAL NORM of dining out *en famille* is steadily becoming more acceptable in Britain, and visiting a restaurant may no longer entail endless searches for a baby-sitter. Many places welcome junior diners, and some actively encourage families, at least during the

L'Artiste Musculé wine bar-bistro *(see p578)*, London

Ice cream parlor sign

day or early evening. Formal restaurants sometimes cultivate a more adult ambience at dinner time, and some impose age limits. If you want to take young children to a restaurant, ask when you book. Italian, Spanish, Indian, fast-food restaurants and ice cream parlors nearly always welcome children, and sometimes provide special menus or high chairs for them. Even traditional English pubs, which were once a strictly adult preserve, are now relaxing their rules to accommodate families and may even provide special rooms or play areas.

The places that welcome children are indicated in the pubs guide *(see pp608–11)*. The restaurant listings also indicate which establishments cater to children's needs.

DISABLED ACCESS

AS IN MOST WALKS of life, restaurant facilities in Britain could be better for disabled visitors, but things are gradually improving. Modern premises usually take account of mobility problems, but it's always best to check first if you have special needs.

PICNICS

EATING OUTSIDE is becoming more popular in Britain, though it is more likely that you will find tables outside pubs in the form of a beer garden, than outdoor restaurants. One inexpensive option is to make up your own picnic; most towns have good delicatessens and bakeries where you can buy supplies, and in Britain you do not usually have to worry about shops closing at midday as they often do on the Continent.

Look for street markets to pick up fresh fruit and local cheeses at bargain prices. Department stores like Marks & Spencer and supermarkets such as Sainsbury's and Tesco often sell an excellent range of prepacked sandwiches and snacks; large towns usually have several sandwich bars to choose from. Your hotel or guest house may also be able to provide a packed lunch. Ask for it the night before.

An option for a cooler day is a hot take-out meal; fish and chips with salt and vinegar all wrapped in paper is not only a British cliché but also a national institution.

Eating alfresco at Grasmere in the Lake District

Choosing a Restaurant

Tʜᴇ ʀᴇsᴛᴀᴜʀᴀɴᴛs in this guide have been selected across a wide range of price categories for their good value, exceptional food and interesting location. This chart lists the restaurants by region, starting with London. Use the color-coded thumb tabs, which indicate the regions covered on each page, to guide you to the relevant sections of the chart.

	CREDIT CARDS	CHILDREN WELCOME	FIXED-PRICE MENU	VEGETARIAN	OUTDOOR TABLES
LONDON					
WEST END & WESTMINSTER: *Mildred's*. **Map** 4 E5. **(£)** 58 Greek St W1. 0171-494 1634. Excellent international vegetarian food. Table-sharing is the norm. Have a drink in the local pub first; staff will find you. ● Sun.				●	■
WEST END & WESTMINSTER: *L'Artiste Musculé*. **Map** 5 C1. **(£)** 1 Shepherd Market W1. 0171-493 6150. French-style bar and pavement café with additional seating in the basement. Intimate atmosphere. Daily specials chalked on the blackboard. ● public hols.	AE DC MC V		■	●	■
WEST END & WESTMINSTER: *Harbour City*. **Map** 4 E5. **(£)(£)** 46 Gerrard St W1. 0171-439 7859. Astonishing *dim sum* is served at lunchtimes by urbane staff. Very popular with local Cantonese families and business people.	AE DC MC V	●	■		
WEST END & WESTMINSTER: *Jade Garden*. **Map** 4 D5. **(£)(£)** 15 Wardour St W1. 0171-287 0626. A popular lunch time *dim sum* place. Patient service and top-quality food. At dinner time, try the fish on the *à la carte* menu. ● public hols.	AE MC V	●	■		
WEST END & WESTMINSTER: *Melati*. **Map** 4 D5. **(£)(£)** 21 Great Windmill St W1. 0171-734 6964. Authentic Indonesian cuisine on three bustling floors with swift service. Try the Singapore *laksa*. Book ahead, or be prepared to line up. ● public hols.	AE DC MC V	●	■	●	
WEST END & WESTMINSTER: *Alfred*. **Map** 4 D5. **(£)(£)(£)** 245 Shaftesbury Ave WC2. 0171-240 2566. This new breed British restaurant serves imaginative modern dishes as well as traditional classics. Decor has a stylish 1940s feel. ● public hols.	AE DC MC V	●	■		■
WEST END & WESTMINSTER: *Bahn Thai*. **Map** 4 E5. **(£)(£)(£)** 21A Frith St W1. 0171-437 8504. The mainstream Thai dishes are excellent. Try *tom yum* (soup) or *pad Thai* (noodles). Chili heat of dishes is marked on the menu. The wine list is unusually good, as is the Thai beer. ● public hols.	AE DC MC V	●		●	
WEST END & WESTMINSTER: *Bertorelli's*. **Map** 4 E5. **(£)(£)(£)** 44A Floral St WC2. 0171-836 3969. This slick Italian operation in Covent Garden is used to pretheater diners. Upstairs a grander restaurant, downstairs a simpler café. ● Sun.	AE DC MC V			●	
WEST END & WESTMINSTER: *Bistrot Bruno*. **Map** 4 D5. **(£)(£)(£)** 63 Frith St W1. 0171-734 4545. Oustandingly creative cookery using eclectic combinations of ingredients. Bruno's cooking is influenced by the flavors of his native South of France. Informal atmosphere. Fish dishes are especially recommended. ● Sat L, Sun.	AE DC MC V				
WEST END & WESTMINSTER: *Café Fish*. **Map** 6 E1. **(£)(£)(£)** 39 Panton St SW1. 0171-930 3999. This seafood restaurant-wine bar offers simple appetizers, creamy main courses and bargain house champagnes. ● Sun.	AE DC MC				■
WEST END & WESTMINSTER: *Gay Hussar*. **Map** 4 E5. **(£)(£)(£)** 2 Greek St W1. 0171-437 0973. London's only Hungarian eaterie. Specialties include chilled wild cherry soup, stuffed cabbage, pressed boar's head and cold pike. ● public hols.	AE		■		
WEST END & WESTMINSTER: *Gopal's*. **Map** 4 D5. **(£)(£)(£)** 12 Bateman St W1. 0171-434 1621. Small but excellent Indian restaurant for the curry lover. Unusual dishes include *meenu* – fish curry from Karnataka. ● public hols.	AE DC MC V		■	●	

Price categories include a three-course meal for one, half a bottle of house wine, and all unavoidable extra charges such as cover, service, VAT **£** under £15 **££** £15–£25 **£££** £25–£35 **££££** £35–£50 **£££££** over £50	**CHILDREN WELCOME** Restaurants that offer smaller portions and high chairs for children. Special menus sometimes available. **FIXED-PRICE MENU** A good value fixed-price meal, at lunch, dinner or both, usually of three courses. **VEGETARIAN** Vegetarian specialties served, sometimes for both appetizers and main courses. **CREDIT CARDS** Indicates which credit cards are accepted: *AE* American Express; *DC* Diners Club; *MC* Master Card/Access; *V* Visa.	**CREDIT CARDS**	**CHILDREN WELCOME**	**FIXED-PRICE MENU**	**VEGETARIAN**	**OUTDOOR TABLES**
WEST END & WESTMINSTER: *Al Hamra*. **Map** 5 C1. **£££** 31–33 Shepherd Market W1. (0171-493 1954. There are over 40 *meze* dishes to sample at this smart Lebanese restaurant, plus lots of grills. Service is formal. In summer there is a large open-air terrace. Great atmosphere. ● *Dec 25 , Jan 1.*		AE DC MC V	●		●	■
WEST END & WESTMINSTER: *Manzi's*. **Map** 4 E5. **£££** 1–2 Leicester St WC2. (0171-734 0224. Old-fashioned and run by the family since 1928, Manzi's offers seafood cooked to order. House wine is the best value. ● *public hols.*		AE DC MC V				
WEST END & WESTMINSTER: *Orso*. **Map** 4 F5. **£££** 27 Wellington St WC2. (0171-240 5269. Brisk, but friendly service at this media and theater meeting place. The food is modern and constantly changing. Noted for its pasta and bold, colorful sauces. ● *public hols.* ▮						
WEST END & WESTMINSTER: *Sri Siam*. **Map** 4 E5. **£££** 14 Old Compton St W1. (0171-434 3544. Perfect for a Thai first-timer. Try the mixed appetizers, and any of the seafood dishes. The set lunch menu is a bargain. ● *public hols.*		AE DC MC V		■	●	
WEST END & WESTMINSTER: *Stephen Bull*. **Map** 3 B4. **£££** 5–7 Blandford St W1. (0171-486 9696. Stylish decor and excellent modern-international food, such as crab and orange ravioli with basil, cream and cuttlefish risotto. ● *Sat L, Sun.* ⓖ		MC V	●			
WEST END & WESTMINSTER: *Alastair Little*. **Map** 4 E5. **££££** 49 Frith St W1. (0171-734 5183. Modern-international dishes in this spartan setting include tournedos with *polenta*, plus anything with a relish. ● *Sat L, Sun, public hols.* ⓖ		AE MC V		■		
WEST END & WESTMINSTER: *Le Caprice*. **Map** 5 C1. **££££** Arlington House, Arlington St SW1. (0171-629 2239. Simple, modern grills attract stars to this high-profile sister of The Ivy *(see below)*. No thick sauces. Book well in advance. ● *public hols.* ⓖ		AE DC MC V				
WEST END & WESTMINSTER: *Greenhouse*. **Map** 5 B1. **££££** 27A Hay's Mews W1. (0171-499 3331. This elegant restaurant spruces up old-fashioned British food such as faggots (meatballs) in gravy and steamed sponge puddings. ● *Sun D, Tue–Sat L.*		AE DC MC V				
WEST END & WESTMINSTER: *The Ivy*. **Map** 4 E5. **££££** 1 West St WC2. (0171-836 4751. A fashionable spot for first-night parties. Modern-international favorites include fishcakes with arugula and Parmesan salad. ⓖ		AE DC MC V				
WEST END & WESTMINSTER: *Quaglino's*. **Map** 6 D1. **££££** 16 Bury St SW1. (0171-930 6767. Terence Conran's bustling flagship offers Modern-international food in a very stylish setting. Very popular, book in advance to guarantee a table. The service can sometimes be terse. ● *public hols.* ▶		AE DC MC V		■		
WEST END & WESTMINSTER: *Pied-à-Terre*. **Map** 4 D4. **£££££** 34 Charlotte St W1. (0171-636 1178. The decor is stark but the French menu (seafood and meat) is sybaritic. The food is of the highest quality, although a formal atmosphere prevails. ● *Sat L, Sun, mid-Aug–Sep 1.*		AE DC MC V		■		
WEST END & WESTMINSTER: *Suntory*. **Map** 6 D1. **£££££** 72–73 St. James's St SW1. (0171-409 0201. Immaculate presentation and impeccable service from Britain's top Japanese restaurant. Private *tatami* rooms are available. ● *public hols.*		AE DC MC V		■		

For key to symbols see back flap

<table>
<tr><td colspan="2">

Price categories include a three-course meal for one, half a bottle of house wine, and all unavoidable extra charges such as cover, service, VAT
£ under £15
££ £15-£25
£££ £25-£35
££££ £35-£50
£££££ over £50

</td><td colspan="2">

CHILDREN WELCOME
Restaurants that offer smaller portions and high chairs for children. Special menus sometimes available.
FIXED-PRICE MENU
A good value fixed-price meal, at lunch, dinner or both, usually of three courses.
VEGETARIAN
Vegetarian specialties served, sometimes for both appetizers and main courses.
CREDIT CARDS
Indicates which credit cards are accepted: AE American Express; DC Diners Club; MC Master Card/Access; V Visa.

</td></tr>
</table>

	CREDIT CARDS	CHILDREN WELCOME	FIXED-PRICE MENU	VEGETARIAN	OUTDOOR TABLES
SOUTH KENSINGTON & HYDE PARK: *Hard Rock Café.* **Map** 5 B2. **££** **150 Old Park Lane W1.** 0171-629 0382. Teenagers and would-be youths line up for this joint to eat good char-grilled burgers to the compelling beat of rock music. Part rock museum, this is a place you'll either love or hate. ● *public hols.* ⚡	AE MC V	●		●	
SOUTH KENSINGTON & HYDE PARK: *Ognisko Polskie.* **Map** 2 E4. **££** **55 Prince's Gate SW7.** 0171-589 4635. This Polish restaurant and bar features mainly hearty fare of meat with dumplings or *sauerkraut* with a good selection of vodkas. ● *public hols.*		●	■		
SOUTH KENSINGTON & HYDE PARK: *Le Suquet.* **Map** 2 F5. **£££** **104 Draycott Ave SW3.** 0171-581 1785. Le Suquet is a lively but relaxed French seafood hang-out. Highlights include foil-wrapped sea bream, scallops in garlic and seafood platter.	AE DC MC V				
SOUTH KENSINGTON & HYDE PARK: *St Quentin.* **Map** 2 F5. **£££** **243 Brompton Rd SW3.** 0171-581 8377. The decor matches the rich French food: confit of duck, chicken in cream, *foie gras.* Expensive, but the set menus provide an escape.	AE DC MC V		■		
SOUTH KENSINGTON & HYDE PARK: *Bombay Brasserie.* **Map** 2 D5. **££££** **Courtfield Close, Courtfield Rd SW7.** 0171-370 4040. Unusual regional specialties in a grand setting. The lunch buffet is a good value. Mainly North Indian menu includes some unusual specialties like tandoori trout. Atmosphere is redolent of the Raj. ● *public hols.* ♿	DC MC V		■	●	
SOUTH KENSINGTON & HYDE PARK: *Clarke's.* **Map** 1 C3. **££££** **124 Kensington Church St W8.** 0171-221 9225. The flavors of Britain, California and Italy fuse at this char-grill restaurant. Dinners feature fresh herbs and wild plants. ● *Sat, Sun.* ♿ ▯	MC V		■		
SOUTH KENSINGTON & HYDE PARK: *Fifth Floor.* **Map** 5 A3. **££££** **Harvey Nichols, Knightsbridge SW1.** 0171 235 5250. Stylish store restaurant popular with business diners and lunching ladies who appreciate the startlingly good British food. ● *Sun.* ♿	AE DC MC V	●	■	●	
SOUTH KENSINGTON & HYDE PARK: *Salloos.* **Map** 5 A2. **££££** **62–64 Kinnerton St SW1.** 0171-235 4444. This up-market and expensive Pakistani restaurant offers a serene dining room, precise cooking of lamb dishes and faultless service. ● *public hols.* ▯	AE DC MC V		■		
SOUTH KENSINGTON & HYDE PARK: *Bibendum.* **Map** 2 F5. **£££££** **Michelin House, 81 Fulham Rd SW3.** 0171-581 5817. A simple but splendid modern-international menu, a suitably pricey wine list and a gorgeous setting. The superb risottos are especially recommended. Book well in advance to guarantee a table. ● *Sun L.* ♿ ▯	MC V		■		
SOUTH KENSINGTON & HYDE PARK: *Le Gavroche.* **Map** 3 B5. **£££££** **43 Upper Brook St W1.** 0171-408 0881. The high temple of *haute cuisine.* The Roux brothers' HQ is formal, clubby, expensive. Eating here is a sophisticated, memorable experience. The food is flawless and the service first-class. ● *Sat, Sun, public hols.* ▯	AE DC MC V		■		
SOUTH KENSINGTON & HYDE PARK: *Hilaire.* **Map** 2 F5. **£££££** **68 Old Brompton Rd SW7.** 0171-584 8993. The modern-international cuisine here features unconventional sauces. The supper menu (after 9:30pm) is a good value. ● *Sat L, Sun.* ▯	AE DC MC V	●	■		
SOUTH KENSINGTON & HYDE PARK: *The Restaurant.* **Map** 5 A2. **£££££** **Hyde Park Hotel, 66 Knightsbridge SW1.** 0171-259 5380. Celebrated chef Marco Pierre White reigns here, with his own brand of *haute cuisine.* Plush and pricey. ● *Sat L, Sun, public hols.*	AE DC MC V		■		

....

SOUTH KENSINGTON & HYDE PARK: *Turner's*. Map 2 F5. £££££ AE DC MC
87–89 Walton St SW3. (0171-584 6711.
Clever, modern-international menu for a fashionable clientele: turbot
with butter beans, guinea fowl with pistachio nuts. ● *Sat L, public hols.*

REGENT'S PARK & BLOOMSBURY: *Wagamama*. Map 4 E4. £
4 Streatham St, WC1. (0171-323 9223.
Japanese high-tech noodle restaurant where diners eat together at long trestle
tables. Excellent value. Worth the wait. ● *25 Dec, 1 Jan.*

REGENT'S PARK & BLOOMSBURY: *Museum Street Café*. Map 4 E4. £££
47 Museum St WC1. Map 13 B1. (0171-405 3211.
Char-grilling combines with trendy Italian ingredients like arugula and
pesto near the British Museum. Bring your own wine. ● *Sat, Sun.*

THE CITY: *Place Below*. Map 7 C2. ££
St. Mary-le-Bow Church, Cheapside EC2. (0171-329 0789.
Lunchtime crowds pack the crypt of this church (built by Wren), for soups,
salads, hot vegetarian dishes and delicious desserts. ● *Sat, Sun.*

FARTHER AFIELD: *Nazrul, Spitalfields*. Map 8 F1. £
130 Brick Lane E1. (0171-247 2505.
One of Brick Lane's many budget Bangladeshi restaurants – furnishings
are basic, but the prices are low and portions generous. ● *Dec 25, 26.* ●

FARTHER AFIELD: *Rasa, Stoke Newington*. £ AE DC MC V
55 Stoke Newington Church St N16. (0171 249 0344.
The best South Indian vegetarian restaurant in Britain. The dishes faithfully
reproduce the village cookery of Kerala. Service is charming. ● ● ●

FARTHER AFIELD: *Malabar, Notting Hill*. Map 1 B3. ££ MC V
27 Uxbridge St W8. (0171-727 8800.
Stylish Malabar offers outstanding Indo-Pakistani cuisine. Some dishes
are unusual; try char-grilled chicken livers. ● *1 week after Aug public hol.*

FARTHER AFIELD: *Osteria Antica Bologna, Wandsworth*. ££ AE MC V
23 Northcote Rd SW11. (0171 978 4771.
An ideal party venue. Try the *assagi* – a selection of vegetable and
fish dishes – for a cheap but satisfying Italian meal. ● *Mon L, Tue L.* ●

FARTHER AFIELD: *Anna's Place, Highbury*. £££
90 Mildmay Park N1. (0171-249 9379.
Simple, traditional Swedish menu including superb traditional
bread and great desserts. Book ahead. ● *Sun, Mon, Aug.* ●

FARTHER AFIELD: *Kensington Place, Kensington*. Map 1 C3. £££ MC
201–205 Kensington Church St W8. (0171-727 3184.
This austere and noisy open-plan restaurant boasts both conventional
and unusual fare, from steak to braised squid. ● *Aug, public hols.* ●

FARTHER AFIELD: *Peasant, Islington*. Map 7 B1. £££ MC V
240 St. John St EC1. (0171-336 7726.
This converted pub produces simple, robust Italianate meals that put
many grander Italian restaurants to shame. ● *Sat L, Sun, public hols.*

FARTHER AFIELD: *Quality Chop House, Clerkenwell*. Map 7 B1. £££
94 Farringdon Rd EC1. (0171-837 5093.
British favorites such as salmon fishcakes and, of course, chops are
offered in this beautifully restored Victorian diner. Book ahead. ● *Sat L.*

FARTHER AFIELD: *RSJ, Southwark*. Map 7 A4. £££ AE MC V
13A Coin St SE1. (0171-928 4554.
Well-executed French dishes near the South Bank Centre and Old Vic
Theatre. The Loire wine list is superb. ● *Sat L, Sun, public hols.* ● ●

FARTHER AFIELD: *Wilson's, Kensington*. Map 1 A5. £££ MC V
236 Blythe Rd W14. (0171-603 7267.
The best "Scottish" restaurant in London. Dishes are mostly Anglo-
Gallic, using Scotch beef and salmon. ● *Sat L, Sun D, public hols.*

FARTHER AFIELD: *Aubergine, Chelsea*. £££££ AE DC MC V
11 Park Walk SW10. (0171-352 3449.
Fashionable Provençal restaurant, which is constantly busy – book ahead
to try some of the most imaginative dishes in town. ● *Sat L, Sun.* ●

<table>
<tr><td colspan="2">

Price categories include a three-course meal for one, half a bottle of house wine, and all unavoidable extra charges such as cover, service, VAT
£ under £15
££ £15-£25
£££ £25-£35
££££ £35-£50
£££££ over £50

</td><td colspan="6">

CHILDREN WELCOME
Restaurants that offer smaller portions and high chairs for children. Special menus sometimes available.
FIXED-PRICE MENU
A good value fixed-price meal, at lunch, dinner or both, usually of three courses.
VEGETARIAN
Vegetarian specialties served, sometimes for both appetizers and main courses.
CREDIT CARDS
Indicates which credit cards are accepted: *AE* American Express; *DC* Diners Club; *MC* Master Card/Access; *V* Visa.

</td></tr>
</table>

	CREDIT CARDS	CHILDREN WELCOME	FIXED-PRICE MENU	VEGETARIAN	OUTDOOR TABLES
FARTHER AFIELD: *Chez Max, Earl's Court.* £££££ 168 Ifield Rd SW10. 0171-835 0874. Two lively brothers from Essex cook fabulous provincial Lyonnais dishes in this cramped and busy bistro. ● *Mon, Sat L, Sun.*	MC V		■		●
FARTHER AFIELD: *L'Incontro, Pimlico.* **Map** 5 B4. £££££ 87 Pimlico Rd SW1. 0171-730 6327. Venetian risottos, seafood and stunning pasta are the specialties of this upper-class hang out. Wine list prices are steep. ● *Sat L, Sun L.*	AE DC MC V	●		●	
FARTHER AFIELD: *River Café, Hammersmith.* £££££ Thames Wharf Studios, Rainville Rd W6. 0171-381 8824. Leader of the Italian new-wave. Char-grilled fish spiced with herbs, sun-dried tomatoes, arugula and pine nuts. ● *public hols.*	MC V	●		●	■
FARTHER AFIELD: *Leith's, Notting Hill.* **Map** 1 B2. £££££ 92 Kensington Park Rd W11. 0171-229 4481. Good-food guru Prue Leith offers British specialties such as ox tongue, while her superb vegetarian menu has no peers. ● *23, 27 Dec.*	AE DC MC V		■	●	
FARTHER AFIELD: *La Tante Claire, Chelsea.* **Map** 5 A5. £££££ 68 Royal Hospital Rd SW3. 0171-351 0227. Book ahead for this top-notch French restaurant. Rich dishes are the norm, such as stuffed pig's trotter (foot). ● *Sat, Sun, public hols.*	AE DC MC V		■		

THE DOWNS AND CHANNEL COAST

	CREDIT CARDS	CHILDREN WELCOME	FIXED-PRICE MENU	VEGETARIAN	OUTDOOR TABLES
AMBERLEY: *Queen's Room, Amberley Castle* ££££ On B2139, Amberley, W Sussex. 01798 831992. A romantic medieval fortress provides a dramatic backdrop for "castle cuisine," a mix of ancient and modern British recipes.	AE DC MC V		■		
BOUGHTON LEES: *Eastwell Manor* £££ Eastwell Park, Boughton Lees, nr Ashford, Kent. 01233 635751. A grand parkland setting graces this dynamic hotel restaurant where the service is formal but friendly. *(See also p545.)*	AE DC MC V	●	■	●	■
BRIGHTON: *Food for Friends* £ 17–18 Prince Albert St, Brighton, E Sussex. 01273 202310. This wholefood café in the Lanes offers friendly service, generous helpings and imaginative cooking amid pine and potted plants.	AE DC MC V	●		●	
BRIGHTON: *Terre à Terre* £ 7 Pool Valley, Brighton, E Sussex. 01273 729051. Close to the pavilion, pier and the Lanes, this vegetarian brasserie has an imaginative international menu, serving delicacies such as char-grilled *haloumi* (sheep's cheese) with capers. ● *Mon (Nov–Mar).*		●		●	■
BRIGHTON: *Black Chapati* ££ 12 Circus Parade, New England Rd, Brighton, E Sussex. 01273 699011. Adventurous and eclectic "Indian" cooking fizzes with original ideas in a stark café setting just outside the town center. The service is efficient, and the atmosphere friendly and welcoming. ● *Sun D, Mon.*	AE MC V			●	■
BROCKENHURST: *Le Poussin* £££ The Courtyard, Brookley Rd, Brockenhurst, Hants. 01590 23063. New Forest produce such as venison and wild pork appears on the menu in robust provincial French-style fare. ● *Sun D, Mon, Tue.*	MC V	●	■		■
EAST GRINSTEAD: *Gravetye Manor* ££££ Vowels Lane, East Grinstead, W Sussex. 01342 810567. Classic food is served in this plush Elizabethan mansion, a luxury hotel in gorgeous grounds. Menu prices don't include VAT.	MC V		■	●	

EDENBRIDGE: *Honours Mill* ££££
87 High St, Edenbridge, Kent. 📞 01732 866757.
Watch your head: the beams are low. Well-tried French classics are
daringly adapted in this quiet, friendly restaurant. ● *Sat L, Sun D, Mon.*

	AE	●	■		
	MC				
	V				

HAMPTON WICK: *Le Petit Max* £££
97A High St, Hampton Wick, Middx. 📞 0181 977 0236.
First-class ingredients and proficient cooking transforms this French café
into a bistro by night. Bring your own wine. ● *Tue–Sat L, Sun D, Mon.* ❱

			■		

HASLEMERE: *Morels* £££
23–27 Lower St, Haslemere, Surrey. 📞 01428 651462.
Accomplished modern French cooking blends with Mediterranean flavors
in an attractive, intimate dining room. ● *Sat L, Sun, Mon.* ♿ ⇗ 🍷

	AE	●	■		
	DC				
	MC				
	V				

HASTINGS: *Rösers* £££
64 Eversfield Pl, St Leonards, Hastings, E Sussex. 📞 01424 712218.
Freshness is the watchword here: sausages and bread are made on the
premises. With the sea so close, fish is a specialty. ● *Sat L, Sun, Mon.* 🍷

	AE		■	●	
	DC				
	MC				
	V				

HORSHAM: *Jeremy's at the Crabtree* ££
Brighton Rd, Lower Beeding, nr Horsham, W Sussex. 📞 01403 891257.
Vivaciously modern European cooking produces memorable results
in this civilized but unpretentious Georgian inn. ● *Sun D.* ♿ ⇗

	MC		■		
	V				

HURSTBOURNE TARRANT: *Esseborne Manor* £££
On A343, N of Hurstbourne Tarrant, Hants. 📞 01264 736444.
Well-flavored and sophisticated English country cooking is offered in
this stylish Victorian manor-house hotel. Good value set lunch. ♿ 🍷

	AE		■	●	
	DC				
	MC				
	V				

JEVINGTON: *Hungry Monk* £££
Between Polegate and Friston, E Sussex. 📞 01323 482178.
This restaurant's popularity rests partly on its picturesque 15th-century
setting, but reliable food is a factor too. ● *Mon–Sat L, Sun D.* ⇗ ❱ 🍷

	AE	●	■	●	

KINGSTON-UPON-THAMES: *Ayudhya* £££
14 Kingston Hill, Kingston, Surrey. 📞 0181 549 5984.
Eclectic Thai cuisine spanning well-known favorites plus exotic
dishes such as chicken in screw-pine leaf. ● *Mon L.* ♿ ⇗ ❱

	AE				
	DC				
	MC				
	V				

NEW MILTON: *Marryat, Chewton Glen* ££££
Christchurch Rd, New Milton, Hants. 📞 01425 275341.
A gastronomic shrine in a tranquil New Forest country-house hotel.
The luxuriant conservatory restaurant overlooks lovely gardens. ♿ ⇗ 🍷

	AE	●	■	●	■
	DC				
	MC				
	V				

PULBOROUGH: *Stane Street Hollow* £££
Codmore Hill, Pulborough, W Sussex. 📞 01798 872819.
A Swiss theme dominates this cottage restaurant. Helpings are copious,
service is efficient and amenable, and much is homegrown. 🍷

		●	■	●	

RICHMOND: *Nightingales* £££
Nightingale Lane, Richmond, Surrey. 📞 0181 940 7471.
A superb Thames view adds to the pleasure of mostly traditional
English cooking at this Victorian hotel. ● *Sat L, Sun D, Mon, Tue.* ⇗

	AE	●	■	●	
	DC				
	MC				
	V				

RIPLEY: *Michels'* £££
13 High St, Ripley, Surrey. 📞 01483 224777.
Ambitious menus change with the seasons. Picturesque setting. In summer
you can have drinks in a walled garden. ● *Sat L, Sun D, Mon.* ♿

	AE	●	■	●	■
	MC				
	V				

ROMSEY: *Old Manor House* £££
21 Palmerston St, Romsey, Hants. 📞 01794 517353.
Italianate influences enhance ingredients including venison and homemade salami in this brick-and-timber Tudor building. ● *Sun D, Mon.* 🍷

	AE		■		
	MC				
	V				

RYE: *Landgate Bistro* ££
5–6 Landgate, Rye, E Sussex. 📞 01797 222829.
Local produce like Romney Marsh lamb or freshly caught fish figures
imaginatively in this pleasant cottage-style restaurant. ● *L, Sun, Mon.*

	AE	●	■	●	
	DC				
	MC				
	V				

STORRINGTON: *Manleys* £££
Manleys Hill, Storrington, W Sussex. 📞 01903 742331.
French cooking with Austrian touches at this cottage restaurant where
service is calm and efficient. ● *Sun D, Mon.* ♿ 🍷

	AE	●	■	●	
	MC				
	V				

For key to symbols see back flap

Price categories include a three-course meal for one, half a bottle of house wine, and all unavoidable extra charges such as cover, service, VAT	CHILDREN WELCOME — Restaurants that offer smaller portions and high chairs for children. Special menus sometimes available.	CREDIT CARDS	CHILDREN WELCOME	FIXED-PRICE MENU	VEGETARIAN	OUTDOOR TABLES
£ under £15	FIXED-PRICE MENU — A good value fixed-price meal, at lunch, dinner or both, usually of three courses.					
££ £15–£25	VEGETARIAN — Vegetarian specialties served, sometimes for both appetizers and main courses.					
£££ £25–£35	CREDIT CARDS — Indicates which credit cards are accepted: AE American Express; DC Diners Club; MC Master Card/Access; V Visa.					
££££ £35–£50						
£££££ over £50						

SURBITON: *Chez Max* £££
85 Maple Rd, Surbiton, Surrey. ☎ 0181 399 2365.
Meals at this French-style, family-run restaurant favour fish dishes but include spicy duck in filo pastry with apricot sauce. ● *Sat L, Sun, Mon.* &

	CREDIT CARDS	CHILDREN WELCOME	FIXED-PRICE MENU	VEGETARIAN	OUTDOOR TABLES
	AE DC MC V		■		

TUNBRIDGE WELLS: *Thackeray's House* £££
85 London Rd, Tunbridge Wells, Kent. ☎ 01892 511921.
The novelist's home is now a double-decker restaurant and wine bar where local produce is given a Gallic touch. ● *Sun D, Mon.* & ⏀

	CREDIT CARDS	CHILDREN WELCOME	FIXED-PRICE MENU	VEGETARIAN	OUTDOOR TABLES
	MC V		■	●	■

WHITSTABLE: *Whitstable Oyster Fishery Co* £££
Royal Native Oyster Stores, Whitstable, Kent. ☎ 01227 276856.
The name suggests what it does best, but other fishy things appear on the menu in this Victorian building by the harbor. ● *Sun D, Mon.* &

	CREDIT CARDS	CHILDREN WELCOME	FIXED-PRICE MENU	VEGETARIAN	OUTDOOR TABLES
	AE DC MC V	●		●	■

WICKHAM: *Old House* £££
The Square, Wickham, Hants. ☎ 01239 833049.
French-inspired food with exotic touches, served in the timber-framed former stable-block of a Georgian hotel. ● *Mon & Sat L, Sun.* &

	CREDIT CARDS	CHILDREN WELCOME	FIXED-PRICE MENU	VEGETARIAN	OUTDOOR TABLES
	AE DC MC V	●	■		

WOOLTON HILL: *Hollington House* ££££
Church Rd, Woolton Hill, Hants. ☎ 01635 255100.
Flamboyant country-house hotel with wood-paneled dining room offers inventively modish international dishes. Good Australian wines. & ⏀

	CREDIT CARDS	CHILDREN WELCOME	FIXED-PRICE MENU	VEGETARIAN	OUTDOOR TABLES
	AE DC MC V	●	■	●	■

EAST ANGLIA

ALDEBURGH: *Regatta* ££
171–173 High St, Aldeburgh, Suff. ☎ 01728 452011.
Seafaring decor reflects the fish specialties which are always cooked with care. Sometimes there's local game on the menu. The ingredients are always top quality, and the service is friendly. ● *Mon, Tues (Oct–Easter).* & ⚡

	CREDIT CARDS	CHILDREN WELCOME	FIXED-PRICE MENU	VEGETARIAN	OUTDOOR TABLES
	AE MC V	●		●	

BROXTED: *Whitehall* ££££
Church End, Broxted, Essex. ☎ 01279 850603.
Stylishly presented modern cooking in a fine Elizabethan manor house. Luxurious hotel accommodation. Attentive service but high prices. &

	CREDIT CARDS	CHILDREN WELCOME	FIXED-PRICE MENU	VEGETARIAN	OUTDOOR TABLES
	AE DC MC V	●	■		

BURNHAM MARKET: *Fishes'* ££
Market Pl, Burnham Market, Norf. ☎ 01328 738588.
Located on the 18th-century village green, this restaurant provides reliable fish specialties: the best of the catch at fair prices. Try potted shrimp or something from the smokehouse. ● *Sun D, Mon.* &

	CREDIT CARDS	CHILDREN WELCOME	FIXED-PRICE MENU	VEGETARIAN	OUTDOOR TABLES
	AE DC MC V		■		

BURY ST. EDMUNDS: *Mortimer's* ££
31 Churchgate St, Bury St. Edmunds, Suff. ☎ 01284 760623.
Straightforward seafood fresh from the market. There's a huge menu and good white wines. Can get very busy. ● *Sat L, Sun.* & ⚡

	CREDIT CARDS	CHILDREN WELCOME	FIXED-PRICE MENU	VEGETARIAN	OUTDOOR TABLES
	AE DC MC V	●			

CAMBRIDGE: *Twenty-two* £££
22 Chesterton Rd, Cambs. ☎ 01223 351880.
Courteous service complements pleasingly inventive food in Victorian setting. Three-course menus change every month. ● *L, Mon.* ⚡ ⏀

	CREDIT CARDS	CHILDREN WELCOME	FIXED-PRICE MENU	VEGETARIAN	OUTDOOR TABLES
	AE MC V		■	●	

CAMBRIDGE: *Midsummer House* ££££
Midsummer Common, Cambs. ☎ 01223 69299.
An intimate restaurant serving fixed-price menus of great complexity. Desserts are luscious and elaborate. ● *Sat L, Sun D, Mon.* ⏀

	CREDIT CARDS	CHILDREN WELCOME	FIXED-PRICE MENU	VEGETARIAN	OUTDOOR TABLES
	AE MC V	●	■	●	■

COLCHESTER: *Warehouse Brasserie* ££
12A Chapel St North, Colchester, Essex. ☎ 01206 765656.
A popular restaurant with an emphasis on fish and vegetarian dishes. Lots of local produce; some light main courses. ● *Sun D.* & ⚡

	CREDIT CARDS	CHILDREN WELCOME	FIXED-PRICE MENU	VEGETARIAN	OUTDOOR TABLES
	MC V	●	■	●	

DEDHAM: *Le Talbooth* ££££
Gun Hill, Dedham, Essex. [01206 323150.
Standards stay high at this long-established Tudor restaurant by the River
Stour. Creative cooking that is popular with locals and visitors alike. ■

AE
MC
V

DISS: *Weaver's Wine Bar* ££
Market Hill, Diss, Norf. [01379 642411.
A charming timbered setting for a cheerful, *ad hoc* restaurant with
the day's dishes chalked on a blackboard. ● *Sat L, Sun, public hols.* ■

DC
MC
V

ELY: *Old Fire Engine House* £££
25 St Mary's St, Ely, Cambs. [01353 662582.
Local produce inspires hearty British cooking in the old fire station
by the cathedral. Friendly, unfussy atmosphere. ● *Sun D.* ■

MC
V

ERPINGHAM: *Ark* ££
The Street, Erpingham, Norf. [01379 586247.
The relaxing, informal atmosphere at this old brick cottage complements
the hearty and wholesome country fare. ● *Tue–Sat L, Mon.* ■

FRESSINGFIELD: *Fox and Goose* ££
On B1116, Fressingfield, Suff. [0137 986 247.
This remote country pub serves a wide range of inventive British and
international dishes. Children are welcomed. ● *Mon, Tue.* ■

HARWICH: *Pier at Harwich* ££
The Quay, Harwich, Essex. [01255 241212.
A bustling harbourside stop-over with nautical decor and excellent fish
served with chips. Comfortable rooms are also available. ■

AE
DC
MC
V

HINTLESHAM: *Hintlesham Hall* ££££
On A1071, Hintlesham, Suff. [01473 652268.
Presentation is the key to success at this hotel west of Ipswich.
Excellent cheese-board. *(See also p548.)* ● *Sat L.* ■

AE
DC
MC
V

HUNTINGDON: *Old Bridge* £££
1 High St, Huntingdon, Cambs. [01480 52581.
A handsome riverside inn with an airy restaurant offering British and
Mediterranean fare, and splendid English cheeses. Good teas too. ■

AE
DC
MC
V

IPSWICH: *Kwok's Rendezvous* ££
23 St Nicholas St, Ipswich, Suff. [01473 256833.
Peking and Szechuan cuisine emerge from the kitchen of this 17th-century
Georgian townhouse. Favorite is Peking duck. ● *Sat L, Sun.* ■

AE
MC
V

KING'S LYNN: *Rococo* £££
11 Saturday Market Pl, King's Lynn, Norf. [01553 771483.
Local produce is served with panache in a cheerful yellow dining room.
Try Norfolk shrimp or specially reared duck. ● *Sun, Mon L.* ■

AE
MC
V

NORWICH: *Adlard's* £££
79 Upper St. Giles St, Norwich, Norf. [01603 633522.
A deceptively humdrum setting belies high-quality cooking of great
flair. The cuisine is mostly classical French. ● *Sun, Mon.* ■

AE
MC
V

ORFORD: *Butley Orford Oysterage* £
The Square, Orford, Suff. [01394 450277.
Café-restaurant with its own smokehouse and oyster-beds. Enjoy a
snack or meal in a delightful Suffolk village. ● *Sun–Thu D (Nov–Mar).*

STONHAM: *Mr Underhill's* ££££
On A140, Stonham, Suff. [01449 711206.
Charm and enthusiasm augment the Mediterranean cooking here. There
is a delicious range of set menus. ● *Tue–Sat L, Sun D, Mon.* ■

DC
MC
V

SUDBURY: *Mabey's Brasserie* ££
47 Gainsborough St, Sudbury, Suff. [01787 3742948.
This civilized brasserie offers excellent cooking at realistic prices. Watch
the chefs in action in the open-plan dining area. ● *Sun, Mon.* ■

AE
MC
V

WELLS-NEXT-THE-SEA: *Moorings* ££
6 Freeman St, Wells-next-the-Sea, Norf. [01328 710949.
Abundant local fish and vegetables typify the dishes at this quayside
restaurant run by an affable *patronne.* ● *Tue, Wed, Thu L.* ■

For key to symbols see back flap

Price categories include a three-course meal for one, half a bottle of house wine, and all unavoidable extra charges such as cover, service, VAT **£** under £15 **££** £15-£25 **£££** £25-£35 **££££** £35-£50 **£££££** over £50	**CHILDREN WELCOME** Restaurants that offer smaller portions and high chairs for children. Special menus sometimes available. **FIXED-PRICE MENU** A good value fixed-price meal, at lunch, dinner or both, usually of three courses. **VEGETARIAN** Vegetarian specialties served, sometimes for both appetizers and main courses. **CREDIT CARDS** Indicates which credit cards are accepted: *AE* American Express; *DC* Diners Club; *MC* Master Card/Access; *V* Visa.	CREDIT CARDS	CHILDREN WELCOME	FIXED-PRICE MENU	VEGETARIAN	OUTDOOR TABLES

WEST MERSEA: *Le Champenois* **£££**
20–22 Church Rd, West Mersea, Essex. **(** 01206 283338.
An authentic taste of France in the Essex marshes. Inventive fish dishes surface amid solid Gallic classics. Comfortable rooms. ● *Tue L, Sun D.* &
Credit cards: AE MC V

THAMES VALLEY

BRAY: *Waterside Inn* **£££££**
Ferry Rd, Bray, Berks. **(** 01628 20691.
Renowned pillar of French classic cuisine in an idyllic riverside setting.
The set lunches are excellent. ● *Mon, Tue L, Sun D (Nov–Mar).* & ▯
Credit cards: DC MC V

CHADLINGTON: *Manor* **£££**
Chadlington, Oxon. **(** 01608 676711.
Satisfying fare in a peaceful Cotswold mansion. Five-course menus offer traditional favorites, but unusual things crop up too. ● *L.* ▨ ▯
Credit cards: MC V

CHINNOR: *Sir Charles Napier* **£££**
Spriggs Alley, nr Chinnor, Oxon. **(** 01494 483011.
Service is informal, but the food is good in this Chiltern pub-restaurant.
The garden has eccentric sculptures. ● *Sun D, Mon.* & ▨ ▯
Credit cards: MC V

COOKHAM: *Alfonso's* **££**
19–21 Station Hill Parade, Cookham, Berks. **(** 0162 85 25775.
Intimate, family-run restaurant full of friendly enthusiasm and Iberian specialties (such as Serrano ham and lambs' kidneys in sherry). Some excellent *Rioja* wines are available. ● *Sat L, Sun.* & ▶ ▯
Credit cards: AE DC MC V

DINTON: *La Chouette* **££**
Westlington Green, Dinton, Bucks. **(** 01296 747422.
Belgian gastronomic flair in this beautiful 16th-century building.
The *patron* also offers live jazz and Trappist beers. ● *Sat L, Sun.* &
Credit cards: MC V

GODSTOW: *Trout* **££**
Godstow, Wolvercote, Oxon. **(** 01865 54485.
A trout stream runs past this charming creeper-covered medieval pub north of Oxford. Peacocks strut outside; inside it is always civilized. &

GORING: *Leatherne Bottel* **££££**
On B4009, Goring, Oxon. **(** 01491 872667.
A glorious riverside setting accounts for the popularity of this relaxing place. Fresh local ingredients are presented with Oriental touches. &
Credit cards: AE MC V

GREAT MILTON: *Le Manoir aux Quat'Saisons* **£££££**
Church Rd, Great Milton, Oxon. **(** 01844 278881.
Raymond Blanc's gastronomic pleasure palace is a rural idyll. The superb food is fresh, inventive and fully flavored. A memorable experience, but not cheap. *(See also p549.)* & ▨ ▯
Credit cards: AE DC MC V

GREAT MISSENDEN: *La Petite Auberge* **££££**
107 High St, Great Missenden, Bucks. **(** 01494 865370.
An intimate restaurant producing reliable provincial French cooking.
Service is efficient but unobtrusive. ● *L, Sun.* & ▶
Credit cards: MC V

HEMEL HEMPSTEAD: *Gallery* **£**
Old Town Hall, High St, Hemel Hempstead, Herts. **(** 01442 232416.
This informal bistro above the arts complex offers a good variety of light snacks and specials. Pretheater dinners are popular. ● *Sun, Mon D.* ▨
Credit cards: MC V

KINTBURY: *Dundas Arms* **££**
53 Station Rd, Kintbury, Berks. **(** 01488 658263.
This old riverside pub serves an appetizing range of bar snacks and traditional dishes, competently prepared. ● *Sun, Mon D.* & ▨ ▯
Credit cards: AE MC V

MELBOURN: *Pink Geranium* £££ AE MC V
Station Rd, Melbourn, nr Royston, Herts. ☎ 01763 260215.
Assured cooking is served in this pretty thatched cottage by the church.
The atmosphere is welcoming, the decor pink. ● *Sat L, Sun D.* ⓺ ⓩ ❱

OXFORD: *Browns* £ AE MC V
5–11 Woodstock Rd, Oxford. ☎ 01865 511995.
A lively, informal restaurant serving a tempting range of snacks and
fuller meals amid bentwood furnishings and potted plants. ⓺ ⓩ ❱

OXFORD: *Nosebag* £
6 St. Michael's St, Oxford. ☎ 01865 721033.
Excellent salads, soups and imaginative light dishes are served to lines
of hungry students on the upper floor of a quaint building. ● *Mon D.* ⓩ

OXFORD: *Al-Shami* ££ AE MC V
25 Walton Crescent, Oxford. ☎ 01865 310066.
This bustling Lebanese restaurant serves *falafel, tabouleh, ful medames*
and other favorites, with authentic desserts to follow. ⓺ ❱

OXFORD: *Cherwell Boathouse* ££ AE DC MC V
Bardwell Rd, Oxford. ☎ 01865 52746.
A romantic punting spot on the River Cherwell. The fixed-price menus
are Mediterranean with a twist. ● *Sun D, Mon & Tue L.* ⓺ ⓩ ❱ ⓨ

SHINFIELD: *L'Ortolan* £££££ AE DC MC V
Old Vicarage, Church Lane, Shinfield, Berks. ☎ 01734 883783.
L'Ortolan is one of Britain's best restaurants. The setting is charming,
although the modern French and British dishes are very pricey. Set
menus represent better value. ● *Sun D, Mon.* ⓺

SPEEN: *Old Plow* ££ AE MC V
Flowers Bottom, Speen, Bucks. ☎ 01494 488300.
An informal bistro in a picturesque former pub. Much is homemade,
and all is fresh – no microwaves! ● *Sun D, Mon.* ⓺ ❱

STONOR: *Stonor Arms* ££ AE MC V
On B480, Stonor, Oxon. ☎ 01491 638345.
A restaurant and brasserie near Henley-on-Thames. Good local produce
is cooked with flair then served in the conservatory. ⓺ ⓨ

STREATLEY: *Swan Diplomat* ££££ AE DC MC V
High St, Streatley, Berks. ☎ 01491 873737.
A Thames-side business hotel serving expert if conservative food in a
delightful setting. There are some Scandinavian dishes. ● *Sat L, Sun D.* ⓺

WATLINGTON: *Well House* £££ AE DC MC V
34–40 High St, Watlington, Oxon. ☎ 01491 613333.
Well-presented dishes such as lamb and apricot pie are offered in this
old brick and flint house. ● *Sat D, Sun D, Mon L.* ⓺ ⓩ

WOBURN: *Paris House* ££££ AE DC MC V
Woburn Park, Woburn, Beds. ☎ 01525 290692.
French classics star at this smart mock-Tudor building in the grounds
of Woburn Abbey. Try the hot raspberry soufflé. ● *Sun D, Mon, Feb.*

WOBURN SANDS: *Spooners* ££ AE MC V
61 High St, Woburn Sands, Milton Keynes, Bucks. ☎ 01908 584385.
This Victorian terraced house makes an agreeable place for a light lunch
or a substantial meal in the evenings. The steaks are especially tasty.
Warm, friendly atmosphere. ● *Sun, Mon.* ⓺ ⓩ

WOODSTOCK: *Feathers* ££££ AE DC MC V
Market St, Woodstock, Oxon. ☎ 01993 812291.
Superior cooking matches the surroundings of a fine historic building.
British fare is warmed with Mediterranean flavors. *(See also p550.)* ⓺

WESSEX

AVEBURY: *Stones* £
Avebury, Wilts. ☎ 01672 539514.
Health food fans rave about the dishes at this self-service vegetarian
restaurant beside the ancient stone circle. Some lovely soups and
British cheeses on the menu. ● *D, Mon–Fri (Nov–Feb).* ⓺ ⓩ

	CREDIT CARDS	CHILDREN WELCOME	FIXED-PRICE MENU	VEGETARIAN	OUTDOOR TABLES

Price categories include a three-course meal for one, half a bottle of house wine, and all unavoidable extra charges such as cover, service, VAT
£ under £15
££ £15–£25
£££ £25–£35
££££ £35–£50
£££££ over £50

CHILDREN WELCOME
Restaurants that offer smaller portions and high chairs for children. Special menus sometimes available.
FIXED-PRICE MENU
A good value fixed-price meal, at lunch, dinner or both, usually of three courses.
VEGETARIAN
Vegetarian specialties served, sometimes for both appetizers and main courses.
CREDIT CARDS
Indicates which credit cards are accepted: AE American Express; DC Diners Club; MC Master Card/Access; V Visa.

BATH: *Moon and Sixpence* ££ 6A Broad St, Bath, Avon. 01225 460962. This popular bistro and wine bar serves inexpensive lunchtime dishes and good-value dinners. The downstairs conservatory is particularly pleasant in summer.	MC V	●	■	●	
BATH: *Hole in the Wall* £££ 16 George St, Bath, Avon. 01225 425242. The new management has made dynamic changes in this famous cellar. Sample modern British cooking at its best. ● *Sun.*	AE MC V		■	●	
BATH: *Priory* ££££ Weston Rd, Bath, Avon. 01225 331922. This palatial but relaxing country-house hotel in lovely gardens offers French and English cooking in a variety of themed rooms.	AE DC MC V	●	■	●	■
BEAMINSTER: *Bridge House* ££ 3 Prout Bridge, Beaminster, Dorset. 01308 862200. This ancient clergy house dishes up old favorites and inventive adaptations in a civilized setting. Good value rooms.	AE DC MC V		■	●	
BLANDFORD FORUM: *La Belle Alliance* £££ White Cliff Mill St, Blandford Forum, Dorset. 01258 452842. Complex recipes are created in this late Victorian building. There are well-equipped rooms if you want to stay. ● *Mon–Sat L, Sun.*	AE MC V		■		
BOURNEMOUTH: *Chez Fred* £ 10 Seamoor Rd, Westbourne, Bournemouth, Dorset. 01202 761023. Fred's fish and chips and wicked desserts, like treacle sponge, are his claim to fame. The service is friendly, the atmosphere lively. ● *Sun.*		●			
BOURNEMOUTH: *Sophisticats* £££ 43 Charminster Rd, Bournemouth, Dorset. 01202 291019. Pleasant, long-standing, owner-run restaurant near town center. Dishes eschew fashion; steaks and local fish are superb. ● *Mon–Sat L, Sun.*				●	
BRADFORD-ON-AVON: *Woolley Grange* £££ Woolley Green, Bradford-on-Avon, Wilts. 01225 864705. A delightful Jacobean country-house hotel with everything from children's chicken nuggets to enterprising international cuisine. The atmosphere is informal, and the service excellent.	AE DC MC V	●	■	●	■
BRISTOL: *Harveys* £££ 12 Denmark St, Bristol, Avon. 01179 275034. The 13th-century cellars of Bristol's famous wine-shipper are the setting for this sophisticated restaurant. ● *Sat L, Sun, public hols.*	AE DC MC V		■	●	
BRISTOL: *Lettonie* £££ 9 Druid Hill, Stoke Bishop, Bristol, Avon. 01179 686456. Enterprising cosmopolitan fare. The Hungarian *patron* incorporates Eastern European elements in the menu. The atmosphere is both lively and bohemian ● *Sun, Mon.*	AE MC V	●	■		
CLEVEDON: *Murrays* £ 91 Hill Rd, Clevedon, Avon. 01275 874058. A coffee-shop and bistro combine the best of both worlds. Dishes include Italian savories and home-baked cakes. ● *Sun, Mon D, public hols.*			■	●	
COLERNE: *Lucknam Park* £££ Off A420, Colerne, Wilts. 01225 742777. A luxurious country-house hotel offering suitably posh cooking. The atmosphere is discreet and formal. Gentlemen are required to wear a jacket and tie. A memorable experience.	AE DC MC V		■	●	■

DEVIZES: *Wiltshire Kitchen* £
11 St. John's St, Devizes, Wilts. 01380 724840.
Breakfast, lunch and tea pose no strain on the purse strings at this popular corner-shop restaurant. All the food is freshly prepared.

MAIDEN NEWTON: *Le Petit Canard* £££ MC V
Dorchester Rd, Maiden Newton, Dorset. 01300 320536.
Bold Pacific Rim cooking (char-grills and stir-fries) using fresh local produce features in this candlelit restaurant. ● Mon–Sat L, Sun, Mon.

MELKSHAM: *Toxique* £££ AE DC MC V
187 Woodrow Rd, Melksham, Wilts. 01225 702129.
Subtle seasonal flavorings ring the changes in this listed farmhouse. Quality is never sacrificed to profit. ● Mon–Sat L, Sun D, Mon, Tue.

SALISBURY: *Harpers* £ AE DC MC V
6–7 Ox Row, Market Place, Salisbury, Wilts. 01722 333118.
Light, friendly, first-floor restaurant offers unpretentious roasts, casseroles and daily specials. Unimaginative but tasty fare. Wonderful views over historic Salisbury. ● Sun (winter).

SHEPTON MALLET: *Bowlish House* £££ MC V
Wells Rd, Shepton Mallet, Somer. 01749 342022.
A Georgian merchant's house with peaceful gardens. Dinner is a relaxed, unstuffy experience. Modern British cuisine. ● Mon–Sat L, Sun.

SHIPTON GORGE: *Innsacre* ££ MC V
Shipton Lane, Shipton Gorge, Dorset. 01308 456137.
A converted 17th-century farmhouse offers a rural idyll with fresh and appetizing seasonal produce. ● L, Sun, Mon, public hols.

STON EASTON: *Ston Easton Park* ££££ AE DC MC V
On A37, Ston Easton, Somer. 01761 241631.
Straightforward menus characterize this splendid country-house hotel. The modern European cookery justifies the expense. An experience that will not be a disappointment. (See also p552.)

STURMINSTER NEWTON: *Plumber Manor* £££ AE DC MC V
Hazelbury Bryan Rd, Sturminster Newton, Dorset. 01258 472507.
Oil paintings adorn this hotel dining room, but they won't distract from the food. The fish is superb, and the desserts very tempting. ● Mon, Sat L.

TAUNTON: *Castle* £££ AE DC MC V
Castle Green, Taunton, Somer. 01823 272671.
A dignified but unostentatious creeper-clad hotel makes a fine setting for consistently excellent modern British fare. (See also p552.)

WARMINSTER: *Bishopstrow House* ££££ AE DC MC V
On B3414, Warminster, Wilts. 01985 212312.
Light lunches and dinners in the elegant Georgian surroundings of this country-house hotel. Try the impressive cheeseboard.

WEST BAY: *Riverside* ££ MC V
Off A35 nr Bridport, Dorset. 01308 422011.
Fish is the mainstay of this long-established restaurant, but there's a good selection of casual snacks. Book ahead. ● Sun D, Mon, Nov–Mar.

WEST BEXINGTON: *Manor* ££ AE DC MC V
Beach Rd, West Bexington, Dorset. 01308 897785.
A delightful range of bar and restaurant food in an old stone inn with nice guestrooms and a garden for children. Close to Chesil Beach.

DEVON AND CORNWALL

BARNSTAPLE: *Lynwood House* £££ AE MC V
Bishops Tawton Rd, Barnstaple, Devon. 01271 43695.
Family-run Victorian house hotel offering real home cooking. Good fish soup and seafood pot dishes. Comfy rooms. ● Sun.

CALSTOCK: *Danescombe Valley* ££££ AE DC MC V
Lower Kelly, Calstock, Corn. 01822 832414.
Book for Anna's legendary four-course, fixed-price dinners. They justify making a diversion. The setting is a beautiful Regency house on the River Tamar. (See also p553.) ● Fri–Tue L, Wed–Thu (Oct–Apr).

For key to symbols see back flap

Price categories include a three-course meal for one, half a bottle of house wine, and all unavoidable extra charges such as cover, service, VAT **£** under £15 **££** £15-£25 **£££** £25-£35 **££££** £35-£50 **£££££** over £50	**CHILDREN WELCOME** Restaurants that offer smaller portions and high chairs for children. Special menus sometimes available. **FIXED-PRICE MENU** A good value fixed-price meal, at lunch, dinner or both, usually of three courses. **VEGETARIAN** Vegetarian specialties served, sometimes for both appetizers and main courses. **CREDIT CARDS** Indicates which credit cards are accepted: *AE* American Express; *DC* Diners Club; *MC* Master Card/Access; *V* Visa.			

	CREDIT CARDS	CHILDREN WELCOME	FIXED-PRICE MENU	VEGETARIAN	OUTDOOR TABLES
CHAGFORD: *Gidleigh Park* **£££££** Chagford, Devon. 【 01647 432367. Imaginative details mark out from the crowd this first-class country-house hotel and restaurant. Pricey, a special occasion place. *(See also p553.)* 🔊 📠 🍷	AE DC MC V	●	■		
DARTMOUTH: *Billy Budd's* **££** 7 Foss St, Dartmouth, Devon. 【 01803 834842. A cheerful bistro specializing in fish dishes with Oriental touches. Simple crêpes and pasta are available for lunch. ● *Sun, Mon.* 🔊	MC V			●	
DARTMOUTH: *Carved Angel* **££££** 2 South Embankment, Dartmouth, Devon. 【 01803 832465. One of Britain's best restaurants occupies a Tudor building on the quayside. The high prices may seem somewhat excessive but they are all-inclusive. ● *Sun D, Mon.* 🔊 🍷		●	■	●	
EAST BUCKLAND: *Lower Pitt* **££** Off A361 nr S Molton, Devon. 【 01598 760243. A restaurant with rooms in a 16th-century longhouse on the edge of Exmoor. Fresh country food is informally served. ● *L, Sun, Mon.* 📠	AE MC V			●	■
HELFORD: *Riverside* **££££** Off B3293, Helford, Corn. 【 01326 231443. This idyllic restaurant-with-rooms overlooks Helford estuary. Cooking hails from provincial France. ● *Mon–Sun L, Nov–early Mar.* 🔊 🍷			■		■
KINGSBRIDGE: *Queen Anne, Buckland-Tout-Saints* **£££** Goveton, Kingsbridge, Devon. 【 01548 853055. Refined cuisine served in a handsome Queen Anne house in lovely grounds. Good British produce is cooked with Gallic finesse. 📠	AE DC MC V	●	■	●	■
LEWDOWN: *Lewtrenchard Manor* **£££** Off A30, Lewdown, Devon. 【 01556 783256. This Elizabethan manor house hotel with mouthwatering fixed-price menus makes a gloriously romantic retreat. ● *Mon–Sat L.* 🔊 📠 🍷	AE DC MC V		■		
LIFTON: *Arundell Arms* **£££** Off A30, Lifton, Devon. 【 01566 784666. An attractive sporting inn in a peaceful village. Local fish and game appear on the fixed-price menus. Bar snacks are also available for lunch and dinner. Convivial atmosphere. 🔊 📠	AE DC MC V		■	●	
MARY TAVY: *Stannary* **££££** On A386 nr Tavistock, Devon. 【 01822 810897. A marvelously inventive vegetarian restaurant in an elegant Victorian setting. ● *Tue–Sat L, Sun, Mon, Tue , Wed (Oct–Mar).* 📠 🍷	AE MC V		■	●	
PADSTOW: *Seafood Restaurant* **££££** Riverside, Padstow, Corn. 【 01841 532485. A much-loved Mecca for fish-lovers in a charming harborside location. A particularly wonderful setting in the summer months. Stylish accommodation. *(See also p554.)* ● *Sun, mid-Dec–Feb.* 🔊 🍷	AE MC V	●	■		
PLYMOUTH: *Yang Cheng* **££** 30A Western Approach, Plymouth, Devon. 【 01572 6601790. Relaxed, attentive Chinese restaurant serving Cantonese specialties. *Dim sum*, fish and shellfish dishes are the high points. ● *Mon.* 🌙	AE MC V	●	■	●	
PLYMOUTH: *Chez Nous* **££££** 13 Frankfort Gate, Plymouth, Devon. 【 01752 266793. An unobtrusive town center bistro with above-average *cuisine spontanée*, recognized by a coveted Michelin rosette. ● *Sun, Mon.* 🔊 🌙 🍷	AE DC MC V		■		

PORT ISAAC: *Slipway* ⓔⓔ | AE MC V
Harbour Front, Port Isaac, Corn. [01208 880264.
In season, this 16th-century chandlery offers a perfect sample of
North Cornwall's fishy fare. ● Mon (Oct–Mar) Jan–Feb. 🔥 🌿

PORTHOUSTOCK: *Volnay* ⓔⓔⓔ
Off B3293, Porthoustock, nr St. Keverne, Corn. [01326 280183.
A cozy restaurant on the eastern Lizard Peninsula. Italian and classic
French influences dominate: olives, anchovies and pesto. ● L, Mon.

ST. IVES: *Tate St. Ives Coffee Shop and Restaurant* ⓔⓔ
Porthmeor Beach, St.. Ives, Corn. [01736 793974.
Admire the views from this art-gallery brasserie while tucking into health
food dishes made with local produce including fish and shellfish. 🔥 🌿

ST. IVES: *Pig'n'Fish* ⓔⓔⓔ | MC V
Norway Lane, St Ives, Corn. [01736 794204.
Mostly fish, but the pig is there too in smoked sausages and pot roast
loin. Try the *bourride* (garlicky fish soup). ● Sun, Mon (Nov–mid-Mar).

SOUTH MOLTON: *Whitechapel Manor* ⓔⓔⓔⓔ | AE DC MC V
Off A361, South Molton, Devon. [01769 573377.
The setting is a Grade I Elizabethan manor. There's nothing archaic about
the food though, which is fresh and light; modern British. 🌿 🍷

TAVISTOCK: *Horn of Plenty* ⓔⓔⓔⓔ | AE MC V
Gulworthy, Tavistock, Devon. [01822 832528.
A restaurant-with-rooms overlooking the Tamar valley. The menu is
cosmopolitan. Try the "pot luck" menu on Mondays that offers a
choice of three appetizers, main courses and desserts. ● Mon L. 🔥 🌿

TORQUAY: *Mulberry Room* ⓔ
1 Scarborough Rd, Torquay, Devon. [01803 213639.
This friendly tea room offers snacks and delicious lunches (dinners on Fri
and Sat) and Sunday roasts. Try the bread and cakes. ● Mon, Tue. 🔥 🌿

TORQUAY: *Table* ⓔⓔⓔ | MC V
135 Babbacombe Rd, Babbacombe, Torquay, Devon. [01803 324292.
Small is beautiful in this end-of-terrace house. The cooking uses foreign
influences and never loses flavor or integrity. ● Tue–Sun L, Mon. 🔥 🌿 🍷

TOTNES: *Willow* ⓔ
87 High St, Totnes, Devon. [01803 862605.
Vegetarian specialties from around the globe, including Mexican, Indian,
Caribbean and Italian, make this place cosmopolitan and ecclectic.
Warm, welcoming atmosphere. ● D Mon & Tue (Thu in summer), Sun. 🔥 🌿

WHIMPLE: *Woodhayes* ⓔⓔⓔ | AE DC MC V
Off A30 nr Exeter, Devon. [01404 822237.
This charming Georgian country-house hotel shares its excellent
six-course dinners of local produce with nonresidents. Convivial
atmosphere and efficient service. ● L (nonresidents). 🔥 🌿

WINKLEIGH: *London House* ⓔⓔ | MC V
Winkleigh, Devon. [01837 83202.
English-style five-course dinners are a real treat in this 18th-century restaurant.
Food and accommodations are excellent value. ● Sun D. 🔥 🌿 🌙

THE HEART OF ENGLAND

ABBERLEY: *Brooke Room, The Elms* ⓔⓔⓔ | AE DC MC V
Stockton Rd, Abberley, H & W. [01299 896666.
Traditional and more daring choices are the bill of fare at this elegant
Queen Anne mansion. Lovely decor and rooms. ● Mon–Sat L. 🔥

BIRMINGHAM: *Chung Ying Garden* ⓔⓔⓔ | AE DC MC V
17 Thorp St, Birmingham. [0121 6666622.
A flamboyant Cantonese food palace offering a giant range of specialties,
including *dim sum* and noodle dishes. ● Sun D. 🔥 🌙

BISHOP'S TACHBROOK: *Mallory Court* ⓔⓔⓔⓔ | AE DC MC V
Off B4087 nr Leamington Spa, Warw. [01926 330214.
Classic French and British cuisine weighs in at a hefty price at this manor-
house hotel, but the results are impressive. Beautiful gardens. 🔥 🍷

	CREDIT CARDS	CHILDREN WELCOME	FIXED-PRICE MENU	VEGETARIAN	OUTDOOR TABLES

Price categories include a three-course meal for one, half a bottle of house wine, and all unavoidable extra charges such as cover, service, VAT
£ under £15
££ £15–£25
£££ £25–£35
££££ £35–£50
£££££ over £50

CHILDREN WELCOME
Restaurants that offer smaller portions and high chairs for children. Special menus sometimes available.
FIXED-PRICE MENU
A good value fixed-price meal, at lunch, dinner or both, usually of three courses.
VEGETARIAN
Vegetarian specialties served, sometimes for both appetizers and main courses.
CREDIT CARDS
Indicates which credit cards are accepted: *AE* American Express; *DC* Diners Club; *MC* Master Card/Access; *V* Visa.

	CREDIT CARDS	CHILDREN WELCOME	FIXED-PRICE MENU	VEGETARIAN	OUTDOOR TABLES
BRIMFIELD: *Poppies* **££££** The Roebuck, Brimfield, H & W. ☎ *01584 711230.* A deceptively simple setting (a village pub) and a relaxed atmosphere conceal highly sophisticated British cooking. ● *Sun, Mon.* ▯	AE MC V		■	●	
BROADWAY: *Collin House* **££** On A44, Broadway, H & W. ☎ *01386 858354.* This modest Cotswold country house welcomes nonresidents. Light lunches are offered in the bar; an imaginative *carte* in the dining room, including crab and ginger souffle. In summer you can eat *alfresco.* ৬	MC V		■	●	■
BROADWAY: *Lygon Arms* **££££** Broadway, H & W. ☎ *01386 852255.* This country cousin of London's Savoy maintains the *haute cuisine* and luxury. Heraldic trappings adorn the Great Hall. ৬	AE DC MC	●	■	●	■
BURTON UPON TRENT: *Dovecliff Hall* **£££** Dovecliff Rd, Stretton, Burton upon Trent, Staffs. ☎ *01283 531818.* A Georgian country house in extensive grounds by the River Dove. An elegant setting. Accomplished, modern British food. ● *Sat L, Sun D, Mon.* ৬	AE DC MC V	●	■	●	■
CHELTENHAM: *Le Champignon Sauvage* **£££** 24 Suffolk Rd, Cheltenham, Glos. ☎ *01242 573449.* Gallic dishes with startling ingredient combinations: sardine and *tapenade* (olive and anchovy paste), rabbit and black pudding. A delight to the palate. ● *Sat L, Sun.* ৬ ▯	AE DC MC V		■		
CHELTENHAM: *Epicurean* **££££** 81 The Promenade, Cheltenham, Glos. ☎ *01242 222466.* A suave split-level establishment discreetly houses a tapas bar downstairs, a chic bistro at ground level, and a formal restaurant upstairs. A place to suit every pocket and occasion. ● *Sun.* ◗	AE DC MC V		■	●	
CHESTER: *Francs* **£** 14 Cupping St, Chester, Ches. ☎ *01244 317952.* An ever-popular brasserie where French rock beats out over tasty *plats du jour.* Sundays are family days and under-10s eat free. Book ahead. ৬ ◗	AE MC V	●	■	●	
DORRINGTON: *Country Friends* **£££** On A49 nr Shrewsbury, Shrops. ☎ *01743 718707.* Simple, reliable English cooking in a pleasant mock-Tudor setting. Fixed-price menu available. Log fires burn in winter. ● *Sun, Mon.* ৬ ⧓	AE MC V		■	●	
KENILWORTH: *Restaurant Bosquet* **££££** 97A Warwick Rd, Kenilworth, Warw. ☎ *01926 52463.* This Victorian house offers serious classic French food with rich sauces and fresh seasonal produce. ● *Tue–Sat L, Sun, Mon.* ৬ ▯	AE MC V	●	■		
LEAMINGTON SPA: *Piccolino's Pizzeria* **£** 5 Spencer St, Leamington Spa, Warw. ☎ *01926 422988.* A jovial family-owned place serving home-cooked Italian favorites – pizza and pasta of course, and other dishes at inexpensive prices. ◗	MC V	●		●	
LEAMINGTON SPA: *Sachers* **£** 14 The Parade, Leamington Spa, Warw. ☎ *01926 421620.* There is live jazz 1930s-style in this relaxed brasserie, concealed behind a cake shop. Stylish mahogany and glass decor. ● *Sun.* ⧓ ◗	MC V	●		●	
LOWER SLAUGHTER: *Lower Slaughter Manor* **££££** Off A429, Lower Slaughter, Glos. ☎ *01451 820456.* Renowned restaurant in a beautiful Cotswolds manor. The menu is based on French classics, modernized by the latest influences from all over the globe. Highly recommended. ⧓	AE MC V		■	●	

MALVERN WELLS: *Croque-en-Bouche* ££££ MC V
221 Wells Rd, Malvern Wells, H & W. [01684 565612.
A dedicated couple manage and cook here. The results are distinctive
and varied international dishes. ● *Wed–Sat L, Sun–Tue.* & ≠ ❚

MIDDLEWICH: *Tempters* £ MC V
11 Wheelock St, Middlewich, Ches. [01606 835175.
A split-level wine bar with wooden tables. Daily specials are chalked on
the blackboard; sandwiches available at lunchtime. ● *Sun D, Mon.* &

MOLLINGTON: *Crabwall Manor* ££££ AE DC MC V
Parkgate Rd, Mollington, Ches. [01244 851666.
Corporate business trade diminishes the personal touch, but the
modern British cooking is well-executed. (*See also p556.*) ● *Sat L.* & ≠ ❚

MORETON-IN-MARSH: *Marsh Goose* £££ AE MC V
High St, Moreton-in-Marsh, Glos. [01608 652111.
A relaxing place with a maze of small rooms. Menus feature French
and British country cooking. Service is formal in the evening. & ≠

PRESTBURY: *White House* ££££ AE DC MC V
The Village, Prestbury, Ches. [01625 829376.
The smart decor matches the upscale cosmopolitan food here. There's
a conservatory for summer evenings. Attractive rooms. ● *Sun D, Mon L.* &

ROSS-ON-WYE: *Meader's* £
1 Copse Cross St, Ross-on-Wye, H & W. [01989 562803.
Friendly Hungarian business; you can sample authentic goulash and
galuska (dumplings) without breaking the bank. ● *Sun, Mon L.* & ≠

ROSS-ON-WYE: *Pheasants* £££ AE DC MC V
52 Edde Cross St, Ross-on-Wye, H & W. [01989 565751.
A cheerful, homey restaurant in a former 17th-century tavern offers
honest, robust food and personal service. ● *Sun, Mon.* & ≠ ❘❙ ❚

STRATFORD-UPON-AVON: *Opposition* ££ MC V
13 Sheep St, Stratford-upon-Avon, Warw. [01789 269980.
A bustling bistro with live music offering simple pretheater suppers.
The day's specials are chalked on blackboards. ● *Sun L.* ❘❙

STRATFORD-UPON-AVON: *Sir Toby's* ££ AE MC V
8 Church St, Stratford-upon-Avon, Warw. [01789 268822.
This rustic 17th-century setting fits the Shakespearian location. A varied menu
with pretheater dinners available and varied inexpensive meals. Call in
advance to check opening times, which vary. ● *Wed–Sat L, Sun–Tue.* &

STROUD: *Oakes* ££ AE MC V
169 Slad Rd, Stroud, Glos. [01453 759950.
Enjoy the modern British and French cooking in this Gothic setting of
Cotswold stone. Traditional English desserts like bread and butter pudding
earn high praise. ● *Sun D, Mon.* &

WATERHOUSES: *Old Beams* ££££ DC MC V
Waterhouses, Staffs. [01538 308254.
French-style, classically based cooking from a restaurant-with-rooms
near Alton Towers. Good wines by the glass. ● *mid-January–Feb.* & ≠ ❚

EAST MIDLANDS

BASLOW: *Fischer's at Baslow* £££ AE DC MC V
Baslow Hall, Calver Rd, Baslow, Derby. [01246 583259.
Whether you eat in the smart dining room or more casually at Café Max,
the cooking is top notch. Handy for Chatsworth. ● *Sun.* & ≠ ❚

BECKINGHAM: *Black Swan* ££ MC V
Hillside, Beckingham, Lincs. [01636 626474.
This 17th-century coaching inn is a mite cramped, but it is intimate; the
quality of the modern British dishes is high and the service is always
friendly and efficient. ● *Tue–Sat L, Mon.* & ≠

BIRCH VALE: *Waltzing Weasel* £££ AE MC V
New Mills Rd, Birch Vale, Derby. [01663 743402.
Hearty English fare (roasts, chops, game pie and Stilton) is served,
accompanied by panoramic views of Kinder Scout. Attractive rooms. &

For key to symbols see back flap

Price categories include a three-course meal for one, half a bottle of house wine, and all unavoidable extra charges such as cover, service, VAT.
£ under £15
££ £15–£25
£££ £25–£35
££££ £35–£50
£££££ over £50

CHILDREN WELCOME
Restaurants that offer smaller portions and high chairs for children. Special menus sometimes available.

FIXED-PRICE MENU
A good value fixed-price meal, at lunch, dinner or both, usually of three courses.

VEGETARIAN
Vegetarian specialties served, sometimes for both appetizers and main courses.

CREDIT CARDS
Indicates which credit cards are accepted: *AE* American Express; *DC* Diners Club; *MC* Master Card/Access; *V* Visa.

	CREDIT CARDS	CHILDREN WELCOME	FIXED-PRICE MENU	VEGETARIAN	OUTDOOR TABLES
BOTTESFORD: *La Petite Maison* **£££** 1 Market St, Bottesford, Leic. **(** 01949 842375. Local supplies of game, fruit and cheese are one reason for this bistro's success; attractive Victorian decor is another. ● *Sun D, Mon.* &	AE MC V	●	■	●	■
BUXTON: *Dandelion Days* **£** 5 Bridge St, Buxton, Derby. **(** 01298 22843. A popular and busy little health food café. Sandwiches, salads and daily specials show plenty of inspiration. Generous portions. ● *Mon.*		●		●	
GREAT GONERBY: *Harry's Place* **£££££** 17 High St, Great Gonerby, Lincs. **(** 01476 61780. Top-quality local produce is transformed into short but striking menus by the energetic *patron* of these small premises. ● *Sun, Mon.* &	MC V				
HAMBLETON: *Hambleton Hall* **££££** Off A606 nr Oakham, Leic. **(** 01572 756991. Splendid views over Rutland Water are a good start to the menu of ornate concoctions with lobsters and *foie gras*. Such memorable feasts don't come cheap. Stylish accommodations. *(See also p558.)* &	AE MC V	●	■	●	■
HAYFIELD: *Bridge End* **£££** 7 Church St, Hayfield, Derby. **(** 01663 747321. A 19th-century guesthouse restaurant on the edge of the Peak District and the Pennine Way. Adventurous British cooking. ● *Tue–Sat L, Sun D, Mon.* &	AE DC MC V	●		●	
HOLDENBY: *Lynton House* **£££** Holdenby, Northnts. **(** 01604 770777. An Italianate version of that archetypal English institution, the old rectory. Inventive antipasti and good fish. A mouthwatering selection of delicious desserts. ● *Mon L, Sat L, Sun.* &	AE MC V		■	●	■
HORTON: *French Partridge* **£££** On B526, Horton, Northnts. **(** 01604 870033. This coaching-inn restaurant offers considered cooking. After 30 years, the menu is still evolving and never stale. ● *L, Sun, Mon.* &			■	●	
LEICESTER: *Bobby's* **£** 154–6 Belgrave Rd, Leicester. **(** 0116 2660106. Vegetarian Gujarati and South Indian dishes make an interesting, good-value treat. The combinations of freshly ground spices make this place unique. Unlicensed, so bring your own alcohol. ● *Mon.* &	AE MC V	●	■	●	
LEICESTER: *Welford Place* **££** 9 Welford Pl, Leicester. **(** 0116 247 0758. Meals are served in this former gentleman's club from breakfast until cocoa time. The atmosphere is mannish, but not exclusive. &	AE DC MC V	●	■	●	
LINCOLN: *Wig and Mitre* **££** 29 Steep Hill, Lincoln. **(** 01522 535190. This operates on similar lines to its sibling, Welford Place *(see above)*. Diners appreciate its flexibility and long opening hours. &	AE DC MC V	●	■	●	■
LINCOLN: *Jew's House* **£££** 15 The Strait, Lincoln. **(** 01522 524851. A fascinating old building close to the cathedral. Serving food *à la française*. Wonderful, calorific handmade chocolates. ● *Sun, Mon L.*	AE DC MC V	●	■	●	
NEWARK: *Gannets Bistrot* **£££** 35 Castlegate, Newark, Notts. **(** 01636 702066. A cheery ground-floor café by the castle with a garden extension and an upstairs bistro. It is plain, simple, and affordable. The staff is very friendly, and the atmosphere bohemian. ● *Sun, Mon.*	MC V	●		●	

NOTTINGHAM: *Saagar* — £€€ | AE MC V
473 Mansfield Rd, Sherwood, Nottingham. (0115 9622014.
North "Indian" cookery from the Punjab, Kashmir and Pakistan. Menus
change frequently and new recipes spice up the choice. & 》

NOTTINGHAM: *Sonny's* — ££ | AE MC V
3 Carlton St, Hockley, Nottingham. (0115 9473041.
Blend of simple snack-bar and restaurant offering roasted peppers or
Cajun cod. The atmosphere is laid-back and fashionable. & 彡 》

PAULERSPURY: *Vine House* — £££ | MC V
100 High St, Paulerspury, Northnts. (01327 811267.
Seventeenth-century house just off the A5. Unusual ingredients, modern
British influences and informal. Pleasant rooms. ● Sat L, Sun, Mon L. 》

PLUMTREE: *Perkins Bar Bistro* — ££ | AE DC MC V
Old Railway Station, Plumtree, Notts. (01602 373695.
This bistro serves a mix of British game and fish with French sauces.
Good bar snacks include beer mugs of shrimp. ● Sun, Mon. 彡

RIDGEWAY: *Old Vicarage* — ££££ | AE MC V
Ridgeway Moor, Ridgeway, Derby. (01742 475814.
High-quality meat, vegetables and fresh herbs produce insistent flavors
at this stone-built Victorian house. A conservatory bistro offers cheaper
menus, and there's plenty of vegetarian choices. ● Sun D, Mon. 彡 》 ▌

ROADE: *Roadhouse* — ££ | AE MC V
16 High St, Roade, Northnts. (01604 863372.
This family business offers imaginative British cooking. Most dishes
have complex sauces. Game features during winter. ● Sat L, Sun D. &

STOKE BRUERNE: *Bruerne's Lock* — £££ | AE MC V
5 The Canalside, Stoke Bruerne, Northnts. (01604 863654.
A fast-evolving modern British restaurant by the side of the Grand
Union Canal. An original setting, and good food. Personal service is
the keynote. ● Sat L, Sun D, Mon. &

STRETTON: *Ram Jam Inn* — £ | AE DC MC V
Great North Rd, Stretton, Leic. (01780 410776.
This roadside haven has provided hospitality since 1750. Hearty snacks
and freshly prepared hot dishes are served all day, every day. & 彡 》

TIDESWELL: *Poppies* — £ | AE DC MC V
Bank Sq, Tideswell, Buxton, Derby. (01298 871083.
This attractive little place uses ingredients like juniper berries, filo pastry
and feta cheese. Simple rooms. ● Sun D, Wed, Mon–Thu (Nov–Mar). & 彡

LANCASHIRE AND THE LAKES

AMBLESIDE: *Sheila's Cottage* — £ | AE MC V
The Slack, Ambleside, Cumbria. (015394 33079.
Tasty baking is served in this converted stable-block cottage. A range of
tea breads and cakes supplements savory dishes such as Cumbrian
sugar-baked ham or Solway shrimp. ● Sun, Mon D. & 彡

AMBLESIDE: *Zeffirelli's* — £ | MC V
Compston Rd, Ambleside, Cumbria. (015394 33845.
An unusual enterprise combining stores, café, a movie theater and a
trendily decorated pizzeria serving pizzas, salads and pasta. ● L. & 彡

AMBLESIDE: *Rothay Manor* — ££ | AE DC MC V
Rothay Bridge, Ambleside, Cumbria. (015394 33605.
This elegant Regency hotel mainly serves traditional English dishes.
A lunch buffet and splendid teas are excellent values. & 彡 ▌

APPLETHWAITE: *Underscar Manor* — £££ | AE MC V
Off A66 nr Keswick, Cumbria. (017687 75000.
A sumptuous Italianate house in peaceful gardens sets the scene for
ambitious food. Beautifully decorated rooms make a romantic retreat. 彡

BIRTLE: *Normandie* — ££££ | AE DC MC V
Elbut Lane, Birtle, G Man. (0161 764 3869.
The modern European dishes here are serious stuff; unfussy, but cooked
and seasoned perfectly. North country reliability and value. & ▌

Price categories include a three-course meal for one, half a bottle of house wine, and all unavoidable extra charges such as cover, service, VAT
£ under £15
££ £15–£25
£££ £25–£35
££££ £35–£50
£££££ over £50

CHILDREN WELCOME
Restaurants that offer smaller portions and high chairs for children. Special menus sometimes available.

FIXED-PRICE MENU
A good value fixed-price meal, at lunch, dinner or both, usually of three courses.

VEGETARIAN
Vegetarian specialties served, sometimes for both appetizers and main courses.

CREDIT CARDS
Indicates which credit cards are accepted: *AE* American Express; *DC* Diners Club; *MC* Master Card/Access; *V* Visa.

	CREDIT CARDS	CHILDREN WELCOME	FIXED-PRICE MENU	VEGETARIAN	OUTDOOR TABLES
BLACKPOOL: *September Brasserie* ££ 15–17 Queen St, Blackpool, Lancs. 01253 23282. Amid the flotsam of Blackpool's eateries, this brasserie is a beacon of hope. It produces some highly innovative robust dishes. ● *Sun, Mon.*	AE DC MC V	●	■	●	
BOWNESS-ON-WINDERMERE: *Porthole Eating House* £££ 3 Ash St, Bowness-on-Windermere, Cumbria. 015394 42793. Summer crowds fail to jade this Italian restaurant. It maintains its pleasing simplicity of style and concentrates on a good value. ● *L, Tue.* ◗ ▮	AE DC MC V	●		●	■
BRAITHWAITE: *Ivy House* £££ Off A66 nr Keswick, Cumbria. 017687 78338. This Georgian hotel is in the center of the village. Striking decor. Dinners have panache. Comfortable accommodations. ● *L, Jan.* ⚅ ▮	AE DC MC V	●	■	●	
BRAMPTON: *Farlam Hall* ££££ On A689, Brampton, Cumbria. 016977 46234. Fixed-price dinners are offered to nonresidents. It's a fine country house, part 17th-century, part Victorian, on lovely grounds. The food is rich and formal in this welcoming family-run operation. ● *L.* ♿	AE MC V		■		
CARTMEL: *Uplands* £££ Haggs Lane, Cartmel, Cumbria. 015395 36248. This peaceful hotel serves excellent value set lunches of local produce; the views toward Morecambe Bay are delightful and make a perfect *digestif.* A place to come back to, year after year. ● *Mon.* ♿ ⚅	AE MC V		■		
CLEVELEYS: *Bay Tree* £ 44 Victoria Rd West, Cleveleys, Lancs. 01253 865604. An attractive vegetarian and wholefood restaurant with wide-ranging menus; weekend meals are particularly good. ● *Tue–Fri D, Mon.* ⚅		●	■	●	
CLITHEROE: *Auctioneer* ££ New Market St, Clitheroe, Lancs. 01200 27153. Themed menus change regularly in this cottagey converted pub; it might be Tuscany this week, Loire Valley the next. ● *Mon.* ⚅	AE MC V	●	■	●	
COCKERMOUTH: *Quince and Medlar* £ 13 Castlegate, Cockermouth, Cumbria. 01900 823579. Adventurous vegetarian cooking in a modest house near the castle. The award-winning menu is well worth sampling. The inventiveness of the dishes is excellent. ● *Tue–Sun L, Mon.* ⚅	MC V			●	
GRASMERE: *Michael's Nook* ££££ Grasmere, Cumbria. 015934 35496. This opulently furnished country-house hotel offers zestful, wide-ranging cooking. Soups and poultry feature on most menus. ♿ ⚅ ▮	AE DC MC V		■		
GRASMERE: *White Moss House* ££££ On A591 at Rydal Water, Cumbria. 015394 35295. Classy set dinners are served unpompously in this comfortable country-house hotel. A traditional setting and attentive service in a house that once belonged to the poet William Wordsworth. ● *L, Sun.* ♿ ⚅ ▮	MC V		■		
KENDAL: *Moon* ££ 129 Highgate, Kendal, Cumbria. 01539 729254. A creative bistro with many vegetarian specialties. The style is pleasantly informal, but ingredients are always up to the mark. ● *Mon–Sun L.* ♿ ⚅	MC V	●		●	
LANGHO: *Northcote Manor* £££ On A59 nr Blackburn, Lancs. 01254 240555. This solid Victorian hotel and conference center provides traditional English (including Lancashire) recipes, and modern European cooking. ♿	AE DC MC V	●	■	●	

LECK: *Cobwebs*	£££times£	MC V		■	●	

LECK: *Cobwebs*   ££££   MC V
Off A65 at Cowan Bridge, Lune Valley, Lancs. 015242 72141.
A country-house atmosphere; set dinners have unusual combinations
of ingredients. Cheeses are excellent. ● *Wed–Sat L, Sun–Tue.*

LIVERPOOL: *Armadillo*   ££   AE MC V
20–22 Mathew St, Liverpool. 0151 236 4123.
Popular city-center eatery in an old warehouse. The food is inventive
and tasty with interesting vegetarian choices. ● *Sun, Mon L.*

LONGRIDGE: *Paul Heathcote's*   ££££   AE MC V
104–106 Higher Rd, Longridge, Lancs. 01772 784969.
The relaxed style of this British restaurant is deceptive, as the food is
prepared with slick technique and innovative talent. ● *Mon.*

MANCHESTER: *Siam Orchid*   ££   MC V
54 Portland St, Manchester. 0161 236 1388.
Manchester's best Thai restaurant has a great range of dishes, including
many vegetarian choices. There's also influences from other parts of southeast Asia. Beware the fiery sauces; cool them with *Singha* beer.

MANCHESTER: *Moss Nook*   ££££   AE DC MC V
B5166 nr airport, Manchester. 0161 437 4778.
Moss Nook offers a superb presentation of gastronomic medleys. Try the
vast *menu surprise*, or one of the many desserts. ● *Sat L, Sun, Mon.*

MELMERBY: *Village Bakery*   £   AE DC MC V
On A686 nr Penrith, Cumbria. 01768 881515.
An 18th-century barn is the setting for this shop and eatery. Organic
and vegetarian snacks are available all day. ● *D, Sun (Nov–Mar).*

NEAR SAWREY: *Ees Wyke*   ££
On B52 nr Hawkshead, Cumbria. 015394 36393.
The views towards Esthwaite Water are one attraction; charming hosts
and excellent, good-value dinners another. This is a place that you will
not forget in a hurry. ● *L, Jan–Feb.*

POULTON-LE-FYLDE: *River House*   ££££   MC V
Skippool Creek, Thornton-le-Fylde, Lancs. 01253 883497.
This restaurant-with-rooms prides itself on its details (cheeses,
teas, and *petits fours*) being as good as the main courses. ● *Sun D.*

SPARK BRIDGE: *Bridgefield House*   £££   MC V
Off A5084 nr Ulverston, Cumbria. 01229 885239.
It is worth making an effort to taste the cooking at this country-house
hotel. Book ahead for a set 5-course gourmet dinner. ● *L.*

ULLSWATER: *Sharrow Bay*   ££££
Nr Howtown, Ullswater, Cumbria. 017684 86301.
One of Britain's greatest country-house hotels. Mealtimes are a gastro-
nomic blowout – even the teas are a banquet. *(See also p561.)*

WATERMILLOCK: *Rampsbeck Country House*   £££   MC V
On A592 nr Pooley Bridge, Cumbria. 017684 86442.
Rampsbeck's dining room occupies a fine stretch of lakeshore, but the
modern British food is ambitious enough to hold the attention. The
service is pleasant and deserves a mention.

WINDERMERE: *Miller Howe*   ££££   AE DC MC V
Rayrigg Rd, Windermere, Cumbria. 015394 42536.
This restaurant is also a beautiful hotel, but the elaborate and theatrical
dishes are the main reason for visiting. ● *Dec–Mar.*

WITHERSLACK: *Old Vicarage*   £££   MC V
Church Rd, Witherslack, Cumbria. 015395 52381.
This idyllic country-house hotel serves dinner at 8pm, a mouthwatering
affair using Cumberland produce. Book ahead. ● *Mon–Sat L.*

YORKSHIRE AND HUMBERSIDE

ASENBY: *Crab and Lobster*   ££   AE MC V
Off A168 nr Thirsk, N Yorks. 01845 577286.
A great seafood pub just off the A1. Blackboards reflect the unpredictability
of fresh catches. The place hums with activity. ● *Sun D.*

Price categories include a three-course meal for one, half a bottle of house wine, and all unavoidable extra charges such as cover, service, VAT ⓔ under £15 ⓔⓔ £15-£25 ⓔⓔⓔ £25-£35 ⓔⓔⓔⓔ £35-£50 ⓔⓔⓔⓔⓔ over £50	**CHILDREN WELCOME** Restaurants that offer smaller portions and high chairs for children. Special menus sometimes available. **FIXED-PRICE MENU** A good value fixed-price meal, at lunch, dinner or both, usually of three courses. **VEGETARIAN** Vegetarian specialties served, sometimes for both appetizers and main courses. **CREDIT CARDS** Indicates which credit cards are accepted: *AE* American Express; *DC* Diners Club; *MC* Master Card/Access; *V* Visa.	CREDIT CARDS	CHILDREN WELCOME	FIXED-PRICE MENU	VEGETARIAN	OUTDOOR TABLES
BOLTON ABBEY: *Devonshire Arms* ⓔⓔⓔ On A59 nr Ilkley, N Yorks. 📞 01756 710441. A luxurious country-house hotel. All types flock in to enjoy the stylish restaurant, excellent bar snacks, and luscious teas. ⓔ ⓔ ⓔ		AE DC MC V	●	■	●	
BRADFORD: *Bombay Brasserie* ⓔ Simes St, Bradford, W Yorks. 📞 01274 737564. This upscale Indian restaurant specializes in Bengali fish and vegetarian dishes, though there's plenty else to try. Tandooris are a strong point. ▶		MC V	●	■	●	
BRADFORD: *Restaurant 19* ⓔⓔⓔⓔ North Park Rd, Heaton, Bradford, W Yorks. 📞 01274 492559. This Victorian terraced house conceals an ornate confection of a dining-room serving startling and ambitious food. The set dinners are a good value and simply described. Handsome bedrooms. ● *L, Sun.* ▮		AE DC MC V		■		
ELLAND: *Bertie's Bistro* ⓔⓔ 7 Town Hall Buildings, Elland, W Yorks. 📞 01422 371724. Edwardian decor sets the scene at this popular bistro. Delectable appetizers, filling stews always available. Try and save some room for desserts such as *Bertie's Bombe*, which is pure indulgence. ● *L, Mon.* ⓔ ▶ ▮		MC V	●		●	
HARROGATE: *Betty's* ⓔⓔ 1 Parliament St, Harrogate, N Yorks. 📞 01423 502746. Betty's serves breakfasts, lunches and dinners as well as an eye-popping range of cakes, teas and coffees, all in lovely Edwardian decor. ⓔ		MC V	●		●	
HARROGATE: *Drum and Monkey* ⓔⓔⓔ 5 Montpellier Gardens, Harrogate, N Yorks. 📞 01423 502650. A town-center pub now achieves a more elevated status as a stylish seafood wine bar and restaurant. It's fish or nothing here. ● *Sun.* ⓔ		MC V	●			
HEADIS: *Bryan's* ⓔ 9 Weetwood Lane, Headingley, Leeds, W Yorks. 📞 0113 2785679. A traditional fish and chip restaurant of the best Yorkshire sort. Beef dripping and fresh fish are the secrets behind perfect results. Traditional, delicious desserts like treacle pudding round off the meal. ⓔ ⓔ ▶		MC V	●	■	●	■
HETTON: *Angel Inn* ⓔⓔ Off B6265 nr Skipton, N Yorks. 📞 01756 730263. This convivial beamed restaurant is more than a village pub, but the bar and brasserie food stay down to earth. ● *Mon–Sat L, Sun D.* ⓔ ⓔ ▮		MC V		■	●	
ILKLEY: *Box Tree* ⓔⓔⓔⓔ 35–37 Church St, Ilkley, W Yorks. 📞 01943 608484. Cuisine is definitely *haute* in this 18th-century farmhouse, recently revitalized by a new and creative chef. ● *Sat L, Sun D, Mon.* ⓔ ⓔ ▶		AE MC V	●	■	●	
LEEDS: *Brasserie Forty-four* ⓔⓔ 44 The Calls, Leeds, W Yorks. 📞 0113 2343232. This waterfront warehouse complex combines bright, sophisticated cooking with stylish accommodations. Lively atmosphere makes this a fun night out. Especially pleasant in summer. ● *Sat L, Sun D.* ⓔ ▶		AE MC V	●	■	●	■
LEEDS: *Haley's* ⓔⓔⓔ Shire Oak Rd, Headingley, Leeds, W Yorks. 📞 0113 2784446. A peaceful Victorian hotel in the university district produces Anglo-French cuisine with exquisite presentation. Light, modern bedrooms. ● *L, Sun.*		AE DC MC V		■	●	
LIVERSEDGE: *Lillibet's* ⓔⓔⓔ 64 Leeds Rd, Liversedge, W Yorks. 📞 01924 404911. This neat stone hotel offers dinners spanning three courses with equal flair, mixing traditional and new ideas. ● *Sat L, Sun, Mon L.* ⓔ		AE MC V	●	■		

LOW LAITHE: *Dusty Miller* £££ AE MC V
On B6165 nr Pately Bridge, N Yorks. (01423 78837.
These elegant surroundings and Nidd Valley views cost a bit, but the
cooking is careful, using top-grade ingredients. ● *L, Sun, Mon.* ▶

RIPLEY: *Boar's Head* £££ AE MC V
Ripley, N Yorks. (01423 771888.
This coaching inn provides comfortable accommodation and food with
finesse; the desserts use exotic fruits. Service is amiable. ⬧

RIPON: *Old Deanery* £££ AE DC MC V
Minster Rd, Ripon, N Yorks. (01765 603518.
This restaurant and brasserie has a historic setting by the cathedral. Local
ingredients are given saucily French treatment. ● *Sat L, Sun D, Mon.* ⬧ ☰

SETTLE: *Blue Goose* ££ MC V
Market Pl, Settle, N Yorks. (01729 822901.
The cooking in this Victorian town house turned wine bar is fairly simple
at lunchtime, more sophisticated and Gallic-inspired by night. ● *Sun.*

SHEFFIELD: *Greenhead House* £££ MC V
84 Burncross Rd, Chapeltown, Sheffield, S Yorks. (0114 2469004.
Four-course menus give a taste of France in the smart dining room of
this stone house. Homemade soups a specialty. ● *L, Sun, Mon.* ⬧ ☰

STADDLEBRIDGE: *McCoy's* £££ AE DC MC V
On A19 nr Northallerton, N Yorks. (01609 882671.
Eccentricity is a virtue in this restaurant-with-rooms. The basement bistro is
open all week, the French-inspired restaurant opens only at dinnertime. ▣

WHITBY: *Magpie Café* £ MC V
14 Pier Rd, Whitby, N Yorks. (01947 602058.
This house by the harbor serves superlative fish and chips with good
cheer. Don't miss the diverse and unusual desserts. ● *late Nov–Mar.* ☰

WINTERINGHAM: *Winteringham Fields* ££££ AE MC V
Winteringham, Humberside. (01724 733096.
This hotel has an interior of carefully achieved, opulent Victoriana.
The same attention is lavished on the modern British cooking, some of
the best in Britain. *(See also p563.)* ● *Sat L, Sun, Mon L.* ⬧ ☰ ▣

YORK: *Taylor's Tea Rooms* £ MC V
46 Stonegate, York. (01904 640348.
A wide range of Yorkshire and Swiss specialties, homemade cakes
and light lunches are served in this medieval building. ● *D.* ☰

YORK: *Melton's* ££ MC V
7 Scarcroft Rd, York. (01904 634341.
This small restaurant in a Victorian terrace is a good value and welcoming,
serving varied Anglo-French food. ● *Sun D, Mon L.* ⬧ ☰ ▣

NORTHUMBRIA

ALNWICK: *John Blackmore's* £££ AE DC MC V
1 Dorothy Foster Court, Narrowgate, Alnwick, Northum. (01665 604465.
This stone house near the castle presents a wide range of options
using substantial appetizers and creamy sauces. ● *L, Sun, Mon.* ⬧ ☰

BERWICK UPON TWEED: *Funnywayt'mekalivin* ££ MC V
41 Bridge St, Berwick upon Tweed, Northum. (01289 308827.
Appealing four-course dinners are offered along with simple bed-
and-breakfast and lunch most days. ● *Mon–Tue D, Sun.* ☰

CONSETT: *Pavilion* ££ AE DC MC V
2 Station Rd, Consett, Co Durham. (01207 503388.
Bustling Cantonese restaurant serving generous helpings from an extensive
Chinese menu. The service is efficient and unobtrusive. Friendly
atmosphere and a good value. ● *Sun–Wed L.* ▶

DARLINGTON: *Victor's* ££ AE DC MC V
84 Victoria Rd, Darlington, Co Durham. (01325 480818.
Unprepossessing surroundings do not detract from this cheerful, good-
value, intimate place. A place with a cozy atmosphere and discreet
service. Cooking is eclectic. ● *Sun, Mon.* ⬧ ▶

Price categories include a three-course meal for one, half a bottle of house wine, and all unavoidable extra charges such as cover, service, VAT
£ under £15
££ £15-£25
£££ £25-£35
££££ £35-£50
£££££ over £50

CHILDREN WELCOME
Restaurants that offer smaller portions and high chairs for children. Special menus sometimes available.

FIXED-PRICE MENU
A good value fixed-price meal, at lunch, dinner or both, usually of three courses.

VEGETARIAN
Vegetarian specialties served, sometimes for both appetizers and main courses.

CREDIT CARDS
Indicates which credit cards are accepted: *AE* American Express; *DC* Diners Club; *MC* Master Card/Access; *V* Visa.

	CREDIT CARDS	CHILDREN WELCOME	FIXED-PRICE MENU	VEGETARIAN	OUTDOOR TABLES
DARLINGTON: *Cottage Thai* £££ 94–96 Parkgate, Darlington, Co Durham. (01325 361717. Handy for the station and theater, this simple place offers Thai classics like *tom yum* soups, and red and green curries. ● *Sun.* ⬤ ⤢ ❱	AE MC V	●	■	●	
EAST BOLDEN: *Forsters* £££ 2 St Bedes, Station Rd, East Boldon, T & W. (0191 519 0929. A family-run enterprise run on Neo-Classical French *auberge* lines, welcoming and unpretentious but with plenty of sparkle. The food is never disappointing. ● *L, Sun, Mon.*	AE DC MC V		■		
GATESHEAD: *Fumi* ££ 248 Durham Rd, Gateshead, T & W. (0191 477 1152. A Japanese outpost offering plenty of fresh *sushi, tempura* and noodle soup dishes. Service is courteous. ● *L, Mon.* ⬤ ⤢ ❱	MC V	●		●	
GATESHEAD: *Eslington Villa* £££ On A6127, Low Fell, T & W. (0191 487 6017. Reliable classic cooking figures in this attractive, graciously furnished hotel. Guests are greeted with *bonhomie.* ● *Sat L, Sun D.* ⬤ ⤢	AE DC MC V	●	■		
HEXHAM: *Black House* £££ Dipton Mill Rd, Hexham, Northum. (01434 604744. Artful combinations of flavor and texture lie behind the stable door of these converted farmhouse outbuildings. ● *L, Sun, Mon.* ⬤ ⤢	MC V			●	
NEWCASTLE UPON TYNE: *Courtney's* ££ 5–7 The Side, Newcastle, T & W. (0191 232 5537. Fresh local meat, game and exotic fish feature in this brasserie. Modern-international cuisine gives flavor and color. A laid-back atmosphere with jazz played in the background. ● *Sat L, Sun.* ⬤ ❱	AE MC V		■		
NEWCASTLE UPON TYNE: *Fisherman's Lodge* ££££ Jesmond Dene, Jesmond, T & W. (0191 281 3281. The food here combines the modern and classical for excellent results. Lunchtime snacks are a good value. ● *Sat L, Sun.* ⬤ ⤢ ❱	AE DC MC V		■	●	■
NEWCASTLE UPON TYNE: *21 Queen St* ££££ 19–21 Queen St, Princes Wharf, Quayside, Newcastle, T & W. (0191 222 0755. A cool, stream-lined setting for complex, well-crafted cooking in this Conran-influenced restaurant. Even the humblest of vegetables are turned into a *tour de force.* Unruffled service. ● *Sat L, Sun.* ⬤ ❱ ▪	AE DC MC V		■		
ROMALDKIRK: *Rose and Crown* ££ On B6277 nr Barnard Castle, Co Durham. (01833 650213. This handsome coaching inn offers a splendid mix of pub, good-value bar meals and undaunting restaurant. Well worth making a detour for. Good selection of ales. ● *Mon–Sat L, Sun D.* ⤢	MC V		■		■
SEATON BURN: *Horton Grange* ££££ off A1 at Stannington, T & W. (01661 860686. This pleasant stone farmhouse hotel offers local English produce. Decor and cooking are sophisticated, light and elegant. ● *L, Sun.* ⬤ ⤢	MC V	●	■		
STOKESLEY: *Chapters* £££ 27 High St, Stokesley, N Yorks. (01642 711888. A successful duo of informal bistro and more serious dining room. Cooking is French with global crosscurrents. Attractive guest rooms.	AE DC MC V				
WHITLEY BAY: *Le Provençale* ££ 183 Park View, Whitley Bay, T & W. (0191 251 3567. Hearty, traditional French cooking. The decor is reassuringly staid, service very pleasant. ● *Mon–Wed L, Sat L, Sun D, Tue D.* ⬤	AE DC MC V		■		

WYLAM: *Laburnum House* £££ AE MC V
Wylam, Northum. 01661 852185.
This village restaurant has daily specials chalked on a blackboard.
Fresh fish is impressive. Unpretentious but tasty food served with
jovial *bonhomie*. Inexpensive rooms are available. *L, Sun.*

NORTH WALES

ABERSOCH: *Riverside* ££ AE DC MC V
On A499 nr Pwllheli, C & M. 01758 712419.
High teas and oven-fresh lunches and dinners are served in the rustic
dining area. Homey and welcoming. *mid-Nov–Mar.*

ABERSOCH: *Porth Tocyn* £££ MC V
Abersoch, C & M. 01758 713303.
Few fail to be charmed by this coastal hotel. There are light alternatives
to the menu. *(See also p564.)* *mid-Nov–Easter.*

CAPEL COCH: *Tre-Ysgawen Hall* £££ AE DC MC V
On B5111 nr Llangefni, Anglesey. 01248 750750.
A firm classical training tailors the modern French cooking at this
massive country-house hotel. Service is courteous and attentive.

CHIRK: *Starling's Castle* £££ AE DC MC V
Bronygarth, nr Chirk, Wrexham. 01691 718464.
This 18th-century farmhouse serves traditional terrines and soups with
Mediterranean-style dishes. Attractive bedrooms. *Mon–Sat L.*

COLWYN BAY: *Café Niçoise* £££ AE DC MC V
124 Abergele Rd, Colwyn Bay, A & C. 01492 531555.
This French-style bistro comes complete with accordion music and Paris-
ian scenes. Provincial cooking inspires the menus. *Mon–Wed L, Sun.*

DEGANWY: *Paysanne* ££ MC V
Station Rd, Deganwy, A & C. 01492 583848.
This bustling Gallic bistro serves daily specials and three-course
provincial dinners; on Saturdays it's *à la carte*. *Mon–Sat L, Sun, Mon.*

DOLGELLAU: *Dylanwad Da* ££
2 Ffôs-y-Felin, Dolgellau, A & C. 01341 422870.
A bright little neighborhood bistro with pine tables serving the likes of
Welsh lamb and port, plum and ginger pie. *L, Sun–Wed (Nov–Mar).*

EYTON: *Plassey Bistro* £
Eyton, nr Wrexham. 01978 780905.
Set amid a complex of Edwardian farm buildings and craft workshops,
Plassey offers good bar snacks and blackboard specials. Slow roasted
Welsh lamb is a delicious specialty. *Mon.*

GLANWYDDEN: *Queen's Head* ££ MC V
Off B5115 nr Llandudno Junction, A & C. 01492 546570.
Popular country pub offering Welsh lamb, local mussels and soups.
Traditional puddings also appear on a long list of desserts.

HARLECH: *Castle Cottage* ££ AE MC V
Pen Llech, Harlech, C & M. 01766 780479.
Despite modern extensions, this is one of the oldest buildings in Harlech.
Menus have Welsh and English elements. Fresh local produce gives the
dishes an authentic flavor. Bedrooms available. *Feb.*

HAWARDEN: *Swiss Restaurant Imfeld* ££ AE DC MC V
68 The Highway, Hawarden, Flint. 01244 534523.
Swiss specialties and *Gemütlichkeit* are served up in this cozy place.
Gourmet evenings and fondue nights are featured occasionally. *L, Mon.*

LLANBEDR: *Llew Glas Brasserie* £ AE DC MC V
Llanbedr, C & M. 01341 241555.
A beamed cottage is the setting for simple dishes like pot roast Welsh
lamb. Snacks served all day. *L, Sun–Wed (Nov–Mar), Tue (Jun–Sep).*

LLANBERIS: *Y Bistro* £££ MC V
43–45 High St, Llanberis, C & M. 01286 871278.
Hungry walkers flock to this restaurant at the foot of the Snowdon
railroad. A good range of hearty, spicy main courses. *L, Sun.*

For key to symbols see back flap

Price categories include a three-course meal for one, half a bottle of house wine, and all unavoidable extra charges such as cover, service, VAT **£** under £15 **££** £15–£25 **£££** £25–£35 **££££** £35–£50 **£££££** over £50	**CHILDREN WELCOME** Restaurants that offer smaller portions and high chairs for children. Special menus sometimes available. **FIXED-PRICE MENU** A good value fixed-price meal, at lunch, dinner or both, usually of three courses. **VEGETARIAN** Vegetarian specialties served, sometimes for both appetizers and main courses. **CREDIT CARDS** Indicates which credit cards are accepted: *AE* American Express; *DC* Diners Club; *MC* Master Card/Access; *V* Visa.	**CREDIT CARDS**	**CHILDREN WELCOME**	**FIXED-PRICE MENU**	**VEGETARIAN**	**OUTDOOR TABLES**

	CREDIT CARDS	CHILDREN WELCOME	FIXED-PRICE MENU	VEGETARIAN	OUTDOOR TABLES
LLANDRILLO: *Tyddyn Llan* **£££** On B4401 nr Corwen, Denbigh. **[** 01490 440264. This Georgian farmhouse hotel produces distinctive, high-quality cooking using local ingredients such as Welsh black beef and fish. *(See also p565.)* **&**	DC MC V	●	■	●	■
LLANGOLLEN: *Gales* **£** 18 Bridge St, Llangollen, Wrexham. **[** 01978 860089. A wine bar, restaurant and guesthouse. Food is served in a paneled bar with church pews; bedrooms are furnished with antiques. ● *Sun.* **& ▯**	MC V	●		●	
LLANSANFFRAID GLAN CONWY: *Old Rectory* **££££** Llanrwst Rd, Llansanffraid Glan Conwy, A & C.. **[** 01492 580611. Great care is lavished on the four-course dinners here. Inside there are many paintings and antiques. ● *Dec 20–Feb 1.* **& ⇄ ▯**	AE DC MC V		■		
MENAI BRIDGE: *Jodie's* **£** Telford Rd, Menai Bridge, Anglesey. **[** 01248 714864. Wine bar food is served in a conservatory and garden overlooking the Menai bridge. Also serves vegetarian dishes. ● *Sun L, Mon L.* **& ⇄**				●	
NORTHOP: *Soughton Hall* **£££** Off A5119, Northop, Flint. **[** 01352 840811. Great cooking matches this hotel's palatial setting: an 18th-century bishop's palace in parkland. Service and dress are formal. ● *Sun.* **⇄**	AE MC V		■	●	
PORTMEIRION: *Portmeirion* **£££** Off A487 nr Minffordd, C & M. **[** 01766 771228. The intriguing folly village boasts one delightful hotel, where an apt Mediterranean frivolity breezes through the menus. ● *Mon L.* **⇄ ▯**	AE DC MC V	●	■	●	■
PWLLHELI: *Plas Bodegroes* **£££** Nefyn Rd, Pwllheli, C & M. **[** 01758 612363. This elegant Georgian country house takes full advantage of excellent local ingredients to produce accomplished British cooking for its award-winning five-course dinners. Fish especially good. *(See also p565.)* ● *L, Mon.*	MC V	●			

SOUTH AND MID-WALES

	CREDIT CARDS	CHILDREN WELCOME	FIXED-PRICE MENU	VEGETARIAN	OUTDOOR TABLES
ABERAERON: *Hive on the Quay* **££** Cadwgan Pl, Aberaeron, Pembroke. **[** 01545 570445. Honey is the specialty at this summertime café, which serves wholesome teas and lunches (dinners too, in high summer) in a homey setting of stripped pine and lots of potted plants. ● *mid-Sept–May.* **&**	MC V	●		●	■
BRECHFA: *Ty Mawr* **£££** Brechfa, Carmarthen. **[** 01539 729254. Small, rustic hotel with good home baking. Local produce is treated to international flourishes. ● *Mon–Wed L, Tues, Sun D, mid-Jan–Feb.* **& ⇄**	AE MC V	●	■	●	
CARDIFF: *La Brasserie/Champers/Le Monde* **££** 60 St Mary St, Cardiff. **[** 01222 372164. Bustling complex of French brasserie (fish and grills), tapas bar and pub-like fish restaurant with friendly atmosphere and good wines. **& ▶**	AE DC MC V	●	■	●	
CARDIFF: *Chikako's* **££** 10–11 Mill Lane, Cardiff. **[** 01222 665279. Minimalist decor complements carefully prepared food in this Japanese enclave. Ingredients are imported or grown in their garden. ● *L.* **⇄ ▶**	AE MC V		■		
CLYTHA: *Clytha Arms* **££** Nr Abergavenny, B Gwent. **[** 01873 840206. Country pub where France and Wales meet in fare such as laverbread *(see p37)* or oysters with leeks. ● *Sun D, Mon L.* **& ⇄**	MC V	●	■	●	■

COWBRIDGE: *Off the Beeton Track*   £
1 Town Hall Sq, Cowbridge, V of Glam. (01446 773599.
Home-baked cakes, simple lunches and afternoon teas precede more
elaborate evening fare. Sauces are a strong point. ● *Sun D, Mon D.* & ⚡
AE MC V

CRICKHOWELL: *Nantyffin Cider Mill Inn*   ££
Brecon Rd, Crickhowell, Powys. (01873 810775.
This unpretentious 16th-century stone inn offers undemanding dishes
like pie and mash, plus local game and seafood. ● *Mon (Nov–Mar).* &
MC V

FREYSTROP: *Jemima's*   ££
Nr Haverfordwest, Pembroke. (01437 891109.
Short but dashing menus with a love of seasonal flavors and high-quality
ingredients in this bistro and restaurant. ● *Sun D, Tue, Wed (winter).* ⚡
AE MC V

GOODWICK: *Tate's Brasserie*   ££
Bay View House, Main St, Goodwick, Pembroke. (01348 874190.
A wide-ranging menu of daytime snacks, bar meals and evening *à la carte*
makes use of local produce and international inspiration. ● *Tue L.* & ⚡

LLANDEWI SKIRRID: *Walnut Tree Inn*   £££
On B4521 nr Abergavenny, B Gwent. (01873 852797.
This popular, informal bistro offers a vast selection of eclectic food,
unpretentiously served but carefully prepared. ● *Sun, Mon.* &

LLANWRDA: *Seguendo di Stagioni*   £££
Harford, nr Pumpsaint, Caerphilly. (01558 650671.
The Italian owner's enthusiasm rubs off on food and guests alike. Ask
what he recommends, and what to drink with it. ● *Sun D, Mon.* 🌙 ❚
MC V

LLYSWEN: *Griffin Inn*   ££
On A470, Llyswen, Powys. (01874 754241.
Shooting and fishing are the attractions in the Wye Valley, home of this
15th-century inn; the fare reflects this. Rooms available. ● *Sun D.* & ⚡
AE DC MC V

MATHRY: *Ann FitzGerald's Farmhouse Kitchen*   ££
Off A487 nr Mabwys Fawr, Caerphilly. (01348 831347.
Interesting dishes with strong flavors are the mark of this restaurant.
Good wines and Welsh cheeses. ● *L (winter).* & ⚡
MC V

NANTGAREDIG: *Four Seasons, Cwmtwrch Farm*   ££
On B4310, Carmarthen. (01267 290238.
Local produce receives honest farmhouse treatment in this family-run
restaurant. Welsh lamb and smoked salmon are featured. ● *Sun.*

NEWPORT: *Cnapan*   ££
East St, Newport, Caerphilly. (01239 820575.
This Georgian restaurant-with-rooms is open all day for coffee and tea.
Lunch and dinner menus include Welsh specialties. ● *Sun D, Tue.* & ⚡
MC V

PONTFAEN: *Tregynon Country Farmhouse*   ££
Off B4313, Gwaun Valley, Newport. (01239 820531.
The food here is delicious and carefully considered (home-smoked bacon
and health foods). Inexpensive, rural accommodation. ● *L.* ⚡
MC V

PORTHGAIN: *Harbour Lights*   ££
Off A487 at Croesgoch, Pembroke. (01348 831549.
This old seaside cottage offers generous local fare with fresh herbs,
Welsh cheeses and lots of laverbread *(see pp36–7).* ● *Dec–mid-Feb.* & ⚡
MC V

SWANSEA: *La Braseria*   ££
28 Wind St, Swansea. (01792 469683.
This Spanish restaurant is especially popular at lunchtime for a good value
set lunches garnished with chips, salads and garlic bread. ● *Sun.* & 🌙
AE DC MC V

SWANSEA: *Number One Wind Street*   ££
1 Wind St, Swansea. (01792 456996.
The style in this modern restaurant is regional French, translated into
Welsh by using local meat and seafood to good effect. ● *Mon–Tue D, Sun.* &
AE MC V

TRELLECH: *Village Green Brasserie*   ££
Trellech, nr Monmouth. (01600 560119.
Eclectic cuisine from around the world in this 400-year-old former
priory. Fixed-priced meals only for Sunday lunch. ● *Sun D, Mon.* &
MC V

Price categories include a three-course meal for one, half a bottle of house wine, and all unavoidable extra charges such as cover, service, VAT. **£** under £15; **££** £15–£25; **£££** £25–£35; **££££** £35–£50; **£££££** over £50	**CHILDREN WELCOME** Restaurants that offer smaller portions and high chairs for children. Special menus sometimes available. **FIXED-PRICE MENU** A good value fixed-price meal, at lunch, dinner or both, usually of three courses. **VEGETARIAN** Vegetarian specialties served, sometimes for both appetizers and main courses. **CREDIT CARDS** Indicates which credit cards are accepted: AE American Express; DC Diners Club; MC Master Card/Access; V Visa.	**CREDIT CARDS**	**CHILDREN WELCOME**	**FIXED-PRICE MENU**	**VEGETARIAN**	**OUTDOOR TABLES**

WELSH HOOK: *Stone Hall* **££**
Off A40 nr Wolf's Castle, Pembroke. (01348 840212.
French cooking with unusual touches (seaweed pancakes and coconut sauce) reigns in this hotel-restaurant in wooded grounds. ● L, Mon. &
AE MC V | ● | ▪ | | |

WHITEBROOK: *Crown at Whitebrook* **££**
Nr Monmouth, Monmouth. (01600 860254.
This 17th-century outpost of provincial France can be found deep in the Wye Valley; it is now run as a restaurant-with-rooms. ● Sun D, Mon L. ⇄ ▯
AE DC MC V | ● | ▪ | ● | ▪ |

THE LOWLANDS

ANSTRUTHER: *Cellar* **£££**
24 East Green, Anstruther, Fife. (01333 310378.
One of this fishing port's oldest buildings. Only top-quality produce is used; fresh seafood dominates the menu. ● Sat L, Sun, Mon. ⇄ ▯
AE MC V | | ▪ | | |

AYR: *Fouters Bistro* **£**
2A Academy St, Ayr, Strathclyde. (01292 261391.
Lively bistro in a vaulted basement. Ingredients are Scottish, cooking mostly provincial-French, with vegetarian dishes. ● Sun, Mon. ⇄ ▯
AE DC MC V | ● | ▪ | ● | |

CANONBIE: *Riverside Inn* **£££**
On A47 nr border, Dumfries & Galloway. (0138 73 71512.
Consistently good cooking ensures the popularity of this 17th-century inn overlooking the Esk. You can eat in the bar or restaurant. ● Sun. ⇄ ▯
MC V | ● | | ● | ▪ |

CUPAR: *Ostlers Close* **£££**
25 Bonnygate, Cupar, Fife. (01334 655574.
Fish play a large part in the menus at this tiny place, but plenty of meat or game dishes get expert French treatment too. Wild mushrooms are one of their delicious specialties. ● Sun, Mon. & ⇄ ▯
AE MC V | | | | |

EDINBURGH: *Cruise Ship* **£**
The Shore, Leith, Edinburgh. (0131 555 4445.
This boat is the most conspicuous of many eating places around Leith docks. Fare is simple – steak, fish, chicken or vegetable dishes. ⇄ ▯
AE MC V | ● | | ● | ▪ |

EDINBURGH: *Henderson's* **£**
94 Hanover St, Edinburgh. (0131 225 2131.
This institution has a wide range of vegetarian specialties. Cakes and unusual cheeses accompany salads and hot dishes. ● public hols. ⇄ ▯
AE MC V | ● | | ● | |

EDINBURGH: *Kalpna* **£**
2–3 St Patrick Sq, Edinburgh. (0131 667 9890.
Indian vegetarian cookery in a calming environment near the university. Flavors are mild and service variable. ● Sat L, Sun. & ⇄ ▯
MC V | ● | ▪ | ● | |

EDINBURGH: *Seeds* **£**
53 West Nicolson St, Edinburgh. (0131 667 8729.
A friendly health food vegetarian café centrally located near Edinburgh University. Good quality ingredients, impeccably flavored. & ⇄
| ● | | ● | |

EDINBURGH: *Indian Cavalry Club* **££**
3 Atholl Pl, Edinburgh. (0131 228 3282.
The last days of the Raj resurface in this fine Indian restaurant near Haymarket. Dishes are rich Anglo-Indian favorites. & ⇄ ▯
AE DC MC V | ● | ▪ | ● | |

EDINBURGH: *Atrium* **£££**
10 Cambridge St, Edinburgh. (0131 228 8882.
An ultrastylish interior by the Traverse Theatre complements the light, simple, but exciting cooking here. This is the cutting edge of modern British cookery; Mediterranean influences dominate. ● Sat L, Sun. & ⇄ ▯
AE MC V | ● | | ● | |

EDINBURGH: *Martin's* — £££ — AE DC MC V
70 Rose St, North Lane, Edinburgh. 📞 0131 225 3106.
City center premises attract business folk and shoppers for a range of
imaginative, French-inspired cooking. ● Sat L, Sun, Mon.

EDINBURGH: *Vintners Rooms* — £££ — AE MC V
87 Giles St, Leith, Edinburgh. 📞 0131 554 6767.
This unusual candlelit restaurant is housed in a wine warehouse. Both
cooking and service are admirably unpretentious. Light lunches are
served in the wine bar. ● Sun.

EDINBURGH: *Waterfront Wine Bar* — £££ — MC V
1C Dock Place, Leith, Edinburgh. 📞 0131 554 7427.
Best of the Leith waterfront bar-restaurants with a cozy bar, excellent
wine list, and conservatory restaurant serving modish fare.

GLASGOW: *Buttery* — £££ — AE DC MC V
652 Argyle St, Glasgow. 📞 0141 221 8188.
Attractive turn-of-the-century pub converted into an elegant dining
room. Simpler food is served downstairs in the Belfry. ● Sat L, Sun.

GLASGOW: *Ubiquitous Chip* — £££ — AE DC MC V
12 Ashton Lane, Glasgow. 📞 0141 334 5007.
The lighthearted individuality suggested by the name reveals itself most
in the upstairs bistro. The food throughout is good, with well-rehearsed
and hugely varied treatments of Scottish fare. ● public hols.

GLASGOW: *Camerons, Glasgow Hilton* — ££££ — AE DC MC V
1 William St, Glasgow. 📞 0141 204 5511.
This is theme-park Scotland, but both food and service are beyond
reproach at this business hotel and restaurant. ● Sat L, Sun.

GLASGOW: *One Devonshire Gardens* — ££££ — AE DC MC V
1 Devonshire Gardens, Glasgow. 📞 0141 339 2001.
French and British inspiration at this sumptuous hotel-restaurant.
The atmosphere is pleasantly relaxed. (See also p569.) ● Sat L.

GULLANE: *La Potinière* — £££
Main St, Gullane, Lothn. 📞 01620 843214.
The cooking here is splendid, bursting with flavor. Very good
value. The husband and wife team who run it create a warm,
convivial atmosphere. ● Wed, Fri–Sat L, Sun–Thu D.

LARGS: *Nardini's* — £ — AE DC MC V
The Esplanade, Largs, Strath. 📞 01475 674555.
A splendid Art Deco interior sets the scene of this seafront lounge café.
Breakfasts, cakes, Italian and British dishes are served all day. This is
the perfect place to sit back, read the paper and relax.

LINLITHGOW: *Champany Inn* — ££££ — AE DC MC V
Champany, nr Linlithgow, Lothn. 📞 0150 683 4388.
Wines spring to the fore here, but the food is good too, whether a per-
fect Angus steak, or more ornate dishes with sauces. ● Sat L, Sun.

MOFFAT: *Well View* — £££
Ballplay Rd, Moffat, D & G. 📞 01683 20184.
Modern French cooking with some Scottish elements is served in this
family-run Victorian hotel. The atmosphere is peaceful. ● Sat L.

PORTPATRICK: *Knockinaam Lodge* — ££££ — AE DC MC V
Off A77 nr Portpatrick, D & G. 📞 01776 810471.
An idyllic location overlooking the sea. Cooking is fashionable,
French and modern, with casseroles and fish. ● Jan–Mar.

ST. ANDREWS: *Brambles* — £ — MC V
5 College St, St Andrews, Fife. 📞 01334 75380.
Popular self-service café specializing in health food and vegetarian recipes,
though meat and fish also appear. Good baking too. ● D, Sun (winter).

ST. ANDREWS: *Peat Inn* — ££££ — AE DC MC V
On B940 nr St Andrews, Fife. 📞 01334 840206.
Highly accomplished modern cooking with regional produce and seasonal vegetables has established this fine hotel-restaurant as one of the
best in Britain. Lunch is a bargain. ● Sun, Mon.

For key to symbols see back flap

<table>
<tr><td colspan="2">

Price categories include a three-course meal for one, half a bottle of house wine, and all unavoidable extra charges such as cover, service, VAT
£ under £15
££ £15–£25
£££ £25–£35
££££ £35–£50
£££££ over £50

</td><td colspan="6">

CHILDREN WELCOME
Restaurants that offer smaller portions and high chairs for children. Special menus sometimes available.
FIXED-PRICE MENU
A good value fixed-price meal, at lunch, dinner or both, usually of three courses.
VEGETARIAN
Vegetarian specialties served, sometimes for both appetizers and main courses.
CREDIT CARDS
Indicates which credit cards are accepted: AE American Express; DC Diners Club; MC Master Card/Access; V Visa.

</td></tr>
</table>

		CREDIT CARDS	CHILDREN WELCOME	FIXED-PRICE MENU	VEGETARIAN	OUTDOOR TABLES
SWINTON: *Wheatsheaf*	££	MC V	●		●	■
Main St, Swinton, Borders. 01890 860257. This country inn offers imaginative cooking served in a traditional dining room or conservatory. Bedrooms available. ● Mon. &						
TROON: *Highgrove House*	£££	AE MC V	●	■	●	■
Old Loans Rd, Troon, Strath. 01292 312511. Watery prospects over the Firth of Clyde accompany informal meals from a wide-ranging menu in this retired sea captain's house. Bedrooms available.						

THE HIGHLANDS AND ISLANDS

		CREDIT CARDS	CHILDREN WELCOME	FIXED-PRICE MENU	VEGETARIAN	OUTDOOR TABLES
ABERDEEN: *Henry J Bean's Bar and Grill*	£				●	
Windmill Brae, Aberdeen, Grampn. 01224 574134. Cheerful, relaxed bar and restaurant. Good-quality burgers are the mainstay; other American dishes include BBQ ribs or Cajun chicken. ● Sun L. & ❯						
ABERFOYLE: *Braeval Old Mill*	£££	MC V		■		
On A81 nr Aberfoyle, Central. 01877 382711. Set four-course dinners offer dishes of carefully prepared local meat, game and fish, followed by tempting desserts. ● Tue–Sat L, Sun D, Mon. & ♦						
ALEXANDRIA: *Georgian Room, Cameron House*	££££	AE DC MC V		■	●	
Off A82, Loch Lomond, Alexandria, Strath. 01389 55565. This large, comfortable hotel caters to the well-heeled leisure market of fishing and golf. The food is attractive and rich. ● Sat L, Sun L. &						
ALYTH: *Drumnacree House*	£££	MC V	●	■		
St. Ninians Rd, Alyth, Tays. 01828 632194. The smokehouse and garden provide produce for a mixed bag of cooking styles used with great enthusiasm and flair. An eclectic range of original ideas to tempt any palate. ● L, Sun, Mon. &						
AUCHMITHIE: *But 'n' Ben*	££	MC V	●			
Off A92 nr Arbroath, Tays. 01241 877223. Twin cottages in a working fishing village. The day's catch figures at lunch and dinner, and there are splendid high teas. ● Sun D, Tue. &						
BALLATER: *Darroch Learg*	££	DC MC V	●	■		
Braemar Rd, Ballater, Grampn. 0133 97 55443. A Victorian shooting lodge. The fare is local, the cooking modern Scottish using a wide range of ingredients, delicately seasoned. ● Jan. &						
BALLATER: *Green Inn*	£££	MC V	●		●	
9 Victoria Rd, Ballater, Grampn. 0133 97 55701. Scottish produce is given the full works at this refurbished former pub. Service is friendly and informed. Rooms available. ● Sat L. &						
CAIRNDOW: *Loch Fyne Oyster Bar*	£££	DC MC V	●			■
Clachan Farm, Ardkinglas, Cairndow, Strath. 01499 600236. This splendid place offers a warm welcome with platters of shellfish, overlooking the lochside oyster beds. ● Mon–Thu D (Nov–Mar). &						
DUNKELD: *Kinnaird*	£££££	AE MC V	●		●	■
Kinnaird Estate, off B898 nr Dunkeld, Tays. 01796 482440. This estate hotel produces ornate food of great originality. Lunch is more affordable. ● Feb. & ♦						
FORT WILLIAM: *Crannog*	££	MC V	●		●	
Town Pier, Fort William, Highl. 01397 705589. Nothing detracts from the simple pleasure of eating exquisitely fresh seafood overlooking a panoramic loch view. Helpings are generous. The atmosphere is warm, welcoming, and the service efficient. & ❯						

INVERNESS: *Culloden House* £££££
Off A96 at Culloden, Highl. ☎ 01463 790461.
The food is Scottish country-house style, with sauces, jellies, sorbets and
mousses interspersing hearty meat, game and fish dishes. Rooms available.

AE DC MC V

KILBERRY: *Kilberry Inn* ££
Kilberry by Tarbert, Argyll, Strath. ☎ 01880 770223.
This low white croft (former post office, now pub) in a quiet coastal village
serves traditional British farmhouse cooking. ● *Sun, mid-Oct–Easter.* ⚡

MC

KILLIECRANKIE: *Killiecrankie* £££
Off A9 nr Pitlochry, Tays. ☎ 01796 473220.
Excellent bar meals supplement more ambitious dinnertime fare in this
attractive hotel. It's hearty stuff, with a few Oriental dishes. ♿ ⚡

MC V

KINCLAVEN: *Ballathie House* £££
Off B9099 nr Stanley, Tays. ☎ 01250 883268.
A warm, hearty hotel in a huge estate on the Tay. The restaurant
serves appropriate fare like venison, and of course, salmon. ♿ ⚡

AE DC MC V

KINCRAIG: *Boathouse* £
Loch Insh, Kincraig, Highl. ☎ 01540 651 272.
Food is served all day at this log-cabin restaurant – fresh fish, haggis or
steak. Snacks are also available. ● *Nov–Dec, Mon–Wed (winter).* ♿ ⚡

MC V

KINGUSSIE: *Cross* £££
Tweed Mill Brae, Ardbroilach Rd, Kingussie, Highl. ☎ 01540 661166.
A small but expertly prepared range of local produce greets diners at this
19th-century tweed mill. Attractive bedrooms. ● *Tue, Dec–Feb.* ♿ ⚡ ❚

MC V

KYLE OF LOCHALSH: *Wholefood Café* £
Plockton Rd, Kyle of Lochalsh, Highl. ☎ 01599 534388.
All-day counter service offering snacks or casseroles, with waitress service
in the evenings. A pleasant menu that even the most hardened meat-
eater will enjoy. Plenty of choice for vegetarians. ● *mid-Oct–Easter.* ♿ ⚡

MC V

KYLESKU: *Kylesku* ££
On A894 by Lairg, Highl. ☎ 01971 5022331.
Lochs and mountains provide a splendid backdrop to this hotel. The
repertoire is limited, but fresh fish is always a good option. ♿ ⚡

MC V

OBAN: *Knipoch* ££££
On A816 nr Oban, Strath. ☎ 01852 316251.
Dinners range from three to five courses. Huge arrays of vegetables
and flamboyant desserts are features. ● *L, mid-Nov–mid-Feb.* ⚡ ❚

AE DC MC V

PERTH: *Number Thirty-three* £££
33 George St, Perth, Tays. ☎ 01736 633771.
Stylish furnishings decorate this seafood restaurant. Snacks in the Oyster
Bar are an alternative to the heftier restaurant menu. ● *Sun, Mon.* ♿

AE MC V

PORT APPIN: *Airds* £££££
Off A828, Loch Linnhe, Strath. ☎ 0163 173 236.
This hotel restaurant has a fine waterfront location and cheerful interior
to complement the splendidly flavored dinners. *(See also p573.)* ⚡ ❚

AE MC V

ST. MARGARET'S HOPE: *Creel* ££
Front Rd, St. Margaret's Hope, S. Ronaldsay, Orkney. ☎ 01856 831311.
Excellent, honest cooking. Seafood predominates, but you might try that
seaweed-fed lamb. ● *Mon–Sat L, Sun D, Mon–Fri (Nov–Mar).* ♿

MC V

TIRORAN: *Tiroran House* £££££
Off B8035 nr Gruline, Isle of Mull, Strath. ☎ 01681 705 232.
Stylish, convivial country-house hotel with a sound range of British
dishes. Local produce is prominent in the set dinners, including the
herbs, salads and estate-raised beef and lamb. Friendly Scottish welcome,
and good service. ● *L, late Oct–mid-May.* ⚡

ULLAPOOL: *Altnaharrie Inn* ££££££
Ullapool, Highl. ☎ 01854 633230.
Set dinners stretch to five courses, with fresh fish straight from boat
or creel. Cooking is modern but not over trendy. Wild ingredients from
field and hedgerow add interest. Dining here is a real pleasure.
(See also p573.) ● *L, late Oct –Easter.* ⚡

AE V

For key to symbols see back flap

British Pubs

N O TOUR OF BRITAIN could be complete without some exploration of its public houses *(see pp34–5)*. These are a great social institution, descendants of centuries of hostelries, ale-houses and stagecoach stops. Some have colorful histories or fascinating decor. Today they still occupy a central role in the community, staging quiz games and folk dancing. Many of those listed below are lovely buildings or have attractive settings. Most serve a variety of beers, spirits and wine by the glass.

A "free house" is independent and will stock several leading regional beers, but most pubs are "tied" – this means that they are owned by a brewery and only stock that brewery's selection.

Many pubs offer additional attractions such as live music and beer gardens with picnic tables. Traditional pub food is often served at lunchtime, and increasingly food is served in the evenings too. Traditional pub games take many forms, including cribbage, shove ha'penny, skittles, dominoes and darts.

LONDON

BLOOMSBURY: *Lamb*
94 Lamb's Conduit St, WC1.
Unspoiled Victorian pub with cut-glass "snob screens" and theatrical photographs. Small courtyard at the rear.

CITY: *Black Friar*
174 Queen Victoria St, EC4.
Eccentric inside and out, with intriguing Art Nouveau decor. Attentive service.

CITY: *Olde Cheshire Cheese*
Wine Office Court, Fleet St EC4.
Authentic 17th-century inn haunted by the shades of Johnson, Pope and Dickens. Restored to its plain, bareboarded glory with open fires in winter.

HAMMERSMITH: *Dove*
19 Upper Mall, W6.
One of the most attractive of West London's riverside pubs, where you can watch rowing crews from the terrace. Very crowded in fine weather.

HAMPSTEAD: *Spaniards Inn*
Spaniards Lane, NW3.
Famous Hampstead landmark dating from the 18th century, once part of a tollgate. Attractive garden.

KENSINGTON: *Windsor Castle*
114 Campden Hill Rd, W8.
A civilized Georgian inn with traditional oak furnishings and open fires. The walled garden attracts well-heeled, youngish crowds in summer. Hearty English food.

SOUTHWARK: *George Inn*
77 Borough High St, SE1.
Quaint coach house with unique galleried courtyard, now owned by the National Trust *(see p25)*. Rooms ramble upstairs and downstairs, and the overflow sits outside. Morris men and Globe Players may be seen at times.

THE DOWNS AND CHANNEL COAST

ALCISTON: *Rose Cottage*
Off A27 nr Lewes, Sussex.
Charming, vine-covered cottage inn decorated with rustic bygones. Limited room inside.

ALFRISTON: *Star*
Alfriston, Sussex.
This quaint old inn, once a pilgrim hostel, is now a stylish hotel but is full of character.

CHALE: *Wight Mouse Inn*
On B3399, Chale, Isle of Wight.
Cheerful, family-oriented inn with large gardens. Bric-a-brac dangles from the ceilings.

FLETCHLING: *Griffin*
Off A272, Fletchling, Sussex.
Sophisticated but very laid-back country inn with a 1930s air, which serves imaginative food. Attractive accommodation.

RYE: *Mermaid*
Mermaid St, Rye, Sussex.
Famous historic building in a steep cobbled street, full of paneling, frescoes and antiques.

SMARDEN: *Bell*
Off A274, Smarden, Kent.
An ancient brick-and-beam pub among orchards. Traditional games, inglenook fireplaces and flagstone floors *(see p546)*.

WALLISWOOD: *Scarlett Arms*
Off A29 nr Ewhurst, Surrey.
Workers' cottages converted into a relaxing pub with beams, log fires and trestle tables.

WINCHESTER: *Wykeham Arms*
75 Kingsgate St, Winchester, Hants.
Classy, idiosyncratic town center pub/hotel with fascinating decor. Excellent food, wine and accommodations *(see p547)*.

EAST ANGLIA

CAMBRIDGE: *Boathouse*
14 Chesterton Rd, Cambridge.
One of the best of Cambridge's waterside pubs, overlooking Jesus Green. For entertainment in summer, sit and watch barges and punts glide past; oars hang in the bars.

HOLYWELL: *Olde Ferry Boat*
Off A1123 at Needingworth, Cambs.
The Great Ouse reaches almost to the door of this picturesque thatched pub. Inside it is comfortably modernized, with cozy bedrooms. Wide range of food, and a resident ghost called Juliette.

LITTLEBURY: *Queens Head Inn*
High St, Littlebury, Essex.
This Tudor village pub has kept plenty of its original character. It offers outstanding real ales and food in a welcoming atmosphere.

SNAPE: *Golden Key*
Priory Lane, Snape, Suffolk.
Pretty gardens, stylish interior and appetizing food are a draw at this inn. Very popular during the Aldeburgh Festival *(see p63)*.

SNETTISHAM: *Rose & Crown*
Off A149 nr Heacham, Norfolk.
Former coaching inn with four attractive bars and plenty of room for children to play in the garden.

SOUTHWOLD: *Crown*
High Street, Southwold, Suffolk.
Popular seaside haunt with nautical decor and oak paneling. Excellent food and Adnam beers *(see p548)*.

STIFFKEY: *Red Lion*
On A149, Norfolk.
Recently reopened after being used as a doctor's office, this old brick-and-flint building has been very well renovated.
👤 🍴 🛏 🅿 🎵

TILLINGHAM: *Cap & Feathers*
South St, Tillingham, Essex.
Smoked meat and fish are offered at this 15th-century pub near the salt marshes. It plays a central role in village life. 👤 🛏 🅿

THAMES VALLEY

BARLEY: *Fox & Hounds*
High St, Barley, Herts.
Look for the tall chimney and the hunting scene sign. Both food and real ales are excellent. Disabled visitors welcome. 👤 🍴 🛏 🅿

BROOM: *Cock*
23 High St, Broom, Bedfordshire.
Charming 17th-century inn called "the pub with no bar" (place your orders at the hatch, and the beer comes straight from the cellar casks). 👤 🍴 🛏 🅿 🎵

BURFORD: *Lamb*
Sheep St, Burford, Oxon.
This picture-postcard Cotswolds inn has roses around the door and mullioned windows. Food is good, as is the service and atmosphere.
👤 🍴 🛏 🅿

FAWLEY: *Walnut Tree*
Off B4155 nr Henley, Buckinghamshire.
A splendid base for enjoying the Chilterns. You can even hitch your horse up in the parking lot.
👤 🍴 🅿

GREAT TEW: *Falkland Arms*
Off B4022 nr Chipping Norton, Oxon.
This partly thatched and vine-covered inn is in an idyllic corner of rural England. It is delightfully straightforward and simply decorated, with mugs and jugs and gleaming harnesses.
👤 🍴 🛏 🅿 🎵

OXFORD: *Turf Tavern*
Bath Pl, St. Helen's Passage, Oxford.
Tiny pub in the heart of the old collegiate quarter gives you an idea of cloistered quadrangles. Sit outside in fine weather. 👤 🍴 🛏

WATTON-ON-STONE:
George & Dragon
High St, Watton-on-Stone, Herts.
Attractive pink building dating back to 1603. Smart but also welcoming; plenty of locals use it, and there are newspapers to read.
👤 🍴 🛏 🅿 🎵

WEST ILSLEY: *Harrow*
Off A34 nr Newbury, Berkshire.
A stylish, white-tiled inn by the village pond, catering to hikers and racing folk. Upscale food.
👤 🍴 🅿

WESSEX

ABBOTSBURY: *Ilchester Arms*
Market St, Abbotsbury, Dorset.
The pub is a main feature of this honey-colored village near Chesil Beach. Warm, rambling rooms are smartly done up with prints. The restaurant has a conservatory extension. 👤 🍴 🅿

BATHFORD: *Crown*
2 Bathford Hill, Bathford, Avon.
This hilly village has enjoyed its namesake hostelry since its 18th-century heyday. Now it is stylish inside, with ambitious food.
👤 🍴 🛏

CROSCOMBE: *Bull Terrier*
On A371 nr Wells, Somerset.
One of Somerset's oldest pubs (originally a priory), this inn is much loved for good food, and has welcoming service. Try the Bull Terrier best bitter, and the walk to the Bishop's Palace at Wells.
👤 🍴 🅿

FORD: *White Hart*
On A420 nr Chippenham, Wiltshire.
A delightful trout-stream setting adds a lot to this lovely 16th-century pub-hotel. It is very popular in summer. Good walks nearby, and a swimming pool for residents. 👤 🍴 🛏

NORTON ST. PHILIP: *George*
On A366, Somerset.
This famous old pub sheltered the Duke of Monmouth before the Battle of Sedgemoor. It is a splendid half-timbered building with good food and an ancient galleried courtyard. 👤 🍴 🛏

SALISBURY: *Haunch of Venison*
1 Minster St, Salisbury, Wiltshire.
Once the church house for St. Thomas's, this ancient pub dates back 650 years. The severed, mummified hand of an 18th-century cardplayer is displayed among more cheerful clutter in its genuinely antique interior. 👤 🍴

STANTON WICK:
Carpenters Arms
Off A368, Avon.
A row of pretty converted miners' cottages contain this welcoming place with log fires. Excellent food and occasional live music are major attractions. 👤 🍴 🛏 🅿 🎵

DEVON AND
CORNWALL

BROADHEMBURY: *Drewe Arms*
Off A373, Devon.
Fresh fish is one reason to come to this thatched village pub, but the West Country ales, garden and atmosphere add to its appeal.
👤 🍴 🛏 🅿

DARTMOUTH: *Cherub*
13 High St, Dartmouth, Devon.
Dartmouth's oldest building, dating from 1380 and once a wool-merchant's house. Local fish prominent on the menu. 👤 🍴

KNOWSTONE: *Masons Arms*
Off A361 nr South Molton, Devon.
One of Devon's favorite inns, with plenty of local life and welcoming hosts. The rustic decor includes farm tools and a bottle collection. The big fireplace has a bread oven. Good bar food.
👤 🍴 🛏 🅿 🎵

LYDFORD: *Castle Inn*
Off A386, Devon.
Pretty, pink-washed Tudor inn by a ruined castle and scenic river gorge. Staff are friendly, food is imaginative, and there's lots of historic interest. Good value rooms (*see p554*). 👤 🍴 🛏 🅿

MYLOR BRIDGE: *Pandora*
Off A39 nr Penryn, Cornwall.
Medieval thatched pub by the waterside. Popular with boating folk and crowded in summer. Bags of atmosphere. 👤 🍴 🛏

PORT ISAAC:
Port Gaverne Hotel
Off B3314 nr Pendoggett, Cornwall.
Gorgeous seafront setting. A 17th-century building with slate floors, paneling and maritime decor. Excellent wine list. Good rooms available. 👤 🍴 🛏 🅿

TREGADILLETT: *Eliot Arms*
Off A30 nr Launceston, Cornwall.
Cluttered with harnesses, old postcards, prints, books and china, and a curious collection of clocks.
👤 🍴 🛏 🅿

THE HEART OF
ENGLAND

ALDERMINSTER: *Bell*
On A34 nr Stratford-upon-Avon, Warwickshire.
Coach house conveniently near Stratford. A civilized place to stop for a meal with well-kept beers. Good wines too. 👤 🍴 🛏 🅿

For key to symbols see back flap

BICKLEY MOSS:
Cholmondeley Arms
On A49, Cholmondeley, Cheshire.
Food draws the crowds to this
Victorian school room pub near
the castle grounds. Lots of period
interest inside. 🚶 🍴 🍺

BLOCKLEY: *Crown*
High St, Blockley, Gloucestershire.
Smart Elizabethan pub in a
gorgeous Cotswolds village. The
food and courtyard gardens are
a great draw. 🚶 🍴 🍺

BRETFORTON: *Fleece*
The Cross, Bretforton,
Hereford & Worcester.
Astonishing medieval house
owned by the National Trust, first
licensed in 1848. A living museum
of rural antiquities such as dough-
proving tables and cheese molds.
Food is simple, wines limited, but
beers are excellent. Lots of community gatherings for Morris
dancing. 🚶 🍴 🍺 🎵

CAULDON: *Yew Tree*
Off A523 nr Ashbourne, Staffs.
An extraordinary collection of
musical machines is on display
(working polyphons, pianolas,
symphonions), along with many
other fascinating bygones. The
interior is homey, with battered
furnishings and traditional pub
games. Simple snacks and beers.
🚶 🍴 🎵

TUTBURY: *Olde Dog & Partridge*
On A50 nr Burton-on-Trent, Staffs.
Imposing Tudor coach house,
agreeably modernized into bars
and family-oriented eating areas.
Pleasant service. 🚶 🍴 🍺 🎵

WENLOCK EDGE:
Wenlock Edge Inn
Hilltop, Much Wenlock, Shropshire.
There's a wood-burning stove and
friendly bar owner; Monday night
is story night. Good walks nearby
and rooms available. 🚶 🍴 🍺

EAST MIDLANDS

BIRCHOVER: *Druid Inn*
Main St, Birchover, Derbyshire.
Vine-covered village pub with a
large menu of good fresh food.
Excellent walking center with Row
Tor Rocks (allegedly a place of
Druid rituals) and Lathkil Dale
nearby. 🚶 🍴 🍺 🎵

FOTHERINGHAY: *Falcon*
Main St, Fotheringhay, Northants.
A splendid pub, now modernized
to serve a range of excellent food.
The public bar keeps its original
character and local clientele.
🚶 🍴 🍺 🎵

GLOOSTON: *Old Barn*
Andrews Lane, Glooston, Leicestershire.
Sixteenth-century inn with
tastefully renovated interior and
several cozy rooms. Better-than-
average food and hand-pumped
ales. Rooms available. 🚶 🍴 🍺

MONSAL HEAD:
Monsal Head Hotel
On B6465, Derbyshire.
Former stable block with horsy
decor. Magnificent view of the
steep Wye valley from the hotel
lounge; good walking country.
🚶 🍴 🍺

NOTTINGHAM:
Olde Trip to Jerusalem
Brewhouse Yard, Nottingham.
Unique pub built onto sandstone
caverns once used as a meeting
place for crusaders. One of the
oldest in Britain. 🍴 🍺

STAMFORD: *George*
71 High St, Stamford, Lincolnshire.
Splendid old coach house with
vestiges of a Norman pilgrim hos-
pice. Now very elegant, it offers
an excellent range of food with
Italian wines. Pretty cobbled courtyard and croquet lawn. 🚶 🍴 🍺

UPTON: *Cross Keys*
Main St, Upton, Nottinghamshire.
Beamed pub with hanging baskets
and pictures. Good bar food with
fresh fish. The restaurant is in the
old dovecote. 🚶 🍴 🍺 🎵 🎵

LANCASHIRE AND
THE LAKES

CARTMEL FELL: *Mason's Arms*
Off A5074 at Bowland Bridge sign,
Cumbria.
Lively, distinctive pub with an
immense range of bottled beers,
real ales, cider and country wines.
Good walks nearby. 🚶 🍴 🍺

ELTERWATER: *Britannia Inn*
Off A593 nr Ambleside, Cumbria.
Unadorned rustic interior and
open fires in the Langdale valley.
An excellent walking or touring
base with rooms. 🚶 🍴 🍺 🎵

GARSTANG: *Th'Owd Tithebarn*
Off Church St, Garstang, Lancashire.
A converted barn with rustic decor
by the canal. You may see Morris
dancing here. 🚶 🍴 🎵

LANGDALE:
Old Dungeon Ghyll
On B5343, Langdale, Cumbria.
Dramatic setting by the waterfall
in the Langdale Pikes. A walking
and climbing base with rooms,
plain but cozy. 🚶 🍴 🍺 🎵 🎵

LIVERPOOL: *Philharmonic*
36 Hope St, Liverpool.
One of the most characterful
Merseyside haunts, a Victorian
setting with plasterwork, stained
glass and mahogany. 🚶 🍴

MANCHESTER: *Lass o' Gowrie*
36 Charles St, Manchester.
Popular student dive with a gaslit
bar and its own brewery in the
cellar. Lively at weekends. 🚶 🍴

NEAR SAWREY:
Tower Bank Arms
B5285, Near Sawrey, Cumbria.
This pretty village is a mecca for
Beatrix Potter fans. The pub backs
on to her house, Hill Top. Well-
preserved interior. 🚶 🍴 🍺

YORKSHIRE AND
HUMBERSIDE

ASKRIGG: *Kings Arms*
Off A684 nr Bainbridge, N Yorks.
The rustic interior is used as the
set in a TV series. Good bar food,
wines and beers are other reasons
to find it *(see p562)*. 🍴 🍺 🎵

COXWOLD: *Fauconberg Arms*
Coxwold, N Yorks.
"Olde worlde" pub with antique
oak settles and Windsor armchairs
to sit on, and plenty of beer, wine,
and good things to eat. 🚶 🍴 🎵

FLAMBOROUGH: *Seabirds*
On B1255, Flamborough, Humbs.
The white chalk cliffs nearby are a
marvelous place for birdwatching.
Interesting interior. The fish is the
highlight of the menu. 🚶 🍴 🍺

GOATHLAND: *Mallyan Spout*
Off A169, Goathland, N Yorks.
Traditional moorland inn with a
relaxing air and good food. The
open fires make it popular with
walkers. Good rooms. 🚶 🍴 🍺

HULL: *Olde White Harte*
Off 25 Silver St, Hull, Humbs.
This ancient tavern lies behind a
modern "White Hart." The interior
offers inglenook fireplaces and
copper-topped bar. 🚶 🍴 🍺

LOW CATTON: *Gold Cup*
Off A166 at Stamford Bridge, Humbs.
The farm animals around add an
authentic touch to this rural pub
with comfortable, relaxing bars
and good food. 🚶 🍴 🎵

MOULTON: *Black Bull*
Off A1 nr Scotch Corner, N Yorks.
This pleasant old place puts
masses of energy into the food,
bar snacks and good wines. The
atmosphere is upscale. 🍴 🍺

NORTHUMBRIA

BLANCHLAND: *Lord Crewe Arms*
Blanchland, Northumb.
Moorland inn with priests' holes,
13th-century fireplaces and ghosts.
Popular with walkers; good food
and rooms *(see p563)*. 🏃 🍴 🛏 🖊

CRASTER: *Jolly Fisherman*
Off B1339 nr Alnwick, Northumb.
Unassuming local pub with
beautiful sea views. The local oak-
smoked kippers are a specialty of
the house. Excellent cliff-top
walks. 🏃 🍴 🛏 🖊

GRETA BRIDGE: *Morritt Arms*
Off A66 nr Scotch Corner, Co Durham.
A fine stone coach house with a
splendid, spacious interior with oak
settles and stuffed fish. Attractive
riverside setting. 🏃 🍴 🛏 🖊

NEW YORK:
Shiremoor House Farm
Off A191, New York, Tyne & Wear.
A skillful conversion from some
derelict farm buildings, it is now
comfortable and stylish. Has
interesting food, and families
welcome. 🏃 🍴 🛏

NEWCASTLE UPON TYNE:
Crown Posada
31 The Side, Newcastle upon Tyne.
A Victorian pub with an ornate
interior of gilt mirrors and stained
glass. It is a city pub for drinkers,
so no children are allowed. 🖊

SEAHOUSES: *Olde Ship*
On B1340, Seahouses, Northumb.
Maritime curiosities festoon this
harbor-front inn. From the window
you can see the Farne Islands.
Good coastal walks. 🏃 🍴 🛏 🖊

NORTH WALES

BEAUMARIS: *Olde Bulls Head*
Castle St, Beaumaris, Anglesey.
A 500-year-old building with
fascinating details inside including
a 17th-century water clock,
cutlasses and a witch's ducking
stool. 🏃 🍴 🖊

BODFARI: *Dinorben Arms*
Off A541, Bodfari, Denbighshire.
Hillside pub with excellent bar
food, lots of whiskies and a
pleasant range of terraces for
admiring the views. 🏃 🍴 🛏

CAPEL CURIG: *Bryn Tyrch Hotel*
On A5 nr Betws-y-Coed, A & C.
Popular with walkers and climbers
exploring the Snowdonia National
Park. Serves vegetarian bar food.
🍴 🛏

GLANWYDDEN: *Queen's Head*
Off B5115, The Glanwydden, A & C.
Excellent pub food is a major
draw at this village pub. It can get
crowded in season. 🏃 🍴 🛏

MAENTWROG: *Grapes*
On A496, Maentwrog, A & C.
Coaching inn with lovely views
and a walled garden. Much of the
furniture was salvaged from
unused chapels. 🏃 🍴 🛏 🖊

SOUTH AND
MID-WALES

ABERYSTWYTH: *Halfway Inn*
On A4120, Pisgah, Cardiganshire.
Rheidol Valley pub where you can
tap your ale from the cask. Events
include sheep-shearing contests.
Comfy rooms. 🏃 🍴 🛏 🖊 🎵

CRICKHOWELL: *Bear*
Brecon Rd, Crickhowell, Powys.
Old inn with splendid food and
excellent range of drinks. Period
features and interesting decor.
Bedrooms available. 🏃 🍴 🛏

EAST ABERTHAW: *Blue Anchor*
On B4265, East Aberthaw, V of Glam.
Charming thatched pub with low-
ceilinged, intimate warrenlike
rooms and open fires. Estuary
walks. 🏃 🍴 🛏

HAY-ON-WYE: *Old Black Lion*
26 Lion St, Hay-on-Wye, Powys.
A 13th-century inn with ambitious
restaurant food. Lots of local
sporting activities (fishing, riding,
golf), plus bookstores. 🏃 🍴 🛏

NEVERN: *Trewern Arms*
On B4582, Nevern, Pembrokeshire.
Appealing riverside inn in a pretty
village. The slate-floored bar is
crammed with agricultural and
domestic bygones. 🏃 🍴 🛏 🖊

PENALLT: *Boat Inn*
Long Lane, Penallt, Monmouthshire.
A mecca for music and ale right
on the border; drinks are served
in Wales. Old railroad bike tracks
and canoeing. 🏃 🍴 🛏

THE LOWLANDS

EDINBURGH: *Bow Bar*
80 West Bow, Edinburgh.
Bar of mahogany and mirrorglass,
with malts and real ales. No
children, games, music or wine.

EDINBURGH:
Cafe Royal Circle Bar
West Register St, Edinburgh.
Refurbished in Victorian style –

tiled portraits of Scottish worthies,
leather seating and chandeliers.
Scottish ales and simple food.

ELIE: *Ship*
The Harbour, Elie, Fife.
Atmospheric quayside pub with
nautical decor and attractive views.
Summer barbecues are a feature.
🏃 🍴 🛏 🖊 🎵

GLASGOW: *Horseshoe*
17–19 Drury St, Glasgow.
Busy Victorian pub with a long
bar and plenty of period features.
Good value bar snacks. Karaoke
in the evenings. 🏃 🍴 🛏

ISLE OF WHITHORN:
Steam Packet
Isle of Whithorn, Dumfries & Galloway.
Superb setting on a lovely harbor
scene. Pleasant eating areas and
real ales. Boat trips from the
harbor. 🏃 🍴 🛏 🎵

THE HIGHLANDS
AND ISLANDS

APPLECROSS: *Applecross Inn*
Shore St, Applecross, Wester Ross,
Highland.
Spectacularly located beyond
Britain's highest mountain pass,
this pub overlooks Skye. Local sea-
food is served, and there is music
most evenings. 🏃 🍴 🛏 🖊 🎵

AUCHTERLESS: *Towie Tavern*
On A947 nr Turriff, Grampian.
White pebbled stucco pub
concentrates on the restaurant
aspect of its trade. Friendly
atmosphere, good fish. 🏃 🍴 🖊

DUNDEE: *Fishermans Tavern*
12 Fort St, Broughty Ferry, Tayside.
Award-winning real ales and lots
of malts too. Good seafront and
Tay rail bridge views. Rooms
available. 🏃 🍴 🛏 🖊

ISLE OF SKYE:
Tigh Osda Eilean Iarmain
Off A851, Isle of Ornsay, Isle of Skye.
Welcoming hotel bar. Lots of malts
and good bar food. Gorgeous
setting. 🏃 🍴 🛏

LOCH LOMOND: *Byre*
A821, Brig o'Turk, Central.
This used to be a cowshed.
Now it's a comfortable place on
the edge of a forest park, with
excellent food. 🏃 🍴 🛏

ULLAPOOL: *Ferry Boat*
Shore St, Ullapool, Highland.
Good whiskies and bar lunches,
and fine views over the harbor.
A two-roomed bar with a coal fire
and big windows. 🏃 🍴 🎵

For key to symbols see back flap

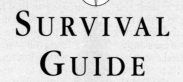

SURVIVAL
GUIDE

PRACTICAL INFORMATION

MILLIONS ANNUALLY seek out what the British often take for granted – the country's ancient history, colorful pageantry, and spectacularly varied countryside. The range of facilities offered to visitors in Britain has expanded and improved considerably over the past few years. To enjoy Britain fully, it is best to know something about the nuts and bolts of British life: when to visit, how to get around, where to find information and what to do if things go wrong. Whether

A mounted sentry, London

or not you find Britain an expensive country will depend a lot on the exchange rate between the pound and your own currency. Prices vary within Britain, and regional differences in some items can be very noticeable. London, not surprisingly, is the most expensive, and the side effects extend to most of southern England, Britain's most affluent region. Entertainment, transportation, food, hotels and consumer items in stores are generally cheaper in other parts of the country.

Weymouth beach, Dorset, on a busy public holiday weekend

WHEN TO VISIT

BRITAIN'S TEMPERATE maritime climate does not produce many temperature extremes *(see p68)*. There are many fine days, but it is impossible to predict rain or shine reliably in any season. Weather patterns shift constantly, and the climate can differ widely in places only a short distance apart. The southeast is generally drier than elsewhere. But wherever you are going be sure to pack a mix of warm and cool clothes and an umbrella. Always get an up-to-date weather forecast before you set off on foot to remote mountain areas or moorland. Walkers can be surprised by the weather, and the Mountain Rescue services are often called out due to

A sign for the Mountain Rescue

unexpectedly severe conditions. Weather reports are given on television and radio, in newspapers or by phone services *(see p637)*.

Britain's towns and cities are all-year destinations, but many attractions open only between Easter and October. Some hotels are crammed at Christmas and New Year. The main family vacation months, July and August, and public holidays *(see p65)* are always busy. Spring and autumn offer a compromise between some good weather and a relative lack of crowds. The information at the beginning of each attraction listed in this guide gives opening days.

INSURANCE

IT IS SENSIBLE to take out travel insurance to cover cancellation or curtailment of your trip, theft or loss of money and possessions and the cost of any medical treatment *(see p620)*. It is better to arrange this in advance, although you can organize it on your trip if necessary. If your country has a reciprocal medical arrangement with Britain (for example, Australia, New Zealand and the EU), you can obtain free treatment under the National Health Service, but there are a number of forms to fill out. Certain benefits covered by medical insurance will not be included. North American and

Canadian health plans or student identity cards may give you some protection against costs, but check the small print. If you want to drive a car in Britain, it is illegal to drive without third-party insurance and it is advisable to take out fully comprehensive insurance.

ADVANCE BOOKING

OUT OF SEASON, you should have few problems booking accommodations or transportation on short notice, but in tourist season, if you have set your heart on a popular West End show, luxury hotel, well-known restaurant or specific flight or tour, try to book ahead. Contact the **British Tourist Authority** (BTA) in your country, or a travel agent for advice and information.

TOURIST INFORMATION

TOURIST INFORMATION is available in many towns and public places, including airports, main rail and bus stations and at some places of historical interest. These bureaus will be able to help you on almost anything in their area. Watch for the tourist information symbol, which can indicate anything from a large and busy central

The most common English tourist information sign

◁ **Fishing boats in Scarborough port, North Yorkshire**

office to a simple kiosk or even a bulletin board in a parking area.

Free leaflets are generally offered but a charge may be made for more detailed maps and booklets. Most tourist offices can suggest guided walks, and nearly all will reserve accommodations for you on request. During the busy vacation periods it is worth asking about the *Book-a-bed-ahead* plan for places you intend to visit. Tourist office addresses and phone numbers are listed throughout

BTA's magazine

this guide. The **BTA's** monthly magazine, *In Britain,* which is available from tourist offices, contains articles about places to visit and includes a useful events calendar.

DISABLED TRAVELERS

THE FACILITIES for disabled visitors to Britain are steadily improving: recently designed or newly renovated buildings and public spaces now offer elevators and ramps for wheelchair access (information given in the headings for each entry in this book); specially designed toilets; grab rails; and for the hearing impaired, earphones. Given advance notice, British Rail *(see p638),* ferry or bus staff will help any disabled

passengers. Ask a travel agent about the Disabled Persons Railcard, which entitles you to discounted rail fares. Many banks, theaters and museums can now provide aids for the visually or hearing impaired. Specialized tour operators, such as **Holiday Care Service,** cater to the physically handicapped visitor. If renting a car, Hertz offers hand-controlled vehicles for rent without any extra cost *(see p637).* For permission to use any of the disabled parking spaces, you need to display a special sign in your car. For more general information, contact **RADAR** or **Mobility International.**

One of the best series for disabled travelers is *Access* by Pauline Hephaistos, published by Survey Projects. You could also try *Holidays in the British Isles: a Guide for Disabled People* (RADAR), and *The World Wheelchair Traveler* by Ann Tyrrell and Susan Abbott (AA).

RADAR
0171-637 5400.

Mobility International
0171-403 5688.
North America
(503) 343-1284.

Holiday Care Service
01293 774 535.

Lorna Doone Cottage and National Trust Information Centre, Somerset

A visit to HMS Victory (p155)

TRAVELING WITH CHILDREN

BRITAIN IS NOT the easiest or most welcoming place for young children, but things are slowly changing.

Peak vacation times – Easter, July and August – and school vacations have most to offer in the way of entertainment for children. Many places have something child oriented going on at Christmas too, particularly pantomimes. Discounts for children, or family tickets, are now widely available for travel, theater shows and other entertainments.

Choose accommodations that welcome children, or opt for efficiency apartments with durable furnishings and room to run around. Many hotels now provide baby-sitting or baby-listening services, and may offer reductions or free accommodations for very young children (see pp536–73).

Restaurants are becoming less child-phobic than they used to be and many now provide high chairs and special child menus (see pp574–607). Italian eateries are often the most friendly and informal. Even the British pub, once resolutely child-free, is now relenting with beer gardens and family rooms. People under 18 are not permitted near the bars and must not buy or consume alcohol. The annual publication *Family Welcome* (HarperCollins) is available from newsstands and lists those places where children are welcome.

PUBLIC TOILETS

ALTHOUGH MANY older-style supervised public toilets still exist, these have largely been replaced by the modern free-standing, coin-operated "Superloos." Young children should never use these toilets on their own.

STUDENT TRAVELERS

FULL-TIME STUDENTS who have an International Student Identity Card (ISIC) are often entitled to discounts on things like travel, sports facilities and entrance fees. North American students can also get medical coverage but it may be very basic (see p620). If you don't have an ISIC, they are available from **STA Travel**, or the **National Union of Students**.

An **International Youth Hostel Federation** card enables you to stay in Britain's hundreds of youth hostels. Inexpensive accommodations are also available (out of term) at many of the university halls of residence – such as the **University of London** – a good way of staying in city centers on a tight budget. If you are exploring the wilder regions of Britain, sleeping quarters can be found in camping barns (dormitory-style bunkhouses), which, though spartan, cost very little. For information on working in Britain, contact **BUNAC**.

Great British Heritage Pass

BUSINESS HOURS

MANY BUSINESSES and stores are closed on Sundays, although opening is now legal. Monday to Friday hours are generally 9 or 10am to 5 or 5:30pm, but store hours can vary, with late shopping one evening a week, and lunchtime or even half-day closing – usually a Wednesday.

Museums in London often open later on weekends but those outside the capital may have more inflexible hours, sometimes closing during the morning, or for one day a week – often on Mondays.

On public holidays, known as bank holidays in Britain, banks, offices, most stores, restaurants and attractions will generally close.

ADMISSION CHARGES

THESE VARY WIDELY from a nominal 50p to over £10 for the popular attractions. In general, tourist attractions are becoming much more elaborate. Museums now combine entertainment with education, and are livelier than they ever used to be. Along with this move, however, is a corresponding rise in admission fees. But reductions are often available for groups, senior citizens, children or students (proof of identity will be required). North American citizens may buy a Great

The privately owned, admission-charging, Hever Castle (see p175)

A Cotswold church, one of hundreds of parish churches open to the public free of charge

British Heritage Pass, which gives access to over 600 sights, available from travel agents and British Airways offices *(see p634).* A few local authority museums and art galleries are free, but donations are always welcome, and are sometimes requested in ways that are hard to refuse. Other sights are in private hands, run either as a commercial venture or on a charitable basis, and in some cases, even as a personal hobby. Stately homes open to the public may still belong to the gentry who have lived there for centuries; a charge is made to defray the enormous costs of upkeep. Many of these beautiful houses have added safari parks or garden centers to encourage and attract more visitors, such as Woburn Abbey *(see p216).*

Britain's thousands of small parish churches are among the country's greatest architectural treasures. None of the churches charge an entrance fee, although some, sadly, are locked because of vandalism.

Increasingly, many of the great cathedrals expect a donation from visitors who are not attending services.

Information leaflets, National Trust

ENGLISH HERITAGE AND THE NATIONAL TRUST

MANY OF BRITAIN'S historic buildings, parks, gardens, and vast tracts of countryside and coastline are cared for by **English Heritage** (EH), the **National Trust** (NT) or the **National Trust for Scotland** (NTS). We identify NT and NTS properties at the beginning of each entry. Entrance fees are often high, so if you wish to visit several stately homes, it may be worth taking out annual membership allowing free access thereafter to any NT or NTS property (remember many are closed in winter).

Many of the NT's properties are "listed." These are buildings or sites that are recognized as having special architectural or historical interest and therefore fully protected from alterations and demolition.

ENGLISH HERITAGE

The sign and symbol of English Heritage

USEFUL ADDRESSES

BUNAC
16 Bowling Green Lane,
London EC1R.
📞 *0171-251 3472.*

English Heritage
429 Oxford St,
London W1R.
📞 *0171-973 3000.*

Youth Hosteling International
📞 *(212) 932-2300 (US).*

National Trust (NT)
36 Queen Anne's Gate,
London SW1H.
📞 *0171-222 9251.*

National Trust for Scotland (NTS)
5 Charlotte Sq,
Edinburgh EH2.
📞 *0131 226 5922.*

National Union of Students
📞 *0171-272 8900.*

STA Travel
Priory Hse, 6 Wrights Lane,
London W8.
📞 *0171-937 9962.*

University of London Union
Malet St, London WC1.
📞 *0171-580 9551.*

USEFUL PUBLICATIONS

BOTH THE REGIONAL and national tourist boards produce comprehensive lists of local attractions and registered accommodations. For route planning, excellent, clear, large-format road atlases are produced by the RAC and AA *(see p636)*. For rural exploration, *Ordnance Survey* maps are ideal.

MEDIA

BRITISH NATIONAL newspapers fall into two categories: broadsheets – quality papers, such as *The Times* or *The Guardian* – and tabloids, heavy on gossip, such as *The Sun* or *The Daily Mirror.*

The Sunday newspapers are more expensive than dailies but are packed with supplements of all kinds, including sections on the arts, driving, restaurants, entertainment, travel, listings and reviews.

Specialty periodicals are available at newsstands on just about every topic from hamster-keeping to hi-fi. For a more in-depth analysis of current events buy *The Economist, New Statesman & Society* or *The Spectator,* while *Private Eye* satirizes public figures. There are a few foreign magazines and newspapers available in large towns, often at main railroad stations, but mostly in London. One of the most popular is the *International Herald Tribune,* which is available on the day of issue.

Television is undergoing an upheaval in Britain as satellite and cable networks invade the airwaves. Still more influential,

A local newsstand and sub-post office at Arisaig, Scotland

however, is the state-run BBC (British Broadcasting Corporation), which operates two TV channels and maintains its reputation for producing some of the best television in the world, without commercial breaks. The BBC's two commercial rivals are ITV and Channel Four, the former tending toward popular soap operas and game shows and the latter catering to more minority tastes (art films and offbeat documentaries).

Standard British three-pin plug

There are also regional variations – such as programs in Welsh and Gaelic – which exist throughout Britain.

The BBC also has a number of radio stations, ranging from pop music (Radio One) to the middlebrow Radio Four – a mix of current affairs, drama and news. There are many local commercial radio stations.

Full TV and radio schedules are listed in daily newspapers and several listings magazines; one of the best is the *Radio Times,* a weekly publication found at most newsstands.

SMOKING

IT IS NOW forbidden to smoke in many public places in Britain. These include most public transportation systems, taxis, some British Rail stations, theaters and movie theaters. The exception to the anti-smoking trend is pubs. ASH (Action on Smoking and Health) advises on smoke-free venues (0171-935 3519).

Some of Britain's national newspapers

WORKING RESTRICTIONS

RESIDENTS OF THE EU can work in Britain without a permit, while Commonwealth citizens under the age of 27 may work part-time for up to two years in the UK. Before arriving in Britain, North American students can get a blue card through their university, which enables them to work for up to six months. BUNAC *(see p617)* is a student club which will organize exchange programs for students to work abroad.

ELECTRICITY

THE VOLTAGE IN Britain is 220/240 AC, 50 Hz. Electrical plugs have three square pins and take fuses of 3, 5 and 13 amps. Visitors will need an adaptor for North American or continental appliances that have been brought from home, such as portable computers, hair driers and tape recorders. Most hotels will have two-pronged European-style sockets for shavers only.

Clock, the Old Royal Observatory, Greenwich *(see p131)*

TIME

BRITAIN IS ON Greenwich Mean Time (GMT) during the winter months, five hours ahead of Eastern Standard Time and ten hours behind Sydney. From the middle of March to October, clocks are set forward one hour to British Summer Time (equivalent to Central European Time). To check the correct time, you can dial 123 to contact the Speaking Clock service.

CUSTOMS AND IMMIGRATION

A VALID PASSPORT is needed to enter Britain. Visitors from the European Union (EU), the United States, Canada, New Zealand and Australia do not require visas to enter the country. Nor are inoculations or vaccinations necessary. When you arrive at any British air or seaport you will find separate lines at immigration control – one for European Union nationals, and several others for everyone else. As a result of Britain's membership of the European Union, anyone who arrives in Britain from a member country can pass through a blue channel – but random checks are still being made to detect entry of any prohibited goods, particularly drugs, indecent material and weapons. Never, under any circumstances, carry luggage or parcels through customs for someone else.

Travelers entering from outside the EU still have to pass through customs channels. Go through the green channel if you have nothing to declare over the customs allowances for overseas visitors, and the red channel if you have goods to declare. If you are unsure of importation restrictions go through the red channel.

Limits on the quantities of alcohol are: two liters of still table wine plus one liter of alcoholic drink over 22 percent vol, or two liters of alcoholic drink not over 22 percent vol; for tobacco products the limits are: 200 cigarettes or 50 cigars. You are allowed up to £36 worth of other goods

(caption for left margin image) ghland malt

including gifts, souvenirs, cider and beer. No live animals may be imported into the UK without a permit since Britain is still free of rabies. Animals found will be impounded and may be destroyed. Non-EU residents can get a VAT refund on goods bought in Britain *(see p626).*

HM Customs and Excise
New King's Beam Hse,
22 Upper Ground, London SE1.
📞 0171-620 1313.
Contact for information regarding import or export restrictions.

The mosque in Regent's Park *(see p105),* **London**

RELIGIOUS ORGANIZATIONS

Baptist
London Baptist Association,
1 Merchant St, London E3.
📞 0181-980 6818.

Buddhist
Buddhist Society,
58 Eccleston Sq, London SW1.
📞 0171-834 5858.

Church of England (Episcopal)
St. Paul's Cathedral, London EC4.
📞 0171-248 2705.

Evangelical Alliance
Whitefield Hse, 186 Kennington Park Rd, London SE11.
📞 0171-582 0228.

Jewish
Liberal Jewish Synagogue,
28 St. John's Wood Rd, London NW8.
📞 0171-286 5181.

United Synagogue (Orthodox),
Woburn Hse, Tavistock Sq, WC1.
📞 0171-387 4300.

Muslim
Islamic Cultural Centre,
146 Park Rd, London NW8.
📞 0171-724 3363.

Quakers
Friends Hse,
173 Euston Rd, London NW1.
📞 0171-387 3601.

Roman Catholic
Westminster Cathedral,
Victoria St, London SW1.
📞 0171-798 9055.

EMBASSIES AND CONSULATES

Australian High Commission
Australia Hse, the Strand,
London WC2.
📞 0171-379 4334.

Canadian High Commission
Macdonald Hse,
1 Grosvenor Sq, London W1.
📞 0171-258 6600.

New Zealand High Commission
New Zealand Hse,
80 Haymarket, London SW1.
📞 0171-930 8422.

United States Embassy
24 Grosvenor Sq, London W1.
📞 0171-499 9000.

CONVERSION CHART

Officially the metric system is used, but imperial measures are still common. Road distances are measured in miles; imperial pints and gallons are 20 percent larger than US measures.

Imperial to metric
1 inch = 2.5 centimeters
1 foot = 30 centimeters
1 mile = 1.6 kilometers
1 ounce = 28 grams
1 pint = 0.5 liters
1 US gallon = 3.8 liters
1 UK gallon = 1.2 US gallon

Metric to imperial
1 millimeter = 0.04 inch
1 centimeter = 0.4 inch
1 meter = 3 feet 3 inches
1 kilometer = 0.6 mile
1 gram = 0.04 ounce
1 kilogram = 2.2 pounds
1 liter = 2.1 US pints

Green and red customs channels at Heathrow airport *(see p634)*

Personal Security and Health

BRITAIN IS A DENSELY POPULATED COUNTRY which, like any other, has its share of social problems. However, it is very unlikely that you will come across any violence. If you do encounter difficulties, never hesitate to contact the police for help. Britain's National Health Service can be relied upon for an emergency or routine treatment. You may have to pay if your country has no reciprocal arrangement with Britain.

HOSPITALS AND MEDICAL TREATMENT

ALL VISITORS to Britain are strongly advised to take out medical insurance against the cost of any emergency hospital care, repatriation and specialists' fees, especially for those visitors from outside the European Union (EU). Emergency medical treatment in a British National Health Service (NHS) emergency room is free, but any kind of additional medical care could prove very expensive.

Residents of the European Union and nationals of some other Commonwealth and European countries are entitled to free medical treatment under the NHS, though the process is bureaucratic. Before traveling, you should obtain a form confirming that your country of origin has adequate reciprocal health arrangements with Britain. But some treatments are not covered and repatriation is not included, so medical insurance is preferable.

If you need to see a dentist while staying in Britain, you will have to pay. The cost varies, depending on your entitlement to NHS treatment, and whether you can find an NHS dentist to treat you. Emergency dental treatment is available in some hospitals, but if you would prefer a private dentist, try looking in the *Yellow Pages (see p622)*.

PHARMACISTS

YOU CAN BUY a wide range of brand-name medicines without prescription from drugstores in Britain. Boots is the best-known and largest supplier, with branches in most towns. Many medicines are only available with a doctor's prescription, which you must take to a dispensing chemist (drugstore) or pharmacist. If you are likely to need drugs, either bring your own or get your doctor to write out the generic name of the drug (as opposed to the brand name). If you are entitled to an NHS prescription, you will be charged a standard rate; without this entitlement you will be charged the full cost of the drug. Remember to ask for a receipt for any insurance claim.

Pharmacy sign

Some pharmacies are open until midnight; for emergencies contact the local hospital. Doctors' offices are normally open mornings and early evenings. You can show up at a hospital emergency room any time. In an emergency, dial 999 for an ambulance.

CRIME

BRITAIN IS NOT a dangerous place for visitors, and it is most unlikely that your stay will be blighted by crime. Practical advice to help you avoid loss or injury is given below. Because of past terrorist attacks, there are occasional security alerts; these are mainly false alarms due to people accidentally leaving bags or parcels lying around. Always co-operate with the authorities if your bag has to be searched or if you are asked to evacuate a building.

SUITABLE PRECAUTIONS

TAKE GOOD CARE of your belongings at all times. Make sure your possessions are adequately insured before you arrive. Never leave them unattended in public places.

Keep your valuables well concealed, especially in crowds. In movies or theaters, keep handbags on your lap, not on the floor. It is always advisable not to carry too much cash or jewelry with you; leave it in your hotel safe instead. Pickpockets love crowded places like bustling markets, busy stores and rush hours. If you are traveling alone at night try to avoid deserted and poorly lit buildings and places such as back

Female police constable

Traffic police officer

Male police constable

Police car

streets and parking lots. By far the safest way of carrying large amounts of cash around is in traveler's checks *(see p625)*. Begging is an increasingly common sight in many British cities, and foreign visitors are frequent targets for hard-luck stories. Requests for money are usually polite; but any abuse should be reported to the police immediately.

WOMEN TRAVELING ALONE

IT IS NOT unusual in Britain for women to travel unaccompanied, or visit a bar or restaurant with a group of female friends. Nor is it especially dangerous, but caution is advisable in deserted places, especially after dark. It is best not to travel alone on public transportation; try to find an occupied car. Call a taxi, especially if you do not know the district very well.

Legally, you cannot carry any offensive weapons around with you in Britain, even for self-defense. These include knives, clubs, guns or tear gas, but personal alarm systems are allowed.

POLICE

THE SIGHT OF a traditional British bobby patroling the streets in a tall hat is now less common than the police patrol car, sometimes with wailing sirens and flashing lights. But the old-fashioned police constable does still exist, particularly in rural areas and crowded city centers, and continues to be courteous, approachable and helpful.

Unlike in many countries, the police in Britain do not carry guns. If you are lost, the

Ambulance

Fire engine

advice to ask a policeman or woman still applies. Traffic wardens may also be able to help you with directions.

In a crisis, dial 999 to get the police, fire and ambulance services, which are on call 24-hours a day. Calls are free from any public or private phone, but they should only be made in real emergencies. In Britain's coastal areas this number will also put you in touch with Britain's voluntary coastguard rescue, the Royal National Lifeboat Institute.

Royal National Lifeboat Institute logo

LOST PROPERTY

IF YOU ARE UNLUCKY enough to lose anything or have anything stolen, you should go immediately to the nearest police station to report your loss. If you plan an insurance claim for any theft, you will need a written report from the local police. All of the main bus and rail stations have lost property offices. Jewelry and large amounts of cash should be kept in your hotel safe, since most hotels disclaim responsibility for valuables not kept in their safe.

DIRECTORY

CRISIS INFORMATION

Police, Fire and Ambulance services
999. Calls are free (24-hour phoneline).

Accident and Emergency Departments
For your nearest Accident and Emergency unit check in phone directory or contact the police.

Childline
0800 1111. Calls are free for children in need of any help (24-hour phoneline).

Emergency Dental Care
0171-837 3646 (24-hour phoneline).

Rape Crisis Centre
0171-837 1600 (24-hour phoneline).

Samaritans
0171-734 2800 (24-hour phoneline for all emotional problems). Look in local telephone directory for nearest branch.

HELPLINES

Alcoholics Anonymous
0171-352 3001.

Disabled Helplines
The Disability Helpline.
01302 310123.
Disabled Living Foundation.
0171-289 6111.

Late-opening Chemists
Contact your local police station or hospital for a list.

Lost Property
Contact your local police station.

National Helpline for Drugs
0171-603 8654.

National Helpline for the Blind
Royal Institute for the Blind.
0171-388 1266.

National Helpline for the Deaf
0171-387 8033.

Pregnancy Advice
01564 793225.

Victim's Helpline
0171-729 1252 (counseling for any victims of crime).

Using the Telephone

Modern BT phone box

THE PHONE SYSTEM in Britain is efficient and inexpensive. You will find public phone booths throughout the entire country. In towns, phones can be found on most street corners, shopping precincts, railroad and bus stations. Rural phone booths are more scarce, but you can come across them in out-of-the-way bus stops and in tiny villages. Most pubs and public buildings are equipped with pay phones. The modern phones now take credit cards as well as coins and phonecards.

TELEPHONE DIRECTORIES

YELLOW PAGES are regional telephone directories listing local businesses and services. There are also local telephone books, such as *The Thomson Local*, which list private and business phone numbers. These should be found at most hotels, post office and libraries. **Talking Pages** is a telephone service run by British Telecom (BT), which gives you the number of a specific kind of shop or service in any area you want.

Yellow Pages logo

Talking Pages logo

CHARGES

CALL COSTS all depend on when, where and for how long you call. The cheapest time to call is from 6pm to 8am Monday to Friday, and throughout the weekend.

USING A CARD PHONE

1 Lift receiver and wait for dial tone.

2 Insert a phonecard, green side up.

3 Display shows how many units are left. Minimum charge is one unit.

4 Some phones accept credit cards. Insert horizontally, with the arrow (if any) facing forward, and slide through.

5 Dial the number and wait to be connected.

6 When your phone card runs out, you will hear a beeping noise. To continue, press the button and the old card will come out. Remove it and put a new card in.

7 If you want to make another call, do not replace the receiver; instead press the follow-on call button.

BT phonecard (far left), sold in shops displaying logo (left)

USING A COIN PHONE

1 Lift the receiver and wait for the dial tone.

2 Insert the money. Any combination of coins can normally be used except for five, two and one pence coins.

3 Dial the number and wait to be connected.

4 The display indicates how much money you have put in and the credit left. A rapid beeping noise means your money has run out. Insert more coins.

5 If you want to make another call, do not replace the receiver; instead press the follow-on call button.

6 When you have finished speaking, replace the receiver. Any coins that were not used will be returned. Pay phones do not always give change, so use 10p and 20p coins for shorter calls.

Sending a Letter

The distinctive Post Office sign

BESIDES MAIN POST OFFICES that offer all the postal services available, there are many branch offices in newsstands, grocery stores and general information centers, particularly in the more isolated areas and smaller towns. In many villages the post office is in the only store. Post offices are usually open from 9am to 5:30pm Monday to Friday, and until 12:30pm on Saturday. Mail boxes – in all shapes and sizes but always red – are found throughout cities, towns and villages.

A Cotswold post office

POSTAL SERVICES

STAMPS CAN BE BOUGHT at any outlet that displays the sign "Stamps sold here." Hotels often have mail boxes in their lobby. When writing to a British address always include the post code, which can be found in phone directories. Letters within the UK can be

Aerograms are all 1st class

2nd-class stamp   1st-class stamp

Special issue commemorative stamps

sent either first or second class. First-class service is more expensive but quicker, with most letters reaching their destination the following day (except Sunday); second-class mail takes a day or two longer.

POSTE RESTANTE

LARGER URBAN post offices have a *poste restante* service where letters can be sent for collection. To use the service be sure to print the surname clearly so it will be filed correctly. Send it to *Poste Restante* followed by the address of the post office. To collect your post you will have to show your passport or other form of identification. Mail will be kept for one month. London's main post office is in William IV Street, WC2. The American Express office at 6 Haymarket, London *(see p86)* has a *poste restante* service for customers.

POST (MAIL) BOXES

THESE MAY BE either free-standing "pillar boxes" or wall safes, both painted bright red. Some pillar boxes have separate slots, one for overseas and first-class mail, another for second-class mail. Initials on the older style post boxes indicate the monarch at the time it was erected.

Post boxes are often embedded in post office walls. Collections are usually made several times a day during weekdays (less often on Saturdays and never on Sundays); times are marked on the box.

A rural post box, embedded in a stone wall

POSTING ABROAD

AIRMAIL PROVIDES a speedy and cost-effective method of communication. Aerograms go first class anywhere in the world and cost the same regardless of destination. It usually takes about three to four days for them to reach cities in Europe, and between four and seven days for destinations elsewhere.

Sending anything by surface mail is more economical but it can take anywhere up to 12 weeks to reach its final destination. To check overseas mail rates, go to your nearest post office and have your letter weighed. Letters and parcels sent to European Union countries cost the same as mail inland.

The Post Office offers an express delivery service called **Parcelforce International**. Available from most main post offices it is comparable in price to many private companies such as **DHL**, **Crossflight** or **Expressair**.

Crossflight
℡ *0181-564 7441.*

Expressair
℡ *0181-897 6568.*

DHL
℡ *0181-818 9000.*

Parcelforce International
℡ *0800 224466.*

Pillar box

Banking and Local Currency

Visitors to Britain usually find that the main banks offer them the best rates of exchange. However, if you do find yourself having to use one of the hundreds of privately owned currency exchanges that are found at nearly every major airport, train station and tourist area, care should be taken to check the commission and minimum charges before completing any transaction. Traveler's checks are by far the safest method of bringing currency to Britain with you.

Lloyds bank with currency exchange facilities

BUREAUX DE CHANGE

Small private currency exchange may be more conveniently located and open when banks are closed. But rates of exchange can vary considerably and commission charges can be high, so it may be worth looking around.

The reputable firms such as **Exchange International**, **Thomas Cook**, **American Express** and **Chequepoint** usually offer good exchange facilities and have branches throughout Britain.

BANKS

Banks generally offer the best rates of exchange for visitors, though commissions may vary considerably.

Every large town and city in Britain will have a branch of at least one of these five main clearing banks – **Barclays**, **Lloyds**, **Midland**, **National Westminster**, and the **Royal Bank of Scotland**.

Many banks have a cash machine from which you can obtain money with a credit card and your personal identification number (PIN); arrange this before you leave home. Some of the most modern machines have easy-to-read computerized instructions in several languages. American Express cards may be used in 24-hour Lloyds and Royal Bank of Scotland cash machines. Once again you will need a PIN number to access your personal account. There is a 2 percent handling charge for each transaction that you make.

If you run out of funds, another way to get money is to contact your own bank and ask them to wire the cash to the nearest British bank. You can also ask branches of Thomas Cook or American Express to do this for you. American visitors can get cash dispatched through **Western Union** to a bank or post office. Take along your passport to claim the money.

Banking hours vary, but the minimum opening times are 9:30am to 3:30pm, Monday to Friday. Many will stay open longer, especially in cities, and some open Saturday mornings. All banks close on Public Holidays (see p614).

CREDIT CARDS

Credit and store cards are widely accepted throughout Britain. But many smaller shops, markets, guesthouses and cafés may not accept them. The main card used throughout Britain is Visa, but other credit cards include Diners Club, American Express, Access and Mastercard.

Eurocheque logo

You can get cash advances with a credit card at any bank displaying the card sign. You will be charged the credit card company's interest rate for obtaining cash.

EUROCHEQUES

With eurocheques, which are available if you have a European bank account, you can write out checks in sterling for the exact amount of a purchase. Your checks are then guaranteed up to a certain amount.

Exchange International
0171-630 1107.

Thomas Cook
0171-408 4179.

American Express
0171-930 4411.
0800 89 23 33

Chequepoint
0171-409 1122.

Western Union
0800 833 833.

British Banks
All these main banks have branches in most of Britain's towns and cities. Most will also offer exchange facilities, but proof of identity may be required.

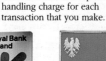

The Royal Bank of Scotland

Royal Bank of Scotland logo

Barclays Bank logo

Lloyds Bank logo

Midland Bank logo

NatWest

National Westminster logo

CASH AND TRAVELER'S CHECKS

Britain's currency is the pound sterling (£), which is divided into 100 pence (p). There are no exchange controls in Britain, so you may bring in and take out as much cash as you like. Scotland has its own bills but they are not always accepted in England and Wales, even though they are legal tender. Traveler's checks are the safest alternative to carrying large amounts of cash.

A Scottish one pound (£1) bill

Always keep the receipts from your traveler's checks separately from the checks themselves because it makes it easier to obtain a refund if they are lost or stolen. Some main banks issue traveler's checks free of commission to their account holders, but the normal rate is about 1 percent. When changing money ask for some smaller bills, since these are easier to use.

Bank Notes
English bills are produced in denominations of £5, £10, £20, and £50. Always get small denominations since some shops may refuse the larger bills.

£50 bill

£20 bill

£10 bill

£5 bill

Coins
Coins currently in use are £1, 50p, 20p, 10p, 5p, 2p and 1p (shown here at actual sizes). There are also a few £2 coins in circulation, issued to commemorate special occasions.

 **1 pound (£1)**

 50 pence (50p)

 20 pence (20p)

 10 pence (10p)

 5 pence (5p)

 2 pence (2p)

 1 penny (1p)

Shopping in Britain

WHILE THE WEST END OF LONDON *(see pp122–3)* is undeniably Britain's most exciting place to shop, many regional centers offer nearly as wide a range of goods. Moreover regional shopping can be less stressful, less expensive, and remarkably varied, with craft studios, farm shops, street markets and factory showrooms adding to the enjoyment of bargain-hunting. Britain is famous for its country clothing: wool, waxed cotton and tweed are all popular along with classic prints such as Liberty or Laura Ashley and tartan. Other particularly British goods include antiques, floral soaps and scents, porcelain, glass and local crafts.

Antique stall at Bermondsey Market

SHOPPING HOURS

IN GENERAL, you can assume most stores in Britain will open during the week from 9am or 10am, and they will close after 5pm or 6pm. Hours on Saturdays may be shorter. Few town center stores open on Sundays, unless it is near Christmas. Some stores open late for one evening a week – Thursday in London's West End – while village shops may close at lunchtime, or for one afternoon each week. Market days vary from town to town; some markets *(see pp122–3)* are held on Sundays.

HOW TO PAY

MOST LARGE STORES all over the UK will accept well-known credit cards such as Access and VISA. Charge cards such as American Express or Diners Club are acceptable in some places, but Marks & Spencer, markets, and some small shops will not take credit cards. Traveler's checks can be used in larger stores, but exchange rates for nonsterling checks may be poor. Take your passport with you for identification. Few places will accept checks drawn on foreign banks (Eurocheques are an exception). Cash is still the most popular way to pay for small purchases.

RIGHTS AND REFUNDS

IF SOMETHING YOU BUY is defective, you are entitled to a refund, provided you have kept your receipt as proof of purchase and return the goods in the same condition as when you bought them, and preferably in the same packaging. This may not always apply to sale goods clearly marked as seconds, imperfect, or shop-soiled. Inspect these carefully before you buy. You do not have to accept a credit in place of a cash refund.

Vivienne Westwood's designer label

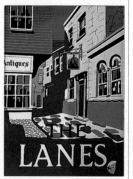

Sign for the Lanes, Brighton
(see p163)

ANNUAL SALES

TRADITIONALLY, sales take place during January, and in June and July, when nearly every shop cuts prices to get rid of slow-selling or imperfect stock. But you may well find special offers at any time of the year. Some shops begin their winter sales just before Christmas. Department stores and fashion houses have some excellent bargains for eager shoppers; one of the most prestigious sales is Harrod's *(see p99)*, where lines will usually form long before opening time.

VAT AND TAX-FREE SHOPPING

VALUE ADDED TAX (VAT) is charged on most goods and services sold in Britain – exceptions include food, books and children's clothes. It is usually included in the advertised price. Visitors from outside the European Union who stay less than three months may claim this tax back. Take your passport with you whenever you go shopping. You must complete a form in the shop when you buy your goods and give a copy to the customs authorities when you leave the country. You may have to show your goods as proof of purchase. If you arrange to have the goods shipped from the store, the VAT should be deducted before you pay.

OUT-OF-TOWN SHOPPING CENTERS

THESE LARGE COMPLEXES, built along the lines of American malls, are rapidly increasing around Britain. The advantages of car access and easy, cheap parking are undeniable, and most centers are accessible by public transportation. The centers usually feature clusters of popular upscale stores, with many services offered such as toilets, cafés, nurseries, restaurants and movies.

A traditional storefront in Stonegate, York *(see p390)*

DEPARTMENT STORES

A FEW BIG DEPARTMENT stores, such as Harrod's, are only found in London, but others have provincial branches. John Lewis, for example, has shops in 22 locations. It sells a huge range of fabrics, clothing and household items, combining quality service with good value. Marks & Spencer, with 303 branches throughout Britain, is even more of a household name, famed for its good-value clothing and prepared food. Debenhams and British Home Stores (BhS) are other well-known general stores with inexpensive clothing and home furnishings. Habitat is a reputable supplier of modern furniture. The sizes of all these stores, and the range of stock they carry, will differ from region to region.

Local Teesdale cheeses

CLOTHING STORES

O NCE AGAIN, London has the widest range, from *haute couture* to cheap and cheerful items ready-made. Shopping for clothing in the regions, however, can often be less tiring. Many towns popular with tourists – Oxford, Bath and York for instance – have independently owned cloth-ing stores where you receive more personal service. Or you could try one of the chain stores such as Principles or Dorothy Perkins for stylish, reasonably priced clothes,

and the Gap and Miss Selfridge for younger and less expensive fashions.

SUPERMARKETS AND FOODSHOPS

S UPERMARKETS are a good way to shop for food. The range and quality of items in stock is usually excellent. Several large chains compete for market share and as a result, prices are generally lower than smaller shops. Sainsbury, Tesco, Asda, Safeway and Waitrose are some of the national names. However, the smaller town-center stores such as local bakeries, greengrocers or markets, may give you a more interesting choice of fresh regional produce, and more personal service.

SOUVENIR, GIFT AND MUSEUM SHOPS

B UYING PRESENTS is a must for most travelers. Most reputable large stores can arrange freight for expensive

The Mustard Shop *(see p187),* **Norwich**

items. If you want to buy things you can carry back in your suitcase, the choice is wide. You can buy attractive, well-made, portable craft items all over the country, especially in areas tourists are likely to visit. For slightly more unusual presents, have a look in museum shops and the gifts available in National Trust *(see p25)* and English Heritage properties.

SECONDHAND AND ANTIQUE SHOPS

B RITAIN'S LONG HISTORY means there are many interesting artifacts to be found. A visit to any of Britain's stately homes will reveal a national passion for antiques. Most towns will have an antique or bric-a-brac (miscellaneous second-hand items) shop or two. Look for auctions – tourist information centers *(see pp614–15)* can help you to locate them. You might like to visit a jumble or flea market in the hope of picking up a bargain.

Book stall, Hay-on-Wye, Wales *(see p447)*

MARKETS

L ARGE TOWNS AND CITIES usually have a central covered market that operates most weekdays, selling everything from fresh produce to pots and pans. The information under each town entry in this guide gives market days. Many towns hold weekly markets in the main square. While you browse among the stalls, look for local fresh produce and the jams and cakes of the Women's Institute stalls.

Entertainment in Britain

L ONDON IS WITHOUT DOUBT the entertainment capital of Britain *(see pp124–7)*, but many regional theaters, opera houses and concert halls have varied programs. Edinburgh, Manchester, Birmingham, Leeds and Bristol in particular have a lot to offer and there are a number of summer arts festivals around the country, such as those at Bath and Cheltenham *(see pp62–3)*. Ticket prices are often cheaper outside the capital.

Punch and Judy show

SOURCES OF INFORMATION

I N LONDON, check the listings magazines, such as *Time Out*, or the *Evening Standard*, London's evening newspaper. All of the quality newspapers *(see p618)* provide comprehensive arts reviews and listings of the cultural events and shows throughout the country, with the largest sections on the weekends. Local newspapers, libraries, or tourist offices *(see p617)* can supply details of regional events. Specialist magazines such as *NME* or *Melody Maker* give up-to-date news of the pop music scene and are available from any newsstand.

THEATERS

B RITAIN HAS AN enduring theatrical tradition dating back to Shakespeare *(see pp310–13)* and beyond. All over the country, amateurs and professionals tread the boards in specially built auditoriums, pubs, clubs and village halls. Productions and performance

standards are generally high, and British actors have an international reputation.

London is the place to enjoy theater at its most varied and glamorous *(see p124)*. The West End alone has more than 50 theaters *(see p125)* ranging from elaborate Edwardian, upholstered in red plush, to exciting modern buildings such as the National Theatre on the South Bank in London.

In Stratford-upon-Avon, the Royal Shakespeare Company presents a year-round program of Shakespeare, as well as avant-garde and experimental plays. Bristol also has a long dramatic tradition, the Theatre Royal *(see p242)*, the oldest working theater in Britain. Some of the best productions outside the capital can be found at the West Yorkshire Theatre in Leeds, the Royal Exchange in Manchester *(see p360)* and the Traverse in Edinburgh.

Street entertainer

Open-air theater ranges from the free street entertainment that is to be found in many city centers, to student performances on the grounds of Cambridge or Oxford colleges or a production at Cornwall's spectacular clifftop amphitheater, the Minack Theatre *(see p262)*. Every fourth year, York also stages a series of open-air medieval mystery plays called the York Cycle. Perhaps the liveliest theatrical tradition in Britain is the Edinburgh Festival *(see p495)*. Seaside resorts put on summer programs of lighthearted entertainment, traditionally stand-up comedy.

Ticket availability varies from show to show. You may be able to buy a ticket at the door, especially for a midweek matinee, but for the more popular West End shows tickets may have to be booked weeks or even months in advance. You can book through agencies and some travel agents, and most hotels will organize theater tickets for you. Booking fees are often charged. Beware of scalpers selling tickets *(see p67)* – these may be counterfeit. There are no age restrictions in Britain's theaters. It is left to your discretion to decide whether a show is suitable for children.

MUSIC

A DIVERSE musical repertoire can be found in a variety of places. Church choral music is a great national tradition and many churches and cathedrals host concerts *(see p193)*. London, Manchester, Birmingham, Liverpool, Bristol and Bournemouth all have their own excellent orchestras.

Rock, jazz, folk and country-and-western concerts are staged periodically in pubs, clubs and sometimes in outdoor spots. Wales has a strong musical tradition, which you will come across in many Welsh pubs; northern England is renowned for its booming brass and silver bands; Scotland, of course, has its famous bagpipers *(see p466)*.

The Buxton Opera House, the Midlands

The multiplex Warner West End cinema, Leicester Square, London

MOVIES

THE LATEST FILMS can be seen in any large town. Check the local papers or the tourist office to find out what is on.

Movies are having a revival, with luxurious multiscreen theaters taking over from the local, single-screen houses. In larger cities a more diverse range of films is often available including more foreign-language productions. These tend to be shown at arts or repertory houses. Mainstream English-speaking films are usually shown by the big chains. Age limits apply to certain films. Young children are allowed to see any feature film which is graded with a U (universal) or PG (parental guidance) certificate. Movie prices vary widely; some are cheaper at off-peak times, such as Mondays or afternoons. For new releases it is advisable to book in advance.

CLUBS

MOST CITIES have some sort of club scene, but London has the most famous ones *(see p124)*. These may feature live music, discos, or DJ or dance performances. Some insist on dress codes or members only, and most have doormen, or "bouncers." Apart from the major cities, Brighton and Bristol have lively clubs.

DANCE

THIS COVERS a multitude of activities: everything from classical ballet and acid-house parties to traditional English Morris dancing or the Scottish Highland fling, which you may come upon in pubs and villages around the country.

Dance halls are rarer than they were, but ballroom dancing is alive and well. Other dance events you may find are ceilidhs (pronounced kay-lee), which is Celtic dancing and music; May Balls often held at universities (invitation only); dinner or tea dances; and square dancing.

Birmingham is home to the Birmingham Royal Ballet and is the best place to see performances outside London. Avant-garde contemporary dance is also performed.

GAY

MOST LARGE communities will have some gay meeting places, mostly bars and clubs. You can find out about them from publications such as the free *Pink Paper* or *Gay Times* on sale in some newsstands, and in gay bars and clubs. London's gay life is centered around Soho *(see p82)* with its many European-style cafés and bars. Outside London, the most active gay scenes are in Manchester and Brighton. Gay Pride is the largest free outdoor festival in Europe.

Three revellers, Gay Pride Festival

CHILDREN

LONDON OFFERS children a positive goldmine of fun, excitement and adventure, but it can be expensive. From the traditional sights to something more unusual such as a discovery center, London has a wide range of activities, many interactive, to interest children of all ages. Kidsline, open from 4pm to 6pm, is a London listings service for children (tel 0171-222 8070).

Outside London, activities for children range from nature trails to fun fairs. Your local tourist office or the local library will have information on things to do with children.

Pirate Ship, Chessington World of Adventures, Surrey

THEME PARKS

THEME PARKS in Britain are enjoyed by children of all ages. Alton Towers has conventional rides plus a car museum, all set in spectacular gardens. Chessington World of Adventures is a huge complex south of London. Based on a zoo, it now includes nine themed areas, such as Calamity Canyon, Transylvania and Circus World. Thorpe Park, in Surrey, is a large watery theme park full of scale model buildings, exciting roller-coaster rides and a peaceful pet farm. Lego Land, the latest park is due to open in April 1996.

Alton Towers
Alton, Staffordshire.
☎ 01538 702200.

Chessington World of Adventures
Leatherhead Rd, Chessington, Surrey.
☎ 01372 727227.

Lego Land
Winkfeld Rd, Windsor, Berkshire.
☎ 01753 622222.

Thorpe Park
Staines Rd, Chertsey, Surrey.
☎ 01932 569393.

Special Vacations and Outdoor Activities

BRITAIN OFFERS MANY special interest vacations or courses where you can learn a new sport or skill, practice an activity you enjoy, or simply have fun and meet people. If you prefer less structured activities, there is a variety of sports you can participate in, from walking in Britain's national parks to sailing on the many waterways and skiing in Scotland, or exploring the country on horseback. Another option is volunteer work on a nature or bird preserve, or an archaeological dig or conservation project.

Horseback riding on a country bridle path *(see p33)*

SPECIAL VACATIONS

A GREAT ADVANTAGE to these vacations is that you can attend the courses alone but without feeling too solitary. There are hundreds of options: any kind of sport – boating, golf, skiing, riding, tennis; arts and crafts such as painting, pottery, calligraphy, jewelry-making; and educational courses on everything from Shakespeare to ecology.

The English and Scottish Tourist Boards *(see p615)* have lists and pamphlets on some of these activities, and can tell you who to contact for more information. Look for their publication, **Activity Holidays** (Jarrold), available from some bookstores.

You can book direct with the organizers, or through a travel agent. Introductory courses generally provide you with all the equipment you need plus accommodation and, often, transportation.

Courses are available at all levels of expertise, for all ages. If you are fit and interested in the countryside, you may like to work on a conservation project for a few days. It can be hard work but worthwhile. Contact the tourist board.

WALKING AND CYCLING

WALKING ALLOWS YOU to experience at first hand the spectacular variety of the British landscape, by yourself or with a club. There is a network of long-distance footpaths and shorter trail routes all over Britain *(see pp32–3)*.

Cyclists may use designated cycle routes and bridle paths *(see p643)* and the quieter rural roads can be a delight. Choose a flat or hilly one depending on your energy and fitness. Be sure to take spare parts with you.

GOLF AND TENNIS

THERE ARE ABOUT 2,000 golf courses in Britain and many clubs welcome visiting players. Weekends are usually busy. Special operators will book packages for you. Greens fees vary widely; many clubs offer temporary membership.

You will find tennis courts in every town and many hotels and some clubs offer temporary membership, but courts in summer are in demand. The **Lawn Tennis Association** can provide more information.

Sailing, Cardigan Bay, Welsh coast

BOATING AND SAILING

MESSING ABOUT IN BOATS is a British obsession. You can sail at many places – the Isle of Wight and the south coast are full of pleasure craft. Inland, the network of rivers, lakes and canals can offer a calmer sort of pleasure. Canal-cruising is very popular *(see p641)* and the Norfolk Broads *(see p184)* provides one of the best inland boating experiences (the **Broads Authority** will provide information). Elsewhere, the Thames and the canals slice through lovely landscape. The Lake District *(see pp340–57)* is another area which is popular with boating enthusiasts.

OTHER WATER SPORTS

WITH SO MUCH coastline, Britain is a place for enjoying the water, even if temperatures are low. The best areas for surfing are the

Walkers and rock climbers, Yorkshire Dales National Park *(see pp370–71)*

West Country and South Wales. Windsurfing is also popular, both on the coast and on lakes. Tuition and equipment rental are available at many resorts, and several also offer water-skiing facilities. Most towns and resorts have public swimming pools, many with water tunnels, slides and wave machines. Scuba diving is popular around rocky parts of the West Country.

FISHING

FISHING IN THE SEA and on rivers is Britain's biggest participating sport. Regulations are very strict, so check for

Solitary sea fisherman, England's southeast coast

details of licenses, open seasons and other restrictions at tourist offices or tackle shops. You may have to join a club, or buy a temporary permit. The best game fishing (salmon and trout) is in the West Country, the Northeast, Wales and Scotland.

SPECTATOR SPORTS

FOOTBALL (SOCCER) is a passion for a large section of the population. League events are held in many large towns once or twice a week in the season. If you want to see a game, ask at the local tourist office, or check the local papers. Rugby Football also has a good following and games are played in cities such as London, Cardiff and Edinburgh. Cricket is the English national game, and matches are played from April to September on village greens throughout the land. Both flat-racing and steeplechasing are very popular and betting is big business. You can find details of race meetings in most national newspapers.

Paragliding over the South Downs *(see p167)*

ADVENTURE SPORTS

ADVENTURE SPORTS are plenti-ful and popular. Among the options are rock-climbing and mountaineering; aero-nautical sports and gliding; ice-skating in many major cities and horseback riding throughout the country. Al-though expensive, it is also possible to try go-karting. Facilities for skiing are limited in the UK but there are winter sports facilities at Scottish resorts such as the Cairngorms.

DIRECTORY

Aircraft Owners and Pilots Association
50A Cambridge St, London SW1V.
📞 0171-834 5631.

Association of Pleasure Craft Operators
35A High St, Newport, Salop TF10.
📞 01952 813572.

Association of British Riding Schools
Old Brewery Yd, Penzance, Cornwall TR18.
📞 01736 69440.

British Activity Holiday Association
22 Green Lane, Hersham, Surrey KT12.
📞 01932 252994.

British Hang-Gliding and Para-gliding Association
The Old School Room, Loughborough Rd,

Leicester LE4.
📞 01162 511322.

British Mountaineering Council
Crawford Hse, Precinct Centre, Booth St East, Manchester M13.
📞 0161 273 5835.

British Surfing Association
Champions Yd, Penzance, Cornwall TW18.
📞 01736 60250.

British Water Ski Federation
390 City Rd, London EC1V.
📞 0171-833 2855.

British Trust for Conservation Volunteers
80 York Way, London N1.
📞 0171-278 4293.

British Waterways
Willow Grange, Church Rd, Watford, Herts WD1.
📞 01923 201239.

Broads Authority
18 Colegate, Norwich,

Norfolk NR3.
📞 01603 610734.

English Golf Union
1–3 Upper King St, Leicester LE1.
📞 01162 553042.

Football Association
16 Lancaster Gate, London W2.
📞 0171-262 4542.

Lawn Tennis Association
Queen's Club, London W14.
📞 0171-381 7111.

National Feder-ation of Anglers
Halliday Hse, 2 Wilson St, Derby DE1.
📞 01332 362000.

National Cricket Association
Lord's Cricket Ground, St John's Wood, NW8.
📞 0171-289 6098.

National Rivers Authority
Rivers Hse, Waterside

Drive, Aztec West, Almondsbury, BS12.
📞 01454 624400.

Outward Bound Trust
Chestnut Field, Regent Pl, Rugby, Warks CV21.
📞 01788 560423.

Racecourse Association
Winkfield Rd, Ascot, Berks SL5.
📞 01344 25912.

Royal Yachting Association
RYA Hse, Romsey Rd, Eastleigh, Hants SO5.
📞 01703 629962.

Rugby Football Union
Rugby Rd, Twickenham, Middx TW1.
📞 0181-892 8161.

Ski Club of Great Britain
118 Eaton Sq, London SW1W.
📞 0171-245 1033.

TRAVEL INFORMATION

S INCE IT IS AN international gateway
for air and sea traffic, traveling
to Britain poses few problems.
By air, travelers have a very
large choice of carriers
serving North America,
Australasia and Europe.
Bus travel is a cheap,
albeit rather slow, form of
transportation from Europe,
while traveling by train has
been transformed with the
advent of the Channel Tunnel – three
hours from Paris to London. Traveling

**British Airways' supersonic
passenger plane, Concorde**

within Britain itself is fairly easy. There
is an extensive network of roads reaching to all parts of the country and renting a car is often the best way
of traveling around. The
InterCity rail network is
very efficient and the network to the smaller
towns, especially around
London, is good. Bus travel
is the cheapest option and
serves most areas but can be
slow. If time is short air travel is possible but expensive.

**Passenger concourse, Waterloo
Station, London**

TRAVELING AROUND
BRITAIN

C HOOSING THE BEST way to
travel around Britain
depends very much on where
and when you want to go,
although the quickest and
most convenient methods are
generally the most expensive.
　Distances between any two
points within mainland Britain
are relatively small (at least
by American or Australian
standards) so air travel usually
makes sense only between
the extremes, such as London
to Edinburgh. For shorter trips,
the time spent getting to and
from airports often outweighs
any savings in actual traveling
time. Rail services are the best
alternative if you want to visit
Britain's major cities, though
fares, especially at peak
times, can be quite expensive.
If you plan to do much
traveling within Britain, a rail
pass can be a very good
value. You can buy a pass
before you arrive in the UK
since several plans cater to
overseas visitors (*see p638*).

Bus networks cover a wide
number of UK destinations,
and are cheaper than trains,
but take longer and may be
less comfortable. Taxis are
available at all major bus or
rail stations to take you to
your hotel; without a car you
will avoid the stress of driving
in congested city centers.
　If you plan a more flexible
vacation, renting your own car
is more feasible than relying
on public transportation. Car
rental can be arranged at all
major airports, large railroad
stations and city center outlets. To get the best deals,
book from abroad. Small local
firms often undercut the large
operators in price, but may not
be as reliable or convenient.
　For detailed exploration of
smaller areas such as Britain's
National Parks or popular

regions like the Lake District
(*see pp346–59*) you may prefer
more leisurely transportation
offered by bike, horse or
narrowboat. Sometimes there
are picturesque local options
like the rowboat ferry between
Southwold and Walberswick
on the Blyth Estuary (*see
p189*). There are also larger
car ferries which travel to
Britain's islands.

**Rowboat ferry on the River Blyth,
Southwold, Suffolk**

CHANNEL TUNNEL

This historic landlink between Britain and France
opened for business in late
1994 and closed one of the
"missing links" in the
European transporta-
tion system. The
sleek new trains
are high-tech and
very comfortable,
producing an experi-
ence more akin to
air travel than rail.
Passengers on
coaches and cars get on a
freight train known as **Le
Shuttle**, which takes 35
minutes to travel between
Calais and Folkestone.

**EURO
TUNNEL**

Eurotunnel logo

For those traveling by rail
there are about 40 scheduled
Eurostar services, operated
by the French, Belgian and
British. They run be-
tween Brussels,
Paris and London
and there is no
need to change
at either end of
the tunnel. There
are two passenger
tunnels – and one
service tunnel –
that lie 25–45 m (82–147 ft)
below the sea bed. All the
tunnels are made of concrete
and iron, and are 31 miles
(50 km) long.

Arriving by Sea, Rail and Bus

IF YOU ARE traveling from Europe by foot, car, or rail you will have to cross the English Channel or North Sea either by ferry or the Channel Tunnel. Ferry services serve a large number of ports on the European mainland and have good linkups with international bus services from most European cities to Britain. The Channel Tunnel means that there is now a nonstop rail link between Britain and Europe. Prices between the ferries and the tunnel services remain very competitive.

Ferry arriving at Dover

FERRY SERVICES FROM EUROPE

A COMPLEX NETWORK of ferry services operates between more than dozen British ports. About 20 car and passenger ferry services travel regularly across the Channel and North Sea routes to many ports in northern and southern Europe *(see pp10–15)*.

Because of the number of areas they reach, ferries can be more convenient for those in cars or on foot than the Channel Tunnel. Fares vary greatly according to the season, time of travel and duration of stay. The shortest crossings are not always the cheapest: you pay for the speed of the journey.

CROSSING TIMES

CROSSING TIMES VARY from just over an hour on the shortest routes to a full 24 hours on services from Spain and Scandinavia. If you take an overnight sailing, you may have to pay extra for sleeping accommodations, but it is often worth booking a cabin on the longer trips to avoid feeling exhausted when you arrive. Fast hovercraft services

between Dover, Boulogne and Calais are run by **Hoverspeed**, while a **Seacat** (catamaran) service crosses between Folkestone and Boulogne. These are the fastest routes across the Channel, taking just over half an hour, and all these craft can carry vehicles. The crossings lack the dip and sway of a conventional ship, and so may be less painful for poor sailors.

SEAPORT BUREAUCRACY

THOSE VISITORS from outside the European Union should allow plenty of time for immigration control and customs clearance at British seaports *(see p619)*. You may not bring pets into Britain, in order to prevent rabies.

A hovercraft crossing the English Channel

INTERNATIONAL BUS TRAVEL

ALTHOUGH BUS TRAVEL is comparably cheaper than other methods of travel, it is not the most comfortable way of traveling across Europe. But if you have a lot of spare time and want to stop off en route it can be convenient. Once you have paid for your ticket you will not have to pay again to use the ferry or the Channel Tunnel.

INTERNATIONAL RAIL TRAVEL

WITH THE ADVENT of the Channel Tunnel, there is now access to the French high-speed rail network, and from there to the rest of the European rail network. Rail travel can be an efficient, comfortable and fast way of traveling across Europe to Britain – in France trains reach speeds of up to 185 mph (300 kmph). The cost is comparable to flying, although it is much more convenient.

Arriving by Air

BRITAIN HAS' ABOUT 130 licensed airports but only a handful of these are equipped for long distance travel. The largest is London's Heathrow, the world's busiest international airport and one of Europe's central routing points for international air travel. It is served by most of the world's leading airlines with direct flights from nearly all the major cities. The other major international airports include Gatwick, Stansted, Manchester, Glasgow, Newcastle, Birmingham and Edinburgh. Smaller airports such as London City, Bristol, Norwich and Cardiff have daily flights to European destinations.

Platform sign for express railway service to London

A British Airways 747 jet at Heathrow Airport

BRITISH AIRPORTS

THE MAJORITY of Britain's largest and best known airports are run by the British Airports Authority – the rest are owned by a local authority or are in private hands. All BAA airports offer up-to-date facilities, including 24-hour banking, shops, cafés, hotels and restaurants. Security is strict at all British airports and it is important never to leave baggage unattended.

If you are starting your visit in London, flights to Gatwick or Heathrow are equally convenient. But if you plan to visit northern England, there are an increasing number of flights going to Birmingham, Newcastle and Manchester, while for Scotland you can fly to Glasgow or Edinburgh.

Heathrow has four terminals and some others have two. Before you fly, check with the airport for which terminal your flight leaves.

During severe weather conditions in the winter months, your flight may be diverted to another airport. If this happens, the airline will organize transportation back to your original destination.

British Airways has flights to nearly all the world's important destinations. Other British international airlines include **Virgin Atlantic**, with routes to the US and the Far East, and **British Midland**, which flies to Western Europe.

The main American airlines offering scheduled services to Britain include **Delta**, **US Air** and **American Airlines**. From Canada, the main carriers are **Canadian Airlines** and **Air Canada**. From Australasia, the national carriers **Qantas** and **Air New Zealand** vie with many Far Eastern rivals.

Britain imposes an airport tax on all departing passengers – currently £5 for domestic and European routes and £10 for long distance flights.

TRANSPORT FROM THE AIRPORT

BRITAIN'S INTERNATIONAL airports lie some way from city centers, but travel to and from them is efficient. Every airport has taxis and these are the most convenient form of door-to-door travel, but they

Arrival terminal at Heathrow Airport

AIRPORT	ℹ INFORMATION	DISTANCE TO CITY CENTER	TAXI FARE TO CITY CENTER	PUBLIC TRANSPORT TO CITY CENTER
Heathrow	0181-759 4321	14 miles (23 km)	£25–30	Tube: 40 min Bus: 1 hr
Gatwick	01293 535353	28 miles (45 km)	£40–45	Rail: 30 min Bus: 70 min
Stansted	01279 680500	37 miles (60 km)	£45–50	Rail: 45 min Bus: 75 min
Manchester	0161 4893000	10 miles (16 km)	£10–12	Rail: 15 min Bus: 30 min
Birmingham	0121 7675511	8 miles (13 km)	£12–15	Bus: 30 min
Newcastle	0191 2860966	5 miles (8 km)	£7–10	Metro: 20 min Bus: 20 min
Glasgow	0141 8871111	10 miles (16 km)	£12–15	Bus: 20 min
Edinburgh	0131 3331000	5 miles (8 km)	£12–15	Bus: 15 min

are also expensive and can be slow if there is traffic congestion – very likely if you travel in the rush hour *(see p636)*. This can also be a problem with taking a coach or bus, although they are a lot cheaper than taxis.

Heathrow and Newcastle are both linked to the center of the city by the Underground *(see p643)*. These are efficient, quick and cheap. Manchester, Stansted and Gatwick have regular express trains that are not too expensive and are a reliable method for traveling into the heart of the city.

National Express Coaches *(see p640)* provide direct connections from major airports to many British destinations. They have regular service between Gatwick and Heathrow.

CHOOSING A TICKET

FINDING THE RIGHT FLIGHT at the right price can be difficult. Promotional fares do come up and it is always worth checking with the airlines direct. Bargain deals are often available from package operators and are advertised in newspapers and travel magazines. Students and under 26s, senior citizens and regular or business travelers may be able to obtain a discount. Children and babies also travel less expensively.

AIR FARES

FARES TO BRITAIN are usually seasonal, the highest being from June to September. The best deals are available from

A modern Forte Crest hotel at Gatwick Airport

November to April, excluding the Christmas period – if you want to travel then, be sure to book well in advance.

APEX (Advance Purchase Excursion) fares are often the best value, though they must be booked up to a month ahead, and are subject to restrictions (such as minimum and maximum stays and no refunds). Charter flights offer even cheaper seats, but have less flexible departure times.

If you choose a discount fare, always buy from a reputable operator, and do not part with cash until you have seen your ticket. Check with the relevant airline to be sure your seat has been confirmed.

Packages may also be worth considering, even if you enjoy independent travel. Airlines and tour operators can put together a great range of flexible deals to suit your needs, sometimes with car rental or rail travel included. This can often work out cheaper than arranging it when you have arrived in Britain.

TRAVELING WITHIN BRITAIN BY AIR

Britain's size means that internal air travel only makes sense over long distances, where it can save a great deal of time – for example, London to Scotland, or to one of the many offshore islands. Air fares can be expensive, but if you book well ahead, fares can be up to three times cheaper than if you just turn up at the airport – although you are still always guaranteed a seat. The British Airways shuttle flights that operate between London and cities such as Glasgow, Edinburgh and Manchester are extremely popular with business travelers. At peak times of the day, flights leave every hour, while at other times there is usually a flight every two hours. Bad weather can cause delays or diversions during the winter months. Even on domestic flights, security is stringent, and you should never leave your bags unattended.

DIRECTORY

AIRLINE NUMBERS

Air Canada
(*(800) 776-3000.*

American Airlines
(*(800) 433-7300.*

British Airways
(*(800) 247-9297.*

British Midlands
(*0181-745-7321.*

Continental Airlines
(*(800) 231-0856.*

Delta Airlines
(*(800) 241-4141.*

Qantas
(*(800) 227-4500.*

TWA
(*(800) 892-4141.*

Virgin Atlantic
(*(800) 862-8621.*

Award-winning exterior of Stansted Airport

Traveling Around by Car

THE MOST STARTLING difference for most foreign motorists is that in Britain you drive on the left, with corresponding adjustments at traffic circles and junctions. Distances are measured in miles. Once you adapt, rural Britain is an enjoyable place to drive, but traffic density in towns and at busy holiday times can cause long delays – public holiday weekends near the south coast can be particularly horrendous. An extensive network of toll-free highways and trunk roads has now cut traveling time to most parts of the country.

No stopping

Speed limit applies

WHAT YOU NEED

TO DRIVE IN BRITAIN you need a current driving license with an international driving permit. In any vehicle you drive you must carry proof of ownership or a rental agreement plus any insurance documents.

ROADS IN BRITAIN

PEAK RUSH-HOUR traffic can last from 8–9:30am and 5–6:30pm on weekdays in the cities; at these times traffic can grind to a halt. In the country a good road map is essential; the AA or RAC motoring atlases are user-friendly. For exploration of more rural areas, the Ordnance Survey series is the best.

A highway sign in miles

London	32
Cambridge	25
Newmarket	30
M 11	
Bishops Stortford	4
Dunmow (A120)	8

On all road maps B roads are secondary roads and A roads, often two-lane highways, are main routes. B routes are often less congested and more enjoyable to use. Rural areas

are crisscrossed by a web of tiny lanes. Highways are marked with M followed by their identifying number.

ROAD SIGNS

SIGNS are now generally standardized in line with Europe. Directional signs are color-coded: blue for highways, green for major routes and white for minor routes. Signs in Britain are not consistent and city suburbs can be confusing. Brown signs indicate places of interest. Advisory or warning signs are usually triangles in red and white, with easy to understand pictograms. Watch for electronic notices on highways that warn of construction, accidents or patches of fog. Railroad crossings often have automatic barriers. If the lights are flashing red it means a train is coming and you must stop. The *UK Highway Code Manual* – available from most good bookstores – is an up-to-date guide to all the current British driving regulations and traffic signs.

RULES OF THE ROAD

SPEED LIMITS are 30–40 mph (50–65 kmph) in urban areas and 70 mph (110 kmph) on highways or two-lane roads – watch out for speed signs on other roads. It is compulsory to wear seat belts in Britain. Drunk-driving penalties are severe – see the *UK Highway Code Manual* for legal limits.

The A30 two-lane highway going through Cornwall

No entry

No right turn allowed

Railroad level crossing

Yield to all vehicles

One-way traffic

Gradient of a road

PARKING

THIS IS THE BANE of the British motorist's life. Parking meters operate during working hours (usually 8am–6:30pm Mon–Sat); keep a supply of coins for them. Some cities have "park and ride" plans, where you can take a bus from an out-of-city parking lot into the center. Other towns have a "disk" parking system; ask the tourist office or a local newsstand for a disk to mark your arrival time. Many lots operate on a pay-and-display system. Avoid double yellow lines at all times; single lines mean you can park in the evenings and on weekends but check carefully. Traffic cops wear distinctive uniforms and will not hesitate to ticket, boot or tow your car away. If in any doubt, find a car park (*see pp642–3*). Outside urban areas and popular tourist zones, parking is not such a problem. Look for the letter P; this indicates legal parking spaces.

Sign for a parking lot

GASOLINE

NORTH AMERICAN visitors may find fuel (gas) very expensive in Britain. Large supermarkets often have the cheapest gas; look for branches of Tesco or Sainsbury with gas stations. Highway service areas are generally more expensive. Gas is sold in three grades: diesel, 4-star and unleaded. Most modern cars in Britain use unleaded gas – any vehicle you rent will probably do so also. Unleaded fuel and diesel are cheaper than 4-star. Most gas stations in Britain are self-service but instructions at the pumps are easy to follow. Green hoses denote unleaded fuel.

EMERGENCY SERVICES

BRITAIN'S MAJOR motoring organizations, the **AA** (Automobile Association) and the **RAC** (Royal Automobile Club), provide a comprehensive 24-hour emergency service, as well as many other automotive services. Both offer reciprocal assistance for members of automobile organizations; before arrival check with your own group to see if you are covered. You can contact the AA or RAC from the roadside SOS phones found on highways. **National Breakdown** is the other major rescue service in Britain, which can sometimes be quicker and cheaper since it uses many local garages.

Most car rental agencies have their own coverage, and their charges include membership of either the AA, the RAC or National Breakdown while you are driving. Be sure to ask the rental company for the service's emergency number.

If you are not a member of an affiliated organization you can still call for rescue service, but it will be expensive. Follow the advice given on your insurance policy or rental agreement. If you have an accident that involves injury or another vehicle, call the police as soon as possible *(see p621)*.

A small rural gas station in Goathland, North Yorkshire

CAR RENTAL

RENTING A CAR in Britain can be expensive. One of the most competitive national companies is **Holiday Autos**, but small local firms may undercut even these rates. Many companies ask you to leave a credit card number; otherwise you may have to part with a substantial cash deposit. You need your driving license and a passport when you rent. Most companies will not rent to novice drivers, and set age limits (usually 21–70). Automatic cars are fairly scarce. If you are touring Britain for three weeks or more, you may find a leasing arrangement cheaper than renting. Remember to add VAT and insurance costs when you check rental rates.

RAC and AA logos

HITCHHIKING

HITCHHIKING is a common practice in Britain, and you are likely to thumb a long-distance lift if you stand near a busy exit road junction. In rural or walking areas like the Lake District, tired hikers may well be offered a lift. It is illegal to hitch on highways or their approach roads. As anywhere, there is a risk in hitchhiking alone, especially for a woman. Ride-sharing is now a common practice. The small-ads magazine *Loot* (sold in newsstands in London, Manchester and Bristol) has a large section for ride seekers.

Traveling Around by Rail

BRITISH RAIL is the national rail network that covers the whole of the country. It is divided into regional sections, which serves over 2,500 stations throughout Britain. The system is efficient and reliable with quiet, modernized trains, particularly on the InterCity services. Traveling across the country, rather than out of London, may involve a number of changes since most lines radiate from London, which has seven major terminals. There is now a fast and efficient rail link with Continental Europe, from Waterloo rail terminal in London through the Channel Tunnel *(see p632)*.

InterCity train speeding through countryside

TICKETS

LARGE TRAVEL AGENTS and all British Rail (BR) stations sell rail tickets. First-class tickets cost about one-third more than standard fares, and generally roundtrip fares are cheaper than one-way tickets.

Allow plenty of time to buy your ticket and always ask about any special offers or reduced fares. There are four types of discounted fares for adults. Apex tickets are available in limited numbers on some long-distance Inter-City routes and have to be booked at least a week in advance. SuperApex fares have to be purchased 14 days in advance and again are available in limited numbers on a few InterCity services. Savers can be used on week-ends and on most weekday trains outside rush hours. Finally, Supersavers can not be used on Fridays, or any peak-hour service to, from or through London.

Ticket offices in rural areas may close on weekends, but small branch lines have a conductor on board who sells tickets. Otherwise buy a ticket beforehand since inspectors can levy on-the-spot fines if you do not have a valid ticket. Many stations have automatic ticket machines.

RAIL PASSES

IF YOU PLAN to do much train traveling around Britain, buy a rail pass. These can be bought from many BR agents abroad, such as **British Rail International**, **Rail Europe** or **CIE Tours International**. A BritRail Flexi-pass allows you to travel on certain days in a given period, while a BritRail Pass gives unlimited travel through-out England, Scotland and Wales for 8, 15, 22 or 28 days. Discounts are also available for under 26-year-olds with a BritRail Youth Pass, or for 16- to 24-year-olds or full-time students with a Young Person's Railcard. For those over the age of 60, the

The distinctive British Rail logo

BritRail Senior Pass or a Senior Rail Card entitles you to a one-third price discount on ordinary or Saver fares.

There are special passes for London transport and a pass that covers London, Oxford, Canterbury and Brighton. Children 5–15 years old pay half fare; the under-5s travel free. Family tickets are also available. Disabled travelers can obtain discounts. Keep a passport-sized photo handy for buying passes. If you have a pass, always show it when you buy a ticket.

GENERAL TIPS

BRITAIN'S FASTEST and most comfortable trains are those on the InterCity routes. These are very popular services and get booked up quickly. It is always advisable to reserve your seat in advance, especially if you want to travel at peak times, such as Friday evenings. InterCity trains have dining cars, air-conditioning and are fast, traveling to Edinburgh from London, for example, in just over four hours.

Porters are rare on British stations, although carts are often available for passengers to help themselves. If you are

Rail terminal, Liverpool Lime Street Station

disabled and need help, contact BR before you travel. A yellow line above a train window indicates a first class compartment. You cannot use these without paying the full fare, even if the train is full.

Check which section of the train to join as they sometimes split through the journey and proceed to different destinations. Trains stop for only a minute at each station, so be ready to get on and off. Some stations are a little way from town centers, but are well marked and nearly always on a bus route. Sunday trains and public holiday services are often a lot slower than normal.

Cover of a BritRail pass

SCENIC TRAIN RIDES

As highway travel made many rural railroads redundant in the mid-20th century, picturesque sections of track, as well as many old steam engines, were rescued and restored to working order by enthusiasts. These services are often privately run. The local tourist office, BR ticket office or travel agents will provide you with information. Most of the lines are short – around 20 miles (32 km) but cover some of the most scenic parts of the country. Lines include the South Devon Steam Railway

(see p277); the Ffestiniog Railway (see pp438–9) in North Wales; the North York Moors Railway (see p380); the Strathspey Steam Railway (see p530) and the La'l Ratty Railway in Cumbria (see p350).

A reconditioned steam train, North Yorkshire

BRITISH RAIL INTERCITY MAP

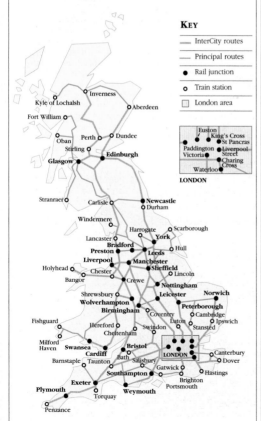

KEY

— InterCity routes
— Principal routes
● Rail junction
○ Train station
□ London area

Inverness
Kyle of Lochalsh
Fort William
Aberdeen
Oban
Perth ○ Dundee
Stirling
Glasgow
Edinburgh

LONDON
Euston
King's Cross
St Pancras
Paddington
Victoria
Liverpool Street
Charing Cross
Waterloo

Stranraer
Carlisle
Newcastle
Durham
Windermere
Harrogate ○ Scarborough
Lancaster
Bradford
York
Preston
Hull
Liverpool
Leeds
Holyhead
Manchester
Sheffield
Bangor
Chester
Lincoln
Crewe
Nottingham
Shrewsbury
Leicester
Norwich
Wolverhampton
Peterborough
Birmingham
Coventry
Cambridge
Fishguard
Hereford
Luton
Ipswich
Cheltenham
Swindon
Stansted
Milford Haven
Swansea
Bristol
Cardiff
Bath
Salisbury
LONDON
Canterbury
Barnstaple
Taunton
Gatwick
Dover
Southampton
Hastings
Exeter
Brighton
Plymouth
Weymouth
Portsmouth
Torquay
Penzance

DIRECTORY

UK RAIL NUMBERS

Apex and SuperApex
0800 450 450 (freephone).

Disabled Information
0171-922 6482.

East Anglia, Southeast
0171-928 5100 (Waterloo).

General Information
0171-387 7070.

Lost Property
0171-922 6477.

Northeast, East Coast, Scotland
0171-278 2477 (King's Cross).

South Wales and West
0171-262 6767 (Paddington).

West Coast, North Wales, East Midlands
0171-387 7070 (Euston).

OVERSEAS RAIL NUMBERS

British Rail International
(212) 575-2667 (New York); (416) 929-3333 (Toronto).

CIE Tours International
(201) 292-3438 or (800) 522-5258 (United States).

Rail Europe
(914) 682-2999 or (800) 848-7245 (United States and Canada).

Traveling around by Coach

IN BRITAIN, coaches refer to the long-distance express buses and those used for sightseeing excursions. What the British refer to as buses, however, covers those vehicles that operate on regular routes with scheduled stops around or between villages, towns and cities. Many coach services duplicate rail routes, but are generally cheaper. Journey times, however, are longer and much less predictable on crowded roads. Modern coaches are comfortable, sometimes with refreshments, toilets and entertainment – in the form of feature films – on board. Some city to city routes, especially at weekends, are so popular that it is a good idea to buy a reserved trip ticket, which guarantees you a seat.

A coach tour, the Royal Mile, Edinburgh

NATIONAL COACH NETWORK

THERE ARE A LOT OF regional coach companies, but by far the largest British coach operator is **National Express** with a nationwide network of over 1,000 destinations *(see pp12–15)*. On the more popular routes – particularly on Friday evenings – it is best to book ahead. National Express offers two levels of service; the faster of the two is the *Rapide* service, which has a host or hostess and catering facilities.

Discounts are available for full-time students or anyone under 25. Senior citizens also qualify for a Discount Coach Card (30 per cent reduction). Britexpass cards lasting 30 days and Tourist Trail Passes are also available for those planning to cover many destinations in a limited period.

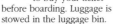

A Britexpass card

You can buy these from most travel agents in North America – via **British Travel Associates** – or while in the UK, at the major international airports, **Victoria Coach Station** and most large travel agents. The other coach operator is **Scottish Citylink**, with regular services between London, the North and Scotland. Some services run direct from Heathrow or Gatwick airports. Allow plenty of time to buy your ticket before boarding. Luggage is stowed in the luggage bin.

British Travel Associates
[800 327 6097 *(in US)*.

National Express
[0171-730 0202.

Scottish Citylink
[0131 557 5717.

Victoria Coach Station
[0171-730 3466.

COACH TOURS

DOZENS OF COACH TOURS are available in the UK, for all interests, age groups and destinations. Some include a tour guide. They may last anywhere from a couple of hours to two weeks or more, touring coast or countryside and visiting places of interest. Some are highly structured, organizing every last photo opportunity or cup of tea; others leave you to sightsee or shop at your own pace. You can opt for a prearranged route, or commission your own itinerary for a group.

Coach tours are popular, but may leave you feeling somewhat herded. Groups always travel at the pace of their slowest member, which can mean a lot of waiting. But at the same time all the stress of organizing a similar trip for yourself is taken away. Some coach operators will pick up passengers from their hotels and then drop them back.

Any large town will have a selection of coach companies. Check the local *Yellow Pages (see p622)*, or ask your hotel or the local tourist office. You can also book coach trips direct from overseas through a specialty travel agent.

Seaside resorts and tourist sites are destinations for many day trips, especially in high season. In some of the more popular rural areas, such as the Lake District, special small buses operate for ease of movement. You can book

A *Rapide* coach, Victoria Coach Station, London

these in advance, or just turn up before the coach leaves, although the tour is likely to be fully booked, especially in tourist season. The local tourist information point or travel agent will be able to tell you where these trips leave from, the cost and may even sell you tickets. It is customary to tip the guide after your tour.

REGIONAL BUSES

REGIONAL BUS SERVICES are run by a large number of companies, some private and some operated by local authorities. Bus services to remote rural areas tend to be sporadic and expensive, with some buses running just once a week and many isolated villages having no service at all. Only a few rural buses are equipped for wheelchairs.

As a general rule, you can assume that the farther you get from a city, the fewer the buses and the more expensive the fare. It is therefore unwise to rely on local buses for transportation, and if you want to see a lot of the country, renting a car is a better option. But if you do have the time, local buses can be a pleasant and expensive and often sociable way of traveling around Britain's lovely countryside.

Most buses run with just one operator – the driver. All drivers prefer you to have the correct fare, so always have a selection of low denomination coins handy. Some routes do not operate on Sundays and public holidays, and those that do are much reduced.

Always check your routes, schedules and fares at the local tourist office or bus station before you depart on a bus. This will prevent your being stranded somewhere with no return transportation.

The Trossach Trundler exploring the Trossachs, Scotland

Traveling Britain's Coasts and Waterways

BRITAIN HAS THOUSANDS OF MILES of inland waterways and hundreds of islands scattered along its coastline. Cruising along a canal in the beautiful Midlands countryside or traveling on one of the small local ferries to a remote Scottish island are both wonderful experiences. Canal boats can be rented and lots of ferries run between Britain's offshore islands.

A barge on the Welsh Backs, Bristol, Avon

CANALS

AS INDUSTRIAL PRODUCTION grew in the 18th century, it became vital to find a cheap and effective way of transporting heavy loads. Canals fulfilled this need and a huge network was built, linking most industrial areas in the north and sea ports.

The arrival of the railroads and their immediate success with freight made most canals redundant, but there are still some 2,000 miles (3,200 km) left, most in the old industrial heartland of the Midlands.

Today these canals lure the travelers who are content to cruise on old-fashioned, slow narrowboats, taking their time to enjoy the wildlife, the views and the canalside inns, originally built to satisfy the bargees' thirsts and to supply stabling for the horses that pulled the barges. These canal holidays can be very relaxing if you have the time.

If you wish to hire a narrowboat, you can book with a specialty travel firm or contact **British Waterways**.

British Waterways
☎ 01923 21036.

LOCAL FERRIES

BRITAIN'S LOCAL FERRIES can offer anything from a ten-minute river journey to a seven-hour sea cruise.

Many of Scotland's ferries are operated by **Caledonian MacBrayne**. They sail to many different destinations, such as the Isle of Skye to the Kyle of Lochalsh, or the five-hour journey from Oban to Loch Boisdale in the Western Isles. They offer a variety of different ticket types, from unlimited travel tickets for a specific period of time, to island-hop passes or all-inclusive coach tour and ferry tickets. Not all the island ferries take cars.

A car ferry traveling from Oban to Loch Boisdale

River ferries make an interesting alternative to the more usual forms of transport. The ferry across the Mersey, between the cities of Liverpool and Birkenhead, is still used by many people commuting to work. London's river trips, such as the one that runs from Westminster to Tower Bridge *(see p118),* offer a different perspective on the city and make a change from tubes, buses and cars. Local tourist information centers can give you information about ferries in their area.

Caledonian MacBrayne
☎ 01475 650100.

Traveling within Cities

U RBAN PUBLIC TRANSPORTATION in Britain is efficient and can be fun – children love London's double-decker buses. Fares are a good value, bearing in mind that you avoid the expense and difficulty of parking a car. Most of the larger cities have good bus services. London, Newcastle and Glasgow also have subway systems, and Manchester and Blackpool have trolleys. Taxis are available at every train station and at stands near hotels and city centers. The best way to see many cities is on foot, but whatever way you choose, try to avoid the rush hours from 8am to 9:30am, and 4:30pm to 6:30pm.

Local buses traveling along Princes Street, Edinburgh

LOCAL BUSES

T HE DEREGULATION of bus services has led to a complex system with many buses often duplicating services on the busiest routes. On most buses you pay the driver as you enter. They will not always accept bills so keep a selection of coins handy. Credit cards and checks are not accepted. The fare depends on the distance you travel. If you are exploring a city by bus, a daily pass is a good idea. Many of the larger cities have daily or weekly passes that can be used on all public transportation in that city; these can often be bought from newsstands. Check with the tourist office for schedules and fares. All-night services are only available in major cities, from about 11pm until early morning. You cannot use a day pass on these.

A London double-decker bus

In London night buses are prefixed with the letter N and all of them pass through Trafalgar Square.

Be on your guard when traveling alone late at night, when there may be few other passengers aboard.

Bus designs have become more innovative in the last few years. The old "big red bus" with a conductor still exists in London, but has been joined by a plethora of modern vehicles of all shapes, colors and sizes, with automatic doors and comfortable interiors. Many are small single-deckers, able to weave in and out of traffic more easily.

Many cities have bus lanes, intended to bypass car traffic jams during the rush hours. These can be effective but your trip may still take a long time. Schedules are hard to keep to, so regard timetables as guidelines. At some stops, called request stops, the driver will not halt unless you signal that you want to get on or off. If you want to board, raise your arm as the bus approaches the stop; if you want to get off, ring the bell once before your stop.

Destinations are shown on the front of buses. If you are not sure which stop you need, ask the driver or conductor to alert you and stay on the lower deck. Always keep your ticket until the end of the trip in case an inspector boards, who can impose an on-the-spot fine if you are without a valid ticket. Stops can often be quite a long distance apart.

DRIVING IN CITIES

T O PREVENT CONGESTION in city centers, parking is strictly controlled, and even minor infringements can result in heavy fines or your car being booted or towed away. You will have to pay a hefty fine to have it released. Always be sure to check the parking regulations carefully on the meters and signs before leaving your vehicle. If you are not sure how long you are likely to stay, try to find a parking lot where you will be charged as you leave. Many visitors prefer not to drive in British cities but there is nothing daunting about it if you obey the rules *(see p636)*.

A tradition parking met

TAXIS

I N LARGE TOWNS there are plenty of taxis to be found at taxi stands and train stations. Some operate by radio so you have to phone. The local *Yellow Pages (see p622)*, pubs, restaurants and hotels will all have a list of taxi numbers. Prices are usually controlled, but competition is fierce and many firms undercut licensed taxis. Always ask the price before you start your trip if there is no taxi meter. If you are not sure of the correct fare ask the local tourist information point.

Licensed taxi drivers undergo strict tests and all licensed cabs must carry a "For Hire" sign, which is lit up whenever they are free. Be careful if you use unlicensed minicabs; some may be in bad repair or uninsured. Do not accept an

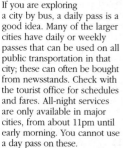

An illegally parked car immobilized by a boot

unbooked minicab ride in the street. The famous London black cabs are almost as much of an institution as the big red bus. These are the safest cabs to use in London since all the drivers are licensed and they are forbidden to drive their cab with damaged bodywork. They also know where they are going. Even these are changing, however, and you will see cabs of many colors, many covered with advertising. The newer cab designs are equipped to carry wheel-chairs. If a cab stops for you in London, it must by law take you anywhere within a radius of 6 miles (10 km) so long as it is

One of London's black cabs

within the Metropolitan Police District. This includes most of London and Heathrow Airport.

All licensed cabs will have meters that start ticking as soon as the driver accepts your business. The fare will increase minute by minute or for each 311 m (1,020 ft) traveled. Surcharges are added for each piece of luggage, each extra passenger or late hours. Most drivers expect a tip of between 10 and 15 percent of the fare. If you have a complaint, note the serial number found in the back of the cab.

GUIDED BUS TOURS

IN MOST MAJOR tourist cities, sightseeing bus tours are available. Weather permitting, a good way to see the cities is from a traditional open-topped double-decker bus. Private tours can be arranged with many companies. Contact the tourist information center.

TROLLEYS

AFTER A LONG ABSENCE (apart from a few nostalgic remnants in Blackpool) trolleys are making a comeback in clean, energy efficient and more modern guises. One of the best trolley systems in Britain is Manchester's Metrolink.

LONDON UNDERGROUND

THE UNDERGROUND in London, known as the tube, is one of the largest systems of its kind in the world. It has over 270 stations, each of which is clearly marked with the London Underground logo. The only other cities to have a subway system are Glasgow and Newcastle, but both are small. London tube trains run every day, except Christmas Day, from about 5:30am until just after midnight, but some of the outlying sections have less frequent service. Fewer trains run on Sundays.

The 11 tube lines are color-coded and maps called *Journey Planners* are available at every station, while maps of the central section are displayed in each train. Most tube trips between central destinations in London can be completed with only one or two changes of train. Smoking is not permitted on the Underground.

Newcastle's tube system is limited to the city center but Glasgow's skirts around the center. Both are clean and efficient, running the same hours as London's.

A London Underground sign outside a station

A trolley along Blackpool's famous promenade

WALKING IN CITIES

ONCE YOU GET USED to traffic on the left, Britain's cities can be safely and enjoyably explored on foot.

There are two types of pedestrian crossing: striped zebra crossings and push-button crossings at traffic lights. At a zebra crossing traffic should always stop for you, but at push-button crossings cars will not stop until the lights change in your favor. Look for instructions written on the road; these will tell you from which direction you can expect the traffic to come. More and more cities and towns are creating traffic-free zones for pedestrians.

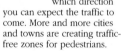

Cycling under the Bridge of Sighs, Oxford

CYCLING

Cycling is a popular pastime in Britain. Even in the smallest town there is usually some place you can rent bikes. Whether you cycle in towns or the countryside, a helmet is recommended. Cyclists may not use highways or their approach roads, nor can they ride on sidewalks, footpaths or pedestrianized zones. Many city roads have cycle lanes and their own traffic lights. You can take a bike on most trains for a charge. Never leave your bike unlocked.

General Index

Acknowledgments

DORLING KINDERSLEY would like to thank the following people whose contributions and assistance have made the preparation of this book possible.

MAIN CONTRIBUTOR
Michael Leapman was born in London in 1938 and has been a professional journalist since he was 20. He has worked for most British national newspapers and now writes about travel and other subjects for several publications, among them *The Independent*, *Independent on Sunday*, *The Economist* and *Country Life*. He has written 11 books, including *the* award-winning *Companion Guide to New York* (1983, revised 1995) and *Eyewitness Travel Guide to London*. In 1989 he edited the widely praised *Book of London*.

ADDITIONAL CONTRIBUTORS
Paul Cleves, James Henderson, Lucy Juckes, John Lax, Marcus Ramshaw.

ADDITIONAL ILLUSTRATIONS
Christian Hook, Gilly Newman, Paul Weston.

DESIGN AND EDITORIAL ASSISTANCE
Eliza Armstrong, Moerida Belton, Josie Barnard, Hilary Bird, Louise Boulton, Roger Bullen, Margaret Chang, Deborah Clapson, Elspeth Collier, Gary Cross, Cooling Brown Partnership, Guy Dimond, Fay Franklin, Angela-Marie Graham, Danny Farnham, Joy Fitzsimmons, Ed Freeman, Andrew Heritage, Annette Jacobs, Steve Knowlden, Charlie Hawkings, Martin Hendry, Nic Kynaston, Pippa Leahy, James Mills Hicks, Marianne Petrou, Chez Pitchall, Mark Rawley, Jake Reimann, Carolyn Ryden, David Roberts, Alison Stace.

ADDITIONAL PHOTOGRAPHY
Max Alexander, Peter Anderson, Steve Bere, June Buck, Michael Dent, Philip Dowell, Mike Dunning, Chris Dyer, Andrew Einsiedel, Philip Enticknap, Jane Ewart, DK Studio/Steve Gorton, Frank Greenaway, Stephen Hayward, John Heseltine, Ed Ironside, Dave King, Neil Mersh, Robert O'Dea, Stephen Oliver, Vincent Oliver, Roger Phillips, Karl Shone, Chris Stevens, Jim Stevenson, Clive Streeter, Harry Taylor, David Ward, Mathew Ward, Stephen Wooster, Nick Wright, Colin Yeates.

PHOTOGRAPHIC AND ARTWORK REFERENCE
Christopher Woodward of the Building of Bath Museum, Franz Karl Freiherr von Linden, NRSC Air Photo Group, The Oxford Mail and Times and Mark and Jane Rees.

PHOTOGRAPHY PERMISSIONS
DORLING KINDERSLEY would like to thank the following for their assistance and kind permission to photograph at their establishments: Banqueting House (Crown copyright by kind permission of Historic Royal Palaces); Cabinet War Rooms; Paul Highnam at English Heritage; Dean and Chapter Exeter Cathedral; Gatwick Airport Ltd; Heathrow Airport Ltd; Thomas Woods at Historic Scotland; Provost and Scolars Kings College; Cambridge; London Transport Museum; Madame Tussaud's; National Museums and Galleries of Wales (Museum of Welsh Life); Diana Lanham and Gayle Mault at the National Trust; Peter Reekie and Isla Roberts at the National Trust for Scotland; Provost Skene House; Saint Bartholmew the Great; Saint James's Church; London St. Paul's Cathedral; Masters and Wardens of the Worshipful Company of Skinners; Provost and Chapter of Southwark Cathedral; HM Tower of London; Dean and Chapter of Westminster; Dean and Chapter of Worcetser Cathedral and all the other churches, museums, hotels, restaurants, shops, galleries and sights too numerous to thank individually.

PICTURE CREDITS
t = top; tl = top left; tlc = top left center; tc = top center; tr = top right; cla = center left above; ca = center above; cra = center right above; cl = center left; c = center; cr = center right; clb = center left below; cb = center below;

crb = center right below; bl = bottom left; b = bottom; bc = bottom center; bcl = bottom center left; br = bottom right; d = detail.

Every effort has been made to trace the copyright holders and we apologize in advance for any unintentional omissions. We would be pleased to insert the appropriate acknowledgements in any subsequent edition of this publication.

Works of art have been reproduced with the permission of the following copyright holders: © ADAGP, Paris and DACS, London 1995: 157t; © Alan Bowness, Hepworth Estate 263bl; © DACS, London 1995: 93c; © D. Hockney: 1970–1 93tr, 1990–3 397t; © Roy Lichtenstein/DACS, London 1995: 73bl and 493c; © Estate of Stanley Spencer 1995 all rights reserved DACS 221t; © Angela Verren-Taunt 1995 all rights reserved Dacs: 263br.

The work of Henry Moore, *Large Two Forms*, 1966, illustrated on page 399b has been reproduced by permission of the Henry Moore Foundation.

The publisher would like to thank the following individuals, companies and picture libraries for permission to reproduce their photographs:

ABBOT HALL ART GALLERY AND MUSEUM, Kendal: 358b(d); ABERDEEN ART GALLERIES 526t; ABERDEEN AND GRAMPIAN TOURIST BOARD 465ca; ACTION PLUS: 67t; 466t; Steve Bardens 66bl, 420c; David Davies 67cr; Glynn Kirk 66tl; Peter Tarry 66cla, 67bl; Printed by kind permission of MOHAMED AL FAYED: 99t; AMERICAN MUSEUM, Bath: 247tl; ANCIENT ART AND ARCHITECTURE COLLECTION: 42cb, 44ca, 44clb, 45ca, 45clb, 46bl, 46br, 48crb, 51ca, 218tl, 221br, 425t; THE ARCHIVE & BUSINESS RECORDS CENTRE, University of Glasgow: 469t; T. & R. ANNAN AND SONS: 502b(d); ASHMOLEAN MUSEUM, OXFORD: 47t; MUSEUM OF AUTOMATA, YORK: 393b.

BARNABY'S PICTURE LIBRARY: 60tr; BEAMISH OPEN AIR MUSEUM: 410c, 401b, 411ca, 411cb, 411b; BRIDGEMAN ART LIBRARY, LONDON: Agnew and Sons, London 309t; Museum of Antiquities, Newcastle upon Tyne 44tl; Apsley House, The Wellington Museum, London 26tl; Bibliotheque Nationale, Paris *Neville Book of Hours* 308tl(d); Birmingham City Museums and Gallery 305t; Bonham's, London, *Portrait of Lord Nelson with Santa Cruz Beyond*, Lemeul Francis Abbot 54cb(d); Bradford Art Galleries and Museums 49clb; City of Bristol Museums and Art Galleries 242c; British Library, London, *Pictures and Arms of English Kings and Knights* 4t(d), 39t(d), *The Kings of England from Brutus to Henry* 26bl(d), *Stowe manuscript* 40tl(d), *Liber Legum Antiquorum Regum* 46tl(d), *Calendar Anglo-Saxon Miscellany* 46–7t(d), 46–7c(d), 46–7b(d), *Decrees of Kings of Anglo-Saxon and Norman England* 47clb, 49bl(d), *Portrait of Chaucer*, Thomas Occleve 49br(d), *Portrait of Shakespeare*, Droeshurt 51bl(d), *Historia Anglorum* 40bl(d), 222tl(d), *Chronicle of Peter of Langtoft* 269b(d), *Lives and Miracles of St Cuthbert* 405tl(d), 405cl(d), 405cr(d), *Lindisfarne Gospels* 405br(d), *Commendatio Lamentabilis intransitu Edward IV* 422b(d), *Histoire du Roy d'Angleterre Richard II* 424t(d), 523b; Christies, London 431t; Claydon House, Bucks, *Florence Knightingale*, Sir William Blake Richmond 148t; Department of Environment, London 48tr; City of Edinburgh Museums and Galleries, *Chief of Scottish Clan*, Eugene Deveria 470bl(d); Fitzwilliam Museum, University of Cambridge, *George IV as Prince Regent*, Richard Cosway 165cb, 198bl, *Flemish Book of Hours* 336tl(d); Giraudon/Musee de la Tapisserie, with special authorization of the city of Bayeux 47b,167b; Guildhall Library, Corporation of London, *The Great Fire*, Marcus Willemsz Doornik 53bl(d), *Bubbler's Melody* 54br(d), *Triumph of Steam and Electricity*, The Illustrated London News 57t(d), *Great Exhibition*, *The transept from Dickenson's Comprehensive Pictures* 56–7, *A Balloon View of London as seen from Hampstead* 107c(d); Harrogate Museum and Art Gallery, North Yorkshire 374t;

Holburne Museum and Crafts Study Centre, Bath 53t;
Imperial War Museum, *London Field Marshall Montgomery*,
J. Worsley 27cbr(d); Kedleston Hall, Derbyshire 24c, 24br;
King Street Galleries, London, *Bonnie Prince Charlie*, G.
Dupré 468tl; Lambeth Palace Library, London, *St. Alban's
Chronicle* 49t; Lever Brothers Ltd, Cheshire 335cra;
Lincolnshire County Council, Usher Gallery, Lincoln, *Portrait
of Mrs. Fitzherbert after Richard Cosway* 165b; London
Library, *The Barge Tower from Ackermann's World in
minature*, F. Scoberl 55t; Manchester City Art Galleries 361b;
David Messum Gallery, London 433b; National Army
Museum, London, *Bunker's Hill*, R. Simkin 54ca; National
Gallery, London, *Mrs Siddons the Actress*, Thomas
Gainsborough 54t(d), 149ca; National Museet, Copenhagen
46ca; Phillips, the International Fine Art Auctioneers, *James I*,
John the Elder Decritz 52b(d); Private Collections: 8–9,
26ca(d), 34tl, 48–9, 55cla, 55bl, 56cdb, Vanity Fair 57br, 149t,
Ellesmere Manuscript 174b(d), *Armada: map of the Spanish
and British Fleets*, Robert Adam 277t, 382t, 408b; Royal
Geographical Society, London 149cb(d); Royal Holloway &
Bedford New College, the *Princes Edward and Richard in
the Tower*, Sir John Everett Millais 121b; Smith Art Gallery
and Museum, Stirling 482b; Tate Gallery, London: 56crb,
223t; Thyssen-Bornemisza Collection, Lugo Casta, *King
Henry VIII*, Hans Holbein the Younger 50b(d); Victoria and
Albert Museum, London 24t(d), 56b, 190t, 337cr, 379b,
Miniature of Mary Queen of Scots, by a follower of Francois
Clouet 497br, 523t(d); Walker Art Gallery, Liverpool 364c;
Westminster Abbey, London, *Henry VII Tomb effigy*, Pietro
Torrigiano 26br(d), 40bc(d); The Trustees of the Weston Park
Foundation, *Portrait of Richard III*, Italian School 49cla(d);
Christopher Wood Gallery, London, *High Life Below Stairs*,
Charles Hunt 25c(d); reproduced with permission of the
British Library Board: *Cotton Faustina BVII folio 85* 49cr,
109cl; © The British Museum: 42cr, 43cb, 73tl, 83c, 105,
108–9 all except 109t and 109bl; © The Bronte Society: 398
all; Burton Constable Foundation: Dr. David Connell 388t.

Cadogen Management: 86b; CADW – Welsh Historic
Monuments (Crown Copyright), 460t; Camera Press: Cecil
Beaton 94bl; Cardiff City Council: 458tr, 459t, 459c; F.K.B.
Carlson: 35bcl; Colin de Chaire: 183c; Trustees of the
Chatsworth Settlement: 320b, 321b; Museum of Childhood,
Edinburgh: 496b; Bruce Coleman Ltd: 31br; Stephen Bond
280b; Jane Burton 31cra; Mark N. Boulton 31cl; Patrick
Clement 30clb; Peter Evans 530tl; Paul van Gaalen 236tl;
Sir Jeremy Grayson 31bl; Harald Lange 30bc; Gordon
Langsbury 531t; George McCarthy 30t, 31bl, 228b, 269br;
Paul Meitz 514clb; Dr. Eckart Pott 30bl, 514t; Hans
Reinhard 30cb, 31tc, 280t, 480tl; Dr. Frieder Sauer 520t;
N. Schwiatz 31clb; Kim Taylor 31tl, 514cra; Konrad Wothe
514ca; Joe Cornish: 389b; courtesy of the Corporation of
London: 115b; Doug Corrance: 471b; John Crook: 157b.

1805 Club: 27t; 1853 Gallery, Bradford 397t; English
Heritage: 132b, 194c, 194b, 195b, 234–5b, 249b,
336br, 337b, 380t, 405tr, 405c; Avebury Museum 42ca;
Devizes Museum 42br, drawing by Frank Gardiner 409br;
Salisbury Museum 42t, 42bl; Skyscan Balloon Photography
43t, 248b; 380t; 409bl; English Life Publications Ltd,
Derby: 328tl, 328tr, 329t, 329b; Et Archive: 41tc, 41cr,
52cb, 53clb, 58crb, 148b; Bodleian Library, Oxford 48crb;
British Library, London 48tl, 48ca; Devizes Museum 42cl,
43b, 248c; Garrick Club 422tl(d); Imperial War Museum,
London 58clb(d), 59br; Labour Party Archives 60br;
London Museum 43cla; Magdalene College 50ca; National
Maritime Museum, London 39b; Stoke Museum
Staffordshire Polytechnic 41bc, 52tl; Victoria & Albert
Museum, London 50t(d); Eureka!: 399t; Mary Evans Picture
Library: 9 inset, 34tr, 40br, 41tl, 41cl, 41bl, 41br, 44bl,
44br, 46cb, 47cla, 51t, 51cb, 51br, 53crb, 54bl, 55br, 56tl,
58ca, 59ca, 59crb, 81cb, 106t, 107t, 119b, 143 inset,
148cb, 149b, 173c, 175c, 181b, 192c, 208bl, 214tl, 217c,
217bl, 217br, 220bl, 225 inset, 265t, 283 inset, 322b, 335t,
335cla, 359tr, 406t, 433tl, 468b, 485bl, 498bl, 500b, 501t,
521b, 613 inset.

Chris Fairclough: 281b, 338b, 640b; Paul Felix: 220c;
Ffotograff © Charles Aithie: 421t; Fishbourne Roman
Villa: 45t; Louis Flood: 470br; Foreign and British Bible
Society: Cambridge University Press 423c; Fotomas
Index: 107cra.

Glasgow Museums: Burrell Collection 506–7 all except
506tl; Art Gallery & Museum, Kelvingrove 505t, 517b,
529b(d); Saint Mungo Museum of Religious Life and Art
503tl; Museum of Transport 504cr; John Glover: 62cr,
146cb, 191b; The Gore Hotel, London: 540c.

Sonia Halliday and Laura Lushington Archive: 395t; Robert
Harding Picture Library: 168t, 534t; Jan Baldwin 271b;
M H Black 272t; Teresa Black 621cb; Nigel Blythe 632ca;
L. Bond 323b; Michael Botham 32br; C Bowman 629c; Lesley
Burridge 290tr; Martyn F Chillman 291bc; Philip Craven
103t, 186b, 311b; Nigel Francis 205b, 635b; Robert Francis
66–7; Paul Freestone 212b; Brian Harrison 515b; Van der
Hars 524t; Michael Jenner 45b, 515c; Norma Joseph 65b;
Christopher Nicholson 239t; B. O'Connor 33ca; Jenny Pate
147bc; Rainbird Collection 47crb; Roy Rainsford 33b, 154t,
284b, 324cr, 356t, 372t, 461b; Walter Rawling 21t; Hugh
Routledge 2–3; Peter Scholey 285t; Michael Short 291br;
James Strachen 370b; Julia K. Thorne 472bl; Adina Tovy
61tl, 472br; Andy Williams 165t, 220br, 332c, 418t, 510;
Adam Woolfitt 20t, 20c, 44tr, 45crb, 246b, 258, 270ca, 291bl,
425bl, 454tl, 530tr; Harewood House: 396c; Paul Harris: 32t,
62cl, 287bl(d), 324b, 353b, 612–3, 630c, 630b; Harrogate
International Centre: 375b; Heathrow Airport Ltd: 619b;
Crown copyright is reproduced with the permission of the
Controller of HMSO: 73br, 120bl, 120br, 121tl; Cathedral
Church of the Blessed Virgin Mary and St. Ethelbert in
Hereford: 302b; Hertfordshire County Council: Bob Norris
58–9; John Heseltine: 74t, 104, 109t, 110, 236tr, 236c, 455tl;
Historic Royal Palaces (Crown Copyright): 159 all; Historic
Scotland (Crown Copyright): 483c, 492tr, 492c; Peter
Hollings: 334bl; Barry J. Holmes: 63t; Neil Holmes: 244b(d),
246c, 270t, 359b, 415tl, 415tr, 437b, 643t; Angelo Hornak
Library: 392tl, 392bl, 392br, 395br; Reproduced by
permission of the Clerk of Records, House of Lords: 469c;
David Martin Hughes: 142–3, 150; Hulton-Deutsch
Collection: 22tr, 27cl, 27cr, 53cla, 54c, 56c, 57cb, 58tl 58tr,
58b, 59t, 60ca, 60bl, 148ca, 155c, 219b, 286t, 334c, 335crb,
336bl, 363b, 383b, 384br, 423t, 481b, 508tl, 522b;
Hunterian Art Gallery: 505b; Hutchison Library: Catherine
Blacky 34cb; Bernard Gerad 467t; Hutton in the Forest:
Lady Inglewood 344t.

The Image Bank, London: Derek Berwin538t; David Gould
343b; Romilly Lockyer 74bl; Colin Molyneux 455bl;
Stockphotos/Steve Allen360c, Trevor Wood 270b; Simon
Wilkinson 166b; Images Colour Library: 30cla, 43c, 207b,
220t, 235t, 236bl, 237b, 322t, 324cl, 325t, 339c, 638t, 638b;
Horizon/Robert Estall 424c; Landscape Only 33cb, 234,
351, 425br; Ironbridge Museum: 301b.

Jarrold Publishers: 198br, 215t(D), 290bl; Michael Jenner:
290tl, 326b, 514b; Jorvik Viking Centre, York: 391t.

Royal Botanic Gardens, Kew: 76ca.

Frank Lane Picture Agency: 386b(d); W Broadhurst 240b;
Michael Callan 228crb; Andrew Lawson: 22ca, 23c, 230br,
231tl, 231tr, 231br; Leeds Castle Enterprises: 151b; Leighton
House, Royal Borough of Kensington: 128br; published by
kind permission Dean and Chapter of Lincoln 326t, 327cb,
327bl; Lincolnshire County Council: Usher Gallery, Lincoln:
c 1820 by William Ilbery 327bl; Llangollen International
Musical Eisteddfod 436c; London Ambulance Service: 621ca;
London Film Festival: 62t; London Transport Museum: 82t;
Longleat House: 252t.

Maldom Millenium Trust: 195t; Mansell Collection, London:
27clb, 40tr, 52ca, 55cb, 247tr, 309bl, 335clb, 388b; Nick
Meers: 18t, 224–5; Metropolitan Police Service: 621t;

Archie Miles: 226ca; Simon Miles: 338tr; Minack Theatre: Murray King 262b; Mirror Syndication International: 76b, 89b, 112; BTA/Juilian Nieman 34ca; Philip Russell 354–5; Museum of London: 44crb, 113t.

National Fishing Heritage Centre, Grimsby: 389t; National Gallery, London: 73tr, 84–5 all; National Gallery Of Scotland: *The Reverend Walker Skating on Duddington Loch*, Sir Henry Raeburn 490c(d); National Library Of Wales: 422tr, 425c(d), 453b; National Museum Of Film And Television, Bradford: 397c; Board of Trustees of the National Museums and Galleries on Merseyside: Liverpool Museum 365t; Maritime Museum 363t; Walker Art Gallery 332b, 364tl, 364tr, 364b, 365c; National Museums of Scotland: 491t, 497bl; National Museum of Wales: 422c; By courtesy of the National Portrait Gallery, London: *First Earl of Essex*, Hans Peter Holbein 337t(d), Angus McBean 83b; National Sound Archive, London – The trademark His Master's Voice is reproduced by kind permission of EMI Records Limited: 99c; National Tramway Museum, Crich: 325c; National Trust Photographic Library: *Bess of Hardwick (Elizabeth, Countess of Shrewsbury)*, Anon 320tl(d); Mathew Antrobus 288br, 376cl, 377bl; Oliver Benn 25br, 264c, 277bl, 376b; John Bethell 265c, 265bl, 265br, 289t; Nick Carter 241b; Joe Cornish 442; Prudence Cumming 253c; Martin Dohrn 50crb; Andreas Von Einsidedel 25bl, 288cb, 289ca; Roy Fox 257t; Geoffry Frosh 273t; Jerry Harpur 230t, 230bl; Derek Harris 230clb, 253t; Nick Meers 252b, 253b, 306b, 615b; Rob Motheson 276t; Cressida Pemberton Piggot 540t; Ian Shaw 22cb, 446t; Richard Surman 289br, 348b; Rupert Truman 289br, 365b; Andy Tryner 288bl; Charlie Waite 377t; Jeremy Whitaker 289bc, 379t, 446b; Mike Williams 288ca, 377c; George Wright 230crb, 276c; National Trust For Scotland: 464b, 486b, 487c, 494b, 508tr, 509tl, 509tr, 509br; Glyn Satterley 503tr; Lindsey Robertson 509bl; National Waterways Museum at Gloucester: 287bc, 287br; NHPA: Martin Garwood 381ca; Nature Photographers: Andrew Cleave 228cla; E A James 31cla, 346t; Hugh Miles 407t; Owen Newman 31ca; William Paton 514crb; Paul Sterry 30crb, 30br, 31cb, 31crb, 220c, 241t, 373t, 514cla; Roger Tidman 183b; Network Photographers: Laurie Sparham 466b; New Shakespeare Theatre Co: 125t; Norfolk Museums Service: Norwich Castle Museum 187b.

Palace Theatre Archive: 124c; Photos Horticultural: 22b, 23t, 147tlc, 147cra, 147cb, 147crb, 230ca, 231c; Pictures: 632t; Popperfoto: 27br, 59bl, 60clb, 60crb, 61bl, 88tl, 146tr, 189t, 268cl, 430b; AFP/Eric Feferber 61br; SG Forester 67br; Port Merion Ltd: 440tl; Press Association: Martin Keene 62b; Public Record Office (Crown Copyright): 48b.

Rob Reichenfeld: 160t, 161c, 161b, 286b, 626b, 631t; Rex Features Ltd: 27ca, 41tr, 60tl, 61bc, 222c, 223br; Barry Beattie 245cl; Peter Brooke 27bc, 624br; Nils Jorgensen 26c, 629t, 636c; Eileen Kleinman 629br; Hazel Murray 61tr; Tess, Renn-Burrill Productions 255b; Richard Young 60tl; Nick Rogers 61tc; Tim Rooke 64cr, 66tr; Sipa/Chesnot 27bl; Today 21c; The Ritz, London: 83t; Royal Academy Of Arts, London: 86ca; Royal Collection © 1995 Her Majesty Queen Elizabeth II: *The Family of Henry VIII*, Anon 38(d), 87c, 88tr, 88bl, 89t, 222tr, 223tl(d), 223tr, 223bl, *George IV, in full Highland dress*, Sir David Wilkie 471t; David Cripps 89c; John Freeman 88br; Royal College Of Music, London: 98c; Royal Pavilion, Art Gallery and Museums, Brighton: 164c, 164bl, 164br, 165cl, 165cr; Royal Shakespeare Theatre Company: Donald Cooper 313c(d).

St. Alban's Museums: Verulamium Museum 218b; Sartaj Balti House: Clare Carnegie 397b; Scottish National Gallery of Modern Art: Roy Lichtenstein In the Car 493c; Scottish National Portrait Gallery: on loan from the collection of the Earl of Roseberry, *Execution of Charles I*, Unknown Artist 52–3; S4C (Channel 4 Wales): 423b; Sidmouth Folk Festival: Derek Brooks 273b; Skyscan Balloon Photography: 248t; Southbank Press Office: 126t; Sporting Pictures: 66cra, 66bc, 66br, 67cl, 344b; Still Moving Pictures: Doug Corrance 534b; Wade Cooper 469b; Derek Laird 468c; Robert Lees 65t; STB 530br, 531c, Paisley Museum 501b, Paul Tomkins 515tr;
S.J. Whitehorn 481t; Tony Stone Images: 34–5, 536–7; Richard Elliott 64b; Rob Talbot 339ca; David Woodfall 426.

Tate Gallery, London: 73bl, 93 all except tl, 263c, 263bl, 263br; Rob Talbot: 339cb; Tuille House Museum, Carlisle: 344c.

Courtesy of the Board of Trustees of the Victoria And Albert Musuem, London: 72b, 100–101 all except 100t.

Charlie Waite: 535t; © Wales Tourist Board: 419c, 420b, 424–5, 454br, 455tr, 455br; Roger Vitos 454tl, 454bl; The Wallace Collection, London: 106cb; David Ward: 511b, 529t; Frederick Warne & Co: 353t(d); Courtesy of the Trustees of The Wedgwood Museum, Barlaston, Staffordshire, England: 297b; Jeremy Whitaker: 214tr, 214c, 215b; Whitbread Plc: 34bl; Whitworth Art Gallery, University of Manchester: courtesy of Granada Television Arts Foundation 361c; Christopher Wilson: 390bl; Wilton House Trust: 251b; Winchester Cathedral: 157t; Woburn Abbey – by kind permission of the Marquess of Tavistock and Trustees of the Bedford Estate: 50–1, 216t; Timothy Woodcock Photolibrary: 5b; Photo © Woodmansterne, Watford, UK: Jeremy Marks 116t, 117t.

York Castle Museum: 391cb; Dean & Chapter York Minster: 395cla, 395ca, 395cl; Peter Gibson 395cra, 395cr, 395cl; Jim Korshaw 392tr; Reproduced by couresty of the Yorkshire Museum: 394c; Yorkshire Sculpture Park: Jerry Hardman Jones 399b.

ZEFA: 64t, 126b, 249t, 255t, 472c, 627t, 634c, 636bl; Bob Croxford 63cr; Weir 183t.

Cover: All special photography except Robert Harding Picture Library/Rosehaven Ltd: front top.

Front Endpaper: All special photography except Robert Harding Picture Library/Andy Williams tl, Adam Woolfitt bl; National Trust Photographic Library/Joe Cornish clc; Tony Stone Images/David Woodfall cl, Timothy Woodcock Photolibrary brl.

Back Endpaper: All special photography except John Heseltine tl, br.

Central London

**REGENT'S PARK
AND BLOOMSBURY**
See pp104–109
Street Finder maps 3, 4

**SOUTH KENSINGTON
AND HYDE PARK**
See pp96–103
Street Finder maps 2, 5

**WEST END AND
WESTMINSTER**
See pp78–95
Street Finder maps 4, 6

REGENT'S
PARK

MARYLEBONE ROAD EUSTON

GLOUCESTER PLACE
BAKER STREET
HARLEY STREET
PORTLAND PLACE
GREAT PORTLAND STREET
CLEVELAND STREET
MORTIMER STREET
TOTTENHAM CO
GOWER

WIGMORE STREET
OXFORD

OXFORD STREET
BROOK STREET
REGENT STREET
CONDUIT ST
WARDOUR

BAYSWATER ROAD
MARBLE ARCH
PARK LANE
MOUNT ST
BERKELEY ST
PICCADILLY
ST JAMES'S ST
PALL MA

KENSINGTON PALACE GDNS
KENSINGTON
HYDE PARK
Round
Pond
SERPENTINE ROAD
Serpentine
GARDENS
ROTTEN ROW
HYDE
PARK
CORNER
GREEN
PARK
THE
JAM
PA

KENSINGTON ROAD
KNIGHTSBRIDGE
KNIGHTSBRIDGE
BROMPTON ROAD
GROSVENOR PLACE
BUCKINGHAM
PALACE
GARDENS
*Buckingham
Palace*
BUCKINGHAM GATE

*Victoria and
Albert Museum*
EXHIBITION ROAD
LOWER
GROSVENOR
PLACE
VICTORIA
VAUXHALL
ROCHESTER ROW
BRI